Advance praise for

New England Court Records
A Research Guide for Genealogists and Historians

by Diane Rapaport

"What an amazing resource! Librarians, historians and genealogists should run, not walk, to buy this book. Diane Rapaport has done us all a great service."

> — **Mary Beth Norton, Pulitzer Prize finalist, Professor of History, Cornell University, and author of** *In the Devil's Snare: The Salem Witchcraft Crisis of 1692*

"Diane Rapaport has written a scholarly and monumental research guide to New England court records. Anyone researching New England ancestors will want this reference book in their library. It is highly recommended."

> — **Kip Sperry, Professor of Family History, Brigham Young University, Certified Genealogist, and Fellow, American Society of Genealogists**

"Ms. Rapaport has created the first-of-its-kind guide to federal and state court records for all of the New England states. She has covered the basic terminology and structure so even a beginning genealogist or historian can jump right in to discover the treasures that lie within these court documents. This book is your key to unlock the door."

> — **Scott Andrew Bartley, editor,** *The Mayflower Descendant* **and** *Vermont Genealogy*

"This remarkable work offers a thorough guide to court records all over New England, and much more: explanations of legal terminology, extensive bibliographies, and colorful examples that entertain as well as inform."

> — **Jane Fletcher Fiske, Fellow, American Society of Genealogists, and author of** *Gleanings from Newport Court Files 1659-1783* **and** *Rhode Island General Court of Trials 1671-1704.*

"New England court records are full of interesting detail about our forebears and their culture. Diane Rapaport's book makes it easy for everyone—beginners and experienced researchers alike—to find and use these valuable resources."

— **Helen Schatvet Ullmann, Certified Genealogist, Fellow, American Society of Genealogists, and Associate Editor of** *The New England Historical and Genealogical Register*

"Diane Rapaport's extensive *New England Court Records* reveals a trove of legal sources, shows where to find the material (not always where you'd predict), and explains how to use it. Genealogists and historians be advised: this fascinating guide may take your research in unexpected directions."

— **Marilynne K. Roach, author of** *The Salem Witch Trials: A Day-to-Day Chronicle of a Community Under Siege*

"*New England Court Records* combines three valuable reference tools into one book. Part I (Understanding the Basics) is a boon to researchers with no formal training in legal concepts and terminology. Part II tells where to find court records for each New England state. And Part III (Sampling the Sources) gives ideas and inspiration, no matter what state you're researching. A great book!"

— **Helen A. Shaw, MA, professional genealogist and editor,** *Old Broad Bay Family History Association Newsletter*

NEW ENGLAND COURT RECORDS

A Research
Guide for
Genealogists
and
Historians

DIANE RAPAPORT

BURLINGTON, MASSACHUSETTS

Copyright © 2006 by Diane Rapaport

All rights reserved. No part of this book may be reproduced or transmitted in any form or by any means, electronic or mechanical, including photocopying, recording or by any information storage and retrieval system, without written permission from the author, except for the inclusion of brief quotations in a review.

Published by:

Quill Pen Press, LLC

35 Corporate Drive, 4th Floor

Burlington, Massachusetts 01803

781-685-4990 (Toll-free 1-866-784-5573)

info@QuillPenPress.com

www.QuillPenPress.com

Courthouse images from the author's collection of vintage picture postcards appear throughout this book and on the front and back covers. Front cover: Rutland, Vermont, ca. 1907. Back cover: Rockland, Maine, ca. 1913, and Northampton, Massachusetts.

Front cover background features detail from a decision of the Superior Court of Judicature at Plymouth, Massachusetts, 1718. *Courtesy of New England Historic Genealogical Society*. Portions of Chapter 18 are reprinted from Diane Rapaport, "Tales from the Courthouse: The Case of the Purloined Pigs," *New England Ancestors* 5 (Winter 2004): 54-55, with permission of the New England Historic Genealogical Society. For more information about *New England Ancestors* magazine and the New England Historic Genealogical Society, please visit *www.NewEnglandAncestors.org*.

Publisher's Cataloging-in-Publication Data

Rapaport, Diane

New England court records: a research guide for genealogists and historians /

by Diane Rapaport. – 1st ed.

p. cm.

Includes bibliographical references and index.

ISBN-13: 978-1-933623-07-8

ISBN-10: 1-933623-07-1

1. Court records—Research—New England.

2. New England—Genealogy—Library Resources.

3. New England—Genealogy—Archival Resources.

4. New England—Genealogy—Handbooks, Manuals, etc.

5. New England—History—Sources.

929.10974

Library of Congress Control Number: 2005908261

Cover design by Judith Arisman

Production by Arrow Graphics, Inc.

Printed by Thomson-Shore, Inc.

To my father, Willis "Bill" Neff,
who brought the past to life.
1927-2004

———◆———

CONTENTS

———•—•—

Preface	xi
Acknowledgments	xiii
Introduction	xv

PART I: UNDERSTANDING THE BASICS

Chapter 1 American Legal System — 3
    Sources of Law — 3
    Common Law: Created by Courts — 4
    Trial and Appellate Courts — 5
    State and Federal Courts — 6

Chapter 2 New England Courts — 7
    State Courts — 7
    Federal Courts — 9

Chapter 3 Types of Court Records — 11
    Civil and Criminal Lawsuits — 11
    Specialized Court Records — 31
    Appeals — 34

Chapter 4 Where to Look for Court Records — 47
    Reliable Sources — 47
    Published Records — 48
    Original Records — 49
    Court Records to be Discovered — 50

PART II: GETTING SPECIFIC, STATE BY STATE

Chapter 5 Finding and Using the Resources in *Part II* — 55
    Organization of *Part II* — 55
    Research Tips — 56

Chapter 6 Connecticut State Courts — 63
    Court History Timeline — 63
    Connecticut Courts Today — 65
    Where to Find Court Records — 66
        Statewide or General Sources — 66
        Fairfield County — 72
        Hartford County — 78
        Litchfield County — 86
        Middlesex County — 91

New Haven County   95
New London County   100
Tolland County   106
Windham County   108

Chapter 7 Maine State Courts   115
Court History Timeline   115
Maine Courts Today   118
Where to Find Court Records   119
  Statewide or General Sources   119
  Androscoggin County   123
  Aroostook County   125
  Cumberland County   126
  Franklin County   128
  Hancock County   129
  Kennebec County   131
  Knox County   133
  Lincoln County   135
  Oxford County   138
  Penobscot County   139
  Piscataquis County   141
  Sagadahoc County   142
  Somerset County   143
  Waldo County   144
  Washington County   145
  York County   146

Chapter 8 Massachusetts State Courts   153
Court History Timeline   153
Massachusetts Courts Today   157
Where to Find Court Records   158
  Statewide or General Sources   158
  Barnstable County   166
  Berkshire County   169
  Bristol County   172
  Dukes County   177
  Essex and (Old) Norfolk County   178
  Franklin County   185
  Hampden County   188
  Hampshire County   190
  Middlesex County   195
  Nantucket County   202
  Norfolk County   204
  Plymouth County   208
  Suffolk County   212
  Worcester County   223

Chapter 9 New Hampshire State Courts   229
   Court History Timeline   229
   New Hampshire Courts Today   231
   Where to Find Court Records   232
      Statewide or General Sources   232
      Belknap County   237
      Carroll County   239
      Cheshire County   240
      Coos County   241
      Grafton County   242
      Hillsborough County   244
      Merrimack County   247
      Rockingham County   249
      Strafford County   252
      Sullivan County   254

Chapter 10 Rhode Island State Courts   257
   Court History Timeline   257
   Rhode Island Courts Today   259
   Where to Find Court Records   260
      Statewide or General Sources   260
      Bristol County   266
      Kent County   267
      Newport County   270
      Providence County   273
      Washington County   279

Chapter 11 Vermont State Courts   285
   Court History Timeline   285
   Vermont Courts Today   286
   Where to Find Court Records   287
      Statewide or General Sources   288
      Addison County   293
      Bennington County   295
      Caledonia County   297
      Chittenden County   298
      Essex County   301
      Franklin County   301
      Grand Isle County   303
      Lamoille County   303
      Orange County   304
      Orleans County   305
      Rutland County   307
      Washington County   309
      Windham County   310
      Windsor County   312

Chapter 12 **Federal Courts in New England**   317
 Court History Timeline   317
 Federal Courts Today   320
 Where to Find Court Records   321
  General Sources   321
  Connecticut   328
  Maine   331
  Massachusetts   333
  New Hampshire   336
  Rhode Island   337
  Vermont   339

PART III: SAMPLING THE SOURCES

Chapter 13 Indexes to Court Records:
 People of Color in Colonial *Rhode Island*   345

Chapter 14 Computer Database:
 Slander in Nineteenth-Century *Maine*   349

Chapter 15 Federal Court Records:
 Bankruptcy in Post-Civil War *Vermont*   359

Chapter 16 Justice of the Peace Records:
 Local Justice in Cornwall, *Connecticut*   369

Chapter 17 Law Library Resources:
 Will Contest in Twentieth-Century *New Hampshire* 377

Chapter 18 Old-Fashioned Research:
 Scandal in Seventeenth-Century *Massachusetts*   387

APPENDIX

Contact Information   395
 State Courts   395
 Federal Courts   415
 Archives and Other Repositories   416
 Law Libraries   427
 Publishers   430
Glossary   432
Recommended Reading   441

INDEX   447

PREFACE

ourt records open windows to the past. Through the pages of court records, we meet long-ago people from all walks of life and experience their passions and concerns, sometimes in their own words. No other source offers genealogists and historians such a wealth of information. Luckily for today's researchers, many old New England court records survive, on ink-splotched scraps of brittle paper or reels of microfilm, and in published volumes, CDs and Internet web sites.

Court records are central to my own work. As many readers already know, I write the "Tales from the Courthouse" column for *New England Ancestors* magazine,[a] highlighting true colonial court cases—amusing, poignant, and sometimes shocking—of remarkable men and women nearly lost to history. These feisty characters prove that human nature changes little, no matter how many centuries pass, and I enjoy sharing their stories.

Although I appreciate court records for the human-interest stories they contain, I began studying legal cases for a very different reason: to become a lawyer. Thirty years ago, after receiving a B.A. degree in American history, I went to law school, graduated with a *Juris Doctor* (J.D.) degree, and worked as a trial lawyer for several years in Minneapolis, Minnesota. Eventually I moved to Massachusetts, where I became a partner in a Boston law firm.

During those years of practicing law, I occasionally pursued genealogical research and continued studying colonial history in my spare time. One day, reading a history of my own town, Lexington, Massachusetts, I ran across mention of a seventeenth-century incident that I never learned about in college—the sale of Scottish prisoners to New England colonists in the mid 1600s. Those unwilling immigrants, captured during the English Civil War, labored at towns and farms all over New England, and one of the Scotsmen settled in Lexington. Intrigued, I began investigating the fate of the Scottish war prisoners, not realizing how this quest would change my career.

The Lexington Scotsman, William Munro, arrived at Boston harbor with a shipload of other Scottish war prisoners in 1652. His name now appears on landmarks all over Lexington, and town histories suggest that Munro was a seventeenth-century success story, rags to near-riches, Scottish prisoner to colonial landowner. Most of what I read about William Munro—where he bought land and whom he married and when his children were born—revealed little about the kind of man he was. As a lawyer, I naturally wondered whether court records might offer more detail, although I suspected that previous historians and genealogists had long ago mined this obvious source of information about one of Lexington's leading families. Thus, I had modest expectations when I decided to check court records at the Massachusetts Archives, not imagining that anything significant would turn up.

As you probably can guess, I uncovered a wonderful cache of court files about William Munro, material apparently overlooked for hundreds of years, some of it in Munro's

---

[a] *New England Ancestors* is a publication of the New England Historic Genealogical Society, Boston, Massachusetts.

own words. For the first time, in the pages of a lawsuit titled *Row v. Bacon*, I could visualize William Munro, this stubborn Scotsman in a quest for justice against an arrogant foe. The case did not involve famous people or enormous amounts of money. It would not have garnered much publicity in its day (had newspapers been available to report on it). But this lawsuit—the "Case of the Purloined Pigs," as I like to call it—was hard-fought and emotional, as only a neighborhood dispute can be, and the jumble of faded handwritten documents spoke volumes about the character of the participants.

By then I was hooked on old court records, and I continued scouring seventeenth-century case files for clues about the other Scottish war prisoners. I found a treasure trove of information about these forgotten men, and my first article about this research, "Scots for Sale: The Fate of the Scottish Prisoners in Seventeenth-Century Massachusetts," appeared in *New England Ancestors* magazine.[b] More articles and my "Tales from the Courthouse" series followed, until finally I turned to research and writing as a full-time career. New England court records remain my most important research source, and the inspiration for this book.

As a former trial lawyer, I bring a unique insider's perspective to court records research. I also understand the needs of historical and genealogical researchers, who may have little experience with court records because:

- They assume that legal documents are difficult to read, full of "legalese," understandable only by trained lawyers. Court records come in many forms, some more complicated than others, but anyone can learn to read them for historical or genealogical purposes.

- They doubt that their own law-abiding ancestors ever found themselves in court. Early New England, however, was a very litigious place, and many people had occasion to appear in court as parties or witnesses. Anyone who thinks that the "litigation explosion" is a modern phenomenon should read the old court records!

- They do not know where to look. No comprehensive guide to New England court records has ever been available—until now.

I wrote this book to provide the answers that you need. *New England Court Records: A Research Guide for Genealogists and Historians* contains substantial detail, useful for experienced researchers, but with enough of the basics about courts and their records so that beginners—such as history students or those new to genealogy—can use court records with confidence.

Read the *Introduction* first, for an overview of the book's features, and be sure to review *Chapter 5: Finding and Using the Resources in Part II*, before you turn to the state-by-state source listings. Most readers will be surprised to learn that original New England court records are available in public and private repositories throughout the United States—not just in courthouses—and that published sources are plentiful. Finally, in the last chapter of this book, revisit *Row v. Bacon* for an unexpected twist to the story—a reminder that some of your best finds in the old court records may be pure serendipity, no matter how carefully you plot your research. Who knows what discoveries await you!

---

[b] Diane Rapaport, "Scots for Sale: The Fate of the Scottish Prisoners in Seventeenth-Century Massachusetts," *New England Ancestors* 4 (Winter 2003): 30-32.

ACKNOWLEDGMENTS

———◆•◆———

No one can write a reference manual—particularly a book spanning nearly four centuries—without help. *New England Court Records: A Research Guide for Genealogists and Historians* is no exception, although I did not realize, at the beginning, what a massive research project lay ahead. I expected to find court records in courthouses and archives, and in microfilm and books, but I underestimated the enormous volume of material available to researchers, the scattered nature of those resources, and the logistical challenges that I would face in organizing this information.

Luckily, hundreds of people were eager to assist—court clerks, archivists, librarians, historians, genealogists, lawyers, judges, and members of local historical and genealogical societies. So many individuals and institutions responded to my inquiries, with such generosity and enthusiasm, that I can never thank them all by name—the list would go on and on, and inevitably I would overlook someone. All of these people contributed to making this book more complete and accurate, but I, of course, am responsible for any errors or omissions that remain.

I am profoundly grateful to everyone who helped to make this book a reality, but I owe special thanks to:

The people who reviewed and commented on sections of the manuscript at various stages of production, contributing immeasurably to the finished book: Scott Andrew Bartley, who read the Vermont chapter and also saved me hours of research in back issues of *The Mayflower Descendant*; Jane Fletcher Fiske, whose transcriptions of early Rhode Island court records inspired a chapter in my book; Walter V. Hickey, the self-described "kid in a candy store" at the National Archives and Records Administration, Northeast Region, who introduced me to the fascinating world of federal court records and made me wish that I could be an archivist; Milli S. Kenney-Knudsen, whose familiarity with New Hampshire archives and fine eye for editorial detail enhanced that state's chapter; Melinde Lutz Sanborn, who shared her unparalleled knowledge of Massachusetts colonial court records and her zeal for genealogical research; Helen A. Shaw, whose experience with Maine court records, especially the old files in Lincoln County, helped me with the Maine chapter; Kip Sperry, who provided information about the LDS Family History Centers and the Genealogical Society of Utah; and Helen Schatvet Ullmann, who offered encouragement and advice about Connecticut resources.

The New England Historic Genealogical Society, particularly D. Brenton Simons and Ralph J. Crandall, who recognized the need for a court records guidebook and urged me to launch this project; and archivist Timothy Salls, who searched for court records in the Society's manuscript collections and provided images for the book cover and some of the illustrations.

Others who went "above and beyond" in their efforts to assist my research for this book:

In Connecticut: Mark H. Jones, Bruce Stark and Mel E. Smith, Connecticut State Archives; Barbara Austen, Connecticut Historical Society; Virginia Apple, Connecticut

Judicial Branch; Michael Gannett, Cornwall Town Historian, and the Cornwall Historical Society.

In Maine: Jeffrey D. Henthorn, Administrative Office of the Courts; Roy Wells, Maine State Archives; Dana Lippitt, Bangor Museum & Center for History; and Eve Anderson, Thomaston Historical Society.

In Massachusetts: Elizabeth Bouvier, Judicial Archives, Supreme Judicial Court; Michael Comeau and Jennifer Fauxsmith, Massachusetts Archives; Stuart Culy and Jean Nudd, National Archives and Records Administration, Northeast Region; Dana L. Leavitt, Massachusetts Superior Court; Glendon J. Buscher, Jr., Esq., Massachusetts Land Court; Kaari Tari, Westford Town Clerk; Jean Williams, Cary Memorial Library, Lexington.

In New Hampshire: Frank C. Mevers and Brian N. Burford, New Hampshire Division of Archives and Records Management.

In Rhode Island: Kenneth S. Carlson, Rhode Island State Archives; and Andrew Smith, Rhode Island Judicial Records Center.

In Vermont: Tanya L. Marshall, Vermont Judicial Records Program, Vermont State Archives; Paul J. Donovan, Vermont Department of Libraries; and Paul Carnahan, Vermont Historical Society Library.

I saved the most important thanks for last: to my husband David Rapaport, whose love and support never wavered during the long months of writing this book (even when I spent much of our summer vacation editing the manuscript). I hope that he knows—now and always—how much I appreciate him.

INTRODUCTION

In early New England, courts and judges played a central role in the lives of all citizens. "Going to law" was the common remedy for disputes large and small—from the complicated business affairs of trans-Atlantic merchants to neighborhood squabbles over insulting remarks or wandering livestock. But few modern-day Americans ever enter a courthouse, and their trial experience may be limited to a brief stint of jury duty or watching "Court TV." Unless you happen to be a lawyer, you probably know little about New England courts, the types of court documents available, or how to find those records.

Part I: Understanding the Basics provides those fundamentals, so that anyone—from novice researchers to experienced historians or genealogists—can learn to read and use court records. This part of the book explains basic concepts about American law, the types of courts in New England, legal documents that you are likely to encounter and the specialized terminology that you need to know. If you want more detail, however, check the *Glossary* and *Recommended Reading* in the *Appendix* at the back of the book.

Then, when you are ready to begin court records research, turn to *Part II: Getting Specific, State by State*. There you will find separate chapters for each New England state—Connecticut, Maine, Massachusetts, New Hampshire, Rhode Island and Vermont—and a chapter about the federal courts operating in the region. Each chapter summarizes the history and structure of the courts in that jurisdiction—from the seventeenth to the twenty-first centuries—followed by an extensive list of court records available at hundreds of sources—in courthouses and archives, books, microfilm, and the latest digital/electronic resources (which you can access without leaving home!). Read the research tips in *Chapter 5* to make the most effective use of these resources, and check the *Appendix* for complete contact information.

For some practical research examples, review *Part III: Sampling the Sources.* Six chapters highlight court records from each New England state—different sources and a variety of time periods—with step-by-step methods that you can apply to your own genealogical or historical research projects. Learn about specialized indexes and computer databases, and types of records that deserve more attention from researchers—such as federal bankruptcy papers, local justice of the peace files and law library resources.

Finally, to stay current on the latest research sources, visit *QuillPenPress.com* for free online updates of *New England Court Records*, including new listings for *Part II*. Keep me posted on your discoveries, so that the next edition of this book will be even better!

PART I

UNDERSTANDING

THE BASICS

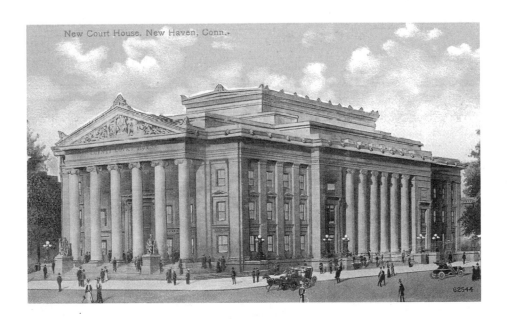

The image on the preceding page, from a vintage picture postcard,
depicts the county courthouse in New Haven, Connecticut, ca. 1915.
Courtesy of the Connecticut Judicial Branch.

CHAPTER 1

---◆·◆---

AMERICAN LEGAL SYSTEM

When English settlers landed on New England shores in the 1600s, they brought centuries-old legal traditions and a strong commitment to the rule of law. As they struggled to build homes and feed their families in the new colonies, transplanted Englishmen quickly established courts modeled on the institutions of the old country. These early courts were surprisingly sophisticated for a rough-hewn society—with jury trials, literate judges and careful recordkeeping—and they laid the foundation for America's current system of law and justice.

Over the years, American courts have changed and evolved—those specifics appear in the chapters of *Part II*—but certain features of the legal system remain relatively constant. Researchers need to understand these basic concepts:

- American law comes from many sources, including the Constitution and the three branches of government: legislative, executive and judicial.

- Courts create legal rules—known as the *common law*—in the process of deciding individual cases.

- The extent of a court's lawmaking power depends upon whether it is a *trial* or *appellate* court.

- Each state—*and* the federal government—has its own legal system, laws and courts.

Sources of Law

The Constitution

After the American Revolution, the former colonies joined as the United States of America and ratified a Constitution that became the "supreme Law of the Land." People sometimes disagree, of course, about how to interpret the Constitution's provisions, and this important document does not contain all of the legal rules governing the United States. The Constitution establishes a framework, however, for organizing the federal government and resolving disputes: a three-part division of powers among the legislative, executive and judicial branches, which create and interpret the law. In addition to the federal Constitution, each state has its own constitution and government, with the same division into legislative, executive and judicial branches. Both state and federal governments have lawmaking power.

Legislative Power

Legislatures—composed of representatives elected by the people—enact laws called *statutes*. The legislative branch also controls many details about how the other two branches of government operate. For example, Congress can create and abolish federal courts, as well as executive agencies, and determine the scope of their power.

Executive Power

The executive branch (headed by the President of the United States, or the governor in each state) is charged with enforcing the law. Some statutes enacted by the legislature are very specific, but others require further interpretation, so agencies of the executive branch can create legally-binding rules and regulations. The President and most governors also issue executive orders, which have the force of law.

Executive agencies sometimes exercise "quasi-judicial" powers, conducting hearings and issuing decisions in their areas of expertise—such as environmental law, or certain regulated industries, like food and drugs or public transportation. These *administrative law* sources, although important in determining legal rights and responsibilities, are beyond the scope of this book. *See Appendix: Recommended Reading* for more information about the history of executive agencies (created in the late nineteenth century) and the role of administrative law in America's legal system.

Judicial Power

The courts—the third branch of government—exercise judicial power under state and federal constitutions and play a complex role in developing the law. Courts have the power of *judicial review*, to determine whether acts of the legislative and executive branches are constitutional. Courts interpret and apply the Constitution, statutes and administrative regulations to resolve disputes between litigants—individuals, corporations, different branches of government, etc. In the process of deciding individual cases, courts also create *common law*.

Common Law: Created by Courts

As courts respond to conflict in specific cases, they develop a body of decisions to guide their resolution of future disputes. This common law system, inherited from English legal tradition, offers fairness and stability through the doctrine of *precedent* or *stare decisis* (Latin for "let the decision stand"). Under this doctrine, courts must follow the holding or legal principle of a past case in deciding new cases with similar circumstances. Published court decisions or *reporters* (explained more fully in *Chapters 3, 4* and *17*) allow judges, lawyers and other researchers to study earlier cases, determine precedent applicable to a current case, or evaluate the legal impact of future conduct.

The common law grows and develops over time, giving courts flexibility to react and adapt to changing conditions. When automobiles replaced horse-drawn carriages in the early twentieth century, for example, courts gradually altered the common law of negligence as new cases raised novel legal issues. Advances in science and technology constantly challenge courts to rethink the common law. Where precedent no longer meets the needs of an evolving society, courts may create new common law rights and duties.

Civil Law: Different Meanings

The common law system serves English and American courts well, but many other countries (in Europe, Latin America, Africa and Asia) have chosen a *civil law* system, based on principles from Roman law. In a civil law court, judges apply and interpret detailed codes of written laws, and their decisions have little weight in future cases.

The term civil law has an entirely different meaning in our common law system. In American courts, a *civil* case is a lawsuit to enforce a private or individual right, as distinguished from a *criminal* case, which is a lawsuit by the government to punish offenses against the public. Civil courts and records, when mentioned in this book, mean "not criminal," and should not be confused with the civil law system of other countries.

Law and Equity

Courts of our common law system distinguish between cases *at law* or *in equity*. Although the differences between law and equity kept legal scholars busy for centuries, the distinction no longer has much practical significance. Researchers should be aware of the terms, however, because early New England courts sometimes maintained separate records for the two types of lawsuits.

A case *at law* generally seeks monetary damages. A case *in equity* seeks *equitable relief* where money cannot adequately redress a wrong, and irreparable injury will result unless relief is granted. For example, the court may issue an *injunction*, ordering the defendant to *do* something (such as reinstating an employee who was fired), or to *stop* or refrain from doing something (*e.g.*, to cease the demolition of historic buildings).

Trial and Appellate Courts

In the American legal system, a court's lawmaking power depends upon whether it is a *trial* or *appellate* court. Most disputes between litigants are decided at the trial court level. There, the parties present evidence, the judge (or jury) determines the facts and applies the applicable law to reach a verdict, and the court issues a decision or *judgment* resolving the case. Generally decisions of a trial court are not binding on any other tribunal, and the losing party can ask an appellate court to review the judgment, to determine whether the trial court made an error of law. In recent years, many state courts have established a second appellate level—an intermediate appeals court—in addition to the "supreme" court of last resort.

Appellate courts usually do not hold new trials or hear evidence (although some courts in New England's history exercised dual trial and appellate functions, as described in the chapters of *Part II*). Instead, when a case is appealed, a panel of appellate court judges reviews the records generated by the trial court, and the parties (or their lawyers) debate the legal points in written *briefs* and oral argument. The appellate court then issues a decision *affirming* or *reversing* the trial court judgment, or ordering other relief. That decision not only resolves the case for the specific litigants, but may set a binding precedent in future cases, which other judges in the court system must follow. Many appellate court decisions are published in bound books called *reporters*.

State and Federal Courts

Each of the New England states—indeed, each of the fifty states—has its own legal system, laws and courts. Although these state systems are similar, and many generalizations can be made, they are not identical. Federal courts, established in 1789, also function within each state. *Chapter 2* explains basic concepts about state and federal courts. *See Part II* of this book, with separate chapters about the federal system and each state, for more information.

CHAPTER 2

NEW ENGLAND COURTS

In colonial New England, court day was a major event, turning the local tavern into a temporary courthouse, doubling a town's population overnight as people arrived from distant farms and frontier outposts. Wealthy gentlemen mingled with petitioners and witnesses of modest means—lumberjacks, sailors, blacksmiths, goodwives, servants, Indians—and jurors took their seats on benches in the tavern's best parlor. Judges in rich clothing (beaver-skin hats with feather plumes, gold-laced collars, perhaps a scarlet cloak) peered down from a long table on a specially-prepared platform, as the clerk dipped his quill pen into the ink pot and called out cases from a docket list.

Courts no longer meet in taverns, of course, and crowds seldom gather at today's courtrooms. Few people know what happens inside their own local courthouse, or how that courthouse differs from another in the next town. This chapter explains the basics that historians and genealogists should understand about the New England court system—the types of courts and the cases that they handle—before embarking on court records research.

State Courts

Types of State Courts

Part II of this book details court evolution from colonial times, and the current structure of the judicial branch, in each New England state. Court names vary, but each state is divided into a hierarchy of trial and appellate courts.

Multi-Level Court System

Generally each county has a multi-level trial court system—*municipal* or *district* courts handling small cases and misdemeanors, and one or more *superior* county courts with general jurisdiction over larger civil cases and serious crimes. Special *limited-jurisdiction* courts also resolve matters involving probate, family relations, land, etc. At the appellate level, some New England states have only one *supreme* court; others have *intermediate appellate* courts to share the burden of appeals from trial court judgments.

General Court

New England researchers inevitably encounter references to a *General Court*. This name is a frequent source of confusion, because it refers to the state legislature, a branch of government that is separate and distinct from the judiciary. Massachusetts and New Hampshire still call their legislature the General Court, and the name was used for the body of elected representatives in many of the New England colonies.

In the colonial days, legislative and judicial functions tended to blur, since legislators often performed double duty as judges of the trial and appeals court sessions. The General Court also sometimes acted much like a traditional court—hearing appeals, or accepting petitions directly from individuals on matters now normally handled by the judiciary. Sources of early General Court records are noted in the state chapters of *Part II*.

Types of Cases Handled by State Courts

New England state courts (and their colonial predecessors) have always handled a wide variety of cases. Although the substance and sources of the law differ from state to state, certain legal matters traditionally fall under state and local jurisdiction.

Civil Cases

Civil cases are court proceedings to enforce, redress, or protect a private or individual right. Issues decided by state courts include:

Torts: Defamation (slander and libel), negligence, nuisance, etc.

Commercial transactions: Contracts, sale of goods and services, debt collection, insurance, etc.

Family relations: Divorce, paternity and termination of parental rights, adoption and custody of children, name change, mental health and commitment, delinquency, etc.

Property issues: Title to real estate, zoning, landlord/tenant issues, inheritance and probate, trusts, guardianship and conservatorship, etc.

Other: Rights or duties under the state constitution, statutes, administrative regulations, common law, etc.

Criminal Cases

Most criminal cases—proceedings by the government to punish offenses against the public—are heard in state courts. The two basic categories of criminal cases are:

Felonies: Serious crimes, such as murder, burglary, rape, arson, etc., usually punished by more than one year in prison, or death.

Misdemeanors: Crimes less serious than felonies, usually punished by a fine or a brief term of confinement.

Other Matters

State (or colonial) courts also exercised jurisdiction over other matters, such as:

Admiralty and maritime cases: Disputes involving seamen's wages, contracts, salvage, whaling, prize cases, smuggling, etc. Colonial courts heard these cases until 1697, when royal vice-admiralty courts were established. Since 1789, admiralty matters have been handled by federal courts.

Naturalization: Both state and federal courts heard naturalization cases (granting United States citizenship) from 1789. Since 1991, however, most new citizens seek naturalization through an agency of the federal executive branch. *See Chapter 3* for further information.

Federal Courts

For historical and genealogical research from 1789 to the present, federal courts may be a source of relevant records. State and federal courts *both* operate within each of the New England states, and sometimes their functions overlap.

Types of Federal Courts

Today, the federal courts serving the New England states are:

U.S. District Courts, which handle trials of most federal cases, civil and criminal. Each state is a separate federal district.

U.S. Courts of Appeals, which handle appeals from U.S. District Courts. The United States has twelve regional Circuit Courts of Appeals, two in New England:

- **First Circuit**, based in Massachusetts, which serves Maine, Massachusetts, New Hampshire, Rhode Island (and Puerto Rico).

- **Second Circuit**, based in New York, which serves Connecticut, Vermont (and New York).

Specialized bodies, such as the **U.S. Bankruptcy Court**, exercise limited jurisdiction at one or more locations in each federal district.

U.S. Supreme Court, *see below*.

See also Chapter 12 for more information about the history and structure of the federal court system.

Types of Cases Handled by Federal Courts

Jurisdictional issues are too complex for a book of this scope, but in general, the federal courts hear the following types of disputes:

- Lawsuits in which the **United States is a party**
- Cases alleging **violation of the Constitution or a federal law**
- Disputes involving **citizens of different states**
- **Specialized matters**, such as:
    - Admiralty
    - Bankruptcy
    - Copyright
    - Federal Tax
    - Naturalization

United States Supreme Court

The Supreme Court, located in Washington, D.C., is the highest appellate court in the American legal system. Established in 1789, the Supreme Court originally heard appeals from the lower federal courts and cases from state courts about federal statutes. For the first century, Supreme Court justices also "rode circuit," presiding at trials with federal Circuit Court judges in the various states.

As the caseload of the federal courts increased, Congress gradually restricted the cases that could be reviewed by the Supreme Court. Now the Supreme Court hears a limited number of appeals annually from federal or state courts, usually involving important questions of federal law or Constitutional issues.

CHAPTER 3

TYPES OF COURT RECORDS

New England court records vary considerably in form and terminology, but you do not need a law school education to decipher them. This chapter describes the basic types of court records that you are likely to encounter, with numerous illustrations to help you recognize and make effective use of these documents in your own research. Read this information, and *Chapter 4*'s preview of where to find court records, before you plunge into the extensive resources of *Part II: Getting Specific, State by State*.

Civil and Criminal Lawsuits

Most of the records described in this book involve lawsuits—civil or criminal proceedings by one party against another in court. Often the parties resolve their differences and settle the case outside of court, but many lawsuits result in a trial, and sometimes one or more appeals to a higher authority by the party dissatisfied with the lower court's decision.

All of these court proceedings leave a paper trail—documents created by the *plaintiff* (who started the civil action) or the *defendant* (the one being sued civilly or prosecuted criminally), as well as by court and government officials or witnesses. These papers, court records, are maintained by the *court clerk* (sometimes called the *register*) until the action is resolved, and generally for some period of time afterward. Eventually, closed court records are transferred elsewhere for storage, preserved as archival records, or destroyed. (The varying state policies for records retention, where available, are explained in *Part II*. Ironically, researchers often can access court records from the seventeenth century more easily than twentieth-century records!) Some courts are making the transition to electronic recordkeeping, but most records of interest to today's genealogists and historians started out as paper documents.

Although different court actions—civil, criminal, probate, etc.—produce many kinds of records, three basic types are common to most cases: docket books, record books, and file papers.

Docket Books

Docket books contain chronological entries by the court clerk about each case. Sometimes early New England clerks kept separate civil and criminal docket books, or recorded civil entries in the front of the volume, and criminal entries in the back.

Civil Cases generally are numbered sequentially (although new case or docket numbers may be assigned later in the docket book if the matter is not resolved in one court session). Docket book entries include information about the names and roles of the parties (*e.g.*, *plaintiff*, *defendant*, *appellant*, *appellee*, *libellant*, *petitioner*, *respondent*, *claimant*, etc.; *see Appendix: Glossary*, for definitions). A brief summary of what happened at the court session usually follows: trial, jury verdict, court judgment, or continuance to another term. Sometimes the docket book lists papers filed with the clerk, court costs, or details about *executions* ("executing" on a judgment means seizing and selling property of a defendant to pay the plaintiff). For examples of civil docket book pages, *see Fig. 3.1, below*, and *Fig. 15.1* in *Chapter 15*.

Criminal Cases have similar docket book entries, although sometimes numbers are not assigned, and some of the terminology is different (for example, the court's judgment may be called a *sentence*). In early docket books, the defendant's race or origin ("Negro," "Indian," "Scotch," etc.) might be noted, or the master's name, if the defendant was a slave or servant.

Petitions in the docket book usually include the petitioner's name and reason for the petition (divorce, naturalization, adoption, insolvency, sale of land to pay debts of estate, etc.), as well as the action taken by the court.

Other Court Business, such as disbursement of funds to sheriffs or clerks to cover expenses of the court, may appear in the docket book at the end of the entries about a particular court session.

Since many courts retain docket books permanently, they may be the easiest court records to find—and probably the most important source to check first if no index is available. By reviewing docket books of the relevant time period, researchers often can locate names, case numbers, or court session dates that may help to access file papers.

Note: The term *docket* also means a court calendar, listing cases to be heard in a particular court session and the case numbers assigned to them. Today's courts often maintain their dockets electronically, in a computer database.

Record Books

Record books look so similar to docket books that researchers may have trouble distinguishing them; court clerks and archivists use both terms almost interchangeably. Both types of books provide comparable information: basic facts about cases or court sessions (dates of hearing, parties, juror lists, orders, judgments, etc.). The main difference is that record book entries tend to be more detailed, summarizing testimony and other information from the file papers, or copying the full text of court orders and judgments. *See Figs. 3.2-3.4, below*, for examples.

In early New England, while court was in session, clerks often took preliminary notes in a *waste book*, to be transcribed later into the permanent record book (sometimes called a *minute book*) as a chronological narrative of the court proceedings. Record books do not always include the case numbers, however, so researchers wanting to access file papers may need to trace a lawsuit through the docket books.

File Papers

The individual documents filed at various stages of a case are called file papers (also *case files* or *file packets*). The number of file papers accompanying any particular case can range from one or two documents to thousands of pages, although early files seldom were voluminous. These papers often contain details not summarized in the docket or record books and offer a wealth of information for genealogists and historians.

File papers can be more difficult to find than the other types of court records, but well worth the effort. Researchers usually must look for the originals, however, since file papers are less likely than docket or record books to be microfilmed or reproduced in published sources. Unfortunately, courts sometimes destroy original file papers without making copies. Even when preserved, file papers may wind up in scattered collections, separated from related documents, or they may languish unprocessed and largely inaccessible in an archival vault. *Part II* provides more details about where to look.

Civil File Papers

In a civil (non-criminal) case, the court file papers typically include:

Complaint
Document that starts a civil action, stating the basis for the plaintiff's claim, and a demand for relief. *See Fig. 3.5, below*.

Summons
Court order telling person to appear in court, *e.g.*, to answer a *complaint*, usually delivered (*served*) by a sheriff or constable. *See Fig. 3.6, below*. Similarly, a *subpoena* orders a witness to give evidence in court. *See Figs. 3.7* and *3.8, below*.

Writ of Attachment
Court order directing a sheriff or constable to seize the defendant's property, to guarantee his appearance in court. *See Fig. 3.9, below*. Both the *summons* and *writ of attachment* (often combined into one document) contain much useful information for genealogical and historical research, sometimes including details such as: case number; date and location of court session; names, residences and occupations of the parties; type of case, with summary of claim against defendant and the amount of damages sought; and name of judge or justice of the peace. On the reverse side of the writ, the *sheriff's return* itemizes property seized.

Interrogatories

Written questions submitted by one party in a lawsuit to the other party, which must be answered in writing as part of the *discovery* process before trial. Interrogatories are commonly used in modern litigation, and they appear in court records as early as the 1800s. *See Fig. 14.4, Chapter 14*, for an example of interrogatories in a nineteenth-century Maine slander case.

Deposition

Sworn testimony taken outside of court and recorded in writing, to be used as evidence in a court case. *See Fig. 3.10, below*. Depositions often provide a colorful glimpse of community life and personalities, and reveal facts difficult to find elsewhere—family relationships, ages of the witnesses, etc. In colonial days, depositions were written summaries, generally prepared by magistrates or other officials, paraphrasing the testimony of witnesses, similar to today's *affidavit*. Modern depositions are verbatim transcripts of testimony, recorded by a court reporter or stenographer.

Motion

Written (or oral) request that the court make a specific ruling or order. Parties communicate with the court by filing motions before, during and after a trial, on a variety of matters, such as:

- **Motion to amend** a document previously filed. The plaintiff, for example, may want to correct errors or add new claims to a complaint.
- **Motion to compel discovery**, to force the opponent to answer interrogatories or provide other information.
- **Motion to dismiss** the case before trial because of settlement or a procedural defect (lack of jurisdiction, failure to state a claim, etc.).
- **Motion in limine**, asking before trial to exclude certain evidence.
- **Motion to continue** (postpone) some action in the case.

Judgment

Court's final decision in a case, usually specifying the amount of money awarded as damages. *See Fig. 3.11, below*.

Bill of Costs

Itemized statement of expenses incurred by one party in a lawsuit, such as filing fees, sheriff's charges for serving documents, costs for making copies of court documents, witness fees (a calculation based on how far the witness traveled, and the number of days spent in court). The winning party may be awarded "costs" as part of the judgment. *See Fig. 14.2, Chapter 14*, for a bill of costs from a nineteenth-century Maine slander case.

Bond

Written promise to do some act or to pay money to court for specific purpose, such as appeal or bail. A *bastardy bond*, for example, was paid by an alleged father, to guarantee that the illegitimate child did not become a public charge. *See Fig. 3.12, below*.

Writ of Execution

Court order (similar to *writ of attachment*, but issued *after* trial) directing a sheriff or constable to seize and sell the defendant's property to satisfy a judgment. (Winning a lawsuit does not guarantee payment!) *Sheriff's return*, on the back of the document, sometimes provides detail about the property seized (such as boundary lines and owners of neighboring land, or amounts and types of crops, etc.). *See Fig. 3.13, below,* and *Figs. 16.3* and *16.4* in *Chapter 16.*

Criminal File Papers

File papers in a criminal case are similar to civil ones—*depositions, bonds* or *bills of costs,* for example—but researchers also may encounter these criminal court records:

Warrant
Court order requiring a sheriff or constable to arrest someone and bring him to court for questioning about an alleged offense. Like the comparable *summons* in a civil case, the warrant often contains much useful information, including the accused's name, residence and occupation. *See Fig. 3.14, below.*

Indictment
Formal charge (also known as a *presentment*) issued by a grand jury to the court, accusing someone of an offense. An indictment is similar to a *complaint* in a civil case, except that the government is the complaining party in a criminal action. Sometimes the indictment is called a *true bill,* and may include the names of the jurors or witnesses, as well as information about the defendant and his alleged offense. In *Fig. 3.15, below,* a 1731 grand jury on Martha's Vineyard "presented" three men for "pedlering and seling goods contarary to Law" and another for "Seling Strong Drink." *Fig. 3.16, below,* illustrates a Vermont grand jury's decision *not* to indict, returning *no bill* after hearing evidence against a teenager arrested for bringing a pistol to school in 1857.

Sentence
Court's *judgment* in a criminal case, finding defendant guilty and specifying the legal consequences, such as amount of monetary fine, length of time to be served in prison, etc.

Recognizance
Written contract to keep the peace for a specified period of time, or to appear in court on a certain date, etc., or otherwise to pay money or suffer a penalty, *e.g.,* a bail *bond.*

Mittimus
Court order directing sheriff to deliver a person to prison.

Inquest
Coroner's investigation, sometimes with a jury, into the death of someone who died in prison or under suspicious circumstances. Inquest papers may include sworn testimony of witnesses.

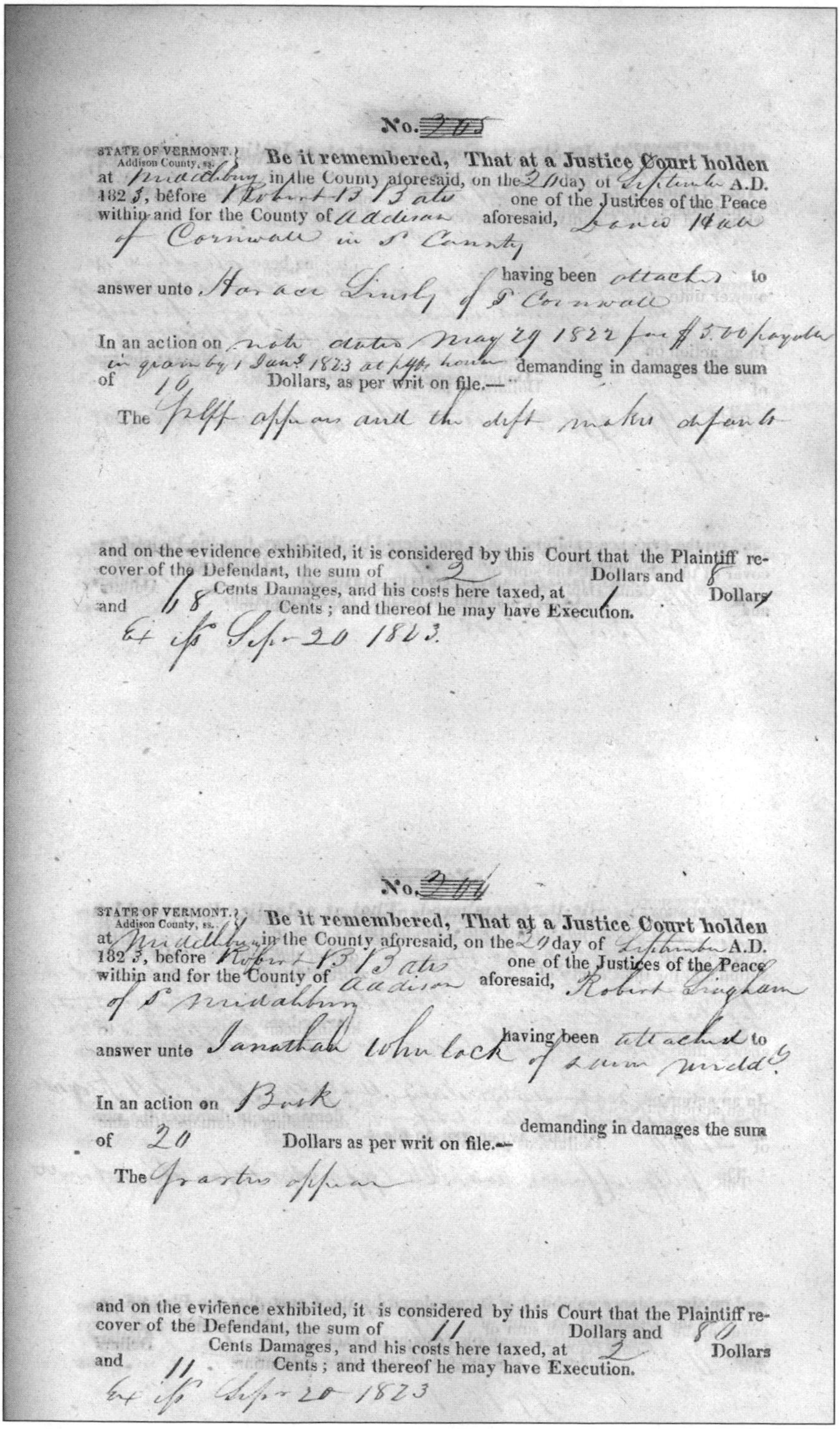

No. *[205]*

STATE OF VERMONT,
Addison County, ss.

Be it remembered, That at a Justice Court holden at *Middlebury* in the County aforesaid, on the *21* day of *September* A.D. 182*3*, before *Robert B. Bates* one of the Justices of the Peace within and for the County of *Addison* aforesaid, *Daniel Hall* *of Cornwall in s.d County*

answer unto *Horace Finly of s.d Cornwall* having been *attached* to

In an action on *note dated May 29 1822 for $5.00 payable in grain by 1 Jan.y 1823 at s.d house* demanding in damages the sum of *10* Dollars, as per writ on file.—

The *plff appears and the deft makes default*

and on the evidence exhibited, it is considered by this Court that the Plaintiff recover of the Defendant, the sum of *2* Dollars and *8* Cents Damages, and his costs here taxed, at *1* Dollars and *68* Cents; and thereof he may have Execution.

Ex ifs Sep.r 20 1823.

No. *[206]*

STATE OF VERMONT,
Addison County, ss.

Be it remembered, That at a Justice Court holden at *Middlebury* in the County aforesaid, on the *29* day of *September* A.D. 182*3*, before *Robert B. Bates* one of the Justices of the Peace within and for the County of *Addison* aforesaid, *Robert Bingham* *of s.d Middlebury*

answer unto *Janathan Whitlock of s.d middl.y* having been *attached* to

In an action on *Book* demanding in damages the sum of *20* Dollars as per writ on file.—

The *parties appear*

and on the evidence exhibited, it is considered by this Court that the Plaintiff recover of the Defendant, the sum of *11* Dollars and *8* Cents Damages, and his costs here taxed, at *2* Dollars and *11* Cents; and thereof he may have Execution.

Ex ifs Sep.r 20 1823

Fig. 3.1. Page from Justice Court Docket Book, Addison County, Vermont, 1819-1827, docket #205 and #206. *Courtesy of Vermont State Archives.*

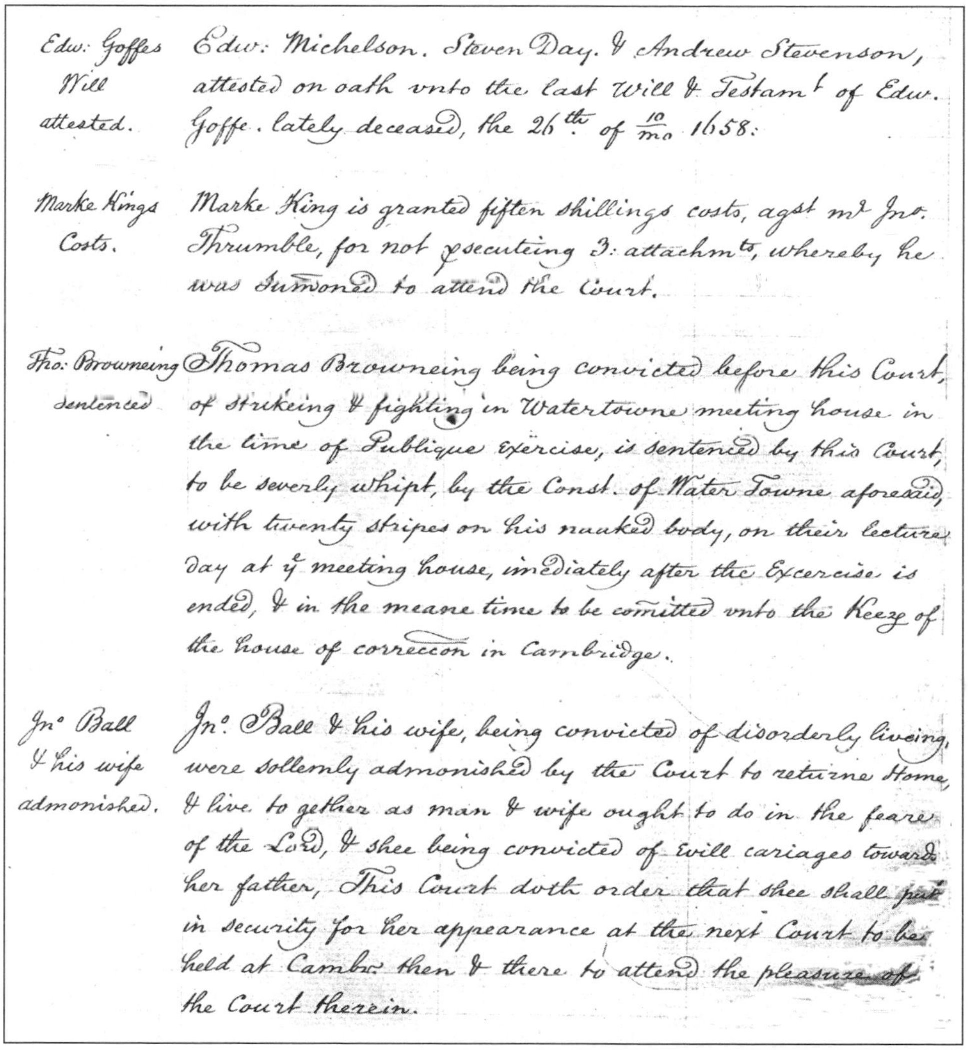

Edw: Goffes Will attested.	Edw: Michelson. Steven Day. & Andrew Stevenson, attested on oath vnto the last Will & Testam.t of Edw. Goffe. lately deceased, the 26.th of $\frac{10}{mo}$ 1658:
Marke Kings Costs.	Marke King is granted fiften shillings costs, agst mr Jno. Thrumble, for not prosecuteing 3: attachm.ts, whereby he was summoned to attend the Court.
Tho: Browneing sentenced	Thomas Browneing being convicted before this Court, of strikeing & fighting in Watertowne meeting house in the time of Publique Exercise, is sentenced by this Court, to be severly whipt, by the Const. of Water Towne aforesaid, with twenty stripes on his naaked body, on their lecture day at ye meeting house, imediately after the Excercise is ended, & in the meane time to be comitted vnto the Keep of the house of correccon in Carnbridge.
Jno Ball & his wife admonished.	Jno: Ball & his wife, being convicted of disorderly liveing, were sollemly admonished by the Court to returne Home, & live to gether as man & wife ought to do in the feare of the Lord, & shee being convicted of evill cariages toward her father, This Court doth order that shee shall put in security for her appearance at the next Court to be held at Cambr then & there to attend the pleasure of the Court therein.

Fig. 3.2. Detail from Middlesex County (Massachusetts) Court Record Books, 1649-1663, 1671-1686. 3 vols. Pulsifer Transcript, 1:166. Court session in Charlestown, December 28, 1658. *Courtesy of Judicial Archives/Massachusetts Archives.*

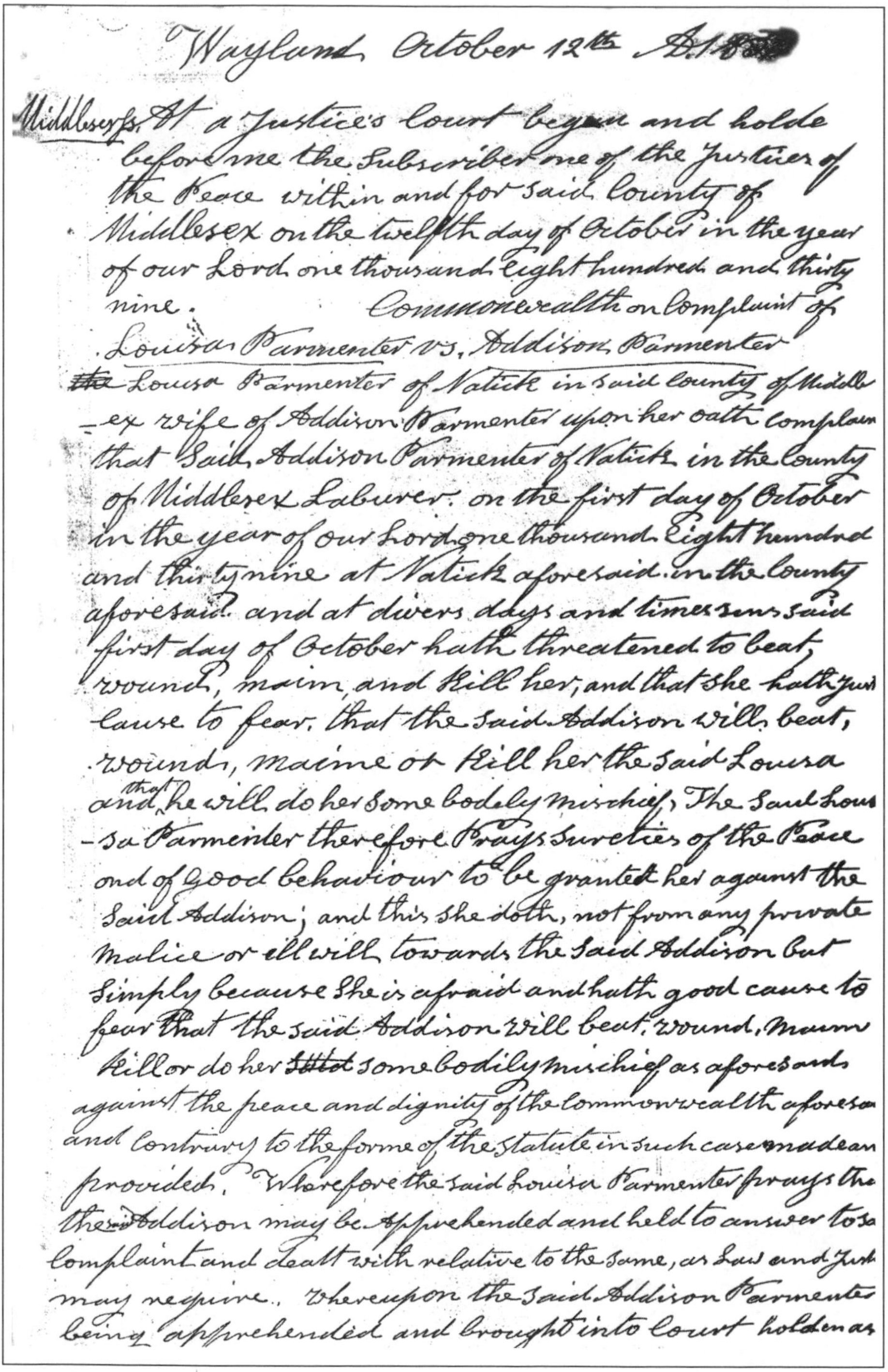

Wayland, October 12th A.D.

Middlesex ss. At a Justice's Court begun and holden
before me the Subscriber one of the Justices of
the Peace within and for said County of
Middlesex on the twelfth day of October in the year
of our Lord one thousand eight hundred and thirty
nine. Commonwealth on Complaint of
Louisa Parmenter vs. Addison Parmenter
Louisa Parmenter of Natick in said County of Middle
-sex wife of Addison Parmenter upon her oath complain
that said Addison Parmenter of Natick in the County
of Middlesex Laborer on the first day of October
in the year of our Lord one thousand eight hundred
and thirty nine at Natick aforesaid in the County
aforesaid and at divers days and times since said
first day of October hath threatened to beat,
wound, maim, and kill her, and that she hath just
cause to fear that the said Addison will beat,
wound, maime or kill her the said Louisa
and that he will do her some bodily mischief, The said Loui
-sa Parmenter therefore prays Sureties of the Peace
and of good behaviour to be granted her against the
said Addison; and this she doth, not from any private
malice or ill will towards the said Addison but
simply because she is afraid and hath good cause to
fear that the said Addison will beat, wound, maim
kill or do her some bodily mischief as aforesaid
against the peace and dignity of the commonwealth aforesa
and contrary to the forme of the statute in such case made and
provided. Wherefore the said Louisa Parmenter prays the
the said Addison may be Apprehended and held to answer to s
complaint and dealt with relative to the same, as Law and Just
may require. Whereupon the said Addison Parmenter
being apprehended and brought into Court holden as

Fig. 3.3. Page from Record Book of Justice of the Peace David Heard, Wayland,
Massachusetts, October 12, 1839, in case of Natick woman, Louisa Parmenter,
whose ex-husband "threatened to beat, wound, maim, and kill her."
Courtesy of Wayland (Massachusetts) Historical Society.

70

UNITED STATES COMMISSIONER'S RECORD OF

(Erase and supply words as the facts require.) The W. H. Anderson Co., Law Book Publishers, Cincinnati, Ohio.

United States of America,　　　　　District of *Mass.* SS.　　　　Division

No. *148*

THE UNITED STATES OF AMERICA

vs.

Ng Yuk Cown

Before me, *John L. Rice* a United States Commissioner for said District, complaint and affidavit was made — ~~or made and certified copy of complaint was presented~~ — on this *ninth* day of *April*, 1915, by *John A. McCabe, U.S. Chinese Inspector* charging in substance that on ~~or about this~~ *ninth* day of *April*, 1915, at *Spam* *Northampton* in said District, the defendant, *Ng Yuk Cown* in violation of ~~Section~~ , ~~Chapter~~ , ~~Act~~ of the Revised Statutes of the United States ~~Penal Code~~, did ~~unlawfully~~ *is a Chinese person being and remaining in the United States unlawfully*

~~Complaint approved by the U.S. District Attorney on~~ , 19 .

On *April 9*, 1915, issued warrant to *John J. Mitchell* U.S. Marshal, *returnable before me.*

On *April 9*, 1915, warrant returned, indorsed as follows:

"Received this warrant on the *9th* day of *April*, 1915, at *Springfield* and executed the same by arresting the within named *Ng Yuk Cown* at ~~said~~ *Springfield* on the *9th* day of *April*, 1915, and have *his body* now in court, as within I am commanded.

John J. Mitchell U.S. Marshal.

District of *Mass.*

By *Edward J. Snyden*, Deputy."

On , 19 , issued subpœna for the following witnesses on behalf of U. S.:

On , 19 , said subpœna was returned, indorsed as follows: "Received this writ , 19 , and on or before , 19 , served the same on the within named by leaving a certified copy thereof with each of them personally; and on the within named by leaving such copy at the usual place of residence of each of them. The other person within named not found.

, U. S. Marshal.

District of

By , Deputy."

On , 19 , issued subpœna for the following witnesses in behalf of U. S. (or) defendant:

On , 19 , said subpœna was returned, indorsed as follows: "Received this writ , 19 , and on or before , 19 , served the same on the within named by leaving a certified copy thereof with each of them personally; and on the within named by leaving such copy at the usual place of residence of each of them. The other person within named not found.

, U. S. Marshal.

District of

By , Deputy."

On *April 9*, 1915, defendant was brought before me, the said United States Commissioner, at my office in the *City of Springfield* in said District, by *Edward J. Snyden* Deputy U. S. Marshal; and the complaint was then and there fully read and explained to the said defendant, who thereupon, for plea, said he is "~~not~~ guilty" as charged in said complaint.

John A. McCabe, Chinese Inspector appeared for the U. S. *Daniel E. Leary* appeared for defendant.

And thereupon, ~~in preliminary trial to determine whether there exists probable ground to believe said defendant guilty as charged, the following~~

FEES OF U. S. COMMISSIONER.
(See Act of May 28, 1896.)

Drawing complaint, with oath and jurat to same, 50c.　**50**

Copy of complaint, with certificate to same, 30c.　**30**

Issuing warrant of arrest, 75c; Entering marshal's return, warrant of arrest, 15c.　**90**

Issuing subpœna or subpœnas in said case, 25c.; with 5c for each of witnesses in addition to the first, c.; Ent. return of subp., 15c.

Drawing temporary bond of defendant and sureties, taking acknowledgment of same and justification of sureties, 75c.　**75**

Issu'g temp'y commitment and making copy of same, $1.00; Ent. ret. of temp. commit., 15c.

Administering oaths to U. S. witnesses on trial, 10c. each and J. witnesses for defendant.　**40**

Hearing and deciding on May , 191 , and reducing the testimony to writing when required by law or order of court, per diem, $5.00　**5 60**

Same, for one additional day on the day of , 191 , because the hearing could not be completed in one day, per diem, $5.00

Drawing final bond of defendant and sureties, taking acknowledgment of same, and justification of sureties, 75c.

Issuing final commitment and making copy of same, $1.00; Ent. return of final commit., 15c.

Recognizance of all witnesses in the case, defendant being held for court, 50c.

Oath to U. S. witnesses as to attendance and travel, 5c. each

Order, in duplicate, to pay first witness on behalf of U. S., 30c., and 5c. for each of additional U. S. witnesses.　**60**

Transcr. of proceed., required by order of court, and transm. of original papers to court, 60c.

Copy of warrant of arrest, with certificate to same, when defendant is held for court and original papers are not sent to court, 40c.

Examination and certificate under Section 1042, R. S., and all services connected therewith (date of commitment to serve sentence, , 19 ; period of imprisonment named in sentence, ; amount of fine and costs, $), $3.00　**8 45**

Fees of Witnesses, Guards, etc. (name of each)

John A. McCabe U. S.
John G. Sullivan Employee
Thos. W. G. Mallog

Ng Yuk Cown, May 14, 1915

Fig. 3.4. Page from U.S. Commissioner's Record of Proceedings in Criminal Cases, Springfield, Massachusetts, 1913-1918. Case #148, against Ng Yuk Cown, under Chinese Exclusion Act. NARA Record Group 21. *Courtesy of U.S. National Archives and Records Administration, Northeast Region.*

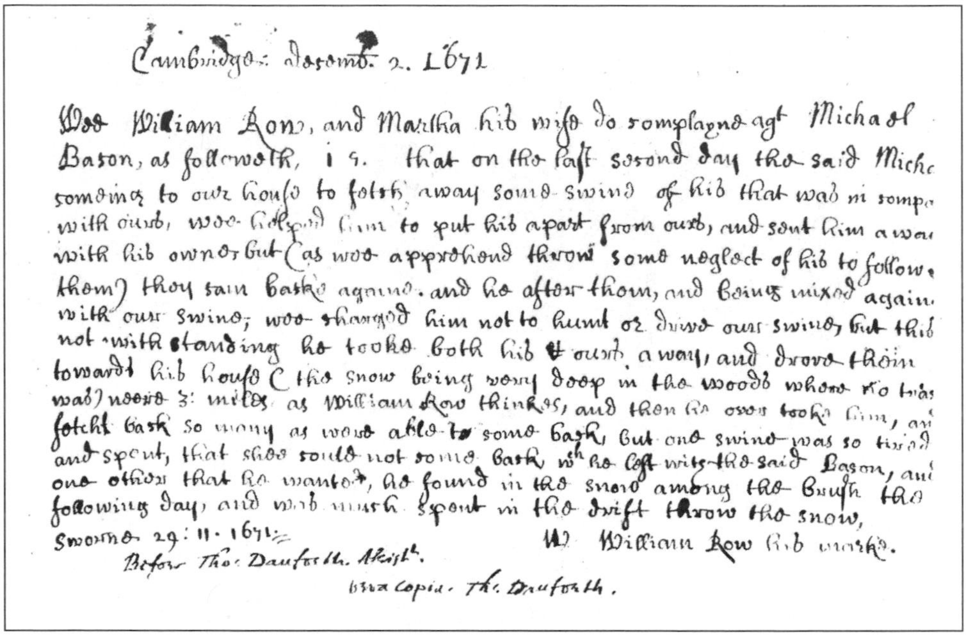

Cambridge: decemb. 2. 1671

Wee William Rowe, and Martha his wife do complayne agt Michael Bacon, as followeth, i.e. that on the last second day the said Michae comeing to our house to fetch away some swine of his that was in compa with ours, wee helped him to put his apart from ours, and sent him awa with his owne, but (as wee apprehend throu' some neglect of his to follow them) they cam backe againe. and he after them, and being mixed again with our swine, wee charged him not to hunt or drive our swine, but this not withstanding he tooke both his & ours away, and drove them towards his house (the snow being very deep in the woods where he was was) neere 3: miles as William Row thinkes, and then he over tooke him, an fetcht back so many as were able to come back, but one swine was so tired and spent, that shee could not come back wch he left with the said Bacon, an one other that he wanted, he found in the snow among the brush the following day, and was much spent in the drift throw the snow,

Sworne 29: 11. 1671. W William Row his marke.

Before Tho: Danforth. Assist.

Vera copia. Th: Danforth.

Fig. 3.5. Complaint of "William Row and Martha his wife" against Michael Bacon, December 2, 1671. Middlesex County (Massachusetts) Folio Collection 2, 59-2. *Courtesy of Judicial Archives/Massachusetts Archives.*

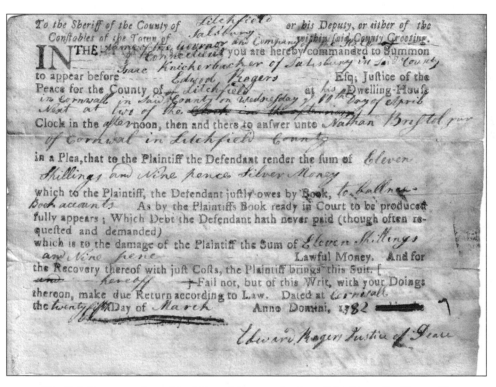

Fig. 3.6. Summons issued by Edward Rogers, Justice of the Peace for Cornwall, Connecticut, in case of *Nathan Bristol, Jr. v. Isaac Knickerbacher*, March 25, 1782. "Court Summons" box, Folder 2, Document 7. *Courtesy of Cornwall (Connecticut) Historical Society.*

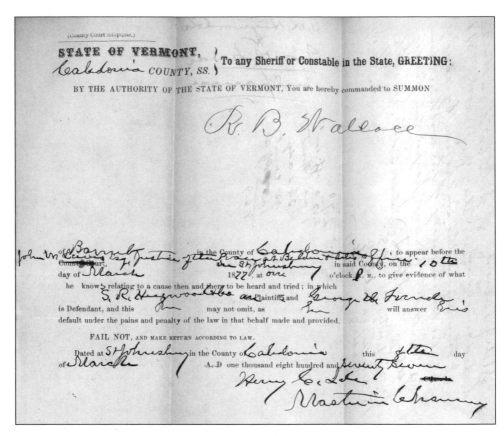

Fig. 3.7. Subpoena for witness R. B. Wallace, to testify at trial of *Heywood v. French*, Caledonia County, Vermont, March 1877. *Courtesy of Vermont State Archives.*

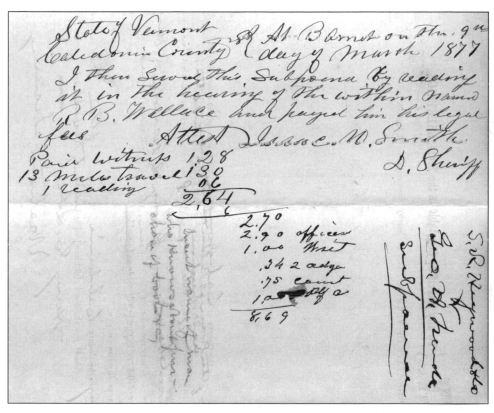

Fig. 3.8. Reverse side of Figure 3.7, the sheriff's return, which states that he "served this Subpoena by reading it in the hearing of…R. B. Wallace and payed him his legal fees," March 9, 1877. *Courtesy of Vermont State Archives.*

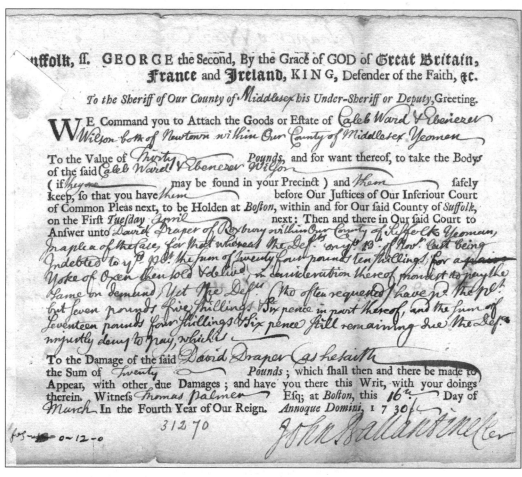

Fig. 3.9. Writ of Attachment, Inferior Court of Common Pleas, Suffolk County, Massachusetts, directed to Sheriff of Middlesex County, March 16, 1730. Suffolk Files, Vol. 230: p. 105, #31270.
Courtesy of Judicial Archives/Massachusetts Archives.

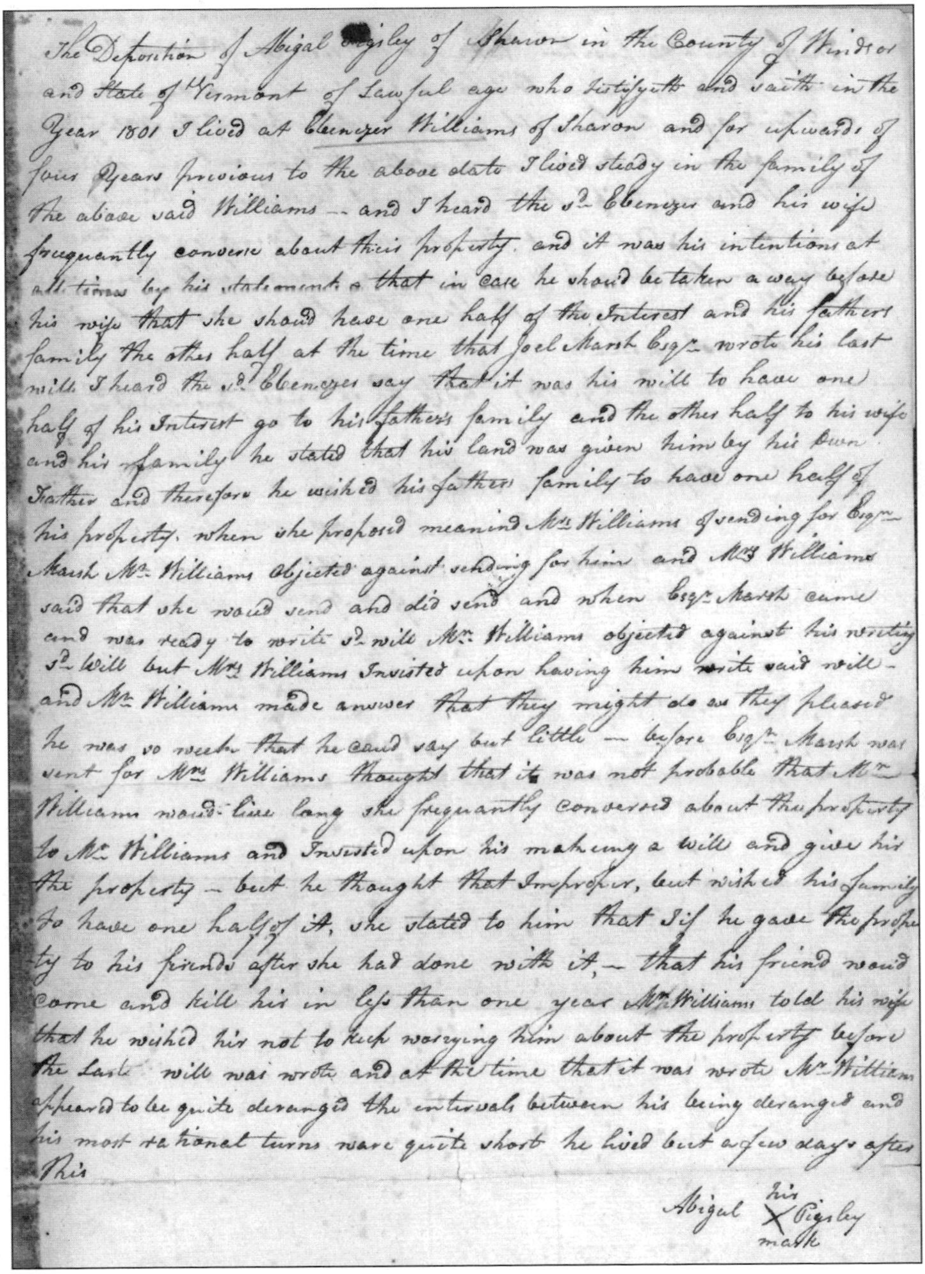

The Deposition of Abigal Pigsley of Sharon in the County of Windsor
and State of Vermont of Lawful age who testifyeth and saith in the
Year 1801 I lived at Ebenezer Williams of Sharon and for upwards of
four years previous to the above date I lived steady in the family of
the above said Williams — and I heard the sd Ebenezer and his wife
frequently converse about their property. and it was his intentions at
all times by his statement a that in case he should be taken away before
his wife that she should have one half of the Interest and his fathers
family the other half at the time that Joel Marsh Esqr wrote his last
will I heard the sd Ebenezer say that it was his will to have one
half of his Interest go to his fathers family and the other half to his wife
and his family he stated that his land was given him by his own
father and therefore he wished his fathers family to have one half of
his property. when she proposed meaning Mrs Williams of sending for Esqr
Marsh Mr Williams objected against sending for him and Mrs Williams
said that she would send and did send and when Esqr Marsh came
and was ready to write sd will Mr Williams objected against his writing
sd Will but Mrs Williams Insisted upon having him write said will —
and Mr Williams made answer that they might do as they pleased
he was so weak that he could say but little — before Esqr Marsh was
sent for Mrs Williams thought that it was not probable that Mr
Williams would live long she frequently conversed about the property
to Mr Williams and Insisted upon his making a will and give his
the property — but he thought that Improper, but wished his family
to have one half of it, she stated to him that if he gave the property to his friends after she had done with it, — that his friend would
come and kill his in less than one year Mr Williams told his wife
that he wished his not to keep worrying him about the property before
the last will was wrote and at the time that it was wrote Mr Williams
appeared to be quite deranged the intervals between his being deranged and
his most rational turns were quite short he lived but a few days after
this

                                                        Abigal his
                                                             X Pigsley
                                                           mark

Fig. 3.10. Detail from deposition of Abigal Pigsley, 1808, concerning
the will of Ebenezer Williams of Sharon, Vermont.
Courtesy of Vermont State Archives.

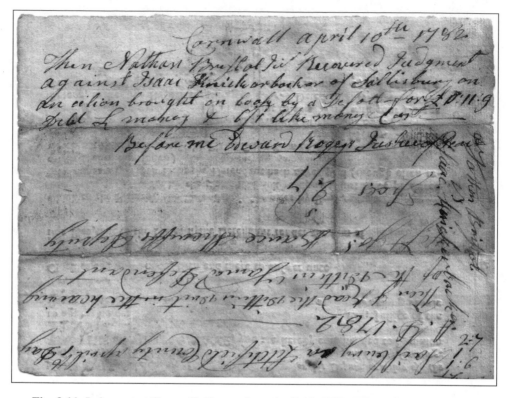

Fig. 3.11. Judgment at Cornwall, Connecticut, April 10, 1782: "Then Nathan Bristol Jr Recovered Judgment against Isaac Knickerbacher of Sallisbury...Before me Edward Rogers Justice of Peace." "Court Summons" box, Folder 2, Document 7. *Courtesy of Cornwall (Connecticut) Historical Society.* *See Chapter 16* for more justice of the peace records from the Society's collection.

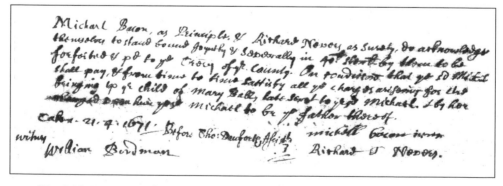

Fig. 3.12. Bastardy Bond of Michael Bacon, 1671, "to sattisfy all ye charges arising for the bringing up ye child of Mary Ball." Middlesex County (Massachusetts) Folio Collection, 1670, 55-2. *Courtesy of Judicial Archives/Massachusetts Archives.*

Fig. 3.13. Writ of Execution issued by J. Buckingham, Justice of the Peace for Hartford County, Connecticut, November 26, 1750. MSS A T 32. *Courtesy of New England Historic Genealogical Society.*

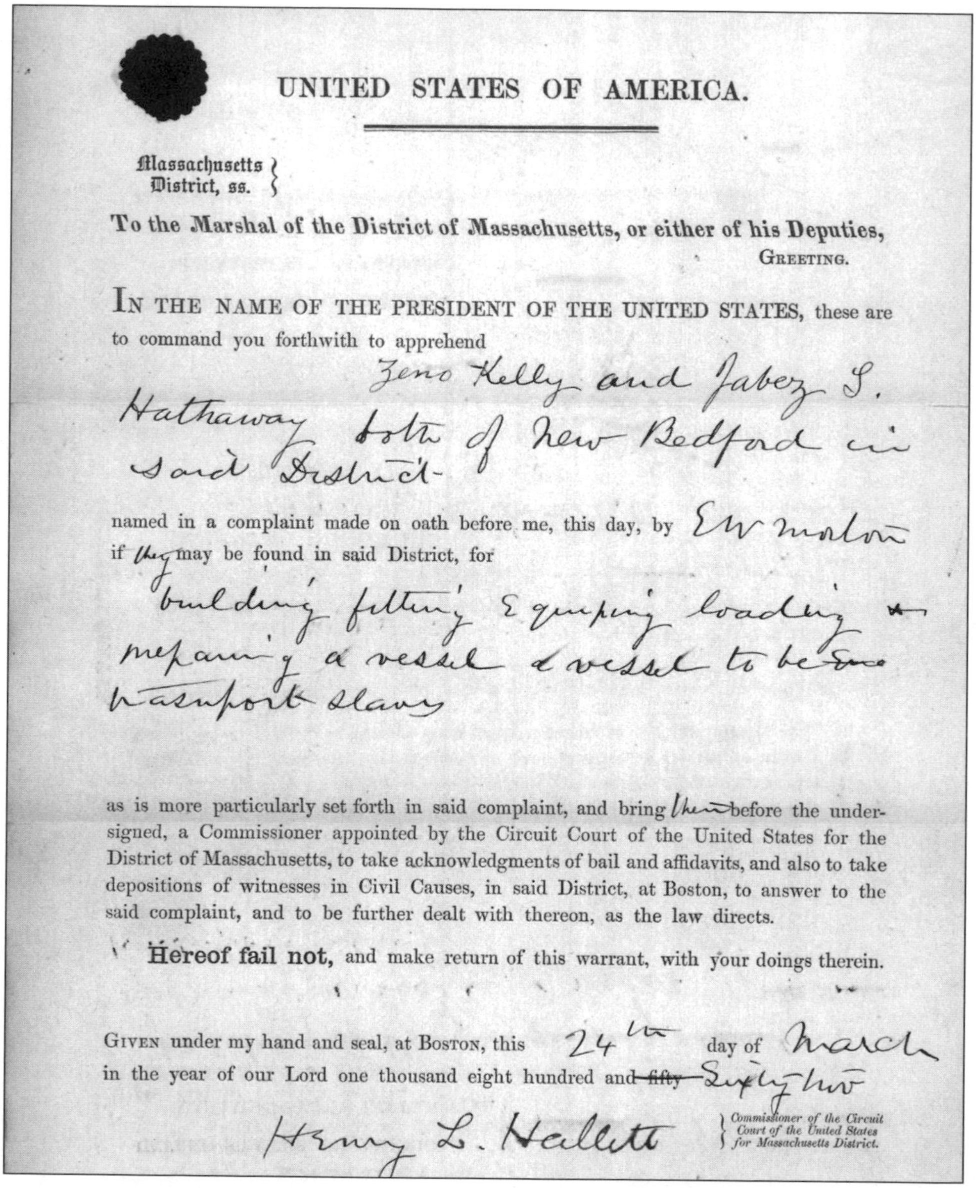

UNITED STATES OF AMERICA.

Massachusetts }
District, ss. }

To the Marshal of the District of Massachusetts, or either of his Deputies,
GREETING.

IN THE NAME OF THE PRESIDENT OF THE UNITED STATES, these are
to command you forthwith to apprehend

Zeno Kelly and Jabez S. Hathaway both of New Bedford in said District

named in a complaint made on oath before me, this day, by *E.W. morton*
if *they* may be found in said District, for

building fitting & equiping loading & preparing a vessel & vessel to be used transport slaves

as is more particularly set forth in said complaint, and bring *them* before the under-
signed, a Commissioner appointed by the Circuit Court of the United States for the
District of Massachusetts, to take acknowledgments of bail and affidavits, and also to take
depositions of witnesses in Civil Causes, in said District, at Boston, to answer to the
said complaint, and to be further dealt with thereon, as the law directs.

Hereof fail not, and make return of this warrant, with your doings therein.

GIVEN under my hand and seal, at BOSTON, this *24th* day of *March*
in the year of our Lord one thousand eight hundred and ~~fifty~~ *Sixty two*

Henry L. Hallett

} Commissioner of the Circuit
} Court of the United States
} for Massachusetts District.

Fig. 3.14. Warrant issued by Henry L. Hallett, Commissioner of the U.S. Circuit Court
for the District of Massachusetts, at Boston, to apprehend suspected slave traders,
on March 24, 1862. NARA Record Group 21. *Courtesy of U.S. National
Archives and Records Administration, Northeast Region.*

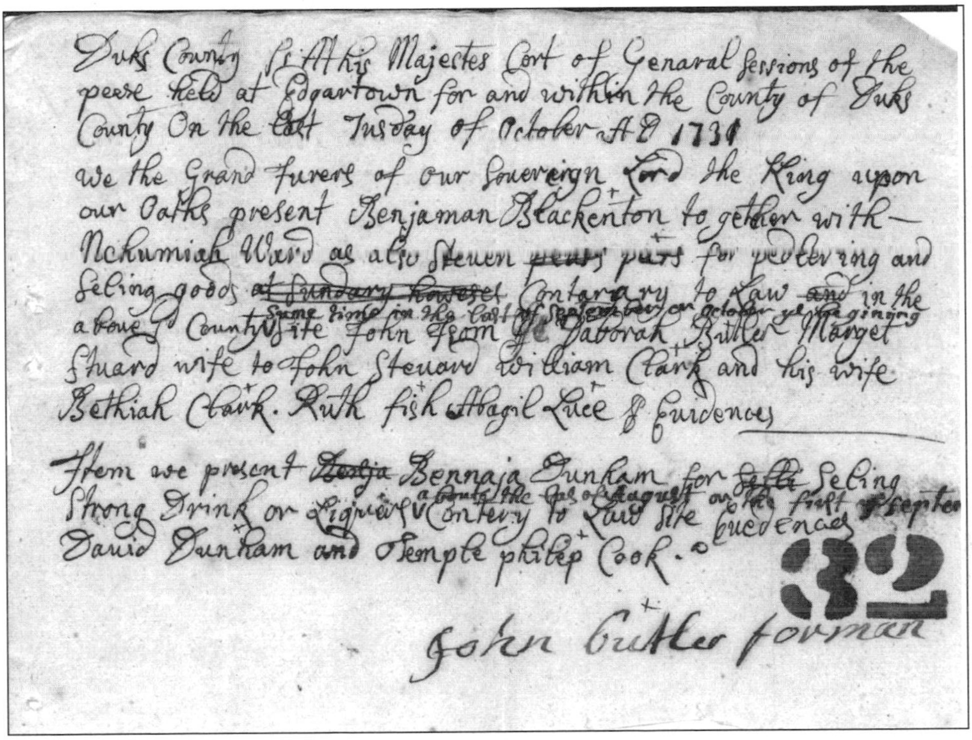

Duks County ss At his Majestes Cort of Genaral Sessions of the
peese held at Edgartown for and within the County of Duks
County On the last Tusday of October AD 1731
we the Grand Jurers of our Soveraign Lord the King upon
our Oaths present Benjaman Blackenton to gether with—
Nehumiah Ward as also Steven ~~pears~~ pars for pedlering and
seling goods ~~at sundary houses~~ Contarary to Law ~~and~~ in the
same time in the last of September or October ye beginging
above sd County Evidences John Team ye Daborah Butler Marget
Stuard wife to John Steuard William Clark and his wife
Bethiah Clark. Ruth fish Abagil Luce Evidences

Item we present ~~Beatja~~ Bennaja Dunham for ~~selli~~ seling
about the last of August or the first of Septem
Strong Drink or Liquers Contery to Law sd Evedences
David Dunham and Temple philep Cook.

32

John Butler forman

Fig. 3.15. Presentment of grand jury for General Sessions of the Peace, Dukes County, Massachusetts, "[o]n the last Tusday of October AD 1731," signed by foreman John Butler. MSS A T 32.
Courtesy of New England Historic Genealogical Society.

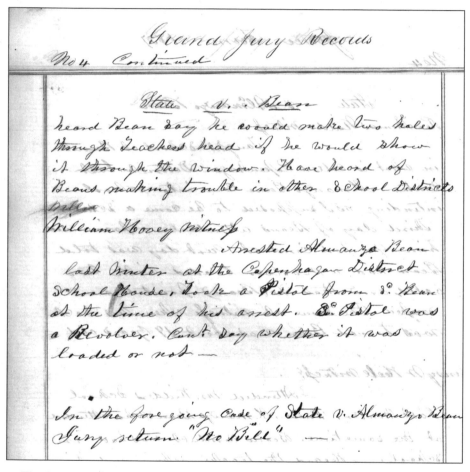

Fig. 3.16. Detail from #4 of Grand Jury Docket, Caledonia County Court, Vermont, June 1857 term, returning "No Bill" in case of *State v. Alamanzo Bean*. *Courtesy of Vermont State Archives.*

Specialized Court Records

Probate and Family

Today's probate courts focus on a variety of issues, but wills and estates have always been central to their work. Many other books explain the typical probate process and how to interpret wills (*see Appendix: Recommended Reading*), so this chapter highlights only the basic types of documents that researchers should know. Then, in *Part II*, the state-specific chapters tell how probate courts evolved in the hierarchy of New England judicial systems, and where to find probate records.

Types of Probate

Probate cases involve people who died *testate* or *intestate*.

Testate means that the deceased person (*testator*) left a *will* directing how to distribute his estate after death. Family members present the will in court, shortly after the testator's death, to be *allowed*, *proved*, or *probated*. The person chosen to carry out provisions of the will is an *executor*.

Intestate means that the deceased did not leave written instructions for distributing his property. The court appoints an *administrator*, whose identity will appear in a written court order or other court records.

Probate Records

Probate courts usually maintain **docket books** and/or **record books**, as described above. **File papers** (also called *estate papers* in probate cases) include:

Estate Inventory
The administrator oversees preparation of a detailed list or *estate inventory* of the deceased's real and personal property. *See Fig. 3.17, below.*

Accounts
Courts often require periodic *accounts* of payments and distributions made from the estate.

Petition
To pay off the deceased's debts, the executor or administrator may *petition* the probate court to allow sale of land or other property in the estate. *See Fig. 3.18, below.*

Settlement or Decree of Distribution
The document showing how the estate is divided up after payment of debts may be called a *settlement* or a *decree of distribution*.

Other types of cases, typically handled by probate courts (or by the General Court in colonial days, and/or family courts in later years) include guardianship, adoption, name change, divorce, custody of minors, and abuse protection or prevention. *See Fig. 3.19*, an adoption and name change petition, and *Fig. 3.20*, a colonial divorce petition, *below*. Probate disputes sometimes lead to lawsuits, accompanied by the types of *civil* file papers discussed above.

Naturalization

Since 1789, any state or federal court had the power to *naturalize* a person (grant United States citizenship). The federal government established an administrative procedure for naturalization in 1991—through the Immigration and Naturalization Service, which was reorganized in 2003 as the U.S. Citizenship and Immigration Services, a bureau of the U.S. Department of Homeland Security.[1] *See* the state and federal chapters of *Part II*, and *Appendix: Recommended Reading*, for more information about naturalization and where to find related court records, which contain much valuable data for genealogical and historical research.

In addition to **docket** or **record books**, court naturalization records include:

Declaration of Intention
Shortly after arrival, immigrants often filed a declaration of intention, also known as *first papers* or *primaries*, at a court in the port of entry. Before 1906, the declaration usually included name, place of birth, port and date of entry, and signature. After 1906, it might also include residence, occupation, date of birth, nationality, country of emigration, last foreign residence, name of ship, marital status, etc. *See Fig. 3.21*, *below*, which includes a photograph.

Final Papers
These court records, filed after the *declaration of intention* (sometimes years later), include:

- **Petition for Naturalization**
  Formal request for citizenship. Before 1906, the petition usually included name, residence, occupation, place and date of birth, port and date of entry. After 1906, it might also include nationality, country of emigration, last foreign residence, length of U.S. residence, name of ship, marital status, information about spouse and children, personal description and (after 1940) a photograph. *See Fig. 3.22, below*.

- **Naturalization Deposition or Affidavit**
  Testimony of two witnesses in support of petition. Information usually included names and addresses of witnesses and applicant, length of residence, and a statement about the applicant's character.

- **Oath of Allegiance**
  Usually contained name, date, residence, and country of origin.

---

[1] In 1906, Congress established the Bureau of Immigration and Naturalization to regulate naturalization procedures nationwide; this agency created new standardized forms and collected copies of naturalization records issued by courts. State and federal courts continued to perform naturalizations. Since 1991, however, most new citizens seek naturalization through the federal administrative procedure.

- **Certificate of Naturalization**
  Issued by court when citizenship granted, containing information such as name, address, date, place and date of birth, nationality, country of emigration, and sometimes information about spouse and children, personal description and photograph (after 1929). *See Fig. 3.23, below.*

Bankruptcy

Bankruptcy cases involve people who are *insolvent* (unable to pay their debts). The law is complicated and changeable—Congress enacted new bankruptcy legislation as recently as 2005—but bankruptcy cases can be divided into two basic types:

Voluntary Bankruptcy is a case started by an insolvent person or company, asking to be relieved of most debts and to undergo a liquidation or reorganization in favor of creditors.

Involuntary Bankruptcy is a case started by creditors, to force a debtor into bankruptcy.

The United States District Courts began overseeing bankruptcy cases when Congress passed the first Bankruptcy Act in 1800. Before that, state courts often handled petitions for relief by debtors, and state "insolvency" courts continued to operate until nearly the twentieth century.[2] Special federal Bankruptcy Courts, created in 1978, now hear cases in each New England state. *See Appendix: Recommended Reading* for more historical background. *Chapter 12* in *Part II* explains where to find many New England bankruptcy records (now primarily at the National Archives-Northeast Region in Waltham, Massachusetts).

Bankruptcy court records, often overlooked by genealogists and historians, are a goldmine of information. **Docket** or **record books** provide basic information, but researchers should seek out **file papers** for an unparalleled look at business practices and lifestyles of the past two centuries. Types of bankruptcy records include:

- Detailed lists of property owned by debtor
- Claims and proofs of debt, submitted by creditors
- Depositions and affidavits of debtors and creditors
- Transcripts of bankruptcy court proceedings
- Certificates of discharge (releasing debtor from responsibility for debts)
- Records describing distribution of bankrupt's assets to creditors.

See Chapter 15, and *Figs. 15.1 to 15.5*, for details from bankruptcy cases in nineteenth-century Vermont.

---

[2] In 1803, Congress repealed the Bankruptcy Act of 1800. The next federal bankruptcy law, the Act of 1841, lasted until its repeal thirteen months later, in 1843. Shortly after the Civil War, Congress passed the Act of 1867, which continued with only minor changes until 1878. Twenty years later, the Act of 1898 brought bankruptcy under federal jurisdiction again, and subsequent legislative changes have continued into the twenty-first century.

Land

Researchers often assume that land deeds are court records, since the local registry or recorder of deeds is typically located at the county courthouse. In most jurisdictions, however, the registry of deeds is part of the executive, rather than judicial, branch of government. Court cases sometimes involve land—title disputes, distribution of real estate assets in bankruptcy, divorce or probate proceedings, etc.—so researchers may encounter land records in the case file papers, including:

Abstract of Title

Summarizes history of title to a parcel of real estate, with prior owners, *liens* (claims) by creditors against the property, *mortgages*, etc., often including maps and boundary descriptions (plot plans or surveys).

Deed

Also known as a *conveyance*, transferring title to real estate. *See Fig. 3.24, below.*

Lease

Similar to a *deed*, transferring limited rights to real estate for a period of time, creating a landlord/tenant relationship.

Mortgage

Document giving house or property as security for repayment of loan. Lender can *foreclose* or take the property if the borrower defaults.

See Appendix: Recommended Reading for more information about land records. *Note*: Some states have special courts for resolving certain land disputes—the Massachusetts Land Court (with statewide jurisdiction), the Vermont Environmental Court (which hears appeals of municipal zoning decisions), or Housing Courts in Connecticut and Massachusetts (which handle landlord/tenant matters). *See* the chapters in *Part II* for more details.

Appeals

In every lawsuit, someone ends up dissatisfied. Usually that unhappy litigant is the losing party, but occasionally the winner objects to the result (the damage award was too small, for example, or the court did not grant all of the relief requested). The next step may be an appeal to a higher court.

Appellate Court Records

Appellate courts, like trial courts, maintain **docket** and **record books**, summarizing the steps in a proceeding, the documents filed and the outcome of the appeal. **File papers** for an appeal may duplicate records in the court below, since the trial court usually transfers either the original case file or copies of certain evidence to the higher court. Other appellate records vary in form and content, depending upon the jurisdiction and time period, but may include:

Notice of Appeal
The *appellant* (party appealing lower court decision) begins an appeal by filing a notice with the court, requesting *reversal* of the judgment, a new trial, or other relief.

Appeal Bond
In early New England appeals, the *appellant* typically posted a bond (often double the amount in controversy) pending the court's decision.

Trial Transcript
Verbatim recording of trial testimony (modern practice), or summary of evidence in lower court.

Briefs
Written arguments by parties or their lawyers, debating the applicable law and summarizing relevant trial evidence. The *appellant's* brief usually argues that the trial court made an error of law in deciding the case. The brief of the *appellee* or *respondent* (party opposing the appeal) answers the appellant's arguments, and usually requests that the judgment be *affirmed*. *Note*: In early court records, arguments and summaries of evidence are more likely to appear in the appellant's *notice of appeal* and in an *answer* or *reply* by the respondent, rather than in separate briefs.

Decision or **Opinion**
Written decision of the appellate court, usually summarizing evidence, explaining legal reasoning, and granting or denying relief, *e.g.*, *reversing* the trial court's judgment (sending the case back to the lower court for a new trial or for reconsideration of certain legal issues) or *affirming* the result below (letting it stand).

Appellate Case Reports

Since the late 1700s, many state and federal appellate court opinions have been published in books called *reporters*, allowing attorneys and judges to study the evolving body of *common law*. These case reports (most published by the "West National Reporter System" and available at law libraries) tend to be overlooked by researchers outside the legal profession, but they contain much information useful for historians and genealogists, too, such as:

- Case name, court, and decision date
- Synopsis of case
- Topic "headnotes," summarizing legal principles stated in case
- Names of parties, attorneys and judges involved in case
- Full court decision, often quoting from trial evidence and court file papers.

Researchers can use the published reports to find cases about parties or subjects of interest, before trying to locate original court records at courthouses or archives. Sometimes the published court opinions are the only source of information about a case, where the court files may be lost or destroyed. *See Chapter 17* in *Part III: Sampling the Sources*, which walks you through some simple research techniques using the "West National Reporter System" and other law library resources.

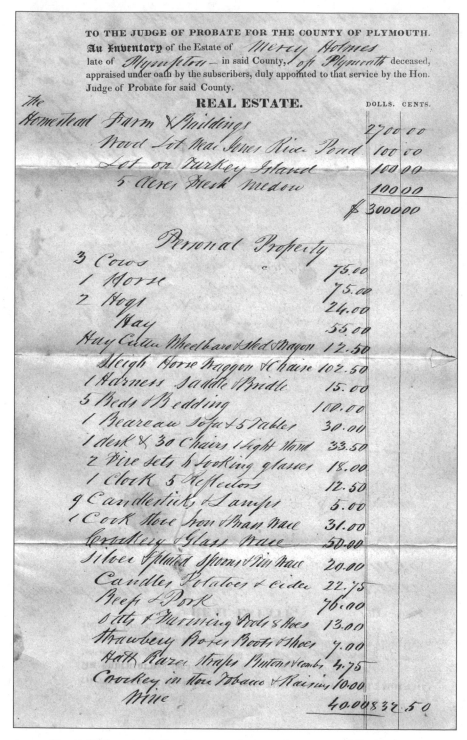

TO THE JUDGE OF PROBATE FOR THE COUNTY OF PLYMOUTH.

An Inventory of the Estate of *Mercy Holmes*
late of *Plympton* — in said County, *of Plymouth* deceased,
appraised under oath by the subscribers, duly appointed to that service by the Hon.
Judge of Probate for said County.

REAL ESTATE.	DOLLS.	CENTS.
The Homestead Farm & Buildings	2700	00
Wood Lot near Jones River Pond	100	00
Lot on Turkey Island	100	00
5 Acres Fresh Medow	100	00
	$3000	00

Personal Property

3 Cows	75.00	
1 Horse	75.00	
2 Hogs	24.00	
Hay	55.00	
Hay Cutter Wheelbarow & Sled Wagon	12.50	
Sleigh Horse Waggon & Chaise	102.50	
1 Harness Saddle & Bridle	15.00	
5 Beds & Bedding	100.00	
1 Beareau Sofa & 5 Tables	30.00	
1 desk & 30 Chairs 1 light stand	33.50	
2 Fire sets & looking glasses	18.00	
1 Clock 5 Reflectors	12.50	
9 Candlesticks & Lamps	5.00	
1 Cook Stove Iron & tin ware	31.00	
Crockery & Glass ware	50.00	
Silver & plated Spoons & tin ware	20.00	
Candles Potatoes & cider	22.75	
Beef & Pork	76.00	
Oats & Farming tools & Hoes	13.00	
Strawbery Boxes Boots & shoes	7.00	
Hatt Razer straps Buttons & combs	4.75	
Crockery in store Tobacco & Raisins	10.00	
Wine	40.00	832.50

Fig. 3.17. Inventory of real estate and personal property, 1843, for estate
of Mercy Holmes. Plymouth County Probate Court, #10511.
Courtesy of Judicial Archives/Massachusetts Archives.

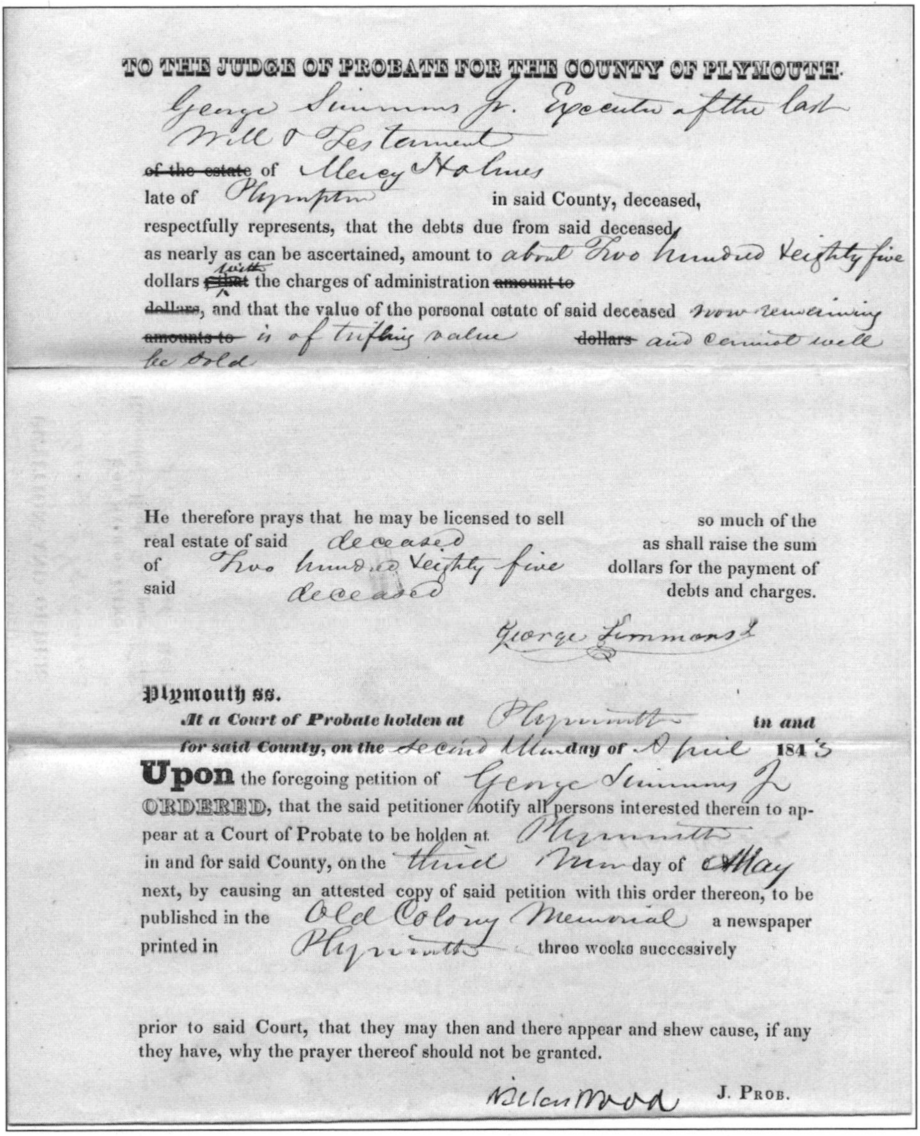

TO THE JUDGE OF PROBATE FOR THE COUNTY OF PLYMOUTH.

George Simmons Jr. Executor of the last Will & Testament

~~of the estate~~ of *Mercy Holmes*

late of *Plympton* in said County, deceased,

respectfully represents, that the debts due from said deceased, as nearly as can be ascertained, amount to *about Two hundred & eighty five* dollars ~~that~~ *with* the charges of administration ~~amount to~~ ~~dollars,~~ and that the value of the personal estate of said deceased *now remaining* ~~amounts to~~ *is of trifling value* ~~dollars~~ *and cannot well be sold*

He therefore prays that he may be licensed to sell   so much of the real estate of said   *deceased*   as shall raise the sum of   *Two hundred & eighty five*   dollars for the payment of said   *deceased*   debts and charges.

George Simmons

Plymouth ss.

At a Court of Probate holden at *Plymouth* **in and for said County, on the** *second Monday of* *April* 184*3*

Upon the foregoing petition of *George Simmons Jr.*

ORDERED, that the said petitioner notify all persons interested therein to appear at a Court of Probate to be holden at *Plymouth* in and for said County, on the *third Mon* day of *May* next, by causing an attested copy of said petition with this order thereon, to be published in the *Old Colony Memorial* a newspaper printed in *Plymouth* three weeks successively

prior to said Court, that they may then and there appear and shew cause, if any they have, why the prayer thereof should not be granted.

Wm Wood J. PROB.

Fig. 3.18. Petition of George Simmons, Jr., for sale of land, April 1843, from estate of Mercy Holmes. Plymouth County Probate Court, #10511. *Courtesy of Judicial Archives/Massachusetts Archives.*

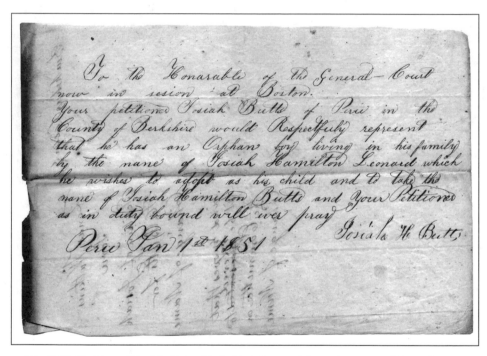

Fig. 3.19. Petition of Josiah Butts, Berkshire County, Massachusetts, to Massachusetts General Court, January 1, 1851, for adoption of orphan child and name change. SC1 Acts 1851 Ch. 249. *Courtesy of Massachusetts Archives.*

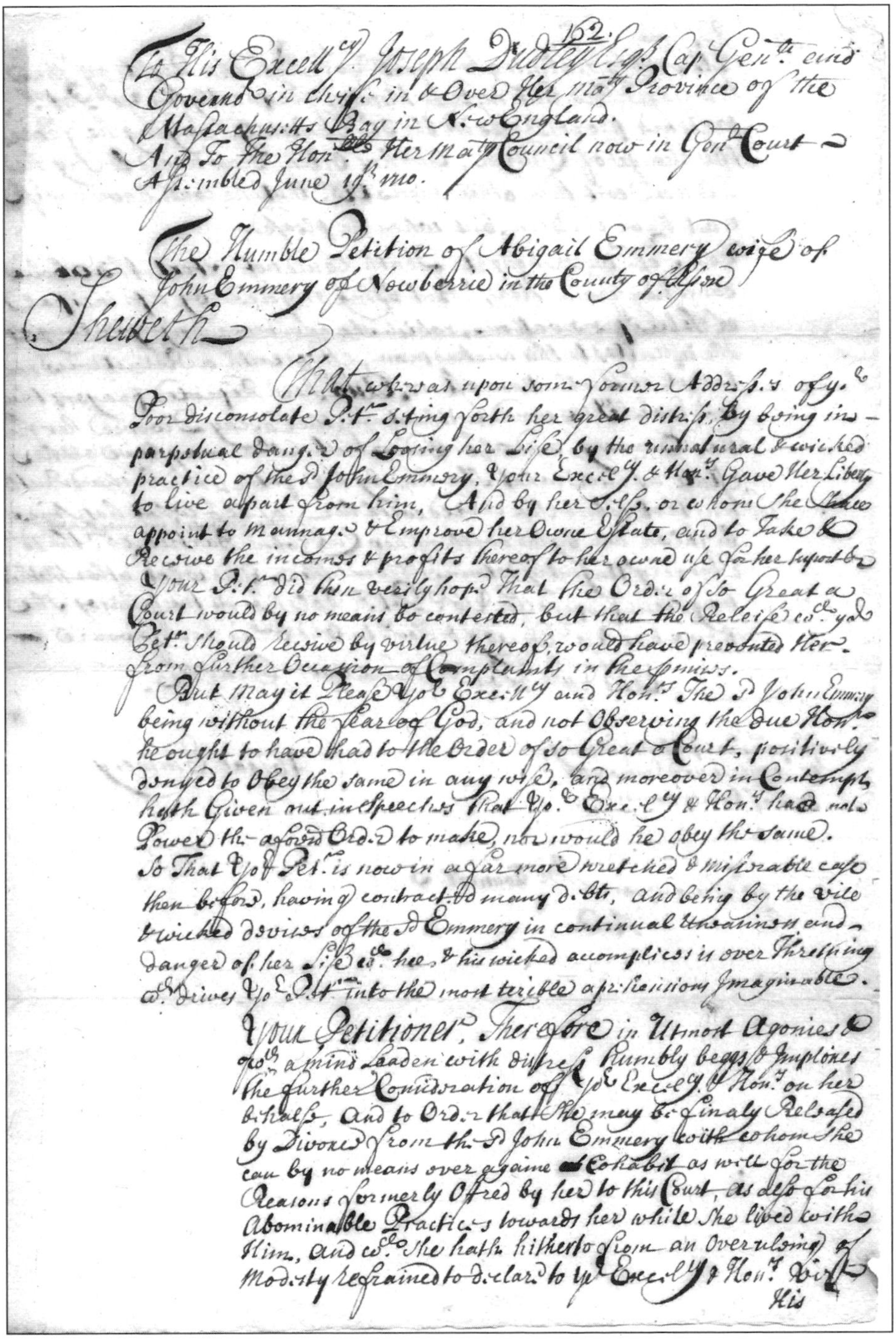

Fig. 3.20. Petition of Abigail Emmery, Newbury, Massachusetts, 1710, to the Massachusetts Governor and Council, seeking divorce due to "purpetual danger of Loosing her Life by the unnatural & wicked practice" of her husband. SC1 45X, Massachusetts Archives Collection, Vol. 9: p. 162. *Courtesy of Massachusetts Archives.*

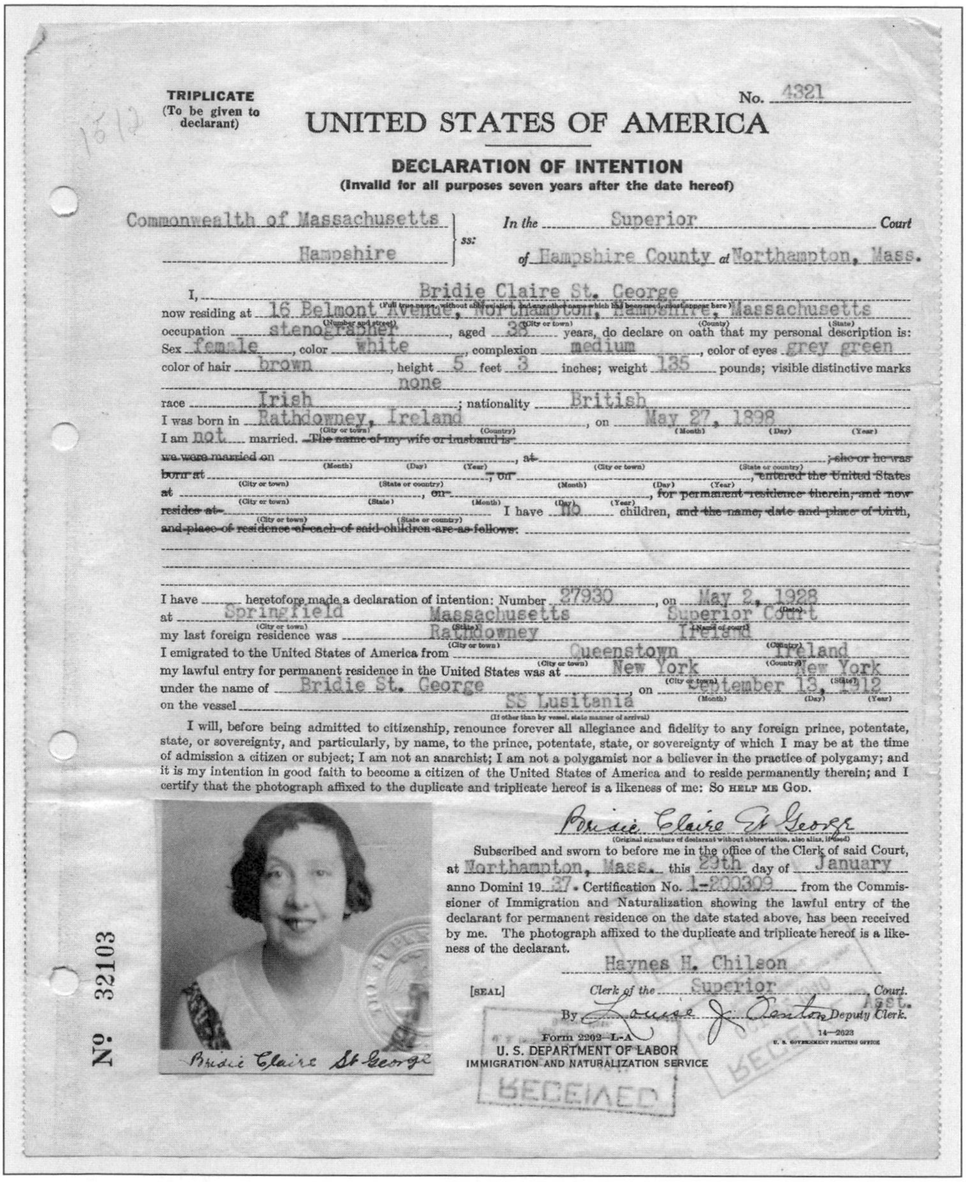

Fig. 3.21. Declaration of Intention of Bridie Claire St. George, 1937, Hampshire County Superior Court, Massachusetts. Vol. 37: p. 22. *Courtesy of Judicial Archives/Massachusetts Archives.*

ORIGINAL
(To be retained by
Clerk of Court)

UNITED STATES OF AMERICA

No. 3955

PETITION FOR NATURALIZATION
[Under General Provisions of the Nationality Act of 1940 (Public, No. 853, 76th Cong.)]

To the Honorable the _____ Superior _____ Court of Hampshire County _____ at Northampton, Mass. _____

This petition for naturalization, hereby made and filed, respectfully shows:

(1) My full, true, and correct name is _Bridie Claire St. George_ (Full, true name, without abbreviation, also maiden name)

(2) My present place of residence is _16 Belmont Ave. Northampton, Hampshire, Mass._ (Number and street) (City or town) (County) (State) (3) My occupation is _Milliner_

(4) I am _43_ years old. (5) I was born on _May 27, 1898_ in _Rathdowney, Queens Co., Ireland_ (Month) (Day) (Year) (City, district, province, or state) (Country)

(6) My personal description is as follows: Sex _F._, color _Wh._, complexion _Med._, color of eyes _Hazel_, color of hair _Br._
height _5_ feet _2_ inches, weight _135_ pounds, visible distinctive marks _none_, race _White_
present nationality _British_ (7) I am _not_ married; the name of my wife or husband is _____

we were married on _____ (Month) (Day) (Year) (City or town) (State or country)

he or she was born on _____ (Month) (Day) (Year) (City or town) (County, district, province, or state) (Country) at _____ (Country) on _____ (Month) (Day) (Year) for permanent residence in the United States

and entered the United States at _____ (City or town) (State) on _____ (Month) (Day) (Year) and was naturalized on _____ (Month) (Day) (Year)

at _____ (City or town) (State) certificate No. _____ or became a citizen by _____

(8) I have _no_ children; and the name, sex, date and place of birth, and present place of residence of each of said children who is living, are as follows: _____

(9) My last place of foreign residence was _Rathdowney, Queens Co., Ireland_ (City or town) (Country, district, province, or state) (10) I emigrated to the United States from _Queenstown, Ireland_ (City or town) (Country) (11) My lawful entry for permanent residence in the United States was

at _New York, New York_ under the name of _Bridie St. George_ (City or town) (Name of vessel or other means of conveyance)

on _Sept. 13, 1912_ on the _SS Lusitania_ (Month) (Day) (Year)

as shown by the certificate of my arrival attached to this petition.

(12) Since my lawful entry for permanent residence I have _not_ been absent from the United States, for a period or periods of 6 months or longer, as follows:

DEPARTED FROM THE UNITED STATES			RETURNED TO THE UNITED STATES		
Port	Date (Month, day, year)	Vessel or Other Means of Conveyance	Port	Date (Month, day, year)	Vessel or Other Means of Conveyance

(13) I declared my intention to become a citizen of the United States on _January 29, 1937_ in the _Superior_ (Month) (Day) (Year) (Name of court)

Court of _Hampshire County_ at _Northampton, Mass._ (14) It is my intention in good faith to become a (City or town) (State)

citizen of the United States and to renounce absolutely and forever all allegiance and fidelity to any foreign prince, potentate, State, or sovereignty of whom or which at this time I am a subject or citizen, and it is my intention to reside permanently in the United States. (15) I am not, and have not been for the period of at least 10 years immediately preceding the date of this petition, an anarchist; nor a believer in the unlawful damage, injury, or destruction of property, or sabotage; nor a disbeliever in or opposed to organized government; nor a member of or affiliated with any organization or body of persons teaching disbelief in or opposition to organized government. (16) I am able to speak the English language (unless physically unable to do so). (17) I am, and have been during all of the periods required by law, attached to the principles of the Constitution of the United States and well disposed to the good order and happiness of the United States. (18) I have resided continuously in the

United States of America for the term of 5 years at least immediately preceding the date of this petition, to wit, since _Sept. 13, 1912_ (Month) (Day) (Year)

and continuously in the State in which this petition is made for the term of 6 months at least immediately preceding the date of this petition, to wit, since

Sept. 13, 1912 (19) I have _not_ heretofore made petition for naturalization: No. _____ (Month) (Day) (Year)

on _____ (Month) (Day) (Year) at _____ (City or town) (County) (State) in the _____ (Name of court)

Court, and such petition was dismissed or denied by that Court for the following reasons and causes, to wit: _____

and the cause of such dismissal or denial has since been cured or removed.

(20) Attached hereto and made a part of this, my petition for naturalization, are my declaration of intention to become a citizen of the United States (if such declaration of intention be required by the naturalization law), a certificate of arrival from the Immigration and Naturalization Service of my said lawful entry into the United States for permanent residence (if such certificate of arrival be required by the naturalization law), and the affidavits of at least two verifying witnesses required by law.

(21) Wherefore, I, your petitioner for naturalization, pray that I may be admitted a citizen of the United States of America, and that my name be changed to _____

(22) I, aforesaid petitioner, do swear (affirm) that I know the contents of this petition for naturalization subscribed by me, that the same are true to the best of my own knowledge, except as to matters therein stated to be alleged upon information and belief, and that as to those matters I believe them to be true, and that this petition is signed by me with my full, true name: SO HELP ME GOD.

Bridie Claire St. George
(Full, true, and correct signature of petitioner, without abbreviation)

U. S. DEPARTMENT OF JUSTICE
IMMIGRATION AND NATURALIZATION SERVICE
Form N-405
(Old 2204-1-D)
[Edition of 1-13-41]

c16—19120

Fig. 3.22. Petition for Naturalization of Bridie Claire St. George, 1937,
Hampshire County Superior Court, Massachusetts. Vol. 37: p. 22.
Courtesy of Judicial Archives/Massachusetts Archives.

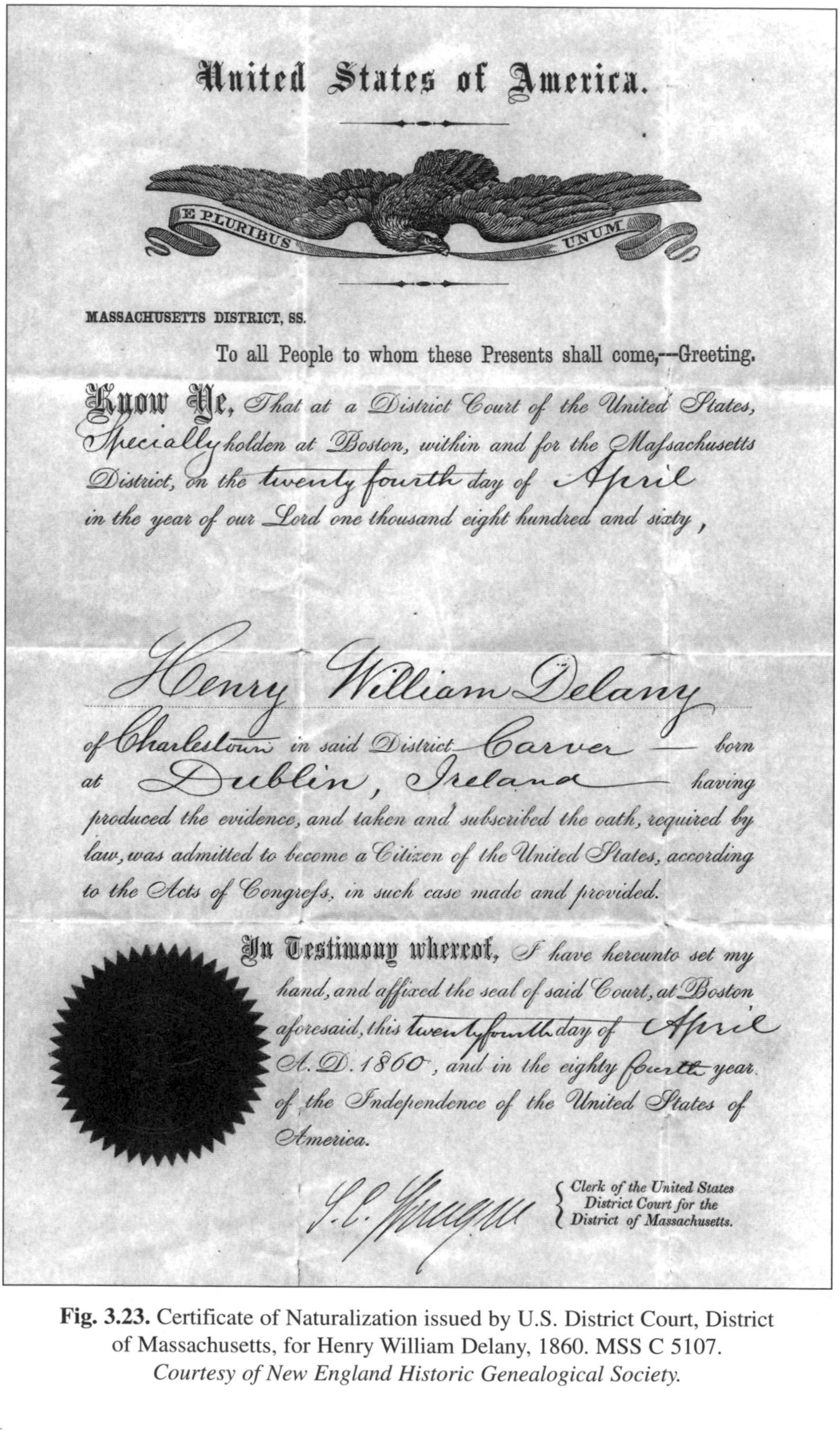

United States of America.

E PLURIBUS UNUM

MASSACHUSETTS DISTRICT, SS.

To all People to whom these Presents shall come,---Greeting.

Know Ye, That at a District Court of the United States, Specially holden at Boston, within and for the Massachusetts District, on the twenty fourth day of April in the year of our Lord one thousand eight hundred and sixty,

Henry William Delany

of Charlestown in said District Carver born at Dublin, Ireland having produced the evidence, and taken and subscribed the oath, required by law, was admitted to become a Citizen of the United States, according to the Acts of Congress, in such case made and provided.

In Testimony whereof, I have hereunto set my hand, and affixed the seal of said Court, at Boston aforesaid, this twenty fourth day of April A. D. 1860, and in the eighty fourth year of the Independence of the United States of America.

Clerk of the United States District Court for the District of Massachusetts.

Fig. 3.23. Certificate of Naturalization issued by U.S. District Court, District of Massachusetts, for Henry William Delany, 1860. MSS C 5107.
Courtesy of New England Historic Genealogical Society.

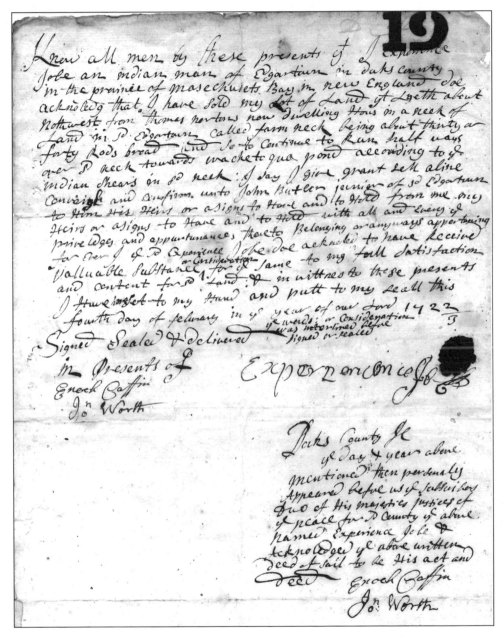

Fig. 3.24. Land deed from "Experience Jobe, an Indian man of Edgartown,"
Masssachusetts, to John Butler, Jr., February 4, 1722/3.
Courtesy of New England Historic Genealogical Society.

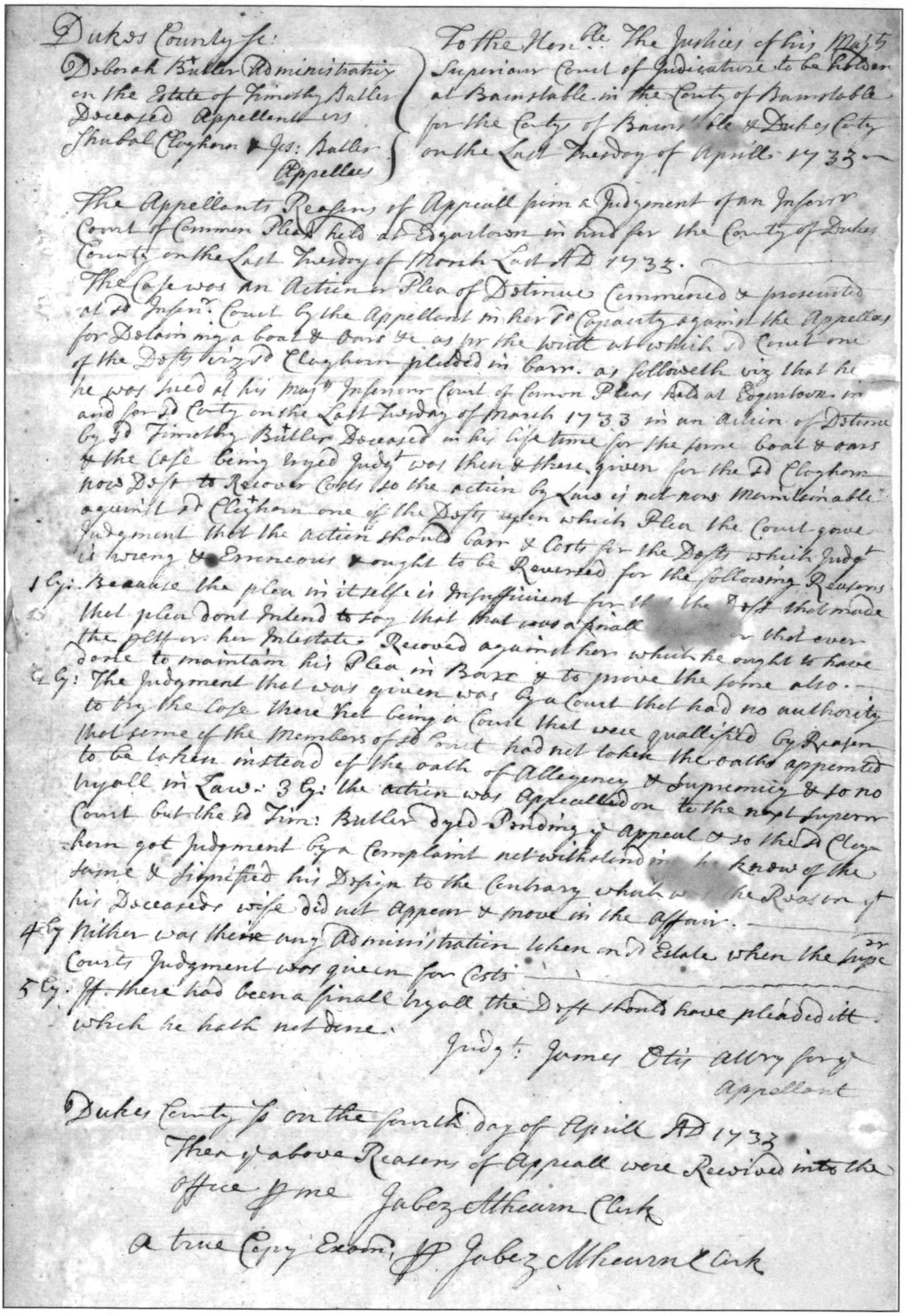

Fig. 3.25. Detail from "Reasons of appeal" of Deborah Butler, April 4, 1732, to the Superior Court of Judicature, appealing a judgment of the Court of Common Pleas, Dukes County, Massachusetts, in favor of Shubal Claghorn and J. Butler. *Courtesy of New England Historic Genealogical Society.*

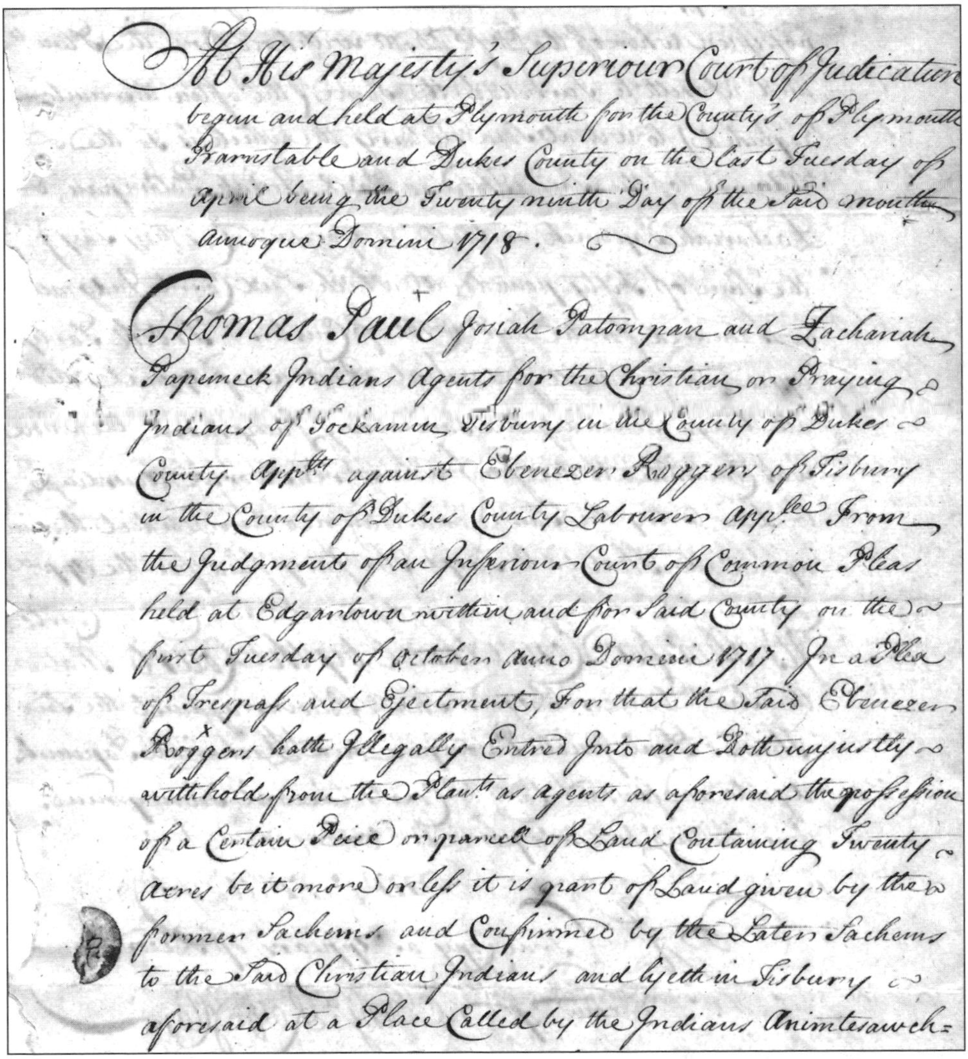
At His Majesty's Superiour Court of Judicature
begun and held at Plymouth for the County's of Plymouth
Barnstable and Dukes County on the last Tuesday of
April being the Twenty ninth Day of the Said month
Annoque Domini 1718.

Thomas Paul Josiah Patompan and Zachariah
Papemeck Indians Agents for the Christian or Praying
Indians of Tockamin Tisbury in the County of Dukes
County Applts against Ebenezer Roggers of Tisbury
in the County of Dukes County Labourer Applee From
the Judgment of an Inferiour Court of Common Pleas
held at Edgartown within and for Said County on the
first Tuesday of October Anno Domini 1717 In a Plea
of Trespass and Ejectment, For that the Said Ebenezer
Roggers hath Illegally Entred Into and Doth unjustly
withhold from the Plaintfs as agents as aforesaid the possession
of a Certain Peice or parcell of Land Containing Twenty
Acres be it more or less it is part of Land given by the
former Sachems and Confirmed by the Later Sachems
to the Said Christian Indians and Lyeth in Tisbury
aforesaid at a Place Called by the Indians Animtesawch=

Fig. 3.26. Detail from decision of Superior Court of Judicature at Plymouth, Massachusetts, 1718, on appeal from Inferior Court of Common Pleas, Dukes County, in land dispute case of *Thomas Paul, Josiah Patompan and Zachariah Papemeck* (native American "agents for the Christian, or Praying, Indians of Tockamin, Tisbury") *v. Ebenezer Roggers* of Tisbury.
Courtesy of New England Historic Genealogical Society.

pute as to overcome the preference we would ordinarily have for the application of New Hampshire law to determine the rights of persons negligently injured on New Hampshire highways. Guenther, Changing Choice of Law Rules in Intrafamily and Other Tort Actions: Comments on Thompson v. Thompson, 7 N.H.B.J. 19, 24 (1964); Leflar, Conflict of Laws in 1964 Annual Survey of American Law 69, 86–87.

We have read the recent, scholarly and well-structured treatise on conflict of laws. Cavers, The Choice-of-Law Process (1965). While we cannot accuse the author of agreeing with the result reached in this case, his discussion of principles of preference in solving conflict problems makes the thoughtful think and exposes the pitfalls of the past. See page 9, n. 24, pages 177–180 and also pages 293–312 for an analysis of Dym v. Gordon, 16 N.Y.2d 120, 362 N.Y.S.2d 463, 209 N.E.2d 792 (1965).

Defendant's exception sustained.

All concurred.

Stanley J. BARTIS, Ex'r, Appellant,

v.

John C. BARTIS et al., Appellees.

Supreme Court of New Hampshire.

Hillsboro.

Argued Nov. 2, 1965.

Decided Jan. 31, 1966.

Will contest. From decree of probate court disallowing will, appeal was taken. The Court, Loughlin, J., dismissed appeal and exceptions to certain rulings during course of trial and to denial of motion to set aside decree were reserved and transferred by the presiding justice. The Su-

preme Court, Wheeler, J., held that finding that will was procured by undue influence was supported by evidence.

Exceptions overruled.

1. Wills ⚖️166(1)

Finding that will was procured by undue influence was supported by evidence.

2. Appeal and Error ⚖️1078(1)

Exceptions taken during trial but not briefed or argued would be considered waived.

———◆———

Clancy & O'Neill, Nashua (Frank B. Clancy, Nashua, orally), for appellant.

Stein, Cleaveland & Rudman, Nashua, (Morris D. Stein, Nashua, orally), for appellees John C. and William J. Bartis.

Charles J. Flynn, Nashua, guardian ad litem (by brief and orally), for minor children of Mildred B. Laforest.

WHEELER, Justice.

Appeal from a decree of the probate court disallowing the will of Lena M. Bartis, late of Nashua, upon proof in solemn form. Trial by the Court (Loughlin, J.), who found "on all the evidence that the will was procured by undue influence" and dismissed the appeal. The appellant's exceptions to certain rulings during the course of the trial and to the denial of his motion to set aside the decree were reserved and transferred by the Presiding Justice.

The contested will was executed on December 27, 1961. Mrs. Bartis deceased on May 6, 1962, survived by three sons, all of whom are parties to these proceedings, a daughter Agnes B. Fezolla, and children of a deceased daughter Mildred Laforest, who were represented by the guardian ad litem. By the will Agnes B. Fezolla was bequeathed $6,000, John C. Bartis $5,000, and William J. Bartis $4,000. Certain war

Figure 3.27. Example of appellate case report published in West National Reporter System, from New Hampshire Supreme Court's opinion in *Bartis v. Bartis*, 216 A.2d 784 (N.H. 1966). *Courtesy of West.*

CHAPTER 4

WHERE TO LOOK FOR COURT RECORDS

Now that you know more about the types of court records, where should you look? In years past, the answer was simple: the courthouse. Anyone who wanted to see old records went to a courthouse and asked the court clerk for access, which probably meant digging through dusty boxes and file packets in a back room or cellar. Today, researchers have more options. While a limited number of original documents are still available at courthouses, most New England court records have found their way into state archives or other public and private repositories. Genealogists and historians also can access a vast array of published source materials, sometimes without even leaving home.

Part II of this book, *Getting Specific, State by State*, will help you to make sense of this multitude of sources. Separate chapters—for each New England state and the federal courts—provide a "Court History Timeline" in each jurisdiction and explain how today's courts are organized. Then, each chapter offers an extensive list of sources—statewide and by county—in the "Where to Find Court Records" section. **Original records** (including rare antiquarian case reports) appear first—with details about court records at hundreds of courts and archives—followed by **published records**—books, microform and digital/electronic sources (CD-ROM and Internet).

Reliable Sources

Everyone knows that some research sources are more reliable than others. Usually a *primary* source (created at the time of an event) is better than a *secondary* synthesis of information from other sources. *Original* records generally are preferred over *published* works. But evaluating the reliability of court records requires closer scrutiny.

Affidavits or trial transcripts may be original primary sources, but the genealogical or historical value of the information contained within the record may depend upon other issues—the veracity of the witness, for example, or whether she had firsthand knowledge of the facts. Sometimes a court record, although written contemporaneously with the event it describes, is merely an abstract or synthesis of other court documents—in a record book, for example—and its reliability depends upon the skill and thoroughness of the court official who created it.

In some cases, published court records are virtually as reliable as the originals. Microfilm or facsimile reproductions may look just like original records. Sometimes microfilm or printed transcripts are the *only* way to read certain early records (where the originals have since disappeared or deteriorated and are no longer accessible), and archivists often insist that researchers use copies when originals are in fragile condition. Reading a transcribed version is also, of course, much easier than trying to interpret a handwritten original (as anyone who has tried to decipher early American script can attest).[3]

Some print volumes of court records are so meticulously transcribed or abstracted that researchers may use them with confidence. Judges and lawyers rely upon published case opinions—from the highly-regarded West reporters, for example—even though the cases contain secondary summaries of trial evidence and editorial material, as well as the court decision. Simplistic distinctions—between *primary* and *secondary* or *original* and *published* court records—do not substitute for careful analysis of the source.

Published Records

Books and Journals

Many court documents, especially for the colonial period, have been transcribed and published. *See* "Books and Journals" in the "Where to Find Court Records" section of each state and federal chapter for lists of titles. The reference librarian at your local public library can help to locate copies, and many resources are also available at the archives, historical societies and other repositories listed in *Part II*. Some published sources can be purchased new or secondhand; check with your local bookstore or online sellers such as *Amazon.com* or *Abebooks.com*.

Appellate court decisions from the eighteenth to twenty-first centuries—state and federal—can be found in published volumes, called *reporters*, from the "West National Reporter System." West also publishes *digests*, containing abstracts and indexes of appellate court opinions. These materials are all available at law libraries; *see Appendix: Contact Information-Law Libraries* for law libraries in the New England area. (Law libraries in other regions of the United States may stock some of these reporters and digests, too, or allow computer access to the CD-ROM and Internet versions. Contact a law librarian first to confirm availability.) *Chapter 17* in *Part III: Sampling the Sources* explains how to use law library resources.

Microform

Vast collections of court records, filmed from the originals and published primarily by the The Church of Jesus Christ of Latter-day Saints (LDS) through the Genealogical

---

[3] *See* Kip Sperry's excellent book, *Reading Early American Handwriting* (Baltimore, Md.: Genealogical Publishing Co., 1998), for help with old documents.

Society of Utah, are available for viewing at more than 5,000 branches of the LDS Family History Library (FHL) worldwide. Check "Microform" in the "Where to Find Court Records" section of each *Part II* chapter.[4] Most microform titles in this book appear exactly as listed in the FHL catalog; you can obtain more information about a particular title (including the number and contents of reels or fiche) by doing a "title" search at the FHL catalog (online at *www.familysearch.org*), or by contacting an LDS Family History Center (*see Appendix: Contact Information-Publishers*). Many other libraries, including most state archives, offer access to certain Genealogical Society of Utah microform, although the titles in their catalogs may differ from the FHL titles. Consult an archivist or reference librarian to locate microform with the content that you need.

Digital/Electronic Sources

The most exciting development in court-records research is the recent proliferation of digital/electronic resources—CD-ROM and Internet databases—allowing historians and genealogists to do their research by computer, at home or anywhere. West case reporters and digests are available on CD-ROM or searchable online from computers at law libraries. Many other court records can be accessed through free or low-cost electronic databases, and detailed state-by-state and federal sources are listed under "Digital/Electronic Sources" in the chapters of *Part II*.

Original Records

Only a small percentage of court records have been published, so serious researchers may need to look for the original documents—at courthouses, state and federal archives or record centers, state historical societies and other repositories. These locations, and specifics about their court record holdings, appear in the "Where to Find Court Records" section of each chapter in *Part II*.

Courthouses

New England courthouses generally hold only *recent* original case files. Many courts maintain original docket/record books or indexes on a permanent basis, however, and those records are useful in locating basic information—such as parties to a case, dates of trial or case file numbers—which may help to access court records at other repositories.

State and Federal Archives or Record Centers

The major repositories of original court records in most New England states are the state and federal archives or record centers. **Record centers** often serve as offsite storage for the more recent court documents, while the courts retain legal custody. Access

---

[4] In *Part II*, microform identified with the abbreviation "GSU" was published by the Genealogical Society of Utah (Salt Lake City), the microfilming arm of the LDS Family and Church History Department. Except as noted, all microform cited in this book is microfilm, rather than microfiche.

to record centers is limited; typically researchers must make prior arrangements with a court clerk to retrieve documents stored there. **State and federal archives** generally maintain the older "archival" records transferred from courts or record centers to the custody of a state or federal agency. Researchers usually deal directly with the archives staff, rather than with court clerks, for access to these records.

State Historical Societies and Other Repositories

Significant numbers of court records have found their way into other public and private institutions, but researchers often overlook these resources. State historical societies, for example, hold court records in many manuscript collections, especially from early years or for courts at the local level (town justice of the peace, etc.). *See* the chapters of *Part II* for further information. *Part II* also lists court records at approximately one hundred fifty other repositories—local historical societies, universities, museums and libraries—collections seldom accessed, because few people know about them.

Court Records to be Discovered

Although this book is the first "comprehensive" guide to New England court records, it is not the last word on where to find these valuable historical and genealogical resources. In preparing this book, I contacted virtually every court in New England, all the major state and federal archives, and hundreds of other institutions large and small, but I soon realized that original court records are housed in so many public and private repositories that I would be unable to find them all. More court records are undoubtedly waiting to be discovered in forgotten boxes throughout New England.

Recently, for example, the town of Westford, Massachusetts discovered tins of folded handwritten papers—including local court records from the 1800s—in a moldy basement vault at the town hall. Workers at New Hampshire's Cheshire County courthouse stumbled across boxes of eighteenth-century documents, which are now being inventoried for transfer to the state archives. Volunteers at the Lincoln County courthouse in Maine are undertaking a similar effort. My inquiries prompted many people to take a closer look at records in their neighborhoods, and some wonderful finds appear in the listings of *Part II*, such as eighteenth-century justice of the peace records at Cornwall, Connecticut's historical society (described in *Chapter 16, Part III: Sampling the Sources*).

Your own town may hold similar treasures. Look for them, and report your findings to Quill Pen Press, so that additional sources can be included in the next edition of *New England Court Records*. In the meantime, be sure to visit *QuillPenPress.com* for free source updates.

Fig. 4.1. Naturalization records, 1790 and 1792, Lincoln County courthouse, Wiscasset, Maine. *Photograph courtesy of Helen A. Shaw.*

PART II

GETTING SPECIFIC,
STATE BY STATE

Portland, Maine., "New Cumberland County Court House." "Now in process of erection."

The image on the preceding page, from the author's collection of vintage picture postcards, depicts the Cumberland County courthouse in Portland, Maine, ca. pre-1907.

CHAPTER 5

FINDING AND USING THE RESOURCES IN *PART II*

After learning the basics in *Part I*, you are ready to get specific about court records, state by state. The chapters of *Part II* explain the courts in each New England state and tell you where to find court records, from the seventeenth to the twenty-first centuries. *Part II* contains substantial detail—hundreds of sources—but there is plenty of guidance to keep you from feeling overwhelmed. PLEASE READ THIS CHAPTER BEFORE YOU BEGIN RESEARCH!

Organization of *Part II*

Separate chapters (6 to 11) cover each New England state—Connecticut, Maine, Massachusetts, New Hampshire, Rhode Island and Vermont. *Chapter 12* focuses on the federal courts in New England. Each chapter follows the same organizational structure, with three major sections: **Court History Timeline**, **Courts Today**, and **Where to Find Court Records**. Review the features of each section, before you consult *Chapters 6 to 12,* to make the most effective use of *Part II*.

Court History Timeline

Each chapter begins with a timeline summarizing how the courts evolved, from the earliest colonial days to modern times. The names of courts—and their duties—changed many times over the centuries, but this timeline provides key facts to simplify your research. Check the timeline whenever you encounter unfamiliar court names in a document, or to learn what courts operated in a particular jurisdiction during a time period of interest.

Courts Today

After the **Court History Timeline**, each chapter outlines the hierarchy of today's courts, from the highest appellate level and the trial court divisions, to other specialized courts—such as probate or family courts in the states, or bankruptcy courts in the federal system. You may need to visit or contact one of these courts in your search for court records. Understanding the current court structure, as well as the role of predecessor courts, makes dealing with court personnel more productive.

Where to Find Court Records

The largest section of each *Part II* chapter is **Where to Find Court Records**. Each state chapter starts with **Statewide or General Sources**, listing original and published court records (and related reference material) in the following categories:

- **Courts**
- **State Archives**
- **Federal Archives**
- **State Historical Society**
- **Other Repositories**
- **Books and Journals**
- **Microform**
- **Digital/Electronic Sources**
    - **CD-ROM**
    - **Internet**

After **Statewide or General Sources**, each state chapter (*6* to *11*) lists court records by **County**, repeating the same categories. Similarly, *Chapter 12* begins with **General Sources** of federal court records, followed by listings of other relevant sources by **State**—again divided into "Courts," "Federal Archives," "Other Repositories," "Books and Journals," etc. Headers at the top of each page help you to quickly locate relevant sections of the book.

Research Tips

Where should you begin? The following tips will help you to search for court records in the *Part II* chapters, whatever your research topic. See how these tips apply to two hypothetical projects:

- **Genealogical** research about an ancestor married in **Salem, Massachusetts, 1750**.
- **Historical** research about slander cases in **Hartford, Connecticut, 1800s**.

Focus on County or Geographical Area

If you are researching court records of a particular state, try to determine **counties** or **towns** of interest. The "Where to Find Court Records" section of each state chapter begins with "Statewide or General Sources," but most court records are listed under individual county names. For example:

- **Salem, Massachusetts, 1750**: Turn to the Essex County section of the Massachusetts chapter (*Chapter 8*) for relevant records.
- **Hartford, Connecticut, 1800s**: Check the Hartford County section of the Connecticut chapter (*Chapter 6*).

"Statewide or General Sources" may, of course, offer useful guidance too, so do not overlook that section in *Chapters 6* and *8*.

Each state chapter begins with a map of the present-day counties, and original incorporation dates are listed in each county section under "Where to Find Court Records." Political boundaries, however, evolved over time—counties added or subdivided, new towns established, border areas transferred from one state or colony to another, towns and counties renamed, etc. Those myriad changes are beyond the scope of this book, but specialized references are listed in the "Books and Journals" sections of each *Part II* chapter. Excellent sources of New England county and town information include Marcia D. Melnyk, *Genealogist's Handbook for New England Research*, 4th ed. (Boston: New England Historic Genealogical Society, 1999), and Alice Eichholz, ed., *Red Book: American State, County and Town Sources*, 3rd ed. (Provo, Utah: Ancestry, 2004).

Identify Courts Operating During the Relevant Time Period

Court names and jurisdictions changed frequently. Review the "Court History Timeline" of the state or federal chapter to learn what courts operated during the time period of interest. For example:

- **Salem, Massachusetts, 1750**: The timeline in *Chapter 8*, for example, shows that courts of the Provincial period still operated in Massachusetts by 1750—local justices of the peace, County Courts, and the Superior Court of Judicature—so you should watch for records with those court names while researching an ancestor from Salem.
- **Hartford, Connecticut, 1800s**: The timeline in *Chapter 6* indicates that Connecticut County Courts were abolished in 1855; after that date, look for slander cases in Municipal or Superior Courts of Hartford County, or after 1870 in the Hartford Court of Common Pleas.

Consider Federal Court Records, for Research from 1789-Present

Remember that state and federal courts *both* operate within each of the New England states, and sometimes their functions overlap. Check *Chapter 12* for details about the history and structure of the federal courts and where to find their records. Do federal courts apply to our hypothetical examples?

- **Salem, Massachusetts, 1750**: Since the federal courts did not exist in 1750, they would not be relevant to a search for the Salem ancestor, unless he likely lived past 1789.
- **Hartford, Connecticut, 1800s**: For nineteenth-century slander cases, federal court records cannot be ruled out. If a Hartford slander involved citizens of different states, the case might wind up in federal court. Review *Chapter 2* and the types of cases handled by state and federal courts.

Look for Published Sources

For most historians and genealogists, particularly those who live outside New England, published sources are the best place to start research. With the help of this book, and a home computer or reference librarian in your neighborhood, you can access a surprising array of court record information. Check published sources before making a long research trip. *See* "Books and Journals," "Microform," and "Digital/Electronic Sources" in the "Where to Find Court Records" section of each state and federal chapter. For example:

- **Salem, Massachusetts, 1750**: *Chapter 8* lists several published sources that may lead to a 1750 Salem ancestor.
    - In the "Essex County" section, under "Books and Records," Melinde Lutz Sanborn's two-volume *Essex County, Massachusetts, Probate Index, 1638-1840,* may be helpful, and that work is also available on microform and an online database (check the "Microform" and "Digital/Electronic Sources" sections). If you find something in Sanborn's index, you can read the corresponding probate records on microform.
    - The "Microform" section lists several titles of the relevant time period—not only probate files, but also records of the Court of General Sessions of the Peace and the Inferior Court of Common Pleas. *Note*: Most microform in *Part II*—identified with the abbreviation "GSU"—was published by the Genealogical Society of Utah (Salt Lake City), the microfilming arm of The Church of Jesus Christ of Latter-day Saints (LDS). *See Appendix: Contact Information-Publishers* to find an LDS Family History Center in your area, where you can arrange to borrow microform.
- **Hartford, Connecticut, 1800s**
    - The "Hartford County" section of *Chapter 6* lists no published sources that appear relevant to slander cases.
    - "Books and Journals" under "Statewide and General Sources" in that chapter, however, looks more promising. Connecticut Supreme Court decisions for the 1800s are available in official reports and the "West National Reporter System" at law libraries (*see also* "Microform" and "Digital/Electronic Sources"), and special West "digests" offer indexing by topic. *See Chapter 17* in *Part III: Sampling the Sources*, for a closer look at how to use law library resources for genealogical and historical research.

Visit the Courthouse for Recent Records

Unless you are searching for pending cases or relatively recent records, a courthouse visit may be disappointing. Few New England courthouses have adequate filing space, so closed case files and older records often go to offsite storage or to state archives and records centers. Many courts routinely destroy certain records. Until recently, Vermont did not even require courts to retain records. In Massachusetts, the Superior Court may destroy certain records from the nineteenth and twentieth centuries after retaining only two to ten percent as a "sample." Record retention and sampling guidelines, where available, appear in the "Where to Find Court Records" sections of the state chapters in *Part II*.

Consider whether a courthouse visit is warranted for the hypothetical examples:

- **Salem, Massachusetts, 1750**
  - Turn to the "Essex County" section of *Chapter 8*, under "Courts," and you will see that the Essex Superior Court maintains divorce record books from 1785 onsite; perhaps those records might be useful.
  - None of the other Essex County courthouses, however, appear to retain substantial collections of older records. You may have better luck checking the state archives, or other research sources listed in the "Essex County" section of the chapter, rather than making a courthouse trip.
- **Hartford, Connecticut, 1800s**
  - A glance at "Courts" in the "Hartford County" section of *Chapter 6* shows no courthouses with relevant nineteenth-century records. The Hartford Probate District Court maintains record books and/or computer records about cases from the 1600s, and other probate courts in the county also keep older records onsite, but slander cases are unlikely to wind up in those files.
  - Federal court records might be relevant to the slander research, but *Chapter 12* advises researchers to check federal archives or other sources, instead of the courts, for records before 1970.

Note: Some courts (particularly probate) keep records longer than the minimum retention periods or maintain copies, microfilm, indexes, or original docket/record books. Specifics about each court's record holdings—most courts responded to my inquiries—appear in the "Courts" section of the state chapters under the county name.[5] If you have questions for a state or federal court clerk, *see Appendix: Contact Information-State Courts* and *Federal Courts*.

Remember that Some Court Records are Confidential

Certain court records—juvenile cases, commitments, medical and psychiatric evaluations, tax returns, adoptions, etc.—may not be viewed by researchers, except under limited circumstances. Restrictions vary from state to state. Check state judiciary websites, in the "Where to Find Court Records" section of each chapter (under "Statewide or General Sources: Digital/Electronic Sources"), or contact court clerks for more details.

Understand that the Registry of Deeds is Not Part of the Judicial Branch

Although typically located in county courthouses, the registry of deeds is not part of the court system. Land deeds and related records about property ownership are beyond the scope of this book, except as included in other court records (trials involving real estate, divorce and probate matters, etc.). *See Chapter 3*, or *Appendix: Recommended Reading*, for more information about land records.

---

[5] Where only a court name and location appears in the "Courts" sections of *Part II*, information about that court's records was unavailable when this book went to press. Contact the court clerk directly for further detail.

Call Ahead or Make an Appointment to Visit Courts and Archives

Contact information for courts, archives and other repositories is contained in the *Appendix* at the back of this book. Since hours of operation, staffing, availability of records, etc. vary greatly from one institution to another, call or write before you visit. Busy courts handling current cases may not be able to accommodate walk-in requests, and records may need to be ordered from off-site storage. Advance planning will make your research trip more productive.

Access Most Original Court Records at State and Federal Archives

You can access most original New England court records at the major public archives (except in Vermont, where most archival state court records are not yet consolidated in state archives custody). Check for details in *Part II* about court records at "State Archives" or "Federal Archives" (in the "Statewide or General Sources" and county sections of *Chapters 6 to 11*, or in the "General Sources" and state sections of *Chapter 12*). To continue our research examples:

- **Salem, Massachusetts, 1750**: Turn to "State Archives" in the "Essex County" section of *Chapter 8* for archival court records that might mention a 1750 Salem ancestor. There you will find several listings of court records at the Massachusetts Judicial Archives—mid-eighteenth-century appellate court docket books relating to Essex County, for instance—which may be worth a trip. Contact the Head of Archives, Supreme Judicial Court, for more information (*see Appendix: Contact Information-State Courts* and *Archives and Other Repositories*).
- **Hartford, Connecticut, 1800s**
  - Turn to "State Archives" in the "Hartford County" section of *Chapter 6*. The Connecticut State Archives holds numerous nineteenth-century County Court and Justice of the Peace records, which might include slander cases.
  - Similarly, *Chapter 12* lists records from federal courts for the relevant time period, at the U.S. National Archives and Records Administration.

Check Other Public and Private Repositories

After the listings for state and federal archives, each chapter in *Part II* details many other repositories, large and small, public and private, with original New England court records in their collections. Be sure to review these record descriptions, because you may find documents that will solve your research problems. Full contact information for all of these repositories is contained in the *Appendix* at the back of the book. Would any of these repositories help in our hypothetical research?

- **Salem, Massachusetts, 1750**: In the "Essex County" section of *Chapter 8*, check "Other Repositories," which lists records from the Peabody-Essex Museum in Salem. Maybe these will lead to new information about an eighteenth-century Salem ancestor.

- **Hartford, Connecticut, 1800s**: Continue the search for Hartford slander cases by checking under "State Historical Society" in the "Hartford County" section of *Chapter 6*. The Connecticut Historical Society holds Justice Court dockets in its manuscript collection, a possible source of slander case records.

Good luck with your search!

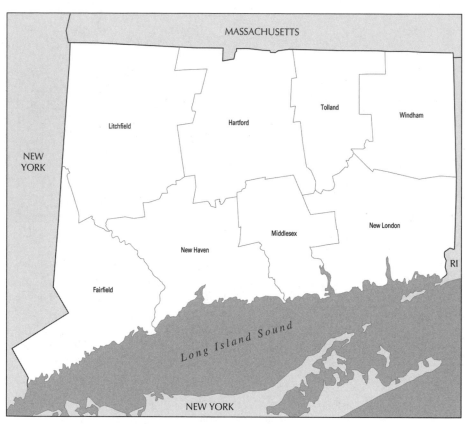

Fig. 6.1. Map of Connecticut Counties. *National Atlas of the United States.* 2005. *http://nationalatlas.gov*

CHAPTER 6

CONNECTICUT STATE COURTS

Court History Timeline

Colonial Courts

Connecticut court history began with three colonies: Connecticut, New Haven and Saybrook.

1638   **Particular Court** (or **Quarter Court**) was established for **Connecticut** Colony, meeting quarterly in Hartford, for trial of civil and criminal cases and appeals from town courts. Special particular courts sometimes met later in Fairfield and New London. **General Court** (**General Assembly**) exercised legislative and judicial powers and served as the colony's highest court, with civil, criminal, divorce and appellate jurisdiction. Both Particular Court and General Court handled probate matters.

1643   **New Haven** became a colony, with its own **General Court**. Governor and magistrates from towns sat twice yearly at New Haven as **Court of Magistrates** to hear major civil and criminal cases, divorces and appeals from town courts. Magistrates tried small civil and criminal cases at **Town** (or **Plantation**) **Courts**. Town deputies (elected legislators) assisted magistrates at town court sessions, with no jury trials.

1662   **Connecticut** (and former **Saybrook** Colony) united under royal charter.

1665-1666   **New Haven** Colony, unable to secure its own charter, was absorbed into **Connecticut** Colony. **General Court** remained highest appellate body and handled some equity matters. Particular Court was replaced by two-level court system: **Court of Assistants**, which met in Hartford for major cases, divorces and appeals (later alternating between Hartford and New Haven); and **County Courts** (Fairfield, Hartford, New Haven and New London), for lesser civil and criminal matters, including probate. **Town** officials continued to handle petty civil cases, misdemeanors, and pre-trial hearings in criminal matters.

1686   **Justices of the Peace** were appointed for minor civil and criminal matters on local level.

1687-1688   **Particular Court** was reestablished during brief administration of Gov. Edmond Andros. Connecticut probate estates valued at more than £50 were filed in Suffolk County, Massachusetts.

1692-1693   **Oyer and Terminer Court** tried witchcraft cases.

1697   Royal **Vice-Admiralty Court** regulated trade and navigation.

1698   **Probate Districts** were established (consisting of original four counties at first), with County Court judge and two justices handling wills, estates, guardianship, etc.

1711   Court of Assistants was replaced by circuit **Superior Court**, meeting twice yearly in each county.

1716   **Probate Courts** were established, each with probate judge and clerk. **Justices of the Peace** presided at county **District Courts** or **Town Courts** for minor civil and criminal cases.

1776-1784   **Maritime Courts** operated during American Revolution.

Courts after Independence

1784   **Supreme Court of Errors** was created, as highest appeals court. **Municipal Courts** were established to handle civil cases at city level, justices of the peace presiding.

1818   Connecticut constitution established **independent judicial branch**. General Assembly no longer had appellate authority.

1819   **Supreme Court of Errors** was held annually in each county.

1855   County Courts were abolished, splitting jurisdiction between **Municipal Courts** and **Superior Courts**. **Commissioners** of Superior Court assisted judges, signing writs and subpoenas and administering oaths.

1870   **Courts of Common Pleas** were established in **Hartford** and **New Haven** counties, and later in other counties.

Twentieth-Century Courts

1921   First **Juvenile Court** was created.

1939   **Trial Justices** replaced justices of the peace for limited criminal jurisdiction at local level.

1941   Single **Court of Common Pleas** was established for entire state.

1960   General Assembly abolished county government. Statewide **Circuit Court** replaced municipal courts and trial justice system.

1965   Supreme Court of Errors was renamed **Supreme Court**.

1974   Circuit Court merged with **Court of Common Pleas**.

1978   Court of Common Pleas and Juvenile Court merged with **Superior Court**, which became sole trial court of general jurisdiction in Connecticut.

1982   Intermediate **Appellate Court** was established to hear appeals from Superior Court and to relieve Supreme Court's overloaded docket.

Connecticut Courts Today

Supreme Court

The Connecticut Supreme Court, the state's highest appellate court, reviews errors of law in cases from Superior Court and certain Appellate Court decisions. Some cases may be appealed directly from Superior Court to Supreme Court; other appeals go first to the intermediate Appellate Court.

Appellate Court

The Connecticut Appellate Court reviews cases from Superior Court to determine whether errors of law have been committed.

Superior Court

The Connecticut Superior Court hears all trials, except probate. The state is divided into:

- 15 **Judicial Districts**, for major civil and criminal trials, and family cases not involving juveniles.
- 22 **Geographical Areas**, for motor vehicle cases and most criminal matters.
- 14 **Juvenile Districts**, for cases involving juveniles.

The four principal Superior Court divisions are:
Civil: Trials by judge or jury, of contract disputes, personal injury claims, etc.
Criminal: Trials of felony or misdemeanor cases.
Housing: Housing cases (*e.g.*, landlord/tenant disputes) in Bridgeport, Hartford, New Haven, Stamford-Norwalk and Waterbury judicial districts; in other judicial districts, housing cases are handled by Civil Division. *Note:* Housing Division records are not covered in this book.
Family: Family matters (*e.g.*, divorce and child custody) and juvenile cases (*e.g.*, delinquency, child abuse, termination of parental rights). *Note:* Juvenile case records are not covered in this book; most are confidential.

Probate District Courts

Connecticut has 123 probate districts, with jurisdiction over estates, trusts, adoptions, conservators, guardianship, name change, etc. For information about current probate districts, *see* "Courts" in each county section, *below*, or *www.jud.state.ct.us/ scripts/prodir1.asp*. For details about historical changes to probate districts and towns, *see Genealogist's Handbook for New England Research* or *A Digest of Early Connecticut Probate Records*, listed in "Statewide or General Sources: Books and Journals," *below*.

Where to Find Court Records
See Appendix for complete contact information.

Statewide or General Sources

Courts

Connecticut Supreme Court, Hartford
Connecticut Appellate Court, Hartford
Supreme Court records and briefs on microfiche, 1986-date; Appellate Court, 1983-date. *See also* "State Archives and Records Center" and other sources, *below*.

Other State Courts
See "Courts" section for each county, *below*.

State Archives and Records Center

Connecticut State Library, **Connecticut State Archives**, Hartford
Record Group 1, Early General Records
> General Court (General Assembly), 1636-1820, including *Conn. Archives: Lotteries and Divorces, Series* 1 & 2, 1718-1820. (Some General Court records also published in *The Public Records of the Colony of Connecticut*; *see* "Books and Journals," "Microform" and "Digital/Electronic Sources," *below*.)
> Supreme Court of Errors, 1784-1901.
> Particular Court, 1639-1665. (Some records also published; *see* "Books and Journals," *below*.)
> Court of Assistants, 1665-1711.
> · Superior Court, 1711-1879.

Record Group 3, Judicial Dept.
> Justice of the Peace Courts, 1729-1936.
> Naturalization records, 1700-1900; microfilm and photocopies. *See also* "Federal Archives and Records Center," *below*.
> "Guide to the Records of the Judicial Dept.," *www.cslib.org/judicial.pdf*.
> "Research Guide to Divorce Records in Connecticut," *www.cslib.org/divorce.htm*.

Record Group 4, Probate Courts
> "Research Guide to Probate Records," *www.cslib.org/probintr.htm*.
> "Research Guide to Conn. Probate Districts," *www.cslib.org/probate/index.htm*.

History and Genealogy Reading Room also provides: Probate indexes and digests, and "Godard Digests" of estate files for many probate districts. *See* "State Archives" section for each county, *below*.

Record Group 5, Records of the Governors
Correspondence re: lawsuits with political ramifications, etc.

Record Group 62, Towns and Boroughs
Includes justice of the peace records.

Record Group 69, Manuscript Collections

Record Group 74, Genealogical Materials

Law and Legislative Reference Unit of Conn. State Library
Official court reports and digests; records and briefs of the U.S. Supreme Court, early 1800s-date; Conn. Supreme Court, late 1700s-date; and Appellate Court, 1986-date.

Superior Court Records Center, Enfield
Court records not yet transferred to Conn. State Archives may be stored at Records Center. Contact court clerks (*see* "Courts" section for each county, *below*, and *Appendix: Contact Information-State Courts*, for access to files at the courthouses or Records Center).

Federal Archives and Records Center

U.S. National Archives and Records Administration (NARA), Northeast Region-Waltham (Boston), Mass.
Donated Materials Group
Naturalization Records of Non-Federal Courts in Conn., 1790-1974. From Conn. state courts, *e.g.*, Superior Courts, Courts of Common Pleas, District Courts, etc., transferred to NARA in 1984.

State Historical Society

Connecticut Historical Society, Hartford
Some manuscript materials are cataloged online, but most are accessed through a card catalog; ask librarian for help with search. Records can be found under subject headings such as: court records, inventories, justice of the peace, lawyers, estate inventories, estate settlements, Connecticut Courts, and Connecticut Governors, *e.g.:*
An account of the life, trial and execution of Lucian Hall, the murderer of Mrs. Lavinia Bacon. Conn., 1844. Book Stacks, 343.1 A169a.
Hoadly, Charles J. Papers, 1885-1908. Manuscript Stacks. Transcriptions and notes from court records, *e.g.*, re: witchcraft cases and first postmortem examination in New England, 1662.
Trumbull, Jonathan, Sr. Papers: Memo Book, 1724-1784. Including Justice of the Peace cases, 1738.

Other Repositories

Brown University Library, Providence, R.I.
Wyllys, Samuel. Papers. Boxes 1-3. 1622-1693. Conn. magistrate's papers, including witness testimony in Oyer and Terminer Courts during witchcraft trials, 1692-1693. *See http://dl.lib.brown.edu/collatoz*. Other Wyllys papers (1694-1726) are located at the Conn. State Library.

Henry Sheldon Museum of Vermont History, Middlebury, Vt.
Sheldon, Henry L. Scrapbook 76. Writs and legal documents, ca. 1880-1900, from Conn. and Vt.

U.S. Citizenship and Immigration Services, U.S. Dept. of Homeland Security, Washington, D.C.
Naturalization certificate files ("C-Files"): Copies of naturalization records from state and federal courts after September 27, 1906, *e.g.*, Declaration of Intention, Petition for Naturalization, and Certificate of Naturalization.
1906-1956: Available on microfilm. Make Freedom of Information/Privacy Act (FOIA/PA) request to U.S. Citizenship and Immigration Services in Washington, D.C.
After 1956: Make FOIA/PA request to the district U.S. Citizenship and Immigration Services office that maintains the records, or office nearest your residence.
See Appendix: Contact Information-Archives and Other Repositories, Washington, D.C.

Yale Law School, New Haven
Reports of cases adjudged by the Superior Court of the state of Connecticut, 1786-1787. Rare Book, MssB C76s 1786-1787.

Books and Journals

Court Records—Abstracts, Transcripts and Indexes

The American Genealogist. Vols. 12-14. List of probate estates handled in Suffolk County, Mass., 1686-1689, including Conn. estates.

Cohn, Henry S. " Connecticut's Divorce Mechanism, 1636-1969," *American Journal of Legal History* XIV, no. 1 (Jan. 1970): 34-54.

Farrell, John T., ed. *The Superior Court Diary of William Samuel Johnson, 1772-1773: With Appropriate Records and File Papers of the Superior Court of the Colony of Connecticut for the Terms, December 1772, through March 1773.* Washington, D.C.: American Historical Assoc., 1942; Millwood, N.Y.: Kraus Reprint Co., 1975.

Manwaring, Charles William. *A Digest of the Early Connecticut Probate Records.* 3 vols. Hartford: R.S. Peck & Co., 1904-1906; Baltimore, Md.: Genealogical Publishing Co., 1995. Vol. 1 explains "daughtering-off" of towns and of probate districts. *See also* "Microform" and "Digital/Electronic Sources," *below.*

Records of the Particular Court of Connecticut, 1639-1663. Collections of the Connecticut Historical Society. Vol. 22. Hartford: Conn. Historical Society, 1928; Bowie, Md.: Heritage Books, 1987.

Records of the Particular Court of Connecticut, Administration of Sir Edmond Andros, Royal governor, 1687-1688. Hartford: Lockwood & Brainard Co., 1935.

Trumbull, J. Hammond, and Charles J. Hoadly. *The Public Records of the Colony of Connecticut, 1636-1776.* 15 vols. Hartford: Case, Lockwood & Brainard, 1850-1890. *See also* "Microform" and "Digital/Electronic Sources," *below.* Includes records of General Court and Particular Courts, wills and inventories, etc.; *e.g.*, "Records of the General and Particular Courts, from April 1636 to December 1649," 1: 1-203.

Trumbull, J. Hammond. *The Public Records of the Colony of Connecticut, from 1665 to 1678; With the Journal of the Council of War, 1675-1678.* 2 vols. Reprint, Salem, Mass.: Higginson Book Co., 1994.

Ullmann, Helen Schatvet, *Hartford County, Connecticut, County Court Minutes: Volumes 3 and 4, 1663-1687, 1697*. Boston: New England Historic Genealogical Society, 2005. Original vol. 3 is in RG 1, Early General Records, Conn. State Library (also known as Early General Records, vol. 56); original vol. 4 is in RG 4, Probate Records, Records of the Hartford Probate Court, Conn. State Library. *See* "State Archives," *above*, and "Microform" in Hartford County section, *below*.

History

Dayton, Cornelia Hughes. *Women before the Bar: Gender, Law and Society in Connecticut, 1639-1789*. Chapel Hill and London: Univ. of N. Carolina Press, 1995.

Ditz, Toby L. *Property and Kinship: Inheritance in Early Connecticut, 1750-1820*. Princeton, N.J.: Princeton Univ. Press, 1986.

Godbeer, Richard. *Escaping Salem: The Other Witch Hunt of 1692*. Oxford Univ. Press, 2004, 2005.

Goodwin, Everett C. *The Magistracy Rediscovered: Connecticut, 1636-1818*. Ann Arbor, Mich.: UMI Research Press, 1981.

Loomis, Dwight, and J. Gilbert Calhoun. *The Judicial and Civil History of Connecticut*. Boston: Boston History Co., 1895.

Maltbie, William M. "The Supreme Court of Errors," *Conn. Bar Journal* 26, no. 4 (Dec. 1952): 357-372.

Tomlinson, R. G. *Witchcraft Trials of Connecticut: The First Comprehensive Documented History of Witchcraft Trials in Colonial Connecticut*. Hartford: Bond Press, 1978.

Law Library Resources

Case Reports: *See Chapter 17*, and *Appendix-Law Libraries* and *Publishers. See also* "Microform" and "Digital/Electronic Sources," *below*.

Connecticut Supreme Court

"Nominative reports." Multiple vols. Court decisions, 1786-1813, *e.g.*, *Kirby's Reports*, *Root's Reports*, *Day's Reports*.

Connecticut Reports. Multiple vols. Enfield, Conn.: Comm. on Official Legal Publications. Court decisions, 1814-date.

Atlantic Reporter. Multiple vols. Eagan, Minn.: West. Court decisions, 1886-date, enhanced with headnotes, key numbers and synopses.

West's Connecticut Digest and *West's Atlantic Digest*. Multiple vols. Eagan, Minn.: West. Summary of Conn. state and federal court decisions, 1764-date, organized alphabetically by topic, with headnotes, key numbers, and multiple indexes (case name, etc.).

Connecticut Appellate Court

Connecticut Appellate Reports. Multiple vols. Enfield, Conn.: Comm. on Official Legal Publications. 1983-date.

Atlantic Reporter. Multiple vols. Eagan, Minn.: West. Court decisions, 1983-date, enhanced with headnotes, key numbers and synopses.

West's Connecticut Digest and *West's Atlantic Digest*. Multiple vols. Eagan, Minn.: West. Digests of Conn. state and federal court decisions, 1764-date, organized alphabetically by topic, with headnotes, key numbers, and multiple indexes (case name, etc.).

Connecticut Superior Court
Connecticut Supplement. Multiple vols. Enfield, Conn.: Comm. on Official
Legal Publications. Selected opinions.
Connecticut Circuit Courts
Connecticut Circuit Court Reports. Multiple vols. Enfield, Conn.: Comm. on
Official Legal Publications. Selected opinions of former Conn. Circuit Court,
1961-1974.
Other Law Library Resources: *Connecticut Practice Series*. Multiple vols. Eagan,
Minn.: West. Updated with pocket parts. Summary of Conn. law, historical
background and case citations.

Research Guides

Cheeseman, Lawrence G., and Arlene C. Bielefield. *The Connecticut Legal Research
Handbook*. Guilford, Conn.: Conn. Law Book Co., 1992.
Melnyk, Marcia. *Genealogist's Handbook for New England Research*, 4th ed. Boston:
New England Historic Genealogical Society, 1999. Contains list of Conn.
towns, counties and probate districts.

Microform

Miscellaneous court records

Conn. Supreme Court reports, 1814-1926, and additional vols. annually; *Kirby's
Reports*, 1785-1788; *Root's Reports*, 1798-1802; *Day's Reports*, 1830-1833.
Microfiche. Kaneohe, Hawaii: Law Library Microform Consortium.
Judd, Sylvester. *Land Lotteries and Divorces of Connecticut 1755-1789 with Index*.
GSU, 1954.
Trumbull, J. Hammond, and Charles J. Hoadly. *The Public Records of the Colony of
Connecticut, 1636-1776*. 15 vols. Hartford: Case, Lockwood & Brainard,
1850-1890. GSU, 1969, 1972. Microfilm. GSU, 1985. Microfiche.

Probate District court records

Estate Record Card Index, 1915-1926. GSU, 1989. Various districts; from records at
Conn. State Archives.
General Index to Probate Records: All Districts in Connecticut 1641-1948. GSU,
1957-1958.
Godard, George Seymour. *Godard's Digests, Analytical and Chronological, of Con-
necticut Probate Papers*. GSU, 1989. Inventories prepared by Conn. State
Library.
Manwaring, Charles William. *A Digest of the Early Connecticut Probate Records*. 3
vols. Hartford: R. S. Peck & Co., 1904-1906. GSU, 1969-1971.
Probate Estate Files, 1881-1915. GSU, 1994. From districts of Andover, Ashford,
Avon, Barkhamsted, Bethany, Bethel, Bozrah, Bristol, Bridgeport, Brooklyn,
Burlington, Canterbury, Canton, Chaplin, Cheshire, Colchester, Coventry,
Eastford, E. Lyme, Easton, E. Windsor, Ellington, Enfield, Farmington,
Granby, Greenwich, Haddam, Hampton, Hartford, Hartland, Harwinton,
Hebron, Kent, Killingly, Killingsworth, Lebanon, Ledyard, Litchfield, Lyme,
Mansfield, Marlborough, Middletown, Milford, Montville and New Haven.
Original records at Conn. State Library.
Probate Files Collection, Early to 1880. GSU, 1977-1979. From districts of Andover,
Ashford, Avon, Barkhamsted, Bethany, Bethel, Bozrah, Bridgeport, Bristol,

Brooklyn, Burlington, Canaan, Canton, Chaplin, Cheshire, Colchester, Coventry, Danbury, Derby, Eastford, E. Lyme, Easton, E. Windsor, Ellington, Enfield, Fairfield, Farmington, Granby, Guilford, Haddam, Hampton, Hartford, Hartland, Harwinton, Hebron, Kent, Killingly, Killingworth, Lebanon, Ledyard, Litchfield, Lyme, Mansfield, Marlborough, Middletown, Milford, Montville, New Haven, New London, New Milford, Newtown, Norfolk, N. Stonington, Norwich, Old Lyme, Old Saybrook, Oxford, Plainfield, Plymouth, Pomfret, Redding, Roxbury, Salem, Sharon, Sherman, Simsbury, Somers, Southington, Stafford, Stamford, Sterling, Stonington, Stratford, Suffield, Thompson, Tolland, Torrington, Voluntown, Wallingford, Waterbury, Westford, Winchester, Windham, Woodbury and Woodstock. Original records at Conn. State Library.

Digital/Electronic Sources

CD-ROM

Atlantic Reporter. Eagan, Minn.: West. Includes Conn. Supreme Court and Conn. Appellate Court opinions, 1945-date.

Connecticut Reporter and West's Connecticut General Statutes Unannotated. Eagan, Minn.: West. Includes Conn. Supreme Court, 1939-date; and Conn. Appellate Court, 1983-date.

Connecticut Reports Archives CD-ROM. 6 disk set. Enfield, Conn.: Comm. on Official Legal Publications. Contains *Kirby's Reports, Root's Reports* (vols. 1-2), *Day's Reports* (vols. 1-5), *Connecticut Reports* (vols. 1-129), *Digest of Decisions Connecticut (Dowling)*, 1st Series (10 vols.), and *Philips Digest* (3 vols.).

Manwaring, Charles William. *Early Connecticut Probate Records, Vols 1-3.* Hartford: R. S. Peck & Co., 1904-1906; Bowie, Md.: Heritage Books, 2002.

West's Connecticut Digest. Eagan, Minn.: West. Digest of state and federal appellate court decisions, 1764-date.

Internet

Connecticut Judicial Branch
   www.jud.state.ct.us
   General information about Conn. state courts.
   www.jud.state.ct.us/external/supapp/archiveAROsup.htm
   Conn. Supreme Court, 2000-date.
   www.jud.state.ct.us/external/supapp/archiveAROap.htm
   Conn. Appellate Court 2000-date.
   www.jud2.state.ct.us/civil_inquiry
   Civil/Family case lookup; to ten years after case closed.
   www.jud.state.ct.us/housing.htm
   Housing case lookup. Tenant eviction cases at Hartford, New Haven, New Britain and Bridgeport districts.
   www.jud2.state.ct.us/Small_Claims
   Small Claims case lookup; one to ten years after case closed.
   www.jud.state.ct.us/faq/courtrec2.html#Access
   "Access Guidelines to Court Records," including guidelines about records that are confidential or closed to the public.

Law Library of Congress *www.loc.gov/law/guide/us-ct.html*
>   Links to Conn. state and federal court opinions.

LexisNexis *www.lexis.com*
>   Conn. Supreme Court, 1786-date; Conn. Appellate Court, 1983-date. Subscription service or available at law libraries and other repositories.

LexisOne *www.lexisone.com*
>   Conn. Supreme Court and Conn. Appellate Court, most recent five years; free.

Loislaw *www.loislaw.com*
>   Conn. Supreme Court, 1899-date; Conn. Appellate Court, 1983-date; some Superior Court decisions. Subscription service.

Public Records of the Colony of Connecticut *www.colonialct.uconn.edu*
>   Early Conn. General Court records.

VersusLaw *www.versuslaw.com*
>   Conn. appellate courts, 1950-date; Mashantucket Pequot Tribal Court, 1992-date; Mohegan Gaming Disputes Court, 1997-date. Subscription service.

Westlaw *www.westlaw.com*
>   Conn. Supreme Court, 1786-date; Conn. Appellate Court, 1983-date. Subscription service or available at law libraries and other repositories. Westlaw CourtEXPRESS offers case research and document retrieval from U.S. courts.

Fairfield County
Founded 1666

Courts

Superior Court—Judicial Districts
Danbury Judicial District, Danbury
Serves Bethel, Brookfield, Danbury, New Fairfield, Newtown, Redding, Ridgefield and Sherman. Civil: docket/record books, file papers, 1978-date. Criminal: docket/record books, 1978-date.
Fairfield Judicial District, Bridgeport
Serves Bridgeport, Easton, Fairfield, Monroe, Stratford and Trumbull.
Stamford-Norwalk Judicial District, Stamford
Serves Darien, Greenwich, New Canaan, Norwalk, Stamford, Weston, Westport and Wilton. Civil: docket/record books, file papers, index; original, microfilm and computer; 1958-date. Criminal: limited; most stored at records center; 1961-date.

Superior Court—Geographical Areas
Geographical Area #1, Stamford
Serves Darien, Greenwich and Stamford. Criminal: docket/record books, file papers, appeals; microfilm and computer; 1990-date.
Geographical Area #2, Bridgeport
Serves Bridgeport, Easton, Fairfield, Monroe, Stratford and Trumbull. Criminal: docket/record books, original and microfilm, 1962-date; original file papers, pending cases; computer, 1998-date.
Geographical Area #3, Danbury
Serves Bethel, Brookfield, Danbury, New Fairfield, Newtown, Redding, Ridgefield and Sherman.

Geographical Area #20, Norwalk
Serves New Canaan, Norwalk, Weston, Westport and Wilton. Criminal: docket/record books, microfilm, 1960s-date.

Probate District Court
Bethel
Microfilmed record books, 1859-date; card index.
Bridgeport
Record books, vols. 1-9, 1782-1840.
Brookfield
Original current estate papers, microfilmed record books, 1800s-date.
Danbury
Microfilm, 1744-date; index.
Darien
Fairfield
Record books, estate papers, appeals, index; original and microfilm; 1648-date.
Greenwich
Record books, appeals, index; original and microfilm; 1835-date.
New Canaan
Microfilmed record books, 1938-date; index.
New Fairfield
Original record books, estate papers, appeals; microfilm offsite.
Newtown
Record books, vols. 1-141; microfilm, 1820-date; index.
Norwalk
Record books, estate papers, appeals, index; original and microfilm; 1802-date.
Redding
Ridgefield
Record books, estate papers, appeals, index; original and microfilm; 1845-date.
Shelton
Record books and estate papers; microfilm and transcripts; 1889-date.
Stamford
Estate papers and appeals: transcripts, 1730-1955; photocopies, 1955-1960; microfilm, 1960-2003; computer, 2004-date; index.
Stratford
Microfilm, 1840-date; staff provides index.
Trumbull
Computer, 1959-date; index.
Westport
Record books, estate papers, appeals; original, transcripts and microfilm; 1836-date.

State Archives

Connecticut State Library, **Connecticut State Archives**, Hartford
Record Group 3, Judicial Dept.
> **Fairfield County court records** Supreme Court of Errors, 1822-1964; Superior Court, 1711-1944; County Court, 1701-1881; Maritime Court, 1777-1783; Court of Common Pleas, 1879-1958; County Commissioners, 1889-1937.

District and Municipal court records Bridgeport City Court, 1884-1909; Brookfield City Court, 1958-1959; Danbury City Court, 1889-1960; Fairfield City Court, 1960; Greenwich City Court, 1956-1960; Greenwich Borough Court, 1889-1939; Monroe City Court, 1954-1960; New Canaan City Court, 1956-1960; Newtown City Court, 1931-1954, 1958-1960; Norwalk Town Court, 1895-1960; Shelton City Court, 1955-1960; Stamford Borough Court, 1883-1962; Stratford City Court, 1960.

Judges' notes, dockets and drafts Fairfield Superior Court, 1863, 1865-1867, 1869, 1871-1872; Judge William Thomas Minor, 1868-1872 (includes Fairfield Superior Court and County Court minutes and notes).

Justice of the Peace courts Danbury, 1892-1922; Darien, 1883-1907; Newtown, 1861-1881.

Coroner's records Fairfield County (Bridgeport), 1883-1979.

Record Group 4, Probate Courts

Probate digests and abstracts

Card, Lester. *Probate Records of Norwalk, 1802-1808*. S. Norwalk, Conn.: By author, n.d.

Mead, Spencer Percival. "Abstracts of Probate Records for the District of Fairfield." Probate Vault 974.62 F15M.

Probate District court records

Bethel Estate papers: original, 1859-1929; microfilm, 1859-1915. Record books: original, 1859-1976; microfilm, 1859-1918.

Bridgeport Estate papers: original and microfilm, 1840-1915. Record books: microfilm, 1840-1916.

Brookfield Record books: microfilm, 1857-1923.

Danbury Estate papers: original and microfilm, 1756-1891. Record books: microfilm, 1739-1916.

Easton Estate papers: original, 1832-1884; microfilm, 1832-1881.

Fairfield Estate papers: original, 1648-1911; microfilm, 1648-1880. Record books: original, 1648-1755; microfilm, 1648-1916.

Greenwich Estate papers: original and microfilm, 1853-1900. Record books: microfilm, 1853-1925.

Newtown Estate papers: original, 1820-1931; microfilm, 1820-1880. Record books: microfilm, 1820-1915.

Norwalk Estate papers: indexes, 1802-1920. Record books: microfilm, 1802-1916.

Redding Estate papers: original, 1839-1902; microfilm, 1839-1880. Record books: microfilm, 1839-1919.

Ridgefield Record books: microfilm, 1841-1916.

Shelton Record books: microfilm, 1889-1917.

Sherman Estate papers: original, 1846-1946; microfilm, 1846-1880. Record books: microfilm, 1846-1931.

Stamford Estate papers: original, 1700-1935; microfilm, 1760-1870. Record books: microfilm, 1728-1916.

Stratford Estate papers: original, 1781-1898; microfilm, 1781-1880. Record books: microfilm, 1840-1917.

Weston Estate papers: original and microfilm, 1832-1875. Record books: microfilm, 1832-1856.

Westport Record books: microfilm, 1835-1916.

State Historical Society

Connecticut Historical Society, Hartford

Connecticut. Danbury Superior Court. Pay order, 1790. Manuscript Stacks, 97864.
    Ordering treasurer to pay Andrew Rowland, State Attorney, for his part in
    trial of Pegg, an African-American woman tried and acquitted of murder.
Read, John. Record books, 1751-1784. Manuscript Stacks, 93839 Items 13-14. Justice
    of the Peace in Danbury and Redding, 1751-1774.
Smith, Seth Samuel. Account book, 1801-1810. Justice of the Peace in Redding.

Other Repositories

Danbury Historical Society, Danbury

Court records: civil docket, 1884-1914; civil cases, 1901-1912; civil short calendar,
    1931-1934; criminal docket, 1896-1931; juvenile court, 1917-1935; nonsuit
    for want of bonds, 1899-1905; foreclosure petitions, 1877-1879; foreclosure
    judgments, 1889-1916; tax liens, 1889-1898; city court cash books, 1889-
    1950.
Probate and land records: transcripts, 1780-1783.

Fairfield Historical Society, Fairfield

Extensive manuscript collection, including legal, probate and land records in: Adams
Family Papers, 1712/13-1889; Andrews Family Papers, 1734/5-1860; Banks Family
Papers, 1746-1929; Beers Family Papers, 1771-1901; Bennett (Bennitt) Family
Papers, 1784-1914; Blakeman, Rufus Papers, 1822-1870; Bradley, William Papers,
1843-1855, 1872; Bradley Family Papers, 1727-1929; Bradley, Henry Collection,
1839-1899; Breed & Mumford Papers, 1698/9-1825; Breed & Susquehannah Co.
Papers, 1754-1966; Brewster, Caleb Papers, 1755-1976; Bulkeley Family Papers,
1713-1943, 1803-1898; Burr Family Papers; Burritt Family Papers, 1793-1854;
Couch Family Papers, 1738/9-1858; Dimon Family Papers, 1724-1834; Fairfield Fam-
ilies Papers, 1693/4-; Fairfield Land Records; Fairfield Municipal Records, 1661-;
Glover, William B. Collection, 1880-1977; Hawley Family Papers, 1721-1892; Hide
(Hyde) Family Papers, 1671-1912; Hopkins Family Papers, 1791-1918; Hull Family
Papers, 1710-1866; Huntington Family Collection, 1811-1907; Jennings Family
Papers, 1756-1925; Lacey Family Papers, 1790-1909; Lyon Family Papers, 1774-
1957; Meeker Family Papers, 1721/2-1950; Merwin Family Papers, 1741/2-1976;
Morehouse Family Papers, 1749/50-1903; Nichols Family Collection, 1794-1970;
Nichols Family Papers, 1728-1894; Ogden Family Papers, 1729/30-1935; Osborn
Family Papers, 1734-1871; Pickett-Overbaugh Papers, 1867-1983; Rowland Family
Papers, 1692-1901; Sanford, Emily Judson Collection, 1807-1968; Sanford Family
Papers, 1775-1882; Seeley Family Papers, 1767-1892; Sherman, Roger Minott
Papers, 1773-1842; Sherwood Family Papers, 1654-1912; Silliman Family Papers,
1726-1894; Stegeman Family Papers, 1850-1961; Sturges, Mary A. Scrapbook, 1893-
1905; Summers-Hill Families Papers, 1733/4-1939; Thorp Family Papers, 1749-1924;
Trinity Church Records, 1790-1954; Turney Family Papers, 1685-1944; Wakeman
Family Papers, 1705-1938, 1957; Wheeler Family Papers, 1693/4-1865; White Fam-
ily Papers, 1767-1917; Wood Family Papers, 1831-1945.

New England Historic Genealogical Society, Boston, Mass.

Card, Lester. "Court records of Theophilus Fitch, J. P., Norwalk, Conn., 1755 to 1768." MSS CT NOR 1912.

_____. "Fairfield County, Conn. Superior Court records. First volume, 1702-1734." MSS CT 8110.

Mead, Spencer P. "Abstract of Probate Records at Fairfield, County of Fairfield, and State of Connecticut, 1704-1757." 1934. MSS CT FAI 29. *See also* "Books and Journals," "Microform" and "Digital/Electronic Sources," *below*.

Trumbull Historical Society, Trumbull

A few original wills, 1690-1900; no index.

Books and Journals

Haslam, Patricia L. "Deaths Untimely: Fairfield County, Connecticut, Superior Court Inquests," *New England Historical and Genealogical Register* 144 (Jan. 1990): 39-47.

Marcus, Ronald. *"Elizabeth Clawson...thou deseruest to dye": An Account of the Trial in 1692 of a Woman From Stamford, Connecticut Who Was Accused of Being a Witch*. Stamford: Stamford Historical Society, 1976.

Mead, Spencer P. *Abstract of Probate Records at Fairfield, County of Fairfield, and State of Connecticut, 1648-1750*. 1929. Salem, Mass.: Higginson Book Co., 1998. *See also* "Other Repositories," *above*, and "Microform" and "Digital/Electronic Sources," *below*.

_____. *Abstracts of Probate Records for the District of Stamford, County of Fairfield and State of Connecticut, 1729-1802*. Greenwich, Conn.: By author, 1919. *See also* "Microform," *below*.

_____. *Abstract of Probate Records for the District of Stamford, County of Fairfield, and State of Connecticut, 1803-1848*. 2 vols. Salem, Mass.: Higginson Book Co., 1997. *See also* "Microform," *below*.

Microform

Miscellaneous court records

Divorce Papers, 1720-1799. GSU, 1990. Superior Court.

Naturalization records

Naturalization Records 1839-1955 (Fairfield County, Connecticut). GSU, 2003. Court of Common Pleas and Superior Court.

Probate District court records
Bethel
Probate Records, 1859-1931. GSU, 1988.
Bridgeport
Probate Records, 1782-1917. GSU, 1949, 1985; Vol. 10, June 15-24, 1840.
Probate Records, 1840-1916. GSU, 1949, 1985.
Brookfield
Probate Records, 1851-1922. GSU, 1986.

Danbury
Probate Records, 1744-1916. GSU, 1948, 1986. Includes towns of Danbury and New Fairfield.

Fairfield
Mead, Spencer P. *Abstract of Probate Records at Fairfield, County of Fairfield, and State of Connecticut, 1648-1757.* GSU, 1941. *See also* "Other Repositories" and "Books and Journals," *above*, and "Digital/Electronic Sources," *below*.

Miscellaneous Wills and Inventories of Richard Smith, Jeremiah Adams and Thomas Skidmore. GSU, 2001. Estates of Thomas Skidmore, 1684, and others.

Probate Records, 1648-1916. GSU, 1949, 1985.

Greenwich
Probate Records, 1853-1927. GSU, 1986.

Huntington
Probate Records, 1889-1917. GSU, 1986.

Newtown
Probate Records, 1820-1922. GSU, 1949, 1986.

Norwalk
Card, Lester L. *Marriage and Probate Records from Norwalk, Connecticut.* GSU, 1941. 1802-1808.

Probate Records, 1802-1916. GSU, 1948, 1988.

Redding
Probate Records, 1839-1920. GSU, 1949, 1986.

Ridgefield
Probate Records, 1841-1917. GSU, 1949, 1986.

Shelton
Probate Records, 1889-1917. GSU, 1986.

Sherman
Probate Records, 1846-1931. GSU, 1986.

Stamford
Mead, Spencer P. *Abstract of Probate Records for the District of Stamford, County of Fairfield, and State of Connecticut, 1729-1848.* GSU, 1941. *See also* "Books and Journals," *above*.

Probate Records, 1728-1916. GSU, 1949, 1985.

Stratford
Probate Records, 1782-1917. GSU, 1949, 1985.

Westport
Probate Records, 1835-1928. GSU, 1949, 1987.

Digital/Electronic Sources

Internet
New England Historic Genealogical Society *www.NewEnglandAncestors.org*
Probate Records of Fairfield County, Connecticut, 1704-1757. Boston: NewEnglandAncestors.org, 2003. From Spencer P. Mead. "Abstract of Probate Records of Fairfield, County of Fairfield, and State of Connecticut." 1934. *See* "Other Repositories," *above*.

Hartford County
Founded 1666

Courts

Superior Court—Judicial Districts
Hartford Judicial District, Hartford
Serves Avon, Bloomfield, Canton, E. Granby, E. Hartford, E. Windsor, Enfield, Farmington, Glastonbury, Granby, Hartford, Manchester, Marlborough, Simsbury, S. Windsor, Suffield, W. Hartford, Windsor and Windsor Locks. Civil: docket/record books (1930s-date), file papers (1940s-date), appeals; original, microfilm and computer; index cards.
New Britain Judicial District, New Britain
Serves Berlin, Bristol, Burlington, New Britain, Newington, Plainville, Plymouth, Rocky Hill, Southington and Wethersfield. Civil: docket/record books, file papers; original and microfilm, 1978-date; computer 2004-date; party-name index.

Superior Court—Geographical Areas
Geographical Area #12, Manchester
Serves E. Hartford, Glastonbury, Manchester, Marlborough and S. Windsor. Criminal: computer printout, latest two to three years.
Geographical Area #13, Enfield
Serves E. Granby, E. Windsor, Enfield, Granby, Simsbury, Suffield, Windsor and Windsor Locks.
Geographical Area #14, Hartford
Serves Avon, Bloomfield, Canton, Farmington, Hartford and W. Hartford.
Geographical Area #15, New Britain
Serves Berlin, New Britain, Newington, Rocky Hill and Wethersfield. Civil and criminal: original file papers; no index.
Geographical Area #17, Bristol
Serves Bristol, Burlington, Plainville, Plymouth and Southington. Civil (small claims): original judgments, to Jan. 1994. Criminal and motor vehicle: docket/record books, file papers (pending cases only), appeals; original, microfilm and computer.

Probate District Court
Avon
Original records, microfilm, 1845-date.
Berlin, New Britain
Record books, index; microfilm, 1824-date.
Bloomfield
Bristol
Record books, estate papers, appeals, index; original (current), microfilm (closed), 1830-date.
Burlington
Record books, estate papers (open matters only), appeals, index; original (wills only) and microfilm, 1834-date.
Canton, Collinsville
Record books, estate papers; microfilm, 1832-date.
E. Granby
Record books, estate papers, index; original and microfilm, 1865-date.

E. Hartford
Estate papers, appeals, index; microfilm, 1887-date.
E. Windsor, S. Windsor
Microfilmed record books, 1900-date (some 1782-1899); alphabetical index.
Enfield
Record books, estate papers, appeals; original for one year after completion, then microfilmed, 1831-date; index cards.
Farmington
Glastonbury
Microfilmed record books, 1975-date; index.
Granby
Record books, estate papers; original and photocopies, 1807-date.
Hartford
Record books, computer, 1600s-date.
Manchester
Estate papers, appeals, index; original and microfilm.
Marlborough
Appeals, other; original and microfilm.
Newington
Record books and estate papers (microfilm), wills (original, off-site storage), 1975-date; index.
Plainville
Record books, estate papers, index; original and microfilm, 1914-date.
Simsbury
Record books, index; original and microfilm, 1769-date.
Southington
Wills (original), other records (computer), 1873-date (prior records in Farmington); index.
Suffield
Record books, 1821-date.
W. Hartford
Record books, microfilm, 1983-date.
Windsor
Transcripts, after 1855.
Windsor Locks
Original and microfilmed records, 1961-date.

State Archives

Connecticut State Library, **Connecticut State Archives**, Hartford
Record Group 1, Early General Records
> **Hartford County court records** Also known as Early General Records Vol. 56. 1663-1677. *See also* "Microform," and transcription by Helen Schatvet Ullmann in "Books," *below*.

Record Group 3, Judicial Dept.
> **Hartford County court records** Supreme Court of Errors, 1820-1977; Superior Court, 1711-1969; County Court, 1666-1881; Maritime Court, 1776-1783; Court of Common Pleas, 1859-1965; County Commissioners, 1890-1950.

District and Municipal court records Berlin City Court, 1951-1960; Bloomfield City Court, 1951-1960; Bristol City Court, 1958-1960; E. Hartford City Court, 1959-1960; Enfield City Court, 1959-1960; Glastonbury City Court, 1951-1960; Hartford City Court, 1804-1960; Manchester City Court, 1956-1960; New Britain City Court, 1951-1960; Newington City Court, 1955-1960; Plainville City Court, 1957-1960; Rocky Hill City Court, 1954-1960; S. Windsor City Court, 1929-1960; Southington City Court, 1955-1960; Suffield City Court, 1955-1960; W. Hartford City Court, 1959-1960; Wethersfield City Court, 1953-1960; Windsor City Court, 1942-1960; Windsor Locks City Court, 1959-1960.

Judges' notes, dockets and drafts Hartford Superior Court, 1863-1866, 1871, 1873.

Justice of the Peace courts Bristol, 1799-1800; E. Windsor, 1785-1801; Farmington, 1763-1795 (*see also* Bristol); Glastonbury, 1773-1796 (*see also* Jonathan Hale Transcript, 974.61 H25cs and Classified Archives, RG 000); Hartford, 1767-1884. *See also* Record Group 62 and 69, *below*.

Coroner's records Hartford County, 1883-1879.

Record Group 4, Probate Courts

Probate District court records
Avon Estate papers: original, 1844-1905; microfilm, 1842-1905. Record books: microfilm, 1844-1919.

Berlin Record books: microfilm, 1824-1917.

Bristol Estate papers: original, 1830-1937; microfilm, 1830-1915. Record books: microfilm, 1830-1917.

Burlington Estate papers: original, 1834-1955; microfilm, 1834-1915. Record books: microfilm, 1835-1927.

Canton Estate papers: original, 1841-1955; microfilm, 1841-1915. Record books: microfilm, 1841-1916.

E. Granby Record books: microfilm, 1865-1955.

E. Hartford Estate papers: original, 1887-1933. Record books: microfilm, 1887-1919.

E. Windsor Estate papers: original, 1782-1899; microfilm, 1782-1915. Record books: microfilm, 1781-1922.

Enfield Estate papers: original, 1831-1928; microfilm, 1831-1915. Record books: microfilm, 1831-1922.

Farmington Estate papers: original, 1769-1948; microfilm, 1769-1915. Record books: microfilm, 1769-1926.

Granby Estate papers: original, 1807-1958; microfilm, 1807-1915. Record books: microfilm, 1807-1924.

Hartford Estate papers: original, 1641-1940; microfilm, 1641-1915. Record books: original, 1677-1850; microfilm, 1636-1917, which also includes Hartford County Court records, 1677-1697. *See also* "Microform" and "Books," *below*.

Hartland Estate papers: original, 1836-1921; microfilm, 1836-1915. Record books: microfilm, 1838-1937.

Manchester Record books: microfilm, 1850-1916.

Marlborough Estate papers: original, 1846-1938; microfilm, 1846-1915. Record books: microfilm, 1846-1937.

Plainville Record books: microfilm, 1910-1928.

Simsbury Estate papers: original, 1769-1906; microfilm, 1769-1880. Record books: microfilm, 1769-1917.

Southington Estate papers: original, 1825-1907; microfilm, 1825-1880. Record books: microfilm, 1825-1918.

Suffield Estate papers: original, 1821-1952; microfilm, 1821-1880. Record books: microfilm, Hampshire County, Mass., including town of Suffield, 1660-1920.

Windsor Record books: microfilm, 1857-1916.

Record Group 62, Towns and Boroughs

Justice of the Peace courts Burlington; Canton; Glastonbury; Hartland, 1718-1919; Marlborough, 1883-1911; Simsbury; Wethersfield; Windsor Locks.

Record Group 69, Manuscript Collections

Justice of the Peace courts Roswell Grant Papers, RG 069:053 (E. Windsor); John Treadwell Papers, RG 069:025 (Farmington); Goslee Family Papers, RG 069:083, and Jonathan Palmer, Jr. Papers, RG 069:087 (Hartford).

Record Group 74, Genealogical Materials

Probate digests and abstracts Lucius Barnes Barbour:

Abstracts of Probate Records from E. Windsor, Conn., 1782-1800. RG 74:36, no. 76.

Genealogical Notes Compiled from E. Hartford and Glastonbury Probate Records, 1800-1830. RG 74:36, no. 75.

Genealogical Notes Compiled from Hartford, Conn. District Probate Records, 1751-1800. RG 74:36, no. 77.

Genealogical Notes Compiled from Hartford, Conn. Probate Records. RG 74:36, no. 78.

Genealogical Notes Compiled from Probate Records, Suffield and Windsor, After 1800. RG 74:36, no. 83.

Genealogical Notes Compiled from Probate Records from Wethersfield, Conn. After 1800. RG 74:36, no. 84.

Index of Vol., Manwaring Digest, 1653-1698. RG 74:36, no. 161.

Index to Hartford Probate Records, 1751-1800. RG 74:36, no. 80.

Index to Hartford Probate Records, Vols. 16-25, and E. Windsor Probate Records, Vols. 1-2. RG 74:36, no. 79.

Notes from Probate Records, Hartford District, 1635-1750. RG 74:36, no. 81.

Federal Archives and Records Center

U.S. National Archives and Records Administration (NARA), Northeast Region-Waltham (Boston), Mass.

City court records, including naturalization records of Hartford, 1875-1876. NARA series 21.8.3.

State Historical Society

Connecticut Historical Society, Hartford

Allyn Family. Papers, 1717-1800. Includes court records kept by Henry Allyn of Windsor.

Chester, John. Complaint, 1669. Re: witchcraft charges against Katherine Harrison of Wethersfield.

Farmington Justice Court Records, 1741-1750. Thomas Hart, Justice of Peace. Microfilm.

Glastonbury Inferior Court Records, 1753-1765. Microfilm.

Important decision for working-men: report of the case of the Thompsonville Carpet Manufacturing Company, versus William Taylor, Edward Gorman, & Thomas Norton, charged with a conspiracy for being concerned in a strike for higher wages.... Hartford: J. B. Eldredge, 1836. Conn. Imprints, 1836 I31r. Hartford County Superior Court.

Phelps, Elisha. Record books, 1805-1818. Justice court dockets for Hartford County.

Phelps, Noah. Record books, 1773-1786. Manuscript Stacks, 73520A. Court records for Hartford County, 1773-1775.

Simsbury Inferior Court Records, 1742-1753. Microfilm.

Southington justice docket, 1792.

Wooley, George W. Legal papers, 1865-1872. Federal court lawsuit of *Cooke & Whitmore v. George W. Wooley* for infringement of patent rights in design of coffins.

Windsor Inferior Court Records, 1719-1734. Matthew Allyn, Justice of Peace. Microfilm.

Windsor Records of [Inferior] Courts Kept by Roger Wolcott, Justice of Peace, 1722-1753. Microfilm.

Other Repositories

Canton Historical Museum, Canton
Admission to Bar of William Edgar Simonds, 1898.
Court records re: case of *W. E. Simonds & Jane Mills v. Miron C. Brockett*, Court of Common Pleas, 1875.
Estate papers re: A. O. and Dr. Ephraim Mills (W. E. Simonds, admin.), 1874-1876.
Wills of Seymour Case, 1872, and Sarah J. Simonds, 1894.

E. Granby Public Library, E. Granby
Copies of probate records in historical room (from originals in town halls and State Library), 18th and 19th centuries.

Historical Society of Glastonbury, Glastonbury
Writs and attachments 1700-1900; grand juror lists, 1785, 1786, 1831-1880; town meeting records, 1690-1737, 1740-1837. Archival collection not fully reviewed and cataloged.

New England Historic Genealogical Society, Boston, Mass.
Windsor (Conn.). Justice of the Peace. Testimony, 1737 January 19, of Capt. George Griswold and John Griswold. MSS C 5159. Re: their ancestry.

Salmon Brook Historical Society, Granby
Criminal: original justice of the peace file papers, 1860-1937.
Probate: original wills, inventories, guardianship papers, etc., 1803-1922.

Other original records: Divorce, 1900; writs, 1785-1845; deeds and title searches, 1696-1920s; ecclesiastical case in civil court, 1849; account book of lawyer Silas Higley, ca. 1840; misc. legal papers, 1795-1900.

All legal documents concern local families and were donated to Society. Some are fairly complete records, others fragmented.

Simsbury Historical Society, Simsbury

Civil and criminal: original file papers, appeals, justice of the peace records, etc., 17th-19th centuries, *e.g.*: McFetridge Collection, which includes writs of attachment and court orders in cases from early 1800s involving Simsbury and Granby residents; and records re: 1808 attempted murder and poisoning of Thomas Chester Clark by Josiah Smith.

Probate: original docket/record books, file papers, appeals; 17th-19th centuries.

University of Connecticut Library, Storrs

International Assoc. of Machinists and Aerospace Workers, Dist. 91, Hartford. Records, 1947-1982. Court records, etc., re: 1960 strike.

Windsor Historical Society, Windsor

"Old Document Project" collection, indexed by date and name. Includes: 17th-century deeds, indentures, land grants, estate inventories, land purchases and land records; 18th-century deeds, quit-claims, summons, complaints, arrest warrants, promissory notes, receipts, contracts, court orders, probate court rulings, wills, bonds, mortgages, leases and indentures; 19th-century quit-claim deeds, wills, court rulings, estate inventories, contracts, probate court decisions, leases, court orders and verdicts, indentures, subpoenas, jury notices and arrest warrants.

Yale University, Beinecke Rare Book and Manuscript Library, New Haven

Allyn, Henry. Record of court cases: Windsor, Conn., 1734-1751. Gen Mss File 270. Justice of the Peace trials.

Books

Ferris, Barbara B., and Grace L. Knox. *Connecticut Divorces: Superior Court Records for the Counties of Litchfield, 1752-1922, and Hartford, 1740-1849*. Bowie, Md.: Heritage Books, 1989. *See also* "Digital/Electronic Sources," *below*.

Manwaring, Charles William. *A Digest of the Early Connecticut Probate Records*. 3 vols. Hartford: R. S. Peck & Co., 1904-1906; Baltimore, Md.: Genealogical Publishing Co., 1995. Vol. 1, 1635-1700; vol. 2, 1700-1729; vol. 3, 1729-1750. *See also* "Microform" and "Digital/Electronic Sources," *below*.

Norris, Anthony J. *A History of the Probate Court for the District of Berlin, Covering the Towns of Berlin and New Britain*. New Britain, Conn.: Campaigns Advertising Services, 1994. Copy at Conn. Historical Society, Book Stacks, 346.05 N853h.

Ullmann, Helen Schatvet. *Hartford County, Connecticut, County Court Minutes: Volumes 3 and 4, 1663-1687, 1697*. Boston: New England Historic Genealogical Society, 2005. Original vol. 3 is in RG 1, Early General Records, Conn. State Library (also known as Early General Records vol. 56); original vol. 4 is in RG 4, Probate Records, Records of the Hartford Probate Court, Conn. State Library. *See* "State Archives," *above*, and "Microform," *below*.

Microform

Miscellaneous court records
Court Expenses, 1814-1847. GSU, 1989. FHL computer #615093. Superior Court.
Divorce Papers, 1725-1849. GSU, 1989. Superior Court.
Probate Records, 1649-1932. GSU, 1949-1954, 1982. First two reels (FHL #4572, 4550) of this 52-reel series include Hartford County Court minute books from the 1600s. *See* transcription by Helen Schatvet Ullmann, in "Books," *above*.
William F. J. Boardman Collection of Manuscripts 1661-1835: land transfers, estates, legal papers, accounts and correspondence of the Boardman and Seymour families, and miscellaneous papers relating to colonial and revolutionary wars, militia, school and ecclesiastical matters principally in Hartford and Wethersfield. GSU, 1954. From originals at Conn. State Library.

Naturalization records
Declarations of Intention, v. 1-3, 1876-1906; Index to Declarations, 1876-1904. GSU, 1983. Court of Common Pleas.
Index to Naturalization Petitions 1834-1898 (Hartford, Connecticut – Superior Court). GSU, 2003.
Index to Naturalization Petitions 1876-1906 (Hartford County, Connecticut – Court of Common Pleas). GSU, 2003.
Index to Naturalization Petitions 1917-1939, 1875-1906 (New Britain, Connecticut – City Court). GSU, 2003.
Index to Naturalization Petitions 1939-1973 (New Britain, Connecticut – Superior Court). GSU, 2003.
Naturalization Record Book, 1876-1876. GSU, 1984. City Court, Hartford.
Naturalization Records, 1834-1906 (Hartford County, Connecticut). GSU, 1983. County Court and Superior Court.
Naturalization Records, 1876-1906; Index to Naturalization, 1876-1906 (Hartford County, Connecticut). GSU, 1983. Court of Common Pleas.
Naturalization Testimony, 1876-1903 (Hartford County, Connecticut). GSU, 1983. Court of Common Pleas.
Naturalization Testimony, v. 1-3, 1868-1898 (Hartford County, Connecticut). GSU, 1983. Superior Court.

Probate District court records
Avon
Probate Records of Avon, Connecticut, from 1836-1874, volume 1. GSU, 1948.
Probate Records, 1844-1930. GSU, 1982.
Berlin
Probate Records, 1824-1919. GSU, 1948, 1982.
Bristol
Probate records, 1830-1919; Index to Probate Records, 1830-1927. GSU, 1948, 1986.
Burlington
Probate Records, 1834-1924. GSU, 1948, 1982.
Canton
Probate Records, 1841-1916. GSU, 1949, 1982.
E. Granby
Probate Records, v. 1, 3, 1865-1955. GSU, 1983.

E. Hartford
Guardian and Ward, 1887-1900. GSU, 1982.
Probate Records, 1887-1919. GSU, 1982.
E. Windsor
Probate Records, 1782-1922. GSU, 1949, 1982.
Enfield
Probate Records, 1831-1916. GSU, 1947-1949, 1982.
Farmington
Probate Records, 1769-1926. GSU, 1948, 1982, 1986.
Granby
Probate Records, 1807-1924. GSU, 1948, 1983.
Hartford
General Index to Probate Files, Hartford Probate District. GSU, 1958.
Manwaring, Charles William. *A Digest of the Early Connecticut Probate Records.* 3
        vols. Hartford: R. S. Peck & Co., 1904-1906. GSU, 1969-1971. *See also*
        "Books," *above*, and "Digital/Electronic Sources," *below*.
*Miscellaneous Wills and Inventories of Richard Smith, Jeremiah Adams and Thomas
        Skidmore.* GSU, 2001. Estates of Jeremiah Adams, Hartford, 1683; Richard
        Smith, Wethersfield, 1680-1715, etc.
Probate Records, 1649-1932. GSU, 1949-1954, 1982.
Hartland
Probate Records, 1836-1936. GSU, 1948, 1987.
Manchester
Probate Records, 1850-1916. GSU, 1983.
Marlborough
Probate Records, 1846-1937. GSU, 1983, 1986.
Plainville
Probate Records, 1910-1928 (Plainville, Connecticut). GSU, 1983, 1988.
Simsbury
Probate Records, 1769-1917. GSU, 1948, 1982.
Southington
Probate Records, 1825-1918. GSU, 1948, 1982.
Wills, Distributions, 1857-1873. GSU, 1982.
Suffield
Probate Records, 1821-1920. GSU, 1949, 1982.
W. Hartford
Probate Records, West Hartford, 1857-1900. GSU, 1982.
Windsor
Probate Records, 1855-1916. GSU, 1982.

Digital/Electronic Sources

CD-ROM
*Early Records of Hartford, Connecticut: Land Records, 1639-1688; Vital Records,
        1644-1730; Probate Records, 1635-1750; Plus Genealogical Notes and a
        Manual of the First Church in Hartford.* Bowie, Md.: Heritage Books, 1995.
Ferris, Barbara B., and Grace L. Knox. *Connecticut Vol. 2: Connecticut Divorces:
        Superior Court Records for the Counties of Litchfield, 1752-1922, and Hart-
        ford, 1740-1849. HB Archives.* Bowie, Md.: Heritage Books, 2000.

Manwaring, Charles William. *Early Connecticut Probate Records, Volumes 1-3*. Hartford: R. S. Peck & Co., 1904-1906; Bowie, Md.: Heritage Books, 2002. *See also* "Books" and "Microform," *above* and "Internet," *below*.

Internet

Ancestry.com *www.Ancestry.com*

Hartford, Connecticut Probate Records, 1635-50, 1700-29, 1729-50. Provo, Utah: Ancestry.com, 2000. Original data from Charles William Manwaring. *A Digest of the Early Connecticut Probate Records*. 3 vols. Hartford.: R. S. Peck & Co., 1904-1906.

Litchfield County

Founded 1751, from Fairfield and Hartford Counties

Courts

Superior Court

Serves Barkhamsted, Bethlehem, Bridgewater, Canaan, Colebrook, Cornwall, Goshen, Hartland, Harwinton, Kent, Litchfield, Morris, New Hartford, New Milford, Norfolk, N. Canaan, Roxbury, Salisbury, Sharon, Thomaston, Torrington, Warren, Washington and Winchester (Winsted).

Litchfield Judicial District, Litchfield

Geographical Area #18, Bantam

Housing: original file papers (current). Criminal: original and microfilm, 1990-date; no index.

Probate District Court

Canaan

Record books, index; original and transcripts, 1858-date.

Cornwall

Record books, estate papers, appeals, index; original and transcripts, 1848-date. (For records before 1742, try Hartford, Woodbury and N. Haven; 1742-1847 in Litchfield.)

Harwinton

Record books, estate papers, index; original and microfilm, 1835-date.

Kent

Record books, estate papers, appeals, index; original and transcripts, 1831-date.

Litchfield

Record books, index; 1743-date.

New Hartford

Record books, estate papers, appeals.

New Milford

Norfolk

Plymouth, Terryville

Record books, estate papers, index; original, microfilm and computer, 1835-date.

Roxbury

Record books, estate papers; original and microfilm, 1842-date; index cards.

Salisbury

Record books, index; 1847-date.

Sharon

Records, index; early 1700s-date.

Thomaston
Torrington
Record books; microfilm, from 1847.
Washington, Washington Depot
Winchester, Winsted
Record books, index; 1838-date.
Watertown
Merged with Woodbury Probate District 2003; some older Watertown probate records still at Watertown Town Hall.
Woodbury
Records, index; microfilm; Woodbury early 1970s-date, Watertown early 1970s-2003.

State Archives

Connecticut State Library, Connecticut State Archives, Hartford
Record Group 1, Early General Records
 Rodger Minott Sherman. 920 Sh560. Justice of the Peace court records.
Record Group 3, Judicial Dept.
 Litchfield County court records Supreme Court of Errors, 1853-1889; Superior Court, 1752-1945; County Court, 1751-1897; Maritime Court, 1782-1787; District Court, 1872-1912; Circuit Court, 1962-1973; Court of Common Pleas, 1877-1949. "County Courts Finding Aids" include: Files, 1751-1855; Minorities Collection, 1753-1854; and Papers by Subject, 1750-1855. *See also* "Digital/Electronic Sources: Internet," *below.*
 District and Municipal court records New Milford City Court, 1958-1960; Salisbury City Court, 1954-1960; Thomaston Town Court, 1876-1899; Torrington City (Justice) Court, 1798-1885; Washington City Court, 1954-1960; Watertown City Court, 1954-1960.
 Judges' notes, dockets and drafts Litchfield Superior Court, 1863, 1868-1869, 1872-1873.
 Justice of the Peace courts Barkhamsted, 1849-1880; Goshen, 1795-1820; Norfolk, 1861-1881; Salisbury, 1757-1850; Torrington, 1789-1927; Winchester, 1874-1888. *See also* Record Group 62 and 69, *below.*
 Coroner's records Litchfield County (Torrington), 1883-1979.
Record Group 4, Probate Courts
 Probate District court records
 Barkhamsted Estate papers: original, 1834-1906; microfilm, 1825-1915. Record books: microfilm, 1825-1923.
 Canaan Estate papers: original, 1844-1912; microfilm, 1844-1915. Record books: 1847-1923.
 Cornwall Record books: 1847-1923.
 Harwinton Estate papers: original, 1835-1924; microfilm, 1836-1915. Record books: microfilm, 1835-1924.
 Kent Estate papers: original, 1831-1928; microfilm, 1831-1915. Record books: microfilm, 1832-1929.
 Litchfield Estate papers: original, 1743-1924; microfilm, 1743-1915. Record books: microfilm, 1743-1916.
 New Hartford Estate papers: original, 1834-1902; microfilm, 1834-1915. Record books: microfilm, 1825-1930.

New Milford Estate papers: original, 1787-1947; microfilm, 1787-1880. Record books: microfilm, 1787-1920.

Norfolk Estate papers: original, 1779-1900; microfilm, 1779-1880. Record books: microfilm, 1778-1917.

Plymouth Estate papers: original, 1833-1926; microfilm, 1833-1880. Record books: 1833-1917.

Roxbury Estate papers: original, 1842-1921; microfilm, 1842-1880. Record books: microfilm, 1842-1927.

Salisbury Record books: microfilm, 1847-1917.

Sharon Estate papers: original, 1755-1939; microfilm, 1755-1880. Record books: microfilm, 1757-1922.

Thomaston Estate papers: original, 1882-1947. Record books: microfilm, 1882-1918.

Torrington Estate papers: original, 1847-1905; microfilm, 1847-1880. Record books: microfilm, 1836-1917.

Washington Record books: microfilm, 1832-1917.

Watertown Record books: microfilm, 1834-1917.

Winchester Estate papers: original, 1838-1912; microfilm, 1838-1880. Record books: 1838-1912.

Woodbury Estate papers: original, 1720-49; microfilm, 1729-1880. Record books: microfilm, 1719-1916.

Record Group 62, Towns and Boroughs

Justice of the Peace courts Cornwall, Sharon, Woodbury.

Record Group 69, Manuscript Collections

Justice of the Peace courts, including: Dwight D. Kilbourne Papers, RG 069:060; Lewis and Henry Norton Papers, RG 069:037; George Catlin Woodruff Papers, RG 069:094.

State Historical Society

Connecticut Historical Society, Hartford

Rankin, Jennett. Memorandum of settlement, 1842. Manuscript Stacks, 93310. Probate records re: estate of Joseph Rankin, Cornwall.

Report of the trial of Edward E. Bradley, indicted for the murder of Lucius H. Foot, before the Superior Court of Connecticut, held at Litchfield, on Tuesday, April 14, 1857.... Hartford: Case, Tiffany & Co., 1857. Conn. Imprints, 1857 B811r.

Terry, Eli, 1772-1852. Petition, 1827 Aug., Plymouth, Conn. To the Superior Court, County of Litchfield [Conn.], Litchfield. Manuscript Stacks, 86202. Re: injunction against Seth Thomas for violation of clock manufacturing agreements.

Other Repositories

Cornwall Historical Society, Cornwall

Approx. 450 justice of the peace records, including writs and constable's returns, 1760-1825; some indexing. *See* examples in *Chapter 16*.

Dedham Historical Society, Dedham, Mass.

Mann, Horace. Papers, 1822-1894 (bulk 1822-1838). Including notes from Tapping Reeves Law School (Litchfield Law School).

Litchfield Historical Society, Litchfield
Numerous manuscripts, partially cataloged by name or date, not by type of record. Searchable electronic database is in process; also the Society is in early stages of project, "Crossroads of Revolution to Cradle of Reform: Litchfield, Connecticut, 1751-1833" (with Va. Center for Digital History at the Univ. of Va.), to create online database of archives and manuscripts collection, as well as related objects and artifacts.
Court records and law-related manuscripts in Society's collection include:
Deeds (six boxes), probate records (one box), pension claims.
"Executions on Judgments and Cases," 1798-1908, seven boxes.
Records of various court clerks, judges and justices of the peace, including extensive personal papers of Frederick Wolcott, and transcripts from Charles Bartlett Andrew's term as judge of Conn. Superior Court in 19th century.
Student notebooks from Litchfield Law School.
"Superior Court Litchfield County" boxes.
"Summonses: American Revolution" (and other periods), two boxes.

Mashantucket Pequot Museum and Research Center, Mashantucket
Overseer ledger, 1884-1914. Mss 24. Superior Court. Re: overseer to Skaghticoke Tribe near Kent.

New Hartford Historical Society, Pine Meadow
Cases before Justice of the Peace, Town of New Hartford, 1911-1931. 2000.1.61.
Court transcript, *Greenwoods Co. v. Town of New Hartford*, 1894. 2000.1.37.
Court transcript, *New Hartford Water Co. v. Village Water Co.*, 1912. 654 pages, with index.

Rosenbach Museum and Library, Philadelphia, Penn.
Attachment, 1758 Aug. 26, New Milford, Conn., against Ephraim Seely. County Court. Signed by Roger Sherman as justice of the peace.

Sharon Historical Society, Sharon
A few copies of probate inventories.

University of Virginia Library, Charlottesville, Va.
Roger Sherman signed document, 1764-1766. Accession #12563-a. Albert H. Small Declaration of Independence Collection. Testimony and other records re: trespass case of *John Davis v. Samuel Galpin*.

Western Reserve Historical Society Library, Cleveland, Ohio
Calhoun, John. Papers, 1773-1787. Docket book and summonses of Justice of the Peace in Washington (Litchfield County).

Yale Law School, New Haven
Slosson, Barzillai. Docket Book: Litchfield County Court, September 1794-March 1808, and Superior Court, January 1795-February 1808. Rare Book, MssA S155 no. 5.

Books and Journals

Burr, Sarah A. W. "Sharon (Conn.) Probate Records," *The American Genealogist* 10: 170-174. Abstracts of first twenty-seven pages of Vol. 2, Sharon Probate Court record book.

Ferris, Barbara B., and Grace L. Knox. *Connecticut Divorces: Superior Court Records for the Counties of Litchfield, 1752-1922, and Hartford, 1740-1849.* Bowie, Md.: Heritage Books, 1989. *See also* "Digital/Electronic Sources," *below.*

Jacobus, Donald L. "Sharon (Conn.) Probate Records," *The American Genealogist* 22: 192-193. Abstracts selected estates from Vols. 2-4, Sharon Probate Court record books.

Russell, Donna Valley. *Sharon Conn., Probate Records, 1757-1783: Towns of Sharon, Kent, Canaan, and Salisbury.* Middletown, Md.: Catoctin Press, 1984.

Stark, S. Judson. *The Wyoming Valley: Probate Record, Liber A. from January 6, 1777 to June 16, 1783.* Wilkes Barre, Penn.: Wyoming Historical and Geological Society, 1923. Includes "Westmoreland in the County of Litchfield in the Colony of Connecticut."

Microform

Miscellaneous court records
Divorce Papers, 1752-1922. GSU, 1989-1990. Superior Court.
Justice Trials, 1783-1818. GSU, 1987. Records of Elijah Rockwell, Justice of the Peace, Colebrook.

Naturalization records
Index to Naturalization Petitions 1790-1906, 1906-1973 (Litchfield County, Connecticut – Court of Common Pleas, and Superior Court). GSU, 2003.

Probate District court records
Canaan
Probate Records, 1847-1923. GSU, 1948, 1987.
Cornwall
Probate Records, 1847-1929. GSU, 1948, 1987.
Harwinton
Probate Records, 1835-1940. GSU, 1948, 1987.
Kent
Probate Records, 1831-1938. GSU, 1948, 1987.
Litchfield
Probate Records, 1743-1917. GSU, 1948, 1987.
New Milford
Probate Records, 1787-1922. GSU, 1949, 1987.
Norfolk
Probate Records, 1779-1918. GSU, 1948, 1987.
Plymouth
Probate Records, 1833-1925. GSU, 1948, 1987.
Roxbury
Probate Records, 1842-1927. GSU, 1949, 1987.
Salisbury
Probate Records, 1847-1917. GSU, 1948, 1987.
Sharon
General Index to Probate Files, Sharon Distrist[sic]*: Abell, Allice to Loucks, Elizabeth.* GSU, 1958.
Probate Records, 1757-1922. GSU, 1948, 1987.
Record of Wills, 1857-1860. GSU, 1987.

Thomaston
Probate Records, 1882-1921. GSU, 1987.
Torrington
Probate Records, 1847-1917. GSU, 1948, 1986-1987.
Washington
Probate Records, 1832-1917. GSU, 1948, 1987.
Watertown
Probate Records, 1834-1917. GSU, 1948, 1987.
Winchester
Probate Records, 1838-1920; General Index, 1838-1958. GSU, 1948, 1987.
Woodbury
Probate Records, 1719-1916. GSU, 1948, 1987.

Digital/Electronic Sources

CD-ROM
Ferris, Barbara B., and Grace L. Knox. *Connecticut Vol. 2: Connecticut Divorces: Superior Court Records for the Counties of Litchfield, 1752-1922, and Hartford, 1740-1849. HB Archives.* Bowie, Md.: Heritage Books, 2000.

Internet
Connecticut State Library, Connecticut State Archives *www.cslib.org/archives.htm*
"County Court Finding Aids," including Litchfield County: Files, 1751-1855; Minorities Collection, 1753-1854; and Papers by Subject, 1750-1855.

Middlesex County
Founded 1785, from Hartford and New Haven Counties

Courts

Superior Court
Serves Chester, Clinton, Cromwell, Deep River, Durham, E. Haddam, E. Hampton, Essex, Haddam, Killingworth, Middlefield, Middletown, Old Saybrook, Portland and Westbrook.
Middlesex Judicial District, Middletown
Civil and family: docket/record books, file papers, appeals; original and microfilm, ca. 1910-date.
Geographical Area #9, Middletown
Criminal: docket/record books, 1962-date (microfilm and computer); original file papers, pending cases.

Probate District Court
Clinton
Microfilmed record books, 1800s-date; index cards.
Deep River
Original wills, copies of estate papers in vols., 1928-date. Earlier records may be located at: Chester (Saybrook), 1780-1949; Guilford, 1719-1780; New London, 1666-1780.
E. Haddam
Original records and transcripts, 1832-date.

E. Hampton
Record books, index; microfilm, 1917-date.
Essex
Original records and index; 1852-date. Earlier Essex records may be located at: Chester (Saybrook), 1780-1853; Guilford, 1719-1780; New London, 1666-1719.
Haddam
Record books, estate papers, appeals; original, microfilm and transcripts, 1830-date.
Killingworth
Record books, index; microfilm, 1834-date.
Middletown
Record books, index; microfilm, 1900-date.
Old Saybrook
Records, 1859-date. Earlier Old Saybrook records may be located at: Essex, 1853-1859; Chester (Saybrook), 1780-1853; Guilford, 1719-1780; New London, 1666-1719.
Portland
Saybrook, Chester
Records, 1780-date. *See also* Districts of Deep River, Essex, Old Saybrook and Westbrook, part of original Saybrook District.
Westbrook
Record books, estate papers, index; original open cases, microfilm offsite; 1854-date. Earlier Westbrook probate records may be located at: Essex, 1853-1854; Chester (Saybrook), 1780-1854; Guilford, 1719-1780; New London, 1666-1719.

State Archives

Connecticut State Library, **Connecticut State Archives**, Hartford
Record Group 3, Judicial Dept.
      Middlesex County court records Supreme Court of Errors, 1819-1934; Superior Court, 1786-1958; County Court, 1785-1855.
      District and Municipal court records Middletown City Court, 1957-1960; Portland City Court, 1954-1960.
      Judges' notes, dockets and drafts Middlesex Superior Court, 1864-1867, 1869-1871, 1874-1875.
      Justice of the Peace courts Chatham, 1832-1839; E. Haddam, 1857-1864; Killingworth, 1927-1936; Middletown, 1790-1826; Saybrook, 1819.
      Coroner's records Middlesex County (Middletown), 1951-1979.
Record Group 4, Probate Courts
      Probate District court records
      Chester Estate papers: original, 1780-1940; microfilm, 1780-1880. Record books: microfilm, 1780-1919.
      E. Haddam Record books: microfilm, 1832-1922.
      E. Hampton Record books: microfilm, 1824-1922.
      Essex Record books: microfilm, 1853-1918.
      Haddam Estate papers: original, 1830-1934; microfilm, 1830-1915. Record books: microfilm, 1830-1919.
      Killingworth Estate papers: microfilm, 1834-1915. Record books: microfilm, 1834-1938.
      Middletown Estate papers: original, 1751-1900; microfilm, 1752-1932. Record books: original, 1752-1759; microfilm, 1752-1917.

Old Saybrook Estate papers: original, 1859-1927; microfilm. Record books: microfilm, 1859-1917.

Westbrook   Estate papers: original, 1854-1930; microfilm, 1854-1880. Record books: microfilm, 1858-1937.

Other archives

Wadsworth Collection. 1718-1921. Includes court and land records, Durham.

State Historical Society

Connecticut Historical Society, Hartford

Brainard family. Papers, 1750-1876. Manuscript Stacks, 98236. Legal records, including summonses and writs, of Haddam justice of the peace and lawyer.

Connecticut. County Court. Records, 1730. Case of *Charles Hazleton v. Josiah Wright* re: Saybrook (Deep River) riot, theft and assault. Published, in part, in *The Connecticut Nutmegger* (1985): 402-409.

Middletown Interior Court Records, 1762-1784. Matthew Talcott, Justice of Peace.

A minute and correct account of the trial of Lucian Hall, Bethuel Roberts, and William H. Bell for murder: at the Middlesex Superior Court, Connecticut, February term, 1844.... Middletown, Conn.: Charles H. Pelton, 1844. Book Stacks, 343.1 M668m.

To the honorable County Court for the County of Middlesex, to be holden at Haddam...April A.D. 1848. Broadsides Collection, 1848 T627th. Petition to dam Wangunk Meadow, Portland, Conn.

To the honorable Superior Court of the state of Connecticut, to be holden at Middletown...February, A.D. 1832: the petition of Charles Miller, of the town of Durham.... Broadsides Collection, 1832 H774h. Bankruptcy petition.

Other Repositories

Middlesex County Historical Society, Middletown

Several hundred incomplete court records, uncataloged, from 1750s into early 20th century.

New England Historic Genealogical Society, Boston, Mass.

Card, Lester. "Saybrook, Connecticut, Probate Records: Index to Volume 1, 1780." CT SAY 10.

Russell Library, Middletown

Extensive collection of Genealogical Society of Utah (Family History Library) microfilm (court, naturalization and probate records) re: Middlesex County. *See* "Microform," *below.*

Western Reserve Historical Society Library, Cleveland, Ohio

Stanley, George W. Docket book, 1819-1841. MS. 3427. Middlesex County, 1819-1837.

Microform

Miscellaneous court records

Court Records, 1786-1797. GSU, 1989. FHL computer #616283. Superior Court.

Divorce Papers, 1786-1797. GSU, 1989. Superior Court.

Naturalization records
Declarations of Intention, 1841-1906. GSU, 1984. Superior Court.
Naturalization Index, 1844-1955. GSU, 1984. Superior Court.
Naturalization Records, 1844-1871. GSU, 1984. County Court and Superior Court.
Naturalization Records, 1844-1909. GSU, 1984. Superior Court.

Probate District court records
Chatham
Probate Records, 1824-1922. GSU, 1948, 1983. District, which included towns of Chatham and Portland, was discontinued in 1915; Chatham was changed to E. Hampton, and Portland became separate district. Records include Portland District, 1915-1922.
Clinton
Probate Records, 1862-1926. GSU, 1983.
E. Haddam
Probate Records, 1741-1922. GSU, 1948, 1982. Contains records of E. Haddam District, 1741-1832, and Colchester District (New London County), 1832-1922.
Probate Records, 1832-1922. GSU, 1948, 1984.
Essex
Probate Records, 1853-1918. GSU, 1984. Includes Old Saybrook District records, 1853-1859.
Haddam
Probate Records, 1830-1919. GSU, 1948, 1984, 1987.
Killingworth
Probate Records, 1834-1937. GSU, 1948, 1984.
Middletown
Land Records, 1851-1933; General Index, 1851-1928. GSU, 1983, 1986. Vol. 6 includes probate records, 1870-1933.
Probate Records, 1752-1917. GSU, 1948, 1984.
Old Saybrook
Probate Records, 1853-1918. GSU, 1984. Old Saybrook District records, 1853-1859, and Essex District.
Probate Records, 1859-1917. GSU, 1987.
Portland
Probate Records, 1824-1922. GSU, 1948, 1983. Records include Chatham District; Portland, originally in Chatham District, became separate district in 1915.
Saybrook
Probate Records, 1780-1920. GSU, 1948, 1983. Saybrook District became Deep River in 1947.
Westbrook
Probate Records, v. 1, 1859-1937. GSU, 1984.

Early American Imprints, Series II. Shaw-Shoemaker (1801-1819). New Canaan, Conn.: Readex Microprint, in cooperation with American Antiquarian Society, 1987-1992. Microfiche. Including:
Swift, Zephaniah. *A vindication of the calling of the special Superior Court at Middletown, on the 4th Tuesday of August, 1815, for the trial of Peter Lung, charged with the crime of murder....* Windham, Conn.: J. Byrne, 1816. Shaw & Shoemaker, 39040.

New Haven County
Founded 1666

Courts

Superior Court—Judicial Districts
Ansonia-Milford Judicial District, Milford and Derby
Serves Ansonia, Beacon Falls, Derby, Milford, Orange, Oxford, Seymour, Shelton and W. Haven.
New Haven Judicial District, Meriden and New Haven
Civil and Family: serves Bethany, Branford, Cheshire, E. Haven, Guilford, Hamden, Madison, Meriden, New Haven, N. Branford, N. Haven, Wallingford and Woodbridge. Small Claims: serves Bethany, Branford, E. Haven, Guilford, Madison, New Haven, N. Branford, Northford and Woodbridge.
Waterbury Judicial District, Waterbury
Civil and family: original docket/record books and file papers, 1900-date; index cards, from 1990s, also index books and computer index.

Superior Court—Geographical Areas
Geographical Area #4, Waterbury
Serves Middlebury, Naugatuck, Prospect, Southbury, Waterbury, Watertown, Wolcott and Woodbury. Criminal: docket/record books, file papers, appeals; original, transcripts, microfilm.
Geographical Area #5, Derby
Serves Ansonia, Beacon Falls, Derby, Orange, Oxford, Seymour and Shelton. Civil: original file papers, 1970-1973; no index. Criminal: some docket books (Milford 1985, Ansonia 1961-date), original file papers (current and past three months), appeals (until appeal disposed); microfilm 1980s; computer, 2001-date; index cards, 1968-1984. Small Claims: original docket/record books, file papers; ca. twenty years; some years have index. Please make all inquiries in writing.
Geographical Area #7, Meriden
Serves Cheshire, Hamden, Meriden, N. Haven and Wallingford. Civil and small claims: docket/record books, file papers; original and computer, 1989-date. Criminal: docket/record books, file papers, appeals; original, microfilm, computer; pending matters.
Geographical Area #22, Milford
Serves Milford and W. Haven.
Geographical Area #23, New Haven
Serves Bethany, Branford, E. Haven, Guilford, Madison, New Haven, N. Branford and Woodbridge. Criminal and motor vehicle: docket/record books, appeals, index; microfilm (original at record center in Enfield), 1962-date.

Probate District Court
Bethany
Record books, index; microfilm off-site, 1854-date.
Branford
Record books, estate papers, appeals, index; original and microfilm offsite, 1850-date.
Cheshire
Record books, estate papers, appeals, index; microfilm, 1680-date.
Derby, Ansonia
Record books, 1868-date.

E. Haven
Guilford
Record books, index; original and microfilm, 1720-date.
Hamden
Madison
Estate papers, appeals, index; original and microfilm, 1834-date.
Meriden
Record books, appeals, index (cards and computer), 1987-date.
Milford
Docket/record books, file papers, appeals, index; original and microfilm, 1832-date.
Naugatuck
Record books, index; microfilm, 1863-date.
New Haven
Docket/record books, file papers, appeals, index; original, microfilm and computer, 1922-date.
N. Branford
N. Haven
Record books, estate papers, appeals; original and microfilm, 1955-date.
Orange
Record books, estate papers, appeals, index; original and microfilm.
Oxford
Record books, wills, index; original and microfilm, 1908-date.
Southbury
Wallingford
Waterbury
Record books, index; original, microfilm, and computer, 1750-date.
W. Haven
Record books, appeals, index; original and microfilm, 1944-date.
Woodbridge
Record books, file papers, 1987-date.

State Archives

Connecticut State Library, **Connecticut State Archives**, Hartford
Record Group 3, Judicial Dept.

> **New Haven County court records**   Superior Court, 1712-1944; County Court, 1666-1862; Maritime Court, 1776-1783; Court of Common Pleas, 1869-1945.

> **District and Municipal court records**   Ansonia City Court, 1958-1960; Branford City Court, 1950-1960; Derby Town Court, 1875-1921; Derby City Court, 1957-1960; Guilford City Court, 1950-1960; Hamden City Court, 1940-1960; Meriden City Court, 1867-1963; Milford Town Court, 1882-1899; Naugatuck City Court, 1954-1960; New Haven City Court, 1784-1960; N. Haven City Court, 1954-1960; Orange City Court, 1929-1960; Seymour City Court, 1955-1960; Wallingford Borough Court, 1886-1943; Wallingford City Court, 1955-1960; Waterbury City Court, 1881-1882; Waterbury District Court, 1883-1895; W. Haven City Court, 1933-1960.

> **Judges' notes, dockets and drafts**   New Haven County Court, 1849-1852; New Haven Court of Common Pleas, 1885-1887, 1889, 1891; Judge William

Thomas Minor, 1868-1872 (includes New Haven Superior Court minutes and notes).

Justice of the peace courts Derby, 1777-1803; Guilford, 1810.

Coroner's records New Haven County (New Haven), 1883-1980; New Haven County (Waterbury), 1917-1979.

Record Group 4, Probate Courts

Probate District court records

Bethany Estate papers: original, 1854-1950; microfilm, 1833-1915. Record books: microfilm, 1855-1915.

Branford Record books: microfilm, 1850-1917.

Cheshire Estate papers: original, 1829-1912; microfilm, 1829-1915. Record books: microfilm, 1829-1920.

Derby Estate papers: original, 1858-1900; microfilm, 1858-1880. Record books: microfilm, 1858-1916.

E. Haven Estate papers: original and microfilm, 1868-1883. Record books: original in vol. 178 of New Haven record books.

Guilford Estate papers: original, 1719-1900; microfilm, 1719-1880. Record books: 1720-1920.

Madison Record books: microfilm, 1834-1917.

Meriden Record books: microfilm, 1836-1916.

Milford Estate papers: original and microfilm, 1832-1900. Record books: microfilm, 1832-1916.

Naugatuck Record books: microfilm, 1863-1916.

New Haven Estate papers: original, 1683-1922; microfilm, 1683-1915. Record books: original, 1647-1922; microfilm, 1647-1915.

Oxford Estate papers: original, 1846-1908; microfilm, 1846-1880. Record books: microfilm, 1846-1917, and microfilm index, 1846-1984.

Wallingford Estate papers: original, 1776-1909; microfilm, 1776-1880. Record books: 1776-1893.

Waterbury Estate papers: original, 1779-1945; microfilm, 1779-1880. Record books: microfilm, 1779-1916.

Record Group 62, Towns and Boroughs

Justice of the Peace courts Southbury, 1788-1915; Wolcott.

Record Group 69, Manuscript Collections

Justice of the Peace courts, including: Wadsworth Papers, RG 069:052 (New Haven).

Federal Archives

U.S. National Archives and Records Administration (NARA), Northeast Region-Waltham (Boston), Mass.

City court records including naturalization records of: Ansonia, 1893-1906; Meriden, 1903-1940; and New Haven, 1843-1923. NARA series 21.8.3.

State Historical Society

Connecticut Historical Society, Hartford

Conspiracy between Joseph Sheldon, and Mrs. Bennett to rob an innocent man: Dr. Bennett's defence to Judge Waldo. New Haven: George Bennett, 1865. Broadsides Collection, Medium 1865 C755c. New Haven divorce trial.

Curtiss, Reuben B. Account book, 1831-1846. Manuscript Stacks, 94929. Accounts of justice of the peace in Oxford, Conn.; mentions African-American woman, Venus.

Other Repositories

James Blackstone Memorial Library, Branford
Blackstone family. Papers, 1702-1835. Includes court records in local case.
Branford, Conn., public papers: Town government, 1823-1882. Includes court records.
Rogers family. Papers, 1750-1910. Records of Branford Probate Court, papers of Justice of the Peace Eli F. Rogers, etc.

Guilford Keeping Society, Guilford
Town of Guilford Archives: Law. Document storage cases #10-14. Justice of the Peace records, 1795-1913, de-accessioned by town in 1974-75. Filed by year with a partial index by name. Liquor, indebtedness, theft, breach of peace, trespass, bigamy, rape, etc.

New Haven Colony Historical Society, New Haven
Conn. Superior Court: Documents for New Haven County. Manuscript Coll. #3.
New Haven County Court records. Manuscript Coll. #28.

Books and Journals

Alcorn, Winifred S. "Abstracts of the Early Probate Records of New Haven, Book I, Part I, 1647-1687," *New England Historical and Genealogical Register* 81 (1927): 121-135.
Dexter, Franklin Bowditch. *Ancient Town Records, Vol. I, New Haven Town Records 1649-1662.* New Haven: New Haven Colony Historical Society, 1917.
_____. *Ancient Town Records, Vol. II, New Haven Town Records 1662-1684.* New Haven: New Haven Colony Historical Society, 1919.
Hoadly, Charles J. *Records of the Colony and Plantation of New Haven, from 1638 to 1649.* Hartford: Case, Tiffany & Co., 1857. *See also* "Microform," *below.*
_____, *Records of the Colony or Jurisdiction of New Haven, from May 1653, to the Union: Together With the New Haven Code of 1656.* Hartford: Case, Lockwood & Co., 1858.
Schmitt, Dale J. "Community and the Spoken Word: A Seventeenth-Century Case," *Journal of American Culture* 132 (Summer 1990): 51-55. New Haven slander case.

Microform

Miscellaneous court records
Divorce Papers, 1712-1899. GSU. Superior Court.
Divorce Papers, No Appearance Files, 1808-1900. GSU, 1990. Superior Court.
Hoadly, Charles J. *Records of the Colony and Plantation of New Haven, from 1638 to 1649.* Hartford: Case, Tiffany & Co., 1857; New Haven: Research Publications, 197-?.
Records of Births, Marriages, and Deaths, 1639-1905. GSU, 1985. Guilford. Vols. A and 1 contain some court minutes.

Naturalization records

Index to Naturalization Petitions 1895-1988 (Waterbury, Connecticut). GSU, 2003-2004. County Court and Superior Court.

Indexes to Naturalization Petitions 1939-1955 and Declarations of Intention 1939-1954 (Meriden, Connecticut – Superior Court). GSU, 2003.

Judges Memorandums [sic] *on Naturalization Petitions, 1903-1906.* GSU, 1984. City Court, Meriden.

Name Index to Declarations Filed, 1844-1923. GSU, 1984. City Court, New Haven.

Name Index to Petitions Filed, 1843-1923. GSU, 1984. City Court, New Haven.

Naturalization Papers, 1867-1878. GSU, 1984. City Court, Meriden; Board of Registration, Meriden; Superior Court.

Naturalization Records, 1893-1906. GSU, 1984. City Court, Ansonia.

Naturalization Records, 1904-1906. GSU, 1984. City Court, Ansonia.

Petitions and Records of Naturalization, 1903-1906. GSU, 1984. City Court, Meriden.

Record of Declarations Filed, 1874-1877. GSU, 1984. City Court, New Haven.

Register of Declarations and Naturalizations Filed, 1900-1906. GSU, 1984. City Court, Ansonia.

Probate District court records

Bethany
Probate Records, 1855-1915. GSU, 1985.

Branford
Probate Records, 1850-1918. GSU, 1985.

Cheshire
Probate Records, 1829-1920. GSU, 1949, 1985.

Derby
Guardianship Records, 1859-1888. GSU, 1985.
Probate Records, 1858-1924. GSU, 1985.

Guilford
Probate Records, 1720-1920. GSU, 1948, 1985.

Madison
Probate Records, 1834-1917. GSU, 1948, 1985.

Meriden
Probate Records, 1836-1916. GSU, 1948, 1984.

Milford
Probate Records, 1832-1916. GSU, 1949, 1985.

Naugatuck
Probate Records, 1863-1916. GSU, 1985.

New Haven
New Haven (Conn.) Probate Records, 1647-1916. GSU, 1949, 1984.

Oxford
Probate Records, 1846-1917; Probate Record Index, 1846-1984. GSU, 1985.

Simsbury
Probate Records, 1769-1917. GSU, 1948, 1982.

Wallingford
Probate Records, 1776-1905. GSU, 1948, 1984.

Waterbury
Probate Records, 1779-1917; General Index to Probate Records, 1779-1928. GSU, 1949, 1987.

Woodbury
Probate Records, 1719-1916. GSU, 1948, 1987.

Early American Imprints, Series I. Evans (1639-1800). New York: Readex Microprint, in cooperation with American Antiquarian Society, 1985. Microfiche. Including: Stanton, Phineas, *A brief historical view, of the several cases and trials that have subsisted between Mr. Adam Babcock, merchant, at New-Haven, in the colony of Connecticut, and Phineas Stanton, Junior, of Stonington....* Norwich, Conn.: John Trumbull, for the author, 1777. Evans, 43376.

Early American Imprints, Series II. Shaw-Shoemaker (1801-1819). New Canaan, Conn.: Readex Microprint, in cooperation with American Antiquarian Society, 1987-1992. Microfiche. Including:
Trial of Joshua Bradley, upon an indictment of forgery. To which are prefixed, the credentials which he exhibited at North-Haven, and other attendant circumstances. Middletown, Conn.: s.n., 1812. Shaw & Shoemaker, 26910.

Digital/Electronic Sources

Internet
Early American Imprints
> *www.readex.com/scholarl/eai_digi.html*
> Evans Digital Edition, Series I. Evans (1639-1800). Chester, Vt.: Readex/Newsbank, Inc., in cooperation with American Antiquarian Society, 2003.
> *www.readex.com/scholarl/earlamim.html*
> Shaw-Shoemaker Digital Edition, Series II. Shaw-Shoemaker (1801-1819). Chester, Vt.: Readex/Newsbank, Inc., in cooperation with American Antiquarian Society, 2004.
> Available at academic libraries. *See also* "Microform," *above*.

New London County
Founded 1666

Courts

Superior Court—Judicial Districts
New London Judicial District, New London and Norwich
Serves Bozrah, Colchester, E. Lyme, Franklin, Griswold, Groton, Lebanon, Ledyard, Lisbon, Lyme, Montville, New London, N. Stonington, Norwich, Old Lyme, Preston, Salem, Sprague, Stonington, Voluntown and Waterford. Civil (at Norwich): docket/record books, file papers, index; original and microfilm, 1978-date.

Superior Court—Geographical Areas
Geographical Area #10, New London
Serves E. Lyme, Groton, Ledyard, Lyme, New London, N. Stonington, Old Lyme, Stonington and Waterford. Civil: original docket/record books, file papers, appeals; housing (three years), small claims (fifteen years). Criminal: docket/record books, appeals; microfilm, 1961-date.
Geographical Area #21, Norwich
Serves Bozrah, Colchester, Franklin, Griswold, Lebanon, Lisbon, Montville, Norwich, Preston, Salem, Sprague and Voluntown. Civil: docket/record books, file papers, appeals.

Probate District Court
Bozrah
Record books, appeals, index; original and microfilm, 1843-date.
Colchester
Record books, index, 1741-date.
E. Lyme, Niantic
Record books, estate papers, appeals; original and microfilm, 1843-date; index, vols. 1-120.
Groton
Record books (microfilm), wills (original), index; 1839-date.
Griswold, Jewett City
Record books, estate papers, index; microfilm, 1991-date.
Ledyard
Record books; microfilm, 1800-date.
Lyme
Record books (microfilm), 1829-1866 from Old Lyme District; original file papers, 1869-date; index.
Montville, Uncasville
Docket/record books (original, vols. 1-16, 1852-1969; microfilm, from vol. 17, 1969-date); index.
New London
Microfilmed records, 1666-1830.
N. Stonington
Record books; current original, microfilm from 1835; index cards.
Norwich
Record books, some indexing; original, transcripts, microfilm, 1748-date.
Old Lyme
Records; original, microfilm, computer, 1830-date.
Salem
Stonington
Records, index; original and microfilm, 1776-date.

State Archives

Connecticut State Library, **Connecticut State Archives**, Hartford
Record Group 000, Classified Archives.
> Roger Hurlbutt, 974.61 N44hu.
Record Group 3, Judicial Dept.
> **New London County court records** Supreme Court of Errors, 1819-1952; Superior Court, 1711-1969; County Court, 1661-1873; Maritime Court, 1781-1784; Court of Common Pleas, 1870-1969; County Commissioners, 1768-1873. "County Courts Finding Aids" include: African-Americans Collection, 1701-1774; Files, 1691-1774; Native-Americans Collection, 1698-1774; and Papers by Subject, 1685-1855. *See also* "Digital/Electronic Sources: Internet," *below.*
> **District and Municipal court records** Groton City Court, 1951-1960; New London City Court, 1784-1960; Norwich Court of Equity, 1716; Norwich City Court, 1959-1960; Stonington Town Court, 1893-1915; Waterford City Court, 1954-1960.

Judges' notes, dockets and drafts New London Superior Court, 1865, 1867, 1871; Judge William Thomas Minor, 1868-1872 (includes New London Superior Court minutes and notes); Judge John Turner Wait, 1845-1876.

Justice of the Peace courts Colchester, 1767-1790; Groton, 1819-1820 (vol. also includes Montville); New London, 1739-1892; Norwich, 1774-1760; Preston, 1807-1934; Stonington, 1769-1855.

Coroner's records New London County (New London), 1883-1979.

Record Group 4, Probate Courts

Probate digests and abstracts

Gallup, Jennie Tefft. "Abstracts of the First Probate Records of Norwich." 2 vols. 1748-1764. Probate Vault 974.62 fN84pr.

Jacobus, Donald L. "New London (Conn.) Probate Records: Abstract of Records Before 1710," *The American Genealogist*, 9:230-233; 10:35-40, 101-104, 166-170, 215-217; 11:30-31, 103-105, 153-157; 12:33-34, 115-116, 151-154; 13:106-110, 164-166, 246-247; 14:16-18, 103-104, 184-186, 246-248; 15:104-106; 17:118-120; 18:121; 19:218; 20:190.

Probate District court records

Bozrah Estate papers: original, 1843-1930; microfilm, 1833-1915. Record books: microfilm, 1843-1929.

Colchester Estate papers: original, 1741-1920; microfilm, 1741-1915. Record books: microfilm, 1741-1922.

E. Lyme Estate papers: original, 1843-1943; microfilm, 1843-1915. Record books: microfilm, 1843-1924.

Groton Record books: microfilm, 1834-1916.

Lebanon Estate papers: original, 1826-1922; microfilm, 1826-1915. Record books: microfilm, 1826-1917.

Ledyard Estate papers: original, 1837-1934; microfilm, 1837-1915. Record books: microfilm, 1837-1923.

Lyme Estate papers: original, 1869-1937; microfilm, 1869-1915. Record books: microfilm, 1869-1919.

Montville Estate papers: original, 1850-1935; microfilm, 1850-1915. Record books: microfilm, 1852-1919.

New London Estate papers: original, 1675-1900; microfilm, 1675-1850. Record books: microfilm, 1675-1915. *Note*: Some records, 1763-1871, destroyed by fire.

N. Stonington Estate papers: original, 1835-1912; microfilm, 1835-1880. Record books: microfilm, 1835-1933.

Norwich Estate papers: original, 1748-1896; microfilm, 1748-1880. Record books: microfilm, 1748-1917.

Old Lyme Estate papers: original, 1855-1945; microfilm, 1830-1880. Record books: microfilm, 1855-1915.

Salem Estate papers: original, 1842-1956; microfilm, 1834-1880. Record books: microfilm, 1842-1929.

Stonington Estate papers: original and microfilm, 1766-1875. Record books: microfilm, 1767-1933.

Voluntown Estate papers: original, 1830-1889; microfilm, 1831-1876. Record books: microfilm, 1830-1890.

Record Group 62, Towns and Boroughs

Justice of the Peace courts, including: New London and Preston.

Record Group 69, Manuscript Collections
>**Justice of the Peace courts**, including; Lyme, 1790-1812 (Richard Ely Selden Papers, RG 069:086); New London, 1739-1892 (Coddington Billings Papers, RG 069:075).

State Historical Society

Connecticut Historical Society, Hartford

Docket/Court of Common Pleas, New London County. Norwich, Conn.: Norwich Print Co., 1880. Book Stacks, 347.461 C752n.

Connecticut. Superior Court. Action of assumpsit, 1822. Manuscript Stacks, 97691. Case to determine whether African-American, formerly owned by William Williams of Groton and now residing in Columbia, Conn., was eligible for support as emancipated slave.

Gallup, Benadam, 1664-1813. Justice of the peace records, and estate of Peleg Lewis.

Harris Family. Papers, 1721-1859. Manuscript Stacks, 41465. Includes deeds and probate records for New London.

Hurlbutt, Ralph. Justice of the Peace records, New London, 1807-1837.

New London County. Justice of the Peace. Book of records, 1788-1817. Manuscript Stacks, 25718. Kept by Henry Champion.

Other Repositories

American Antiquarian Society, Worcester, Mass.

Norwich (Conn.). Records, 1777-1871. Mss. Dept., Misc. mss. boxes "N," Octavo vols. "N." Several court records, including punishments for vagrancy and drunkenness.

Mashantucket Pequot Museum and Research Center, Mashantucket

Depositions, 1732, 1747, 1760. MSS 9. Superior Court; re: land dispute between town of Groton and Mashantucket Pequot Tribe.

Overseer account, June 28, 1854. MSS 11. Superior Court; re: goods provided to Eastern or Paucatuck Pequots.

Overseer records, December 1837-February 12, 1839/Ledger, 1837-1839. MSS 16. Superior Court; re: Mohegan Tribe in Norwich.

Petition, March 11, 1857. MSS 27. Superior Court; re: dispute between Mashantucket Pequots and overseer of tribe.

Record, 1782, 1783, n.d. MSS 10. Register of Probate Records, Town of Stonington; re: death of Thomas Cinnemon, a Mashantucket Pequot who served in the Continental Army.

Report of the Committee on the Sale of Pequot Land, January 23, 1856. MSS 14. County and Superior Courts.

Mystic River Historical Society, Mystic

Probate docket/record books, town of Groton, Jan.-June 1976.

Mystic Seaport, The Museum of America and the Sea, Mystic

Clift Family Collection. Coll. 65. Re: Mystic shipmasters, including documents re: probate court in Groton.

Legal records of the Smack *L.A. Macomber*. Coll. 45. Legal briefs, probate certificates, etc., re: cases before Court of Commissioners of Alabama Claims concerning destruction of Conn. vessel by Confederate warship.

New England Historic Genealogical Society, Boston, Mass.
Gallup, Jennie F. Tefft. "Abstracts of the First Probate Records of Norwich, Conn., 1740-1770." 3 vols. MSS CT NOR 2134. *See also* "Digital/Electronic Sources," *below*.

New London County Historical Society, New London
Diary and court records of 18th-century Justice of the Peace Joshua Hempstead.

Stonington Historical Society, Stonington
Original probate record books, vols. 1-108 (vol. 79 missing), Stonington District; also land records from 1851.

Yale University, New Haven
Beinecke Rare Book and Manuscript Library
Connecticut writs: Norwich, Connecticut, 1742-1762. Gen Mss File 216. 32 writs signed by Isaac Huntington, Justice of the Peace, addressing sheriffs of New London and Windham counties.
Law School Library
Minutes, June 13, 1843-June 14, 1844. Rare Book Room, MssB C76con. County Court.

Books and Journals

Jacobus, Donald L. "New London (Conn.) Probate Records: Abstract of Records Before 1710," *The American Genealogist*, 9:230-233; 10:35-40, 101-104, 166-170, 215-217; 11:30-31, 103-105, 153-157; 12:33-34, 115-116, 151-154; 13:106-110, 164-166, 246-247; 14:16-18, 103-104, 184-186, 246-248; 15:104-106; 17:118-120; 18:121; 19:218; 20:190.
Knox, Grace L., and Barbara B. Ferris. *Connecticut Divorces: Superior Court Records for the Counties of New London, Tolland & Windham, 1719-1910.* Bowie, Md.: Heritage Books, 1987.

Microform

Miscellaneous court records
Divorce Papers, 1719-1875. GSU, 1989. Superior Court.
Land Records, 1646-1906; General Index, 1646-1906. GSU, 1947, 1984, 1987. New London. Vol. 4 includes General Court records.
Records of Trials, 1661-1700, in the County Court of New London County, Connecticut. GSU, 1954.

Naturalization records
Declarations of Intention, 1872-1906. GSU, 1983. Superior Court.
Declarations of Intentions, 1875-1906. GSU, 1983. Court of Common Pleas.
Naturalization Books, 1856-1905. GSU, 1983. Superior Court.
Naturalization Books, 1874-1906. GSU, 1983. Court of Common Pleas.
Naturalization Papers, 1875-1902. GSU, 1983. Court of Common Pleas.

Probate District court records
Bozrah
Probate Records, 1843-1931. GSU, 1948, 1982, 1984.
Colchester
Probate Records, 1741-1922. GSU, 1948, 1982. Contains records of Colchester District, 1832-1922, and E. Haddam District (Middlesex County), 1741-1832.

E. Lyme
Probate Records, 1843-1924. GSU, 1948, 1982, 1987.
Groton
Probate Court Journal, 1839-1850. GSU, 1947.
Probate Records, 1839-1917. GSU, 1947, 1981.
Lebanon
Probate Records, 1826-1917. GSU, 1947, 1982.
Ledyard
Probate Journal, 1837-1857. GSU, 1947.
Probate Records, 1837-1923. GSU, 1982.
Lyme
Probate Records, 1869 1920. GSU, 1981.
Montville
Probate Records, 1852-1919. GSU, 1982.
New London
Probate Records, 1675-1916. GSU, 1982.
Will Books, 1890-1926. GSU, 1982.
N. Stonington
Probate Journals, 1835-1937. GSU, 1981.
Probate Papers on File in Connecticut State Library, Hartford, for North Stonington District, 1828-1912. GSU, 1981.
Probate Records, 1835-1933. GSU, 1981.
Norwich
Probate Records, 1748-1917. GSU, 1947, 1981.
Probate Records, 1830-1889. GSU, 1981.
Records of Court Proceedings, 1748-1852. GSU, 1981.
Old Lyme
Probate Records, 1830-1915. GSU, 1948, 1981. District name changed from Lyme to Old Lyme in 1869.
Salem
Probate Records, 1842-1929. GSU, 1948, 1982.
Stonington
Probate Records, 1767-1933. GSU, 1947, 1981.

Early American Imprints, Series I. Evans (1639-1800). New York: Readex Microprint, in cooperation with American Antiquarian Society, 1985. Microfiche. Including: Stanton, Phineas. *A brief historical view, of the several cases and trials that have subsisted between Mr. Adam Babcock, merchant, at New-Haven, in the colony of Connecticut, and Phineas Stanton, Junior, of Stonington....* Norwich, Conn.: John Trumbull, for the author, 1777. Evans, 43376.

Digital/Electronic Sources

Internet
Connecticut State Library, Connecticut State Archives *www.cslib.org/archives.htm*
"County Court Finding Aids," including New London County: African-Americans Collection, 1701-1774; Files, 1691-1774; Native-Americans Collection, 1698-1774; and Papers by Subject, 1685-1855.

Early American Imprints *www.readex.com/scholarl/eai_digi.html*
>   Evans Digital Edition, Series I. Evans (1639-1800). Chester, Vt.:
>   Readex/Newsbank, Inc., in cooperation with American Antiquarian Society,
>   2003. Available at academic libraries. *See also* "Microform," *above.*

New England Historic Genealogical Society *www.NewEnglandAncestors.org*
>   *Probate Records of Norwich, Connecticut, Volumes 1-3.* Boston: NewEng-
>   landAncestors.org, 2003. From Jennie F. Tefft Gallup. "Abstracts of the First
>   Probate Records of Norwich, Conn., 1740-1770." *See also* "Other Reposito-
>   ries," *above.*

Tolland County
Founded 1785, from Windham County

Courts

Superior Court
Serves Andover, Bolton, Columbia, Coventry, Ellington, Hebron, Mansfield, Somers,
Stafford, Tolland, Union, Vernon and Willington.
Tolland Judicial District, Rockville
Civil: original docket/record books, file papers, 1700s-date; partial index, ca. 1950-
date.
Geographical Area #19, Rockville
Criminal: docket/record books, file papers, appeals; microfilm and computer, last 2
years.

Probate District Court
Andover, Bolton
Record books, index; original, 1789-date.
Ellington, Rockville
Estate papers, index; 1826-date.
Hebron
Records, index; microfilm.
Mansfield, Storrs
Record books, wills, index; original, transcripts, computer, 1810-date.
Stafford, Stafford Springs
Original active files, microfilmed closed files, 1771-date. *Note*: Files for Somers, prior
to merger with Stafford District in 1998, are located at Somers Town Hall. Old Will-
ington probate records are at Stafford, but more recent Willington records at Tolland.
Tolland

State Archives

Connecticut State Library, **Connecticut State Archives**, Hartford
Record Group 3, Judicial Dept.
>   **Tolland County court records** Supreme Court of Errors, 1819-1942; Supe-
>   rior Court, 1787-1945; County Court, 1786-1855.
>   **District and Municipal court records** Coventry City Court, 1955-1962;
>   Rockville (Vernon) City Court, 1955-1960; Stafford Borough Court, 1884-
>   1892; Stafford Springs Borough Court, 1887-1916.

Judges' notes, dockets and drafts Tolland Superior Court, 1864, 1868-1870, 1873-1874.

Justice of the Peace courts Coventry, 1729-1905; Mansfield, 1774-1920; Stafford, 1796-1809; Union, 1774-1802.

Coroner's records Tolland County (Rockville), 1883-1979.

Record Group 4, Probate Courts

Probate District Court records

Andover Estate papers: original, 1851-1946; microfilm, 1851-1915. Record books: microfilm, 1851-1924.

Coventry Estate papers: original, 1849-1932; microfilm, 1849-1915. Record books: microfilm, 1849-1917.

Ellington Estate papers: original, 1826-1920; microfilm, 1826-1915. Record books: microfilm, 1826-1916.

Hebron Estate papers: original, 1789-1897; microfilm, 1851-1915. Record books: microfilm, 1789-1937.

Mansfield Estate papers: original, 1831-1953; microfilm, 1831-1915. Record books: 1831-1918.

Somers Estate papers: original, 1834-1941; microfilm, 1834-1880. Record books: microfilm, 1834-1919.

Stafford Estate papers: original, 1759-1933; microfilm, 1759-1880. Record books: microfilm, 1759-1930.

Tolland Estate papers: original, 1833-1960; microfilm, 1833-1880. Record books: microfilm, 1830-1920.

Record Group 62, Towns and Boroughs

Justice of the Peace courts, including: Columbia, Somers and Tolland.

State Historical Society

Connecticut Historical Society, Hartford

Burnap, Daniel. Papers, 1789-1839. Manuscript Stacks, 96103. Records of justice of the peace in Tolland County.

Connecticut. Superior Court. Action of assumpsit, 1822. Case to determine whether African-American, formerly owned by William Williams of Groton and now residing in Columbia, Conn., was eligible for support as emancipated slave.

Hebron Court Records, 1764-1800.

Other Repositories

Mansfield Historical Society, Storrs

Wills and estate inventories.

Somers Historical Society, Somers

Deeds re: Somers property for following families: Billings, Hall, Kibbe (to Pease, 1852), Morgan, Parsons, Ward.

Wills for Daniel Kibbe, 1791, and Sanford Billings, 1886.

Books

Knox, Grace L., and Barbara B. Ferris. *Connecticut Divorces: Superior Court Records for the Counties of New London, Tolland & Windham, 1719-1910.* Bowie, Md.: Heritage Books, 1987.

Microform

Miscellaneous court records
Depositions, 1892-1893. GSU, 1989. Superior Court; re: lawsuit of *George W. Adams* (Tolland County) *v. Charles I. Rawson* (Oxford, Mass.)
Divorce Papers, 1787-1910. GSU, 1989. Superior Court.
Executions, A-Z, 1772-1891. GSU, 1989. Superior Court.

Naturalization records
Declarations of Intention, 1853-1914. GSU, 1983. Superior Court and County Court.
Naturalization Record Book, 1876-1876. GSU, 1984. City Court, Hartford; includes Tolland County naturalization petitions.
Naturalization Records, 1853-1906; Naturalization Index, 1853-1955. GSU, 1983. Superior Court and County Court.

Probate District Court records
Andover
Probate Records, 1789-1924. GSU, 1948, 1983. Also contains records of Hebron District, 1789-1851.
Coventry
Probate Records, 1849-1917. GSU, 1948, 1983.
Ellington
Probate Records, 1826-1916. GSU, 1948, 1983.
Hebron
Probate Records, 1789-1924. GSU, 1948, 1983. Hebron District, 1789-1851; also records of Andover District.
Probate Records, 1851-1937. GSU, 1983.
Mansfield
Probate Records, 1831-1918. GSU, 1948, 1983.
Somers
Probate Records, 1835-1940. GSU, 1949, 1983.
Stafford
Probate Records, 1759-1931. GSU, 1949, 1983.
Tolland

Probate Records, 1830-1920. GSU, 1949, 1986.

Windham County
Founded 1726, from New London County

Courts

Superior Court
Windham Judicial District, Danielson, Putnam and Willimantic
Civil (Putnam): original docket/record books, file papers, appeals, index.
Geographical Area #11, Danielson
Civil (housing, small claims): docket/record books, file papers; original and computer.
Criminal: docket/record books, file papers (original and microfilm); index (cards prior to 1986, computer 1986-date).

Probate District Court
Ashford
Brooklyn
Record books, 1833-date.
Eastford
Hampton
Record books, index; original and microfilm, ca. 1855-date.
Killingly, Danielson
Record books, estate papers, index; microfilm, 1800s-date.
Plainfield
Record books, index; microfilm, 1747-date.
Pomfret
Records, index; original and microfilm, 1753-date.
Putnam
Record books (original), file papers (original re: adoptions and wills only), index, 1855-date.
Thompson, N. Grosvenordale
Windham, Willimantic
Docket/record books; hand-copied files from 1700s (original in Hartford), typescript from 1800s, more recent documents microfilmed, in storage.
Woodstock
Estate papers, appeals, index; microfilm, 1831-date.

State Archives

Connecticut State Library, **Connecticut State Archives**, Hartford
Record Group 3, Judicial Dept.
    Windham County court records Supreme Court of Errors, 1820-1886; Superior Court, 1726-1947; County Court, 1727-1855; Court of Common Pleas, 1941-1945.
    District and Municipal court records Killingly City Court, 1959-1960; Plainfield City Court, 1954-1960; Putnam City Court, 1950-1960.
    Judges' notes, dockets and drafts Windham Superior Court, 1865, 1867, 1871; Judge William Thomas Minor, 1868-1872 (includes Windham Superior Court minutes and notes).
    Justice of the Peace courts Hampton, 1795; Pomfret, 1792-1903; Windham, 1729-1875.
    Coroner's records Windham County (Putnam), 1883-1979.
Record Group 4, Probate Courts
    Probate District Court records
    Ashford Estate papers: original, 1865-1944; microfilm, 1865-1915. Record books: microfilm, 1830-1927.
    Brooklyn Estate papers: original, 1833-1933; microfilm, 1833-1915. Record books: microfilm, 1833-1917.
    Canterbury Estate papers: original, 1835-1878; microfilm, 1881-1915. Record books: microfilm, 1835-1918.
    Chaplin Estate papers: original, 1850-1926; microfilm, 1850-1915. Record books: microfilm, 1850-1915.
    Eastford Estate papers: original, 1849-1912; microfilm, 1849-1915. Record books: microfilm, 1849-1923.

Hampton Estate papers: original, 1836-1936; microfilm, 1836-1915. Record books: microfilm, 1836-1917.

Killingly Estate papers: original, ca. 1845-1914; microfilm, 1845-1915. Record books: microfilm, 1835-1920.

Plainfield Estate papers: original, 1747-1854; microfilm, 1747-1880. Record books: microfilm, 1747-1918.

Pomfret Estate papers: original, 1752-1935; microfilm, 1752-1880. Record books: microfilm, 1753-1919.

Putnam Record books: microfilm, 1856-1920.

Sterling Estate papers: original, 1852-1920; microfilm, 1852-1880. Record books: microfilm, 1852-1917.

Thompson Estate papers: original, 1832-1945; microfilm, 1823-1880. Record books: microfilm, 1832-1916.

Windham Estate papers: original, 1719-1917; microfilm, 1719-1880. Record books: microfilm, 1719-1918.

Woodstock Estate papers: original, 1831-1929; microfilm, 1831-1880. Record books: microfilm, 1831-1916.

Record Group 62, Towns and Boroughs

Justice of the Peace courts, including Pomfret.

Record Group 69, Manuscripts Collection

Hunt, Chester. Collection. 1818-1879. RG 069:079. Includes writs and court orders of Windham justice of the peace.

Record Group 74, Genealogical Materials

Probate digests and abstracts Lucius Barnes Barbour:

Abstract of Brooklyn Probate Records, 1786-1900. RG 74:36, no. 73.

Abstract of Probate Records, Pomfret District, 1752-1906. RG 74:36, no. 82.

Abstracts of Probate Records, Pomfret and Woodstock Districts, 1752-1902. RG 74:36, no. 86.

Genealogical Notes Compiled from Probate Records, Windham District, 1719-1737. RG 74:36, no. 85.

State Historical Society

Connecticut Historical Society, Hartford

McClellan, John, 1816-1835. Justice of the peace records and dockets of Woodstock lawyer.

Report of the arguments of counsel, in the case of Prudence Crandall, plff....vs. State of Connecticut: before the Supreme Court of Errors, at their session at Brooklyn, July term, 1834.... Boston: Garrison & Knapp, 1834. World Imprints, 1834 P556r.

Windham Justice Court Records, 1754-1761. First Record Book of Samuel Gray, Esq. of Windham, from June 7, 1754 to April 2, 1761. Microfilm.

Other Repositories

Brown University Library, Providence, R.I.

The trial and a sketch of the life of Oliver Watkins, now under sentence of death in Brooklyn (Con.) jail for the murder of his wife, March 22, 1829.... Providence: Brown, 1830. Hay Rider, Box 31 No. 6.

Killingly Historical Society, Danielson
Killingly probate docket/record books (microfilm), 1851-1920; index.

Mashantucket Pequot Museum and Research Center, Mashantucket
Pay order and affidavit, October 13, 1781 and May 7, 1781. Mss 15. Superior Court; re: claim for benefits by widow of a Mashantucket Pequot of Canterbury, for his service in Continental Army.

University of Pennsylvania, Van Pelt Library, Philadelphia, Penn.
Windham County (Conn.) Superior Court. Miscellaneous manuscripts, 1820-1821. Rare Book & Ms Library Manuscripts, Misc Mss. Court memorandum books for Sept. term 1820, Jan. term 1821 and Sept. term 1821.

Woodstock Historical Society, Woodstock
Land deeds and wills, 1700s-1800s; no index.

Yale University, Beinecke Rare Book and Manuscript Library, New Haven
Connecticut writs: Norwich, Connecticut, 1742-1762. Gen Mss File 216. 32 writs signed by Isaac Huntington, Justice of the Peace, addressing sheriffs of New London and Windham counties.

Books and Journals

Hayward, Kendall P. "Windham (Conn.) Probate Records," *The American Genealogist* 23:228-229. Abstract, selected estates from vols. 1-3 of Windham Probate Court record books.
Knox, Grace L.,and Barbara B. Ferris. *Connecticut Divorces: Superior Court Records for the Counties of New London, Tolland & Windham, 1719-1910*. Bowie, Md.: Heritage Books, 1987.
Pasay, Marcella Houle. *Family Secrets: 18th & 19th Century Birth Records Found in the Windham County, CT, County Court Records & Files, at the CT State Library Archives, Hartford*. Bowie, Md.: Heritage Books, 2000.
_____, *The Windham County, CT, County Court Records*. 2 vols. Bowie, Md.: Heritage Books, 2000-2002.
Prior, Eva Jane Covell. *Woodstock, Conn. Estates Found in Pomfret Probate Court Records, May 1752–May 1831*. Woodstock, Conn.: By Author, 1984.

Microform

Miscellaneous court records
Court Expenses, 1826-1883. GSU, 1990. Superior Court.
Divorce Papers, 1726-1907. GSU, 1990. Superior Court.

Naturalization records
Declarations of Intentions, 1855-1906. GSU, 1983. Superior Court and County Court.
Index to Naturalization Records 1927-1974 (Windham County, Connecticut – Superior Court). GSU, 2003.
Naturalization Petition and Record, v. 1, 1906-1913. GSU, 1983. Superior Court.
Naturalizations, 1855. GSU, 1983. County Court.
Naturalizations, 1855-1906. GSU, 1983. Superior Court.

Probate District court records

Ashford

Probate Records, 1830-1928; General Index to Probate Records, 1830-1935. GSU, 1949, 1983.

Brooklyn

Probate Records, 1833-1917. GSU, 1949, 1983.

Canterbury

Probate Records, 1835-1918. GSU, 1947, 1947, 1981.

Chaplin

Probate Records, 1850-1919. GSU, 1986.

Eastford

Probate Records, 1849-1923. GSU, 1949, 1983.

Hampton

Probate Records, 1836-1917. GSU, 1948, 1986.

Records, 1856-1863. GSU, 1986. Wills of Hampton residents and property owners.

Killingly

Probate Records, 1849-1920. GSU, 1949, 1986.

Plainfield

Probate Records, 1747-1918. GSU, 1949, 1983.

Probate Records, 1830-1889. GSU, 1981.

Pomfret

Probate Records, 1754-1919. GSU, 1949, 1983.

Putnam

Probate Records, 1856-1920. GSU, 1983.

Sterling

Probate Records, 1852-1917. GSU, 1983.

Thompson

Probate Records, 1832-1916. GSU, 1949, 1983.

Woodstock

Probate Records, 1831-1916. GSU, 1949, 1983.

Fig. 6.2. Courthouse in Waterbury, Connecticut, ca. 1901–1907,
from the author's collection of vintage picture postcards.

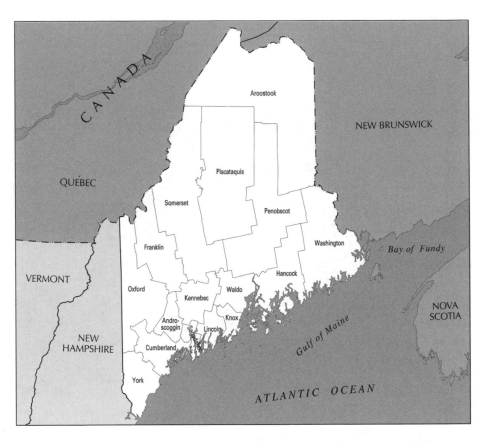

Fig. 7.1. Map of Maine Counties. *National Atlas of the United States.* 2005.
http://nationalatlas.gov.

CHAPTER 7

MAINE STATE COURTS

Court History Timeline

Early Colonial Courts

1636   Province of New Somersetshire held court in Saco.

1639   Sir Ferdinando Gorges obtained charter for Province and County of Maine, dividing province into two parts at the Kennebunk River. **Inferior Court** met three times per year in each part, and **General Court** met annually at Saco. **Commissioners** were appointed in each town to handle civil matters involving less than forty shillings.

1643   Sir Alexander Rigby purchased conflicting grant to area and sent deputy to conduct courts in Casco and Scarborough.

1646   Massachusetts annexed Maine settlements—Kittery, Gorgeana (now York), Wells, Cape Porpoise, Saco, Casco and Scarborough.

1653   **York County Court** was established, under Massachusetts control, for jury trials of civil and criminal cases, probate matters, etc. Annual court sessions generally convened in summer; sometimes additional sessions met in York at first, later alternating between York and Wells. **Commissioners** (similar to later justices of the peace) were appointed in towns.

1658   **Court of Associates** was established (with three or more judges or "associates") to hear civil and criminal cases without a jury, probate matters, appeals from County Court, etc. Sessions convened in Fall and Spring, at York, Scarborough, Wells, Saco or Kittery.

1664-1668   Court sessions were interrupted. Commissioners of King Charles II appointed **justices of the peace**.

Provincial Courts

1677   Massachusetts purchased "Gorges Rights," establishing **Province of Maine**. **County Court** and **Court of Associates** continued, temporarily, as before.

1680   **General Assembly** served as Court of Appeals. **Court of Pleas** replaced Court of Associates, meeting annually in spring, alternately at Wells and York, with magistrates (including President or Deputy-President of Province) presiding. **Court of Sessions** replaced County Court, generally meeting at York, Wells or Kittery, spring and fall. **Town commissioners** held court without jury for minor matters.

1686-1689   England vacated the Massachusetts charter and placed Maine under royal control with new court system. **Governor and Council** in Boston served as supreme court. **Superior Court of Common Pleas** at York had power to try all cases and hear appeals. **Inferior Court of Common Pleas** had jurisdiction over non-capital crimes, misdemeanors and cases not exceeding £10 in value. Judge and two or more justices of the peace presided, with quarterly sessions at York and Wells. **Court of Quarter Sessions**, justices of the peace presiding, also met quarterly at York and Wells.

1689-1692   Massachusetts charter was restored, and Maine returned to previous court system, with **Court of Sessions** and **Court of Pleas**.

1692   Maine became **York County, Province of Massachusetts Bay.** Court system was reformed under new Massachusetts charter. At York, the **Superior Court of Judicature, Court of Assize and General Gaol Delivery,** heard appeals from lower courts, equity cases and trials of serious crimes and civil matters. **Court of Sessions of the Peace** (sometimes called **Court of Quarter Sessions** and later **Court of General Sessions of the Peace**) heard criminal cases. **Inferior Court of Common Pleas** (later **Circuit Court of Common Pleas**) heard civil cases and had limited equity jurisdiction. This court, and the Court of Sessions of the Peace, generally met quarterly at York. **Judge of Probate** was appointed. **Justices of the peace** exercised broad powers at local level, trying civil cases not exceeding forty shillings, punishing misdemeanors and minor crimes, officiating at marriages, issuing licenses, etc.

1697   Royal **Vice-Admiralty Court** regulated trade and navigation.

1703-1704   Maine's courts moved to Boston because of Indian wars.

1713   Special session of Courts of Assize and General Gaol Delivery heard backlog of capital cases.

1735   Inferior courts and General Sessions moved to Falmouth.

1760   New counties were created. **Cumberland County** held court at Fal-
            mouth–Court of General Sessions and Inferior Court of Common Pleas
            (twice per year) and Superior Court of Judicature, Court of Assize and
            General Gaol Delivery (annually in June). **Lincoln County** held lower
            courts at Pownalborough but had no Superior Court, so appeals went
            to Falmouth.

District of Maine Courts

1780   Province of Maine was renamed **District of Maine**, under Massachu-
            setts jurisdiction.

1782   **Supreme Judicial Court**, which replaced Superior Court of Judicature,
            Court of Assize and General Gaol Delivery, met annually in York, Cum-
            berland and Lincoln counties. **Courts of Common Pleas and General
            Sessions of the Peace** were established for counties of York (at York,
            Waterboro and Biddeford), Cumberland (at Falmouth), and Lincoln
            (Hallowell, Pownalborough and Waldoboro).

1789   New counties were established: Hancock and Washington. Supreme
            Judicial Court met for these counties at Pownalborough. Courts of Com-
            mon Pleas and General Sessions of the Peace met annually in each county.

1793   Supreme Judicial Court convened in Wiscasset for Lincoln, Hancock
            and Washington counties.

1819   **Maine** separated from Massachusetts and **became 23rd state**.

Courts after Statehood

1820   New state court structure: **Supreme Judicial Court** had jurisdiction
            over certain civil actions, serious or capital crimes, and appeals. **Circuit
            Court of Common Pleas**, in each county, heard civil and criminal cases.
            Court of Sessions had authority over jails, licenses, highways, taxes, etc.

1821   **Justices of the peace** investigated criminal matters and held trials (civil
            matters not exceeding $20 and criminal matters with a fine of $5 or less).
            Probate Courts were established under county jurisdiction, with
            appeals to Supreme Judicial Court.

1822   Circuit Court of Common Pleas was renamed **Court of Common Pleas**,
            with exclusive jurisdiction over most civil and criminal matters and
            appeals from justices of the peace. Appeals from Court of Common Pleas
            went to Supreme Judicial Court: three terms per year in York, Cumber-
            land, Lincoln, Kennebec, Somerset and Hancock counties; two terms in
            Oxford (expanded to three in 1825), Penobscot and Washington counties.

1825   First **Municipal Court** was created in Portland. Additional municipal
            courts were established in later years, as well as **Police Courts**, in vari-
            ous cities.

1831   Court of Sessions was renamed **County Commissioner's Court**.

1839   **District Courts** replaced Courts of Common Pleas.

1844   **Town Courts** were established in every city, town or plantation, meeting monthly, with one or two justices having same powers as former justices of the peace.

1852   **District Courts** were **abolished**, giving powers to **expanded Supreme Judicial Court**, divided into three Judicial Districts: **Western** (York, Cumberland, Oxford and Franklin counties); **Middle** (Lincoln, Kennebec, Somerset and Waldo counties); and **Eastern** (Piscataquis, Penobscot, Hancock, Washington and Aroostook counties).

1853   Waldo County was transferred to Eastern Judicial District.

1854   Androscoggin County was established in Western Judicial District.

1856   Town Courts were abolished.

1860   Knox County was established in Middle Judicial District.

1866   Fire destroyed Cumberland County probate records in Portland.

1868   **Superior Court** was established in **Cumberland** County, with jurisdiction limited to civil matters not exceeding $500.

1878   **Superior Court** was established in **Kennebec** County (Augusta), taking over criminal matters from Supreme Judicial Court for the county. Superior Court was established in other counties over next fifty years, gradually assuming jurisdiction over criminal and civil trials.

1901   **Supreme Judicial Court** heard appeals (as **Law Court** for entire state) at annual sessions in Augusta, Bangor and Portland.

1961   **District Court** was established in thirty-three judicial districts. Jurisdiction overlapped with **Superior Court**, allowing trials of civil and criminal cases, divorce, etc., in either court.

Maine Courts Today

State Courts

Supreme Judicial Court

Maine's Supreme Judicial Court decides appeals on matters of law in civil and criminal cases from state trial courts or county probate courts.

Trial Courts

Maine has two trial court levels:
- **Superior Court**: One in each county, for jury trials of civil or criminal cases and injunctions (except for family matters, juvenile cases or civil violations).
- **District Court**: Located in thirty-one courthouses throughout the state, for non-jury trials of civil and criminal cases. Family Division hears all divorce and family matters, including child support and paternity. District Court also serves as Juvenile Court and hears contested charges of traffic or civil violations.

County Probate Courts

Maine's Probate Courts, one in each county, are under **county** jurisdiction, separate from the state court system. Judges handle estates and trusts, adoption, name changes, guardianship and protective proceedings, with no jury trials.

Where to Find Court Records
See Appendix for complete contact information.

Statewide or General Sources

Courts

Supreme Judicial Court, Portland
Permanent card index. Law Court appeal records onsite ten years, then to Record Center twenty years, and finally to State Archives. Other records onsite ten years, at Record Center twenty to fifty years, then destroyed.

Superior and District Court—Record Retention Guidelines
The Maine Judicial Branch mandates how long Superior and District Courts must retain records onsite, and what happens to the records thereafter (stored temporarily at the Record Center in Augusta, archived at the State Archives, or destroyed):
Superior Court
> **Criminal**: Permanent card index. Docket books onsite twenty-five years, then to State Archives. File papers re: murder and felony onsite ten years, to Record Center fifteen years, then to State Archives. Other records onsite five to ten years, to Record Center up to forty years, then generally destroyed.
> **Civil**: Permanent card index. Docket books onsite twenty years, then to State Archives. General civil and land file papers onsite ten years, to Record Center ten years, then general civil files destroyed, and land records to State Archives. Divorce records onsite twenty years, then to State Archives.

District Court
> **Criminal and civil**: Permanent card index. Docket books onsite twenty to twenty-five years, then to State Archives. File papers onsite five to ten years, to Record Center up to forty years, then generally destroyed, except land records to State Archives.

Divorce and family: Permanent card index. Docket books and file papers onsite twenty years, then to State Archives.

Some courts retain records longer than the minimum time period; *see* "Courts" section for each county, *below.* Contact court clerks for access to files at courthouses or Record Center; contact State Archives to access archival records.

State Archives

Maine State Archives, Augusta

Original docket books, record books and file papers of all counties operating in Maine, 1636-1929+ (more contemporary materials gradually added), except for Lincoln County (where original court records are retained at courthouse in Wiscasset, and State Archives has microfilm).

Whittier, David Q. "History of the Court System of the State of Maine." Augusta: Maine State Archives, 1971. Archives reading room.

See also "Digital/Electronic Sources," *below*, for computer database indexes.

Federal Archives and Records Center

U.S. National Archives and Records Administration (NARA), Northeast Region-Waltham (Boston), Mass.

Naturalization: Dexigraph collection (negative photostats) of naturalization records from 301 federal and state courts in five New England states (Maine, Mass., N.H., R.I. and Vt.) between 1790 and 1906. Index is available on microfilm, as *Index to New England Naturalization Petitions, 1791-1906*; *see* "Microform," *below*. *Note*: NARA-Waltham staff will search index and provide copies for a fee; need name, residence at time of application, and birth date.

State Historical Society

Maine Historical Society, Portland

Some manuscript collections can be located through Society's online catalog, *www.mainehistory.org/library_search.shtml*, although many are indexed only by card catalog at library. *See, e.g.*:

Libby, Charles Thornton. Papers, 1643-1945. Coll. 1724. Re: law practice, and publication of *Province and Court Records of Maine*, etc.

McDaniel, John. Writ 1771. Coll. S-85/20. Case against Joseph Rounds.

Smith, Samuel Emerson. Docket book, 1821-1827. Coll. 1469. Court of Common Pleas docket book of Smith, Chief Justice, and Ebenezer Thatcher and Sanford Kingsbury, Associate Justices.

Other Repositories

Judicial Archives/Massachusetts Archives, Boston, Mass.

Maine Counties File Papers of Appeals to Mass. Supreme Judicial Court, 1718-1774. Finding aid.

U.S. Citizenship and Immigration Services, U.S. Dept. of Homeland Security, Washington, D.C.

Naturalization certificate files ("C-Files"): Copies of naturalization records from state and federal courts after September 27, 1906, *e.g.*, Declaration of Intention, Petition for Naturalization, and Certificate of Naturalization.

1906-1956: Available on microfilm. Make Freedom of Information/Privacy Act (FOIA/PA) request to U.S. Citizenship and Immigration Services in Washington, D.C.

After 1956: Make FOIA/PA request to the district U.S. Citizenship and Immigration Services office that maintains the records, or office nearest your residence.

See Appendix: Contact Information-Archives and Other Repositories, Washington, D.C.

University of Maine, Orono

Dunn, Charles J. Legal and personal papers, 1833-1986. SpC Box 2039. Maine Supreme Court Judge; collection includes records of cases and estates.

Books

Court Records—Abstracts, Transcripts and Indexes

Frost, John Eldridge. *Maine Probate Abstracts.* 2 vols. Camden, Maine: Picton Press, 1991. Vol. 1, 1687-1775; vol. 2, 1775-1800.

Libby, Charles Thornton, Robert E. Moody, and Neal W. Allen, Jr., eds. *Province and Court Records of Maine.* 6 vols. Portland: Maine Historical Society, 1928-1975; reprint, 1991 (vol. 1 only, with new introduction by Neal W. Allen, Jr.). Maine court records, 1636-1727. *See* prefaces and introductions to vols. for detailed court history. *See also* "Microform," *below.*

Moore, M. J. *Book of Eastern Claims.* Portland: S. M. Watson, 1887-1895. Oakland, Maine: Danbury House, 198-?. Also published in *Maine Historical and Genealogical Register.* Vols. 4-8. List of extinguished and disputed land claims in Maine, 17th and early 18th centuries, transcribed from original records.

Sargent, William M. *Maine Wills, 1640-1760.* Portland: Maine Historical Society, 1887. Baltimore, Md.: Genealogical Publishing Co., 1972. *See also* "Microform" and "Digital/Electronic Sources," *below.*

History

Williamson, Joseph. *Capital Trials in Maine Before the Separation.* Portland: Maine Historical Society, 1890.

Willis, W. *History of the Law, the Courts, and the Lawyers of Maine.* Portland: Bailey & Noyes, 1863.

Wroth, L. Kinvin. "The Maine Connection: Massachusetts Justice Downeast, 1620-1820." In Osgood, Russell K., ed. *The History of the Law in Massachusetts: The Supreme Judicial Court 1692-1992.* Boston: Supreme Judicial Court Historical Society, 1992, 171-206.

Law Library Resources

Case Reports: *See Chapter 17*, and *Appendix-Law Libraries* and *Publishers. See also* "Microform" and "Digital/Electronic Sources," *below.*

Supreme Judicial Court

Maine Reports. Multiple vols. Court decisions, 1820-1965.

Atlantic Reporter. Multiple vols. Eagan, Minn.: West. Court decisions, 1886-date, enhanced with headnotes, key numbers and synopses.

West's Maine Digest and *West's Atlantic Digest*. Multiple vols. Eagan, Minn.: West. Digests of Maine state and federal court decisions, 1820-date, organized alphabetically by topic, with headnotes, key numbers, and multiple indexes (case name, etc.).

Superior Court

Decisions. Multiple vols. Official reports. Selected opinions, 1979-date.

Research Guides

Denis, Michael J. *Maine Towns and Counties: What was What, Where and When*. Oakland, Maine: Danbury House Books, 1988.

Ring, Elizabeth. *Reference List of Manuscripts Relating to the History of Maine*. 2 vols. Orono, Maine: Univ. Press, 1938-1938. Reprint, Salem, Mass.: Higginson Book Co.

Wells, William W., Jr. *Maine Legal Research Guide*. Portland, Maine: Tower Publishing Co., 1989.

Microform

Index to New England Naturalization Petitions, 1791-1906. U.S. National Archives and Records Admin., 1983. M1299. Alphabetical index of individuals naturalized, in state and federal courts of Maine, Mass., N.H., R.I. and Vt. (indicates court and certificate number).

Libby, Charles Thornton, Robert E. Moody, and Neal W. Allen, Jr., eds. *Province and Court Records of Maine*. 6 vols. Portland: Maine Historical Society, 1928-1975. GSU, 1976. Microfilm. Vol. 1-5. GSU, 1984. Microfiche. Maine court records, 1636-1727. *See* prefaces and introductions to vols. for detailed court history.

Maine Supreme Court reports, 1820-1926, and additional vols. annually. Microfiche. Kaneohe, Hawaii: Law Library Microform Consortium.

Sargent, William M. *Maine Wills, 1640-1760*. Portland: Maine Historical Society, 1887; Baltimore, Md.: Genealogical Publishing Co., 1972. GSU, 1969, 1984. Microfilm, microfiche.

Digital/Electronic Sources

CD-ROM

Atlantic Reporter. Eagan, Minn.: West. Includes Maine Supreme Judicial Court opinions, 1945-date.

Maine & New Hampshire Settlers, 1600s-1900s. Family Archives CD-ROM. Novato, Cal.: Broderbund, 2000. Includes: William M. Sargent. *Maine Wills, 1640-1760*. Portland: Maine Historical Society, 1887. Patterson, William D. *The Probate Records of Lincoln County, Maine, 1760-1800*. Portland: Maine Genealogical Society, 1895.

Maine Reporter. Eagan, Minn.: West. Maine Supreme Judicial Court cases reported in *Atlantic Reporter 2d* and *Maine Reporter*, 1945-date.

Internet

Ancestry.com *www.Ancestry.com*

Maine Will Abstracts, 1640-1760. Provo, Utah: MyFamily.com, Inc., 2000. Original data from William M. Sargent. *Maine Wills, 1640-1760.* Portland: Maine Historical Society, 1887.

Law Library of Congress *www.loc.gov/law/guide/us-me.html*
    Links to Maine state and federal court opinions and resources.

LexisNexis *www.lexis.com*
        Maine Supreme Judicial Court, 1820-date. Subscription services or available at law libraries and other repositories.

LexisOne *www.lexisone.com*
        Maine Supreme Judicial Court, most recent five years; free.

Loislaw *www.loislaw.com*
        Maine Supreme Judicial Court, 1923-date. Subscription service.

Maine Archives Interactive
        www.informe.org/sos_archives
        Maine Archives Interactive. Databases: *Early Court Cases from York, Washington and Kennebec Counties* and *Miscellaneous Municipal Records Filed with the State* (municipal and trial justice court records).

Maine Judicial Branch
        www.courts.state.me.us/index.html
        General information about Maine's courts.
        www.courts.state.me.us/opinions/supreme
        Maine Supreme Judicial Court opinions, 1997-date.
        www.courts.state.me.us/opinions/superior/index.html
        Maine Superior Court orders and/or decisions, selected recent cases.
        www.courts.state.me.us/courtservices/citizen_guide/index.html
        "Citizen's Guide to the Courts."

New England Historic Genealogical Society *www.NewEnglandAncestors.org*
        Index to Maine Court Records, 1696-1854. Boston: NewEnglandAncestors.org, 2004. Courtesy of Maine State Archives.

University of Maine School of Law *http://webapp.usm.maine.edu/SuperiorCourt*
        Selected Maine Superior Court opinions, 2000-date.

VersusLaw *www.versuslaw.com*
        Maine appellate courts, 1940-date; Passamaquoddy Tribal Court, 1985-date. Subscription service.

Westlaw *www.westlaw.com*
        Maine Supreme Judicial Court, 1820-date. Subscription service or available at law libraries and other repositories. Westlaw CourtEXPRESS offers case research and document retrieval from U.S. courts.

Androscoggin County
Founded 1854, from Cumberland, Lincoln, Oxford and Kennebec Counties

Courts

Androscoggin County Superior Court, Auburn
Civil and criminal: docket books (original, 1977-1998, and computer, 1998-date); original file papers, 1993-date; card index, early 1900s-1998. Divorces: docket books and file papers, original, 1977-1998 (after 1998, filed in District Court); card index, 1900s-1998.

District Court, Lewiston
Civil: docket books, twenty years; file papers, five years. Criminal: docket books, twenty-five years; misdemeanor file papers, ten years. Divorces and Family Court: original records and docket books, twenty years. Small claims: dockets and file papers, two years.

Androscoggin County Probate Court, Auburn
Original docket/record books; index. *See also* "Digital/Electronic Sources," *below.*

State Archives

Maine State Archives, Augusta
Original records (docket/record books, file papers) of courts operating in Androscoggin County, from earliest proceedings to 1929, and later materials gradually added. *See also* re: Androscoggin County:
Municipal Court records. Including: Auburn, 1895-1965; Lewiston, 1877-1965; Lisbon, 1941-1962; Livermore Falls, 1924-1966.

State Historical Society

Maine Historical Society, Portland
(Two cases): No. 390 Benjamin F. Warner v. Maine Central R. R. Co.; no. 391 George B. Warner v. Maine Central R. R. Co. Stacks 385 M285w. Supreme Judicial Court, Androscoggin County, January Term, 1913. Case re: building fire caused by train passing through Leeds Junction, Wales, Maine.

Other Repositories

Androscoggin Historical Society, Auburn
Criminal cases: newspaper and printed accounts, mostly 19th century, indexed by case name.
Probate: pre-1800 published records. *See also* "Digital/Electronic Sources," *below.*

Pejepscot Historical Society, Brunswick
Civil: docket/record books, file papers; original, 1730s-1900; no index. Criminal: docket/record books; original, 1883-1891, 1919-1921, 1936-37; no index. Probate: file papers; original, 1800-1900; no index.

Poland Historical Society, Poland
George Knight murder trial (transcript), 1856; deeds of Megquier family, 1864-1928. In process of cataloging other records.

Microform

Miscellaneous court records
Accounts Allowed by County Commissioners, 1864-1879, 1884-1914. GSU, 1991. FHL computer #569580.
Assignments and Discharges, 1878-1892. GSU, 1991. FHL computer #588143. Court of Insolvency.

Bills of Constables Fees, 1891-1935. GSU, 1991. FHL computer #570096. Supreme Judicial Court and Superior Court.

Coroners and Sheriffs Bonds, 1891-1918. GSU, 1991. FHL computer #570901. Supreme Judicial Court; includes deputy sheriff's commissions, 1891-1910.

County Commissioners Records, 1854-1941, Index to County Commissioners Records, 1854-1959. GSU, 1991.

Court Attachments, 1854-1895, of Androscoggin County, Maine. GSU, 1956. FHL computer #126571. Supreme Judicial Court and District Courts.

Duputy [sic] *Sheriffs Commissions, 1911-1921.* GSU, 1991. FHL computer #570931.

Insolvency Dockets, 1888-1898. GSU, 1991. FHL computer #588145. Court of Insolvency.

Sheriffs, Stenographer and Clerks Term Bills, 1893-1919. GSU, 1991. FHL computer #570892. Supreme Judicial Court and Superior Court.

Soldiers Discharges, 1863-1865. GSU, 1956. County Court; discharge papers of Civil War soldiers.

Naturalization records

Naturalization Records, 1895-1906. GSU, 1956. Supreme Judicial Court.

Probate court records

Administrators, Executors and Guardians Records, 1854-1979. GSU, 1956, 1992.

Probate of Wills, v. 1-2, 1854-1892. GSU, 1956.

Probate Records, 1854-1919. GSU, 1956, 1992.

Digital/Electronic Sources

Internet

Androscoggin Historical Society *www.rootsweb.com/~meandrhs/probate/probate.html* Abstracts of records at Androscoggin County Probate Court, from 1854.

Aroostook County

Founded 1839, from Penobscot and Washington Counties

Courts

Superior Court

Aroostook County Superior Court–Caribou

Civil and criminal: docket/record books, file papers, alphabetical index; original, 1990-date. No public access to indexes. Court staff will search; fee per name searched.

Aroostook County Superior Court–Houlton (no longer open to public)

Civil and criminal: docket/record books, file papers, alphabetical index; original, 1960-1989. Contact Aroostook County Superior Court in Caribou for access.

District Court

Except as noted, *see* "Superior and District Court—Record Retention Guidelines" in "Statewide or General Sources: Courts," *above.*

Caribou

Civil and criminal: original docket/record books, file papers, alphabetical index.

Fort Kent
Civil: docket/record books, file papers, index; original, 1990-2001; computer, 2001-date. Criminal: docket/record books, index; original and microfilm, 1965-date, computer, 1999-date.
Houlton
Madawaska
Presque Isle

Aroostook County Probate Court, Houlton
Docket/record books, file papers, appeals; original, 1840-date; card index.

State Archives

Maine State Archives, Augusta
Original records (docket/record books, file papers) of courts operating in Aroostook County, from earliest proceedings to 1929, and later materials gradually added. *See also* re: Aroostook County:
Municipal Court records. Including: Caribou, 1918-1962; Fort Fairfield, 1929-1964; Fort Kent, 1911-1962; Houlton, 1911-1962; Presque Isle, 1717-1962; Van Buren, 1939-1962.
Trial Justice Court records. Including: Ashland, 1926-1957; Limestone, 1952-1957; Merrill, 1963-1966.

Microform

Probate Records, 1839-1895. GSU, 1954.
Records of Marriages, Marriage Intentions, Births and Deaths, 1786-1942. GSU, 1954. Mars Hill, Maine, Town Clerk. Includes naturalization papers, with names, courts and dates, 1881-1946.

Cumberland County
Founded 1760, from York County

Courts

Cumberland County Superior Court, Portland
Civil, criminal, and some real estate: docket/record books, file papers, index; original, 1993-date. Divorce: file papers, index; original, 1982-date.

District Court
Bridgton
See "Superior and District Court—Record Retention Guidelines" in "Statewide or General Sources: Courts," *above*.
Portland
Civil and criminal: printout, 1980s-date; file papers (original if pending case, transcript if case recorded).

Cumberland County Probate Court, Portland
Docket/record books, file papers, index; original and microfilm, 1908-date.

State Archives

Maine State Archives, Augusta
Original records (docket/record books, file papers) of courts operating in Cumberland
County, from earliest proceedings to 1929, and later materials gradually
added. *See also* re: Cumberland County:
Municipal Court records. Including: Bridgton, 1919-1953; Brunswick, 1902-1965;
Portland and S. Portland, 1899-1965; Westbrook, 1893-1965.
Trial Justice Court records. Including: Freeport, 1951-1965; Gray, 1954-1965; Scar-
borough (18 vols.), 1939-1965.

State Historical Society

Maine Historical Society, Portland
Philip H Brown, et al. vs. John Rand, et al. M 347.9 B817. Supreme Judicial Court,
Cumberland County, in Chancery, re: estate of J. Bundy Brown, Portland
businessman.
Capen family. Deeds and probate records, 1800-1824. Coll. S-319. Portland.
Cumberland County, Maine. County records, 1780-1803. Coll. 1265. 5 vols., includ-
ing record book of John Frothingham, Notary Public, 1780-1795, and Justice
dockets of Samuel Freeman, 1790-1803.
Cumberland, County, Maine. List of witnesses, 1762. Coll. S-3039. "O'Brian's case"
before Justice Milliken.
Everett, Ebenezer. Court records, 1818-1823. Coll. S-1789. Brunswick Justice of the
Peace.
Lewis family. Papers, 1730-1843. Coll. 36. John Lewis, N. Yarmouth Justice of the
Peace.
Morgan, Jonathan. Court Records, 1823-1840. Coll. 1468. Docket book (1823-1827),
accounts of legal cases (1829-1840), and record book of cases (1826-1828)
kept by Jonathan Morgan, Justice of the Peace, Portland.
Neal, William K. Court records, 1871-1917. Coll. 1266. Portland Justice.
Shepley, Ether. Papers, 1820-1867. Coll. 117/A. Chief Justice of Maine Supreme Judi
cial Court, of Saco and Portland. Record books, 1837-1853, of cases tried.
Thrasher, Ebenezer. Daybook, docket book, and navigation book, 1839-1845; 1800-
1822. Coll. 1159. Includes docket book of Cape Elizabeth, Maine, Justice of
the Peace, 1800-1822.
Webb, Nathan. Papers, 1799-1902. Coll. 1680. Legal papers of lawyer and judge,
Portland.

Other Repositories

Freeport Historical Society, Freeport
Docket book, 1904-1909; index.
Book of lien claims and attachments, 1905-1960; partially indexed.

Judicial Archives/Massachusetts Archives, Boston, Mass.
Mass. Supreme Judicial Court Docket Books [Minute Books], 1702-1797. Originals
and microfilm, including cases from Cumberland County, 1761-1772, 1778-1797.

New Gloucester Historical Society, New Gloucester
Writs, wills, town legal matters, and petitions for ejectment and for help with drunken husband, late 1700s to late 1800s.

Peabody-Essex Museum, Salem, Mass.
Peleg W. Chandler papers, 1829-1908; bulk: 1852-1866. MH-55. Legal papers re: cases of Boston lawyer, including extended probate of estate of William Potter, Brunswick, Maine.

Standish Historical Society, Standish
Original warrants and accounts, 1785-1900; no index.

University of Maine at Orono, Special Collections
Giveen, Thomas M. Account book and papers, 1872-1893. SpC MS 990 sc. Records of court cases by Brunswick lawyer.

Windham Historical Society, Windham
Moses Little Judicial Papers Collection (1817-1843). Justice of the Peace from Windham. Papers found in Windham attic and donated to Society. *See* "Digital/Electronic Sources," *below.*

Microform

County Commissioners Records, 1761-1909. GSU, 1991. FHL computer #554097. Court of General Sessions of the Peace, Court of Common Pleas and Court of County Commissioners.
Court Records, 1829-1866. GSU, 1956. FHL computer #307070. Justice of the Peace Court.
Index of Probate Files, 1850-1899. GSU, 1991.
Index to Cumberland County Records from 1760 to 1886, inclusive. GSU, 1991. Includes Court of County Commissioners 1761-1909.
Probate Docket Books, 1908-1916; Probate Index, 1908-1923. GSU, 1991.

Digital/Electronic Sources

Internet
Windham Historical Society
www.rootsweb.com/~megenweb/cumberland/windham/papers/moses.html
Moses Little Judicial Papers Collection (1817-1843). Justice of the peace records, indexed and abstracted. *See* "Other Repositories," *above.*

Franklin County
Founded 1838, from Kennebec, Oxford and Somerset Counties

Courts

Franklin County Superior Court, Farmington
Civil: original docket/record books, twenty years; file papers, ten years; index (cards, 1925-1999, and computer, 1999-date). Criminal: original docket/record books,

twenty-five years; file papers, five to ten years; index (cards, 1925-1997, and computer 1997-date). Appeals and real estate: original docket books, twenty years; file papers, ten years.

District Court, Farmington
Civil: original docket/record books, twenty years; file papers, five years; computer index, 2002-date. Criminal: original docket/record books, twenty years; file papers, five to ten years; computer index, 1999-date. Small claims/disclosure: original docket books, twenty years; file papers, five years; computer index, 2004-date. Divorce: docket books and file papers; original, twenty years, and computer, 2002-date; index cards, 1965-2002. Real estate: original docket books, twenty years; file papers, five years; computer index, 2002-date. Protective custody: original docket books and file papers, twenty years; computer index, 1998-date. Juveniles: original docket books, twenty years; file papers, ten years; computer index, 1999-date. Protection from abuse and harassment: original docket books, twenty years; file papers, five years.

Franklin County Probate Court, Farmington
Docket/record books, file papers; original, 1838-date.

State Archives

Maine State Archives, Augusta
Original records (docket/record books, file papers) of courts operating in Franklin County, from earliest proceedings to 1929, and later materials gradually added. *See also* re: Franklin County:
Municipal Court records. Including Farmington, 1888-1903, 1909-1967.
Trial Justice Court records. Including: Madison, 1890-1956; New Sharon, 1821-1843 (filed under Mercer).

State Historical Society

Maine State Archives, Portland
Whittier, Benjamin. Court cases, 1804-1806. Coll. S-1812. Municipal court cases of Benjamin Whittier of Farmington.

Microform

Probate Records, 1838-1892, and Index, 1838-1928. GSU, 1954, 2004.

Hancock County
Founded 1789, from Lincoln County

Courts

Hancock County Superior Court, Ellsworth
Civil and criminal: docket/record books, file papers, appeals; original, 1981-date (civil), 1990-date (criminal). In-person requests only.

District Court
Bar Harbor (Closed permanently, July 2005)
Civil and criminal: docket/record books, index; 1969-2005. Contact Ellsworth District Court.
Ellsworth
Civil/family: docket/record books, file papers; original, 1966-2001; computer, 2001-date; alphabetical index. Criminal: original docket/record books, 1966-1987; original file papers, five years; computer, 1987-date (no public terminal).

Hancock County Probate Court, Ellsworth
Docket/record books, file papers, wills (1790-date), name change, guardianship, conservatorship, adoption (1862-date); original and microfilm; index.

State Archives

Maine State Archives, Augusta
Original records (docket/record books, file papers) of courts operating in Hancock County, from earliest proceedings to 1929, and later materials gradually added. *See also* re: Hancock County:
Municipal Court records. Including: Bar Harbor, 1899-1966; Bucksport, 1872-1964; Ellsworth, 1869-1966; Farmington, 1888-1903, 1909-1967.
Trial Justice Court records. Including: Gouldsboro, 1798-1799; Stonington, 1947-1966.

State Historical Society

Maine Historical Society, Portland
Docket of the Supreme Judicial Court for Hancock County. Ellsworth, Maine: American Press, 1890. Stacks 974.11j H191.
Stevens, George. Records 1821-1831. Coll. S-1019. Blue Hill Justice of the Peace.
Tobias L. Roberts et al vs. Fred E. Richards et al: on report. Ellsworth, Maine: Supreme Judicial Court, Hancock County, 1890?. M 347.9 R544. 1890 case re: Round Porcupine Island or Wheeler's Porcupine Island.

Other Repositories

Judicial Archives/Massachusetts Archives, Boston, Mass.
Supreme Judicial Court Docket Books [Minute Books], 1702-1797. Originals and microfilm, including cases from Hancock and Washington counties, 1786-1794.

Winter Harbor Historical Society, Winter Harbor
Scattered probate records.

Books

Gray, Ruth. *Abstracts of Penobscot County Maine Probate Records 1816-1866: Including Abstracts of Probate Records From Hancock County 1790-1816 Relating to That Part of Hancock County Set Off as Penobscot County in 1816*. Camden, Maine: Picton Press, 1990.

Microform

Early American Imprints, Series II. Shaw-Shoemaker (1801-1819). New Canaan, Conn.: Readex Microprint, in cooperation with American Antiquarian Society, 1987-1992. Microfiche. Including: *The trial of Moses Adams, high-sheriff of the county of Hancock: before the Supreme Judicial Court of the commonwealth of Massachusetts, on an indictment for the murder of his wife....* Boston: E.B. Tileston, 1815. Shaw & Shoemaker, 36122, 36123.

Noyes, Benjamin Lake. *Deer Isle, Hancock, Maine Wills Copied from Records of the Probate Court.* GSU, 1965.

Probate Records, 1791-1899; Index 1791-1909. GSU, 1955.

Real Estate Transfers 1931-1944 and Court Cases Hancock County, Maine; and Miscellaneous Maine Military Records and Data on Families. GSU, 1982. Newspaper clippings from Benjamin Lake Noyes collection.

Digital/Electronic Sources

Internet

Early American Imprints *www.readex.com/scholarl/earlamim.html*
Shaw-Shoemaker Digital Edition, Series II. Shaw-Shoemaker (1801-1819). Chester, Vt.: Readex/Newsbank, in cooperation with American Antiquarian Society, 2004. Available at academic libraries. *See also* "Microform," *above.*

Kennebec County
Founded 1799, from Cumberland and Lincoln Counties

Courts

Kennebec County Superior Court, Augusta
Civil (including divorces and small claims appeals): docket/record books, file papers, appeals; original, transcripts and computer, 1991-date; index from 1977, computer, 2001-date. Criminal: docket/record books, file papers, appeals; original, transcripts and computer; felonies, 1993-date, and misdemeanors, 1998-date; index from 1977, computer, 1998-date (before 1977, index in docket book at archives). Fee for record check.

District Court
Augusta
Civil and protective custody: docket/record books, file papers, appeals; original, twenty years. Small claims: docket/record books, file papers, appeals; original, five years. Criminal: docket/record books, file papers, appeals; original, 1997-date. Juvenile: docket/record books, file papers, appeals; original, ten years.
Waterville
See "Superior and District Court—Record Retention Guidelines" in "Statewide or General Sources: Courts," *above.*

Kennebec County Probate Court, Augusta
Docket/record books, case files, appeals; original and microfilm, 1799-date; computer dockets, 1995-date.

State Archives

Maine State Archives, Augusta

Original records (docket/record books, file papers) of courts operating in Kennebec
County, from earliest proceedings to 1929, and later materials gradually
added, including:

Kennebec County Supreme Court, 1799-1854. *See also* "Digital/Electronic Sources,"
below.

Municipal Court records. Including: Augusta, 1869-1870, 1903-1963; Gardiner, 1928-
1963; Hallowell, 1948-1964; Waterville, 1880-1963; Winthrop, 1903-1964.

Trial Justice Court records. Including: Augusta, 1813-1820; Readfield, 1818-1851.

State Historical Society

Maine Historical Society, Portland

Holmes, John, 1773-1843. Papers. Coll. 29. Includes lawyer's records of court proceedings, 1813-1820, in Norridgewock and Augusta, etc.

*Trial of Dr. Valorous P. Coolidge: for the murder of Edward Mathews, at Waterville,
Maine.* Boston: Boston Daily Times, 1848?. Stacks M 343.1 C779, QJ M
343.1 C779.

Other Repositories

Massachusetts Historical Society, Boston, Mass.

Richardson, Edward. Papers, 1776-1819; bulk: 1776. Ms N-792. Including court
records as justice of the peace for Kennebec and Oxford counties.

Vaughn family. Vaughan family papers, 1768-1950. Ms N-83. Including dockets,
1799-1826, Kennebec and Augusta Courts of Common Pleas, and other court
records.

Microform

Early American Imprints, Series II. Shaw-Shoemaker (1801-1819). New Canaan,
Conn.: Readex Microprint, in cooperation with American Antiquarian Society, 1987-1992. Microfiche. Including: *The Trial of David Lynn, Prince Kein
[sic], Jabex Meiggs [sic], Elijah Barton, Adam Pitts, Anson Meiggs [sic],
and Nathaniel Lynn: indicted for the murder of Paul Chadwick: containing...all the evidence....* Augusta: Peter Edes, 1809. Shaw & Shoemaker,
18778. Supreme Judicial Court at Augusta.

Lilly, Georgiana H. *Index to Kennebec County Probate, 1799-1850.* GSU, 1971. Typescript at D.A.R. Library, Washington, D.C.

Marriage Records ca. 1828-1887 and Birth Records 1876-1879. GSU, 1954. Supreme
Court.

Probate Records, 1799-ca. 1930. GSU, 1954, 1992-1993.

Digital/Electronic Sources

Internet

Ancestry.com *www.Ancestry.com*
        Maine Court Records, 1696-1854. Provo, Utah: Ancestry.com, 2003.

Early American Imprints *www.readex.com/scholarl/earlamim.html*
>Shaw-Shoemaker Digital Edition, Series II. Shaw-Shoemaker (1801-1819). Chester, Vt.: Readex/Newsbank, in cooperation with American Antiquarian Society, 2004. Available at academic libraries. *See also* "Microform," *above.*

Maine State Archives
>*www.state.me.us/sos/arc/files/dbinfo.html#CTS*
>*Courts 1696-1854.* Download searchable MS Access 97 database index of early cases from York County Court of Common Pleas (1696-1760), Kennebec County Supreme Court (1799-1854), and Washington County District Court (1839-1846), including depositions and decisions; original records at Maine State Archives. Also available as searchable online database index at Ancestry.com and New England Historic Genealogical Society.
>*www.informe.org/sos_archives*
>Maine Archives Interactive. Databases: *Early Court Cases from York, Washington and Kennebec Counties* or *Miscellaneous Municipal Records Filed with the State* (municipal and trial justice court records).

New England Historic Genealogical Society *www.NewEnglandAncestors.org*
>*Index to Maine Court Records, 1696-1854.* Boston: NewEnglandAncestors.org, 2004. Courtesy of Maine State Archives.

Knox County
Founded 1860, from Lincoln and Waldo Counties

Courts

Knox County Superior Court, Rockland
See "Superior and District Court   Record Retention Guidelines" in "Statewide or General Sources: Courts," *above.*

District Court, Rockland
See "Superior and District Court—Record Retention Guidelines" in "Statewide or General Sources: Courts," *above.*

Knox County Probate Court, Rockland
Docket/record books, file papers, appeals, index; original, transcripts, and microfilm, 1860-date (before 1860, records filed in Waldo or Lincoln counties); computer dockets from 1992. Computer not available to public.

State Archives

Maine State Archives, Augusta
Original records (docket/record books, file papers) of courts operating in Knox County, from earliest proceedings to 1929, and later materials gradually added. *See also* re: Knox County:

Municipal & Town Court records. Including: Rockland, 1855-1965; Thomaston, 1849-1853.

Trial Justice Court records. Including James Malcolm Papers (Cushing and Thomaston, 1783-1894, justice of the peace records); Elizabeth Manning's accounts for probate court work (1821-1822, Cushing).

State Historical Society

Maine Historical Society, Portland
Docket of the Supreme Judicial Court, Knox County. Rockland, Maine: Opinion Office, 1890. Stacks 974.11j K77. Includes "a table of the several terms of the Supreme Judicial Court which have been holden in the County of Knox" (1860-1890), officers of the court, 1890, and manuscript financial accounts.
Dunton, Alvin R., *The true story of the Hart-Meservey murder trial....* Boston: The author, 1882. Stacks QJ M343.1 H251.
Ingraham, Joseph. Docket book 1804-1813. Coll. 1241. Court record book kept by Justice Joseph Ingraham of Thomaston, Maine.
Thomaston, Maine. Docket book 1867. Coll. 1296.

Other Repositories

New England Historic Genealogical Society, Boston, Mass.
John S. Case Papers, 1833-1908. MSS C 1974. Including Rockland estate papers and wills.

Thomaston Historical Society, Thomaston
Cilley Family Papers. Including court records re: lawsuits in early 1800s involving Jonathan Cilley (Thomaston lawyer, Speaker of Maine House of Representatives, and U.S. Congressman), *e.g.* original transcripts of libel case and other trials, depositions re: Albert Hall's alleged theft of government funds, depositions in case of *Ruggles v. Estate of Jonathan Cilley*, etc.
Deposition of Charles Armstrong, 1914. Re: family roots and his whereabouts during the previous several years.
1802 will of Major-General Henry Knox (first U.S. Secretary of War, who lived in Thomaston from 1795 until his death in 1806). Typewritten copy.
Deeds and property transactions, 19th century.

University of Maine at Orono, Special Collections
Judges' docket, Knox County, Dec. term, 1875. SpC MS 764 sc.

Microform

Accounts, 1888-1947. GSU, 1992. FHL computer #652955. Court of County Commissioners.
Commissioners Minutes, 1860-1945. GSU, 1992. FHL computer #652938. Court of County Commissioners.
County Estimates, 1861-1912. GSU, 1992. FHL computer #652905. Court of County Commissioners.
Insolvency Records, v. 1-3, 1884-1900. GSU, 1992. FHL computer #647541. Court of Insolvency.
Petitions, 1891-1931. GSU, 1992. FHL computer #652930. Court of County Commissioners.
Probate Records, 1861-1979; Index to Probate Records, 1860-1928. GSU, 1992.
Sheriffs and Others Bonds, 1870-1905. GSU, 1992. FHL computer #652878. Court of County Commissioners.

Lincoln County
Founded 1760, from York County

Courts

Note: Originals and microfilm of Lincoln County court records from 1760 are retained at the courthouse in Wiscasset (earliest records in the Lincoln County Registry of Deeds vault). Microfilm boxes are labeled, but not indexed. Maine State Archives has copy of microfilm, with a printed list of contents by box number. *See Appendix: Contact Information-State Courts* and *Archives and Other Repositories.*

Lincoln County Superior Court, Wiscasset
Civil: docket/record books, file papers; original, 1900-date; index (computer, 2001-date). Criminal: docket/record books, file papers; original, 1920-date; index (computer, 1998-date).

District Court, Wiscasset
Civil: docket/record books, file papers, 1986-date. Criminal: docket/record books, file papers; 1985-date.

Lincoln County Probate Court, Wiscasset
Docket books, file papers, index; 1760-date.

State Archives and Library

Maine State Archives, Augusta
Microfilmed records (docket/record books, file papers) of courts operating in Lincoln
    County, with printed list of contents by box number, from earliest proceedings
    to 1929, and later materials gradually added. *See also* re: Lincoln County:
Municipal Court records. Including Wiscasset, 1913-1965.
Trial Justice Court records. Including: Waldoboro, 1837-1840 (justice docket of John
    Bulfinch).

Maine State Library, Augusta
Sheepscot manuscripts, 1662-1828. Call #974.1 cL73s. Handwritten. Use restricted to serious research. Includes journal of court decisions, depositions, and other court records.

State Historical Society

Maine Historical Society, Portland
Call, Moses. Court Records, 1846. Coll. S-2055. *Moses Call v. Simon Handley*, Lin-
    coln County Superior Court, including complaint, testimony and verdict. *See
    also* printed appellate brief: *Moses Call & al (in equity) vs. William J. Perkins
    & als : plaintiffs' abstract.* Wiscasset, Maine: Joseph Wood, printer, 1872. M
    347.9 P419. Supreme Judicial Court.
Lincoln County, Maine. Criminal records and civil actions, 1772-1808; 1787. Coll.
    1283. Kept by Nathaniel Thwing.

Patterson, William D. Papers, 1650-1930. Coll. 1. Records of Lincoln County Probate Court, Mass. Supreme Judicial Court, etc.

Pownalborough Courthouse Collection. Coll. 1924. Wide-ranging collection of documents (many stored in trunks and boxes at the courthouse until 1952); finding aids available. Court records include: Files of Jonathan Bowman, Dresden probate judge, with trial and probate records, 1760-1795; "Town of Dresden Affairs" papers, including deeds (1662-1832), wills and estate inventories (1788-1850), writs (1761-1830), depositions, etc.

Riggs, Benjamin. Record of marriage, 1808-1839. Coll. 1288. Georgetown, Maine, kept by Benjamin Riggs, Justice of the Peace. Also record of cases brought before Riggs in 1815-1816. *See also* "Books and Journals," *below*.

Smith, Samuel E. Docket Book, 1821; 1824-1827. Coll 1469. Circuit Court of Common Pleas for Second Eastern Circuit, held at Topsham, Lincoln County, Maine, 1821, Samuel E. Smith, Chief Justice, Ebenezer Thatcher, Sanford Kingsbury, Associate Justices. Also includes accounts, 1824-1827.

Thatcher, Ebenezer. Docket books, 1812-1820. Coll. 1473. Judge of Maine Circuit Court of Common Pleas. Collection includes docket books of courts in Norridgewock (1812, Somerset County) and Wiscasset (1819, Lincoln County), kept by justices Ebenezer Thatcher and Nathan Weston.

Wood, Oliver. Marriage records, 1784-1798. Coll. 1206. Marriages and cases of judge in Norridgewock and vicinity, then Lincoln County.

Other Repositories

Boothbay Region Historical Society, Boothbay Harbor
Misc. manuscripts from Collection #8: Box #3, Reed documents, 1809-1900, including fifteen wills; Box #15, re: division of towns and water system controversy; Box #17, Beath, Kelley and Blake documents, 1700s-1800s, including deeds and will; Box #19, Justin (Webber) Smith's legal documents, 1748-1957; Box #26, Benjamin and James Pinkham of Dover papers, 1840s-1915, including legal documents; Box #30, Hodgdon family legal papers, 1820-1921; Box #33, estate matters; Box #34, legal papers of Alfred Wadsworth estate (1844-1849), Seavey (1863-1913), and Nellie Baker (1891-1926).

Jefferson Historical Society, Jefferson
Approx. fifty vols. of *Maine Reports* (published cases of Supreme Judicial Court of Maine) from 1820-1953 (with some gaps).

Judicial Archives/Massachusetts Archives, Boston, Mass.
Mass. Supreme Judicial Court Docket Books [Minute Books], 1702-1797, originals and microfilm, including cases from Lincoln County, 1761-1772, 1778-1797.

New England Historic Genealogical Society, Boston, Mass.
Avery, James. Account book of court judgments by James Avery, 1785-1798. Records of confession processes from 5 May 1787 to 22 June 1794. MSS C 4907, 4997. Court records of Justice of the Peace.

Commissioners Records of Lincoln County, Maine, 1759-1777. MSS/ME 88 6. Transcription by Georgiana Lilly. *See also* "Digital/Electronic Sources," *below*.

University of Maine at Orono, Special Collections
Lincoln County. County Clerk. County documents, 1808-1880. SpC MS 773 sc.
Includes records re: appointment of jurors in 1808, and judgments, 1818-1880.

Books and Journals

Fredricks, Katherine M. E. *Bar-Bits from Old Court Records in Lincoln County, Maine*. Wiscasset: County Commissioners of Lincoln County, 1960.
Kelley, Judith Holbrook, and Clayton Rand Adams. *Marriage Returns of Lincoln County, Maine to 1866*. Maine Genealogical Society, Special Publication, No. 39. Rockport, Maine: Picton Press, 2001, 2002.
New England Historical and Genealogical Register. Boston: New England Historic Genealogical Society, 80:24. Record of marriage, 1808-1839. Georgetown, Maine, kept by Benjamin Riggs, Justice of the Peace.
Patterson, William D. *The Probate Records of Lincoln County, Maine, 1760-1800*. Maine Genealogical Society, Special Publication, No. 6. Portland: Maine Genealogical Society, 1895; Camden, Maine: Picton Press, 1991. *See also* "Microform" and "Digital/Electronic Sources," *below*.

Microform

Miscellaneous court records
Book of Record in the Office of Justice of the Peace for the County of Lincoln, 1804-1838. GSU, 1991. Includes complaints, warrants, oaths, marriages, etc. of Hezekiah Prince.
Court Records, 1761-1989. GSU, 1991. FHL computer #581614. Court of General Sessions and Court of County Commissioners.
Noyes, Benjamin Lake, ed. *Miscellaneous Genealogical Papers Deer Isle, Hancock County, Maine*. GSU, 1982. Includes records, 1760-1795, from Court of Common Pleas at Pownalborough.
Record of Marriages, 1828-1866. GSU, 1991. Supreme Judicial Court.
Records of Soldiers Discharge, 1866-1890. GSU, 1991. Supreme Judicial Court.

Probate records
Patterson, William D. *The Probate Records of Lincoln County, Maine, 1760-1800*. Portland: Maine Genealogical Society, 1895. GSU, 1982, 1985. Microfilm, microfiche.
Probate Records, 1760-1957. GSU, 1954, 1992.
[Second Prospectus of] Probate Records of Lincoln County, Maine. Maine Genealogical Society, 1894. Washington, D.C.: Library of Congress Photoduplication Service, 1984.

Digital/Electronic Sources

CD-ROM
Maine & New Hampshire Settlers, 1600s-1900s. Family Archives. Novato, Cal.: Broderbund, 2000. Includes William D. Patterson. *The Probate Records of Lincoln County, Maine, 1760-1800*. Portland: Maine Genealogical Society, 1895.

Internet
Ancestry.com *www.Ancestry.com*
>*Lincoln County, Maine: Probates, 1760-1800.* Provo, Utah: Ancestry.com, 2001. Original data from William D. Patterson. *The Probate Records of Lincoln County, Maine, 1760-1800.* Portland: Maine Genealogical Society, 1895.

New England Historic Genealogical Society *www.NewEnglandAncestors.org*
>*Commissioners Records of Lincoln County, Maine, 1759-1777.* Boston: www.NewEnglandAncestors.org, 2003. *See also* "Other Repositories," *above.*

Oxford County
Founded 1805, from Cumberland and York Counties

Courts

Oxford County Superior Court, S. Paris
Civil records: original docket/record books, file papers, 1990-date; index. Criminal records: original docket/record books, 1976-date; original file papers, 1990-date; index. Divorce records: original file papers, 1981-date; index.

District Court
Rumford
See "Superior and District Court—Record Retention Guidelines" in "Statewide or General Sources: Courts," *above.*
S. Paris
Civil and criminal: docket/record books, file papers, appeals; original, 1965-date; computer index (most civil records, criminal since 1999).

Oxford County Probate Court, S. Paris
Docket/record books, file papers, appeals, index; original and microfilm, pre-1800-date.

State Archives

Maine State Archives, Augusta
Original records (docket/record books, file papers) of courts operating in Oxford County, from earliest proceedings to 1929, and later materials gradually added. *See also* re: Oxford County:
Municipal Court records. Including Fryeburg, 1945-1966; Norway, 1882-1966.
Trial Justice Court records. Including: Bethel, 1890-1900; Brownfield, 1793-1794; Buckfield, 1869-1886; Fryeburg, 1795-1799; Norway, 1830-1839, 1873-1882; Rumford, 1860-1864; Waterford, 1820-1828.

State Historical Society

Maine Historical Society, Portland
Continued docket, Supreme Judicial Court, Oxford County. Paris, Maine: 1855. Stacks 974.11j Ox2.1. March term, 1855. Includes list of practitioners at the Oxford bar and manuscript notations.
S. J. Court docket, Oxford County. Stacks 974.11j Ox2.2 . September term, 1874.

Other Repositories

Hamlin Memorial Library, Paris
Thomas Clark papers, 1775-1852. Including legal documents.

Massachusetts Historical Society, Boston, Mass.
Richardson, Edward. Papers, 1776-1819. Ms N-792. Including records as Justice of the Peace for Kennebec and Oxford counties.

University of Maine at Orono, Special Collections
Oxford County Records, 1825-1834. SpC MS 822 sc. Writs of attachment and summonзсз.

Microform

Deeds, Eastern District, 1806-1957; Index to Deeds, 1805-1902. GSU, 1954, 2004. Registry of Deeds and Justice of the Peace. Vols. 125-266 include records from Supreme Judicial Court, insolvency assignments, abstract of will, etc.
Index to Probate Records Previous to the Year 1900 (Oxford County, Maine). GSU, 1954.
Probate Dockets, 1820-1867. GSU, 1956.
Probate Estate Records Pre 1820-1899 and Indexes 1820-1980, Oxford County, Maine. GSU, 2003-2004.
Probate of Wills and Letters Testamentary (Probate Records vol. 1), 1836-1865. GSU, 1956.
Probate Records 1805-1872 and Indexes Pre 1820. GSU, 1954.
Probate Records, 1810-1885. GSU, 1956.

Penobscot County
Founded 1816, from Hancock County

Courts

Penobscot County Superior Court, Bangor
Civil: docket/record books, file papers, appeals; original, some transcripts; 1976-date (1960-1975, at archives). Criminal: docket/record books, file papers, appeals; original, some transcripts; 1991-date (1976-1990, storage facility, and 1960-1975, at archives).

District Court
Except as noted, *see* "Superior and District Court—Record Retention Guidelines" in "Statewide or General Sources: Courts," *above*.
Bangor
Civil: docket/record books, file papers, appeals, index; original, 1998-date; computer, 2001-date. Criminal: docket/record books, file papers, appeals, index; original, 1978-date; computer, 1986-date.
Lincoln
Millinocket

Newport
Civil and criminal: docket/record books, file papers, index; original on site five to ten years; computer, 1965-date.

Penobscot County Probate Court, Bangor
Docket/record books, file papers, index; original, microfilm and transcripts, 1816-date. Search fee.

State Archives

Maine State Archives, Augusta
Original records (docket/record books, file papers) of courts operating in Penobscot County, from earliest proceedings to 1929, and later materials gradually added. *See also* re: Penobscot County:
Municipal Court records. Including Bangor, 1834-1963; Brewer, 1949-1965; Dexter, 1898-1965; Lincoln, 1947-1966; Millinocket, 1909-1963; Old Town, 1883-1962; Orono, 1957-1963.
Trial Justice Court records. Including Dixmont, 1818-1851; Lincoln, 1941-1943.

State Historical Society

Maine Historical Society, Portland
Argument of Bertram L. Smith for the state: in the matter of petition for pardon of David L. Stain and Oliver Cromwell .... Bangor: G. H. Glass & Co., 1900. Defendants convicted in Supreme Judicial Court for the murder of John Wilson Barron at Dexter, February 22, 1878. Includes testimony. *See also* related brief: *State vs. David L. Stain and Oliver Cromwell: argument for the state on the prisoners' motion for a new trial/by Mr. Orville Dewey Baker, Attorney-General*. Augusta: Press of Charles E. Nash, 1888?. Stacks Mk D523b-s.
Joseph P. Bass, Aplt. v. city of Bangor: brief of appellant; law on report. Stacks M 343.1 B293. Brief to Supreme Judicial Court, Penobscot County, 1913.
Inhabitants of Lowell vs. inhabitants of Newport. M 347.9 L951. Supreme Judicial Court, Penobscot County, April Term, 1875. Action for supplies furnished to a pauper.

Other Repositories

Bangor Museum and Center for History, Bangor
Justice of the Peace records for Bangor area, including debt records and marriage intentions, sporadic from 1777-1820; no index.
Summaries of court cases by Judge Jonas Cutting, 1854-1860, *e.g.*, vol. titled "Penobscot County Criminal Term." Table of contents in each vol. Cutting served as Justice in the Supreme Judicial Court of Maine, 1854-1875.
District and Supreme Court Docket book by C.P. Roberts, 1847-1849; no index.

Hampden Historical Society, Hampden
Probate docket/record books (transcripts), 1790-1866.

University of Maine at Orono, Special Collections
Burgess, James H. Probate Court records, 1909-1922. SpC MS 890 sc. Records of
    Bangor lawyer and Justice of the Peace.
Dunn, Charles J., 1872-1939. SpC MS 150. Legal and personal papers, 1833-1986.
    Records of Penobscot County lawyer and Maine Supreme Court judge.
Hillard, Heddle, 1853-1924, collector. Collection, 1832-1878, Folder 4. SpC MS 786
    sc. Includes court records, mainly Penobscot County.

Books

Gray, Ruth. *Abstracts of Penobscot County Maine Probate Records 1816-1866:*
    Including Abstracts of Probate Records From Hancock County 1790-1816
    Relating to That Part of Hancock County Set Off as Penobscot County in
    1816. Camden, Maine: Picton Press, 1990.
Swett, David Livingstone. *Vital Records of Orrington, Maine.* Vol. 10. Rockport,
    Maine: Picton Press, 2003. Includes records of Simeon Fowler, Justice of the
    Peace, 1787-1789.

Microform

Penobscot County, Maine, Towns of Greenbush & Passadunkeag [i.e., Passadumkeag]
    1833-1880: Aaron Haynes, Justice of Peace (Records of); Court Proceedings
    and Latter Part Contains 62 Marriages. GSU, 2003.
Probate Records, 1816-1893; Index 1816-1866. GSU, 1956.

Piscataquis County
Founded 1838, from Penobscot and Somerset Counties

Courts

Piscataquis County Superior Court, Dover-Foxcroft
Civil and criminal: docket books and indexes, original and computer; file papers prior
to 1960, sent to archives or destroyed.

District Court, Dover-Foxcroft
Civil and criminal: docket/record books, file papers; original and computer, 1965-date.

Piscataquis County Probate Court, Dover-Foxcroft
Docket/record books, index; original and microfilm, 1838-date.

State Archives

Maine State Archives, Augusta
Original records (docket/record books, file papers) of courts operating in Piscataquis
    County, from earliest proceedings to 1929, and later materials gradually
    added. *See also* re: Piscataquis County:
Municipal Court records. Including Dover, 1884-1967.

State Historical Society

Maine Historical Society, Portland
Chandler, Charles Parsons, 1801-1857. Papers. Coll. 75. Including court docket books and legal documents of Foxcroft lawyer.

Other Repositories

Dover-Foxcroft Historical Society, Dover-Foxcroft
Extensive archives collection, which Society is cataloging and conserving, *e.g.*:
Piscataquis County, Court of County Commissioners. Bills of Costs, August 1889–August 1899. Original, no index, including names of accused and witnesses, charge, hearing dates, etc.
Piscataquis County, Superior Court. Jury Lists and Summary of Cases, March Term, 1930 (original, indexed); Bills of Costs, March Term, 1981–September Term, 1938 (original, no index), including names of accused and witnesses, charge, hearing dates, etc.
Summons, writs, etc. to sheriff, 1845-1858.

Microform

Probate Records, 1838-1884. GSU, 1955.
Record of Wills, 1856-1879; Old Records, v. X, 1838-1867. GSU, 1955.

Sagadahoc County
Founded 1854, from Lincoln County

Courts

Sagadahoc County Superior Court, Bath
See "Superior and District Court—Record Retention Guidelines" in "Statewide or General Sources: Courts," *above*.

District Court, W. Bath
Civil and criminal: docket books (original from 1965, computer, 1999-date); *see* "Superior and District Court—Record Retention Guidelines" in "Statewide or General Sources: Courts," *above*, re: file papers. In-person requests only.

Sagadahoc County Probate Court, Bath
Docket/record books, file papers, appeals, index; original, 1854-date.

State Archives

Maine State Archives, Augusta
Original records (docket/record books, file papers) of courts operating in Sagadahoc County, from earliest proceedings to 1929, and later materials gradually added. *See also* re: Sagadahoc County:
Municipal Court records. Including: Bath, 1855-1965.

State Historical Society

Maine Historical Society, Portland
*Report in full of the trial of Bartlett, Simms and McGuire, for the robbery of the Bow-
        doinham Bank: before the Supreme Judicial Court, at Bath, Me., at the April
        term, 1867/by J. D. Pulsifer, stenographer to the court.* Portland: B. Thurston
        & Co., 1867. Stacks M B675.2.
Sewall, Jacob S. Docket book, 1838-1841. Coll. 1586. Justice of the Peace records,
        Bath.
Thayer, Henry Otis. The famous Jefferies-Donnell suit, June 24, A.D., 1766: from the
        papers of Henry O. Thayer. Coll. 3037. Undated typescript re: legal rights to
        12,000 acres near Georgetown (Maine) on the Kennebec River. Jefferies was
        from Boston, Donnell from York.

Microform

Probate Records 1854-1901; Docket 1854-1876. GSU, 1954.

Somerset County
Founded 1809, from Kennebec County

Courts

Somerset County Superior Court, Skowhegan
Civil and criminal: docket books, file papers, appeals; original and transcripts, 1960-
date; computer index, 1998-date; index cards before 1998. Divorce: docket books, file
papers, appeals; original and transcripts, 1960-date; index cards.

District Court, Skowhegan
Civil and criminal: original docket/record books, 1999-date (civil), 1998-date
(criminal).

Somerset County Probate Court, Skowhegan
Docket/record books, file papers, appeals, index; original and microfilm, 1800-date.

State Archives

Maine State Archives, Augusta
Original records (docket/record books, file papers) of courts operating in Somerset
        County, from earliest proceedings to 1929, and later materials gradually
        added. *See also* re: Somerset County:
Municipal Court records. Including Pittsfield, 1901-1965; Skowhegan, 1908-1965.
Trial Justice Court records. Including: Anson, 1857-1881; Athens, 1811, 1896-1917;
        Bingham, 1935-1966; Fairfield, 1818-1851, 1883-1888, 1938-1962; Har-
        mony, 1856-1871; Madawaska, 1928-1939; Mercer, 1821-1843; Norridge-
        wock, 1886-1887; Pittsfield, 1880-1883; Solon, 1867-1873, 1890-1900;
        Starks, 1821-1843 (filed under Mercer).

State Historical Society

Maine Historical Society, Portland
Allen, William, Jr. Docket Books, 1816-1834. Coll. 1467. Justice of the Peace, Norridgewock.
Holmes, John, 1773-1843. Papers. Coll. 29. Includes lawyer's records of court proceedings, 1813-1820, in Norridgewock and Augusta, etc.
Thatcher, Ebenezer. Docket books, 1812-1820. Coll. 1473. Judge of Maine Circuit Court of Common Pleas. Collection includes docket books of courts in Norridgewock (1812, Somerset County) and Wiscasset (1819, Lincoln County), kept by justices Ebenezer Thatcher and Nathan Weston.
Webster, John H. Papers, 1859-1888. Coll. S-2035. Including 1859 case v. William Calden for unpaid debt.
Wyman, Lewis. Records, 1856-1897. Coll. 176. Includes Wyman's justice docket, 1858-1876.

Microform

Probate Records, 1810-1885. GSU, 1954.
Records, 1833-1890. GSU, 1954. Court of County Commissioners. Appointments, bonds and marriages.

Waldo County
Founded 1827, from Hancock County

Courts

Waldo County Superior Court, Belfast
See "Superior and District Court—Record Retention Guidelines" in "Statewide or General Sources: Courts," *above*.

District Court, Belfast
See "Superior and District Court—Record Retention Guidelines" in "Statewide or General Sources: Courts," *above*.

Waldo County Probate Court, Belfast
Docket/record books, file papers, appeals; original and microfilm, 1827-date.

State Archives

Maine State Archives, Augusta
Original records (docket/record books, file papers) of courts operating in Waldo County, from earliest proceedings to 1929, and later materials gradually added. *See also* re: Waldo County:
Municipal Court records. Including Belfast, 1883-1966.

Microform

Probate Records and Indexes 1826-1892. GSU, 1954.

Washington County
Founded 1789, from Lincoln County

Courts

Washington County Superior Court, Machias
Civil and criminal: docket/record books, file papers, appeals, index; original and transcripts, 1930-date.

District Court, Calais and Machias
See "Superior and District Court—Record Retention Guidelines" in "Statewide or General Sources: Courts," *above*.

Washington County Probate Court, Machias
Docket/record books, file papers, appeals; original and transcripts, 1785-date.

State Archives

Maine State Archives, Augusta
Original records (docket/record books, file papers) of courts operating in Washington County, from earliest proceedings to 1929, and later materials gradually added, including:
Washington County District Court, 1839-1846. *See also* "Digital/Electronic Sources," *below*.
Municipal Court records. Including Calais, 1851-1964; Eastport, 1903-1964; Machias, 1871-1966.
Trial Justice Court records. Including Baileyville, 1959-1966; Danforth, 1937-1964; E. Machias, 1826-1836; Jonesboro, 1826-1840; Machias, 1826-1840, 1863-1899; Pembroke, 1846-1849; Vanceboro, 1947-1965.

State Historical Society

Maine Historical Society, Portland
Spalding, James A. *Lowell vs. Faxon and Hawkes: a Celebrated Malpractice Suit in Maine*. Easton, Penn.: American Academy of Medicine, 1910. Stacks M343 Sp18.

Other Repositories

Judicial Archives/Massachusetts Archives, Boston, Mass.
Mass. Supreme Judicial Court Docket Books [Minute Books], 1702-1797, originals and microfilm. Including cases from Hancock and Washington counties, 1786-1794.

Massachusetts Historical Society, Boston, Mass.
Warren, John C. *A letter to the Hon. Isaac Parker, chief justice of the Supreme court of the state of Massachusetts: containing remarks on the dislocation of the hip joint, occasioned by the publication of a trial which took place at Machias, in the state of Maine, June 1824...with an appendix of documents from the trial....* Cambridge, Mass.: Hillard & Metcalf, 1826. QM.

New England Historic Genealogical Society, Boston, Mass.

An authentic report of a trial before the Supreme Judicial Court of Maine, for the County of Washington, June term, 1824: Charles Lowell vs. John Faxon & Micajah Hawks, surgeons and physicians, in an action of trespass on the case, for ignorance and negligence in their professional treatment of plaintiff's dislocated hip: with observations on the prejudices and conduct of the inhabitants of Eastport, in regard to this case: the character and testimony of several witnesses, and the novel, and extraordinary positions assumed by the court. Portland: 1825. Rare Book RD101/L65/1825.

Report of the trial of an action, Charles Lowell against John Faxon and Micajah Hawks, doctors of medicine, defendants.... Portland: Printed for J. Adams by David and Seth Paine, 1825. Rare Book RD101/L65/1825.

Microform

Court Records 1821-1892. GSU, 1956. FHL computer #290353. Supreme Judicial Court; misc. cases, including marriage & divorce.

Probate Records 1785-1893. GSU, 1956.

Probate Records of the Northern District of Washington County, 1826-1839. GSU, 1954.

Will Abstracts, v. W-1, 1888-1906. GSU, 1956.

Digital/Electronic Sources

Internet

Ancestry.com *www.Ancestry.com*

 Maine Court Records, 1696-1854. Provo, Utah: Ancestry.com, 2003.

Maine State Archives

 www.state.me.us/sos/arc/files/dbinfo.html#CTS

 Courts 1696-1854. Download searchable MS Access 97 database index of early cases from York County Court of Common Pleas (1696-1760), Kennebec County Supreme Court (1799-1854), and Washington County District Court (1839-1846), including depositions and decisions; original records at Maine State Archives. Also available as searchable online database index at Ancestry.com and New England Historic Genealogical Society.

 www.informe.org/sos_archives

 Maine Archives Interactive. Databases: *Early Court Cases from York, Washington and Kennebec Counties* or *Miscellaneous Municipal Records Filed with the State* (municipal and trial justice court records).

New England Historic Genealogical Society *www.NewEnglandAncestors.org*

 Index to Maine Court Records, 1696-1854. Boston: NewEnglandAncestors.org, 2004. Courtesy of Maine State Archives.

York County
Founded 1652

Courts

York County Superior Court, Alfred

Civil and criminal: docket/record books, file papers, appeals, ten years (unless older cases still pending).

District Court
Except as noted, *see* "Superior and District Court—Record Retention Guidelines" in "Statewide or General Sources: Courts," *above.*
Biddeford
Springvale
Civil: docket books, 1965-2001; computer, 2002-date; index. Criminal: docket books, 1965-1986; computer, 1987-date. Mail requests honored, but if no self-addressed stamped envelope, court charges $5 postage and handling. Other charges for record checks, copies, etc.
York

York County Probate Court, Alfred
Probate and equity: docket/records books, file papers, appeals, index; original and microfilm, 1867-date.

State Archives

Maine State Archives, Augusta
Original records (docket/record books, file papers) of courts operating in York County, from earliest proceedings to 1929, and later materials gradually added, including:
York County Court of Common Pleas, 1696-1760. *See also* "Digital/Electronic Sources," *below.*
Municipal Court records. Including Biddeford, 1933-1965; Kennebunk, 1923-1965; Kittery, 1943-1965; Saco, 1935-1965; Sanford, 1900-1965; S. Berwick, 1911-1965; York, 1930-1962.
Trial Justice Court records. Including Berwick, 1787-1798; Biddeford, 1788-1805; Buxton, 1815-1838; Kennebunk, 1796-1834, 1856-1866; Kittery, 1787-1799; Lebanon, 1787-1794, 1830-1861; Limerick, 1790-1799, 1808-1821, 1899-1910; Limington, 1824-1847; Lyman, 1795-1796; Old Orchard Beach, 1954-1964; Saco, 1793, 1797-1798, 1823-1843; Sanford, 1787-1799, 1810-1844, 1897-1898; Wells, 1788-1792, 1795-1818; York, 1787-1795, 1810-1848; 1902-1929.

State Historical Society

Maine Historical Society, Portland
Frost, William. Accounts and Justice Court Records, 1769-1820. Coll. 911.
Kittery, Maine. Records, 1650-1827. Coll. 1189. Including court docket books of Joshua Hubbard, 1787-1807.
Frank W. Nutter and Frank C. Deering receivers of the Saco Savings Bank, petitioners: in re: Batchelder & Snyder co. vs. Saco Savings Bank. M 347.9 B314. Maine Supreme Judicial Court, York County, 1911?
Parris, Albion K. Docket book, 1831. Coll. 1273. Maine Supreme Court, York.
Parsons, William. Justice docket, 1802-1826. Coll. S-878. Justice of the Peace in Alfred.
Pepperrell, William. Summons, 1724. Coll. S-3040. Ordering witnesses to appear before Justice of the Peace re: injury to Martha Rackly's ram.
Charles Lorenzo Perkins vs. inhabitants of York. M 347.9 P4192. Supreme Judicial Court, York County, September term, 1918. Re: injury to Perkins from driving over hole in road.
Sargent, William. Estate settlement costs, 1825-1826. Coll. S-671.

Shepley, Ether. Papers, 1820-1867. Coll. 117/A. Chief Justice of Maine Supreme Judicial Court, of Saco and Portland. Record books, 1837-1853, of cases tried.
Thayer, Henry Otis. The famous Jefferies-Donnell suit, June 24, A.D., 1766: from the
papers of Henry O. Thayer. Coll. 3037. Undated typescript re: legal rights to
12,000 acres near Georgetown (Maine) on the Kennebec River. Jefferies was
from Boston, Donnell from York.
York County, Maine. Court cases, 1865-1878. Coll. 1274. Cases before Trial Justice
George W. S. Putnam.
York County, Maine. Probate minute book, 1766-1771. Coll. 1277.
Wells, Nathaniel. Papers, 1723-1786. Coll. 1626. Justice of the Peace, Wells.
Woodman Collection. Papers, 1706-1889. Coll. 1589. Re: Buxton, Maine, including
writs, executions, deeds, docket books, estate papers, etc.

Other Repositories

Boston Historical Society and Museum, Boston, Mass.
Summons, May 20, 1742. MS0119/-#DC1484. Re: action of ejectment between Elizabeth Milliken, widow of Boston, and Eliot Vaughn, gentleman of Scarborough. Superior Court of Judicature.

Harvard University, Law School Library, Cambridge, Mass.
Cobb, William. Records of William Cobb, justice of the peace, Limerick, York County,
Maine, 1859-1867. MSS HLS MS 4337.

Judicial Archives/Massachusetts Archives, Boston, Mass.
Supreme Judicial Court Docket Books [Minute Books], 1702-1797, originals and
microfilm; including cases from York County, 1719-1797 (gaps).

Massachusetts Historical Society, Boston, Mass.
Cushing, William. Charge to Grand Jury, 1780. MS S-543. Charge to Grand Jury of
York County, District of Maine, in June 1780, from the chief justice of the Mass.
Supreme Judicial Court.

New England Historic Genealogical Society, Boston, Mass.
Currier, Doris Goodwin. "References to wives, or children, in wills and deeds as
recorded at Alfred, Maine court house." MSS A 2247. Typescript compiled ca. 1954.

Old Berwick Historical Society, S. Berwick
Civil, criminal and probate: docket/record books and file papers, 1771-1895 (mostly
1840s-1890s), with index, *e.g.*: Oakes, Abner. Papers, 1840-1895. Includes court and
legal records of lawyer and judge of S. Berwick.

Old York Historical Society, York
Records (microfilmed): York County Commissioner Record General Session, Vol. 10
(1733)-Vol. 21 (1859-1867); York County Court Records, Vol. 1 (1636-1671), Reel
1-6 (including Vol. 38, p. 114, 1820); Book of York's Gaolers Records, 18th century.

Peabody-Essex Museum, Phillips Library, Salem, Mass.
Curwen family. Papers, 1641-1902. MSS 45. Capt. George Curwen (1610-1684)
papers series includes legal documents re: Cape Porpoise River Falls Mill, Wells.

Portsmouth Athenaeum, Portsmouth, N.H.
Petitions, lists of voters, and other records from York County, 1798-1844. S667. Petitions to Circuit Court of Common Pleas and county commissioner re: construction of roads and railroads, particularly to Portsmouth, N.H. Also voter list (1832-ca. 1840) for Berwick and S. Berwick.

Sanford Historical Committee, Sanford
Civil file papers, #4501-4824, July 1925-July 1926; no index.
Criminal file papers, #8248-9190, Dec. 1929-Dec. 1933; no index.

University of Maine at Orono, Special Collections
Edwin A. Churchill Papers, 1987-2000. SpC MS 777. Re: Churchill's work as expert witness for state of Maine in three court cases, Moody Beach lawsuit (*Edward B. Bell, et al. v. Town of Wells, et al.*), Wells Beach lawsuit (*Lisle Eaton, et al. v. Inhabitants of the town of Wells*), both before Supreme Judicial Court of Maine, and *State of New Hampshire v. State of Maine*. Records include detailed historical research and court documents.
Hill Family Papers, 1698-1842 (bulk 1720-1770). SpC MS 245. Including records of Berwick justice of the peace.

University of New Hampshire, Special Collections, Durham, N.H.
Deering, Roger. Legal papers, 1652-1713. MS 37. Appeal to Superior Court of Judicature from decision of Inferior Court of Common Pleas at York, depositions, etc.

Books

Anderson, Joseph Crook. *York County, Maine, Will Abstracts, 1801-1858.* 2 vols. Maine Genealogical Society, Special Publication: No. 27. Camden, Maine: Picton Press, 1997.
Ayer, Harry B. *Index to the Probate Records of the County of York, Maine: From January 1, 1901, to January 1, 1911.* Biddeford, Maine: Press of the Biddeford Journal, 1911.
Collections of the Maine Historical Society. Portland: Maine Historical Society, 1831, 1865. 1:269-286. Extracts from York County Court records. Appendix: 532-542, includes record of court held at Saco in 1640.
Documentary History of the State of Maine: Collections, 2d ser. 24 vols. Portland: Maine Historical Society, 1869-1916. Many transcribed cases and court records, *e.g.*: *The Trelawny Papers*, vol. 3, including cases of *Cleeve v. Winter* (1640), 3:208-214, 225-242, 260-266, 269-272, and *Mackworth v. Winter* (1641), 3:266-269; *The Baxter Manuscripts*, vols. 4-6, 9-24, including court cases from 1680s at 6:29, 204, 216-218, and case from 1781-1783 at 20:439-463.
Frost, John Eldridge. *Maine Probate Abstracts.* 2 vols. Camden, Maine: Picton Press, 1991. Vol. 1, 1687-1775; vol. 2, 1775-1800.
Index to the Probate Records of the County of York, Maine: From January 1, 1901 to January 1, 1917. Biddeford, Maine: Press of the Biddeford Journal, 1918.
Sargent, William M. *Maine Wills, 1640-1760.* Portland: Maine Historical Society, 1887; Baltimore, Md. Genealogical Publishing Co., 1972. *See also* "Microform" and "Digital/Electronic Sources," *below.*

Supplement to Probate Index, York County: From January 1, 1901, to January 1, 1911. Maine: s.n., 1911-1916.

York Deeds. Vol. 5. Portland: J.T. Hull, 1889. Includes records of Court of Sessions of the Peace, Inferior Court of Common Pleas and Court of Quarter Sessions, 1680-1686, 1690-1699.

Microform

Probate Bonds, 1843-1868. GSU, 2001.

Probate Records, 1687-1938; Index to Probate Records, 1687-1900. GSU, 1953-1954, 2001.

Sargent, William M. *Maine Wills, 1640-1760.* Portland: Maine Historical Society, 1887; Baltimore, Md.: Genealogical Publishing Co., 1972. GSU, 1969, 1984. Microfilm, microfiche.

Suffolk County (Mass.) Court Files, 1629-1797. GSU, 1972. 1,639 reels. Re: many different courts and counties, including Maine, with several index systems (alphabetical, chronological, by subject and geography, etc.).

Digital/Electronic Sources

CD-ROM

Maine & New Hampshire Settlers, 1600s-1900s. Novato, Cal.: Broderbund, 2000. Includes William M. Sargent, *Maine Wills, 1640-1760.* Portland: Maine Historical Society, 1887.

Internet

Ancestry.com *www.Ancestry.com*

> *Maine Court Records, 1696-1854.* Provo, Utah: Ancestry.com, 2003.
>
> *Maine Will Abstracts, 1640-1760.* Provo, Utah: MyFamily.com, Inc., 2000. Original data from William M. Sargent. *Maine Wills, 1640-1760.* Portland: Maine Historical Society, 1887.

AncestryandGenealogy.com *www.ancestryandgenealogy.com/freedataancforn.asp*

> *Lost Babes, Fornication Abstracts.* AncestryandGenealogy.com, 2005. Free database, abstracting birth and marriage records from fornication cases in York County courts, 1689-1699.

Maine State Archives

> *www.state.me.us/sos/arc/files/dbinfo.html#CTS*
>
> *Courts 1696-1854.* Download searchable MS Access 97 database index of early cases from York County Court of Common Pleas (1696-1760), Kennebec County Supreme Court (1799-1854), and Washington County District Court (1839-1846), including depositions and decisions; original records at Maine State Archives. Also available as searchable online database index at Ancestry.com and New England Historic Genealogical Society.
>
> *www.informe.org/sos_archives*
>
> Maine Archives Interactive. Databases: *Early Court Cases from York, Washington and Kennebec Counties* or *Miscellaneous Municipal Records Filed with the State* (municipal and trial justice court records).

New England Historic Genealogical Society *www.NewEnglandAncestors.org*

> *Index to Maine Court Records, 1696-1854.* Boston: NewEnglandAncestors.org, 2004. Courtesy of Maine State Archives.

Fig. 7.2. Courthouse in Skowhegan, Maine, ca. 1911,
from the author's collection of vintage picture postcards.

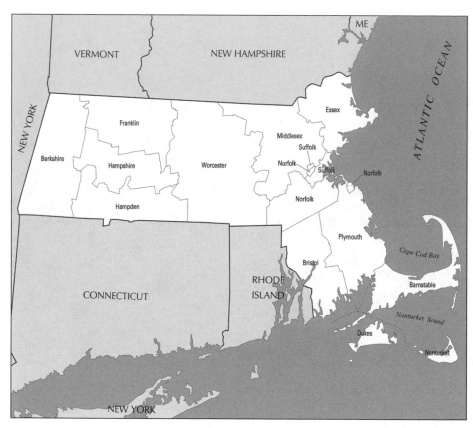

Fig. 8.1. Map of Massachusetts Counties. *National Atlas of the United States*. 2005. *http://nationalatlas.gov*

CHAPTER 8

MASSACHUSETTS STATE COURTS

Court History Timeline

Early Colonial Courts

Massachusetts court history began with two colonies: **Plymouth** and **Massachusetts Bay**.

1620 Pilgrims founded **Plymouth** Colony. They soon elected a governor and assistants, who met as **Court of Assistants**. The **General Court**, composed of voting freemen, served as court and legislature.

1630 **Massachusetts Bay** Colony was established under royal charter. Like Plymouth, Massachusetts Bay formed a **General Court**, which met quarterly as legislature, with some judicial functions in early years, *e.g.*, hearing petitions for equitable relief and other private business, including name changes and adoptions. **Court of Assistants** (governor, deputy-governor and eighteen assistants) tried jury cases—civil and criminal claims exceeding £10 damages or fine, divorce, capital crimes or banishment—and heard appeals from lower courts. Later, Court of Assistants also heard **admiralty** cases, without a jury. Assistants came to be known as "magistrates," in both Massachusetts Bay and Plymouth. A single magistrate resolved minor civil and criminal cases, and performed marriages, in a **Magistrates Court** in his own town.

1636 **Quarter Courts** were established for Massachusetts Bay in Ipswich, Salem, Newtown (Cambridge) and Boston. Magistrates or "other persons of worth" tried civil cases up to ten shillings and criminal cases concerning life, limb or banishment.

Plymouth established the **Grand Enquest**, a special grand jury of freemen who heard accusations of criminal conduct and referred cases to the Court of Assistants or General Court.

1638   **Commissioners of Small Causes** were appointed in Massachusetts Bay to resolve small civil matters and misdemeanors in towns without a resident magistrate.

1643   **County Courts** replaced Massachusetts Bay Quarter Courts, for counties of Essex, (Old) Norfolk, Middlesex and Suffolk (other counties were added later). Composed of magistrates from each county sitting with a jury, County Courts met quarterly for civil and criminal cases up to £10 damages or fine, probate matters, and county business (*e.g.*, tavern licenses, jails, roads and bridges, etc.). Juries decided questions of fact, and judges decided issues of law and equity. Appeals went to **Court of Assistants**. *Note*: Old Norfolk County consisted of Dover, Portsmouth, Hampton, Exeter (**New Hampshire**, then under Massachusetts jurisdiction), and Salisbury and Haverhill (Massachusetts).

1646   Massachusetts Bay annexed **Maine** settlements—Kittery, Gorgeana (now York), Wells, Cape Porpoise, Saco, Casco and Scarborough.

1665   Plymouth established **Town "Select" Courts** (three to five selectmen presiding) to resolve small civil cases and disputes over damage to Indian crops.

1679   New Hampshire union with Massachusetts ended; New Hampshire became royal province.

1684   First Massachusetts charter was vacated, placing colony under royal control.

1685-1689 General Court was abolished. **Governor** and **Council** replaced Court of Assistants, and **Superior Court of Judicature for the Dominion** became highest trial and appellate court in 1687. **County** Court jurisdiction was divided between **Courts of Common Pleas** for civil cases, and **General Sessions** for criminal cases. **Justices of the Peace**, appointed by Governor and Council, heard small cases at local level, and many also presided at County Courts. Plymouth Colony became **Plymouth, Barnstable** and **Bristol Counties**, Massachusetts.

1689-1692 "Glorious Revolution" ended royal Dominion government, and courts reverted briefly to previous forms.

Provincial Courts

1692   Massachusetts became royal province under new charter. **General Court** was restored as legislature. **Governor** and **Council** had authority over divorces and probate appeals. Except for those matters, **Superior Court of Judicature** was highest appellate body, and also trial court for capital criminal cases, civil cases over £10, and some equity matters. The Superior Court of Judicature, Court of Assize and General Gaol Delivery **met as circuit court in each county**, with a grand jury and trial juries.

At **county** level, jury trials were held in quarterly **Courts of General Sessions of the Peace** (for criminal cases and county government), and **Inferior Courts of Common Pleas** (for civil cases between forty shillings and £10). These courts also heard appeals (generally new trials) from cases tried by **Justices of the Peace**, who assumed powers of former magistrates. Justices of the Peace tried misdemeanors and civil cases less than forty shillings and bound criminal defendants over to the grand jury in the Courts of General Sessions. Governor and Council appointed special **Probate Judges** for each county.

1692-1693   Special **Oyer and Terminer Court** tried Salem witchcraft cases.

1697   Royal **Vice-Admiralty Court** regulated trade and navigation.

1775-1776   Massachusetts court sessions were interrupted during Revolution, while British troops occupied Boston. After Declaration of Independence, **Maritime Courts** with admiralty jurisdiction sat at Plymouth, Ipswich and N. Yarmouth until adoption of Constitution.

Courts after Independence

1780   Superior Court of Judicature was renamed **Supreme Judicial Court**, continuing as circuit court in the counties. **Courts of Common Pleas** (civil) and **General Sessions** (criminal) held jury trials as before in each county.

1783   **Probate Court** was established in each county, with appeal to Supreme Judicial Court (instead of to Governor and Council as before). Jurisdiction included wills, administration of estates, guardians for minors and "distracted persons," etc.

1785   Jurisdiction over **divorce** trials was transferred from Governor and Council to **Supreme Judicial Court**.

1789   **Admiralty** jurisdiction was transferred to new **U.S. District Court**.

1799   **Municipal Court of the Town of Boston** was created to hear Boston **criminal** cases.

1804   Reports of Supreme Judicial Court decisions began to be published.

1813   **Boston Court of Common Pleas** was established, to hear Boston **civil** cases (instead of circuit Court of Common Pleas for Suffolk County).

1821   Maine separated from Massachusetts, and courts reorganized: Statewide **Court of Common Pleas for the Commonwealth** became middle-tier trial court for civil and criminal cases. At local level, **Justices of the Peace** and newly-created **Police, Municipal and District Courts** continued to handle small cases.

1851   Jurisdiction over name changes and adoptions was transferred from General Court to county **Probate Court**.

1856   **Insolvency Court** was established.

1858   Probate Court and Insolvency Court merged into **Probate and Insolvency Court**.

1859   Most of Supreme Judicial Court's trial jurisdiction was transferred to new statewide **Superior Court**, which replaced Court of Common Pleas. Municipal Court of the Town of Boston was abolished. **Supreme Judicial Court** continued to handle divorce, capital cases, some equity matters, etc., in addition to appeals.

1866   **Boston Municipal Court** (different from previous Municipal Court of the Town of Boston) replaced Boston Police Court, handling criminal and civil cases.

1870s   **District Court** jurisdiction expanded to misdemeanors and general civil cases (but not equity), gradually replacing Justices of the Peace and Police Courts.

1880s-1890s **Superior Court** jurisdiction expanded to equity, torts, divorce, capital cases, etc. (previously handled by Supreme Judicial Court).

1898   **Court of Registration** was created to resolve land title and real estate disputes.

Twentieth-Century Courts

1900   Court of Registration was renamed **Court of Land Registration**.

1904   Court of Land Registration became **Land Court**.

1906   **Boston Juvenile Court** was established. Juvenile sessions elsewhere continued to be held at District Courts until 1969.

1921   Uniform statewide **District Court** system was established, merging jurisdiction of Justices of the Peace and Police Courts.

1922   **Probate and Insolvency Court** began hearing divorces; **Superior Court** retained concurrent jurisdiction over divorce cases.

1969   **Juvenile Court** was created in Springfield and Worcester; eventually most counties had Juvenile Courts.

1971   First **Housing Court** was established in Boston.

1972   New intermediate **Appeals Court** relieved burden on **Supreme Judicial Court**.

1978   Courts reorganized, creating unified state court system. **Probate and Family Court** replaced Probate and Insolvency Court. Other trial courts were organized into departments, *e.g.*, **Superior Court** Department, **District Court** Department, etc. *See* "Massachusetts Courts Today," *below*.

Massachusetts Courts Today

Supreme Judicial Court

The Supreme Judicial Court is the highest court in Massachusetts and the oldest continuously-operating appeals court in the Western Hemisphere. Chief justice and six associate justices preside.

Appeals Court

Intermediate Appeals Court handles most appeals from departments of Trial Court and certain state agencies. (Some appeals, such as first-degree murder convictions, bypass Appeals Court and go directly to Supreme Judicial Court.) Three-judge panels hear cases in Boston and in other Massachusetts locations.

Trial Court

Superior Court

The Superior Court is the highest trial court level, with locations in each county. Jurisdiction includes: civil cases over $25,000, first-degree murder and other criminal cases, equitable relief, labor disputes seeking injunction, medical malpractice tribunals, and appeals of certain administrative proceedings.

District Court

Most counties have several District Court locations (except Dukes, Nantucket and Suffolk counties, which each have one District Court). District Court handles criminal cases (all misdemeanors, and felonies punishable by sentence up to five years), civil cases under $25,000, small claims up to $2,000, housing, juvenile and mental health matters, etc.

Boston Municipal Court

The Boston Municipal Court (BMC) performs functions similar to District Court, in Suffolk County only, with eight BMC divisions in the Boston area (Chelsea, however, has District Court); *see* "Courts" section for "Suffolk County," *below*. The BMC has jurisdiction over most criminal offenses not requiring state prison sentence and a wide range of civil cases.

Probate and Family Court

Each county has at least one Probate and Family Court location, with jurisdiction over probate matters (wills, administrations, guardianship, conservatorship and change of name, etc.), family matters (divorce, paternity, child support, custody, visitation, adoption, termination of parental rights, abuse prevention, etc.), and general equity jurisdiction.

Land Court

Land Court exercises statewide jurisdiction over registration, confirmation and tax foreclosure, mortgage foreclosure, zoning, land use issues, etc. Decisions are appealed to Appeals Court. *Note*: Registries of Deeds are not part of the court system, although they maintain registered land records for the Land Court.

Housing Court

Housing Court has six courthouse locations and generally tries residential housing cases—zoning, nuisance, landlord/tenant, evictions, etc., including criminal cases—without juries. *Note*: Housing Court records are not covered in this book.

Juvenile Court

Juvenile Court is divided into eleven divisions in more than forty locations, with general jurisdiction over delinquency, children in need of services, adoption, guardianship, termination of parental rights, etc. *Note*: Juvenile Court records are not covered in this book; most are confidential.

Where to Find Court Records
See Appendix for complete contact information.

Statewide or General Sources

Courts

Supreme Judicial Court, Boston
All Supreme Judicial Court records are permanent. For location of pre-1990 records, contact Head of Archives; provide party names and year, if possible.

Appeals Court, Boston
Dockets (paper, 1972-1988, and computer, 1988-date); briefs, transcripts, etc. (original and microfiche), 1972-date. Provide party names and year, if possible, when seeking access.

Land Court, Boston
See "Trial Court Record Retention Guidelines," *below*. Provide party names and geographical location, if possible, when seeking access.

Other State Courts
See "Trial Court Record Retention Guidelines" and "Courts" section for each county, *below*.

Trial Court Record Retention Guidelines
Supreme Judicial Court Rule 1:11 provides the following guidelines:
Superior Court
Permanent records: all records before 1860, docket books, divorce and naturalization records, and records of Barnstable, Dukes, Essex and Nantucket counties. Other records more than ten to twenty years old may be destroyed after "sample" maintained. Sampling guidelines vary by county; *see* "Courts" section for each county, *below*.
District Court and Boston Municipal Court
Permanent records: all records before 1800, docket books, divorce, naturalization and paternity records. Other records more than two to twenty years old may be destroyed after "sample" maintained: 1800-1969, 5% sample; from 1970, 2% sample.
Probate and Family Court
Permanent records: all records before 1900, docket and record books, and adoption records. Other records more than twenty years old (with some exceptions) must be retained as microform, then originals may be destroyed.
Land Court
Permanent records: all land registration and foreclosure papers, docket books, and cases appealed to Supreme Judicial Court or Appeals Court. Other records more than ten to twenty years old may be destroyed after "sample" maintained: before 1970, 5% sample; from 1970, 2% sample.
Note: Some courts retain records longer than the minimum time period; *see* "Courts" section for each county, *below*. For more information about sampling criteria or access to Trial Court records, contact court clerks or Head of Archives, Supreme Judicial Court; *see Appendix: Contact Information-State Courts.*

State Archives and Library

Judicial Archives/Massachusetts Archives, Boston
Judicial Archives (operated by the Division of Archives and Records Preservation, Supreme Judicial Court of Mass.) shares storage and research facilities with the Mass. Archives (operated by the Secretary of the Commonwealth). Original court records include:
Supreme Judicial Court (and its predecessors): 1629-1950, Suffolk County; 1629-1793, all Mass. counties.
Superior Court (and its predecessors): pre-1860.
District and Municipal Court (and predecessors): pre-1800.
County probate records: pre-1900.
Justice of the Peace records.
Naturalization records, including abstracts from state and local courts: 1885-1931.
Divorce records.
Records from special courts, *e.g.*, Land Court records, 1898-1972.
See specifics in "State Archives" section for each county, *below*. Some records are available on microform. Looseleaf notebooks at Archives front desk also provide more detail about court records (although the notebooks are not updated regularly). Later court records, subject to sampling and retention guidelines, may be available. Contact Head of Archives, Supreme Judicial Court, for current information; *see Appendix: Contact Information-State Courts.*
Massachusetts Archives holds court-related collections, including:
General Court files, from 1629.

Secretary of State's records, Acts & Resolves, with published returns of names changed at county Probate Courts, from 1851.

Massachusetts Archives Collection, 328 vols. of colonial, provincial and Revolutionary records, *e.g.*, vol. 9, *Domestic Relations*, 1643-1774; vols. 15A-19B, *Estates*; vols. 38B-44, *Judicial*, 1640-1774; vols. 45-46, *Lands*, 1622-1739; vols. 81-86, *Minutes of Council*, 1689-1776; vol. 140, *Revolutionary Misc.*, 1775-1778 (incl. divorces); vols. 164-179, *Revolution Council Papers*, 1775-1783; vol. 281, *Estates of Absentees*, 1781-1791; vol. 282, *Judicial*, 1671-1799; vol. 303, *Petitions*, 1659-1786. *See also* "Microform" and "Digital/Electronic Sources," *below*.

State Library of Massachusetts, Boston

Pauper cases argued and determined in the Supreme Judicial Court, 1805-1826. Ms. 72.

Federal Archives and Records Center

U.S. National Archives and Records Administration (NARA), Northeast Region-Waltham (Boston)

Naturalization: Dexigraph collection (negative photostats) of naturalization records from 301 federal and state courts in five New England states (Maine, Mass., N.H., R.I. and Vt.) between 1790 and 1906. Index is available on microfilm, as *Index to New England Naturalization Petitions, 1791-1906; see* "Microform," *below*. *Note*: NARA-Waltham staff will search index and provide copies for a fee; need name, residence at time of application, and birth date.

State Historical Society

Massachusetts Historical Society, Boston

Cushing, William. Judicial notebook, 1783. Special Colls. Cushing, and P-406, microfilm. Notebook of Chief Justice of Supreme Judicial Court re: *Commonwealth v. Jennison*, ruling that slavery was unconstitutional.

Devens, Charles. Notebooks, 1841-1882. Ms. N-1114. 71 vols. of lawyer and judge of Mass. Superior and Supreme Courts, including docket books, case notes, trial calendars, etc.

Endicott family. Endicott family papers, 1612-1958. Ms. N-1182. Includes papers re: William C. Endicott, Sr.'s service as Supreme Judicial Court justice, etc.

Mysteries of Crime: As Shown in Remarkable Capital Trials/ by a Member of the Massachusetts Bar. Boston: S. Walker, 1870. KF221.M8 M95 1870.

The official report of the trial of John C. Best for murder: Superior Court of Massachusetts.... Boston: Boston Attorney-General, 1903. 1901 trial for murder of George E. Bailey. Book KF.

Paine, Robert Treat. Papers, 1659-1862. Ms. N-641; P-392, microfilm. Includes minutes of trials (Boston Massacre and Shays' Rebellion), etc., and other legal papers of Mass. attorney-general and Supreme Judicial Court justice.

Papers related to the criminal prosecution of Theodore Lyman, Jr. by Daniel Webster, 1828-1876. Ms. S-416. Supreme Judicial Court.

A Report of the evidence and points of law, arising in the trial of John Francis Knapp, for the murder of Joseph White, esquire: Before the Supreme Judicial Court of the Commonwealth of Massachusetts. Salem: W. & S. B. Ives, 1830. E187.

Other Repositories

Boston College Law School Library, Newton Centre
Supreme Judicial Court. Records and briefs.

Boston University Law School Library, Boston
Supreme Judicial Court. Records and briefs.

Dartmouth College, Hanover, N.H.
Brown, Nelson Pierce, 1878-1946. Trial notes. 25 vols. Cases as judge of Mass.
    Superior Court.

Harvard University, Cambridge
Law School Library
Justice of the Peace docketbook, 1791-1797. MSS HLS MS 4235. 2 vols. Cases in
    Mass. and N.H. Courts of Common Pleas.
Supreme Judicial Court. Records and briefs.
Houghton Library
Lowell, John. Papers, 1629-1894 (inclusive), 1764-1803 (bulk). MS Am 1582. Legal
    documents re: various Mass. courts, including depositions and testimony.
    Electronic finding aid: *http://nrs.harvard.edu/urn-3:FHCL.Hough:hou01686.*

New England Historic Genealogical Society, Boston
Davenport, Bennett Franklin. Papers, 1636-1923 (bulk 1876-1880). MSS 382. Also
    microform. Includes court records.
Glover, Nathan Holbrook. Papers, 1647-1982 (bulk 1686-1744, 1793-1927). MSS
    319. Includes various Mass. estate papers (wills, 1702-1958), court cases
    (1719-1853), etc.
Legal Papers. To be cataloged; typed guide lists items by surname. Contact NEHGS
    Archivist.

Social Law Library, Boston
[Colonial journal of a number of different cases from different courts of Massachu-
    setts], 1773-1783. Rare books KFM2478.C65 1773. Transcripts or reports by
    unidentified eyewitness to cases in Supreme Judicial Court, Superior Court
    of Judicature, Court of Common Pleas, Maritime and Admiralty Courts.
Mass. Appeals Court records and briefs; microform, 1972-date. Main Deposit Collec-
    tion. Organized by *Massachusetts Appeals Court Reports* vol., then alpha-
    betical by case title.
Mass. Supreme Judicial Court records and briefs (including information about pro-
    ceedings in lower courts that led to appeal); microform and bound volumes,
    1840-date. Main Deposit Collection. Organized by *Massachusetts Reports*
    vol., then alphabetical by case title.
Philip and Francis Sears Collection of Law Books. 300 vols. from personal library of
    19th-century Boston lawyers, including early Mass. case reports, lawyers
    diaries, etc.

Supreme Judicial Court Historical Society, Boston
Papers re: Small Loans Case of former Supreme Judicial Court Assoc. Justice Francis
    Quirico.

Papers of former Supreme Judicial Court Chief Justice Paul M. Liacos, including draft decisions, opinions, orders, research memoranda, etc.
Supreme Judicial Court draft decision of Hon. John Wilkes Hammond, who served on court 1898-1914.

U.S. Citizenship and Immigration Services, U.S. Dept. of Homeland Security, Washington, D.C.
Naturalization certificate files ("C-Files"): Copies of naturalization records from state and federal courts after September 27, 1906, *e.g.*, Declaration of Intention, Petition for Naturalization, and Certificate of Naturalization.
1906-1956: Available on microfilm. Make Freedom of Information/Privacy Act (FOIA/PA) request to U.S. Citizenship and Immigration Services in Washington, D.C.
After 1956: Make FOIA/PA request to the district U.S. Citizenship and Immigration Services office that maintains the records, or office nearest your residence.
See Appendix: Contact Information-Archives and Other Repositories, Washington, D.C.

University of Massachusetts, Amherst, W. E. B. Du Bois Library
"Suffolk Files" microfilm; *see Suffolk County (Mass.) Court files, 1629-1797*, in "Microform," *below*.
Supreme Judicial Court records, 1780-1800. Microfilm.

Books and Journals

Court Records—Abstracts, Transcripts and Indexes
The Acts and Resolves, Public and Private, of the Province of the Massachusetts Bay.... 21 vols. Boston: Wright & Potter, 1869-1922. Vol. 7 (Resolves, 1692-1702) and Vol. 8 (Resolves, 1703-1707) contain editorial notes of Abner C. Goodell, Jr., reprinting excerpts from records of various Mass. courts.
Collections of the Massachusetts Historical Society. Boston: Mass. Historical Society, 1792-. Including: 4th series, Vol. 8: case of *Randolph v. Mather* (1687). 5th series: 3:438-442, brief in 1781 slave case; 9:123-140, records re *Estate of John White* (1684) from *Trumbull Papers*.
Colonial Society of Massachusetts publications, including:
Vol. 5: *Transactions, 1897, 1898*. Boston: 1902. John Noble. "The Records and Files of the Superior Court of Judicature, and of the Supreme Judicial Court: Their History and Places of Deposit."
Vol. 6: *Transactions, 1899, 1900*. Boston: 1904. John Noble. "The Case of Maria in the Court of Assistants, 1681."
Vol. 8: *Transactions, 1902-1904*. Boston: 1906. Admiralty cases in early 18th-century Mass.
Holmes, Oliver Wendell, and Harry C. Shriver. *The Judicial Opinions of Oliver Wendell Holmes: Constitutional Opinions, Selected Excerpts and Epigrams as Given in the Supreme Judicial Court of Massachusetts (1883-1902)*. Buffalo, NY: Dennis & Co., 1940.
Hutchinson, Thomas, and Lawrence Shaw Mayo. *The History of the Colony and Province of Massachusetts-Bay*. Cambridge: Harvard Univ. Press, 1936. Vol. 2, Appendix: 366-391, includes testimony of Anne Hutchinson in 1637.
Index of Probates in All Abstracts of Title Filed to July 1, 1910, in the Land Court. Boston: Wright & Potter, 1910.

List of Persons Whose Names Have Been Changed in Massachusetts, 1780-1892. Boston: Wright & Potter, 1893.

Noble, John, and John F. Cronin, eds. *Records of the Court of Assistants of the Colony of the Massachusetts Bay, 1630-1692.* 3 vols. Boston: County of Suffolk, Rockwell & Churchill Press, 1901-1928. *See also* "Microform," *below.*

Quincy, Joseph, Jr. *Reports of Cases Argued and Adjudged in the Superior Court of Judicature of the Province of Massachusetts Bay, Between 1761 and 1772, by Joseph Quincy, Jr....* Boston: Little, Brown & Co., 1865; N.Y.: Russell & Russell, 1969. *Note:* New edition, by Daniel R. Coquillette and Neil L. York, eds., is forthcoming from Colonial Society of Mass.

Shurtleff, Nathaniel B., ed. *Records of the Governor and Company of the Massachusetts Bay in New England.* 5 vols. in 6. Boston: W. White, 1853-1854. *See also* "Microform," *below.* Vol. 1, 1628-1641; vol. 2, 1642-1649; vol. 3, 1644-1657; vol. 4 (1), 1650-1660; vol. 4 (2), 1661-1674; vol. 5, 1674-1686. Includes early Court of Assistants and Quarter Court records, as well as General Court.

Toppan, Robert N., ed. "Andros Records." *Proceedings* XIII. Worcester, Mass.: American Antiquarian Society, 1900: 237-268.

———. "Council Records of Massachusetts under the Administration of President Joseph Dudley," *Proceedings,* 2d. ser., XIII. Boston: Mass. Historical Society, 1899: 222-286.

Williams, Ephraim, and Dudley A. Tyng. *Reports of Cases Argued and Determined in the Supreme Judicial Court of the Commonwealth of Massachusetts: From September 1804 to March Term, 1822.* 17 vols. Boston: Tileston and Weld, 1808-1823. *See also* "Microform," *below.*

Wroth, L. Kinvin, and Hiller B. Zobel, eds. *Legal Papers of John Adams.* 3 vols. Cambridge: Belknap Press of Harvard Univ. Press, 1964.

History

Law in Colonial Massachusetts 1630-1800. Boston: Colonial Society of Massachusetts and University Press of Virginia, 1984.

Nelson, William E. *Americanization of the Common Law: The Impact of Legal Change in Massachusetts Society, 1760-1830.* Cambridge: Harvard Univ. Press, 1975.

Osgood, Russell K., ed. *The History of the Law in Massachusetts: The Supreme Judicial Court 1692-1992.* Boston: Supreme Judicial Court Historical Society, 1992.

Law Library Resources

Case Reports: *See Chapter 17,* and *Appendix-Law Libraries* and *Publishers. See also* "Microform" and "Digital/Electronic Sources," *below.*

Massachusetts Supreme Judicial Court

Massachusetts Reports. Multiple vols. Boston: Office of Reporter of Decisions, Supreme Judicial Court of Mass. Court decisions, 1804-date.

North Eastern Reporter. Multiple vols. Eagan, Minn.: West. Court decisions, 1885-date, enhanced with headnotes, key numbers and synopses.

West's Massachusetts Digest. Multiple vols. Eagan, Minn.: West. Summary of Mass. state and federal court decisions, 1761-date, organized by topic and key number, and indexed by case name, etc.

Massachusetts Appeals Court

Massachusetts Appeals Court Reports. Multiple vols. Boston: Office of Reporter of Decisions, Supreme Judicial Court of Mass. 1972-date.

North Eastern Reporter. Multiple vols. Eagan, Minn.: West. 1972-date, enhanced with headnotes, key numbers and synopses.

West's Massachusetts Digest 2d. Multiple vols. Eagan, Minn.: West. Summary of Mass. state and federal court decisions, 1972-date, organized alphabetically by topic, with headnotes, key numbers, and multiple indexes (case name, etc.).

Massachusetts Superior Courts

Massachusetts Law Reporter. Multiple vols. Boston: Office of Reporter of Decisions, Supreme Judicial Court of Mass. Selected cases, 1993-date.

Massachusetts Appellate Division (appellate level of state District Court)

Massachusetts Appellate Division Reports. Multiple vols. Boston: Office of Reporter of Decisions, Supreme Judicial Court of Mass. 1936-date.

West's Massachusetts Digest 2d. Multiple vols. Eagan, Minn.: West. Summary of Mass. state and federal court decisions, including Mass. Appellate Div., 1990-date, organized alphabetically by topic, with headnotes, key numbers, and multiple indexes (case name, etc.).

Other Law Library Resources: *Massachusetts Practice Series.* Multiple vols. Eagan, Minn.: West. Updated with pocket parts. Summary of selected Mass. law subjects, including historical background and case citations.

Research Guides and Bibliographies

Bowen, Richard LeBaron. *Massachusetts Records: A Handbook for Genealogists, Historians, Lawyers and Other Researchers.* Rehoboth, Mass.: By author, 1957.

Galvin, William Francis, Secretary of the Commonwealth. *Historical Data Relating to Counties, Cities and Towns in Massachusetts.* Boston: New England Historic Genealogical Society, 1997.

Hindus, Michael S., et al. *The Records of the Massachusetts Superior Court and Its Predecessors: An Inventory and Guide.* Boston: Archives Division, Office of the Secretary of the Commonwealth, 1977.

Jeffrey, William. *Early New England Court Records: A Bibliography of Published Materials.* Cambridge: Ames Foundation, Harvard Law School, 1954.

Melnyk, Marcia D. *Genealogist's Handbook for New England Research.* 4th ed. Boston: New England Historic Genealogical Society, 1999. Contains list of Massachusetts towns and counties.

Menand, Catherine S. *A Research Guide to the Massachusetts Courts and Their Records.* Boston: Mass. Supreme Judicial Court, Archives and Records Preservation, 1987.

Neary, Mary Ann, et al. *Handbook of Legal Research in Massachusetts.* Boston: Mass. Continuing Legal Education, 2002.

Microform

Miscellaneous court records

Colony Records, 1629-1777. GSU, 1974. Mass. General Court.

Divorce Index, 1952-1970. GSU, 1974.

Divorce Records, 1760-1786. GSU, 1973. Various Mass. counties.

Massachusetts State Archives Collection, Colonial Period, 1622-1776. GSU, 2002-2003. Vols. 1-94. Includes court records. *See also* "State Archives and Library," *above*, and "Digital/Electronic Sources," *below*.

Massachusetts State Archives Collection, Colonial and Post Colonial Period, 1626-1806. GSU, 2002. Vols. 240-328. Includes court records. *See also* "State Archives and Library," *above*, and "Digital/Electronic Sources," *below*.

Massachusetts Supreme Court reports, 1804-1926, and additional vols. published annually. Also *Quincy's Reports*, 1761-1772; *Thacher's Criminal Cases*, 1823-1843; *Davis' Land Court Cases*, 1898-1908; *Cushing's Election Cases*, 1780-1852; *Russell's Election Cases*, 1853-1902; *Massachusetts Contested Election Cases*, 1903-1942. Kaneohe, Hawaii: Law Library Microform Consortium. Microfiche.

Noble, John, and John F. Cronin, eds. *Records of the Court of Assistants of the Colony of the Massachusetts Bay, 1630-1692.* 3 vols. Boston: County of Suffolk, Rockwell & Churchill Press, 1901 1928; GSU, 1970, 1988. *See also* "Books and Journals," *above*.

Shurtleff, Nathaniel B., ed. *Records of the Governor and Company of the Massachusetts Bay in New England.* 5 vols. in 6. Boston: W. White, 1853-1854; GSU, 1970, 1984, 1986. Microfiche, microfilm. *See also* "Books and Journals," *above*.

Suffolk County (Mass.) Court Files, 1629-1797. GSU, 1972. 1,639 reels, with several index systems (alphabetical, chronological, by subject and geography, etc.) re: many different courts and counties.

Wheildon, William Wilder. *Blue Laws and their Origin: their Birth in Massachusetts and Not in Connecticut; samples of punishment under the early laws; a severe penalty for using profane language.* 1886 (8 leaves); Ann Arbor, Mich.: Univ. Microfilms, 1987. Microfiche.

Williams, Ephraim, and Dudley A. Tyng. *Reports of Cases Argued and Determined in the Supreme Judicial Court of the Commonwealth of Massachusetts: From September 1804 to March Term, 1822.* 17 vols. Boston: Tileston and Weld, 1808-1823; GSU, 1986. *See also* "Books and Journals," *above*.

Naturalization records

Index to New England Naturalization Petitions, 1791-1906. U.S. National Archives and Records Admin., 1983. M1299. Alphabetical index of individuals naturalized, in state and federal courts of Maine, Mass., N.H., R.I. and Vt. (indicates court and certificate number).

Indexes to Returns of Naturalizations, 1920-1923, 1924-1925, 1920-1925. GSU, 1994. Mass. courts.

Returns of Naturalization Before Various Massachusetts Courts, 1885-1931. GSU, 1993.

Digital/Electronic Sources

CD-ROM

Massachusetts Cases, LawDesk. Eagan, Minn.: West. Cases, 1885-date, as reported in *North Eastern Reporter*.

Massachusetts Decisions. Eagan, Minn.: West. Mass. Supreme Judicial Court cases, 1899-date; Appeals Court, 1972-date; and District Court and Appellate Div., 1990-date; as reported in *North Eastern Reporter*.

North Eastern Reporter, 2d. Eagan, Minn.: West. Includes Mass. cases.

West's Massachusetts Digest, 2d. Eagan, Minn.: West. Summary of state and federal court decisions, 1933-date.

Internet

LexisNexis *www.lexis.com*

> Mass. Supreme Judicial Court, 1804-date; Appeals Court, 1972-date; Superior Court, 1993-date. Subscription service or available at law libraries and other repositories.

LexisOne *www.lexisone.com*

> Mass. Supreme Judicial Court and Appeals Court, most recent five years; free.

Loislaw *www.loislaw.com*

> Mass. Supreme Judicial Court, 1899-date; Appeals Court, 1972-date; Appellate Div. of District Court, 1980-date; Superior Court, 1995-date. Subscription service.

Massachusetts Archives *www.sec.state.ma.us/ArchivesSearch/RevolutionarySearch.asp*

> Massachusetts Archives Collection (1629-1799) Search, by personal name, place or subject, from eighteen archive vols. *See also* "State Archives and Library" and "Microform," *above.*

Massachusetts Lawyers Weekly *www.masslaw.com/masjc.cfm*

> Full-text Mass. Supreme Judicial Court and Appeals Court opinions since 1997 available free; decisions from 1993 available to subscribers only.

Massachusetts Supreme Judicial Court and Appeals Court

> *www.ma-appellatecourts.org*
> Public case information: Supreme Judicial Court and Appeals Court dockets. Search by docket number, party, attorney, lower court or lower court judge. 1988-date (some dockets from 1970s). Also current court calendars.
> *http://massreports.com/slipops*
> Slip Opinions: current Supreme Judicial Court and Appeals Court opinions (posted at 10 am on day opinion released, and removed after two weeks), including procedural history of case and list of appellate attorneys.

Massachusetts Trial Court

> *www.mass.gov/courts/courtsandjudges/courts/trialcourt.html*
> General information about Trial Court.
> *www.mass.gov/courts/courtsandjudges/courts/landcourt/lchist3.html*
> Buscher, Glendon J., Jr., Esq. "A Brief History of the Land Court." 1998, 2004.
> *www.mass.gov/courts/courtsandjudges/courts/landcourt/evolution_title.html*
> Buscher, Glendon J., Jr., Esq. "The Nature and Evolution of Title." 2003.

Social Law Library *www.socialaw.com/slips.htm?sid=121*

> Mass. Supreme Judicial Court, Appeals Court and Superior Court, latest two years.

VersusLaw *www.versuslaw.com*

> Mass. appellate courts, 1930-date. Subscription service.

Westlaw *www.westlaw.com*

> Mass. Supreme Judicial Court, 1804-date; Appeals Court, 1972-date; Appellate Div. of the District Court, 1990-date; Superior Court, 1993-date. Subscription service or available at law libraries and other repositories. Westlaw CourtEXPRESS offers case research and document retrieval from U.S. courts.

Barnstable County

Founded 1685, from Plymouth Colony.
Note: Courthouse fire destroyed records in 1827.

Courts

Barnstable Superior Court, Barnstable
Civil and criminal: docket/record books, file papers, appeals, index; original from 1827; transcripts in Supreme Judicial Court appeals only; computer, 2000-date. Naturalization: 1827-1991; index. Divorce: original, 1827-date; index. All Barnstable County Superior Court records are permanent.

District Court
Barnstable
Serves Barnstable, Yarmouth and Sandwich. Civil: docket/record books (original, mid to late 1800s date), file papers (original, last ten years), some appeals; index, 1980-date. Criminal: docket/record books (original, mid-to-late 1800s-date), file papers (last ten years), some appeals; index, 1980-date.
Falmouth
Serves Falmouth, Mashpee and Bourne. Civil and criminal: docket/record books, file papers, appeals, index; original, 1996-date.
Orleans
Serves Brewster, Chatham, Dennis, Eastham, Orleans, Harwich, Truro, Wellfleet and Provincetown. *See* "Trial Court Record Retention Guidelines" for District Court in "Statewide or General Sources: Courts," *above*.

Barnstable Probate and Family Court, Barnstable
Docket/record books, file papers, index; original, 1686-date; microfilm, 1900-1976.

State Archives

Judicial Archives/Massachusetts Archives, Boston
Barnstable County Court records include:
Court of Common Pleas, 1783-1859 (from 1827 at Barnstable Superior Court).
Court of General Sessions of the Peace, 1783-1791.
Supreme Judicial Court (and its predecessors): file papers of appeals to SJC, 1718-1774, with finding aid; docket books/minute books, 1702-1797, originals and microfilm, including cases from Barnstable and Dukes County, 1720-1797.
Contact Head of Archives, Supreme Judicial Court, for current information.

Other Repositories

Boston Athenaeum, Boston
Freeman, Nathaniel. *A Charge to the Grand Jury at the Court of General Sessions of the Peace: Holden at Barnstable...March term, A.D. 1802....* Boston: Manning & Loring, 1802. Tract B465 no. 16.

Bourne Archives, Bourne
Jane Toppan collection, 1902-1985. Murder trials, Barnstable Superior Court.

Cape Cod Community College, W. Barnstable
Baker family. Collection of papers, ca. 1819-1911. Dennis, Mass.; Probate Court, etc.

Falmouth Historical Society, Falmouth

Numerous legal, estate and land transfer papers in family manuscript collections, ca. 1700-1900s, indexed by name, including:

Eldred/Eldredge families collection of papers, ca. 1800-1902. Estate and court records.

Hinckley family. Collection of papers, ca. 1729-1890. Misc. papers re: justice of the peace, lawyer, and estate administrator.

Town, State Papers. Herring Dispute Collection, 1794-1830. Re: fish regulation and land use issues.

Library of Congress, Manuscript Div., Washington, D.C.

Chamberlayne, Charles Frederic. Journal, 1885-1887. Judge's journal of county court cases.

Gifford family. Collection of papers, ca. 1675-1960. Including court records, estate and guardianship papers, etc., for Falmouth, Mass. family.

New England Historic Genealogical Society, Boston

Gustavus Adolphus Hinckley Papers, 1883-1905. MSS 419. Including Barnstable County probate records, 1685-1742.

Books and Journals

Bartley, Scott Andrew. "Barnstable County Probate Index, 1686 to 1850." *The Mayflower Descendant* 53:29-45, 149-170; 54:31-47. Covers "Abraham" to "Brackett."

Roberts, Gary Boyd. *Mayflower Source Records: Primary Data Concerning Southeastern Massachusetts, Cape Cod, and the Islands of Nantucket and Martha's Vineyard, from The New England Historical and Genealogical Register*. Baltimore, Md.: Genealogical Publishing Co., 1997. *See also* "Digital/Electronic Sources," *below*. Includes probate records.

Microform

Miscellaneous court records

Court Records, 1827-1859. GSU, 1992. Court of Common Pleas.

Court Records, 1859-1932. GSU, 1992. Superior Court.

Plaintiff Index, 1885-1913. GSU, 1992. Superior Court.

Selective Service Records, and Exemptions as Aliens for 1917-1918. GSU, 1992. Superior Court.

Naturalization records

Declarations of Intention, 1907-1935. GSU, 1992. Superior Court.

Naturalizations, 1907-1933. GSU, 1992. Superior Court.

Probate court records

Probate and Guardianship records, 1674-1950. GSU, 1992.

Probate Records, 1686-1894. GSU, 1972.

Wills, Inventories, etc, 1637 to 1685, County of Barnstable. GSU, 1972.

Digital/Electronic Sources

CD-ROM

Family Tree Maker Genealogies of Mayflower families: 1500s-1800s. Novato, Cal.:
    Broderbund, 1997. Includes Gary Boyd Roberts. *Mayflower Source Records:
    Primary Data Concerning Southeastern Massachusetts, Cape Cod, and the
    Islands of Nantucket and Martha's Vineyard, from The New England Histor-
    ical and Genealogical Register.* Baltimore, Md.: Genealogical Publishing
    Co., 1997. With probate records.
Hinckley, Gustavus Adolphus, and Robert J. Dunkle. *Records of Barnstable, Massa-
    chusetts [1600s-1800s].* Boston: New England Historic Genealogical Soci-
    ety, 2001. Includes probate records.

Berkshire County
Founded 1761, from Hampshire County

Courts

Berkshire Superior Court, Pittsfield
Supreme Judicial Court Rule 1:11 requires permanent retention of docket books,
divorce and naturalization records, and all other Berkshire Superior Court records
before 1860. Other records more than ten to twenty years old may be destroyed after
"sample" maintained: 1860-1969, 10% sample; from 1970, 2% sample. For more
information about sampling criteria or access to records, contact court clerk or Head
of Archives, Supreme Judicial Court.

District Court
Northern Berkshire, N. Adams
Serves Adams, Cheshire, Clarksburg, Florida, Hancock, New Ashford, N. Adams,
Savoy, Williamstown and Windsor. (Pittsfield District Court has concurrent jurisdic-
tion in Hancock and Windsor.) *See* "Trial Court Record Retention Guidelines" for
District Court in "Statewide or General Sources: Courts," *above.*
Pittsfield
Serves Becket, Dalton, Hancock, Hinsdale, Lanesborough, Lenox, Peru, Pittsfield,
Richmond, Washington and Windsor. (Northern Berkshire District Court has concur-
rent jurisdiction in Hancock and Windsor; Southern Berkshire District Court has
concurrent jurisdiction in Becket and Lenox.) Civil and criminal: all dockets and
index cards at court; original file papers at court for ten years, then to offsite storage,
and destroyed after twenty years, except for samplings, etc. as required.
Southern Berkshire, Great Barrington
Serves Alford, Becket, Egremont, Great Barrington, Lee, Lenox, Monterey, Mt. Washington, New Marlborough, Otis, Sandisfield, Sheffield, Stockbridge, Tyringham and
W. Stockbridge. (Pittsfield District Court has concurrent jurisdiction in Becket and
Lenox.) Civil and criminal: original docket/record books.

Berkshire Probate and Family Court, Pittsfield
Docket/record books, file papers, appeals, index; 1761-date, probate; 1922-date,
divorce.

State Archives

Judicial Archives/Massachusetts Archives, Boston
Berkshire County Court records include:
Court of Common Pleas, 1761-1859.
Court of General Sessions of the Peace, 1761-1827.
Divorce: original Supreme Judicial Court record books, ca. 1785-1887; original Superior Court records and index card file, from 1888; Superior Court microfilm, 1888-1927.
Naturalization: Superior Court, original, 1812-1991, microfilm, 1937-1945; Pittsfield District Court, original records, 1885-1906; card indexes.
Probate: record books, vols. 1-58, 1761-1865, microfilm; index in each vol.
Supreme Judicial Court (and its predecessors): docket books/minute books, 1702-1797, originals and microfilm, including cases from Berkshire County, 1758-1771, 1778-1796.
Contact Head of Archives, Supreme Judicial Court, for current information.

Other Repositories

Berkshire Athenaeum, Pittsfield Public Library, Pittsfield
Extensive collection of Berkshire County court records on microfilm and other research resources, including:
Index cards of researcher Elmer Shepard, who transcribed information from Berkshire probate records. *See* "Master Index to the Elmer I. Shepard Collection in the Local History Dept., Berkshire Athenaeum, Pittsfield, Mass." Berkshire Family History Assoc.: 1993. Computer printout.
Edward R. Knurow Manuscript Collection and Index. Includes court references and record abstracts. Digital and microform access in progress.

Stockbridge Library Association, Stockbridge
Field family. Papers, 1803-1941. Including transcripts of court cases.

University of Massachusetts, Amherst
Taylor, Charles J., compiler. Great Barrington historical documents collection, 1731-1904. MS 104. Includes Court of Common Pleas cases, estate papers, etc.

Books

Bailey, Frederic W. *Early Massachusetts Marriages Prior to 1800: As Found on Ancient Court Records of the Counties of Middlesex, Hampshire, Berkshire and Bristol.* Worcester, Mass.: By author, 1914; Baltimore, Md.: Genealogical Publishing Co., 1979. *See also* "Microform," *below.*
Brown, Irene Quenzler. *The Hanging of Ephraim Wheeler: A Story of Rape, Incest, and Justice in Early America.* Cambridge: Belknap Press of Harvard Univ. Press, 2003. *See also* Early American Imprints in "Microform" and "Digital/Electronic Sources," *below.*

Microform

Miscellaneous court records

Bailey, Frederic W. *Early Massachusetts Marriages Prior to 1800: As Found on Ancient Court Records of the Counties of Middlesex, Hampshire, Berkshire and Bristol.* Worcester, Mass.: By author, 1914; Baltimore, Md.: Genealogical Publishing Co., 1979; GSU, 2003. *See also* "Books," *above.*

Divorce Record Indexes, 1847-1940. GSU, 1986. Superior Court and Supreme Judicial Court.

Divorce Records, 1877-1887. GSU, 1986. Supreme Judicial Court.

Divorce Records, 1887-1916. GSU, 1986. Superior Court.

Records, 1760-1860; Indexes, 1761-1854. GSU, 1971, 1991. Court of Common Pleas.

Revolutionary War Pension Papers, 1818-1825, Berkshire County, Massachusetts. GSU, 1986. Court of Common Pleas and Supreme Judicial Court.

Naturalization records

Naturalization Declarations and Petitions, 1848-1885. GSU, 1986. Superior Court, Court of Common Pleas and Supreme Judicial Court.

Naturalization Declarations of Intention, 1906-1945; Index 1829-1936. GSU, 1986, 2000. Superior Court.

Naturalization Index, 1815-1906. GSU, 1986. Superior Court.

Naturalization Petitions and Records, 1891-1934, 1937-1945, (Index 1826-1938, Berkshire County, Massachusetts). GSU, 1986, 2000. Superior Court.

Naturalization Record Index Cards, 1815-1985, Berkshire County, Massachusetts. GSU, 1986. Court of Common Pleas, Superior Court and Supreme Judicial Court.

Naturalization Records, 1843-1856, Berkshire County, Massachusetts. GSU, 1986. Court of Common Pleas and Supreme Judicial Court.

Naturalization Records, 1866-1941, Berkshire County, Massachusetts. GSU, 1986. Superior Court.

Naturalization Records, 1874-1906. GSU, 1995. District Court, Adams.

Naturalization Records, 1885-1906. GSU, 1992. District Court, Great Barrington.

Naturalization Records Index, Petitions and Oaths, and Declarations and Intentions; 1885-1906. GSU, 1991. District Court.

Previous Declarations and Petitions for Naturalization [Docket Book], 1856-1887, Berkshire County, Massachusetts. GSU, 1986. Superior Court, Court of Common Pleas and Supreme Judicial Court.

Probate and insolvency records

Certificates of Discharge, 1879-1899. GSU, 1991. Court of Insolvency.

Court Dockets, 1860-1899. GSU, 1991. Court of Insolvency.

Inheritance Tax Records, v. 1-2, 1907-1921. GSU, 1991. Probate Court.

Miscellaneous Statistics, Land Transfers, Church Records and Vital Statistics for Great Barrington, 1666-1870. GSU, 1961. From typescript at Mason Public Library, Great Barrington; includes abstracted index of Berkshire probate records.

Probate Records, 1761-1917. GSU, 1971, 1991. Probate Court.

Record of Adjournments, 1894-1907. GSU, 1991. Probate Court and Court of Insolvency.

Records of Assignments, v. 2, 1878-1910. GSU, 1991. Court of Insolvency.

Early American Imprints, Series II. Shaw-Shoemaker (1801-1819). New Canaan, Conn.: Readex Microprint, in cooperation with American Antiquarian Society, 1987-1992. Microfiche. Including: *Report of the Trial of Ephraim Wheeler for a Rape Committed on the Body of Betsy Wheeler, His Daughter, a Girl Thirteen Years of Age: Before the Supreme Judicial Court, Holden at Lenox, Within and for the County of Berkshire, on the Second Tuesday of September, 1805....* Stockbridge, Mass.: H. Willard, 1805. Shaw & Shoemaker, 9720. *See also* "Books," *above*, and "Digital/Electronic Sources," *below*.

Digital/Electronic Sources

Internet
Early American Imprints *www.readex.com/scholarl/earlamim.html*
> Shaw-Shoemaker Digital Edition, Series II. Shaw-Shoemaker (1801-1819). Chester, Vt.: Readex/Newsbank, in cooperation with American Antiquarian Society, 2004. Available at academic libraries. *See also* "Microform," *above*.

Bristol County
Founded 1685, from Plymouth Colony

Courts

Bristol Superior Court, Taunton
Civil: original docket/record books (1918-date), file papers and appeals (pending and disposed, ten years); index. Criminal: original docket/record books (1930-date), file papers and appeals (1852-date); index. Divorce: original docket/record books, file papers, appeals, 1888-1930; index.
Note: Supreme Judicial Court Rule 1:11 requires permanent retention of docket books, divorce and naturalization records, and all other Bristol Superior Court records before 1860. Other records more than ten to twenty years old may be destroyed after "sample" maintained: 1860-1889, 20% sample; 1890-1919, 10% sample; 1920-1969, 5% sample; from 1970, 2% sample; equity cases 1897-1974, 30% sample. For more information about sampling criteria or access to records, contact court clerk or Head of Archives, Supreme Judicial Court.

District Court
Except as noted below, *see* "Trial Court Record Retention Guidelines" for District Court in "Statewide or General Sources: Courts," *above*.
Attleboro
Serves Attleboro, Mansfield, N. Attleboro and Norton.
Fall River
Serves Fall River, Freetown, Somerset, Swansea and Westport.
New Bedford
Serves Acushnet, Dartmouth, Fairhaven, Freetown, New Bedford and Westport. Civil: docket/record books, file papers, appeals, index; original and computer, 1982-date. Criminal: docket/record books, file papers, appeals; original, computer and microfilm, 1977-date; some indexed. Juvenile: docket/record books, file papers, appeals; original and computer, 1994-date; no index. Small claims: docket/record books, file papers, appeals, index; original and computer, 1984-date.

Taunton
Serves Berkley, Dighton, Easton, Raynham, Rehoboth, Seekonk and Taunton. Civil
and criminal: docket/record books, file papers, appeals, index; original, 1976-date
(civil), 1989-date (criminal).

Bristol Probate and Family Court, Taunton (also New Bedford and Fall River)
Civil and probate/family: docket/record books, file papers, index; original and computer, 1687-date (some in storage).

State Archives

Judicial Archives/Massachusetts Archives, Boston
Bristol County Court records include:
Court of Common Pleas (and its predecessors): 1652-1859.
Court of General Sessions of the Peace: 1697-1827.
Divorce records: original Supreme Judicial Court record books, ca. 1785-1887;
    original and microfilm of Superior Court divorce dockets, from ca. 1888.
Naturalization: Superior Court records, 1805-1991, and microfilm, 1805-1945; Fall
    River District Court, New Bedford District Court, and Taunton District Court
    (formerly Police Court), 1885-1906; card and microfilm indexes.
Probate: record books, 1687-1900 and file papers, 1687-1881; index, 1687-1966.
    Microfilm.
Supreme Judicial Court (and its predecessors): docket books/minute books, 1702-
    1797, originals and microfilm, including cases from Bristol County, 1719-
    1796 (gaps).
Contact Head of Archives, Supreme Judicial Court, for current information.

Other Repositories

Boston Historical Society and Museum, Boston
Bill of costs [facsimile], April 1703. MS0119/-#DC1478. *Thomas Wait v. David Lad*,
Court of Common Pleas.

New England Historic Genealogical Society, Boston
Andrews, John. Deposition, 1737 October 25. MSS C 5154. Taunton land dispute
    between Thomas Macomber and Richard Godfrey.
Leonard, Samuel. Documents re: Samuel Leonard of Raynham, Mass. MSS A 2414.
    Includes 1745 affidavit, Bristol Superior Court.
White, Samuel. Affidavit, 1767 February 20. MSS C 2756. Court action of Seth
    Williams, Taunton.
Wilbour, Benjamin F. "Little Compton, Rhode Island, Wills," 1945. MSS A 801.
    Abstract of original probate records of Taunton, Mass. and Little Compton,
    R.I. *See also* "Digital/Electronic Sources," *below*.

Old Colony Historical Society, Taunton
Manuscript collection of court records from the mid-17th-20th centuries, including:
Justice of the Peace Records
        Baylies, Francis. Collection of Legal Papers.
        Clap, Thomas. Court Records and Marriages, 1729-1768. Mss. Box 25 #1.

Danforth, Thomas. Docket Book, 1826-1829, and Indenture. Mss. Box 25#8, 8A. Town of Norton.

Ellis, James P. Account Book, 1875-1877. Vfile EL59J.

Leland, S. Court and Land Records of Norfolk County, Mass., 1845-1847. Mss. Box 25, #10.

Tisdale, James. Marriage records (1795-1809), Account Book (1823-1847), and Court Records (1798). Mss. Box 25 #13.

Other Court Records

Burt, Abel. Testimony in the case of *Hornick v. Crosman*, 28 March 1692. Vfile B95A1692.

Commonwealth of Mass. v. Emily Brow, Media Lewis, Mary Camata, and Raymond O'Brien, District Court, Taunton, Mass., 24 March 1945.

George Cornell v. William Thomas, Jr., 18 August 1733. Vfile C815G 8/18/1733.

Robert Crossman v. Mr. Strong, c.1700. Vfile C884R 1700.

Dean, Hannah (Mrs. Isaac Dean). Testimony re: estate of father, James Leonard, 1735. Vfile IR6W 1735.

Docket of Grand Jury Cases, dated 8 April 1707. Vfile B776CJ.

Hammond, Benjamin. Testimony re: slave owned by Capt. Benjamin Claghorn, 1 March 1730. Vfile H185B 3/1/1730.

Haskins, William. Testimony in the case of Robert Crossman's dam, 14 October 1707. Vfile H273W 10/14/1707.

Leonard, Phillip. Finding of the jury into the death of, 1696. Vfile J979 1696.

Leonard, Uriah. Testimony re: estate of father, James Leonard, 1735. Vfile IR6W 1735.

Robinson, Judith. Testimony as to time of her mother's death in 1726, 9 December 1745. Vfile R556J 1745.

Smith, Regard. Testimony re: hiring John Archbill (Archibald), a Scotsman, for twenty weeks in 1653. Vfile Sm64R 11/11/1653.

Lott Strange v. John Williams, 13 September 1733. Vfile St81L 9/13/1733.

Constable Records

Constabulary Assessment, 20 August 1698. Vfile C765 8/20/1698.

Miscellaneous Manuscript Records related to Fees, Jury Notification, Court Expenses for the Years 1802, 1811-1818. Vfile B776CJ.

Pratt, Micah. Constable Papers, 1770-1777. Vfile P888M 1770-1777.

Old Dartmouth Historical Society, New Bedford Whaling Museum, New Bedford

Dartmouth (Mass.: Town). Records, 1674-1912. Bristol County judges of probate and Court of Common Pleas, etc.

Worth, Henry Barnard. Papers, 1714-1942. Includes transcripts of court and probate records for Dartmouth, New Bedford, Acushnet, Freetown, Westport, Nantucket and Fairhaven; French spoliation claims (1847, 1885-1906), court dockets, etc.

Books and Journals

The Acts and Resolves, Public and Private, of the Province of the Massachusetts Bay.... 21 vols. Boston: Wright & Potter, 1869-1922. Vol. 7 (Resolves, 1692-1702) and Vol. 8 (Resolves, 1703-1707) contain editorial notes of Abner C.

Goodell, Jr., reprinting excerpts from records of various Mass. courts., *e.g.,* Inferior Court of Quarter Sessions, Bristol County, 1695/6 (7:492).

Bailey, Frederic W. *Early Massachusetts Marriages Prior to 1800: As Found on Ancient Court Records of the Counties of Middlesex, Hampshire, Berkshire and Bristol.* Worcester, Mass.: By author, 1914; Baltimore, Md.: Genealogical Publishing Co., 1979. *See also* "Microform," *below.*

Rounds, H. L Peter. *Abstracts of Bristol County, Massachusetts, Probate Records.* 2 vols. Baltimore, Md.: Genealogical Publishing Co., 1987-1988, 2001. Vol 1, 1687-1745; vol. 2, 1745-1762. *See also* "Digital/Electronic Sources," *below.*

_____. "Bristol County Probate Abstracts." *The Mayflower Descendant* 45:13-24, 159-164; 46:39-44, 171-174; 47:13-18, 133-138; 48:59-64, 129-134; 49:22-33, 125-143. Continuation of his previous 2-vol. work, *above,* ending with Probate Records, vol. 20, 1768.

Microform

Miscellaneous court records

Attleboro, Massachusetts, Jurors Record, 1841-1918. GSU, 1969.

Bailey, Frederic W. *Early Massachusetts Marriages Prior to 1800: As Found on Ancient Court Records of the Counties of Middlesex, Hampshire, Berkshire and Bristol.* Worcester, Mass.: By author, 1914; Baltimore, Md.: Genealogical Publishing Co., 1979; GSU, 2003. *See also* "Books," *above.*

Bristol County, Massachusetts, Docket Books for Divorce Records, 1909-1918. GSU, 2000. Superior Court.

Court of Common Pleas, Records 1696-1868. GSU, 1972.

Court of General Sessions, Records, 1702-1738. GSU, 1972.

Court Records, 1714-1814 (approx.). GSU, 1972. Court of Common Pleas.

Court Records, 1797-1861. GSU, 1972. Supreme Judicial Court; mostly civil cases.

Court Records (Miscellaneous) 1780-1868. GSU, 1972. Circuit Court of Common Pleas.

Divorce Records, 1862-1889. GSU, 1992. Supreme Judicial Court.

Divorce Records, 1887-1908. GSU, 1992. Superior Court.

Indexes (1840-1909) and Vital Records (1843-1908). GSU, 1969. Fall River.

Naturalization records

Civil Docket Books with Naturalizations, 1884-1895. GSU, 1988. District Court, Taunton.

Naturalization Card File, 1885-1906. GSU, 1988. District Court, Taunton.

Naturalization Declarations, 1901-1906; Index Cards, 1885-1906. GSU, 1992. District Court, Taunton.

Naturalization Declarations of Intention, 1896-1906. GSU, 1988. District Court, Taunton.

Naturalization Docket Books (1904-1906)—Primary Declarations and Final Applications (1988). District Court, Attleboro.

Naturalization Index, 1805-1906. GSU, 1988. Court of Common Pleas.

Naturalization Index, 1907-1992; Declaration of Intentions, 1906-1930. GSU, 1992. Superior Court.

Naturalization Index, ca. 1852-1885. GSU, 1992. Supreme Judicial Court.

Naturalization Index–Declarations and Petitions, Previous to 1856. GSU, 1992. Court of Common Pleas and Supreme Judicial Court.

Naturalization Petition Packets and Index, 1885-1906. GSU, 1988. District Court, Taunton.

Naturalization–Petitions and Records, 1805-1856. GSU, 1992, 1993. Court of Common Pleas and Supreme Judicial Court.

Naturalization Primary Declarations, 1885-1906. GSU, 1988. District Court, Taunton.

Naturalization Records, 1904-1906. GSU, 1992. District Court, Attleboro.

Naturalization Records–Declarations of Intention (1870-1885, 1931-1945 and Petitions (1856-1945). GSU, 1992, 2000. Superior Court.

Naturalization Records from Various District Courts-Primary Declarations, 1906-1909. GSU, 1993. District Court, Taunton, Fall River, New Bedford, and Attleboro.

Naturalization Records–Preliminary Petitions, 1927. GSU, 1993. Superior Court.

Naturalization Records–Primary Declarations, 1852-1885. GSU, 1993. Superior Court and Court of Common Pleas.

Naturalization Records–Primary Declarations and Final Applications, 1885-1906. GSU, 1993. District Court, Fall River.

New Bedford, Massachusetts, Record of Applications for Naturalization, 1886-1900. GSU, 1969.

Record of Final Applications for Naturalization, 1896-1906. GSU, 1988. District Court, Taunton.

Probate records

Bristol County (Mass.) Probate Records 1690-1881. GSU, 1969.

Extracts from the Probate Records of Bristol County, Mass., Relating to the Hail, Mason and Other Families, 1691-1809. GSU, 1954. From typescript at Conn. State Library, Hartford.

Probate Records 1687-1916; Index, 1687-1926. GSU, 1968.

Digital/Electronic Sources

CD-ROM

Family Tree Maker's Family Archives Genealogical Records: Massachusetts Town, Probate and Vital Records, 1600s-1900s. Cambridge, Mass.: The Learning Co., 1999. Includes: H. L Peter Rounds. *Abstracts of Bristol County, Massachusetts, Probate Records.* 2 vols. Baltimore, Md.: Genealogical Publishing Co., 1987-1988, 2001.

Internet

Bristol Registry of Deeds *www.newbedforddeeds.com*
    Online search of Mass. Land Court records re: Bristol County, 1994-date.

New England Historic Genealogical Society *www.NewEnglandAncestors.org*
    Little Compton, Rhode Island, Wills. Boston: NewEnglandAncestors.org, 2003. Abstract of original probate records of Taunton, Mass. and Little Compton, R.I., by Benjamin F. Wilbour. "Little Compton, Rhode Island, Wills." 1945. *See also* "Other Repositories," *above.*

Dukes County
Founded 1683, as a New York county, and 1695, as a Massachusetts county

Courts

Dukes Superior Court, Edgartown
All Dukes County Superior Court records are permanent. Indexes are available. Civil, criminal, divorce, juvenile: original docket/record books, file papers, to date, including: Quarter Court, 1665-1692; Court of General Sessions of the Peace, 1692-1827; Court of Common Pleas, 1692-1859; Superior Court, from 1859; Divorce records, 1800s-1920s; Naturalization, 1790-1976. Contact Head of Archives, Supreme Judicial Court, or Dukes Superior Court clerk for current information. Please make appointment for visit.

District Court, Edgartown
Serves Edgartown, Oak Bluffs, Tisbury, W. Tisbury, Aquinnah (formerly Gay Head), Gosnold and Elizabeth Islands. *See* "Trial Court Record Retention Guidelines" for District Court in "Statewide or General Sources: Courts," *above.*

Dukes Probate and Family Court, Edgartown
Probate file papers from 1690.

State Archives

Judicial Archives/Massachusetts Archives, Boston
Dukes County Court records include:
Probate: 1690-1932, microfilm.
Supreme Judicial Court (and its predecessors): docket books/minute books, 1702-1797, originals and microfilm, including cases from Barnstable and Dukes County, 1720-1797 (gaps).
Contact Head of Archives, Supreme Judicial Court, for current information.

Other Repositories

Library of Congress, Washington, D.C.
Peter Force Papers. Records, 1712-1812, re: Inferior Court of Common Pleas and Superior Court of Dukes County; includes unpublished finding aid.

Martha's Vineyard Historical Society, Edgartown
Court records copied from files at Dukes County Courthouse. Also ca. 1,000 deeds and wills, 1660-1950, with card index by name, filed by date.

New England Historic Genealogical Society, Boston
Dukes County court records, ca. 1662-1744 (bulk 1720s-1730s), *e.g.*, writs, deeds, testimony, appeals, etc., re: residents of Martha's Vineyard, including Native Americans. Some records uncataloged. Contact NEHGS Archivist.

Microform

Probate Records, 1790-1938. GSU, 1972.

Digital/Electronic Sources

CD-ROM
Family Tree Maker Genealogies of Mayflower families: 1500s-1800s. Novato, Cal.: Broderbund, 1997. Includes Gary Boyd Roberts. *Mayflower Source Records: Primary Data Concerning Southeastern Massachusetts, Cape Cod, and the Islands of Nantucket and Martha's Vineyard, from The New England Historical and Genealogical Register.* Baltimore, Md.: Genealogical Publishing Co., 1997. With probate records.

Essex and (Old) Norfolk County
Both counties were founded 1643. (Old) Norfolk consisted of New Hampshire towns Dover, Portsmouth, Hampton, Exeter (under Massachusetts jurisdiction until 1679), and Salisbury and Haverhill (annexed to Essex County in 1680).

Courts

Essex Superior Court, Salem (also Lawrence and Newburyport)
All Essex County Superior Court records are permanent. *See* "Trial Court Record Retention Guidelines" for Superior Court in "Statewide or General Sources: Courts," *above*. Also, divorce: Supreme Judicial Court record books, ca. 1785-1887, at courthouse; SJC file papers, and Superior Court files papers, ca. 1887-1927, stored offsite. For access to records, contact court clerk or Head of Archives, Supreme Judicial Court.

District Court
Except as noted below, *see* "Trial Court Record Retention Guidelines" for District Court in "Statewide or General Sources: Courts," *above*.
Gloucester
Serves Essex, Gloucester and Rockport. Civil, criminal and juvenile: original docket record books, file papers, index; 1988-date (civil), 1973-date (criminal), 1985-date (juvenile).
Haverhill
Serves Boxford, Bradford, Georgetown, Groveland and Haverhill. Civil and criminal, including restraining orders: docket/record books, file papers; original, last ten years; computer, 2000-date.
Ipswich (Moved to Newburyport courthouse, 2004)
Civil and criminal: docket/record books, file papers, index; original, 1970s-date (perhaps older dockets in storage). Call ahead. In-person research only.
Lawrence
Serves Andover, Lawrence, Methuen and N. Andover.
Lynn
Serves Lynn, Marblehead, Nahant, Saugus and Swampscott.
Newburyport
Serves Amesbury, Merrimac, Newbury, Newburyport, Rowley, Salisbury and W. Newbury. Civil and criminal: original docket/record books, file papers; index.
Peabody
Serves Lynnfield and Peabody. Civil and criminal: original docket/record books, file papers.

Salem

Serves Beverly, Danvers, Manchester by the Sea, Middleton and Salem. Original naturalization records, etc.

Essex Probate and Family Court, Salem (also Lawrence)
Original probate cases #58038-78954 (1881-1896), probate court divorce file papers (1922-1944), and domestic cases #32040-44219 (1965-1972) in offsite storage. More recent records at courthouse. Some digital/electronic records also available.

State Archives

Judicial Archives/Massachusetts Archives, Boston
Essex County court records include:
Consolidated index to Court of Common Pleas, 1749-1859; Superior Court, 1859-1904; Supreme Judicial Court, 1797-1904; and Witchcraft Trial W.P.A. Transcript. Microfilm.
Court of Common Pleas, Court of General Sessions of the Peace, and Superior Court (and their predecessors): docket/record books, file papers, 1600s-1800s (gaps), offsite storage (*see* Peabody-Essex Museum in "Other Repositories," *below*) and microfilm.
Divorce records: Superior Court divorce indexes, 1887-1927, and Probate Court divorce indexes, 1922-1944. Microfilm of Supreme Judicial Court record books, 1797-1920, and consolidated index for 1785-1904 divorces.
Naturalization: Lawrence and Lynn/Salem Superior Court records, 1907-1982 (*see* Head of Archives, Supreme Judicial Court, re: pre-1907); Gloucester, Lawrence and Newbury District Courts, 1886-1906 (gaps); Lynn District Court, 1885-1906; card and microfilm indexes.
(Old) Norfolk County: files, 1654-1685. Microfilm.
Probate: original probate record files #1-58037 (1638-1881); index vols. 1638-1840, (*see* docket books for 1841-1881) and index vols. 1881-1896. Vault 400. Also docket and record books, 1638-1915. Microfilm.
Supreme Judicial Court (and its predecessors): docket books/minute books, 1702-1797, originals and microfilm, including cases from Essex County; docket books, 1797-1988; record books, 1797-1930; file papers, 1695-1899.
Contact Head of Archives, Supreme Judicial Court, for current information.

State Historical Society

Massachusetts Historical Society, Boston
Dane, Nathan. Nathan Dane Papers, 1663-1834. Ms. N-1090. Legal papers of Beverly, Mass. lawyer, including docket books of Court of Common Pleas, 1782-1812.
Salem Witchcraft Papers, 1692. Ms. N-859.
Pickering, John. Papers, 1803-1811. Ms. N-707. Records of Salem/Boston lawyer re: Supreme Judicial Court cases and legal opinions of Judge Edmund Trowbridge.
Trial of Benjamin Shaw, Benjamin Alley Junior, Jonathan Buffum, and Preserved Sprague, for Riots and Disturbance of the Public Worship, in the Society of Quakers, at Lynn, Massachusetts, Before the Court of Common Pleas, Held at Ipswich, Massachusetts, March 16, 1822. Salem: Cushing & Appleton, 1822. Box 1822.

Trowbridge, Edmund. Testimony, 10 June 1762. Misc. Bd. 1762 June 10. Trowbridge, Mass. Attorney General testified against Solomon Newhall in bribery case before Superior Court of Judicature, Ipswich.

Other Repositories

Boston Athenaeum, Boston
Tyley, Samuel, et al. Notarial records: Boston, of Samuel Tyley, Ezekiel Goldthwait, and Ezekiel Price, 1748 Dec. 2-1754 March 11. Mss L3. Includes deposition records re: 1740 trial of Capt. Thomas Chapman, Marblehead, for murder of Samuel Majory, Salem.

Dartmouth College Library, Hanover, N.H.
Massachusetts. Commissioner of Probate. Commission, 1694 April 3, to Phillip English. Rauner Manuscript #694253. Re: Pudeater estate, Salem.

Gloucester Archives, Gloucester
City clerk copies of letters, notices, etc., 1889-1906. CC2. Includes naturalization notices, 1889-1899.
Index to deeds, 1898-1908. 3 vols. Essex County Registry of Deeds South: records, partially cross-indexed to Land Court numbers.
Legal records, 1651-1910.
Notices of applications, 1885-1900. CC34. Re: naturalization applications.
Trustee writs, 1835-1909. CC13. Re: cases in Gloucester Police Court, Justice of the Peace Court, District Court, etc.

Hagley Museum and Library, Manuscripts and Archives Dept., Greenville, Del.
Writ of *John Cookson vs. Peter Bennet*, 1719 Mar 9. Call #2017. Essex County Court of Common Pleas.

Harvard Business School, Baker Library, Boston
Selected receivership records from the Municipal Court, Boston, Mass., 1799-1844 (inclusive). Mss. 781 1825-1844. Including Oriental Bank, Boston, and Nahant Bank, Lynn, which went into receivership after panic of 1837.

Lynn Museum and Historical Society, Lynn
Records, 1811. MS/G1. Essex County Circuit Court of Common Pleas.
Records, 1875-1889. MS/G7. Police Court, Lynn.

New England Historic Genealogical Society, Boston
Cogswell, Dorothea Bates. Papers, 1647-1975 (bulk: 1710-1853). MSS 405. Includes court and probate records of Cogswell, Russell and Northend families, of Gloucester, Ipswich and Rowley.
Rolfe, Benjamin, clerk. Summons issued to Robert Hooper of Marblehead, Mass., 1738 April 26. Mss C 2458. Superior Court of Judicature at Ipswich.

Newburyport Archival Center, Newburyport Public Library, Newburyport
Wills from Marcia E. Little Collection of Early New England and Newbury Families (copied from handwritten books and bound as "New England and Newbury Wills," vols. II-VII, and IX).
Also numerous published court records (*e.g.*, Essex County and Maine).

N. Andover Historical Society, N. Andover

Archival material re: town of Andover is not fully indexed, but majority of documents accessible via computer database; formats include original manuscripts, copies and microfilm.

Forbes Rockwell Research: wills, inventories and probate, etc., 1665-1822.

"Alpha Run" of family records: 1710-1942, including wills, land deeds, court summons, bonds, birth certificates and one guardianship authorization.

Peabody-Essex Museum, Phillips Library, Salem

Library retains on deposit the original records of the Essex County courts from 1636-1820, including the Essex County Quarterly Court, General Sessions of the Peace and Court of Common Pleas, as well as special Court of Oyer and Terminer that heard the 1692 Salem witchcraft trials. Microfilm of Essex probate record books also available, 1636-1914. Manuscript collections include:

Bowditch, Joseph. Papers, 1699-1941. MSS 156. Business papers series (1737-1779) includes court records re: Bowditch's activities as sheriff, court clerk, and justice of the peace, etc.

Curwen family. Papers, 1641-1902. MSS 45. Salem. Capt. George Curwen (1610-1684) papers series includes: legal documents re: Cape Porpoise River Falls Mill, Wells, Maine; court papers as judge in Essex County; duties in Oyer and Terminer Court during "witch trials," etc. Rev. George Curwen (1683-1717) and family papers series includes documents re: Samuel Curwen (1715-1802) as Salem justice of peace, etc.

Dunlap, Andrew. Papers, 1754-1847. MSS 150. Salem/Boston attorney and legislator; papers (1814-1835) re: marine and shipping cases, mutiny, piracy, etc.

Hudson family. Papers, 1741-1914. MSS 174. Newburyport; legal documents, court and estate records, etc.

Loring, George Bailey. Papers, 1831-1904. MSS 183. Salem; legal documents and estate records, etc.

Osgood family. Papers, 1661-1932. MSS 189. Salem estate records, wills, etc.

Page, Samuel. Papers, 1777-1871 (bulk 1785-1813). MSS 177. Danvers and Danversport; court and estate records, etc.

Pickman, Benjamin. Papers, 1698-1904. MSS 5. Legal papers of various families.

Prince family. Papers, 1732-1839. MSS 72. Salem; papers re: John Prince's legal work as clerk for Essex County courts, justice of the peace, etc.

Prince, John. Papers, 1759-1887. MSS 73. Marblehead; misc. legal papers.

Saltonstall, Leverett. Papers, 1715-1845. MSS 243. Salem; papers re: marine and civil litigation, etc.

Sanderson, Elijah and Jacob. Papers, 1780-1827; bulk: 1789-1820. MSS 246. Papers of Salem cabinetmakers, including court case of *Elijah Sanderson and Caleb Burbank v. John Waters*.

Stearns and Sprague family papers, 1718-1889. MSS 192. Includes legal and court records re: Salem family.

Topsfield Historical Society collection, 1661-1970. MSS 231. Includes papers re: legal cases, probate, and petitions to the Land Court re: Ipswich land.

Waters, Joseph G. Papers, 1759-1913. MSS 93. Salem lawyer, judge and legislator; papers re: Salem law practice, Essex County Court of Common Pleas, Salem Police Court, maritime cases, estate papers, etc.

Topsfield Historical Society, Topsfield
Original family papers (wills, deeds, etc.), from 1600s. *See also* Peabody-Essex Museum, *above*.

Vermont Historical Society, Barre, Vt.
Royce-Washburn papers. MSC-50. Re: law practice of Reuben Washburn of Lynn, Mass. and Ludlow, Vt.

Books and Journals

Court Records—Abstracts, Transcripts and Indexes

Dow, George Francis, ed. *The Probate Records of Essex County, Massachusetts*. 3 vols. Salem: The Essex Institute, 1916-1920; Newburyport: Parker River Researchers, 1988. Vol. 1, 1635-1664; vol. 2, 1665-1674; vol. 3, 1675-1681. *See also* "Microform," *below*.

_____. *Records and Files of the Quarterly Courts of Essex County, Massachusetts*. 9 vols. Salem: The Essex Institute, 1911-1975. *See also* "Microform" (vols. 1-8) and "Digital/Electronic Sources" (vols. 1-9), *below*. Vol. 1, 1636-1656; vol. 2, 1656-1662; vol. 3, 1662-1667; vol. 4, 1667-1671; vol. 5, 1672-1674; vol. 6, 1675-1678; vol. 7, 1678-1680; vol. 8, 1680-1683; vol. 9, 1683-1686.

Essex Antiquarian. 13 vols. Salem: The Essex Antiquarian, 1897-1909. Including: vols. 1-13, Old Norfolk County Records (1648-1681), continued in *Historical Collections of the Essex Institute; see below*; vols. 3-9, 12-13, Salem Quarterly Court Records and Files, 1637-1659; vols. 8-13, Ipswich Court Records and Files, 1638-1658.

Essex County, Massachusetts Probate Records: Part I. Boston: Research Publication Co., 1903.

Historical Collections of the Essex Institute. Vols. 1-8. Salem: H. Whipple for Essex Institute, 1859-1868. (*See also Essex Institute Historical Collections*. Vols. 9 *et seq*. Salem: Essex Institute Press, 1869-ca. 1993.) Including: vols. 7 and 8, Essex County Court Records (1636-1641); vols. 11 and 13, James Kimball, "Gleanings from the Files of the Court of General Sessions of the Peace;" vols. 50-51, Essex County probate records (1635-1648); vols. 56-68, 70, Old Norfolk County Records (1648-1681), part 2, continued from *Essex Antiquarian; see above*.

Hutchinson, Thomas. *A Collection of Original Papers Relative to the History of the Colony of Massachusetts-Bay*. Boston: Thomas & John Fleet, 1769; Albany, N.Y.: Prince Society, 1865, 2:1-25. Essex County Court opinion by Samuel Symonds, Assistant, in *Giddings v. Brown*.

Hutchinson, Thomas, and Lawrence Shaw Mayo. *The History of the Colony and Province of Massachusetts-Bay*. Cambridge: Harvard Univ. Press, 1936, 2:19-47, includes court documents from the witchcraft proceedings after 1692.

Sanborn, Melinde Lutz. *Ages From Court Records 1636 to 1700: Volume I, Essex, Middlesex, and Suffolk Counties, Massachusetts*. Baltimore, Md.: Genealogical Publishing Co., 2003.

_____. *Lost Babes: Fornication Abstracts from Court Records, Essex County, Massachusetts, 1692-1745*. Derry, N.H.: By author, 1992. *See also* "Digital/Electronic Sources," *below*.

_____. *Essex County, Massachusetts, Probate Index, 1638-1840.* 2 vols. Boston: By author, 1987. *See also* "Microform" and "Digital/Electronic Sources," *below*.

History

Boyer, Paul, and Stephen Nissenbaum. *Salem-Village Witchcraft: A Documentary Record of Local Conflict in Colonial New England.* Boston: Northeastern Univ. Press, 1993.

Norton, Mary Beth. *In the Devil's Snare: The Salem Witchcraft Crisis of 1692.* New York: Alfred A. Knopf, 2002.

Roach, Marilynne K. *The Salem Witch Trials: A Day-by-Day Chronicle of a Community Under Siege.* New York: Cooper Square Press, 2002; Taylor Trade Publishing, 2004.

Microform

Miscellaneous court records

Court Records, 1636-1641. GSU, 1971.

Court Records, 1638-1692: Indexes to Court Records/Papers, 1636-1695. GSU, 1971. County Court.

Court Records, 1648-1681. GSU, 1971. County Court (Old Norfolk County).

Court Records, 1686-1726. GSU, 1971. Inferior Court of Common Pleas.

Court Records, 1692-1796. GSU, 1971. Court of General Sessions of the Peace.

Court Records, 1749-1782. GSU, 1971. Inferior Court of Common Pleas.

Court Records, 1782-1811, 1821-1859. GSU, 1971. Court of Common Pleas.

Court Records, 1797-1826. GSU, 1971. Supreme Judicial Court.

Court Records, 1811-1821. GSU, 1971. Circuit Court of Common Pleas.

Court Records, 1859-1865. GSU, 1971. Superior Court.

Dow, George Francis, ed. *Records and Files of the Quarterly Courts of Essex County, Massachusetts.* 8 vols. Salem: The Essex Institute, 1911-1922; GSU, 1971, 1972. *See also* "Books and Journals," *above*, and "Digital/Electronic Sources," *below*.

Essex County Courts File Papers, 1636-1694 (Inclusive). Watertown: Mass.: General Microfilm Co., 1990.

Essex County, Massachusetts, Births, Marriages, and Deaths, 1636-1795. GSU, 1971. County Court and Court of General Sessions of the Peace.

Essex County, Massachusetts, Vital Records (Births, Marriages, Deaths) 1860-1910. GSU, 2004. County Court.

Execution Records, 1686-1783. GSU, 1977. Inferior Court of Common Pleas and County Court.

List of Persons Warned from the Town of Danvers, 1752-1770. GSU, 1971. Court of General Sessions of the Peace.

Public Notary Book, 1723-1769. GSU, 1971.

Town Records, 1638-1858. GSU, 1971. Salisbury; includes early court records.

Town Records, 1642-1861. GSU, 1971. Amesbury; includes early court records.

Witchcraft Papers, 1655-1750. GSU, 1971. Court of Assistants and Superior Court of Judicature.

Naturalization records

Declaration Records (1906-1945) at Salem and Lynn by the Essex County Superior Court. GSU, 1999.

Naturalization Declaration Records (1920-1945) at Lawrence, Massachusetts, Superior Court. GSU.

Naturalization Index (1906-1939) of the Essex County Superior Court Sitting at Salem/Lynn and Lawrence. GSU, 1999.

Naturalization Petitions (1920-1945) at Lawrence, Massachusetts, by Essex County Superior Court. GSU, 1999.

Naturalization Records Index, 1906-1982 (at Lawrence): Essex County (Massachusetts) Superior Court. GSU, 1999.

Naturalization Records Index, 1906-1982 (at Salem/Lynn): Essex County (Massachusetts) Superior Court. GSU, 1999.

Petition Records (1907-1945) at Salem and Lynn by the Essex County Superior Court. GSU, 1999.

Richardson, Arthur. *Naturalizations, Essex County, Mass. 1794-1820.* GSU, 2001.

Probate and insolvency records

Dow, George Francis, ed. *The Probate Records of Essex County, Massachusetts.* 3 vols. Salem: The Essex Institute, 1916-1920; Newburyport: Parker River Researchers, 1988; GSU, 1988.

Essex County, Massachusetts, Probate Records and Indexes 1638-1916. GSU, 1971, 2000, 2001. Probate Court and Court of Insolvency.

Miscellaneous Probate Records and Deeds, 1779-1846. GSU, 1971.

Probate Records 1638-1691. GSU, 1971.

Pulsifer, David. *Records of the County of Norfolk, in the Colony of Massachusetts.* GSU, 1971. Copied from original records, 1647-1714. (Old) Norfolk County.

Sanborn, Melinde Lutz. *Essex County, Massachusetts, Probate Index, 1638-1840.* 2 vols. Boston: By author, 1987. GSU, 1994. Microfiche.

Will of Richard Dole, Snr. of Newbury, Essex County, Massachusetts dated 25 March 1698. Probated Sept 16, 1699. GSU, 1971. From typescript transcription at D.A.R. Library, Washington, D.C.

Early American Imprints, Series I. Evans (1639-1800). New York: Readex Microprint, in cooperation with American Antiquarian Society, 1985. Microfiche. Including: Maule, Thomas. *Nevv-England Pesecutors* [sic] *mauld vvth their own weapons…imprisonment and tryal of Thomas Maule of Salem, for publishing a book….* New York: William Bradford, 1697. Evans, 801.

Early American Imprints, Series II. Shaw-Shoemaker (1801-1819). New Canaan, Conn.: Readex Microprint, in cooperation with American Antiquarian Society, 1987-1992. Microfiche. Including:

Jackman, Joseph. *The sham-robbery, committed by Elijah Putnam Goodridge, on his own person, in Newbury, near Essex bridge, Dec. 19, 1816: with a history of his journey to the place where he robbed himself: and his trial with Mr. Ebenezer Pearson, whom he maliciously arrested for robbery: also the trial of Levi & Laban Kenninston….* Concord, N.H.: By author, 1819. Shaw & Shoemaker, 48361.

Report of the evidence & arguments of counsel at the trial of Levi and Laban Kenniston before the Supreme Judicial Court: on an indictment for the robbery of Major Elijah Putnam Goodridge on the evening of the 19th of December, 1816. Boston: J.T. Buckingham, 1817. Shaw & Shoemaker, 41954, 41955. Re: Ipswich case.

Digital/Electronic Sources

CD-ROM

Massachusetts Probate Records: Middlesex & Essex Counties–Selected Years. Provo, Utah: Ancestry.com, MyFamily.com, Inc., 2000. Index to Essex County records, 1640-1840.

Internet
Ancestry.com *www.Ancestry.com*
> Sanborn, Melinde Lutz. *Essex County, Massachusetts, Probate Index, 1638-1840.* 2 vols. Boston: By author, 1987; Provo, Utah: Ancestry.com.
> _____. *Essex County Probate Records, Part 1, and Supplement.* Orem, Utah: Ancestry, 1998; Provo, Utah: Ancestry.com.

AncestryandGenealogy.com
> *www.ancestryandgenealogy.com/freedataessexprobate.asp*
> Sanborn, Melinde Lutz. *Essex County, Massachusetts, Probate Index.* AncestryandGenealogy.com, 2005.
> *www.ancestryandgenealogy.com/freedataancforn.asp*
> _____. *Lost Babes, Fornication Abstracts.* AncestryandGenealogy.com, 2005. Abstracts of birth and marriage records from fornication cases in Essex County courts, 1636-1745.

Early American Imprints
> *www.readex.com/scholarl/eai_digi.html*
> Evans Digital Edition, Series I. Evans (1639-1800). Chester, Vt.: Readex/Newsbank, in cooperation with American Antiquarian Society, 2003.
> *www.readex.com/scholarl/earlamim.html*
> Shaw-Shoemaker Digital Edition, Series II. Shaw-Shoemaker (1801-1819). Chester, Vt.: Readex/Newsbank, in cooperation with American Antiquarian Society, 2004.
> Available at academic libraries. *See also* "Microform," *above.*

Essex Registry of Deeds (Northern District) *www.lawrencedeeds.com/dsSearch.asp*
> Online search of Land Court records re: Essex County, N. District, 1999-date.

Essex Registry of Deeds (Southern District) *www.salemdeeds.com/goget.asp?type=lc*
> Online search of Land Court records re: Essex County, S. District, 1991-date.

Salem Witch Trials Documentary Archive and Transcription Project
> *http://etext.lib.virginia.edu/salem/witchcraft/texts/transcripts.html*
> Court records from Salem witchcraft trials, 1692.
> *http://etext.virginia.edu/salem/witchcraft/Essex*
> Dow, George Francis, ed. *Records and Files of the Quarterly Courts of Essex County, Massachusetts.* 9 vols. Salem, Mass.: The Essex Institute, 1911-1975. *See also* "Books and Journals" and "Microform," *above.*

Franklin County
Founded 1811, from Hampshire County

Courts

Franklin Superior Court, Greenfield
Civil: original dockets, file papers, appeals, 1885-date; index cards, 1882-date; computer dockets, 2000-date. Criminal: original dockets, file papers, appeals, 1901-date;

computer dockets, 2000-date. Divorce: dockets, 1913-1923; index cards, 1880-1923; other divorce records in offsite storage. Naturalization: index cards, 1842-1995.

Note: SJC Rule 1:11 requires permanent retention of all docket books, divorce and naturalization records, and all other Franklin Superior Court records prior to 1860. Other records more than ten to twenty years old may be destroyed after "sample" maintained: 1860-1969, 10% sample; from 1970, 2% sample. For more information about sampling criteria or access to records, contact court clerk or Head of Archives, Supreme Judicial Court.

District Court
Greenfield
Serves Ashfield, Bernardston, Buckland, Charlemont, Colrain, Conway, Deerfield, Gill, Greenfield, Hawley, Heath, Leyden, Monroe, Montague, Northfield, Rowe, Shelburne, Sunderland and Whately. Civil: original docket/record books, file papers, appeals; index. *See* "Trial Court Record Retention Guidelines" for District Court in "Statewide or General Sources: Courts," *above*. Criminal: original docket/record books, file papers, ca. 1896-date; index. No record searches by mail or telephone due to lack of staffing.
Orange
Serves Athol, Erving, Leverett, New Salem, Orange, Shutesbury, Warwick and Wendell. Civil and criminal: original docket sheets, 1950-date; original file papers and appeals, 1980-date; index.

Franklin Probate and Family Court, Greenfield
Dockets (original, 1814-2000, computer, 2001-date); original file papers and appeals. Index ledgers, 1812-1984; index cards, 1984-2000; computer index, 2001-date. Information available in person, or by mail.

State Archives

Judicial Archives/Massachusetts Archives, Boston
Franklin County court records include:
Court of Common Pleas: docket books, 1823-1859; file papers, 1812-1859.
Court of General Sessions of the Peace: file papers, 1812-1828.
Divorce record books: Supreme Judicial Court, original and microfilm, 1872-1887; Superior Court, original and microfilm, 3 vols., from 1887.
Justice of the Peace: file papers, 1816-1896 (gaps).
Naturalization: Superior Court records, 1853-1976; microfilm, 1906-1945. Pre-1907 papers filed chronologically/alphabetically.
Probate: docket books, 1810-1971; record books, 1812-1894; index, 1812-1965. Microfilm.
Supreme Judicial Court: file papers, 1816-1863.
Contact Head of Archives, Supreme Judicial Court, for current information.

Other Repositories

Memorial Libraries, Deerfield
Collections at Pocumtuck Valley Memorial Assn. Library (PVMA) and Historic Deerfield Library (HD) include:
Franklin County Court records, 1825-1826, incomplete. Civil cases; no index. PVMA.
Franklin County Probate Court, 1812-1894. Microfilm; index. HD.

Hampshire County Inferior Court of Common Pleas, 1677-1790. Microfilm; index. HD.
Hampshire County Probate Court, 1660-1820. Microfilm; index. HD.
Williams, John. 1751-1816. Records of his civil court cases in Deerfield, 1787-1800.
        3 docket vols.; no index. PVMA.

New England Historic Genealogical Society, Boston
"Greenfield, Mass. Records." n.d. Handwritten transcription by unknown compiler.
        MSS MS 70 GRE 31. *See also* "Digital/Electronic Sources," *below*.

Shelburne Historical Society, Shelburne Falls
Wills and land deeds, 18th-20th centuries, mixed with other papers and not cataloged.

Microform

Miscellaneous court records
County Commissioners Dockets and Records, 1732-1867. GSU, 1986.
Court of Common Pleas, Dockets, 1823-1865, Records, 1812-1858. GSU, 1972.
Franklin County, Massachusetts, Divorce Records 1872-1933. GSU, 2000. Supreme
        Judicial Court.
Franklin County, Superior Court Divorce Docket, 1888-1923. GSU, 1991.
*Record of Proceedings Kept by Henry Bassett, One of the Justices of the Peace for the
        County of Franklin 1816-1838.* GSU, 1973. Ashfield.
Records of Philip Phillips, Justice of the Peace, 1790-1792. GSU, 1973. Ashfield.
Superior Court Records, 1859-1867. GSU, 1972.
Supreme Judicial Court, Index, 1816-1888, Dockets, 1816-1888, Records, 1816-1871.
        GSU, 1972.

Naturalization records
Applications for Naturalization, 1886-1900. GSU, 1993. Greenfield.
Applications for Naturalization (Final Declarations), 1899-1906. GSU, 1991. District
        Court, Orange.
Franklin County, Massachusetts, Naturalization Declarations 1906-1945. GSU, 2000.
        Superior Court.
*Naturalization Index, 1896-1906; Naturalization Files (Primary and Final Declara-
        tions), 1891-1906.* GSU, 1991. District Court, Greenfield.
Naturalization Indexes (1811-1991). GSU, 1991. Superior Court.
Naturalization Records-Petitions (1907-1945). GSU, 2000. Superior Court.

Probate court records
Franklin County Probate Files, ca. 1812-1915. GSU, 1991, 1992.
Probate Dockets, Records, and Indexes, 1810-1971. GSU, 1972, 1991.

Digital/Electronic Sources

Internet
Franklin Registry of Deeds *www.masslandrecords.com*
        Online search of Land Court records re: Franklin County, 1900-date.
New England Historic Genealogical Society *www.NewEnglandAncestors.org*

Abstracts of Probate Records, Greenfield, Massachusetts. Boston: NewEng-landAncestors.org, 2004. From handwritten transcription, compiler unknown, at NEHGS. *See* "Other Repositories," *above.*

Hampden County
Founded 1812, from Hampshire County

Courts

Hampden Superior Court, Springfield
Civil and criminal: docket/record books, file papers, index; original, 1930-date. Divorce: dockets and file papers (after 1887) in offsite storage. No phone calls for record checks accepted.
Note: Supreme Judicial Court Rule 1:11 requires permanent retention of docket books, divorce and naturalization records, and all other Hampden Superior Court records before 1860. Other records more than ten to twenty years old may be destroyed after "sample" maintained: 1860-1889, 20% sample; 1890-1919, 10% sample; 1920-1969, 5% sample; from 1970, 2% sample. For more information about sampling criteria or access to records, contact court clerk or Head of Archives, Supreme Judicial Court.

District Court
Except as noted below, *see* "Trial Court Record Retention Guidelines" for District Court in "Statewide or General Sources: Courts," *above.*
Chicopee
Serves Chicopee. Civil, criminal and juvenile: original docket/record books, file papers, appeals; index.
Holyoke
Serves Holyoke.
Palmer
Serves Brimfield, E. Longmeadow, Holland, Hampden, Ludlow, Monson, Palmer, Wales and Wilbraham.
Springfield
Serves Longmeadow, Springfield and W. Springfield. Original naturalization records.
Westfield
Serves Agawam, Blandford, Chester, Granville, Montgomery, Russell, Southwick, Tolland and Westfield.

Hampden Probate and Family Court, Springfield
Original probate file papers, 1812-1915, in off-site storage. More recent records at courthouse.

State Archives

Judicial Archives/Massachusetts Archives, Boston
Hampden County Court records include:
Divorce: Supreme Judicial Court record books (original), and divorce index (microfilm).
Naturalization: Superior Court records, 1812-1991; microfilm, 1906-1945; card/micro-film index (includes Springfield District Court records).
Probate: record books, 1806-1919 (microfilm).
Contact Head of Archives, Supreme Judicial Court, for current information.

Other Repositories

American Antiquarian Society, Worcester

Boise, Patrick. Trial notebook, 1850-1857. Mss. Dept., Octavo vols. "B." Summaries of Hampden County cases, as Trial Justice and as Justice of the Peace.

Hampshire County (Mass.). Court records, 1677-1696; 1786-1826. Mss. Dept., Folio vols. "H." Northampton and Springfield, 1677-1696, with numerous references to John Pynchon; and list of Hampshire County Justices of Common Pleas Court, and Justices of the Peace, ca. 1786-1826.

Memorial Libraries, Deerfield

Childs, Jonathan R. 1822-1857. Records of criminal court in Chicopee, Mass., 1853-1854, incomplete. No index.

Microform

Miscellaneous court records

Court Dockets for Divorce Proceedings, ca. 1871-ca. 1886. GSU, 1986. Supreme Judicial Court.

Court of Common Pleas Index, 1812-1861, Hampden County, Massachusetts. GSU, 1986-1987.

Court of Common Pleas, Records, 1812-1859. GSU, 1972. Court of Common Pleas.

Court Records, 1638-1812. GSU, 1972. Court of General Sessions of the Peace and other courts.

Court Records, 1816-1914. GSU, 1986. Supreme Judicial Court; includes probate records.

Court Records, 1859-1894, and Index, 1859-1861. GSU, 1986. Superior Court.

Divorce Index Cards, 1831-1936, to Hampden County Superior Court Records. GSU, 1986.

Divorce Proceedings Dockets, 1887-1918. GSU, 1986. Superior Court.

Hampden County Superior Court Records, 1894-1916. GSU, 1986.

Superior Court Civil Case Indexes, 1859-1915, Hampden County, Massachusetts. GSU, 1987.

Naturalization records

Hampden County Naturalization Petitions, Declarations, and Orders, 1927-1945. GSU, 1986, 1999. Superior Court.

Index to Naturalization Records (Primary and Final) in Various Hampden County Courts, 1812-1853. GSU, 1986.

Naturalization Certificates of Intention, 1875-1893. GSU, 1986. Superior Court.

Naturalization Declarations of Intention, 1906-1931. GSU, 1986, 1999.

Naturalization Docket (1896-1906), and Naturalization Records Index (1896-1906), Hamdpen [sic] County, Massachusetts. GSU, 1990. District Court of Eastern Hampden, Palmer.

Naturalization Index cards, 1906-1986, 1812-1906, to Hampden County Superior Court Records, 1812-1986. GSU, 1986.

Naturalization Papers and Indexes, 1885-1906, Springfield, Massachusetts. GSU, 1990. Police Court.

Naturalization Papers of Primary Declarations, 1853-1877. GSU, 1986. Court of Common Pleas and Superior Court.

Naturalization Papers, Primary and Final, 1853-1874. GSU, 1986. Court of Common Pleas and Superior Court.

Naturalization Papers: Pending (1851-1890), and Dismissed (1886-1887). GSU, 1986. Superior Court.

Naturalization Petitions Index (Hampden County): 1906-1989. GSU, 1998-1999. From Mass. Archives.

Naturalization Petitions of Military Personnel, 1918. GSU, 1986. Superior Court.

Naturalization Primary and Final papers, 1853-1906. GSU, 1986. Superior Court.

Naturalization Records, 1879-1906, Superior Court, Hampden County, Massachusetts. GSU, 1986-1987.

Naturalization Records of Final Admission and Primary Declaration, 1840-1852, Court of Common Pleas, and Supreme Judicial Court, Hampden County. GSU, 1986-1987.

Primary Declarations and Naturalizations, 1852-1855, Hampden County, Massachusetts. GSU, 1990. Police Court, Springfield.

Records of Naturalization and Final Admission, 1875-1880. GSU, 1986. Superior Court.

Records of Naturalizations and Declarations, 1885-1906, Holyoke, Massachusetts. GSU, 1990. Police Court.

[Springfield, Massachusetts] Naturalization Index, March 4, 1886-August 22, 1906. GSU, 1990. District Court.

Probate and insolvency records

Affidavits of Trust of Administrator Appointments, 1900-1901, Hampden County. GSU, 1988.

Court Records, 1816-1914. GSU, 1986. Supreme Judicial Court; includes probate records.

Grants of Property, 1881-1894, Hampden County. GSU, 1988. Court of Insolvency.

Index of Public Administration, Insolvent Files, 1812-1986. GSU, 1986.

Index of Wills Filed Without Petition, 1812-1986. GSU, 1986.

Index to Public Administrations, 1812-1986. GSU, 1986.

Probate Docket Books, 1812-1916, and Indexes, 1812-1867. GSU, 1987.

Probate Records Index, 1812-1986. GSU, 1986.

Probate Records of Hampden County and City of Springfield, 1806-1919. GSU, 1971.

Probate Records, 1809-1881, Hampden County, Massachusetts. GSU, 1987-1988, 1996.

Probate Records, 1814-1929. GSU, 1988.

Digital/Electronic Sources

Internet

Hampden Registry of Deeds *http://registryofdeeds.co.hampden.ma.us* or *www.mass-landrecords.com* Online search of Land Court records re: Hampden County, 1987-date.

Hampshire County

Founded 1662, from Middlesex County

Courts

Hampshire Superior Court, Northampton

Civil and criminal: docket/record books, file papers (original, and transcripts if appeal); 1990-date (civil), 1985-date (criminal); some indexing, on computer, 1993-

date. Divorce: docket/record books, file papers; original, 1960s, and older file papers in offsite storage.

Note: Supreme Judicial Court Rule 1:11 requires permanent retention of docket books, divorce and naturalization records, and all other Hampshire Superior Court records before 1860. Other records more than ten to twenty years old may be destroyed after "sample" maintained: 1860-1969, 10% sample; from 1970, 2% sample. For more information about sampling criteria or access to records, contact court clerk or Head of Archives, Supreme Judicial Court.

District Court
Northampton
Serves Chesterfield, Cummington, Easthampton, Goshen, Hatfield, Huntington, Middlefield, Northampton, Plainfield, Southampton, Westhampton, Williamsburg and Worthington. Civil: docket/record books, file papers, appeals, index; original, 1975-date. Criminal: docket/record books, file papers, appeals, index; original, 1919-date. Juvenile: docket/record books, file papers, index; original, 1942-1995.
Ware
Serves Amherst, Belchertown, Granby, Hadley, S. Hadley, Pelham, Ware, and all of MDC Quabbin Reservoir and Watershed Area. *See* "Trial Court Record Retention Guidelines" for District Court in "Statewide or General Sources: Courts," *above*.

Hampshire Probate and Family Court, Northampton
Docket/record books, file papers, appeals, index; original and microform, late 1600s-date; computer, 2000-date.

State Archives

Judicial Archives/Massachusetts Archives, Boston
Hampshire County Court records include:
Court of Common Pleas: 1677-1859.
Court of General Sessions of the Peace: file papers, 1677-1859.
District Court and Justice of the Peace: docket and testimony books.
Divorce: original Supreme Judicial Court record books (to 1887) and Superior Court divorce records (from 1888).
Naturalization: Superior Court, 1849-1988; Northampton and Ware District Courts, 1885-1906; card indexes.
Probate and Insolvency Courts: 1838-1890s; includes index.
Supreme Judicial Court: file papers of appeals to Supreme Judicial Court, 1718-1774, with finding aid; docket books/minute books, 1702-1797, originals and microfilm, including cases from Hampshire County, 1722-1797 (gaps).
Contact Head of Archives, Supreme Judicial Court, for current information.

State Historical Society

Massachusetts Historical Society, Boston
Harvey, Joseph. Joseph Harvey legal documents, 1799-1802. Ms. N-1371. Default judgments (defendant failed to appear) before Hampshire County Justice of the Peace.
Wait family. Legal documents, 1717-1773. Ms. S-285. Hatfield and Hampshire County cases, estate settlement, will, etc.

Other Repositories

American Antiquarian Society, Worcester
Hampshire County (Mass.). Court records, 1677-1696; 1786-1826. Mss. Dept., Folio vols. "H." Northampton and Springfield, 1677-1696, with numerous references to John Pynchon; and list of Hampshire County Justices of Common Pleas Court, and Justices of the Peace, 1786-1826.

Harvard University, Law School Library, Cambridge
Record of cases before the magistrate of Agawan [sic], Springfield, Massachusetts, 1638-1702. MSS HLS MS 4344. Original manuscript of the Pynchon court record; *see* "Books" and "Digital/Electronic Sources," *below*, for published versions.

Historic Northampton Museum and Education Center, Northampton
Hawley, Joseph (Justice of the Peace). Court action, 27 May 1685, Petition by Joseph Hawley, Jr. for children of David Wilton. Will, 1693. Deeds, 1681, 1699.
Page from "Booke of Records of Executions and their returnes belonging to Hampshire, 1671, Springfield."
18th century legal documents, described in finding aid; and wills of Samuel and Sarah Baker of Northampton (1793), and Joseph Hawley of Hadley (1775).
19th century warrants and legal documents.
Museum has finding aids and searchable database.

Memorial Libraries, Deerfield
Collections at Pocumtuck Valley Memorial Assn. Library (PVMA) and Historic Deerfield Library (HD) include:
Hampshire County Inferior Court of Common Pleas, 1677-1790. Microfilm; index. HD.
Hampshire County Probate Court, 1660-1820. Microfilm; index. HD.
Williams, John. 1751-1816. Records of his civil court cases in Deerfield, 1787-1800. 3 docket vols.; no index. PVMA.

New England Historic Genealogical Society, Boston
Corbin manuscript collection. Microfilm. Transcriptions of Walter E. Corbin and Lottie Squier Corbin, including abstracts and excerpts from Hampshire County probate, court and land records. *See also* "Digital/Electronic Sources," *below*.

Yale University Library, New Haven, Conn.
Strong, Simeon. Record book, 1769-1800. MssA. Justice of the Peace for Hampshire County.

Books

The Acts and Resolves, Public and Private, of the Province of the Massachusetts Bay.... 21 vols. Boston: Wright & Potter, 1869-1922. Vol. 7 (Resolves, 1692-1702) and Vol. 8 (Resolves, 1703-1707) contain editorial notes of Abner C. Goodell, Jr., reprinting excerpts from court records, *e.g.*: Court of Oyer and Terminer, at Northampton, 1696 (7:528-530).

Bailey, Frederic W. *Early Massachusetts Marriages Prior to 1800: As Found on Ancient Court Records of the Counties of Middlesex, Hampshire, Berkshire and Bristol*. Worcester, Mass.: By author, 1914; Baltimore, Md.: Genealogical Publishing Co., 1979. *See also* "Microform," *below*.

Smith, Joseph H. *Colonial Justice in Western Massachusetts (1639-1702): The Pynchon Court Record.* Cambridge: Harvard Univ. Press, 1961.

Microform

Miscellaneous court records

Bailey, Frederic W. *Early Massachusetts Marriages Prior to 1800: As Found on Ancient Court Records of the Counties of Middlesex, Hampshire, Berkshire and Bristol.* Worcester, Mass.: By author, 1914; Baltimore, Md.: Genealogical Publishing Co., 1979; GSU, 2003.

Court Records, 1677-1728. GSU, 1972. County Court, Court of Quarter Sessions, Court of General Sessions of the Peace and Inferior Court of Common Pleas.

Court Records, 1728-1783. GSU, 1972. Inferior Court of Common Pleas and Court of General Sessions of the Peace.

Court Records, 1766-1771, 1776-1790. GSU, 1972. Court of General Sessions of the Peace.

Court Records, 1783-1853. GSU, 1972. Court of Common Pleas and Court of General Sessions of the Peace. Vol. A includes record of executions, 1715-1764.

Court Records, 1797-1954. GSU, 1988. Supreme Judicial Court.

Court Records, 1854-1916. GSU, 1988. Superior Court.

Court Records, Civil, 1854-1859. GSU, 1972. Court of Common Pleas.

Court Records, Criminal, 1852-1859. GSU, 1972. Court of Common Pleas.

Court Records Index Cards, 1677-ca. 1830. GSU, 1995. Inferior Court of Common Pleas and Court of Sessions.

Divorce Dockets, 1888-1918. GSU, 1988. Superior Court.

Divorce Index cards (A thru Z), 1758-1789. GSU, 1995. Court of Sessions and Supreme Judicial Court.

Divorce Index, 1790-1960, Superior Court, Hampshire County, Massachusetts. GSU, 1987. Superior Court.

Divorce Records Index Cards, 1758-1960. GSU, 1995. Superior Court.

Divorce Records Index Cards (A to end), 1812-1887. GSU, 1995. Supreme Judicial Court.

Index to Attorneys Admitted to the Bar, 1743-1925, Hampshire County, 1743-1925. GSU, 1987. Superior Court, Supreme Judicial Court, Court of Sessions and Court of Common Pleas.

Index to Common Pleas, v. 1-33, May term 1798-Oct. term 1853. GSU, 1995.

Index to Divorces Found in Court of Sessions Volumes, 1758-1789. GSU, 1987.

Index to General Sessions and Common Pleas, Volumes 1-24, inclusive, 1677 to Jan. 18, 1798. GSU, 1987.

Index to Marriages, 1758-1789, in the Court of Sessions, Hampshire County, 1758-1789. GSU, 1987.

Index to Superior Court Records, 1853-1986, Hampshire County. GSU, 1987.

Records, 1800-1837. GSU, 1972. Court of Sessions.

Waste Book of Hampshire County, Massachusetts. GSU, 1958. Court records, 1663-1667.

Naturalization records

Final Naturalization Docket, 1903-1906. GSU, 1990. District Court, Ware.

Naturalization Dockets, 1885-1906. GSU, 1988. District Court, Northampton.

Naturalization Index, 1859-present. GSU, 1996. Superior Court. From Mass. Archives.
Naturalization Records, 1849-1934; General Index, 1836-1986. GSU, 1987, 1988.
  Superior Court.

Probate court records

Court Records, 1638-1812. GSU, 1972. Court of General Sessions of the Peace and
  other courts.
Index to Estate Files, 1660-1988. GSU, 1989.
Probate Records, 1660-1916; Index, 1660-1971. GSU, 1988-1989.
Probate Records, 1797-1869. GSU, 1971.
Probate Records for Hampshire County, 1660-1820. Holyoke, Mass.: New England
  Archives Center, 1969.

Early American Imprints, Series II. Shaw-Shoemaker (1801-1819). New Canaan,
Conn.: Readex Microprint, in cooperation with American Antiquarian Society, 1987-
1992. Microfiche. *See also* "Digital/Electronic Sources," *below*. Including:
A report of the trial of Andrew Wright, printer of the Republican spy, on an indictment
  for libels against Governor Strong: before the Hon. Theophilus Parsons,
  Chief Justice of the Supreme Court of the Commonwealth of Massachusetts,
  at Northampton, Sept. term 1806. Northampton: Andrew Wright, 1806. Shaw
  & Shoemaker, 11267.
Report of the trial of Dominic Daley and James Halligan for the murder of Marcus
  Lyon: before the Supreme Judicial Court begun and holden at Northamp-
  ton...April 1806.... Northampton: S. & E. Butler, 1806. Shaw & Shoemaker,
  11268.

Digital/Electronic Sources

CD-ROM

Dunkle, Robert J., ed. *The Corbin Collection Volume 1: Records of Hampshire*
  County, Massachusetts. Boston: New England Historic Genealogical Soci-
  ety, 2003. Transcriptions of Walter E. Corbin and Lottie Squier Corbin,
  including abstracts and excerpts from Hampshire County probate, court and
  land records. *See also* "Other Repositories," *above*.
Families of the Pioneer Valley. W. Springfield, Mass.: Regional Publications, 2000.
  Includes Pynchon court records from 1639.
Stott, Clifford L. *Vital Records of Springfield, Mass. to 1850.* Boston: New England
  Historic Genealogical Society, 2002. Includes Pynchon court records from
  1638/9-1716/7.

Internet

Early American Imprints *www.readex.com/scholarl/earlamim.html*
  Shaw-Shoemaker Digital Edition, Series II. Shaw-Shoemaker (1801-1819).
  Chester, Vt.: Readex/Newsbank, in cooperation with American Antiquarian
  Society, 2004. Available at academic libraries. *See also* "Microform," *above*.
Hampshire Registry of Deeds *www.masslandrecords.com*
  Online search of Land Court records re: Hampshire County, 1994-date.

Middlesex County
Founded 1643

Courts

Middlesex Superior Court, Cambridge and Lowell
Civil: original docket/record books (1911-date), pleadings and file papers (1974-date); transcripts six years; computer (1988-date); index from 1911. Criminal: original docket/record books (1961-date), pleadings and file papers (1975-date); computer (1990-date); index from 1919.
Note: Supreme Judicial Court Rule 1:11 requires permanent retention of docket books, divorce and naturalization records, and all other Middlesex Superior Court records before 1860. Other records more than ten to twenty years old may be destroyed after "sample" maintained: 1860-1889, 20% sample; 1890-1919, 10% sample; 1920-1969, 5% sample; from 1970, 2% sample; equity cases 1892-1974, 30% sample. For more information about sampling criteria or access to records, contact court clerk or Head of Archives, Supreme Judicial Court.

District Court
Except as noted below, *see* "Trial Court Record Retention Guidelines" for District Court in "Statewide or General Sources: Courts," *above.*

Ayer
Serves Ashby, Ayer, Boxborough, Dunstable, Groton, Littleton, Pepperell, Shirley, Townsend, Westford and Devens Regional Enterprise Zone. Civil: original docket books, 1878-date; original file papers and appeals, 1975-date; index, 1989-date. Criminal: docket books, 1897-date; file papers and appeals, 1992-date; index, 1990-date.

Cambridge, E. Cambridge
Serves Arlington, Belmont and Cambridge.

Concord
Serves Concord, Carlisle, Lincoln, Lexington, Bedford, Acton, Maynard and Stow.

Framingham
Serves Ashland, Framingham, Holliston and Hopkinton.

Lowell
Serves Billerica, Chelmsford, Dracut, Lowell, Tewksbury and Tyngsboro. Civil, criminal, juvenile: docket/record books, index; original and computer, 1833-date. Naturalization: docket/record books, index; original, 1897-1906. Civil war pensions: original certificates, 1865; no index.

Malden
Serves Everett, Malden, Melrose and Wakefield.

Marlborough
Serves Hudson and Marlborough.

Natick
Serves Natick, Sherborn, Sudbury and Wayland.

Newton, W. Newton
Serves Newton. Civil: original docket/record books, 1900-date; file papers, 1998-date on site, 1980-1997 offsite. Criminal: original docket/record books, 1900-date; file papers, 1997-date on site, 1982-1996 offsite. Juvenile: original docket/record books, 1900-date; file papers, 1997-date on site, 1982-1996 offsite.

Somerville
Serves Medford and Somerville.

Waltham
Serves Waltham, Watertown and Weston.
Woburn
Serves Burlington, N. Reading, Reading, Stoneham, Wilmington, Winchester and Woburn. Civil: docket/record books. Criminal: original docket/record books, file papers, appeals. Juvenile: original docket/record books, file papers, before October 2003 (after this date, taken over by Juvenile Court).

Middlesex Probate and Family Court, Cambridge, Concord, Lowell and Marlborough *See* "Trial Court Record Retention Guidelines" for Probate and Family Court in "Statewide or General Sources: Courts," *above.*

State Archives

Judicial Archives/Massachusetts Archives, Boston
Middlesex County Court records include:
County Court: 1648-1699.
Court of Common Pleas (and predecessors): 1648-1859
Court of General Sessions of the Peace (and predecessors): 1648-1827.
Divorce: Supreme Judicial Court record books (original, to 1887); Supreme Judicial Court records (microfilm, 1807-1887); Superior Court divorce dockets (original, after 1887); other Superior Court records (microfilm, 1887-1938).
Naturalization: Superior Court, 1842-1984 (microfilm 1906-1945); Lowell Police (District) Court, ca. 1832-1906; Malden and Newton District Courts, 1885-1906; Somerville District Court, 1894-1906; Woburn District Court, 1892-1906. Indexes include cards, microfilm and naturalization dockets.
Probate: file papers, 1648-1871 (#1-45383); original (vault 400) and microfilm; index.
Supreme Judicial Court (and predecessors): file papers of appeals to Supreme Judicial Court, 1718-1774, with finding aid; docket books/minute books, 1702-1797, originals and microfilm, including cases from Middlesex County, 1719-1797 (gaps).
Contact Head of Archives, Supreme Judicial Court, for current information.

State Historical Society

Massachusetts Historical Society, Boston
Argument of Daniel Wells: esq. on the trial of William Wyman, at Lowell, Nov. 1843, on an indictment against himself and others for embezzlement of the funds of the Phoenix bank, Charlestown, Mass., before the Hon. Charles Allen. Greenfield, Mass.: A. Phelps, 1844. Box 1844.
Middlesex County docket book, 1790-1793. Ms. S-745. Justice of the Peace William Swan, Groton.
Russell, James. Legal documents compiled by James Russell, 1692-1701. Ms. N-822. Including Russell's papers as Middlesex County Justice of the Peace.
Savage family. Savage family papers, 1688-1927; bulk: 1711-1891. Ms. N-99. Including court decisions, 1787-1790, in Middlesex County Court.
Stearns, Isaac. Papers, 1721-1808. Ms. N-960. Including probate and legal documents of Middlesex County Justice of the Peace.

Trial of Michael Martin, for highway robbery: before the Supreme Judicial Court of Massachusetts, for the county of Middlesex, October term, 1821.... Boston: Russell & Gardner, 1821. Book B Martin; Shoemaker 7003.

Other Repositories

American Antiquarian Society, Worcester
Lemmon, Joseph. Papers, 1708-1767. Mss. Dept., Misc. mss. boxes "L," Oversize mss. boxes "L." Records of Charlestown, Mass. Justice of the Peace, etc.
Maynard, Jonathan. Papers, 1791-1834. Mss. Dept., Octavo vols. "M," Misc. mss. boxes "M." Records of Framingham Justice of the Peace, 1791-1812.

American Textile History Museum, Manuscript Collection, Lowell
Massachusetts. Supreme Judicial Court. Statement of agreed facts (undated). Typescript court document re: Wamesit Power Co. and others, in suit against city of Boston for withdrawing water from Sudbury River for city's water supply.

Boston Historical Society and Museum, Boston
Notice of probate, May 7, 1788. MS0119/-#DC1457. Re: will of Joshua Prentiss, late of Holliston. Middlesex Probate Court.
Summary of *Boston v. Westford*, n.d. MS0190/—03. Re: Westford persons in Boston house of corrections, 1832.
Summons, February 2, 1732. # MS0119/-DC1483. Commanding selectmen of Westford to appear before Court of General Sessions re: ill-kept roads.

Concord Free Public Library, Special Collections, Concord
Brooks, Nathan. Nathan Brooks legal papers, 1795-1861 (bulk 1813-1861). Concord lawyer, notary public and justice of the peace.
Hoar, John. An inventory of the estate of...John Hoar late of Lincoln decd. on the sixteenth day of May...: Ms., 1786. Middlesex Probate Court #11592, Series 1.
Ebenezer Hubbard estate papers, 1807-1808.
Records of the Middlesex County criminal cases kept by Justice of the Peace Abiel Heywood at Concord, 1798-1823.
Records of Writs and Executions Kept by Middlesex County Deputy Sheriff Abel Moore. Writs, 1816-1818; executions, 1817-1830.

Harvard University, Cambridge
Lamont Library
Records of the County of Middlesex, in the Commonwealth of Massachusetts, [1648-1686] [microform]. Harvard Depository Film M 443 [Consult Documents/Microtexts desk for HNBVQ7], HOLLIS #001307424. *Note*: Microfilmed from photostatic copy of original records, made before WWII; different from later filming by Genealogical Society of Utah (*see* "Microform," *below*), and believed to contain some papers no longer in original files at Judicial Archives, Massachusetts Archives.
Law School Library
Harris, Nathaniel, *Records of the court of Nathaniel Harris one of His Majesty's Justices of the Peace within and for the County of Middlesex, holden at Watertown from 1734-1761....* Watertown: Watertown Historical Society, 1938. Harvard Depository US 905.97MAS HAR, HOLLIS #003120291.

Middlesex County (Mass.). Records from cases before the county court of Middlesex County, 1649-1663, 4 vols. MSS HLS 1368 (Special Collections). Also available as Law School Microform (Drawer 337).

Lexington Historical Society, Lexington
18th and 19th-century court records, including summons, writs of attachment, testimony, probate, sexual complaint, indenture agreements, etc. Computer database.

Library of Congress, Manuscript Division, Washington, D.C.
Charlestown (Boston, Mass.). Papers, 1633-1855. Includes copies of court records re: Squaw Sachem of Mistick (then in Middlesex County) charging landowners with encroachment; Phoenix Bank (Charlestown) proceedings against William Wyman incidental to bankruptcy; etc.

Lincoln Public Library, Lincoln
Land Court records, 1800-1900. 2004.013. Re: Lincoln.

New England Historic Genealogical Society, Boston
Account book of John and Thomas Greenwood, 1709-1804. MSS A 1052. Includes justice of the peace records of John and Thomas Greenwood of Newton, and Justice John Stone.
Stone, William Eben. Papers, 1016-1937 (bulk 1450-1881). MSS 89. 4 March 1672 petition of Daniel Stone to the Mass. Court of Assistants for compensation re: care he provided eight survivors of a shipwreck. *See also* "Books and Journals," *below*.
Trial of the Case of the Commonwealth versus David Lee Child, for Publishing in the Massachusetts Journal a Libel on the Honorable John Keyes: Before the Supreme Judicial Court, Holden in Cambridge, in the County of Middlesex. Boston: Dutton & Wentworth, 1829. Rare Book KF223/C55.
Wyman, Thomas Bellows. Abstract of Middlesex court files. MSS 596. Handwritten transcription in 2 vols., 1649-1664 and 1664-1675. *See also* "Digital/Electronic Sources," *below*.

New Hampshire Historical Society, Concord, N.H.
Cummings, Oliver. Estate papers, 1717-1833. Deeds, wills, probate papers, etc., Dunstable.

Waltham Public Library, Waltham
Minute books for Justice William Fiske, 1793-1798-1803. *See also* "Microform," *below*.

Wayland Historical Society, Wayland
Record books, Col. David Heard, Wayland Justice of the Peace. Multiple vols., ca. 1839-1863, including cases of drunkenness, theft, adultery, attempted rape, assault and battery, disturbing church service, debt, etc., re: towns of Wayland, Lincoln, Stow, Sudbury, Sherborn, Framingham, Weston and Natick.
Complaint to Justice of the Peace Roby by Jacob Reeves, re: theft of silver spoon, 1761. "Taverns" collection.
Deposition, 1660. #16
Proceedings of 1860 hearing re: flooding of town pastureland by mills.

Register of writs, executions and services, Horace Heard, Wayland deputy sheriff, 1837-1853. #18.

Wills, probate inventories, deeds, etc., 17th-20th centuries.

Westford (Town of)

Recently-discovered tin boxes of town records, 19th-20th centuries; inventory incomplete. Court records include: folder 8-9, probate, 1916; folder 14-6, court action, 1880; folder 17-5, court and lawyer letters, 1882; folder 18-5, juror list, 1883; folder 20-5, probate, 1886; folder 24-6, court (fire inquest), 1869; folder 26-1, juror list, 1890-1891; folder 27-4, Carville lawsuit, 1896; folders 27-7, 27-9, 27-10 and 31-7, District Court, 1896; folder 27-13, District Court, 1897; folder 31-11, District Court, 1895; folders 32-6, 32-14 and 33-9, District Court, 1898-1899; folders 33-3 and 33-5, court expenses, 1904-1905; folder 33-9, District Court, 1900, 1904; folder 33-11, District Court, 1908.

Westford Museum and Historical Society, Westford

Miscellaneous re: Westford, including: files of attorney Charles L. Hildreth; deeds, indentures, records of accidents at Abbot Mill, records from Westford Poor Farm, records of real estate transactions.

Weston Historical Society Museum, Weston

Deeds to Weston property, early-to-mid-1800s; will, 1897.

Books and Journals

The Acts and Resolves, Public and Private, of the Province of the Massachusetts Bay.... 21 vols. Boston: Wright & Potter, 1869-1922. Vol. 7 (Resolves, 1692-1702) and Vol. 8 (Resolves, 1703-1707) contain editorial notes of Abner C. Goodell, Jr., reprinting excerpts from court records, *e.g.: Gibson v. Gove*, 1695-96, 1703/4 (7:497-798, 8:309-310); *Richardson v. Fowl*, Inferior Court of Common Pleas, Middlesex County, 1695 (7:498-500); *Rice and Shepherd v. Brown and Minot*, General Quarter Sessions of the Peace, Charlestown, 1697 (7:586-587).

Bailey, Frederic W. *Early Massachusetts Marriages Prior to 1800: As Found on Ancient Court Records of the Counties of Middlesex, Hampshire, Berkshire and Bristol.* Worcester, Mass.: By author, 1914; Baltimore, Md.: Genealogical Publishing Co., 1979. *See also* "Microform," *below.*

The Cambridge Historical Society Publications. Cambridge: The Society, 1913, 7:70-77. Transcribed 1672 petition of Daniel Stone to the Mass. Court of Assistants for compensation re: care he provided eight survivors of a shipwreck. *See also* New England Historic Genealogical Society in "Other Repositories," *above.*

Collections of the Massachusetts Historical Society, 1st series. Boston: Mass. Historical Society, 1792- 5:45-52. Law cases, Supreme Judicial Court, Concord (1795).

Folsom, Samuel H., and William E. Rogers, eds. *Index to the Probate Records of the County of Middlesex, Massachusetts: 1st ser. from 1648 to 1871, 2d ser. from 1871 to 1909.* 2 vols. Cambridge: 1912-1914. *See also* "Microform" and "Digital/Electronic Sources," *below.*

Gozzaldi, Mary I. *History of Cambridge, Massachusetts, 1630-1877; with a genealogical register, by Lucius R. Paige: comprising a biographical and genealogical record of the early settlers and their descendants; with references to their wills and the administration of their estates in the Middlesex County Registry of Probate.* Cambridge: Cambridge Historical Society, 1930; Salem: Higginson Book Co., 2000. *See also* "Microform," *below.*

Harris, Nathaniel. *Records of the Court of Nathaniel Harris One of His Majesty's Justices of the Peace Within and for the County of Middlesex, Holden at Watertown from 1734 to 1761. Together with a Paper by F. E. Crawford Read Before the Historical Society of Watertown, November 14, 1893.* Watertown: Watertown Historical Society, s.d. Copies available at Concord Free Public Library, Watertown Public Library, etc.

Rodgers, Robert H. *Middlesex County in the Colony of the Massachusetts Bay in New England, Records of Probate and Administration.* 2 vols. Boston: New England Historic Genealogical Society, 1999, 2001. Vol. 1, October 1649-December 1660; vol. 2, March 1660/61-December 1670. (Vol. 3, February 1670/71-June 1676, forthcoming. Rockport, Maine: Picton Press, 2006.)

Sanborn, Melinde Lutz. *Ages From Court Records 1636 to 1700: Volume I, Essex, Middlesex, and Suffolk Counties, Massachusetts.* Baltimore, Md.: Genealogical Publishing Co., 2003.

Microform

Miscellaneous court records

Bailey, Frederic W. *Early Massachusetts Marriages Prior to 1800: As Found on Ancient Court Records of the Counties of Middlesex, Hampshire, Berkshire and Bristol.* Worcester, Mass.: By author, 1914; Baltimore, Md.: Genealogical Publishing Co., 1979; GSU, 2003.

Births, Marriages, and Deaths, 1651-1793. GSU, 1972. Superior Court.

Births, Marriages, and Deaths, 1671-1745. GSU, 1972. Superior Court.

Card Index to Births, Deaths, Wills, and Miscellaneous Court Records, 1600-1799. GSU, 1986.

Colonial County Court Papers, 1648-1798. GSU, 1974.

Court and Sessions Records, 1686-1799. GSU, 1986. Court of General Sessions of the Peace.

Court Records, 1649-1699. GSU, 1972. County Court; transcribed and original records.

Court Records, 1686-1809. GSU, 1972. Court of General Sessions of the Peace and Inferior Court of Common Pleas.

Court Records, 1699-1783. GSU, 1972. Includes Inferior Court of Common Pleas and Court of Common Pleas.

Court Records, 1783-1811, 1821-1847. GSU, 1972. Circuit Court of Common Pleas.

Court Records, 1791-1812. GSU, 1971. Justice of the Peace, Framingham.

Court Records, 1797-1850. GSU, 1972. Supreme Judicial Court.

Court Records, 1808-1831. GSU, 1972. Court of Sessions.

Court Records, 1812-1821. GSU, 1972. Circuit Court of Common Pleas.

Folio Index Cards, 1650-1800. GSU, 1986. County courts.

Middlesex County, Massachusetts, Court Records 1851-1887. GSU, 2000. Supreme Judicial Court; includes divorces.

Middlesex County, Massachusetts, Divorce Docket Books 1887-1938. GSU, 2000. Superior Court.

Militia Complaints, 1802. GSU, 1972. From original records at Waltham Public Library; includes William Fiske's records as Justice of the Peace, 1790-1803.

Minute Books for Justice's Matters, 1793, 1798-1893, GSU, 1972. Justice's Court, William Fiske; from original records at Waltham Public Library.

Naturalization records

Naturalization Declaration Records, 1906-1945. GSU, 1999-2000. Superior Court.

Naturalization Index Cards, 1800-1885. GSU, 1986.

Naturalization Petition Records, 1911-1945. GSU, 2000. Superior Court.

Naturalization Records, 1841-1884. GSU, 1974.

Naturalization Records and Certificates Indexes, 1906-1984. GSU, 1999. Superior Court.

Probate court records

Busiel, Alice E. *Miscellaneous Index and Records (1659-1692) Prior to the Appointment of a Judge of Probate in 1692.* GSU, 1964.

Card Index to Births, Deaths, Wills, and Miscellaneous Court Records, 1600-1799. GSU, 1986.

Folsom, Samuel H., and William E. Rogers, eds. *Index to the Probate Records of the County of Middlesex, Massachusetts: First Series from 1648 to 1871.* Cambridge, Mass: 1914. GSU, 1964.

Gozzaldi, Mary I. *History of Cambridge, Massachusetts, 1630-1877; with a genealogical register, by Lucius R. Paige: comprising a biographical and genealogical record of the early settlers and their descendants; with references to their wills and the administration of their estates in the Middlesex County Registry of Probate.* Cambridge: Cambridge Historical Society, 1930; Salem: Higginson Book Co., 2000. Microfilm title is: *Supplement and index: comprising a biographical and genealogical record of the early settlers and their descendants, with references to their wills and the administration of their estates in the Middlesex County registry of probate.* GSU, 1972.

Index to the Probate Records of the County of Middlesex, Massachusetts: Second Series. Cambridge, Mass: 1912-1953. GSU, 1964. 1870-1949.

Middlesex County (Mass.) Probate Packets [1-4702] (Second Series), 1872-1967. GSU, 1968.

Miscellaneous Town Records, 1700-1919. Waltham, Mass.: Graphic Microfilm of New England, 1969. Natick; includes will from 1700s.

Probate Records 1648-1924 (Middlesex County, Massachusetts). GSU, 1964-1967.

Digital/Electronic Sources

CD-ROM

Massachusetts Probate Records: Middlesex & Essex Counties–Selected Years. Provo, Utah: Ancestry.com, MyFamily.com, 2000. Middlesex County, 1648-1909.

Internet

Ancestry.com *www.Ancestry.com*

Flint, James, comp. *Middlesex County, Massachusetts Probate Index, 1648-1870, 1871-1909.* Provo, Utah: Ancestry.com, 2000. Original data from

Samuel H. Folsom and William E. Rogers, *Index to the Probate Records of the County of Middlesex, Massachusetts: 1st Ser. from 1648 to 1871, 2d Ser. from 1871 to 1909.* 2 vols. Cambridge, Mass: 1912-14.

Sanborn, Melinde Lutz. *Middlesex County, Massachusetts Deponents, 1649-1700.* Provo, Utah: Ancestry.com, 2000-. Index to deponents whose ages were stated in the "Middlesex County Court Folios" at Judicial Archives/Mass. Archives.

AncestryandGenealogy.com *www.ancestryandgenealogy.com/freedataancforn.asp*

Sanborn, Melinde Lutz. *Lost Babes, Fornication Abstracts.* AncestryandGenealogy.com, 2005. Free database, abstracting birth and marriage records from fornication cases in Middlesex County court, 1650-1700.

Middlesex Registry of Deeds (Northern and Southern Districts)

www.masslandrecords.com

Online search of Land Court records re: Middlesex County, Northern District, 1901-date; Southern District, 1987-date.

New England Historic Genealogical Society *www.NewEnglandAncestors.org*

Abstracts of Court Files of Middlesex County, Massachusetts, 1649-1675. Boston: NewEnglandAncestors.org, 2003. From handwritten abstracts by Thomas Bellows Wyman at NEHGS; *see* "Other Repositories," *above.*

Index to the Probate Records of Middlesex County, Massachusetts. Boston: NewEnglandAncestors.org, 2003. From Samuel H. Folsom and William E. Rogers. *Index to the Probate Records of the County of Middlesex, Massachusetts: 1st Ser. from 1648 to 1871.* Vol. 1. Cambridge, Mass: 1912-14.

Nantucket County
Founded 1695, from Dukes County

Courts

Nantucket Superior Court, Nantucket
All Nantucket Superior Court records are permanent. Civil: original docket/record books, file papers, index; original, 1721-date. Criminal: docket/record books, file papers, index; original, 1817-date.

District Court, Nantucket
See "Trial Court Record Retention Guidelines" for District Court in "Statewide or General Sources: Courts," *above.*

Nantucket Probate and Family Court, Nantucket
Civil and probate/family: docket/record books, file papers; original and microfilm, 1706-date; index, card and computer.

State Archives

Judicial Archives/Massachusetts Archives, Boston
Nantucket County Court records include:
Court of Common Pleas: microfilm, 1721-1859.
Court of General Sessions of the Peace: microfilm, 1721-1816.

Naturalization: Superior Court records, 1803-1974; microfilm, 1906-1945; card and microfilm index.

Probate: record books (microfilm, 1706-1867); index in each vol.

Contact Head of Archives, Supreme Judicial Court, for current information.

State Historical Society

Massachusetts Historical Society, Boston

Trial of Barker Burnell, late cashier of the M. & M. Bank, in Nantucket: Court of Common Pleas, June term, 1847, before his honor, Judge Washburn/reported for the Nantucket Inquirer and Weekly Mirror. Boston: B.B. Mussey, 1847.

Other Repositories

Nantucket Historical Association Research Library, Nantucket

Extensive manuscripts collection, with searchable online database, *http://12.46.127.86/dbtw-wpd/WebQueryMS.htm.* Court records include:

Bunker, Winslow papers/Terry collection, 1787-1924. Coll. 160, Folders 3 and 7. Including legal documents of notary public Lauriston Bunker (1849-1934), cases re: ships sailing in Nantucket waters, and 1845 naturalization certificate of John Morrow.

Isaac Coffin papers/Crafts collection, 1659-1836. Coll. 289. Includes records kept by Coffin as Nantucket probate judge.

Folger family. Papers, 1676-1952. Coll. 118. Legal documents of Walter Folger, Jr. (1765-1849), judge of Courts of Common Pleas and General Sessions, and of other family members.

Microfilmed Court and Town Records, 1721-1915. Coll. 414. Includes Nantucket County Superior Court record books, 1721-1847.

Nantucket Relief Association papers. Coll. 72. Includes court and probate records.

Nantucket town and county papers, 1668-1985. Coll. 127. Includes list of Nantucket families in records of Probate Court of Dukes County, 1899-1900; copies of cases from Court of Common Pleas, 1678-1705.

Worth, Henry Barnard. Collection, 1641-1905. Coll. 35. Includes Court records, 1673-1681, and cases re: Native Americans, 1682-1729. *See also* "Microform," *below*.

Old Dartmouth Historical Society, New Bedford Whaling Museum, New Bedford

Worth, Henry Barnard. Papers, 1714-1942. Includes transcripts of court and probate records for Dartmouth, New Bedford, Acushnet, Freetown, Westport, Nantucket and Fairhaven; French spoliation claims (1847, 1885-1906), court dockets, etc.

Books

Bedard, Richard N. *Nantucket Court Records, 1807-1814.* Columbia Falls, Maine: By author, 1989. *Note*: Maine Historical Society Library has copy.

Roberts, Gary Boyd. *Mayflower Source Records: Primary Data Concerning Southeastern Massachusetts, Cape Cod, and the Islands of Nantucket and Martha's Vineyard, from The New England Historical and Genealogical Register.* Baltimore, Md.: Genealogical Publishing Co., 1997. Includes probate records. *See also* "Digital/Electronic Sources," *below*.

Worth, Henry Barnard. *Nantucket lands and landowners*. 2 vols. Nantucket: Nantucket Historical Assoc., 1901-1913. Vol. 2 includes wills and estates. *See also* "Microform," *below*.

Microform

Miscellaneous court records
Court Records, 1721-1816. GSU, 1972. Court of General Sessions of the Peace and other courts.
Court Records, 1721-1859. GSU, 1972. Court of Common Pleas and other courts.
Macy's Collection, 1658-1855 (approx.). GSU, 1972. From manuscripts at Nantucket Historical Association, including court records.

Naturalization records
Naturalization Records: Declarations of Intention (1908-1945); Petitions (1910-1945); Citizenship Petitions Granted (1930-1945). GSU, 1998.

Probate court records
Probate Records, 1706-1867. GSU, 1972.
Worth, Henry Barnard. *Nantucket lands and landowners*. 2 vols. Nantucket: Nantucket Historical Assoc., 1901-1913. GSU, 1968. Vol. 2 contains information about wills and estates.
Worth's Collection, 1589-1921 (approx.). GSU, 1972. Records compiled by Henry Barnard Worth, at Nantucket Historical Assoc., including transcripts of will, and probate records.

Digital/Electronic Sources

CD-ROM
Family Tree Maker Genealogies of Mayflower families: 1500s-1800s. Novato, Cal.: Broderbund, 1997. Includes Gary Boyd Roberts. *Mayflower Source Records: Primary Data Concerning Southeastern Massachusetts, Cape Cod, and the Islands of Nantucket and Martha's Vineyard, from The New England Historical and Genealogical Register*. Baltimore, Md.: Genealogical Publishing Co., 1997. With probate records.

Internet
Nantucket Registry of Deeds *www.masslandrecords.com*
        Online search of Land Court records re: Nantucket County, 1958-date.

Norfolk County
Founded 1793, from Suffolk County

Courts

Norfolk Superior Court, Dedham
Note: Supreme Judicial Court Rule 1:11 requires permanent retention of docket books, divorce and naturalization records, and all other Norfolk Superior Court records before 1860. Other records more than ten to twenty years old may be destroyed after "sample" maintained: 1860-1889, 20% sample; 1890-1919, 10%

sample; 1920-1969, 5% sample; from 1970, 2% sample. For more information about sampling criteria or access to records, contact court clerk or Head of Archives, Supreme Judicial Court.

District Court
Brookline
Serves Brookline. *See* "Trial Court Record Retention Guidelines" for District Court in "Statewide or General Sources: Courts," *above*.
Dedham
Serves Dedham, Dover, Medfield, Needham, Norwood, Wellesley and Westwood. Civil and criminal: original docket/record books (decades-date), original pleadings and file papers (1996-date, civil) (1987-date, criminal); computer dockets, 2001-date (civil), 1997-date (criminal); index cards.
Quincy
Serves Braintree, Cohasset, Holbrook, Milton, Quincy, Randolph and Weymouth. Civil, criminal, land/housing: original docket/record books, file papers, appeals; most matters before 1980-1985 transferred to Archives or destroyed where appropriate; index (twenty to thirty years). Juvenile: original docket/record books, file papers, appeals; 1950-date; index (twenty years). *Note*: In-person requests only.
Stoughton
Serves Avon, Canton, Sharon and Stoughton. Civil and criminal: original docket/record books; 1920-date; index.
Wrentham
Serves Foxborough, Franklin, Medway, Millis, Norfolk, Plainville, Walpole and Wrentham. Civil and criminal: docket/record books, 1898-date; limited card index. Other: inquests (1930s-1970s), insanity (1900-1970), naturalization (1898-1904); no index.

Norfolk Probate and Family Court, Canton
See "Trial Court Record Retention Guidelines" for Probate and Family Court in "Statewide or General Sources: Courts," *above*.

State Archives

Judicial Archives/Massachusetts Archives, Boston
Norfolk County Court records include:
Divorce: original Supreme Judicial Court record books (to 1887) and Superior Court divorce dockets (after 1887).
Naturalization: Superior Court records; Dedham, Quincy, Stoughton and Wrentham District Court, 1885-1906; index.
Supreme Judicial Court (and predecessors): docket books/minute books, 1702-1797, originals and microfilm, including cases from Norfolk County, 1794-1796.
Contact Head of Archives, Supreme Judicial Court, for current information.

State Historical Society

Massachusetts Historical Society, Boston
Adams-Morse Papers, 1680-1856, bulk: 1730-1824. Manuscripts, Adams-Morse. Court records and papers of Henry Adams and son Elijah, who served as justices of the peace for Suffolk and Norfolk counties.

Cornelius Kollock papers, 1807-1840. Ms. N-631. Includes dockets of cases and trial records of Wrentham justice of the peace.

Other Repositories

Boston Athenaeum, Boston
Report of the Trial of John Wade, for Arson, Before the Supreme Judicial Court, Holden at Dedham, Oct. Term, 1835. Dedham: Mann, 1835. B1125 no. 3.

Dedham Historical Society, Dedham
Ames family. Papers, 1726-1880 (bulk 1758-1822). Dedham justice of the peace records and other legal papers, etc.
Mann, Horace. Papers, 1822-1894 (bulk 1822-1838). Records of law practice, cases in Norfolk County Court of Common Pleas, as judge advocate of 1st Div. Mass. Militia, etc.

Harvard Law School Library, Cambridge
Ellms, John B. Attorney's docket, 1842-1844. Re: cases in Canton. HLS MS 4313.
Report of the Case of Rev. Moses Thatcher, vs. Gen. Preston Pond, for slander, in charging him with committing the crime of adultery. Dedham: Dedham Patriot, 1838. Rare Trials Scarlet, HOLLIS #004097872.
Sacco-Vanzetti Case Records, 1920-1928. Manuscripts and microform. Sacco-Vanzetti trial, Dedham, Mass., Superior Court; Supreme Judicial Court. Online finding aid: *http://nrs.harvard.edu/urn-3:HLS.LIBR:law00030. See also* "Books" and "Microform," *below.*

New England Historic Genealogical Society, Boston
Appointment of guardianship to Amos Fuller, Needham, Mass., 1748 May 10. MSS C 1338.
Jury opinion for the case *Wilson v. Fisher*, 1759 February. MSS C 5131. Re: title dispute over land of First Church in Dedham.

Old Colony Historical Society, Taunton
Leland, S. Court and Land Records of Norfolk County, Mass., 1845-1847. Mss. Box 25, #10.

Portsmouth Athenaeum, Portsmouth, N.H.
Hill Family Papers, 1841-1963 (bulk 1890-1920). MS030. Arthur Dehon Hill, lawyer, Suffolk County district attorney, Harvard law professor. Papers include post-trial appeal of Sacco and Vanzetti case, Dedham.

Wellesley Historical Society, Wellesley Hills
Real estate transaction files: ca. 1890-1940; index.
Wills, inventories (small number): varied dates; no index.

Books

Probate Index, Norfolk County, Massachusetts 1793-1900. 2 vols. Dedham, Mass.: Transcript Press, 1910. *See also* "Microform," *below.*

The Sacco-Vanzetti case: Transcript of the Record of the Trial of Nicola Sacco and Bartolomeo Vanzetti in the Courts of Massachusetts and Subsequent Proceedings, 1920-7. New York: H. Holt & Co., 1928-1929.

Microform

Miscellaneous court records
Court records, 1764-1859. GSU, 1972. Supreme Judicial Court.
Court Records, 1793-1811; 1821-1858. GSU, 1972. Court of Common Pleas.
Court Records, 1812-1820. GSU, 1972. Circuit Court of Common Pleas.
Court Records, 1859. GSU, 1972. Superior Court.
Divorce Docket Books (1887-1918); Index to Divorce Records (1887-1923). GSU, 1987. Superior Court.
Record of Marriages in the County of Norfolk Beginning in May 1794. GSU, 1972. Court of General Sessions of the Peace, 1794-1795.
Sacco-Vanzetti case papers, 1920-1928. Bethesda, Md: LexisNexis Academic and Library Solutions. American Legal Manuscripts from the Harvard Law School Library.

Naturalization records
Naturalization Records and Index Cards, 1806-1958. GSU, 1987. Superior Court, Dedham and Quincy.

Probate court records
Probate Docket Books, and Record Books (1793-1916). GSU, 1970, 1987.
Probate Index, Norfolk County, Massachusetts, 1793-1900. 2 vols. Dedham, Mass.: Transcript Press, 1910. GSU, 1985.

Early American Imprints, Series II. Shaw-Shoemaker (1801-1819). New Canaan, Conn.: Readex Microprint, in cooperation with American Antiquarian Society, 1987-1992). Microfiche. Including:
A Correct and Concise Account of the Interesting Trial of Jason Fairbanks, for the Barbarous and Cruel Murder of Elizabeth Fales: at the Supreme Judicial Court, Holden in Dedham, in the County of Norfolk, State of Massachusetts, on Tuesday, August 4, 1801. Boston: s.n., 1801. Shaw & Shoemaker, 363.
A deed of horror trial of Jason Fairbanks, at the supreme judicial court, holden at Dedham, in the County of Norfolk...on August 4, 1801, for the murder of Elizabeth Fales, his sweetheart. Salem: W. Carlton, 1801?. Shaw & Shoemaker, 393.
Impartial account of the trial of Ebenezer Mason on an indictment for the murder of William Pitt Allen: At the Supreme Judicial Court, holden at Dedham...on Thursday the sixth day of August, 1802. Dedham: H. Mann, 1802. Shaw & Shoemaker, 2605.
Report of the trial of Jason Fairbanks, on an indictment for the murder of Elizabeth Fales at the Supreme Court, holden at Dedham...6th, and...7th Days of August, 1801. Boston: Russell & Cutler, 1801. Shaw & Shoemaker, 1228.
Report of the trial of John Boies for the murder of his wife, Jane Boies: at an adjourned term of the Supreme Judicial Court, holden at Dedham, for the county of Norfolk, June 2, 1829. Dedham: H. & W. H. Mann, 1829?. Shaw & Shoemaker, 40248.
Report of the trials of Stephen Murphy and John Doyle before the Supreme Judicial Court at Dedham, Oct. 23, 1817: for the rape of Rebecca Day, Jun., on the 10th Aug. 1817.... Boston: Chester Stebbins, 1817. Shaw & Shoemaker, 41958.

Digital/Electronic Sources

Internet
Early American Imprints *www.readex.com/scholarl/earlamim.html*
>Shaw-Shoemaker Digital Edition, Series II. Shaw-Shoemaker (1801-1819). Chester, Vt.: Readex/Newsbank, in cooperation with American Antiquarian Society, 2004. Available at academic libraries. *See also* "Microform," *above.*

Norfolk Registry of Deeds *www.norfolkdeeds.org*
>Online access to Land Court records re: Norfolk County, including indices 1985-date, scanned documents 1900-date, and complete, but unverified, owners index.

Plymouth County
Founded 1685, from Plymouth Colony

Courts

Plymouth Superior Court, Plymouth
Civil: original docket/record books, 1965-date; file papers, 1975-date. Criminal: original docket/record books, 1920-date; file papers, 1964-1980; some appeals. Juvenile: original appeals, 1948-1975. Divorce: file papers, after 1887, in offsite storage.
Note: Supreme Judicial Court Rule 1:11 requires permanent retention of docket books, divorce and naturalization records, and all other Plymouth Superior Court records before 1860. Other records more than ten to twenty years old may be destroyed after "sample" maintained: 1860-1889, 20% sample; 1890-1919, 10% sample; 1920-1969, 5% sample; from 1970, 2% sample. For more information about sampling criteria or access to records, contact court clerk or Head of Archives, Supreme Judicial Court.

District Court
See "Trial Court Record Retention Guidelines" for District Court in "Statewide or General Sources: Courts," *above.*
Brockton
Serves Abington, Bridgewater, Brockton, E. Bridgewater, W. Bridgewater and Whitman.
Hingham
Serves Hanover, Hingham, Hull, Norwell, Rockland and Scituate.
Plymouth
Serves Duxbury, Halifax, Hanson, Kingston, Marshfield, Pembroke, Plymouth and Plympton.
Wareham, W. Wareham
Serves Carver, Lakeville, Marion, Mattapoisett, Middleboro, Rochester and Wareham.

Plymouth Probate and Family Court, Plymouth and Brockton
Original probate records, 1881-1935 (2nd series, #1-99530) in offsite storage. More recent records at courthouse.

State Archives

Judicial Archives/Massachusetts Archives, Boston
Plymouth County court records at **Judicial Archives** include:
Court of Common Pleas: docket books and file papers, 1687-1859.

Court of General Sessions of the Peace: 1686-1827.

Divorce: original Supreme Judicial Court record books and microfilm, 1813-1889; original and microfilm of Superior Court index and dockets, 1888-1973.

Inquest files: 1813-1827, 1875-1925.

Naturalization: Brockton Superior Court (original, 1812-1990, and microfilm, 1906-1945); Plymouth Superior Court (original, 1812-1984, and microfilm, 1906-1945); Abington/Hingham, Brockton and Plymouth District Courts, 1885-1906. Indexes.

Probate: original file papers, 1685-1881 (vault 400); microfilm of record books, 1685-1881; docket books/index, 1881-1967.

Supreme Judicial Court (and predecessors): file papers of appeals to SJC, 1718-1774, with finding aid; docket books , 1702-1797, originals and microfilm, including cases from Plymouth County, 1719-1797 (gaps); record books, docket books and file papers, 1797-1940.

Contact Head of Archives, Supreme Judicial Court, for current information.

Massachusetts Archives also holds court-related collections, *e.g.*, transcripts of Plymouth Colony archives, 1629-1691, including legislative and court records, deeds and wills.

State Historical Society

Massachusetts Historical Society, Boston

Plymouth County (Mass.). Papers related to the boundary disputes with Suffolk County, Mass., 1640-1821. Ms. S-754. Petitions, court orders, etc.

Winslow family papers II. 1638-1760; bulk: 1638-1680. Ms. N-487. Papers from colonial governors Edward and Josiah Winslow of Plymouth Colony, including court documents.

Other Repositories

Hingham Historical Society, Hingham

Original records from 1640-date, with detailed finding aids for some materials. Includes deeds to houses and land in Hingham and surrounding towns, probate records and wills, and early town records.

Plymouth County Commissioner, Plymouth

Four original vols., 1633-1685, of wills, inventories, probate records, etc.; transcripts of same.

Books and Journals

Court Records—Abstracts, Transcripts and Indexes

Bowman, George E. "Plymouth Colony Wills and Inventories." *The Mayflower Descendant* 1-11. *See also* "Digital/Electronic Sources," *below.*

Greenlaw, Lucy Hall. *Plymouth County Marriages, 1692-1746: literally transcribed from the first volume of the records of the Inferior Court of Common Pleas, and from an unnumbered volume and volume one of the records of the Court of General Sessions of the Peace, Plymouth County, Massachusetts.* Cambridge, Mass.: By author, 1900. Reprinted from Vols. 1-2, *The Genealogical Advertiser.*

Konig, David Thomas. *Plymouth Court Records 1686-1859: The Court of Common Pleas and General Sessions of the Peace.* 16 vols. Wilmington, Del.: Michael Glazier, Inc., in association with the Pilgrim Society, 1978-1981. *See also* "Digital/Electronic Sources," *below.*

Merrick, Barbara L. "Plymouth County Probate Records and Files." *The Mayflower Descendant* 39:123-124; 40:33-36; 41:17-22, 185-188; 42:137-138; 43:209-212; 49:154-157. Continued from early vols. 1-34 (*see* Bowman, George E., *above,* and "Digital/Electronic Sources," *below)* to ca. 1703.

Pope, Charles Henry. *The Plymouth Scrap Book: The Oldest Original Documents Extant in Plymouth Archives Printed Verbatim, Some Reproduced, With a Review of Bradford's History of Plymouth Plantation.* Boston: C.E. Goodspeed, 1918.

Roberts, Gary Boyd. *Mayflower Source Records: Primary Data Concerning Southeastern Massachusetts, Cape Cod, and the Islands of Nantucket and Martha's Vineyard, from The New England Historical and Genealogical Register.* Baltimore, Md.: Genealogical Publishing Co., 1997. Includes probate records. *See also* "Digital/Electronic Sources," *below.*

Roser, Susan E. *Mayflower Deeds & Probates: From the Files of George Ernest Bowman at the Massachusetts Society of Mayflower Descendants.* Baltimore, Md.: Genealogical Publishing Co., 1994.

Sherman, Ruth Wilder, Robert M. Sherman, and Robert S. Wakefield. *An Index to Plymouth County, Massachusetts Warnings Out from the Plymouth Court Records, 1686-1859.* Plymouth: Gen. Society of Mayflower Descendants, 2003.

Shurtleff, Nathaniel B., and David Pulsifer, eds. *Records of the Colony of New Plymouth in New England.* 12 vols. Boston: Press of William White, 1855-1861; facsimile reprint, Bowie, Md.: Heritage Books, Inc., 1998-1999. Vol. 1, Court Orders 1633-1640; vol. 2, Court Orders 1641-1651; vol. 3, Court Orders 1651-1661; vol. 4, Court Orders 1661-1668; vol. 5, Court Orders 1668-1678; vol. 6, Court Orders 1678-1691; vol. 7, Judicial Acts 1636-1692; etc. *See also* "Microform," *below.*

Simmons, C. H. *Plymouth Colony Records.* Camden, Maine: Picton Press, 1996. Re: wills and inventories, 1633-1669.

Wood, Ralph V., Jr. *Plymouth County Massachusetts Probate Index 1686-1881.* Camden, Maine: Picton Press, 1988.

History

Kawashima, Yasuhide. *Igniting King Philip's War: The John Sassamon Murder Trial.* Lawrence, Kan.: Univ. Press of Kansas, 2001. 17th-century trial in Plymouth.

Nelson, William Edward. *Dispute and Conflict Resolution in Plymouth County, Massachusetts, 1725-1825.* Chapel Hill: Univ. of N. Carolina Press, 1981.

Research Guides and Bibliographies

Sherman, Ruth Wilder, and Robert S. Wakefield. *Plymouth Colony Probate Guide: Where to Find Wills and Related Data for 800 People of Plymouth Colony, 1620-1691.* Warwick, R.I.: Plymouth Colony Research Group, 1983.

Microform

Miscellaneous court records

Court Records, 1686-1817. GSU, 1972. Court of General Sessions of the Peace.

Court Records, 1702-1859. GSU, 1972. Court of Common Pleas.
Laws and Court Records, 1623-1676. GSU, 1972.
Notarial Records, 1741-1830. GSU, 1972.
Plymouth Colony Records, Court Orders, 1633-1690. GSU, 1968.
Plymouth County (Mass.) Record Books (Including Divorces), 1813-1950; and Divorce Index, 1918-1930. GSU, 2000. Supreme Judicial Court and Superior Court.
Plymouth County, Massachusetts, Divorce Records Index 1888-1973 and Divorce Records 1798-1812. GSU, 2000. Supreme Judicial Court and Superior Court.
Shurtleff, Nathaniel B., and David Pulsifer, eds. *Records of the Colony of New Plymouth in New England.* Multiple vols. Boston: Press of William White, 1855-61. GSU, 1969, 1972. Microfilm. GSU, 1984. Microfiche.

Naturalization records

Applications for Naturalization, v. 1-2, 1885-1906. GSU, 1988. District Court, Wareham.
Brockton (Massachusetts) Certificates Stub Index, 1907-1990. GSU, 1999. Superior Court.
Brockton (Massachusetts) Declaration Records, 1909-1945. GSU, 1999. Superior Court.
Brockton (Massachusetts) Petition Index and Declaration Index, 1906-1984. GSU, 1999. Superior Court.
Naturalization Card File, 1885-1906. GSU, 1987. Police Court, Brockton.
Naturalization Declarations and Petitions (1907-1945) for the Plymouth, Massachusetts Area. GSU, 1999. Superior Court.
Naturalization Declarations and Petitions (1910-1945) for the Brockton, Massachusetts Area. GSU, 1999. Superior Court.
Naturalization Index cards, Docket Book, and Papers, 1885-1906. GSU, 1988. District Court, Plymouth.
Naturalization Packets and Index, 1885-1906. GSU, 1987-1988. Police Court, Brockton.
Plymouth County (Massachusetts) Declarations of Intention Index, 1906-1984. GSU, 1999. Superior Court.
Plymouth County (Massachusetts) Petition and Records Index, 1906-1984. GSU, 1999. Superior Court.
Plymouth (Massachusetts) Declaration Records, 1906-1945. GSU, 1999. Superior Court.

Probate court records

Plymouth Colony Records, Scrap Book, 1636-1695. GSU, 1972. Includes probate and guardianship records.
Plymouth Colony records, Wills, 1633-1686, Vols. 1-4. GSU, 1968.
Probate Records, 1686-1903; With Index and Docket, 1685-1967. GSU, 1968.

Digital/Electronic Sources

CD-ROM

Family Tree Maker Genealogies of Mayflower families: 1500s-1800s. Novato, Cal.: Broderbund, 1997. Includes Gary Boyd Roberts. *Mayflower Source Records: Primary Data Concerning Southeastern Massachusetts, Cape Cod, and the Islands of Nantucket and Martha's Vineyard, from The New England Historical and Genealogical Register.* Baltimore, Md.: Genealogical Publishing Co., 1997. With probate records.

Konig, David Thomas. *Plymouth Court Records 1686-1859*. Boston: New England
     Historic Genealogical Society, 2002. Courts of Common Pleas and General
     Sessions of the Peace.
Mayflower Descendant Legacy. Wheat Ridge, Col.: Search & ReSearch Publishing
     Corp., 1997. Includes *The Mayflower Descendant*, quarterly magazine of
     Pilgrim genealogy and history published by the Massachusetts Society of
     Mayflower Descendants, Boston, Vols. 1-34 (1899-1937), with transcripts
     and abstracts of 17th-century wills and inventories.
Roser, Susan E. *Mayflower Vital Records, Deeds, and Wills, 1600s-1900s*. Novato,
     Cal.: Broderbund, 1997.

Internet
Plymouth Colony Archive Project *http://etext.lib.virginia.edu/users/deetz*
          http://etext.lib.virginia.edu/users/deetz/Plymouth/texts.html
          Selected excerpts from 17th-century Plymouth colony court records about
          servants, sexual misconduct, and Native Americans.
          http://etext.lib.virginia.edu/users/deetz/Plymouth/probates.html
          Selected probates, 1628-1687.
          http://etext.lib.virginia.edu/users/deetz/Plymouth/wills.html
          Selected wills, 1621-1704.
          http://etext.lib.virginia.edu/users/deetz/Plymouth/willsindex00.html
          Index to Plymouth Colony Wills and Inventories, 1670-1685.

Suffolk County
Founded 1643

Courts

Suffolk Superior Court, Boston
Records include original Superior Court divorce indexes and record books in Civil
Clerk's office; divorce file papers in offsite storage.
Note: Supreme Judicial Court Rule 1:11 requires permanent retention of docket
books, divorce and naturalization records, and all other Suffolk Superior Court records
before 1860. Other records more than ten to twenty years old may be destroyed after
"sample" maintained: 1860-1889, 20% sample; 1890-1919, 10% sample; 1920-1969,
5% sample; from 1970, 2% sample; equity cases 1892-1974, 30% sample. For more
information about sampling criteria or access to records, contact court clerk or Head
of Archives, Supreme Judicial Court.

Boston Municipal Court
Except as noted below, *see* "Trial Court Record Retention Guidelines" for District and
Municipal Court in "Statewide or General Sources: Courts," *above*.
Central, Boston
Criminal: original docket books and general criminal indexes, 1822-date; original file
papers, 1972-date (cases dated before 1972 are sampled); Criminal Div. fully auto-
mated since 1995.
Brighton
Civil: docket/record books, file papers, appeals, index; original, transcript, computer,
1980-date. Criminal: docket/record books, file papers, appeals, index; original and
computer, 1978-date. Juvenile: file papers; original, 1980-1996.

Charlestown
Dorchester
E. Boston
Roxbury
S. Boston
W. Roxbury, Jamaica Plain

Chelsea District Court
Serves Chelsea and Revere (also jury matters for Charlestown, E. Boston and Winthrop). Civil: docket/record books, file papers, appeals, index; original and computer, 1980-date. Criminal: docket/record books, file papers, appeals; original and computer; sample 2% after twenty years or more. Juvenile: docket/record books, file papers, appeals, index; original, 1980-1994.

Suffolk Probate and Family Court, Boston
Docket/record books, file papers, appeals, index; original, microfilm, computer, 1896-date. Older records stored offsite and retrieved only once per week; submit request in advance.

State Archives and Library

Judicial Archives/Massachusetts Archives, Boston
Suffolk County court records include:
County Court: record books, 1680-1692. *See* "Suffolk Files" Collection, *below*, for file papers.
Court of Common Pleas and Superior Court: docket/minute books, 1718-1859; record books, 1692-1860; file papers, 1731-1860.
Court of General Sessions of the Peace: docket/minute books, 1743-1773; record books, 1702-1809; file papers and index, 1707-1778.
Divorce records: "Suffolk Files" Collection, *below*. Supreme Judicial Court record books and file papers, original and microfilm, 1760-1804.
Greenough Collection: 1647-1828; original and microfilm. Misc. court records, with inventory and alphabetical index, many relating to "Suffolk Files." *See also* "Microform," *below*.
Municipal Court of Boston: docket/minute books, record books and file papers, 1800-1860.
Naturalization: Supreme Judicial Court, 1790-1859; Superior Court, 1804-1832, 1856-1888 (gaps); Boston Municipal Court, 1800-1859, with partial index vol. 1822-1957; Chelsea District Court, 1885-1906; Dorchester District Court, 1902-1906 (one docket vol., with papers #1-293). Indexes.
Probate: original and microfilm of file papers, 1643-1894; microfilm of record books, 1900-1916; index.
Suffolk County Miscellaneous and Mixed Files: Court of Common Pleas, Justice of the Peace, Supreme Judicial Court-Suffolk, Vice-Admiralty, 1731-1839.
"Suffolk Files" Collection: 1629-1799; originals and microfilm. File papers from many different courts and counties, on 1,639 microfilm reels, including several index systems (alphabetical, chronological, by subject and geography, etc.). *See also* "Microform," *below*.
Supreme Judicial Court (and predecessors): 1629-1950 including minute/docket books, 1702-1918; record books, 1686-1950; file papers, 1800-1885.
Contact Head of Archives, Supreme Judicial Court, for current information.

State Library of Massachusetts, Boston
Inventory of the estate of James Bowdoin, 1748 Mar. 29. Ms. 19.

State Historical Society

Massachusetts Historical Society, Boston

Adams, John. Notes on the Boston Massacre trials, 1770. In John Davis papers. Special collections.

Adams-Morse Papers, 1680-1856, bulk: 1730-1824. Court records and papers of Henry Adams and son Elijah, who served as justices of the peace for Suffolk and Norfolk counties.

Braman, Jason. Jason Braman account books, 1819-1843. Ms. N-2047 (Tall). Constable's records re: legal cases and court fees.

Chandler, Zachariah. Papers, 1638-1927; bulk: 1638-1783. Call # Z Chandler. Documents of Roxbury cordwainer, including court petitions in dispute with Roxbury town selectmen.

Cooke, Josiah Parsons. Papers, 1810-1830. Ms. N-1025. Re: Boston lawyer, including docket book for Court of Common Pleas, 1816-1819.

Dana Family Papers, 1654-1933; bulk: 1770-1931. Ms. N-1088; P-646, microfilm; 286 bound vols. Including papers of Francis Dana, Chief Justice to Mass. Supreme Court, and Richard Dana, U.S. Attorney for Mass. during Civil War.

Dorr family. Dorr family French spoliation claims, 1796-1889. Ms. N-1129. Re: Boston shipping merchant.

Moses Inglee v. Mrs. George Hayward papers, 1853-1858. Ms. N-1471. Depositions, etc., re: Boston lawsuit for breach of marriage contract.

Longley, Edmund. Papers, 1832-1834. Ms. S-606. Estate of Boston blacksmith.

McCleary family. Papers, 1735-1904. Call # McCleary family. Including legal papers of Boston lawyers who served as justices of the peace and city clerks; also court cases and decisions.

Papers related to the trial of John White Webster, 1850. Ms. N-168.

Plymouth County (Mass.). Papers related to the boundary disputes with Suffolk County, Mass., 1640-1821. Ms. S-754. Includes petitions, court orders, etc.

Sewall, Samuel. Papers, 1672-1790, bulk: 1672-1728. Ms. N-905. Records of magistrate, including Probate Court, 1715-1728.

Sullivan, John L., merchant. Judgment, 1803. Ms. N-49.48. Court of Common Pleas; *Thomas Russell v. Samuel Brown.*

Sumner, Increase. Papers, 1769-1798. Call # I. Sumner. Boston lawyer, Associate Justice of Mass. Supreme Judicial Court, Governor of Mass; papers include evidence taken and court dockets kept as justice, 1782-1794.

Ursuline Convent trial notes, 1834. Call #Ursuline. Trial records, apparently kept by Chief Justice of Mass. Supreme Judicial Court re: mob burning of Charlestown convent.

Withington family. Withington family papers, 1720-1821. Ms. S-214.Includes transcribed inventories of probated estates.

Also numerous published trial reports; search ABIGAIL online catalog (*www.masshist.org*), for keyword "trial" in title, *e.g.*:

The arraignment, tryal, and condemnation, of Capt. John Quelch...for sundry piracies, robberies, and murder, committed...on the coast of Brazil, &c.: who...were found guilty, at the Court-House in Boston, on the thirteenth of

June, 1704.... London: Ben. Bragg, 1705. Court of Admiralty, Boston. DA27-L; facsimile, Oversize AC4 P49.1 v.37.

Benton, Josiah Henry, *A Notable Libel Case; The Criminal Prosecution of Theodore Lyman, Jr., by Daniel Webster in the Supreme Judicial Court of Massachusetts, November Term, 1828.* Boston: C.E. Goodspeed, 1904. B Lyman.

Boston Slave Riot and Trial of Anthony Burns. Boston: Fetridge, 1854. E450.92.

The Charlestown Convent: Its Destruction by a Mob on the Night of August 11, 1834: With a History: Trials of the Rioters: Compiled from Authentic Sources. Boston: Patrick Donahoe, 1870. Book Box 870.

Report of a trial in the Supreme Judicial Court: holden at Boston, Dec. 16th and 17th, 1828, of Theodore Lyman, jr., for an alleged libel on Daniel Webster.... Boston: Putnam & Hunt, 1828. Henry Adams Library, Box 1828, B Lyman

Report of the Case of Geo. C. Hersey: Indicted for the Murder of Betsy Frances Tirrell Before the Supreme Judicial Court of Massachusettss... Boston: A. Williams, 1862. B Hersey.

Trial: Commonwealth vs. J.T. Buckingham: on an indictment for a libel; before the Municipal court of the city of Boston, December term, 1822. Boston: New-England Galaxy, 1822. B Quincy, Box 1822.

The Trial of the British soldiers...for the murder of Crispus Attucks...on March 5, 1770.... Boston: J. Fleming, 1770; Boston: Belcher & Armstrong, 1807. Box 1807. Re: Boston Massacre, 1770. *See also* "Microform" and "Digital/Electronic Sources," *below.*

The trial of Michael Powars for the murder of Timothy Kennedy: before the Supreme Judicial Court of Massachusetts, Boston, April 11, 1820. Boston: Thomas G. Bangs, 1820. Box 1820.

Trial for alleged embracery...; Commonwealth of Massachusetts vs. Ebenezer Clough; Before the Municipal court of Boston Judge Thacher; October term, 1833.... Boston: Beals, Homer & Co., 1833. B Thacher, Box 1833.

Other Repositories

American Antiquarian Society, Worcester

Lechford, Thomas. Notebook, 1638-1641. Mss. Dept., Folio vols. "L." Records of first lawyer in colony of Mass. Bay. *See also* "Books," *below.*

Massachusetts. Court of Common Pleas (Suffolk County). Record book, 1783-1790. Mss. Dept., Octavo vols. "M." By Clerk of Court Ezekiel Price.

American Textile History Museum, Manuscript Collection, Lowell

Stoddard & Lovering. Business records, 1827-1859. Includes court records re: debt collection of Boston textile importers during panic of 1837.

Boston Athenaeum, Boston

Massachusetts. Court of Common Pleas. Docket of continued actions. Jan. term, 1848.

Morris, Robert. Papers, 1820-1874. Mss L602. Legal documents of first African-American lawyer in Boston.

Price, Ezekiel. Business records, 1753-1800. Papers, 1753-1800. Mss. L50. Boston notary public, justice of the peace, clerk of Inferior Court of Common Pleas, etc.

Tyley, Samuel, et al. Notarial records: Boston, of Samuel Tyley, Ezekiel Goldthwait, and Ezekiel Price, 1748 Dec. 2-1754 March 11. Mss L3. Includes Court of Admiralty records.

Also numerous published trial reports in Rare Book collection; search online catalog, *www.bostonathenaeum.org,* for keyword "trial" and limit search to Rare Books. *See, e.g.*:

Braynard, Selden. *Copy of the Record of the Trial of Selden Braynard, in the Municipal Court of Boston, With Some Explanatory Remarks, to Correct Impressions Made by Inaccurate Reports in the Newspapers....* Boston: Beals, 1827. Adams, D30.

The Parkman murder: trial of Prof. John W. Webster, for the murder of Dr. George Parkman, November 23, 1849: Before the Supreme Judicial Court, in the City of Boston.... Boston: Daily Mail Office, 1850. B1445 no. 3.

Trial (Before the Municipal Court) of Charles L. Cook, Late Preacher of the Gospel of the Orthodox and Restorationist Denominations, for Receiving Stolen Goods. Boston: S.N. Dickinson, 1835. Tract B1441 no. 5.

Trial: Boston Gas Light Company versus William Gault, Containing the Arguments of Counsel, and the Charge of the Judge. Boston: Eastburn's Press, 1848. Rare Book LC KF228 .B67 1848.

Trial of Mrs. Kinney for the Alleged Murder of her Husband, George T. Kinney, by Poison. Before the Supreme Court of Massachusetts.... Boston: Times & Notion Office, 1840. Tract B1441 no. 8.

Boston Public Library, Boston

Adlow (Elijah) Papers. Rare Books and Manuscripts. More than 10,000 legal documents, ca. 1711-1904 (gaps), including Supreme Judicial Court records; partially cataloged. Discovered in basement of old Suffolk County Courthouse in 1954 by Chief Justice Elijah Adlow of Boston Municipal Court.

Boston Historical Society and Museum, Boston

Many court records in Manuscript Collection, *e.g.*:

Appeal, October 17, 1718. MS0119.

Appointment of Daniel Souther as guardian of Sarah Gould, April 13, 1785. MS0190/-02. Suffolk Probate Court.

Charge of slander, n.d. Charge against Isaac Waldron, Boston apothecary, for speaking against Simon Bradstreet, Esq. MS0119/-#DC1476. Mass. Court of Assistants.

Citizenship certificates: John Ulmar, 1813; James Nelson, umbrella maker, 1837. MS0190/-02. Suffolk Court of Common Pleas.

Court record of jurors for Superior and Inferior Court, Boston, 1732-1796. MS0107.

Decree in admiralty, October 25, 1686. MS0119/-#DC1463. Re: brigantine *Robert and John*, and Thomas Tyler, Master.

Indictment of Delia Atkins and Levina Vickum for theft, 1798. MS0119/-#DC1322. Indictment of John Ballentine, and others, for pulling down a wharf, 1699. MS0119/- #DC1323. Court of General Sessions of the Peace, Boston.

Also numerous published trial reports in Book Collection. Search Manuscript Collection under keyword "court," or Library Book Collection under keyword "trial." *See* online catalog, *www.bostonhistory.org.*

Harvard Business School, Baker Library, Boston
Selected receivership records from the Municipal Court, Boston, Mass., 1799-1844 (inclusive). Mss. 781 1825-1844. Including Oriental Bank, Boston, and Nahant Bank, Lynn, which went into receivership after panic of 1837.

New England Historic Genealogical Society, Boston
Answer to Richard Ways reasons of appeal from the judgment of the county court held at Boston the 30th of July 1667, tendered by Ephraim Hunt and John Bickness now defendants. MSS 614.

Blake, Samuel. "An account [of] what cases I tried when I was upon the jury at August court, 1753." MSS C 2739. Dorchester.

Cunningham, Nathaniel. Copy of reasons of appeal against Capt. Thomas Smart. MSS C 746. Superior Court of Judicature at Boston, 1720, re: sale or delivery of fish.

Massachusetts. Court of General Sessions of the Peace. MSS C 5142. Boston, July 1710, re: unlicensed liquor sales, etc.

Massachusetts. Inferior Court of Common Pleas (Suffolk County). Accounts of petit jurors, Boston, Mass., 1773 October 1774 April. MSS C 3208.

Otis, Harrison Gray. Motion, 1812 May, Boston, Mass., in suit brought by Susannah Cunningham, plaintiff. MSS C 2651. Motion by Otis, defendant in land title case, to take deposition of John Singleton Copley, residing in London.

[Petition, 1737 July 15], to the honourable his Majesty's Justices of the Court of General Sessions of the Peace within and for the County of Suffolk.... MSS. Re: Stephen Minot's "The George Tavern" on Boston neck.

Service of traverse jurors at the municipal court of the city of Boston, July, August, and September 1823. MSS C 1018. Jurors' names, number of days served, and compensation, certified by Peter O. Thacher, judge.

[Testimony concerning the burning of John Creek's house in Boston, Mass., 1679]. MSS C 97. Handwritten by Edward Rawson.

Will of Samuel Burrell, 1796, Boston. MSS C 742.

Also numerous published trial reports in Rare Book collection; search online library catalog, *www.NewEnglandAncestors.org*, with word "trial" in title search, *e.g.*:

Trial of the Commonwealth, versus Origen Bacheler: for a Libel, on the Character of George B. Beals, Deceased, at the Municipal Court, *Boston, March Term, A.D., 1829....* Boston: John H. Belcher, 1829. KF223/B331.

Peabody-Essex Museum, Salem
Peleg W. Chandler papers. 1829-1908; bulk: 1852-1866. MH-55. Legal papers re: cases in Suffolk County Superior Court and U.S. District Court (Mass.), etc.

Portsmouth Athenaeum, Portsmouth, N.H.
Hill Family Papers, 1841-1963. MS030. Including papers re: Arthur Dehon Hill, Suffolk County district attorney (1908-1909).

University of Chicago, Chicago, Ill.
Quincy, Edmund. Memorandum of bond for Thomas White, Jr., of Braintree, Mass., for his appearance before the Court of General Sessions of Roxbury. Manuscript, 1721 Oct. 16. From Miscellaneous Manuscripts Collection.

University of Massachusetts, Amherst, W.E.B. Du Bois Library
"Suffolk Files" microfilm; *see* Suffolk *County (Mass.) court files, 1629-1797*, in "Microform," *below*.

Winthrop Public Library and Museum, Winthrop
Dawes, Thomas. Appointment, 1814 Mar. 28. Probate Court.
Holmes, Zacheus. Notice, 1862 May 26. Superior Court.
Tewksbury, Henry. Division of the estate of Joseph Belcher, 1817 Jan. 6. Probate Court.
Tewksbury, John. Papers, 1729-1740. Probate Court.

Books

Court Records—Abstracts, Transcripts and Indexes
Abstract and Index of the Records of the Inferiour Court of Pleas (Suffolk County Court) Held in Boston, 1680-1698. Boston: Historical Records Survey, WPA, 1940. *See also* "Microform," *below*.
The Acts and Resolves, Public and Private, of the Province of the Massachusetts Bay.... 21 vols. Boston: Wright & Potter, 1869-1922. Vol. 7 (Resolves, 1692-1702) and Vol. 8 (Resolves, 1703-1707) contain editorial notes of Abner C. Goodell, Jr., reprinting excerpts from court records, *e.g.*: *Turell v. Dyer*, and *Cooke v. Paige*, Court of Pleas and Sessions of the Peace for Suffolk, 1686 (7:508, 511); *Rex v. Chubb*, Superior Court of Judicature, Boston, 1697 (7:591-592); *Rex v. Ray*, Superior Court of Judicature, Boston, 1699 (7:690-691); *Adam v. Saffin*, Superior Court of Judicature, Boston, 1703 (8:269-271); *Cooper v. Stratton & Story*, Superior Court in Suffolk County, 1702-1703 (8:295-298).
Aspinwall, William. *A Volume Relating to the Early History of Boston Containing the Aspinwall Notarial Records from 1644 to 1651*. Boston: Municipal Printing Office, 1903. *See also* "Microform," *below*.
Catalogue of Records and Files in the Office of the Clerk of the Supreme Judicial Court for the County of Suffolk. Boston: A.C. Getchell, 1897.
Chamberlain, Mellen. *A Documentary History of Chelsea, 1624-1824....* 2 vols. Boston: Mass. Historical Society, 1908. Appendix includes court records re: controversies over will of Gov. Richard Bellingham.
Colonial Society of Massachusetts publications, including:
Vol. 3: *Transactions, 1895-1897*. Boston: 1900. Mass. cases from 17th and 18th centuries, including documents from Suffolk Court files. *See also* "Microform," *below*.
Vol. 4: Davis, Andrew M. *Papers Relating to the Land Bank of 1740*. Boston: 1910. Re: Suffolk court files. *See also* "Microform," *below*.
Vols. 29, 30: *Collections: Records of the Suffolk County Court, 1671-1680*. Boston: 1933. *See also* "Microform," *below*.
Hale, Edward Everett, Jr., et al., eds. *Notebook Kept by Thomas Lechford, Esq., Lawyer, in Boston, Massachusetts Bay, from June 27, 1638, to July 29, 1641*. Cambridge, Mass.: John Wilson & Son, Univ. Press, 1885.
Index to the Probate Records of the County of Suffolk, Massachusetts, from the Year 1636 to and Including the Year 1893. 3 vols. Boston: Rockwell and Churchill, City Printers, 1895. *See also* "Microform," *below*.

Index to the Probate Records of the County of Suffolk, Massachusetts, from the Year 1894 to and Including the Year 1909. 2 vols. Boston: Printing Dept., 1911-1913. *See also* "Microform," *below.*

Index to the Probate Records of the County of Suffolk, Massachusetts: from the Year 1910 to and Including the Year 1922. 2 vols. Boston: Printing Dept., 1927. *See also* "Microform," *below.*

Index to the Probate Records of the County of Suffolk, Massachusetts: from the Year 1923 to and Including the Year 1935. 3 vols. Boston: City of Boston Printing Dept., 1941.

Index to the Probate Records of the County of Suffolk, Massachusetts: from the Year 1936 to and Including the Year 1947. 3 vols. Boston: City of Boston Printing Dept., 1951.

Index to the Probate Records of the County of Suffolk, Massachusetts: from the Year 1948 to and Including the Year 1958. 2 vols. Boston: City of Boston Printing Dept., 1961.

Index to the Probate Records of the County of Suffolk, Massachusetts: from the Year 1959 to and Including the Year 1968. 2 vols. Boston: City of Boston Printing Dept., 1969.

Matthews, Nathan. *Commonwealth of Massachusetts: In the Court of Land Registration. Title No. 416. The East Boston Company, petition for registration. Brief for the petitioner, before the master, submitted January 18, 1904.* Boston: G. H. Ellis Co., 1904.

McGhan, Judith, and William B. Trask. *Suffolk County Wills: Abstracts of the Earliest Wills Upon Record in the County of Suffolk, Massachusetts: from the New England Historical and Genealogical Register.* Baltimore, Md.: Genealogical Publishing Co., 1984. *See also* "Microform," *below.*

Sanborn, Melinde Lutz. *Ages From Court Records 1636 to 1700: Volume I, Essex, Middlesex, and Suffolk Counties, Massachusetts.* Baltimore, Md.: Genealogical Publishing Co., 2003.

_____. *Miscellaneous Docket Index, Suffolk County, Massachusetts: Probate Records, 1639-1866.* Rockport, Maine: Picton Press, 1997.

Slafter, Edmund F. *John Checkley; or the Evolution of Religious Tolerance in Massachusetts Bay.* 2 vols. Boston: Prince Society, 1897, 2:1-50. Records from Checkley's libel trial and appeal, Court of General Sessions of the Peace and Supreme Court in Boston, 1724.

History

Silverman, Robert A. *Law and Urban Growth: Civil Litigation in the Boston Trial Courts, 1880-1900.* Princeton, N.J.: Princeton Univ. Press, 1981.

Stapp, Carol Buchalter. *Afro-Americans in Antebellum Boston: An Analysis of Probate Records.* New York: Garland, 1993.

Research Guides and Bibliographies

Menand, Catherine S. *A Guide to the Records of the Suffolk County Inferior Court of Common Pleas, in the Custody of the Social Law Library, Boston, Massachusetts.* Boston: Colonial Court Records Project, Social Law Library, 1981.

Noble, John. *Catalogue of Records and Files in the Office of the Clerk of the Supreme Judicial Court for the County of Suffolk.* Boston: A. C. Getchell, 1897.

Microform

Miscellaneous court records

Abstract and Index of the Records of the Inferiour Court of Pleas (Suffolk County Court) Held in Boston, 1680-1698. Boston: Historical Records Survey, WPA, 1940; GSU, 1970.

Aspinwall, William. *A Volume Relating to the Early History of Boston Containing the Aspinwall Notarial Records from 1644 to 1651*. Boston: Municipal Printing Office, 1903; GSU, 1987.

Catalogue of Records and Files in the Office of the Clerk of the Supreme Judicial Court for the County of Suffolk. 1890. GSU, 1972. Microfilm. Ann Arbor, Mich: Univ. Microfilms, 1989. Microfiche.

Connors, Madaline. *List of names compiled from old records*. GSU, 1973. Typescript compiled from files of Supreme Judicial Court and indexes from other courts.

Court Records, 1680-1692. GSU, 1973. County Court.

Court Records, 1686-1799. GSU, 1973. Superior Court of Judicature and Supreme Judicial Court.

Court Records, 1701-1855. GSU, 1972. Court of Common Pleas.

Court Records, 1702-1780. GSU, 1973. Court of General Sessions of the Peace.

Court Records, 1800-1804. GSU, 1973. Supreme Judicial Court.

Court Records and Account Books, 1718-1772. GSU, 1973. Court of Admiralty.

Davis, Andrew M. *Papers Relating to the Land Bank of 1740*. GSU, 1971. *See also* "Books and Journals," *above*.

Divorce Records, 1888-1915, Divorce Dockets, 1888-1916 and Index to Libellants, 1903-1910. GSU, 1988. Superior Court.

Dockets, 1790-1870. GSU, 1973. Supreme Judicial Court.

Greenough Collection of Old Court Records, 1647-1828. GSU, 1973. Misc. court records, with inventory and alphabetical index, many relating to *Suffolk County (Mass.) court files, 1629-1797, below*.

Index to Dockets, Equity and Probate, 1862-1870. GSU, 1973. Supreme Judicial Court.

Notarial Records of Samuel Cooper, 1795-1804. GSU, 1973. Re: marine loss or damages.

Partitions and Executions, 1694-1856. GSU, 1973. Superior Court of Judicature and Supreme Judicial Court.

Partitions and Executions, 1782-1910. GSU, 1988. Court of Common Pleas and Superior Court; also includes naturalization records of Supreme Judicial Court, 1803-1832.

Publications of the Colonial Society of Massachusetts. Transactions, Vol. 3. Boston: Colonial Society of Mass., 1900. GSU, 1971; FHL #844519 item 1. Mass. cases from 17th and 18th centuries, including documents from Suffolk Court files. *See also* "Books," *above*.

Records of the Suffolk County Court, 1671-1680. Collections, Colonial Society of Mass., Vols. 29, 30. Boston: Colonial Society of Mass., 1933. GSU, 1971.

Suffolk Co., Massachusetts Miscellaneous Papers (Arranged Chronologically) 1679-1808. GSU, 1973.

Suffolk County (Mass.) Court files, 1629-1797. GSU, 1972. 1,639 reels, re: many different courts and counties, with several index systems (alphabetical, chronological, by subject and geography, etc.).

Suffolk County, Massachusetts Court Files, (Misc. Transcripts and Records). GSU, 1973. 1637-1774.

Naturalization records

Naturalization Applications and Papers, 1885-1906, Suffolk County, Massachusetts. GSU, 1988. District Court, E. Boston.

Partitions and Executions, 1782-1910. GSU, 1988. Court of Common Pleas and Superior Court; also includes naturalization records of Supreme Judicial Court, 1803-1832.

Primary and Final Declarations of Intention and Naturalizations, 1864-1888 and Card Index 1856-1884. GSU, 1988. Superior Court.

Probate court records

Index to the Probate Records of the County of Suffolk, Massachusetts, from the Year 1636 to and Including the Year 1893. 3 vols. Boston: Rockwell & Churchill, City Printers, 1895; GSU, 1971.

Index to the Probate Records of the County of Suffolk, Massachusetts, from the Year 1894 to and Including the Year 1909. 2 vols. Boston: Printing Dept., 1911-1913; GSU, 1991.

Index to the Probate Records of the County of Suffolk, Massachusetts: from the Year 1910 to and Including the Year 1922. 2 vols. Boston: City of Boston Printing Dept., 1927; GSU, 1987.

Index to Dockets, Equity and Probate, 1862-1870. GSU, 1973. Supreme Judicial Court.

McGhan, Judith, and William B. Trask. *Suffolk County Wills: Abstracts of the Earliest Wills Upon Record in the County of Suffolk, Massachusetts: from the New England Historical and Genealogical Register.* Baltimore, Md.: Genealogical Publishing Co., 1984; GSU, 1987.

Probate Indices, Suffolk Co., Mass., 1636-1894. GSU, 1941. From manuscript in N.Y. Genealogical and Biographical Society.

Probate Record Books (1900-1916), and Probate Docket Books (1901-1916), Suffolk County, Massachusetts. GSU, 1987.

Probate Records, 1760-1870. GSU, 1973. Supreme Judicial Court.

Public Index of Matters Concerning Domestic Relations, 1972-1983. Boston: Register of Probate, 2000.

Public Index of Matters Concerning Domestic Relations, 1984-1992. Boston: Register of Probate, 2000.

Public Index of Matters Concerning Domestic Relations, 1993-1997. Boston: Register of Probate, 2000.

Public Index of Matters Concerning Probate, 1980-1997. 3 vols. Boston: Register of Probate, 2000.

Suffolk Co., Massachusetts Miscellaneous Papers (Arranged Chronologically) 1679-1808. GSU, 1973.

Suffolk County, Massachusetts, Probate and Deed Indexes, ca. 1640-1800. GSU, 1941. From typescript in N.Y. Genealogical and Biographical Society.

Suffolk County (Massachusetts) Probate Court Records, 1650-1850 (inclusive). Waltham, Mass.: Graphic Microfilm of New England, 19-?.

Suffolk County (Massachusetts) Probate Records, 1636-1899. GSU, 1969-1971.

Suffolk County Probate Court 10-year Index, 1969-1979. 3 vols. Boston: New England Historic Genealogical Society, 1995.

Unified Public Index, 2001-2003. Boston: Register of Probate, 2000.

Early American Imprints, Series I. Evans (1639-1800). New York: Readex Microprint, in cooperation with the American Antiquarian Society, 1985. Microfiche. Including:

The trial of William Wemms,...for the murder of Crispus Attucks..., on...the 5th of March, 1770, at the Superior Court of Judicature, Court of Assize, and general gaol delivery, held at Boston: the 27th day of November, 1770.... Boston: J. Fleming, 1770. Evans, 11683; *see also* related item, Evans, 11580.

The trials of five persons for piracy, felony and robbery...at a Court of Admiralty...held at the court-house in Boston, within His Majesty's province of the Massachusetts-Bay in New-England, on Tuesday the fourth day of October..., 1726. Boston: T. Fleet, for S. Gerrish, 1726. Evans, 2818.

The trials of eight persons indicted for piracy &c.:...At a justiciary Court of Admiralty assembled and held in Boston within His Majesty's province of the Massachusetts-Bay in New-England, on the 18th of October 1717.... Boston: B. Green, for John Edwards, 1718. Evans, 2003.

Early American Imprints, Series II. Shaw-Shoemaker (1801-1819). New Canaan, Conn.: Readex Microprint, in cooperation with the American Antiquarian Society, 1987-1992. Microfiche. Including:

A sketch of the proceedings and trial of William Hardy: on an indictment for the murder of an infant, November 27, 1806; before the Supreme Judicial Court, holden at Boston, ...in the year of Our Lord 1807.... Boston: Oliver & Munroe, 1807. Shaw & Shoemaker, 13599.

Report of the trial of Henry Phillips for the murder of Gaspard Dennegri: heard and determined in the Supreme Judicial Court of Massachusetts, at Boston, on the 9th & 10th Jan. 1817.... Boston: Russell, Cutler & Co., 1817. Shaw & Shoemaker, 41956. Another report of the trial: Boston: Thomas G. Bangs, 1817. Shaw & Shoemaker, 42356.

Trial of a scold the trial of Mrs. Elizabeth Bowlan, who was indicted for being a common barrator, and also a noisy, turbulent brawler and common scold: whose trial came on before the Municipal Court held at Boston, August term, 1813.... Boston: Nathaniel Coverly, 1813. Shaw & Shoemaker, 29966.

Trial of William M'Donnough on an indictment for the murder of his wife Elizabeth M'Donnough: before the Hon. Supreme Judicial Court of the Commonwealth of Massachusetts, at November term, holden at Boston, in the county of Suffolk, on the fourth Tuesday of November, 1817.... Boston: Thomas G. Bangs, 1817. Shaw & Shoemaker, 42328.

The Trial of the British soldiers...for the murder of Crispus Attucks...on March 5, 1770.... Boston: J. Fleming, 1770. Reprint, Boston: Belcher & Armstrong, 1807. Shaw & Shoemaker, 13739. Re: Boston Massacre, 1770.

Digital/Electronic Sources

Internet

AncestryandGenealogy.com *www.ancestryandgenealogy.com/freedataancforn.asp*
Sanborn, Melinde Lutz. *Lost Babes, Fornication Abstracts*. Ancestryand Genealogy.com, 2005. Free database, abstracting birth and marriage records from fornication cases in Suffolk County courts, 1633-1640, 1671-1691.

Early American Imprints
www.readex.com/scholarl/eai_digi.html

Evans Digital Edition, Series I. Evans (1639-1800). Chester, Vt.: Readex/Newsbank, in cooperation with American Antiquarian Society, 2003. *www.readex.com/scholarl/earlamim.html*

Shaw-Shoemaker Digital Edition, Series II. Shaw-Shoemaker (1801-1819). Chester, Vt.: Readex/Newsbank, in cooperation with American Antiquarian Society, 2004.

Available at academic libraries. *See also* "Microform," *above.*

Suffolk Registry of Deeds *www.suffolkdeeds.com*

Online search of Land Court records re: Suffolk County, 1983-date.

Worcester County
Founded 1731, from Middlesex and Suffolk Counties

Courts

Worcester Superior Court, Worcester
Civil and criminal: docket/record books, file papers; original, 1859-date. Equity: docket/record books, 1961-1974; some file papers from 1970s. Divorce: some file papers from 1887 in offsite storage.
Note: Supreme Judicial Court Rule 1:11 requires permanent retention of docket books, divorce and naturalization records, and all other Worcester Superior Court records before 1860. Other records more than ten to twenty years old may be destroyed after "sample" maintained: 1860-1889, 20% sample; 1890-1919, 10% sample; 1920-1969, 5% sample; from 1970, 2% sample. For more information about sampling criteria or access to records, contact court clerk or Head of Archives, Supreme Judicial Court.

District Court
Except as noted below, *see* "Trial Court Record Retention Guidelines" for District Court in "Statewide or General Sources: Courts," *above.*
Clinton
Serves Berlin, Bolton, Boylston, Clinton, Harvard, Lancaster, Sterling and W. Boylston.
Dudley
Serves Charlton, Dudley, Oxford, Southbridge, Sturbridge and Webster.
E. Brookfield
Serves Barre, Brookfield, E. Brookfield, Hardwick, Leicester, New Braintree, N. Brookfield, Oakham, Paxton, Rutland, Spencer, Warren and W. Brookfield. Civil, criminal and juvenile: docket/record books, file papers (original and computer), 1900-date; index, card and computer.
Fitchburg
Serves Fitchburg and Lunenburg.
Gardner
Serves Gardner, Hubbardston, Petersham and Westminster.
Leominster
Serves Holden, Leominster and Princeton.
Milford
Serves Hopedale, Mendon, Milford and Upton; also town of Bellingham in Norfolk County.

Uxbridge
Serves Blackstone, Douglas, Millville, Northbridge, Sutton and Uxbridge.
Westborough
Serves Grafton, Northborough, Shrewsbury, Southborough and Westborough.
Winchendon
Serves Ashburnham, Phillipston, Royalston, Templeton and Winchendon. Civil and criminal: docket/record books; original, 1904-date. Juvenile: some docket/record books (most transferred to Fitchburg Juvenile Court). Motor Vehicle: Docket/record books, mid-1960s.
Worcester
Serves Auburn, Millbury and Worcester. Civil: docket books, 1933-1985 (1865-1932 at storage); file papers, 1980-date. Criminal: docket books, 1940-1985 (1867-1939 at storage); file papers, 1980-date. Criminal and civil index: cards, 1978-1998, computer, 1999-date. Autopsy reports: 1979-1983 at storage, permanent records.

Worcester Probate and Family Court, Worcester
Probate and divorce: docket/record books, file papers, appeals; original, 1925-date (probate), 1950-date (divorce); microfilm, 1731-1881 (probate); computer, 1984-date (all); index, 1731-date. Records from 1925-date available at courthouse; earlier records in offsite storage.

State Archives

Judicial Archives/Massachusetts Archives, Boston
Worcester County court records include:
Court of Common Pleas: 1731-1859.
Court of General Sessions of the Peace: 1731-1827.
Divorce: original Supreme Judicial Court record books, and microfilm, 1797-1887; original Superior Court divorce dockets and index (from 1890), and microfilm, 1887-1936.
Naturalization: Superior Court, 1809-1990, microfilm, 1906-1945, and index vols., 1906-1978+; Webster/Southbridge, Fitchburg, Westborough/Grafton and Worcester Central District Courts, 1885-1906. Indexes.
Probate: microfilm of docket/record books, 1731-1915 (vol. 833); file papers in offsite storage.
Supreme Judicial Court (and predecessors): file papers of appeals, 1718-1774, with finding aid; docket books/minute books, 1702-1797, originals and microfilm, including cases from Worcester County, 1735-1787.
Contact Head of Archives, Supreme Judicial Court, for current information.

State Historical Society

Massachusetts Historical Society, Boston
Dudley Indians. Report, 1889. Report of Justices of Mass. Superior Court to legislature re: Indian land claim.

Other Repositories

American Antiquarian Society, Worcester
Adams, Benjamin. Judicial records, 1802-1830. Mss. Dept., Octavo vols. "A." Uxbridge Justice of the Peace.

Brigham, Elijah. Papers, 1754-1877. Mss. Dept., Mss. Boxes "B," Folio vols. "B." Records of Westborough judge and legislator, including cases as Justice of the Peace, 1791-1793, and in Court of Common Pleas, 1794-1815, etc.

Dana, John Adams. Docket books, 1850-1857. Mss. Dept., Folio vols. "D." Cases heard in Worcester by Dana as trial judge or Justice of the Peace.

Dike, Nicholas. Regimental orderly book, 1776-1777. Mss. Dept., Folio vols. "D." Includes entries as Westminster Justice of the Peace, 1778-1801.

Flagg, Samuel. Records, 1768-1813. Mss. Dept., Folio vols. "F." Vol. 2 contains case records as Worcester Justice of the Peace, 1794-1797.

Knox, Joseph. Papers, 1824-1841. Mss. Dept., Mss. Boxes "K." Legal papers of Hardwick, Mass. attorney re: cases of larceny, arson, disturbing church services, counterfeit bills, assault and battery, indebtedness, etc.

Leicester (Mass.). Records, 1706-1868. Mss. Dept., Octavo vols. "L," Misc. mss. Boxes "L." Includes court records.

Oxford (Mass.). Records, 1687-c. 1851; 1883. Mss. Dept., Misc. mss. Boxes "O," Oversize mss. Boxes "O." Writs, wills and legal documents.

Paine family. Papers, c. 1721-c. 1918. Mss. Dept., Octavo vols. "P," Folio vols. "P," Mss. boxes "P," Oversize mss. boxes "P." Legal records of Worcester family, including French spoliation claims, estate records (1793-1807), justice of the peace records (1798-1811), etc.

Read, Benjamin. Judicial records, 1786-1800. Mss. Dept., Octavo vols. "R." Mendon Justice of the Peace.

Shrewsbury (Mass.). Records, 1723-1877. Mss. Dept., Misc. mss. boxes "S." Court summonses, arrest warrants, papers re: lawsuits in Worcester Court of Common Pleas v. First Congregational Church in Shrewsbury (1834-1835), etc.

Bolton Historical Society, Bolton
100-200 legal documents (wills, estate inventories, deeds/mortgages), most from 18th and 19th centuries. Catalog and index in progress.

Fitchburg Historical Society, Fitchburg
City Records of Poor and Sick, 1800s-1917; deeds and wills, 1760-1880s.

New England Historic Genealogical Society, Boston
Holman, Winifred Lovering. Worcester County probate deeds of Joseph Richards and heirs, 1732-1768. MSS A 5476.

Westminster Historical Society, Westminster
Original court records (probate/family, juvenile, land), 1800s and later.

Books and Journals

Blake, Francis E. *Worcester County, Massachusetts, Warnings, 1737-1788.* Camden, Maine: Picton Press, 1992.

Harlow, George H. *Index to the Probate Records of the County of Worcester, Massachusetts, from July 12, 1731, to January 1, 1920: Series A and B.* 5 vols. Worcester: Oliver B. Wood, 1898-1920. *See also* "Microform" and "Digital/Electronic Sources," *below.*

Pizziferri, Shirley M. (Robinson), and Ruth Q. Wellner. "Worcester County Probate Records/Abstracts." *The Mayflower Descendant* 37:1-2, 173-176; 38:33-38,

165-168; 39:31-34, 157-160; 40:37-38, 155-158; 41:37-44, 175-178; 42:37-40, 133-136; 43:31-36, 175-182; 44:47-50, 175-180; 45:47-50, 165-170; 46:21-24, 145-146; 47:9-12, 105-108; 48:43-46, 149-156; 49:62-76; 50:154-164; 51:105-116; 52:73-79; 53:171-178; 54:13-26. Covers 1731-1746.

Rice, Franklin P. *Records of the Court of General Sessions of the Peace for the County of Worcester, Massachusetts, from 1731-1737*. Worcester: Worcester Society of Antiquity, 1882. *See also* "Microform," *below.*

Voultsos, Mary. *Greeks in Worcester, Massachusetts, 1890-1910*. Worcester: By author, 1991, 1992. Includes naturalization petitions, 1885-1939.

Microform

Miscellaneous court records

Court Records, 1784-1859. GSU, 1972. Court of Common Pleas.

Court Records, 1792-1805. GSU, 1971. Justice of the Peace, Winchendon.

Decision of the Supreme Judicial Court of Massachusetts: in a case relating to the sacramental furniture of a church in Brookfield: with the entire arguments of Hon. Samuel Hoar, Jun. for the plaintiff, and of Hon. Lewis Strong for the defendant. Ann Arbor, Mich: Univ. Microfilms, 1989. Originally published as *Decision of the Brookfield Case*. Boston: Peirce & Parker, 1832.

Justice Docket of 1827-1830, Showing Litigants, Office, Justice, Execution, etc. GSU, 1971. Barre.

Records of the Court of General Sessions of the Peace from the County of Worcester, Massachusetts, 1731-1862. GSU, 1971.

Records of the Inferior Court of Common Pleas for Worcester County, 1731-1784. GSU, 1971, 1972.

Rice, Franklin P. *Records of the Court of General Sessions of the Peace for the County of Worcester, Massachusetts, from 1731-1737*. Worcester: Worcester Society of Antiquity, 1882; GSU, 1971.

Vital records, 1787-1805. GSU, 1971. Justice of the Peace, Westminster; includes civil and criminal case records.

Worcester County, Massachusetts, Court Records (Including Divorces), 1797-1887. GSU, 2000. Supreme Judicial Court.

Worcester County, Massachusetts, Divorce Docket Books, 1891-1936. GSU, 2000. Superior Court.

Worcester County, Massachusetts, Divorce Records Index, 1887-1936. GSU, 2000. Superior Court.

Naturalization records

Naturalization Records (Worcester County): Declarations of Intention, 1909-1945. GSU, 1998.

Naturalization Records (Worcester County): Petitions Indexes (1885-1949) and Petitions (1906-1945). GSU, 1998.

Naturalization Records Index, 1943-1978; Declarations Index, 1943-1978. GSU, 1998.

Returns of Naturalization, Worcester County, 1916-1929. GSU, 1993. Superior Court.

Probate records

Harlow, George H. *Index to the Probate Records of the County of Worcester, Massachusetts, from July 12, 1731, to January 1, 1920: Series A and B*. 5 vols.

Worcester: Oliver B. Wood, 1898-1920; GSU, 1969. *See also* "Books," *above,* and "Digital/Electronic Sources," *below.*

Pease, Janet K. *Worcester County, Massachusetts probate abstracts, 1748-1751.* GSU, 1980. *See also* "Digital/Electronic Sources," *below.*

Probate Records 1731-1916, Index 1731-1881, 1731-1916. GSU, 1971, 2001.

Probate Records, 1798-1854. GSU, 1971. Supreme Judicial Court.

Digital/Electronic Sources

CD-ROM

Early Vital Records of Worcester County, Massachusetts, to about 1850. 2d ed. Wheat Ridge, Col.: Search & ReSearch, 2000. Includes Janet K. Pease. *Worcester County, Massachusetts Probate Abstracts, 1748-1751. See also* "Microform," *above.*

Internet

Ancestry.com *www.Ancestry.com*

> Flint, James, comp. *Worcester County, Massachusetts, Probate Index 1731-1881 Volume 1 & 2 A-Z.* Provo, Utah: Ancestry.com, 2000. Original data from *Index to the Probate Records of the County of Worcester, Massachusetts.* 5 vol. Worcester: Oliver B. Wood, 1898-1920. *See* "Books," and "Microform," *above.*

New England Historic Genealogical Society *www.NewEnglandAncestors.org*

> *Index to the Probate Records of the County of Worcester, Massachusetts.* Boston: NewEnglandAncestors.org, New England Historic Genealogical Society, 2004. From *Index to the Probate Records of the County of Worcester, Massachusetts.* 5 vols. Worcester: Oliver B. Wood, 1898-1920. *See* "Books," and "Microform," *above.*

Worcester Registry of Deeds (Northern District) *www.state.ma.us/nwrod*

> Online search of Land Court records re: Worcester County (Northern District), 1899-date.

Worcester Registry of Deeds (Worcester District) *www.worcesterdeeds.com*

> Online search of Land Court records re: Worcester County (Worcester District), 1951-date.

Fig. 9.1, Map of New Hampshire Counties. *National Atlas of the United States.* 2005.
http://nationalatlas.gov

CHAPTER 9

———— ◆·◆ ————

NEW HAMPSHIRE STATE COURTS

Court History Timeline

Early Colonial Courts

1630s   **Town Courts** operated in Dover, Portsmouth (Strawbery Banke) and Exeter. Massachusetts Bay had jurisdiction over Hampton from 1638.

1641   Dover and Portsmouth united with Massachusetts Bay. *See* Court History Timeline for Massachusetts, *Chapter 8.*

1643   Exeter submitted to Massachusetts jurisdiction. **County Court** was organized for **Norfolk County**, consisting of Dover, Portsmouth, Hampton, Exeter (New Hampshire), and Salisbury and Haverhill (Massachusetts). Norfolk County Court soon split, creating **separate court system for Dover and Portsmouth** (known variously as the "northern division," the County of Dover and Portsmouth, or Piscataqua County). A lower **Court of Associates** in Piscataqua County, composed of local judges called "assistants" or "commissioners," tried criminal and civil cases under £20 and resolved larger cases between sessions of County Court.

   Commissioners to End Small Causes were appointed for each town, with civil and criminal jurisdiction. They decided cases not exceeding 20 shillings (later increased to 40 shillings), performed marriages and took depositions.

1660   **County Court** met biannually in Norfolk County (Hampton in October and Salisbury in April), and annually in Piscataqua County (June, generally alternating between Dover and Portsmouth). Four to seven judges (local and from Massachusetts) presided at each session.

Provincial Courts

1679   Union with Massachusetts ended, and **New Hampshire became royal province**. **Quarter Court**, composed of President and Council, met three times per year (biannually by 1681) at Dover, Hampton or Portsmouth.

1682   Quarter Court was replaced by **Court of Pleas** (also called **Quarter Sessions**, for criminal cases). **Justices of the Peace** handled minor cases, issued arrest warrants, etc. **Court of Chancery** was established for "equity" cases.

1686   Courts reorganized under **Council of New England**, which temporarily governed both Massachusetts and New Hampshire. **Superior Court of Judicature** heard civil cases over £10. **Court of Pleas** resolved smaller civil cases, and **General Sessions of the Peace** handled crimes not punishable by loss of life or limb. **President and Council** in Boston served as Court of Appeals. **Justices of the Peace**, or any member of Council, decided petty matters.

1690-1691   Courts closed following "Glorious Revolution" of 1689. In 1691, during brief reunion with Massachusetts, **Justices of the Peace** held **Quarterly Courts**.

1692   New Hampshire provincial government was reestablished. **Justices of the Peace** continued local courts. In Portsmouth, **Quarter Court of Sessions** heard criminal cases; **Court of Common Pleas** handled civil cases under £20, except title to land; **Supreme Court of Judicature** heard appeals and tried larger cases; **High Court of Chancery** had general equity powers.

1697   Royal **Vice-Admiralty Court** regulated trade and navigation.

1699-1702   Courts reorganized, with court sessions in each county: Quarter Court of Sessions became **Court of General Sessions of the Peace**; Court of Common Pleas became **Inferior Court of Common Pleas**; Supreme Court of Judicature became **Superior Court of Judicature**. High Court of Chancery was abolished. **Justices of the Peace** continued to handle small local matters, but no longer tried jury cases.

State Courts

1789   Basic court structure continued into twentieth century, although some court names changed, as highlighted below. **Admiralty** jurisdiction was transferred to new **U.S. District Court**.

1794   Court of General Sessions of the Peace was abolished. **Inferior Court of Common Pleas** handled both civil and criminal trials.

1813   Inferior Court of Common Pleas merged into new circuit **Court of Common Pleas** (Eastern and Western circuits).

1852   **Police Courts** were established, with same jurisdiction as Justices of the Peace.

1855   Superior Court of Judicature became **Supreme Judicial Court**.

1859   Court of Common Pleas was abolished. Jurisdiction over civil and criminal trials was transferred to Supreme Judicial Court.

1876   Supreme Judicial Court became **Supreme Court**. Fire destroyed probate, deeds and vital records in Coos County.

1901   Courts reorganized, establishing **Superior Court** with jurisdiction over trials (at "trial terms") and **Supreme Court** to hear appeals (at "law terms").

1913-1915   **Municipal Courts** and **District Courts** were established. Municipal Courts eventually merged with District Courts.

New Hampshire Courts Today

Supreme Court

New Hampshire's Supreme Court hears direct appeals from the other state courts.

Superior Court

One Superior Court provides jury trials in each county (except Hillsborough, which has two Superior Court locations). Jurisdiction includes: civil claims of $1,500 or more, when either party requests jury; civil cases over $25,000; felonies; injunctive relief; and misdemeanor appeals from District Court. Both Superior Court and Family Court have jurisdiction over divorce, custody, support and domestic violence, and District Court hears some domestic violence cases.

District Court

District Court is a system of "community courts," located in thirty-six New Hampshire cities and towns. Cases involve families, juveniles, small claims, landlord/tenant matters, minor crimes, and civil cases in which the disputed amount does not exceed $25,000.

Probate Court

One Probate Court operates in each county, with jurisdiction over trusts, wills and estates, adoptions, termination of parental rights, name changes, guardianship, etc. (Some of these functions now are handled by Family Court.)

Family Court

Family Court became a permanent part of the judicial branch in July, 2005, after operating as a pilot program in Grafton and Rockingham Counties during the previous ten years. Projected start date for Family Court in other counties: Carroll, Coos and Sullivan Counties, 2006; Merrimack County, 2007. Cases include divorce, child custody, domestic violence, juvenile delinquency, adoption, guardianship of minors, etc.

Where to Find Court Records
See Appendix for complete contact information.

Statewide or General Sources

Courts

New Hampshire Supreme Court, Concord
Original case files and briefs, 1970-date.
See also N.H. Law Library and other sources, *below*.

District Court—Record Retention Guidelines
Civil and criminal: docket card retained permanently; most other records may be destroyed seven years after final judgment or conviction. Some courts retain records longer than the minimum time period; *see* "Courts" section for each county, *below.*

Other State Courts
See "Courts" section for each county, *below*.

State Archives and Law Library

New Hampshire Division of Archives and Records Management, Concord
Court records include:
> Case records, 1659-1696, V28; 1679-1772, V77-78, V61.
> Card index to case records, 1679-1772, Research Area.
> General Court records, from 1680.
> Probate: Provincial Period, file papers, 1630s-1772, V34-38; also microfilm and indexes. Misc. to 1908. V37.
> N.H. Supreme Court, docket books. V31.

Court-related manuscripts include:
Adultery; Death Penalty; General (Notaries and Justices of the Peace); Municipal
> Courts; U.S. Supreme Court. FC1.
Attorneys Bar Applications, 1903-1924. V43.
Bridges, Delores. Court Case v. Perkins Bass, 1962. DC005001, V74.
Colby, Joseph and Joseph, Jr. *Report of the case of State v. Joseph Colby, Jr.*, 1838;
> *David Hopson v. Joseph Colby, Jr.*, 1825; *Asa Gage v. Joseph Colby, Jr.*,
> 1817. DC005036, V46.
Maine Boundary Dispute Documents to U.S. Supreme Court, 2000. Bx656013 and
> 020134.
Putney, Henry M. Legal brief re: fitness to serve as railroad commissioner, 1909. E-1,
> E-32, V24.
Wyman, Louis C. Court cases, 1950s and 1970s. V73.

New Hampshire Law Library, Concord
N.H. Supreme Court case files and briefs, 1849-1970. 630 bound vols. of original documents (including evidence and transcripts from lower courts); no index.

Federal Archives and Records Center

U.S. National Archives and Records Administration (NARA), Northeast Region-Waltham, Mass. (Boston)
Naturalization: Dexigraph collection (negative photostats) of naturalization records from 301 federal and state courts in five New England states (Maine, Mass., N.H., R.I. and Vt.) 1790-1906. Index is available on microfilm, as *Index to New England Naturalization Petitions, 1791-1906; see* "Microform," *below. Note:* NARA-Waltham staff will search index and provide copies for a fee; need name, residence at time of application, and birth date.

State Historical Society

New Hampshire Historical Society, Concord
*The argument of the Hon. Levi Woodbury before the Hon. Messrs. Henry Hubbard,
    Leonard Wilcox, and Frederick Vose, as referees and arbitrators in the case
    of Isaac Hill against Cyrus Barton, September 29, 1844.* Concord: Farmer's
    Monthly Visitor, 1844. Library 920 B2931wo.
Doe, Charles. Papers, 1841-1890. Chief justice of N.H. Supreme Judicial Court; dock-
    ets, case notes, judicial opinions, etc.
Dudley, John. Family papers, 1728-1853. Probate records and papers re: Superior
    Court of Judicature.
Duncan, Laurence I. Legal papers. 1946-1972. Judge of Superior and Supreme Courts.
    File papers, opinions, briefs, etc.
Hale, Benjamin. Estate settlement papers. 1784.
Kenison, Frank R. Papers, 1941-1978. Chief Justice of N.H. Supreme Court. File
    papers, briefs, etc.
Leach, Edward, and Henry W. Stevens. Legal Papers. Case notes and court records re:
    clients from towns throughout N.H., 1800s.
Misc. N.H. papers, 1781-1865. Deposition, deed, will, etc.
Perley, Ira. Papers. 1817-1877. Re: law practice and cases of lawyer/legislator and
    judge for N.H. Superior Court of Judicature and Supreme Judicial Court.

Other Repositories

American Philosophical Society Library, Philadelphia, Penn.
New Hampshire. Admiralty Court, Proceedings, 1777, relating to the armed brigantine *McClary* vs. the brigantine *Susanna*. Mss. 973.3 N41. 1 vol.; also available on
microfilm, Film 1403.

Dartmouth College Library, Hanover
Chesley, Samuel. Legal papers. 1759-1760. Rauner Manuscript, 759355. Lawsuits
    involving Chesley.
DeGregory, Hugo. Papers, 1949-1966. Rauner Manuscript, MS-746. Lawsuits v. State
    of N.H.

Webster, Daniel. Numerous papers re: Dartmouth College case before N.H. Superior Court of Judicature and appeal to U.S. Supreme Court, 1817. (Search library catalog for subjects "Dartmouth College case" or "Webster, Daniel, 1782-1852-Manuscripts.")

Harvard Law School Library, Cambridge, Mass.
Justice of the Peace docketbook, 1791-1797. MSS HLS MS 4235. 2 vols. Cases in Mass. and N.H. Courts of Common Pleas.
Rindge, Isaac. Ledger book of a court clerk, 1768-1773. HLS MS 6030. Chief clerk of N.H. Court of Common Pleas.

Maine Historical Society, Portland, Maine
Report of the case of the trustees of Dartmouth College against William H. Woodward: argued and determined in the Superior Court of Judicature of the state of New-Hampshire, November 1817: and on error in the Supreme Court of the United States, February 1819 / by Timothy Farrar. Portsmouth, N.H.: John W. Foster; Boston: West, Richardson & Lord, 1819. Stacks 378 D225B-f.

New England Historic Genealogical Society, Boston, Mass.
Bouton, Nathaniel. A list of justices of Court of Sessions, Court of Quarter Sessions of the Peace, and Court of Pleas for province of N.H. from 1692 to 1699. Also a list of grand and petit jurors. MSS A 2323.
Bowman, Fred Q. "Murder Trial Gleanings: New Hampshire, 1822-35." MSS C 1820. Re: use of trial records in genealogy.

U.S. Citizenship and Immigration Services, U.S. Department of Homeland Security, Washington, D.C.
Naturalization certificate files ("C-Files"): Copies of naturalization records from state and federal courts after September 27, 1906, *e.g.*, Declaration of Intention, Petition for Naturalization, and Certificate of Naturalization.
1906-1956: Available on microfilm. Make Freedom of Information/Privacy Act (FOIA/PA) request to U.S. Citizenship and Immigration Services in Washington, D.C.
After 1956: Make FOIA/PA request to the district U.S. Citizenship and Immigration Services office that maintains the records, or office nearest your residence.
See Appendix: Contact Information-Archives and Other Repositories, Washington, D.C.

Vermont Historical Society, Barre, Vt.
Jonathan Dorr Bradley Papers. MS-52. Docket of N.H. Supreme Court, July 1858.

Books and Journals

Court Records—Abstracts, Transcripts and Indexes
Batchellor, Albert S., Henry H. Metcalf, and Otis G. Hammond, eds. *Probate Records of the Province of New Hampshire*. 9 vols. Concord: Rumford Printing, 1907-1941; Bowie, Md: Heritage Books, 1989-1990. *See also New Hampshire Provincial and State Papers*. Vols. 31-39, *below*, and "Microform" and "Digital/Electronic Sources," *below*.
Collections of the New Hampshire Historical Society. Concord, N.H., 1824-. Including "Province Records and Court Papers from 1680 to 1892," 8:1-303; and case of *Livius v. Gov. John Wentworth* (1772), 9:304-363.

Dow, George Francis, ed. *Records and Files of the Quarterly Courts of Essex County, Massachusetts*. 9 vols. Salem, Mass.: The Essex Institute, 1911-1975. Vols. 1-8 also on microfilm, and vols. 1-9 in Internet database (*see* "Microform" and "Digital/Electronic Sources," *below*). Vol. 1, 1636-1656; vol. 2, 1656-1662; vol. 3, 1662-1667; vol. 4, 1667-1671; vol. 5, 1672-1674; vol. 6, 1675-1678; vol. 7, 1678-1680; vol. 8, 1680-1683; vol. 9, 1683-1686. Includes records of Old Norfolk and Piscataqua Counties.

Hammond, Otis G., ed. *New Hampshire Court Records 1640-1692, Court Papers 1652-1668, State Papers Series Vol. 40*. Concord: State of N.H., 1943. *See also* "Microform," *below*.

Kenney-Knudsen, Milli S. *Hard Time in Concord, New Hampshire*. Bowie, Md.: Heritage Books, 2005. N.H. crimes, 1812-1883.

New Hampshire Genealogical Record. Dover, N.H.: Charles W. Tibbetts, 1904-1994. Some issues contain court records, *e.g.*, vol. 8, no. 1, "Minutes of Court of Quarter Sessions, 1683-1688."

New Hampshire Provincial and State Papers. 40 vols. Concord: George E. Jenks, 1867-1943. Vols. 31-39: Probate records. Vol. 40: Court records, 1640-1692, Court papers, 1652-1668. (Published separately; *see* Hammond, Otis G., *above*.) Other court records scattered in vols. throughout, *e.g.*, 1:578-582; 2:512-562; 12:718-720; 13:10; 18:639-642, 654-655, 707-709; 29:158, 301. *See also* "Microform" and "Digital/Electronic Sources," *below*.

Roberts, Richard P. *New Hampshire Name Changes, 1768-1923*. Bowie, Md: Heritage Books, 1996.

Wiltse, Charles M., and Harold D. Moser, eds. *The Papers of Daniel Webster*. 16 vols. Hanover, N.H.: Univ. Press of New England, 1974-1989. Ser. 2 includes legal papers from Webster's N.H. law practice.

History

Page, Elwin L. *Judicial Beginnings in New Hampshire 1640-1700*. Concord: N.H. Historical Society, 1959.

Law Library Resources

Case Reports: *See Chapter 17, and Appendix-Law Libraries and Publishers. See also* "Microform" and "Digital/Electronic Sources," *below*.

New Hampshire Supreme Court

"Nominative reports." Multiple vols. Court decisions, 1803-1816, *e.g., Decisions of the Superior and Supreme Courts of New Hampshire from 1802 to 1809, and from 1813 to 1816* [from the reports of] *Jeremiah Smith*. Boston: Little, Brown, 1879.

New Hampshire Reports. Multiple vols. Concord: Reporter, Supreme Court of N.H. Court decisions, 1816-date.

Atlantic Reporter. Multiple vols. Eagan, Minn.: West. Court decisions, 1886-date, enhanced with headnotes, key numbers and synopses.

West's New Hampshire Digest and *West's Atlantic Digest*. Multiple vols. Eagan, Minn.: West. Digests of N.H. state and federal court decisions, earliest to date, organized alphabetically by topic, with headnotes, key numbers, and multiple indexes.

Other Law Library Resources: *New Hampshire Practice Series*. 16 vols. Dayton, Ohio: Michie, 1984. Updated with pocket parts. Summary of selected N.H. law subjects, including historical background and case citations.

Research Guides

Towle, Laird C. *New Hampshire Genealogical Research Guide*. Bowie, Md.: Heritage Books, 1983. Includes details about each vol. of *New Hampshire Provincial and State Papers*.

Wallace, R. Stuart. "The State Papers: A Descriptive Guide." *Historical New Hampshire* 31 (Fall 1976): 119-128.

Microform

Colonial Court Records, 1638-1772 approx. GSU, 1975.

Court Minutes, 1695-1771. GSU, 1951. Court of General Quarter Sessions.

Court Minutes, 1696-1771. GSU, 1975. Inferior Court of Common Pleas.

Court Minutes, 1699-1771. GSU, 1975. Superior Court of Judicature.

Court Papers, 1659-1696. GSU, 1975.

Court Records, 1648-1681. GSU, 1971. Old Norfolk County, Mass. Including towns now in N.H.

Court Records, 1692-1771. GSU, 1975. Court of General Quarter Sessions, Inferior Court of Common Pleas and Superior Court of Judicature.

Court Records, 1699-1773. GSU, 1975. Superior Court of Judicature.

Court Records, 1714-1774. GSU, 1951. Court of Appeals.

Court Records, 1729-1770. GSU, 1975. Inferior Court of Common Pleas and Court of General Quarter Sessions.

Court Records, 1730-1770. GSU, 1975. Court of General Quarter Sessions and Inferior Court of Common Pleas.

Index to New England Naturalization Petitions, 1791-1906. U.S. National Archives and Records Admin., 1983. M1299. Alphabetical index of individuals naturalized, in state and federal courts of Maine, Mass., N.H., R.I. and Vt. (indicates court and certificate number).

Marsh, Robert E. *New Hampshire Name Changes: Taken from Section Records*. GSU, 1993. From N.H. court records, 1699-1899.

Miscellaneous Province and State Papers, 1641-ca. 1800. GSU, 1975.

New Hampshire Provincial and State Papers. 40 vols. Concord: George E. Jenks, 1687-1943. GSU, 1967, 1975, 1981, 1984. Microfilm, microfiche. Washington, D.C.: Library of Congress Photoduplication Service, 1974. Microfilm. Vols. 31-39, Probate records of the province of New Hampshire; vol. 40, Court records, 1640-1692, Court Papers 1652-1668.

N.H. Supreme Court reports, 1816-1925, and additional vols. annually. Microfiche. Kaneohe, Hawaii: Law Library Microform Consortium.

Province Deeds and Probate Records from 1623-1772. GSU, 1975. Various courts.

Pulsifer, David. *Records of the County of Norfolk, in the Colony of Massachusetts.* GSU, 1971. Copied (in 1852) from original records, 1647-1714. Old Norfolk County deeds, wills, etc., including towns now in N.H.

Smith's Reports (Superior and Supreme Courts), 1796-1816. Microfiche. Kaneohe, Hawaii: Law Library Microform Consortium.

Suffolk County (Mass.) Court Files, 1629-1797. GSU, 1972. 1,639 reels re: many different courts and counties, including N.H., with several index systems (alphabetical, chronological, by subject and geography, etc.).

Digital/Electronic Sources

CD-ROM

Atlantic Reporter. Eagan, Minn.: West. Includes N.H. Supreme Court opinions, 1945-date.

New Hampshire Provincial Probate Records, 1635-1771. Heritage Books Archives. Bowie, Md.: Heritage Books, 1999.

New Hampshire Reporter and West's New Hampshire Statutes. Eagan, Minn.: West. Cases reported in *Atlantic Reporter*, 1945-date.

New Hampshire Provincial and State Papers. 40 vols. Concord: George E. Jenks, 1867-1943; Concord: N.H. Div. of Archives and Records Management, 2004. 2-CD set, with index.

Internet

LexisNexis *www.lexis.com*
> N.H. Supreme Court, 1816-date. Subscription service or fees; also available at law libraries and other repositories.

LexisOne *www.lexisone.com*
> N.H. Supreme Court, most recent five years; free.

Loislaw *www.loislaw.com*
> N.H. Supreme Court, 1874-date. Subscription service.

N.H. Judiciary *www.nh.gov/judiciary*
> General information about N.H. courts.

N.H. Supreme Court *www.courts.state.nh.us/supreme/opinions*
> N.H. Supreme Court, 1995-date.

N.H. Div. of Archives and Records Management
> *www.sos.nh.gov/archives/guide.html*
> Guide to Archives
> *www.sos.nh.gov/archives/Index%20to%20NH%20State%20Papers.pdf*
> Consolidated index to *Provincial and State Papers of New Hampshire.*

Salem Witch Trials Documentary Archive and Transcription Project
> *http://etext.virginia.edu/salem/witchcraft/Essex*
> Dow, George Francis, ed. *Records and Files of the Quarterly Courts of Essex County, Massachusetts.* 9 vols. Salem, Mass.: The Essex Institute, 1911-1975. Includes records of Old Norfolk and Piscataqua Counties.

VersusLaw *www.versuslaw.com*
> N.H. Supreme Court, from 1930. Subscription service.

Westlaw *www.westlaw.com*
> N.H. Supreme Court, 1816-date. Subscription service or fees; also available at law libraries and other repositories. Westlaw CourtEXPRESS offers case research and document retrieval from U.S. courts.

Belknap County

Founded 1840, from Strafford County

Courts

Belknap County Superior Court, Laconia

Laconia District Court
See "District Court—Record Retention Guidelines" in "Statewide or General Sources: Courts," *above*.

Belknap County Probate Court, Laconia

State Archives

New Hampshire Division of Archives and Records Management, Concord
Clerk of Court [Edwin P. Thompson] Letterbook, 1898-1909. 1 vol. V31.
Laconia Municipal Court. V34.
Naturalizations: declarations, 1906-1914, 1944-date (still in boxes); correspondence
        of Clerk of Court with U.S. Dept. of Labor, 1910-1926. V4/V31; files 1842-
        1975 (Boxes 2602-2604, 2908, index in Binder 15); computer index.
Superior Court, etc., 1841-1899 (unprocessed).

Other Repositories

Laconia Historical and Museum Society, Laconia
Large collection of original court records, including deeds, wills, probate inventories,
etc., re: Laconia area, 1790-1930; mostly unprocessed.

New England Historic Genealogical Society, Boston, Mass.
Depositions of Samuel Connor and Nathaniel Thing, 1774 September 17. MSS C
2642. Re: running bounds of Gilmanton, N.H. in 1731.

University of New Hampshire Library, Durham
Harper, John Adams. Account book, 1810-1855. MS 11. Records of Meredith Bridge
(Laconia) lawyer, including Circuit Court of Common Pleas docket, 1813-1816.

Microform

Miscellaneous court records
Court Judgements [sic]*, 1841-1917; Indexes to Judgements* [sic]*, 1841-1921.* GSU,
1976, 1990. Court of Common Pleas, Supreme Judicial Court, Circuit Court, Supreme
Court and Superior Court.

Naturalization records
Belknap County, New Hampshire Naturalization Papers, 1842-1906. GSU, 1976.
        Supreme Judicial Court, Court of Common Pleas, Supreme Court, Circuit
        Court, Superior Court and Police Court of Laconia.
Declarations of Intentions, v. 1-9, 1906-1929. GSU, 1990. Superior Court.
Naturalization Docket of Notices, 1870-1904. GSU, 1990.
Naturalization Petitions and Records, 1907-1930. GSU, 1990. Superior Court.

Probate court records
Probate Records, 1841-1973; Indexes to Probate Records, 1841-1925. GSU, 1951,
1990.

Carroll County
Founded 1840, from Grafton and Strafford Counties

Courts

Carroll County Superior Court, Ossipee
Civil (including equity and domestic relations) and criminal: original file papers, early 19th-century-date; no index. Searches for records prior to 1950 temporarily suspended due to staffing shortage.

District Court
Northern Carroll County, N. Conway
Civil and criminal: original docket/record books, 1950-date; original file papers (civil destroyed after twenty years, criminal destroyed after seven years unless warrant issued); computer, 1993-date; no index. Make requests in writing; fees.
Southern Carroll County, Ossipee
Civil and criminal: dockets (books before 1980, cards 1980-1993, computer 1993-date); original file papers and appeals; index cards. Written request or in-person inspection.

Carroll County Probate Court, Ossipee
Docket/record books, file papers, appeals, index; original, microfilm, computer; 1840-date.

Other Repositories

Syracuse University Library, Syracuse, N.Y.
Carroll County (N.H.). Supreme Court. Law Library, KFN1745.D6 1877. (Restricted access). Includes State Docket, Oct. Term 1875; Equity Docket, Oct. Term 1874; and Civil Docket, Oct. Term 1869.

Microform

Miscellaneous court records
Court Judgements [sic], *1861-1916*. GSU, 1976, 1990. Supreme Judicial Court, Circuit Court, Superior Court.

Naturalization records
Certificates of Naturalization, 1907-1928. GSU, 1990. Superior Court.
Declarations of Intentions, no. 1-250, 1907-1942. GSU, 1990. Superior Court.
Naturalization Petitions and Records, no. 1-157, 1907-1937. GSU, 1990. Superior Court.
Naturalization Records, Minors, v. 1, no. 1-97, 1876-1903. GSU, 1990. Supreme Court and Superior Court.
Naturalization Records, v. 2, 1871-1905. GSU, 1990. Supreme Court and Superior Court.

Probate court records
Probate Papers, 1840-1936; Index to Probate Papers, 1840-1990. GSU, 1990-1991.
Probate Records, 1840-1870. GSU, 1951.
Unfiled Probate Papers, 1840-1936. GSU, 1991.

Cheshire County
Founded 1769/1771

Courts

Cheshire County Superior Court, Keene
Civil, criminal and family: docket/record books, file papers; original, and some transcripts of court proceedings in last ten years, 1787-date; index, ca. 1940-date. Naturalization: 1870-1920. Request by party name or docket number and year of filing. *See also* "State Archives," *below*, re: newly-discovered court records.

District Court
See "District Court—Record Retention Guidelines" in "Statewide or General Sources: Courts," *above*.
Jaffrey-Peterborough, Jaffrey
Keene

Cheshire County Probate Court, Keene
Probate and equity: docket/record books, file papers, appeals. Original records, 1900-date; computer, 1993-date; card index.

State Archives

New Hampshire Division of Archives and Records Management, Concord
Municipal Courts: Hinsdale, 1978-1992+, and Marlborough, 1928.
Probate: 1771-1899. Index cards in Research Area list Box #s.
Other Cheshire County records (recently discovered at courthouse in Keene) will be transferred to state archives in 2006 or 2007, including: docket books and file papers (writs, executions and affidavits, etc.), ca. 1771-1889; justice of the peace record books, ca. 1772-1859; Revolutionary War pension applications, 1820s-1830s; oaths of county officers.

Other Repositories

Boston Athenaeum, Boston, Mass.
The Dublin (N.H.) suit: *Edward F. Abbot, et al v. William F. Bridge, et al*, 1856-1860. Mss. L457. Records of N.H. Supreme Judicial Court case by newly-formed church congregation against established church society and town of Dublin.

Chesterfield Historical Society, Chesterfield
Petitions to Cheshire County Superior Court re: laying out roads, and deposition re: accident, late 1800s.

Dartmouth College Library, Hanover
Bellows, Josiah G. Legal papers, 1870-1882. Rauner Manuscript, MS-668. Walpole attorney and probate judge in Cheshire County.
Vose, Frederick. Legal papers, 1825-1863. Rauner Manuscript, ML-67. Attorney and judge in Walpole and Cheshire County.

Historical Society of Cheshire County, Keene
Justice of the Peace records, 1752-1987. RG40.

Massachusetts Historical Society, Boston, Mass.
Cheshire County (N.H.). Superior Court. Docket, 1804.

New England Historic Genealogical Society, Boston, Mass.
Index to probate records, 1769-1800, Cheshire County, NH. Anonymous typescript.
MSS C 4194.

Microform

Miscellaneous court records
Court Records, 1771-1859. GSU, 1976. Court of Common Pleas.
Court Records, 1772-1855. GSU, 1976. Superior Court of Judicature and Supreme Judicial Court.
Records, 1813-1902. GSU, 1976. Supreme Judicial Court and Superior Court of Judicature.
Road and Session Records, 1772-1901. GSU, 1976.

Naturalization records
Naturalization Records and Petitions, 1860-1945. GSU, 1976. Supreme Judicial, Circuit Court and Superior Court.

Probate court records
Administrations, 1823-1869. GSU, 1951.
Dowers Claims, Settlement of Estates of Widows, 1814-1886. GSU, 1951.
Guardianship Papers, 1824-1853. GSU, 1951.
Index to Probate Records, 1769-1800, Cheshire County, New Hampshire. GSU, 1951.
Index to Probate Records in New Hampshire: Counties of Rockingham, Cheshire, Strafford, Grafton, Hillsboro. GSU, 1973. Re: 1769-1800.
Probate Estate Files, 1769-1885. GSU, 2001-2002.
Wills, 1799-1869. GSU, 1951.
Wills, Inventories, Claims, Accounts 1771-1815. GSU, 1951.

Coos County
Founded 1803, from Grafton County
In 1876, courthouse fire destroyed probate, deeds and vital records.

Courts

Coos County Superior Court, Lancaster
Civil/equity and criminal: original docket/record books, file papers, index; 1887-date.
Naturalization: records and index from 1887.

District Court
Berlin
Civil: docket/record books, file papers; original, 1997-date. Criminal: original docket/record books, file papers; docket cards, 1983-1992; computer, 1992-date.

Colebrook
Civil and criminal: docket/record books, file papers; original, 1993-date.
Gorham
See "District Court—Record Retention Guidelines" in "Statewide or General Sources: Courts," *above*.
Lancaster
Civil and criminal: docket books before 1980, docket cards, 1980-1992; computer dockets, 1992-date.

Coos County Probate Court, Lancaster
Docket/record books, file papers, appeals; original, 1887-2000; computer, 2000-date.

Microform

Court Judgements [sic], *1886-1916*. GSU, 1976, 1992. Supreme Court and Superior Court.
Naturalization Records, 1888-1900; Index to Naturalization, 1886-1930. GSU, 1976. Supreme Court.
Probate Packets, 1885-1931; Probate Index, 1885-1992. GSU, 1992.

Grafton County
Founded 1769/1771

Courts

Grafton County Superior Court, N. Haverhill
Civil, criminal, domestic and equity: docket books and original file papers, 1900-1910; case index cards, docket cards and original file papers, 1910-1995; computer database, 1995-date.

District Court
Haverhill, N. Haverhill
Civil (including writs, small claims, landlord/tenant): original docket/record books, file papers and appeals (retained ten to twenty years, depending upon type of case, then files destroyed); all indexes retained, 1979-date. Criminal: original docket/record books, file papers retained ten years.
Lebanon
See "District Court—Record Retention Guidelines" in "Statewide or General Sources: Courts," *above*.
Littleton
Civil and small claims: docket/record books, file papers, appeals, index; original, 1992-date; computer, 1991-date. Criminal: docket/record books, case file, appeals, index; original, 1983-date; computer, 1991-date. Landlord/tenant: appeals; original, 1988-date; computer, 1991-date; no index.
Plymouth
Civil and criminal: computer dockets, 1990-date; original record books, docket cards, file papers, seven years (landlord/tenant, two years).

Grafton County Probate Court, N. Haverhill
Index books, 1773-1899; original file papers, 1900-date; computer case listings, 1994-date; card index.

Grafton County Family Court, Lebanon, Littleton, N. Haverhill, and Plymouth
Family Court established as pilot program in 1996, for divorce, child custody, domestic violence, juvenile delinquency, adoption, guardianship of minors, etc.

State Archives

New Hampshire Division of Archives and Records Management, Concord
Dartmouth College, *Trustees of Dartmouth College vs. Woodward*, Feb 8, 1817 #75, Bx11294, B07-04. Verdict, Nov. Term 1817, #29.
Haverhill Municipal Court, 1830.
Naturalization: 1773-1906, A-Z, BxA98011-12; Declarations, 1906-1914, 1915-1943, 1944-1965, 1966-1990, BxA98013-14, BXA98021-22; Petitions, 1906, BxA98023-24; index.
Probate: 1775-1899; computer database.
Superior Court, etc.: 1773-1899; computer index.

State Historical Society

New Hampshire Historical Society, Concord
Blair, Henry W. Papers, 1794-1904. Records of court cases and law practice of Plymouth, N.H. lawyer and legislator.

Other Repositories

Dartmouth College Library, Hanover
Court of Common Pleas (Grafton County).
    Docket, 1839. Rauner Manuscript Codex, 000285.
    Docket, 1843. Rauner Manuscript Codex, 002081.
    Records, 1816-1853. Rauner Manuscript, MS 584.
Court of Common Pleas and Superior Court (Grafton County). Court docket, 1831-1835.
Dartmouth College, complainant. Papers in the matter of *Dartmouth College v. Currier*, 1884-1912. N.H. Supreme Court lawsuit.
New Hampshire. Court of Common Pleas. Writs of execution, 1822-1833. Rauner Manuscript, 822358. Court at Haverhill and Plymouth, N.H.

New England Historic Genealogical Society, Boston, Mass.
Index to probate records, 1769-1800, Grafton County, N.H. Anonymous typescript. MSS C 4177.

Microform

Miscellaneous court records
Civil Judgement [sic] *Records, 1859-1964*. GSU, 1991. Supreme Judicial Court, Circuit Court, Supreme Court and Superior Court.
Court Docket, January-May-September 1936. GSU, 1991. Superior Court.

Court Dockets, 1774-1775, 1782-1913. GSU, 1991. Court of Common Pleas, Superior Court of Judicature, Supreme Judicial Court, Circuit Court, Supreme Court and Superior Court.

Court Judgments, 1840-1867, 1876-1881. GSU, 1991. Superior Court of Judicature, Supreme Judicial Court, and Supreme Court; includes divorce cases.

Court Records, 1773-1774, 1782-1820, 1840-1859. GSU, 1991. Court of Common Pleas.

Court Records, 1774-1821, 1836-1837; Court Dockets, 1774-1819, 1833-1851. GSU, 1991. Superior Court of Judicature and Supreme Judicial Court.

Equity Records, 1881-1918. GSU, 1991. Supreme Court and Superior Court; includes divorce cases.

Record of Sheriffs Deputations and Dismissals, 1817-1850. GSU, 1991. Court of Common Pleas.

Sessions Records, 1840-1920. GSU, 1991. Court of Common Pleas, Supreme Judicial Court, Circuit Court, Supreme Court and Superior Court.

Naturalization records

Certificates of Naturalization, no. 475621-475630, 1914-1915. GSU, 1991. Superior Court.

Declarations of Intention, 1906-1929. GSU, 1991. Superior Court.

Naturalization Dockets, 1868-1906. GSU, 1991. Supreme Judicial Court, Supreme Court and Superior Court.

Naturalization Index, 1773-1906, Grafton County, New Hampshire. GSU, 2001. Supreme Court, Supreme Judicial Court and Superior Court.

Naturalization Papers, 1840-1906. GSU, 1991. Court of Common Pleas, Supreme Judicial Court, Circuit Court, Supreme Court, and Superior Court; includes declarations of intention and petitions for naturalization.

Petition and Record, 1907-1921. GSU, 1991. Superior Court.

Petitions for Naturalization, 1839-1862. GSU, 1976. Court of Common Pleas, Superior Court of Judicature and Supreme Judicial Court.

Probate court records

Index to Probate Records, 1769-1800, Grafton County, New Hampshire. GSU, 1951.

Index to Probate Records in New Hampshire: Counties of Rockingham, Cheshire, Strafford, Grafton, Hillsboro. GSU, 1973. Re: 1769-1800.

Probate Records, 1773-1933; Indexes to Probate Records, 1773-1950. GSU, 1951, 1991.

Hillsborough County
Founded 1769/1771

Courts

Superior Court
Hillsborough County Superior Court North, Manchester
Civil and criminal: file papers and index; microfilm, 1901-1971; computer, 1980-1985; original, 1986-date. Marital: file papers and index; microfilm, 1901-1958 and 1971; original 1980-date. Equity: file papers and index; microfilm, 1901-1958 and 1971; computer, 1980-1985; original, 1980-date.

Hillsborough County Superior Court South, Nashua
Civil, criminal, equity and domestic relations: original file papers and appeals, 1992-date; computer index.

District Court
Except as noted below, *see* "District Court—Record Retention Guidelines" in "Statewide or General Sources: Courts," *above*.
Goffstown
Hillsborough
Civil: docket/record books, file papers; original and computer, 1992-date. Criminal: docket/record books (original, 1971-date); file papers (original, 1983-date, and computer, 1992-date), index.
Manchester
Merrimack
Milford
Nashua

Hillsborough County Probate Court, Nashua
Docket/record books, file papers, index; original, 1771-date.

State Archives

New Hampshire Division of Archives and Records Management, Concord
Justice of the Peace: Joshua Atherton, 1792-1806; Wyseman Clagett, 1805-1812. V37.
Naturalization: Manchester Police Court: 1851-1855. Bx057051, 057054; index in Hillsborough County Binder #20. Other: 1859-1871, 1890-1900, V44 and Bx607053; docket books, 1889-1900, V31; intentions and petitions/orders, Bins 840-842; indexes 1820-1997, Research Area Binder #20 and card index.
Probate: published index, 1771-1884; *see* "Books," *below*.
Superior Court, etc.: 1771-1906+ (unprocessed); case records, ca. 1772, V39; docket books, 1794-ca. 1836, V32, V33; judgment books, 1783-ca. 1900, V31 and V32; index in Hillsborough County Binder, and card index; computer database in progress.

State Historical Society

New Hampshire Historical Society, Concord
Briggs, James Franklin. Legal papers, 1841-1892. Hillsborough Bridge lawyer; includes lawsuits, estates, guardianship, etc.
Brooks, Isaac. Legal papers, 1769-1838. Justice of the Peace for Amherst and surrounding towns.

Other Repositories

Dartmouth College Library, Hanover
Darling, Joshua, 1775-1842. Justice's book of records, 1805-1839. Rauner Manuscript Codex, 000359. Court of Common Pleas.

Goffstown Historical Society, Goffstown
Police court records, 1914-1915.
Deeds for land transfers in Range 5, from 1777-1884.

Manchester City Archives and Records Center, Manchester
Legal actions-appeals, 1853-1938. Accession 1998.24.
Legal actions-summonses, 1854-1896. Accession 1998.36. Court of Common Pleas.
Legal actions-warrants for the selection of jurymen, 1851-1874. Accession 1998.37.
    Including jury selection for Supreme Judicial Court, Court of Common Pleas
    and U.S. District Court.
Legal actions-petitions, 1884-1890. Accession 1998.33. N.H. Supreme Court.
Legal actions-bills in equity, 1868-1929. Accession 1998.26. N.H. Supreme Judicial
    Court.
Records of the Police Court/Municipal Court, 1846-1959. Accession 2000.22. Man-
    chester, N.H.

New England Historic Genealogical Society, Boston, Mass.
Index to probate records, 1769-1800, Hillsborough County. Anonymous typescript.
    MSS C 4179.
Pickering, John. Letter, 1782 June 27, Portsmouth, N.H., to the honorable justices of
    the Inferior Court at Amherst. MSS C 2652. Requesting continuance in case
    of defendant Joseph Patterson.
*Trial of Daniel Davis Farmer, for the Murder of the Widow Anna Ayer, at Goffstown,
    on the 4th of April, A.D. 1821.* Concord: Hill & Moore, 1821. Rare Book
    E312.62/A2.

Books

Oesterlin, Pauline J. *Hillsborough County, New Hampshire, Court Records, 1772-
    1799.* Bowie, Md: Heritage Books, 1996.
Patten, Matthew. *The Diary of Matthew Patten of Bedford, N.H.: From Seventeen
    Hundred Fifty-Four to Seventeen Hundred Eighty-Eight.* Bedford: By the
    Town, 1903. Re: Justice of the Peace. *See also* "Microform," *below.*
*The State of New Hampshire, Hillsborough County Register of Probate Index, 1771-
    1884.* Manchester, N.H.: Hillsborough County, 1973. *See also* "Microform,"
    below.

Microform

Miscellaneous court records
Appointments of Justices and Notary Publics, ca. 1888-1943. GSU, 1988. Superior
    Court.
Court Dockets, 1837-1901. GSU, 1988. Supreme Court, Court of Common Pleas,
    Supreme Judicial Court, Superior Court of Judicature and Circuit Court.
Court Executions, v. 1-5, 1782-1816. GSU, 1976. Court of Common Pleas.
Court Judgements [sic]*, 1783-1859.* GSU, 1976. Court of Common Pleas.
Court Judgments, 1855-1901; Plaintiff Index, 1855-1889; Equity Index, 1888-1901.
    GSU, 1976, 1988. Supreme Judicial Court, Circuit Court and Supreme Court.
Court Records, 1772-1827. GSU, 1976. Superior Court of Judicature and Supreme
    Judicial Court.

Execution of Lawsuits 1813-1859. GSU, 1951. Court of Common Pleas.

Judgements [sic], *1901-1916; Equity Index Cards, 1901-1936; Dockets, 1901-1936*. GSU, 1988. Superior Court.

Patten, Matthew. *The Diary of Matthew Patten of Bedford, N.H.: From Seventeen Hundred Fifty-Four to Seventeen Hundred Eighty-Eight*. Bedford, N.H.: By the Town, 1903; GSU, 1974. Re: Justice of the Peace. *See also* Bosworth, Louise Pernet, *Index to Matthew Patten's Diary*. GSU, 1941.

Soldiers Discharges, 1866-1880. GSU, 1988. Supreme Judicial Court.

Writs of Attachment 1849-1894. GSU, 1976. Lyndeborough, N.H..

Naturalization records

Judgements [sic], *1901-1916; Equity Index Cards, 1901-1936; Dockets, 1901-1936*. GSU, 1988. Superior Court; naturalization records included in judgment vols.

Naturalization Dockets, 1901-1906. GSU, 1988. Superior Court.

Naturalization Index, Early-2001 and Naturalization Records 1901-1906, Hillsborough County, New Hampshire. GSU, 2001. Superior Court.

Naturalization Records, 1906-1932; Index, 1906-1929. GSU, 1988. Superior Court.

Records of Naturalizations, 1842-1901; Indexes, ca. 1842-1907. GSU, 1988. Supreme Judicial Court, Court of Common Pleas, Circuit Court, Superior Court of Judicature and Police Courts.

Probate court records

Higbee, Jessie M. *Wills and administrations, Court of Probate, 1771-1775, Hillsboro County, New Hampshire*. GSU, 1974.

Index to Probate Records, 1769-1800, Hillsboro County, New Hampshire. GSU, 1951.

Index to Probate Records in New Hampshire: Counties of Rockingham, Cheshire, Strafford, Grafton, Hillsboro. GSU, 1973. Re: 1769-1800.

Probate Records, 1771-1921; Indexes to Probate Records, 1771-1859, 1885-1961. GSU, 1952, 1987.

Register of Probate Index, 1771-1884. Manchester, N.H.: Hillsborough County, 1973. GSU, 1978.

Merrimack County

Founded 1823, from Grafton, Hillsborough and Rockingham Counties

Courts

Merrimack County Superior Court, Concord

District Court

Except as noted below, *see* "District Court—Record Retention Guidelines" in "Statewide or General Sources: Courts," *above*.

Concord

Civil and criminal: original docket/record books, file papers; criminal records destroyed after seven years, varying retention policies for civil; docket card permanently retained. Pilot project in 2005 for browser-based Internet case management system and scanning court records.

Franklin

Henniker

Hooksett
New London

Merrimack County Probate Court, Concord
Original records, 1823-date; computer, 1993 to date; index.

State Archives

New Hampshire Division of Archives and Records Management, Concord
Note: Computer database of court records, 1823-1852.
Allenstown Municipal Court: correspondence, 1935. B-8, 97, V25.
Allenstown Police Justice Court. E-1, E-105, V25.
Circuit Court: petitions, 1875-1876, and docket books, 1875, 1877-1878. V39.
County Records. V39.
Court of Common Pleas: docket books, 1823-1859, and judgments, 1840-1859, V40;
        index by plaintiff, 1825-1872, and general index, 1872-1883, V31.
Deputations of Deputy Sheriffs. V39.
District Court (Second), 1870-1874. V39.
Equity Court: judgments, 1874-1876, and dockets, 1875-1878. V39. File. FC1.
Naturalization: card index in Research Area, 1847-1948; Court of Common Pleas,
        1846-1860, Supreme Judicial Court, 1860-1873, Supreme Court, 1882-
        1889 and Superior Court, V31; alphabetical files, Bx695091-695104;
        declarations of intention, 1908-1948 (not processed), Bx695111; peti-
        tions/orders, 1906-1929, V51; misc. correspondence, 1940s-1950s (not
        processed), Bx695112.
Pauper Concerns. V29.
Probate: index, 1824-1984; record volumes, 1-421; microfiche of file papers (alpha-
        betical).
Sessions Court (part of Supreme Judicial Court): index, 1823-1864, V31; docket
        book, 1834, and judgments, 1841-1867, 1869-1874, V41; docket books,
        1845-1878, V40.
Superior Court of Judicature: index by plaintiff, 1824-1880, V31; docket books, 1824-
        1855, 1916-1921, V40; judgments, 1840-1858, V39.
Supreme Court: dockets, 1878-1895, V40; judgments, 1890-1899, V41.
Supreme Judicial Court: index by plaintiff, 1890-1900, V31; numerous docket books,
        1824-1921, V39-40; judgments, 1850s-1870s, V39-40.

State Historical Society

New Hampshire Historical Society, Concord
Atkinson, Simeon and Sarah. Estate papers. 1805, 1810. Boscawen, N.H.
Prescott family. Estate papers. Concord.

Microform

Miscellaneous court records
Court Records, 1840-1867. GSU, 1976. Court of Common Pleas and Supreme
        Judicial Court.

Court Records, 1840-1875; Index to Court Records, 1824-1888. GSU, 1976. Superior Court of Judicature, Supreme Judicial Court and Circuit Court.
Court Records, 1876-1900; Index to Court Records, 1890-1900. GSU, 1976. Supreme Judicial Court.

Naturalization records
Naturalization Index, 1850-1948, Merrimack County, New Hampshire. GSU, 2001.
Naturalization Records, 1846-1889. GSU, 1976.

Probate court records
Probate Records, 1823-1972; Probate Indexes, 1823-1973. GSU, 1951, 1988-1989.

Rockingham County
Founded 1769/1771

Courts

Rockingham County Superior Court, Brentwood
Civil: original file papers, 1975-date; docket cards, 1955-1987; index cards, 1920-1987. Criminal: original file papers, 1967-date; docket cards, 1958-1987. Equity/domestic: original file papers, 1970-date; docket cards (equity, 1958-1987, domestic, 1975-1987); index cards, 1920-1987. All cases: computer index and case histories, 1988-date.

District Court
Except as noted below, *see* "District Court—Record Retention Guidelines" in "Statewide or General Sources: Courts," *above.*
Auburn
Derry
Civil: original docket/record books, 1970-date; original file papers and appeals, twenty years; index. Criminal: original docket/record books, 1970-date; original file papers and appeals, ten years; index.
Exeter
Hampton
Plaistow
Civil and criminal: original docket cards and file papers; computer docket, 1991-date.
Portsmouth
Civil, criminal, small claim and landlord/tenant: original docket/record books and file papers.
Salem

Rockingham County Probate Court, Brentwood
Docket/record books, file papers, appeals, index; original, 1924-date; microfilm before 1924.

Rockingham County Family Courts, Brentwood, Derry, Portsmouth and Salem
Family Courts established as pilot program in 1996.

State Archives

New Hampshire Division of Archives and Records Management, Concord
Court records: 1643-1980, including docket books, V29-30, 76; Supreme Judicial
    Court records, 1855-1900 (024131, 024134, 024143, 024163, 025033,
    026151-026153, 026161-026164); index vols. and cards.
Exeter town records, including earliest court records, before 1643.
Merrill, Phinehas (Surveyor). Probate Record Rockingham Co. #9012 (1815).
    DC005001, F3, V74.
Naturalization: 1771-1923, Bin 528-530; records, 1898-1940, V31; intentions,
    petitions/orders, 1906-1991, Bin 611; indexes, 1771-1996, Binder #15, cards
    and computer.
Probate: record vols. and file papers, 1643-1980; indexes, 1643-1919 in Binder #17,
    cards and computer, 1870-1918.

State Historical Society

New Hampshire Historical Society, Concord
Bartlett, Levi. Papers, 1801-1823. Judge, County Court of Common Pleas, Kingston,
    N.H.
Bartlett family. Papers, 1743-1888. Kingston, N.H. judges.
Doe, Joseph. Legal papers, 1748-1840. Justice of the peace and probate records,
    Newmarket, N.H. Legal and financial papers, 1826-1851. Records re: debts
    owed to Doe.
Wiggin, Andrew. Samuel Alcock probate document, 1747 May 8. Portsmouth, N.H.

Other Repositories

Dartmouth College Library, Hanover
*Libel trial. Report of the trial, Timothy Upham vs. Hill & Barton,...at the Court of
    common pleas, Rockingham county, October term, 1830....* Concord: Hill &
    Barton, 1831. Rauner NH Concord, 1831p.
New Hampshire. Court of Common Pleas (Rockingham County). *Portsmouth & Con-
    cord railroad v. William Jones & Wm. P. Jones....* Portsmouth: Portsmouth
    Journal Office, 1851. Rauner Chse Strtr New Eng, P665 3.
New Hampshire. Court of Common Pleas (Rockingham County). Writs of attachment,
    1809-1817. Rauner Manuscript, 002248.
New Hampshire. Superior Court of Judicature. Legal papers. 1907. Complaint of
    drunken and disorderly conduct in Newton, N.H. Rauner Manuscript, 907313.
*Trial of Munroe Colcord, Elihu Colcord, John A. Webster, John Silloway, Stephen
    Eaton and Nathan Eaton, for the murder of Dolly Seaver...at Portsmouth....*
    1845. Rauner Alumni, W852c.

Hampton Historical Society, Hampton
Civil pleadings, early 19th century, no index. Wills, 17th-19th centuries, no index.

Historical Society of Seabrook, Seabrook
Civil and criminal: Seabrook Municipal Court record books, 1931-1947, and miscellaneous file papers, 1937-1952.

Kensington Historical Society, Kensington Public Library, Kensington
Naturalization book, 1858, and writs with promissory notes and lists of goods, 1799-1820, 1849-1854.

New England Historic Genealogical Society, Boston, Mass.
Farrar, Timothy. Papers, 1775-1856. MSS 188. Includes court records of Rockingham
    County judges.
Nevin, James. Will, 1766; codicil, 1769; and probate court ruling, 1769. Portsmouth,
    N.H., MSS C 5094.
Pickering, John. Letter, 1782 June 27, Portsmouth, N.H., to the honorable justices of
    the Inferior Court at Amherst. MSS C 2652. Requesting continuance in case
    of defendant Joseph Patterson.

Portsmouth Athenaeum, Portsmouth
Court of Common Pleas, 1782-ca. 1845. MS042. Summonses, warrants, attachments,
    etc.
Court of Common Pleas, 1817. S354. Record book listing 835 cases.
Peirce Family Papers, 1665-1840 (bulk 1668-1840). MS009. Deeds, wills, estate
    papers, legal documents, etc. of Daniel Peirce, Portsmouth lawyer and justice
    of the peace, and Peter Livius, chief justice of N.H. Supreme Court, etc.
Pickering, William and Valentine. Court Document, 1790. MS042.1. Land dispute
    heard by Justices of the Peace Samuel Penhallow and Nathaniel Adams.
Report of the trial, Timothy Upham vs. Hill & Barton,...at the Court of common pleas,
    Rockingham county, October term, 1830.... 1831. Rare Pamphlet 42778.
William Smith Papers, 1806-1807. S0449. Includes court record re: 1807 case of
    Smith v. Wadley.

Rye Historical Society, Rye
Original juror lists and records of liens against property.

Books

Evans, Helen F. *Abstracts of the Probate Records of Rockingham County, N.H., 1771-*
    1799. 2 vols. Bowie, Md.: Heritage Books, 2000. *See also* "Digital/Electronic Sources," *below.*

Microform

Miscellaneous court records
Court Records, 1648-1681. GSU, 1971. County Court (Old Norfolk County), including towns of Hampton, Exeter and Strawbery Banke (Portsmouth), now in
    Rockingham County.
Court Records, 1772-1819. GSU, 1975. Court of Common Pleas and Circuit Court of
    Common Pleas for the Eastern District.
Equity Records 1774-1820, 1842-1853; Index to Court Records 1771-1900. GSU,
    1975. Superior Court of Judicature, Supreme Judicial Court, Superior Court
    of Judicature for the First Judicial District and Superior Court of Judicature
    at Concord.
Index to Court Records, 1849-1897. GSU, 1975. Epping, N.H.

Records of Writs, 1849-1910. GSU, 1996. Chester, N.H.
Rockingham County Justices of the Peace and Notaries Public, 1894-1930. GSU, 1996.

Naturalization records
Declarations of Intentions, 1906-1929; Declarations Index Cards, 1922-1956. GSU, 1988. Superior Court.
Naturalization Index Cards, 1771-1906. GSU, 1988. Superior Court.
Naturalization Papers, 1926-1939. GSU, 1988. Superior Court.
Naturalization Petitions and Records, 1907-1933; Naturalization Index Cards, 1919-1964. GSU, 1988. Superior Court.

Probate court records
Court Dockets, 1786-1902. GSU, 1988.
Court Minutes, 1772-1773, 1808-1827. GSU, 1988.
Estate Papers, Old Series, 1771-1869. GSU, 1988-1989.
Index to Probate Records in New Hampshire: Counties of Rockingham, Cheshire, Strafford, Grafton, Hillsboro. GSU, 1973. Re: 1753-1800.
Insolvency Records, 1891-1898, 1907, 1931-1948. GSU, 1988.
Inventory of Amount of Property Belonging to the Estate of John Hanscom at the Close of the Settlement, Sept. 11, 1844. GSU, 1988. Includes record of accounts, 1844-1848.
Inventory of the Estate of Jonathan M. Spratt, Taken May 20, 21, 22 & June 19th, 1850. GSU, 1988.
Mixed Records, 1771-1773, Copied from Vol. No. 3: Original Volume is with Colonial Records in Concord, New Hampshire. GSU, 1988.
Philbrook, Mary. *Probate records in Office of Probate Clerk, County of Rockingham, at Exeter, New Hampshire, 1753-1800*. GSU, 1951.
Probate Records, 1771-1969. GSU, 1951-1952, 1988.
Pulsifer, David. *Records of the County of Norfolk, in the Colony of Massachusetts*. GSU, 1971. Copied in 1852 from original records, 1647-1714; including towns of Hampton, Exeter and Strawbery Banke (Portsmouth), now in Rockingham County.
Schedules and Specifications of Martha T. Moses as Guardian of the Children of John Hanscom, 1835-1844. GSU, 1988.
Wills Filed not Probated, 1847-1971; Index to Wills Filed, 1847-1945. GSU, 1988.

Digital/Electronic Sources

CD-ROM
Evans, Helen F. *Abstracts of the Probate Records of Rockingham County, N.H., 1771-1799*. 2 vols. Bowie, Md.: Heritage Books, 2000.

Strafford County
Founded 1769/1773

Courts

Strafford County Superior Court, Dover
Civil, criminal, equity, domestic relations and naturalization: docket/record books, file papers, appeals; original, 1773-date.

District Court
Except as noted below, *see* "District Court—Record Retention Guidelines" in "Statewide or General Sources: Courts," *above.*
Dover
Durham
Civil: docket/record books; original and computer, 1990-date. Criminal: docket/record books; original and computer, 1948-date.
Rochester

Strafford County Probate Court, Dover
Docket/record books, file papers, appeals, index; original, 1770-date.

State Archives

New Hampshire Division of Archives and Records Management, Concord
Dover Town Court: from 1640, in Vol. 1 of Province Deeds.
John Smith estate in Dover, n.d., MD3, F6.
Superior Court, etc.: 1780-1859, 1870-1874 (partially processed); docket books, 1820-1874, V33; partial index, Research Area binder and computer database in progress.

State Historical Society

New Hampshire Historical Society, Concord
Sanborn, Cyrus King. Legal papers. 1845-1887. 38 boxes. Includes court cases of Rochester lawyer.

Other Repositories

New England Historic Genealogical Society, Boston, Mass.
Tuttle, John. Deposition, 1714, July 3. MSS C 2658. Re: property survey near Dover for James Davis.

University of New Hampshire Library, Durham
Docket of the Supreme Court, Strafford County, N.H., September term, 1887. Dover: Foster's Democrat Job Print, 1887. NHamp KFN1712.N45 1877.

Books

Evans, Helen F. *Abstracts of the Probate Records of Strafford County, New Hampshire, 1771-1799.* 2d ed. Bowie, Md.: Heritage Books, 1983.
Hulslander, Laura Penny. *Abstracts of Strafford County, New Hampshire Inferior Court Records, 1773-1783.* Bowie, Md.: Heritage Books, 1987.

Microform

Miscellaneous court records
Court Records, 1648-1681. GSU, 1971. County Court (Old Norfolk County); including town of Dover, now in Strafford County.

Court Records, 1773-1816. GSU, 1976, 1990. Court of Common Pleas.
Court Records, 1773-1874. GSU, 1976. Superior Court of Judicature.
Court Records, 1855-1874. GSU, 1976. Supreme Judicial Court.
Court Records, 1876-1901. GSU, 1976. Supreme Judicial Court.
Court Records, New Series, 1840-1859. GSU, 1976. Court of Common Pleas.
Court Records, v. 1, 1874-1876. GSU, 1990. Circuit Court.
Superior Court Records, 1901-1915; Plantiffs [sic] *Index to Civil, Equity, and Sessions Cases, 1901-1920.* GSU, 1990.

Naturalization records
Naturalization Papers, 1861-1906; Indexes to Petitions for Naturalization, and Declarations of Intention, 1861-1936. GSU, 1976, 1990. Court of Common Pleas, Supreme Judicial Court, Circuit Court, Superior Court, and Police Court of City of Dover.
Naturalization Petition and Record, 1907-1931. GSU, 1990. Superior Court.
Naturalization Records, 1842-1861. GSU, 1990. Court of Common Pleas and Supreme Judicial Court; includes petitions for naturalization and declarations of intention.
Record of Declarations of Intention, 1906-1931. GSU, 1990. Superior Court.

Probate court records
Index to Strafford County, New Hampshire Probate Records, 1769-1800. GSU, 1951.
Index to Probate Records in New Hampshire: Counties of Rockingham, Cheshire, Strafford, Grafton, Hillsboro. GSU, 1973. Re: 1769-1800.
Probate Records, 1773-1946; Probate Indexes, 1773-1989. GSU, 1951, 1989-1991.
Pulsifer, David. *Records of the County of Norfolk, in the Colony of Massachusetts.* GSU, 1971. Copied in 1852 from original records, 1647-1714; including town of Dover, now in Strafford County.

Sullivan County
Founded 1827, from Cheshire County

Courts

Sullivan County Superior Court, Newport

District Court
Claremont
Civil and criminal: original file papers, 1989-date; index cards, before 1993; computer dockets, 1993-date; some file and sound recordings on cassette tape. Records destroyed at earliest possible date.
Newport
See "District Court—Record Retention Guidelines" in "Statewide or General Sources: Courts," *above.*

Sullivan County Probate Court, Newport
Docket/record books, file papers, appeals; original and computer, 1827-date.

State Archives

New Hampshire Division of Archives and Records Management, Concord
Court of Common Pleas: records, 1827-1842, V8; docket books, 1842-1859, V8-9, 42.
Superior/Supreme Court: 1828-1972; case books, V8-9, 32; docket books, V42.
Naturalization: 1800s-1900s; 10 boxes in Bin A68; card index.

State Historical Society

New Hampshire Historical Society, Concord
Gove, Jonathan. Legal papers. 1823-1829. Case notes and legal forms of Acworth,
N.H. Justice of the Peace.

Microform

Miscellaneous court records
Court Records, 1828-1855. GSU, 1976. Superior Court of Judicature.
Court Records, 1855-1905. GSU, 1976. Supreme Court, Circuit Court and Superior
         Court of Judicature.
Records, 1827-1859. GSU, 1976. Court of Common Pleas.

Naturalization records
Naturalization Index, Early-1955, Sullivan County, New Hampshire. GSU, 2001.
         Superior Court, Supreme Court, Supreme Judicial Court and Court of Com-
         mon Pleas.
Naturalizations, 1838-1903. GSU, 1976. Court of Common Pleas, Supreme Judicial
         Court, Circuit Court, Supreme Court and Superior Court.

Probate court records
Probate, Wills and Indexes 1852-1947, Sullivan County, New Hampshire. GSU, 2001.
Probate Records, 1827-1902; General Index, 1827-1874. GSU, 1951.

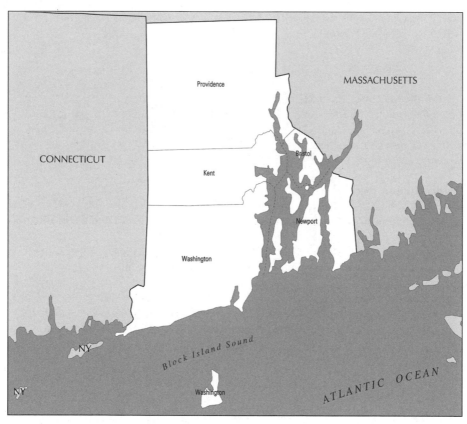

Fig. 10.1. Map of Rhode Island Counties. *National Atlas of the United States.* 2005.
http://nationalatlas.gov

CHAPTER 10

RHODE ISLAND STATE COURTS

Court History Timeline

Colonial Courts

Rhode Island's court history began with four separate towns—**Providence, Portsmouth** (Pocasset), **Newport** and **Warwick** (Shawomct).

1636	**Providence** was founded by Roger Williams and others, who drew up a "compact" to obey "all such orders or agreements as shall be made for the public good."
1638	**Portsmouth** was founded by William Coddington and Anne Hutchinson at Rhode Island (Aquidneck). Settlers elected Coddington as **Judge**, with **elders** to assist him.
1639	Coddington and followers started a new settlement—**Newport**—at the southwest end of the island. Their compact provided that decisions would be made by elders and a judge (Coddington, who could cast a double vote).
1640	**Providence** settlers agreed to a government by "**arbitration**," with five men called "**disposers**," to make decisions, and appeals to town meeting. Rhode Island (**Portsmouth** and **Newport**) formed a joint government, with Coddington as Governor. **Particular Courts** of magistrates and jurors met monthly in each town, deciding cases not involving "life or limb." **Quarter Courts** or **Quarter Sessions** heard appeals, four times per year, in Portsmouth and Newport.
1643	Roger Williams went to England, seeking a charter to form a new colony composed of Providence, Portsmouth and Newport.
1644	England granted a **royal charter**, giving towns power to form a "civil government."
1647	Four towns—Providence, Portsmouth, Newport and Warwick—unified under the charter, with a code of laws to govern the colony. **General**

Court of Elections (later called **General Assembly**) was the colony's legislative body, with some judicial functions, including appeals, divorce, serious criminal cases, etc. **General Court of Trials** met two to four times per year. Initially a circuit court, it had statewide jurisdiction over important civil and criminal cases, maritime disputes and appeals from **Town Courts**.

1663 A **new royal charter** was granted. Governor, deputy governor and ten "assistants" served as magistrates in the **General Assembly**, which had broad legislative, executive and judicial powers. "Governor and Company" could appeal to England in "matters of public controversy" between Rhode Island and other colonies.

1667 Governor and Council, also known as **General Council of Probate** or **Supreme Court of Probate**, heard appeals of probate decisions from **town councils** (until 1813).

1671 General Court of Trials began to meet exclusively at Newport.

1676 **Providence** burned during King Philip's war, destroying many records.

1687-1688 Rhode Island lost charter, and became county in **Dominion of New England**, the royal government of Sir Edmund Andros. General Assembly and General Court of Trials were abolished, replaced by **General Quarter Sessions** and **Inferior Court of Common Pleas**. Town **justices of the peace** decided minor disputes.

1689-1692 "Glorious Revolution" ended Dominion government, and courts reverted to previous forms.

1697 Royal **Vice-Admiralty Court** regulated trade and navigation.

1703 Colony was divided into two counties: Rhode Island (Newport and islands) and Providence Plantations, each with annual **Court of Common Pleas**. **General Court of Trials** was composed of Governor and Council, or upper house of General Assembly. The entire **General Assembly** sat as a court of appeals and heard equity cases.

1716 General Court of Trials was renamed **General Court of Trials and General Gaol Delivery**.

1729 Colony was divided into three counties: Newport, King's and Providence. New court structure: **Superior Court of Judicature** (upper house of **General Assembly**) heard appeals twice yearly at Newport. **Inferior Courts of Common Pleas** handled civil jury trials in each county, with judges appointed by General Assembly. **Courts of General Sessions of the Peace** handled non-capital criminal trials in each county, justices of the peace presiding.

1741 Separate **Equity Court**, with judges elected by the General Assembly, decided appeals from Superior Court.

1743 Equity Court was abolished.

1747	Massachusetts ceded towns of Barrington, Bristol, Cumberland, Little Compton, Tiverton and Warren to Rhode Island. **Superior Court of Judicature, Court of Assize, and General Jail Delivery** was established, to sit twice yearly in each county with chief justice and four associate justices. General Assembly's upper house no longer heard appeals.
1776	Rhode Island **Admiralty Court** was created, for jury trial of prize cases, with appeals to Continental Congress.

Courts after Independence

1789	**Admiralty** jurisdiction was transferred to new **U.S. District Court**. Inferior Courts of Common Pleas became **Courts of Common Pleas** for civil trials only. **Courts of General Sessions of the Peace** continued to hear non-capital criminal trials.
1798	Superior Court of Judicature was renamed **Supreme Judicial Court** (for appeals).
Late 1700s	Towns and cities began to establish **Probate Courts**, which assumed probate jurisdiction previously exercised by town councils.
1838	Courts of General Sessions of the Peace were abolished; jurisdiction was transferred to **Courts of Common Pleas** (which now handled civil and criminal trials).
1844	Supreme Judicial Court became **Supreme Court**.
1862	Massachusetts ceded town of East Providence to Rhode Island.
1893	**Supreme Court** split into: **Appellate Division** for appeals, and **Common Pleas Division** for civil and criminal trials.
1906	Courts reorganized. *See* "Rhode Island Courts Today," *below.*

Rhode Island Courts Today

State Courts

Supreme Court

Rhode Island's Supreme Court hears appeals from cases decided in lower courts.

Superior Court

Each county, except Bristol, has one Superior Court. (Civil and criminal cases for Bristol County are handled by Providence County courts.) Superior Court jurisdiction includes criminal trials (all felonies) and civil trials over $5,000.

District Court

Each county, except Bristol, has one or more District Courts. (Civil and criminal cases for Bristol County are handled by Providence County courts.) District Court hears criminal trials and civil trials under $5,000; civil cases $5,000-$10,000 can be tried either in District Court or Superior Court.

Family Court

Each county, except Bristol, has one Family Court, for family-related matters, including divorce, juvenile, domestic abuse and child support cases. *Note*: Juvenile records are confidential, with limited exceptions. Adoption records are sealed, except as provided by the Passive Voluntary Adoption Mutual Consent Act, Chapter 157.2 of the General Laws of Rhode Island.

Workers' Compensation Court

Workers' Compensation Court hears claims for injuries in the course of employment.

Traffic Tribunal

Traffic Tribunal hears non-criminal traffic cases. *Note:* Traffic Tribunal records are not covered in this book.

Town Courts

Probate Courts

Probate matters—probate of wills, settlement of estates, adoptions, guardianships, name changes, etc.—continue to be handled by Probate Courts at the town and city level.

Municipal Courts

Some towns and cities have Municipal (Police) Courts, for criminal matters relating to traffic and ordinance violations, etc.

Where to Find Court Records
See Appendix for complete contact information.

Statewide or General Sources

Courts

Rhode Island Supreme Court, Providence
Original case files and briefs, 2003-date.

Rhode Island Workers' Compensation Court, Providence
Original dockets, case files and appeals (pending cases, and closed cases for one year); computer files, 1990-date.

Other State Courts
See "Courts" section for each county, *below*.

State Archives, Records Center and Law Library

Rhode Island State Archives, Providence
Early court records include:
Records of the Island of Rhode Island. 1637-1663. 1 vol. C#0206.
Ancient Records of the Colony of Rhode Island and Providence Plantations "Gyles
        Records," 1638-1670, including appendix of records, 1637-1718, and Andros
        court records, 1687-1688. 1 vol. C#0207.
R.I. Colony Records (contains General Court of Trials), 1646-1669. 2 vols. C#0204.
Other court records include:
Admiralty Court. Minute Books/Index, 1727-1743, 1776-1783. 3 vols. C#0018.
Counterfeit Cases, 1741-1743, 1745-1777. C#1238.
Court Clerks' Accounts/Reports, 1820-1845. C#1244.
Court Clerks' Reports, 1820-1868. C#1245.
Court Clerks' Returns, 1747-1832.
Court of Magistrates, Jan. 1850. 1 vol. C#00495.
Equity Court file papers, Sept. 1741-Dec. 1743. 7 vols. C#00371.
Equity Court, Sept. 1741-Dec. 1743. 1 vol. C#00494.
Fines and Recoveries, Court of Trials, 1725-1780. 1 vol. C#00461.
General Assembly, Docket, 1734-1803.
General Council/Supreme Court of Probate, 1798-1803. 1 vol. C#0049.
General Council of Probate, 1755-1777. 1 vol. C#0049.
Grand Jury. Chap Books, Law and Speeches to 1829-1833. C#1246.
Hale, Nathan v. creditors, 1816. C#1242.
Ives, R. H. v. C. J. Hazard, 1857-1863. C#1243.
Land and Public Notary Records, 1648-1776. 8 vols. C#00481.
Probate Court Docket, 1931.
R.I. Law Cases file papers, Oct. 1725-Jan., 1741. 10 vols. C#0036.
Suits, 1730-1743, 1750, 1770-1780. C#1237.
Suits, 1794-1805. C#1237.
Superior Court of Trials, *Tervet v. Weeden*, transcripts, 1886-1887.
Supreme Court. Opinions, 1878, 1881-1883, 1887-1898, 1908-1909, 1935.
Supreme Court. Probate Records, 1871-1890.
Wills and Inventories, 1710-1800, 1802, 1821. C#1236.

Rhode Island Supreme Judicial Court, Judicial Records Center (JRC), Pawtucket
Central repository for State's semi-active, closed and archival court records. Archives
at JRC include early R.I. court records, *e.g:*
        Civil and criminal cases, from 1671.
        Divorce cases, from 1749.
        Naturalization papers, from 1793-1974.
Use Archival Request Forms, at *www.courts.ri.gov/records/forms.htm*, for specific
questions about those records. For questions about recent court records, contact court
clerks or send request by regular mail to JRC (*see Appendix: Contact Information-
State Courts* and *Archives and Other Repositories*).
Note: For most Rhode Island records during years 1671-1746, *see* "Newport County"
section, *below*.

Rhode Island State Law Library, Providence
Briefs from cases argued before R. I. Supreme Court, from 1908. Chronological
    bound vols.; no cumulative indexing.
Decisions of R.I. District Court, 6th Div. (including Providence). Bound vols.

Federal Archives and Records Center

U.S. National Archives and Records Administration (NARA), Northeast Region-
Waltham (Boston), Mass.
Naturalization: Dexigraph collection (negative photostats) of naturalization records
from 301 federal and state courts in five New England states (Maine, Mass., N.H., R.I.
and Vt.), 1790-1906. Index is available on microfilm, as *Index to New England Naturalization Petitions, 1791-1906*; *see* "Microform," *below*. *Note*: NARA-Waltham staff
will search index and provide copies for a fee; need name, residence at time of application, and birth date.

State Historical Society

Rhode Island Historical Society, Providence
Elijah Armstrong Papers, 1772-1821. Mss 265. Justice of the Peace records.
George A. Brayton Papers, 1827-1834. Mss 305. Justice of the Peace records.
Clarke Indian Manuscripts Collection, 1641-1787. Mss 350. Court records, deposi-
    tions and deeds re: R.I. Indians.
Legal Papers, 1701-1852. Mss 533.
Rhode Island Court Records Collection (Sicard Gift), 1780?-1820. Mss 231sg5.
See also "Guide to Manuscripts at the Rhode Island Historical Society Library Relating
to People of Color," *www.rihs.org/mssinv/PeopleofColorweb.htm*, described in *Chapter
13*, which includes references to court and probate records in Society's collections.

Other Repositories

Boston Athenaeum, Boston, Mass.
Hildreth, Richard. *A Report of the Trial of the Rev. Ephraim K. Avery, Before the
Supreme Judicial Court of Rhode Island, on an Indictment for the Murder of Sarah
Maria Cornell, Containing a Full Statement of the Testimony, Together with the
Arguments of Counsel, and the Charge to the Jury*. Boston: Russell, Odiorne & Co.,
D. H. Ela, 1833. Adams, D255; Tract, B1443.

New England Historic Genealogical Society, Boston, Mass.
*The Arguments of Counsel in the Close of the Trial of Rev. Ephraim K. Avery, for the
Murder of Sarah M. Cornell, at a Special Term of the Supreme Court of Rhode Island,
Held from May 6th to June 2d, 1833*. Boston: Daily Commercial Gazette and Boston
Daily Advocate, 1833. Rare Book KF223/A95.

Providence College, Providence
DeCesare, Catherine Osborne. "Courting Justice: Rhode Island Women and the Gen-
eral Court of Trials, 1671-1729." Ph.D. diss., Providence College, 2000. KFR91.W6
D43 2000.

U.S. Citizenship and Immigration Services, U.S. Dept. of Homeland Security, Washington, D.C.
Naturalization certificate files ("C-Files"): Copies of naturalization records from state and federal courts after September 27, 1906, *e.g.*, Declaration of Intention, Petition for Naturalization, and Certificate of Naturalization.
1906-1956: Available on microfilm. Make Freedom of Information/Privacy Act (FOIA/PA) request to U.S. Citizenship and Immigration Services in Washington, D.C.
After 1956: Make FOIA/PA request to the district U.S. Citizenship and Immigration Services office that maintains the records, or office nearest your residence. *See Appendix: Contact Information-Archives and Other Repositories*, Washington, D.C.

University of Rhode Island Library, Kingston
Staples, William R. *History of the criminal law of Rhode Island: charge of Hon. William R. Staples delivered to the Grand Jury of the Court of Common Pleas in Newport and Providence*. 1853. URI RI Coll., KFR561 Z9 C6 1853.

Books and Journals

Court Records—Abstracts, Transcripts and Indexes
Bartlett, John Russell, ed. *Records of the Colony and State of Rhode Island and Providence Plantations*. 10 vols. Reprint, New York: AMS Press, 1968. Court-related records scattered throughout. *See also* "Digital/Electronic Sources," *below*.
Beaman, Nellie C. *Rhode Island Genealogical Register*. Princeton, Mass.: R.I. Families Assoc., 1992 . Includes (in installments) abstracts of wills for all R.I. towns. Vol. 16 contains index, 1636-1840.
Chafee, Zechariah, Jr. "Records of the Rhode Island Court of Equity, 1741-1743." *Publications of the Colonial Society of Massachusetts (Transactions, 1942-1946)*. Boston: 1951. 35: 91-118.
Chapin, Howard Millar. *Documentary History of Rhode Island*. 2 vols. Providence: Preston & Rounds Co., 1916-1919. 2:132-165. Aquidneck Quarter Court Records, 1641-1646.
Farnham, Charles W. *Bar Bills at Crown Point: Some 1761 Law Suits Against Rhode Island Soldiers*. Providence: Roger Williams Press, 1960.
Fiske, Jane Fletcher. *Gleanings from Newport Court Files, 1659-1783*. Boxford, Mass.: By author, 1998.
_____. *Rhode Island General Court of Trials, 1671-1704*. Boxford, Mass.: By author, 1998.
John Albro's Deposition of 1705 as to the Purchase of Aquidneck with Coddington's Deposition of 1687. Providence: Society of Colonial Wars, E. L. Freeman Co., 1938.
Rhode Island Court Records: Records of the Court of Trials of the Colony of Providence Plantations, 1647-1670. 2 vols. Providence: R.I. Historical Society, 1920-1922; Buffalo, N.Y.: Dennis & Co., 1946. *See also* "Microform," *below*.
Rhode Island Land Evidences, Vol. I: 1648-1696, Abstracts. Providence: R.I. Historical Society, 1921, 1970; Clearfield Co., 1998. Includes wills, powers of attorney, etc.

Towle, Dorothy S. *Records of the Vice-Admiralty Court of Rhode Island: 1716-1752*. Washington, D.C.: American Historical Assoc., 1936; Millwood, N.Y.: Kraus Reprint, 1975.

Wakefield, Robert S. *Index to Wills in R.I. Genealogical Register, Volumes 1 through 4*. Warwick, R.I.: Plymouth Colony Research Group, 1982.

Weiner, Frederick Bernays. "Notes on the Rhode Island Admiralty, 1727-1790." *Harvard Law Review* 46 (Nov. 1932): 44-90. Includes selected transcribed admiralty records.

History

Arnold, Samuel Greene. *History of the State of Rhode Island and Providence Plantations*. 2 vols. New York: D. Appleton, 1859-1860.

Durfee, Thomas. *Gleanings from the Judicial History of Rhode Island*. Providence: Sidney S. Rider, 1883.

Eaton, Amasa M. "The Development of the Judicial System in Rhode Island." *Yale Law Journal* 14 (Jan. 1905): 148-170.

Farrell, John T. "The Early History of Rhode Island's Court System." *Rhode Island History* 9 (July 1950): 65-71; 9 (Oct. 1950): 103-117; 10 (Jan. 1951): 14-25.

Law Library Resources

Case Reports: *See Chapter 17*, and *Appendix-Law Libraries* and *Publishers. See also* "Microform" and "Digital/Electronic Sources," *below.*

Rhode Island Supreme Court

Rhode Island Reports. Providence: Supreme Court. Court decisions, 1828-1980.

Rhode Island Reporter. Eagan, Minn.: West. Court decisions, 1980-date, enhanced with headnotes, key numbers and synopses.

Atlantic Reporter. Eagan, Minn.: West. Court decisions, 1886-date, enhanced with headnotes, key numbers and synopses.

West's Rhode Island Digest. Eagan, Minn.: West. 1783-date. *West's Atlantic Digest*. Eagan, Minn.: West. 1764-date. Digests of R.I. state and federal court decisions, organized alphabetically by topic, with headnotes, key numbers, and multiple indexes (case name, etc.).

Research Guides

Ullmann, Helen Schatvet. *A Finding Aid for Rhode Island Town Records*. Acton, Mass.: By author, 2000.

Microform

Admiralty Papers 1726-1786. GSU, 1974. FHL computer #358097.

Briggs, Anthony Tarbox. *Briggs Collection of Cemetery Records, Wills, Record Books of Genealogy and Scrapbooks of Vital Records and Historical Events: with General Index to Surnames, A-Z*. GSU, 1950. From manuscripts at R.I. Historical Society.

Court Minute Books, 1727-1783. GSU, 1974. FHL computer #365918. Court of Admiralty.

Court Records, 1671-1879. GSU, 1973. FHL computer #359634. General Court of Trials; General Court of Trials and General Gaol Delivery; Superior Court of

Judicature, Court of Assize and General Gaol Delivery; Supreme Judicial Court and Supreme Court.

Court Records, 1741-1743. GSU, 1973. FHL computer #359632. Court of Equity.

Genealogy of the Descendants of Zebedee Williams, Son of John Williams. GSU, 1950. Includes equity case of *George W. Williams, et al. v. William H. Herrick, et al.*, in Appellate Div. of R.I. Supreme Court.

General Council Meeting Minutes and Documents. GSU, 1974. Includes probate.

Index to New England Naturalization Petitions, 1791-1906. U.S. National Archives and Records Admin., 1983. M1299. Alphabetical index of individuals naturalized, in state and federal courts of Maine, Mass., N.H., R.I. and Vt. (indicates court and certificate number).

Land and Public Notary Records of Rhode Island, 1648-1795. GSU, 1973.

Petitions to the Rhode Island General Assembly, 1725-1867. GSU, 1973-1974, 1996.

Proceedings of the General Assembly: 1646-1851. GSU, 1974. Includes R.I. Court of Trials.

Records of Rhode Island, 1638-1644. GSU, 1974. FHL computer #838527. Includes R.I. General Court.

Rhode Island Court Records: Records of the Court of Trials of the Colony of Providence Plantations, 1647-1670. 2 vols. Providence: R.I. Historical Society, 1920-1922. GSU, 1981.

Rhode Island Miscellaneous Records, ca. 1600-1900. GSU, 1992. Includes probate records; from James Arnold's collection of notes at Knight Memorial Library, Providence.

R.I. Superior Court rescripts, 1917-1919. Kaneohe, Hawaii: Law Library Microform Consortium. Microfiche.

R.I. Supreme Court reports, 1828-1926, and additional vols. annually. Kaneohe, Hawaii: Law Library Microform Consortium. Microfiche.

Digital/Electronic Sources

CD-ROM

Atlantic Reporter. Eagan, Minn.: West. Includes R.I. Supreme Court opinions, 1945-date.

Bartlett, John Russell, ed. *Records of the Colony and State of Rhode Island and Providence Plantations.* Boston: New England Historic Genealogical Society, 2003.

Rhode Island Reporter and West's Rhode Island General Laws. Eagan, Minn.: West. R.I. cases reported in *Atlantic Reporter*, 1944-date.

Internet

FindLaw *www.findlaw.com/11stategov/ri/rica.html*
> R.I. Supreme Court, 1997-date.

Rhode Island Judiciary
> *www.courts.state.ri.us/supreme/publishedopinions.htm*
> R.I. Supreme Court opinions, 1999-date.
> *www.courts.state.ri.us/superior/publisheddecisions.htm*
> R.I. Superior Court opinions, 2000-date.

LexisNexis *www.lexis.com*
> R.I. Supreme Court, 1828-date, and R.I. Superior Court, 1991-date. Subscription services, or available at law libraries and other repositories.

LexisOne *www.lexisone.com*
>R.I. Supreme Court, most recent five years; free.

Loislaw *www.loislaw.com*
>R.I. Supreme Court, 1828-date, and R.I. Superior Court, 1991-date. Subscription services, or available at law libraries and other repositories.

VersusLaw *www.versuslaw.com*
>R.I. Supreme Court, from 1950. Subscription service.

Westlaw *www.westlaw.com*
>R.I. Supreme Court, 1828-date, and R.I. Superior Court, 1991-date. Subscription services, or available at law libraries and other repositories. Westlaw CourtEXPRESS offers case research and document retrieval from U.S. courts.

Bristol County

Founded 1746/7, from Bristol County, Mass.

Courts

Note: All Bristol County civil and criminal cases, except matters in Probate and Municipal Courts, are handled by courts of Providence County. *See* "Courts" section for Providence County, *below*.

Probate and Municipal Courts
Barrington Probate Court
Docket/record books, file papers, appeals, index; original, 1770-date.
Bristol Probate Court
Original record books (from 1700s), dockets (1890-date), file papers (from 1800s); microfilm, 1988-date; index (computer, 1993-date, cards, 1700s-date).
Bristol Municipal Court
Traffic, parking, zoning: docket sheets, taped transcripts, 1999-date.
Warren Probate Court and Municipal Court
Probate: docket/record books, appeals, index; late 1700s-date. Municipal Court: docket/record books and index; original, 1999-date.

State Archives and Records Center

Rhode Island State Archives, Providence
Court House, Bristol. Receipts/accounts, etc., 1871-1874. C#1297.
Court House, Bristol. Reports, 1818-30, 1858-60. C#1297.
Supreme Court, Bristol. Docket, 1877-1888.

Rhode Island Supreme Judicial Court, Judicial Records Center, Pawtucket
Court of Common Pleas (and predecessor courts). Indexes: plaintiff, 1747-1844; defendant, 1747-1844 (missing). Record Books: 1747-1905.
Court of General Sessions of the Peace. Record Books: 1747-1834.
Supreme Court (and predecessor courts). Indexes: plaintiff, 1747-1840; defendant, 1747-1850 (missing). Record Books: 1747-1777; 1777-1802 (missing); 1802-1893.

Other Repositories

New England Historic Genealogical Society, Boston, Mass.
Papers of the Reynolds family, Bristol. MSS C 1177. Includes original wills, 1757,
   1789 and 1813.
Stetson, Oscar Frank. "Bristol County, Rhode Island Court Records, 1749-1903."
   Typescript transcription of original records. MSS C 601. *See also* "Digi-
   tal/Electronic Sources," *below*.

Microform

Naturalization records
*Bristol (R.I.) Naturalization Records (1890-1902) and index (1896-1998)—, 1890-
1998. GSU, 2002.*

Probate records (Town Councils and Probate Courts)
Barrington
Barrington, Rhode Island Land Evidence Records, 1770-1936. GSU, 1973.
Barrington (R.I.) Probate Indexes, 1770-2002. GSU, 2002.
Barrington (R.I.) Probate Records, 1851-1929. GSU, 2002.
Barrington (R.I.) Town Council Records: vols. 1-4, 1770-1891. GSU, 1973.
Barrington, R.I., Town Records (Incl Probate), 1718-1886. GSU, 1973.
Bristol
Books of Wills and Inventories, 1746-1881. GSU, 1972.
Bristol (R.I.) Probate Bonds, 1817-1890. GSU, 1972.
*Bristol (R.I.) Probate Records (1892-1923) and Index (1700-2002), 1892-1923. GSU,
   2002.*
Bristol (R.I.) Town Council Records, 1760-1877. GSU, 1972.
*Deeds, Wills, Inventories, Administrations, Grand Deeds, Grand Articles 1680-1808.
   GSU, 1972.*
*Inventories (1811-1885) and Administrators Accounts (1811-1877), 1811-1885. GSU,
   1972.*
Letters of Administration, 1815-1906. GSU, 1972.
Warren
Probate Records, 1746-1920. GSU, 1973, 2002.
Town Meeting Records 1746-1881. GSU, 1973.

Digital/Electronic Sources

Internet
New England Historic Genealogical Society *www.NewEnglandAncestors.org*
   Bristol County, Rhode Island, Divorces, 1819-1893. Boston: www.NewEng-
   landAncestors.org, 2002. From typescript transcription of Oscar Frank Stet-
   son. "Bristol County, Rhode Island Court Records, 1749-1903." *See also*
   "Other Repositories," *above*.

Kent County
Founded 1750, from Providence County

Courts

Kent County Superior Court, Warwick
File papers; computer; five years or active cases.

District Court, 3rd Div., Warwick

Kent County Family Court, Warwick
File papers, 2001-date.

Probate and Municipal Courts
Coventry Probate Court and Municipal Court
Probate: 1741-date; some indexes, 1926-date. Criminal (traffic, town ordinance violations): docket/record books, file papers, appeals (original, from 1989; computer, all traffic and most ordinance, 2000-date).
E. Greenwich Probate Court
Docket/record books, file papers; 1700s-date.
Warwick Probate Court
Docket/record books, file papers, appeals; original, late 1700s-date.
Warwick Municipal Court
Criminal: docket/record books, file papers, appeals, index; original and computer, 1980-date. Traffic and housing: docket/record books, file papers, appeals, index; original and computer, 1990-date.
W. Greenwich Probate Court
Docket/record books, file papers, 1741-date; chronological and alphabetical index.
W. Warwick Probate Court
Docket/record books, file papers, index; original, 1913-date.

State Archives and Records Center

Rhode Island State Archives, Providence
Court of Common Pleas, Kent. Docket, 1880-1893.
Court House, Kent. Building Comm. Vouchers, Oct. 1805. C#1297.
E. Greenwich. Probate Records/Deeds, 1740-1741. C#1252.
Justices Court, E. Greenwich. Oct. 1770–May 1867. C#0052.
Supreme Court, Kent. Docket, 1880-1893.

Rhode Island Supreme Judicial Court, Judicial Records Center, Pawtucket
Court of Common Pleas (and its predecessor courts). Indexes: plaintiff and defendant, 1750-1847. Record Books: 1750-1834, 1836-1905.
Supreme Court (and its predecessor courts). Indexes: plaintiff and defendant, 1752-1867. Record Books: 1751-1893.

State Historical Society

Rhode Island Historical Society, Providence
Warwick Town Records Collection, 1647-1844. Mss 221. Court of Trials records, 1659-1674; other court records, 1718-1729; Warwick wills transcriptions, 1703-1761; etc. *Note*: Warwick was part of Providence County until 1750.

Other Repositories

Library of Congress, Washington, D.C.
The law of self-defense: the trial of George W. Congdon for the murder of Christopher G. Wilcox. Providence: S. S. Rider, 1884. Call #LAW Trials (A & E), LC Control #37024943. Court of Common Pleas, 1883.

Books

Beaman, Alden G. *East Greenwich and West Greenwich, Rhode Island, Births from Probate, Grave and Death Records, 1680-1860.* Princeton, Mass.: By author, 1980.
_____. *East Greenwich and West Greenwich, Rhode Island, Marriages from Marriage, Probate, Grave and Death Records, 1680-1860.* Princeton, Mass.: By author, 1980.
Capwell, Helen. *Records of the Courts of Trials of the Town of Warwick, 1659-1674.* The Shepley Press, 1922.
Chapin, Howard M. *The Early Records of the Town of Warwick.* Providence: E. A. Johnson Co., 1926.
Morgan, Marshall, Cherry F. Bamberg and Jane F. Fiske. *More Early Records of the Town of Warwick, Rhode Island: "The Book With Clasps" and "General Records."* Boston: New England Historic Genealogical Society, 2001.

Microform

Naturalization records
Declarations of Intention, 1917-1929. GSU, 1997. Superior Court.
Declarations of Intention, 1929-1951. GSU, 1997. Superior Court.
Naturalization Petitions, 1793-1958. GSU, 1996. Court of Common Pleas, Supreme Court and Superior Court; includes index.
Naturalization Petitions, 1917-1947. GSU, 1997. Superior Court.
Naturalization Petitions, 1923-1960. GSU, 1996. Superior Court; index.

Probate records (Town Councils and Probate Courts)
Coventry
Probate Records, 1764-1878. GSU, 1973.
E. Greenwich
Probate Records (1715-1924) and indexes (1872-2002), 1715-2002. GSU, 1973, 2002.
Town Council Records 1865-1873. GSU, 1973.
Warwick
Court docket 1839-1846. GSU, 1973.
Index for Probate Record Book No. 18. GSU, 1996.
Probate Bonds, 1873-1921. GSU, 1996.
Probate Docket Books, 1839-1925. GSU, 1996.
Probate Letters, 1839-1931. GSU, 1996.
Probate Proceedings, 1876-1938 (1947, 1953, 1955). GSU, 1996.
Probate Records, 1804-1876. GSU, 1973.
Probate Records, 1856-1932. GSU, 1973.
Probate Records, 1918-1931. GSU, 1996.

Town Council Records, 1742-1879. GSU, 1973.
Town Records 1647-1711. GSU, 1973.
Wills, 1703-1917. GSU, 1973, 1996.
W. Greenwich
West Greenwich (R.I.) Probate Records 1743-1915. GSU, 1973, 2002.
West Greenwich (R.I.) Town Council Records, 1741-1901. GSU, 1973.
W. Warwick
Probate Records 1913-1924 (West Warwick, R.I.). GSU, 2003.

Newport County
Founded 1703

Courts

Newport County Superior Court, Newport

District Court, 2nd Div., Newport
Serves Jamestown, Little Compton, Middletown, Newport, Portsmouth, Tiverton.

Newport County Family Court, Newport

Probate and Municipal Courts
Jamestown Probate Court
Docket/record books, 1700-2004; some indexing.
Little Compton Probate Court
Docket/record books, file papers (original and microfilm), name index; 1746-date.
Middletown Probate Court and Municipal Court
Newport Probate Court and Municipal Court
Portsmouth Probate Court
Original docket/record books.
Tiverton Probate Court and Municipal Court
Probate: docket/record books, file papers (original, and some transcripts); 1747-date.
Municipal traffic and ordinance violations: docket/record books, file papers, appeals;
original, 1993-date.

State Archives and Records Center

Rhode Island State Archives, Providence
Court of Common Pleas, Newport. Case doc. 1744-1771, 1820-1827. AG bx. 407c.
Court of Common Pleas, Newport. Docket, 1880-1891.
Court of Magistrates, Newport. Annual Report 1849-1850.
Supreme Court, Newport, Appellate Div. Docket, 1894-1901.
Supreme Court, Newport. *Sisson v. Church*, 1865-1867. AG bx. 407c.

Rhode Island Supreme Judicial Court, Judicial Records Center, Pawtucket
Court of Common Pleas (and predecessor courts). Indexes: plaintiff and defendant,
    1730-1905. Record Books: 1730-1905, and Special Court of Common Pleas,
    1758-1810.
Court of General Sessions of the Peace. Record Books: 1746-1837.

Supreme Court (and predecessor courts). Indexes: plaintiff and defendant, 1671-1905. Record Books: 1671-1750, 1754-1905. *Note:* Newport County "Court Book A" covered General Court of Trials for entire colony, 1671-1721.

State Historical Society

Rhode Island Historical Society, Providence
Newport Town Records Collection, 1729-1829. Mss 208. Misc. court and probate records.

Other Repositories

Library of Congress, Washington, D.C.
The case, Trevett against Weeden...for refusing paper bills in payment for butcher's meat,...tried before the honourable Superior Court, in the county of Newport, September term, 1786.... Providence: John Carter, 1787. Rare Book/Special Collections, AC901.M5./Law Library, KFR401.5.

New England Historic Genealogical Society, Boston, Mass.
Documents concerning Joseph Sanford, 1784-1841. MSS C 5694. Re: Hannah Hall's estate.
Rhode Island. Court of Commissioners. Acts and orders, 1656 May 22. MSS C 1196. Portsmouth.
Wilbour, Benjamin F. "Little Compton, Rhode Island, Wills." 1945. Abstract of original probate records of Taunton, Mass. and Little Compton, R.I. MSS A 801. *See also* "Digital/Electronic Sources," *below.*

Newport Historical Society, Newport
Original Newport town records (which survived confiscation by British and shipwreck during American Revolution), including land evidence, wills and probate records; finding aids. Also rare books and microform records.

University of Rhode Island Library, Special Collections, Kingston
Dismissed with Prejudice. Series I, Court Documents, 1957-1960. MSG #146. *Commerce Oil Refining Corp. v. William W. Miner, et al.* Alleged conspiracy to obstruct development of refinery. Superior Court, Newport; U.S. District Court, District of R.I.; U.S. Court of Appeals.

Books

Beaman, Alden G. *Newport County, Rhode Island, Marriages from Probate Records, 1647-1860.* Princeton, Mass.: R.I. Families Assoc., 1984.
Fiske, Jane Fletcher. *Gleanings from Newport Court Files, 1659-1783.* Boxford, Mass.: By author, 1998.
_____. *Rhode Island General Court of Trials, 1671-1704.* Boxford, Mass.: By author, 1998.
Perry, Amos, and Clarence S. Brigham. *The Early Records of the Town of Portsmouth.* Providence: E. L. Freeman & Sons, 1901.

Microform

Miscellaneous court records

Court Records, 1730-1881. GSU, 1973. FHL computer #79666. Court of Common Pleas and Inferior Court of Common Pleas.

Court Records, 1751-1785, 1813-1833. GSU, 1973. Justices' Court, Middletown; includes some marriages.

Naturalization records

Declarations of Intention, 1890-1929. GSU, 1997. Superior Court.

Declarations of Intention of Naturalization 1888-1905. GSU, 1973. Court of Common Pleas.

Declarations of Intention (Newport County), 1929-1941. GSU, 1997. Superior Court.

Military Petitions for Naturalization (Newport County), 1902-1918. GSU, 1997. Superior Court.

Naturalization Index, 1793-1942. GSU, 1996. Court of Common Pleas, Supreme Court and Superior Court.

Naturalization Index, 1793-1981. GSU, 1996. Court of Common Pleas, Supreme Court and Superior Court.

Naturalization Papers Index, Soldiers and Sailors, 1918-1919. GSU, 1997. Court of Common Pleas.

Naturalization Petitions, 1793-1921. GSU, 1996. Court of Common Pleas.

Naturalization Petitions (Newport County), 1915-1929. GSU, 1997. Superior Court.

Naturalization Petitions (Newport County), 1929-1945. GSU, 1997. Superior Court.

Probate records (Town Councils and Probate Courts)
Jamestown

Land Evidence Records, 1680-1899 (index 1680-1903). GSU, 1973, 2000. Vol. 1 includes wills and probate.

Records of the Town (1744-1796) and the Town Council (1746-1766) of Jamestown, Rhode Island, and Index. GSU, 1990.

Town Council and Probate Records, 1767-1915. GSU, 1973, 2000.

Little Compton

Little Compton, Rhode Island, Probate Records, 1876-1915. GSU, 1999.

Town Council and Probate Records, 1746-1881. GSU, 1973.

Middletown

Probate Docket (1896-1936) and Books (1881-1921), 1881-1936. GSU, 2002.

Probate Records and Bonds, 1850-1907. GSU, 1973.

Town Council Records, 1743-1879. GSU, 1973. Includes probate, wills, inventories, guardianship.

Newport

Administration Bonds and Index, 1728-1775. GSU, 1973.

Miscellaneous Inventories, 1721-1748. GSU, 1973. *Note*: Records damaged; parts lost or unreadable.

Probate Records, 1779-1915; Index to Probate Records, 1779-1973. GSU, 1973, 2000.

Town Council Records, 1702-1776. GSU, 1973.

Portsmouth

Probate Bonds, 1829-1926. GSU, 1973, 1996.

Probate Records, 1824-1919. GSU, 1973, 1996.

Town Council and Probate Records, 1697-1930. GSU, 1973, 1996.

Town Records, 1638-1850. GSU, 1973. Includes wills, inventories, etc.

Tiverton

Durfee, Grace S., and Henry C. Durfee. *Newport County Miscellaneous Records.* GSU, 1969. Includes Tiverton probate records.

Probate and Town Council Records, 1747-1920. GSU, 1972.

Probate Dockets (1882-1918), Estates (1830-1844), and Probate Bonds (1874-1916). GSU, 1996.

Tiverton (R.I.) Probate Records, 1747-1900. GSU, 2002.

Town Council Records, 1776-1929, and Some Probate Records to ca. 1790. GSU, 1996.

Town Meetings, 1697-1906. GSU, 1972. Includes probate.

Digital/Electronic Sources

Internet

New England Historic Genealogical Society *www.NewEnglandAncestors.org*

> *Little Compton, Rhode Island, Wills.* Boston: NewEnglandAncestors.org, 2003. Abstract of original probate records, Taunton, Mass. and Little Compton, R.I. Benjamin F. Wilbour. "Little Compton, Rhode Island, Wills." 1945. *See* "Other Repositories," *above.*

Providence County
Founded 1703

Courts

Providence County Superior Court, Providence

District Court, 6th Div., Providence

Serves Barrington, Bristol, Burrillville, Central Falls, Cranston, Cumberland, E. Providence, Foster, Glocester, Johnston, Lincoln, N. Providence, N. Smithfield, Pawtucket, Providence, Scituate, Smithfield, Warren, Woonsocket.

Providence County Family Court, Providence

Probate and Municipal Courts

Burrillville Probate Court, Harrisville

Docket/record books, file papers, appeals; original and microfilm, 1806-date.

Central Falls Probate Court

Cranston Probate Court and Municipal Court

Cumberland Probate Court and Municipal Court

E. Providence Probate Court

Docket/record books, file papers, appeals; original, 1862-date; computer index.

E. Providence Municipal Court

Civil docket/record books, file papers, appeals; original and computer, 1994-date.

Foster Probate Court

Docket/record books, wills; original, 1781-date; card file index.

Glocester Probate Court, Glocester/Chepachet

Docket/record books, 1815-date; some indexed.

Johnston Municipal Court
Docket/record books, file papers, appeals; original and computer, 1993-date; no index.
Johnston Probate Court
Docket/record books; original, 1898-date.
Lincoln Probate Court
Docket/record books, file papers, appeals, index; original, 1895-date.
N. Providence Probate Court and Municipal Court
N. Smithfield Probate Court
Original docket/record books, 1871-date; index.
Pawtucket Probate Court and Municipal Court
Probate: original docket/record books, 1778-date; index.
Providence Probate Court
Docket/record books, file papers, appeals, index; original and microfilm, 1900-date.
Providence Municipal Court
Scituate Probate Court, N. Scituate
Docket/record books, file papers, appeals, index; 1731-date.
Smithfield Probate Court, Esmond
Woonsocket Probate Court and Municipal Court
Criminal (petty misdemeanors only), housing, building code, zoning, animal control, moving violations: original dockets, 1987-date (moving violations, 1993-date).

State Archives and Records Center

Rhode Island State Archives, Providence
Court of Common Pleas, Providence. Docket, 1870-1872, 1875-1876.
Court House, Providence. Accounts, 1877-1878; minutes, 1876-1878; accounts/vouchers, 1876, 1878. C#1297.
Supreme Court, Providence. Docket, 1872-1893.

Rhode Island Supreme Judicial Court, Judicial Records Center, Pawtucket
Court of Common Pleas (and predecessor courts). Indexes: plaintiff and defendant, 1731-1917. Record Books: 1730-1803, 1805-1901 (1902-1906 missing).
Court of General Sessions of the Peace. Record Books: 1730-1750.
Special Court of Common Pleas. Record Books: 1819-1892.
Supreme Court (and predecessor courts). Indexes: plaintiff, 1747-1906; defendant, 1747-1900 (1901-1906 missing). Record Books: 1747-1905.

State Historical Society

Rhode Island Historical Society, Research Library, Providence
Cranston Town Records Collection, 1780-1925. Mss 193. Some court records, probate book, etc.
Foster Town Records Collection, 1760-1900. Mss 198. Jury warrants, 1800-1887; Justice Court records (bastardy proceedings), 1804-1847; Probate Court records, 1783-1899; writs, 1825-1852, 1866.
Johnston Town Records Collection, 1759-1899. Mss 202. Justice Court records and sheriff's writs, 1757-1768, 1805-1809; Probate Court records, 1759-1823, etc.
Scituate Town Records Collection, 1748-1915. Mss 216. Deposition of Benjamin Angell, 1851, etc.

Smithfield Town Records Collection, 1731-1892. Mss 217. Justice Court records, 1802-1823; petition re: bastard child, 1742, etc.

Warwick Town Records Collection, 1647-1844. Mss 221. Court of Trials records, 1659-1674; other court records, 1718-1729; Warwick wills transcriptions, 1703-1761; etc. *Note*: Warwick was part of Providence County until 1750.

Other Repositories

Brown University Library, Providence
Trial and a sketch of the life of Amos Miner, now under sentence of death for the murder of John Smith late town-sergeant of Boston, tried before the Supreme…Court of Rhode Island, march term, 1833…. Providence, 1833. Hay Rider, Box 32 No. 2. Trial for highway robbery.

Harvard University, Widener Library, Cambridge, Mass.
Report of the case of John Dorrance against Arthur Fenner, tried at the December term, of the Court of common pleas, in the county of Providence, A.D. 1801…. Providence: Wheeler, 1802. Harvard Depository US 14474.2; HOLLIS #006424384.

Library of Congress, Washington, D. C.
Records of the Rhode Island Superior Court, 1844. MMC, MSS4028. Vol. from court session held at Providence.

New England Historic Genealogical Society, Boston, Mass.
Slater, Samuel. Deposition, 1820 October 24. MSS C 5092. N. Providence, R.I.; testimony before Justice of the Peace Stephen Jenks, in trial of *Lydia Croade v. Edmund R. Croade* re: failure to honor promissory note.

Providence City Archives, Providence
First, Second and Third Books of the Town of Providence, 1647-1715. Contain court records and wills. *See also* "Microform," *below*.
Will Book No. 1, 1670-1720/1. Will Book No. 2, 1716-28/29.

University of Rhode Island Library, Kingston
Docket of the Court of Common Pleas for the county of Providence: December term, A.D. 1878. Providence: E. L. Freeman & Co., 1878. URI RI Collection, KFR48 P9 1878.

Books and Journals

Bartlett, John Russell, ed. *Records of the Colony and State of Rhode Island and Providence Plantations*. 10 vols. New York: AMS Press, 1968. *See also,* "Digital/Electronic Sources," *below*.

Bowen, Richard Le Baron. *Index to the Early Records of the Town of Providence*. Salem, Mass.: Higginson Book Co., 2000.

The Early Records of the Town of Providence. 21 vols. Providence: Snow & Farnham, 1892-1915.

Field, Edward. *Index to the Probate Records of the Municipal Court of the City of Providence, Rhode Island: From 1646 to and including the Year 1899*. Providence: Providence Press, 1902. *See also* "Microform" and "Digital/Electronic Sources," *below*.

Rhode Island Court Records: Records of the Court of Trials of the Colony of Providence Plantations, 1640-1670. 2 vols. Providence, 1920-1922.

The Rhode Island Jewish Historical Notes. Providence: R.I. Jewish Historical Assoc. Including:

Adelman, David C. "Jews in the Court Records of Providence 1739-1860." Vol. 1, no. 1 (1954).

Zurier, Melvin L., Esq. "How Jewish Parties Fared in the Rhode Island Supreme Court: 1870-1912, and 1913-1924." Vol. 6, no. 2 (1972); no. 3 (1973).

Microform

Miscellaneous court records

First, Second and Third Books of the Town of Providence: 1647-1715. GSU, 1972. Includes court records, wills, etc.

Early American Imprints, Series II. Shaw-Shoemaker (1801-1819). New Canaan, Conn.: Readex Microprint, in cooperation with American Antiquarian Society, 1987-1992. Microfiche. Including: *Report of the case of John Dorrance against Arthur Fenner: tried at the December term of the Court of Common Pleas, in the county of Providence, A.D. 1801....* Providence: Bennett Wheeler, 1802. Shaw & Shoemaker, 2156.

Rhode Island Court Records: Records of the Court of Trials of the Colony of Providence Plantations, 1647-1670. 2 vols. Providence: R.I. Historical Society, 1920-1922. GSU, 1981.

Naturalization records

Declarations of Intention, 1928-1949. GSU, 1997. Superior Court.
Declarations of Intentions (Providence County), 1917-1927. GSU, 1997. Superior Court.
Naturalization and Citizenship Index. 1793-1892. GSU, 1996. R.I. Supreme Court.
Naturalization and Citizenship Index, 1793-1905. GSU, 1996. Court of Common Pleas.
Naturalization Petitions (Providence County), 1917-1929. GSU, 1997. R.I. Supreme Court.
Naturalization Petitions, 1793-1892. GSU, 1996. Supreme Judicial Court.
Naturalization Petitions, 1820-1893. GSU, 1996-1997. Court of Common Pleas.
Naturalization Records, 1930-1946. GSU, 1997. Superior Court.

Probate records (Town Councils and Probate Courts)
Burrillville
Probate Records, Warrants, Bonds, 1806-1956. GSU, 1973, 2002.
Central Falls
Probate Dockets, 1890-1923. GSU, 1993.
Probate Records, 1733-1917 (Lincoln, Rhode Island). GSU, 1974, 1993. Includes Central Falls, from 1895.
Cranston
Estate Files, early to 1885 (Cranston, Rhode Island). GSU, 2004.
Probate Index: early to 2003 (Cranston, Rhode Island). GSU, 2003.
Probate Records: 1798-1894 (Cranston, Rhode Island). GSU, 1973.
Probate Records: 1888-1916 (Cranston, Rhode Island). GSU, 1973.

Town and Probate Records: 1754-1877 (Cranston and Smithfield, Rhode Island).
GSU, 1973.

Cumberland

Probate Records, 1746-1916. GSU, 1974, 1993.

Probate Records, 1874-1925. GSU, 1993.

E. Providence

East Providence, R.I., Probate Indexes and Records, 1862-1998. GSU, 2002.

East Providence, R.I., Probate Records, 1862-1894. GSU, 1973.

Foster

Probate Records, 1781-1887. GSU, 1973.

Glocester

Probate Records, 1731-1915. GSU, 2000.

Town Council Records, 1731-1892. GSU, 1973.

Johnston

Field, Edward. *Probate Records of the Town of Johnston, Being Copies of Wills Admitted to Probate from January 1, 1875 to June 1, 1898.* GSU, 1973.

Partitions, Dower Agreements and Leases, 1843-1888. GSU, 1973.

Probate Records, 1646-1899. GSU, 1972.

Probate Records, 1759-1898. GSU, 1972.

Probate Records, 1840-1898. GSU, 1992.

Lincoln

Lincoln, Rhode Island, Probate Records, 1895-1915. GSU, 1999.

Probate Records, 1733-1917 (Lincoln, Rhode Island). GSU, 1974, 1993.

N. Smithfield

North Smithfield, Rhode Island, Probate Records (1870-1915) and Indexes (1871 1969), 1870-1969. GSU, 2002.

N. Providence

Court Records, 1874-1886; Probate Index, 1874-1973. GSU, 1973.

Probate Records, 1870-1907 (Pawtucket, Rhode Island). GSU, 1974. *Note*: Part of N. Providence annexed to Pawtucket in 1874.

Probate Records Index, 1700-1996. GSU, 1996.

Records of the Town Council and Court of Probate, 1765-1874. GSU, 1974.

Pawtucket

Probate Docket 1896-1926 and Probate Records 1877-1916 (Pawtucket, Rhode Island). GSU, 1996.

Probate Files, Early to 1885 (Pawtucket, R.I.). GSU, 2003.

Probate Records, 1862-1877 (Pawtucket, Rhode Island). GSU, 1974.

Probate Records, 1870-1907 (Pawtucket, Rhode Island). GSU, 1974.

Probate Records Index, 1700-1996. GSU, 1996.

Providence

Calef, Frank T. *Genealogical Information Copied From Will Books 6-9 of Providence, R.I.* GSU, 1950.

The Providence Probate Records to 1775 with Index. GSU, 1950. Manuscripts at R.I. Historical Society.

City of Providence Letters of Administration and Guardianship, 1804-1899. GSU, 1992.

Commissioners' Probate Reports, 1820-1899. GSU, 1995.

Estate Papers, 1803-1899. GSU, 1992.

Field, Edward. *Index to the Probate Records of the Municipal Court of the City of Providence, Rhode Island: From 1646 to and including the Year 1899.*

Providence: Providence Press, 1902; Washington, D.C.: Library of Congress Photoduplication Service, 1989.

Guardians Accounts 1839-1893, 1899. GSU, 1972.

Probate Docket Books, 1909-1912. GSU, 1994.

Probate Dockets of Estates, 1824-1921, Index, 1900-1925. GSU, 1994. Includes docket entries, 1703 and 1819 (vol. 22), but most entries 1830s.

Probate Inventories of Estates, 1819-1899. GSU, 1992.

Probate Proceedings, 1798-1876. GSU, 1972.

Probate Proceedings, 1876-1920. GSU, 1994.

Probate Records, 1646-1899. GSU, 1972.

Probate Records: Administration Accounts of the City of Providence, 1821-1899. GSU, 1992.

Probate Records: Bond Books of the City of Providence, 1873-1899. GSU, 1992.

Providence (R.I.) Probate Files (1646-1894) and Indexes (1646-1899). GSU, 2000-2002.

Providence, Rhode Island, Wills (1678-1916) and Indexes (1872-1914). GSU, 1972. Includes wills, administrations and guardianships.

Scituate

Probate and Civil records, 1731-1886. GSU, 1973.

Scituate (R.I.) Probate Records, 1881-1919. GSU, 2002.

Smithfield

Probate Records, 1733-1917 (Lincoln, Rhode Island). GSU, 1974, 1993. *Note*: In 1871, part of Smithfield became town of Lincoln.

Town and Probate Records: 1754-1877 (Cranston and Smithfield, Rhode Island). GSU, 1973.

Town Council Journals, 1770-1871. GSU, 1974. Includes probate records.

Woonsocket

Probate Records, 1867-1883. GSU, 1973.

Woonsocket (R.I.) Probate Indexes 1867-2001 and probate files (early to 1885), 1867-2001. GSU, 2002.

Digital/Electronic Sources

CD-ROM

Bartlett, John Russell, ed. *Records of the Colony and State of Rhode Island and Providence Plantations.* New York: AMS Press, 1968; Boston: New England Historic Genealogical Society, 2003.

Early Records of the Town of Providence, Rhode Island. Bowie, Md.: Heritage Books, 1999. Includes probate records and wills.

Internet

Early American Imprints *www.readex.com/scholarl/earlamim.html*
Shaw-Shoemaker Digital Edition, Series II. Shaw-Shoemaker (1801-1819). Chester, Vt.: Readex/Newsbank, in cooperation with American Antiquarian Society, 2004. Available at academic libraries. *See also* "Microform," *above.*

New England Historic Genealogical Society *www.NewEnglandAncestors.org*
Index to Providence, Rhode Island Probate 1646-1899. Boston: NewEnglandAncestors.org, 2002. From Edward Field. *Index to the Probate Records of the Municipal Court of the City of Providence, Rhode Island: From 1646 to and including the Year 1899.* Providence: Providence Press, 1902.

Washington County
Founded 1729, from Newport County

Courts

Washington County Superior Court, Wakefield

District Court, 4th Div., Wakefield
Original civil and criminal file papers, 2003-date; criminal records on computer, 1996-date.

Washington County Family Court, Wakefield

Probate and Municipal Courts
Charlestown Probate Court
Record books, 1738-date; file papers, 1942-date.
Exeter Probate Court
Docket/record books, index; original, 1743-date.
Hopkinton Probate Court
Docket/record books, index; original and microfilm, 1757-date.
Narragansett Probate Court and Municipal Court
Probate: docket/record books, file papers, index; original and microfilm, 1888-date.
Municipal: docket/record books, file papers, appeals; original and computer, 1992-date. Please make requests in writing.
New Shoreham Probate Court, Block Island
Docket/record books, file papers, appeals, index; original and microfilm, 1798-date.
N. Kingstown Probate Court
Docket/record books, index; original and microfilm, late 1600s-date (however, fires in 1870 and 1920 destroyed or damaged some records). In-person searches, or mail requests for copies (include book and page number, stamped self-addressed envelope, and checks for $1.50/page, payable to Town of N. Kingstown).
Richmond Probate Court, Wyoming
Docket/record books, index; original, 1747-date.
S. Kingstown Probate Court, Wakefield
Docket/record books, index; original, 1723-date.
Westerly Probate Court and Municipal Court
Probate: docket/record books, file papers, index; original, transcripts, microfilm and computer, 1600s-date. Criminal and traffic summons: docket/record books, file papers; original, 1990-2000; computer, 2000-date. Make written request.

State Archives and Records Center

Rhode Island State Archives, Providence
Coroner Inquests, Washington County, 1903-1930. Acc. 2003-2.
Court House, Kingston. Accounts/vouchers, 1864, 1872. C#1297.
Court House, Washington County. Accounts/vouchers, 1869-70, 1889. C#1297.

Rhode Island Supreme Judicial Court, Judicial Records Center, Pawtucket
Supreme Court (and predecessor courts). Indexes: plaintiff and defendant, 1747-1916.
    Record Books: 1747-1905.
Court of Common Pleas (and predecessor courts). Indexes: plaintiff and defendant,
    1731-1960. Record Books: 1731-1829, 1831-1905.

State Historical Society

Rhode Island Historical Society, Providence
Brown, Beriah. Papers, 1710-1874. Mss. 109. Re: sheriff of Kings County (later
    Washington County) and Inferior Court of Common Pleas.
Exeter Town Records Collection, 1740-1869. Mss 197. 7 boxes of Justice Court
    records, 1760-1869.
Richmond Town Records Collection, 1800-1907. Mss. 215. Justice Court records,
    1800-1822.

Other Repositories

New England Historic Genealogical Society, Boston, Mass.
Justice of the Peace record, Kingston, R.I., re: Samuel Cranston and property trespass,
1704. MSS C 1334.

Pettaquamscutt Historical Society, Kingston
Court documents, mostly uncataloged and dispersed, including:
Docket book (civil and criminal) of Justice Benjamin Hull, 1814-1816, and his papers,
    1810-1860.
Arrest warrants, mid-18th-late-19th centuries.
Probate court book, S. Kingstown, 1920s-1930s.
Wills (various dates, 1750-1940), etc.

University of Rhode Island Library, Kingston
Colt Family Papers. MSG #78. Legal papers of attorney Samuel P. Colt, 1850-1915.
    Includes estate files of Hannah B. Smith, Ambrose E. Burnside (Civil War
    general and R.I. governor), and Cornelius J. Vanderbilt; and Colt's papers re:
    other estates, civil and divorce cases, real estate matters, etc.
Westerly list: Court of Common Pleas, Washington County, November term, 1881.
    Westerly, R.I.: G.B. & J.H. Utter, 1881. Court calendar.

Books

Beaman, Alden G. *Rhode Island Vital Records, New Series.* 13 vols. Princeton, Mass:
    By author, 1976-. Includes abstracts of Washington County court records,
    from record books.
_____. *Washington County, Rhode Island Births from Probate Records 1685-1860:
    Comprising the Towns of North Kingstown, South Kingstown, Exeter, West-
    erly, Charleston, Richmond, Hopkinton.* Princeton, Mass.: By author, 1978.
_____. *Washington County, Rhode Island Marriages from Probate Records
    1685-1860: Comprising the Towns of North Kingstown, South Kingstown,
    Exeter, Westerly, Charleston, Richmond, Hopkinton.* Princeton, Mass.:
    By author, 1978.

Microform

Miscellaneous court records
Court Records 1731-1880. GSU, 1973. FHL computer #147974. Court of Common Pleas and Inferior Court of Common Pleas.
Court Records, 1747-1901. GSU, 2000. FHL computer #665926. Superior Court of Judicature and Supreme Court.
Court Records 1782-1821. GSU, 1973. Justices' Court, South Kingstown.
Fines and Recoveries, 1725-1750. GSU, 1973. FHL computer #665912.

Naturalization records
Declarations of Intention, 1917-1929. GSU, 1997. Superior Court.
Declarations of Intention, 1930-1952. GSU, 1997. Superior Court.
Declarations of Naturalization Intention, 1881-1900. GSU, 1973. Court of Common Pleas.
Miscellaneous Naturalization Papers, 1875-1928. GSU, 1993. Hopkinton records.
Naturalization Petitions, 1917-1929. GSU, 1997. Superior Court.
Naturalization Petitions, 1930-1945. GSU, 1993. Superior Court.
Westerly, Rhode Island, Naturalized Citizen List (early to 1925). GSU, 1999.
Westerly (Rhode Island) Naturalization Index, Certificates, and Citizenship Papers Filed at Town Clerk's Office, early to 1945. GSU, 1999.

Probate records (Town Councils and Probate Courts)
Charlestown
Charlestown (R.I.) Probate and Town Council Records, 1738-1916. GSU, 2002.
Probate Records, 1798-1878. GSU, 1973.
Town Records, 1738-1889. GSU, 1973. Includes probate.
Exeter
Exeter, Rhode Island, Probate Records and Index: 1878-1915. GSU, 2000.
Probate Bonds 1872-1902. GSU, 1973.
Town Council and Probate Records 1743-1878. GSU, 1973.
Hopkinton
Probate Bonds (1872-1915) and Docket Books (1895-1928). GSU, 1993.
Probate Index Cards, 1757-1993. GSU, 1993.
Probate Records, 1757-1920. GSU, 1973, 1993.
Town Records, 1743-1920. GSU, 1993. Includes administration bonds, 1788-1813; and probate records, 1780-1920.
Narragansett
Narragansett (R.I.) Probate Records (ca. 1800-1915) and Indexes (1884-1915), 1800-1915. GSU, 2000.
N. Kingstown
Probate and Civil Records of the Town 1692-1877. GSU, 1973.
Probate Records (1873-1933) and Probate Index (1896-1997) – North Kingstown, R.I.. GSU, 2003.
Richmond
Probate Bonds 1873-1914. GSU, 1973.
Probate Records, 1747-1877. GSU, 1973.
Probate Records, 1747-1915; Probate Estate Files Indexes, 1747-1977. GSU, 1999.
S. Kingstown
Town Council Records, 1704-1943. GSU, 1973. Includes probate.

Westerly

Administrator's Bonds, 1872-1916. GSU, 1993.

Indexes of Town, Land, Probate, and Vital Records, 1661-1745. GSU, 1993. Probate records in book 2.

Probate Docket, 1908-1911. GSU, 1993.

Probate Records, 1811-1877. GSU, 1973.

Probate Records, 1874-1894. GSU, 1993.

Probate Records Index, 1798-1990. GSU, 1993.

Town Council and Probate Records, 1699-1888. GSU, 1973.

Westerly, Rhode Island, Probate Files (early to 1885). GSU, 1999.

Fig. 10.2. Courthouse in Woonsocket, Rhode Island, ca. 1908, from the author's collection of vintage picture postcards.

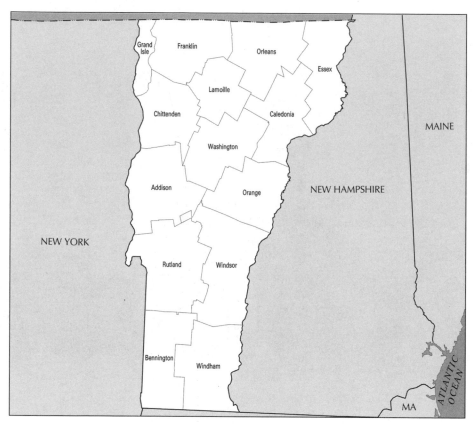

Fig. 11.1. Map of Vermont Counties. *National Atlas of the United States.* 2005.
http://nationalatlas.gov

CHAPTER 11

VERMONT STATE COURTS

Court History Timeline

Courts before Statehood

Before 1764 Massachusetts and New Hampshire granted land to settlers in areas now part of Vermont.

1764 England placed Vermont towns under **New York** jurisdiction (Albany County, 1764-1777). Local **justices of the peace** were appointed. New York issued grants to Vermont land that conflicted with previous land grants.

1766-1775 Vermont counties of Cumberland (1766-1777), Gloucester (1770-1777) and Charlotte (1772-1777) were established. Courts of **General Sessions of the Peace** and **Courts of Common Pleas** operated under New York law.

1775 Protests about conflicting land grants resulted in "Westminster Massacre" (New York authorities fired on unarmed Vermonters at court). New York **courts closed** east of the Green Mountains. The American Revolution began.

1777 Vermont declared independence. The Vermont Constitution provided for **County Courts** in new counties of Cumberland (eastern half of Vermont) and Bennington (western half).

1778 **Superior Court** (predecessor of today's Supreme Court) first met in Bennington. **Probate Districts** were established. **Court of Confiscation** (one in each county) seized and sold Tory estates for Vermont's benefit.

1782 Court system was reorganized. Superior Court was abolished. **Supreme Court** met annually in each county, with jurisdiction over divorce, foreclosures, serious crimes and civil cases in which the State was a party, also hearing appeals from county courts. **County Courts** handled most county matters. **Probate Districts** were created in each county, with appeals to Supreme Court. **Justice of the Peace Courts**, at town and local level, had jurisdiction over small cases.

1788   First **Municipal Court** was established at Vergennes.

Courts after Statehood

1791   Vermont became fourteenth state.

1797   Supreme Court judges were required to issue written decisions (but few were published before 1824). **Court of Chancery** was established to hear "equity" cases, meeting annually in each county, with Supreme Court judges presiding.

1825   Court system was reorganized. **Supreme Court judges assumed dual role**, presiding at County Court sessions (with two assistant judges in each county), and hearing appeals to Supreme Court. Appeals were granted only for issues of law, *i.e.*, no retrial of facts determined in County Court.

1850-1857   State was divided into **four judicial circuits**, with **circuit judge** appointed in each to preside at County Courts and also to hear chancery (equity) cases.

1865   **Municipal Court** was established at Burlington; later municipal courts at Barre, Bellows Falls, Bennington, Brattleboro, Brighton, Montpelier, Rutland, St. Albans, Springfield, Winooski, and in counties of Addison, Caledonia and Orleans.

1906   General Assembly increased number of judges and separated their functions. **Supreme Court** cases were heard only at **Montpelier**, and Supreme Court judges no longer traveled to or presided over County Courts.

1965   **Municipal Courts** disbanded.

Vermont Courts Today

Supreme Court

Vermont's Supreme Court hears appeals from cases decided in lower courts.

Superior Court

One Superior Court provides trials in each county, by a panel of three judges or by a jury with a presiding judge. Superior Court has exclusive jurisdiction over most civil cases and some criminal cases.

District Court

One District Court provides judge or jury trials in each county, hearing predominantly criminal cases. Civil cases include suspension of driver's license, fish and wildlife violations, and appeals of traffic tickets and municipal ordinance decisions.

Family Court

One Family Court, located in each county, hears family-related legal matters, including divorce, juvenile, domestic abuse and child support cases. There are no jury trials. All juvenile proceedings are confidential; public may not access records.

Probate Court

Vermont's southern counties each have two Probate Districts:
- Bennington County (Bennington and Manchester)
- Rutland County (Fair Haven and Rutland)
- Windham County (Marlboro and Westminster)
- Windsor County (Hartford and Windsor).

There is one Probate Court in each of the other counties. Probate Court has jurisdiction over wills, settlement of estates, adoptions, guardianships, name changes, etc. Confidential records include adoptions, involuntary guardianship evaluations, wills, juvenile records and mental health records. Adoption records are retained permanently and sealed for ninety-nine years from the adoptee's birthdate; then the birth certificate is unsealed and becomes a public record.

Environmental Court

Vermont's Environmental Court meets in locations throughout the state, hearing appeals of environmental, land use and zoning cases.

Vermont Judicial Bureau

Hearing officers for the Vermont Judicial Bureau handle traffic tickets and other violations of municipal ordinances. *Note*: Records of the Vermont Judicial Bureau are not included in this book.

Where to Find Court Records
See Appendix for complete contact information.

Until recently, Vermont had no uniform policies for court record retention. Practice varied from court to court, and conflicting jurisdiction at state and local levels created much confusion—some clerks or judges denying public access, reorganizing or purging court files, or giving records to outside parties. Vermont court records, scattered throughout the State in public and private repositories, were difficult to find and use.

That chaotic situation began to change in 2004. The Vermont Judicial Records Program (VJRP), a joint project of the Vermont Court Administrator's Office and the Vermont State Archives, took the first steps to consolidate archival court records. VJRP is inventorying records still held at courthouses or warehoused at the State Records Center by the Department of Buildings and General Services—a massive ongoing effort—and preparing an online database (to be launched with a partial listing of records in 2006).

The Vermont State Archives gained legal custody, in 2005, of all Vermont judicial records dating before 1931, but many of those records will remain in courthouses and other repositories until construction of a proposed new State Archives building with more vault space. In the meantime, while these changes are being implemented, researchers should contact the Vermont State Archives, court clerks, or other repositories listed below for the latest information.

Statewide or General Sources

Courts

Supreme Court of Vermont, Montpelier
Current records only. Case files returned to lower courts after decision; briefs, 2001-date, in temporary storage at Records Center (*see below*). *See also* Vermont Department of Libraries ("Other Repositories") and other sources *below*.

Environmental Court, Barre
Original docket/record books, file papers, appeals, 1996-date; reporter notes, video and audio tapes, 1997-date; computer dockets.

Other State Courts
See "Courts" section for each county, *below*.

State Archives and Records Center

Vermont State Archives, Montpelier
The State Archives has legal custody of Vermont court records dating before 1931, but many of those records remain in scattered public and private repositories, until construction of a new Archives facility. Watch for forthcoming online database at *www.vermont-archives.org* (which will list record series, dates and locations) or contact the State Archives with specific questions. Judicial records currently at the State Archives include:
Henry Stevens Collection. Including court records, 1716-1854. *See* "Books and Journals," *below*, for published guide to collection.
Vermont State Papers. 82 vols. 18th and 19th-century manuscripts, with index, *e.g.*:
        Vols. 12-16. *Courts*. 1778-1799. *See also* "Courts" section for each county, *below.*
        Vol. 27. *Extents*. Early writs of execution, to recover debts due to the State.
        Vol. 37. *Confiscations*. 1777-1782. Court of Confiscations; seizure of Tory estates to finance Revolutionary War.
        Vol. 38. *Miscellaneous*. 1777-1799. Includes depositions.

Vol. 40. *Wolf Certificates* [and Panther]. 1778-1799. Signed by judges and justices of the peace, authorizing bounties.
Vol. 72. *Depositions*. 1808-1841.
Vols. 78-79. *Miscellaneous*. 1800-1866. Includes list of suits prosecuted by state's attorneys.

Vermont Dept. of Buildings and General Services, Records Center, Montpelier
Until the State Archives took custody of pre-1931 court records in 2005, many courts warehoused older records at the State Records Center. Hundreds of boxes (pre-1931, as well as more recent records) remain unopened and unprocessed there, pending review by the Vermont Judicial Records Program. The Records Center microfilmed some court records, generally destroying the originals, but the resulting microfilm is often of poor quality, not well organized, sometimes mixing confidential files with public records. Some indexes are available, but they are incomplete or outdated.

The Records Center does, however, provide useful microfilm of vital records (birth, death and marriage data). Other resources include microfilm of older probate records, by district, and a card index to Vermont naturalizations before 1906. *See* "Vermont Dept. of Buildings and General Services, Records Center" in section for each county, *below*, re: other court records that may be available at the State Records Center. Call first to confirm availability.

Federal Archives and Records Center

U.S. National Archives and Records Administration (NARA), Northeast Region-Waltham (Boston), Mass.
Naturalization: Dexigraph collection (negative photostats) of naturalization records from 301 federal and state courts in five New England states (Maine, Mass., N.H., R.I. and Vt.), 1790-1906. Index is available on microfilm, as *Index to New England Naturalization Petitions, 1791-1906*; *see* "Microform," *below*. *Note*: NARA-Waltham staff will search index and provide copies for a fee; need name, residence at time of application, and birth date.

State Historical Society

Vermont Historical Society, Barre
Much of the manuscript collection is not yet cataloged online but can be accessed by indexes and finding aids in the library. Holdings include:
Docket book for Supreme Court in several counties, 1812-1823. AC 352.0743 V592.
Kellogg, John and Loyal Papers. MS-33. Rutland County jury cases, 1855; court docket, 1848; Supreme Court calendar, 1859; County Court calendar, 1849; Supreme Court docket, 1866.
Kellogg, Loyal C. Court Dockets. Doc Box 56. Vt. Supreme Court dockets, 1860-1866.
Kellogg Papers. Doc Box 72. Includes bound judge's dockets of Chancery Court, 1860-1864, 1866; and Hon. Asahel Peck's docket, Sept. 1866.
Records re: lawsuits, *e.g.*, 1782 treason trials of Timothy and Charles Phelps. *X 974.3 P513.
Royce-Washburn papers. MSC-50. Law practice of Stephen Royce of Berkshire, Vt. and Reuben Washburn of Lynn, Mass. and Ludlow, Vt. Bound manuscript

book with records of estates settled, 1818-22; court records of 1830s-1850s (approx. 2000 individual records); Vt. Supreme Court dockets, 1834, 1839-49; writs, depositions, bail bonds, attorneys' briefs; etc. (various counties).

Vt. Supreme Court:

Court docket, 1812-1823. AC352.0743 V592.

General Term at Woodstock...on the first Tuesday of November, 1858. Woodstock: Davis & Greene, 1858. Pam.

Williams, Charles Kilborn. *Rules of the Court of Chancery of the State of Vermont.* Irasburgh, Vt.: 1840. Pam.

Other Repositories

U.S. Citizenship and Immigration Services, U.S. Dept. of Homeland Security, Washington, D.C.

Naturalization certificate files ("C-Files"): Copies of naturalization records from state and federal courts after September 27, 1906, *e.g.*, Declaration of Intention, Petition for Naturalization, and Certificate of Naturalization.

1906-1956: Available on microfilm. Make Freedom of Information/Privacy Act (FOIA/PA) request to U.S. Citizenship and Immigration Services in Washington, D.C.

After 1956: Make FOIA/PA request to the district U.S. Citizenship and Immigration Services office that maintains the records, or office nearest your residence.

See Appendix: Contact Information-Archives and Other Repositories, Washington, D.C.

University of Vermont, Bailey/Howe Library, Burlington

Kerin, Austin H. *Yankees in Court: Humorous Tales from Vermont Courtrooms.* Brattleboro: Stephen Daye Press, 1937. Special Collections Wilbur, PN6231.L4 K47 1937.

Potash, P. Jeffrey. *Litigious Vermonters: Court Records to 1825.* Burlington: Univ. of Vt., 1979. Special Collections Wilbur, KFV78.P67 1979. Pilot project of National Historical Publications and Records Commission, to microfilm and index Supreme and County Court record books for Chittenden, Windsor, Washington, and Bennington Counties. *Note*: Original court records from that project are now at Vermont State Archives.

Slade, William, ed. *Vermont State Papers....* Middlebury: J. W. Copeland, 1823, 549-556. Special Collections Wilbur, F52.V4. Includes early Vt. Supreme Court decisions.

Vt. Supreme Court reports and digests (*see* "Books and Journals," *below*), in Library's Special Collections.

Vermont Dept. of Libraries, Law Library, Montpelier

Vt. Supreme Court briefs: From cases published in *Vermont Reporter*. Original briefs, 1871-1978. Microfiche, 1978-2001. From unpublished cases, 1994-2002. Law publisher West has briefs, 2003-date, to be scanned for forthcoming database.

Books and Journals

Court Records—Abstracts, Transcripts and Indexes

Proceedings of the Vermont Historical Society for the years 1923, 1924, 1925. Bellows Falls: Vt. Historical Society, 1926, 141-192. Reprint, *The Upper Connecticut:*

Narratives of its Settlement and its Part in the American Revolution. Vol. 2. Montpelier: Vt. Historical Society, 1943, 141-192. Court records of Gloucester County (under N.Y. jurisdiction, 1770-1777).

History

Bandel, Betty. "What the Good Laws of Man Hath Put Asunder." *Vermont History* 46 (Fall 1978): 221-233. History of divorce in Vt.

Bellesiles, Michael A. "The Establishment of Legal Structures on the Frontier: The Case of Revolutionary Vermont." *Journal of American History* (March 1987).

Crockett, Walter H. *Vermont: The Green Mountain State.* New York: Century History Co., 1923, 5:1-473. Vt. courts and legal system.

Hand, Samuel. "Lay Judges and the Vermont Judiciary to 1825." *Vermont History* 46 (Fall 1978): 205-220.

Nuquist, Andrew E., and Edith W. Nuquist. *Vermont State Government and Administration: An Historical and Descriptive Study of the Living Past.* Burlington: Univ. of Vt. Government Research Center, 1966, 218-240. Vt. courts, 1777-1966.

Taft, Russell S. "The Supreme Court of Vermont." *Vermont Legislative Directory.* Montpelier: 1915, 299-321. Also published in other early 20th-century annual eds. of *Directory.*

Thurber, Harris E. "The Vermont Judiciary: A Study in Cultural Adaptation." Ph.D. diss., Princeton Univ., 1955. Chapters 3 and 4, pp. 85-192, discuss structure of courts.

Vermont Historical Society Collections. 2 vols. Montpelier: 1870-1871.

Wheeler, Hoyt Henry. "The Early Jurisdiction and Jurisprudence of the Territory Now Vermont." *Vermont Bar Association Proceedings* 1 (1882): 51-77.

Law Library Resources

Case Reports: *See Chapter 17*, and *Appendix-Law Libraries* and *Publishers. See also* "Microform" and "Digital/Electronic Sources," *below.*

Vermont Supreme Court

"Nominative reports." Court decisions, 1789-1826. *e.g.*:

Slade, William. *Vermont State Papers.* Middlebury: 1823. Earliest cases.

Chipman, Nathaniel. *Report and Dissertations.* Rutland: 1793. Cases 1789-1791.

Tyler, Royall. *Reports of Cases....* 2 vols. New York: 1809. Cases 1800-1803.

Chipman, Daniel. *Reports.* Middlebury: 1824. Vol. 1, citing early cases.

Vermont Reports. Montpelier: Vt. Supreme Court. Court decisions, 1826-date.

Atlantic Reporter. Eagan, Minn.: West. Court decisions, 1885-date, enhanced with headnotes, key numbers and synopses.

West's Vermont Digest. Eagan, Minn.: West. 1764-date. *West's Atlantic Digest.* Eagan, Minn.: West. 1789-date. Digests of Vt. state and federal court decisions, organized alphabetically by topic, with headnotes, key numbers, and multiple indexes (case name, etc.).

Research Guides

Durfee, Eleazer D., and Gregory Sanford. *A Guide to the Henry Stevens, Sr. Collection at the Vermont State Archives.* Montpelier: Vt. Secretary of State's Office, 1989, 1991. Available at libraries, or from Vt. State Archives.

Eicholz, Alice. *Collecting Vermont Ancestors.* Montpelier: New Trails, 1986, 5-6.

Microform

Index to New England Naturalization Petitions, 1791-1906. National Archives and Records Admin., 1983. M1299. Alphabetical index of individuals naturalized, in state and federal courts of Maine, Mass., N.H., R.I. and Vt. (indicates court and certificate number).

Vermont Reports. Vol. 1-127. Montpelier: Vt. Supreme Court, 1826-1970. *N. Chipman's Reports,* 1789-1791; *D. Chipman's Reports,* 1789-1825; *Tyler's Reports,* 1800-1803; *Brayton's Reports,* 1815-1819; *Aiken's Reports,* 1825-1828. Kaneohe, Hawaii: Law Library Microform Consortium. Microfiche.

Digital/Electronic Sources

CD-ROM

Atlantic Reporter. Eagan, Minn.: West. Includes Vt. Supreme Court opinions, 1945-date.

Vermont Reporter and West's Vermont Statutes. Eagan, Minn.: West. Vt. cases as reported in *Atlantic Reporter,* 1944-date.

West's Vermont Digest. Eagan, Minn.: West. Index to state and federal appellate court decisions, 1789-date.

Internet

Catalog of Vermont Archives and Manuscripts *http://arccat.uvm.edu*
    Online catalog of unpublished archival and manuscript collections, including court records, at various Vt. repositories.

Cornell University Law School Legal Information Institute
    www.law.cornell.edu/states/vermont.html#opinions
    Vt. Supreme Court opinions, 1993-date.

Law Library of Congress *www.loc.gov/law/guide/us-vt.html*
    Links to Vt. state and federal court opinions and resources.

LexisNexis *www.lexis.com*
    Vt. Supreme Court, 1826-date. Subscription service or available at law libraries and other repositories.

LexisOne *www.lexisone.com*
    Vt. Supreme Court, most recent five years; free.

Loislaw *www.loislaw.com*
    Vt. Supreme Court, 1924-date. Subscription service.

New England Historic Genealogical Society *www.NewEnglandAncestors.org*
    Bartley, Scott Andrew. "The Vermont Court System: An Historical Overview." Parts 1 and 2. 2000.
    _____. "Vermont Probate Records." 2003.

Vermont Courts Online (service of the Vermont Judiciary)
    http://secure.vermont.gov/vtcdas/user
    Online search of civil and small claims case data from District, Family, and Superior Courts of all Vt. counties (except Superior Courts of Chittenden and Franklin Counties), 1995-date. Fees.

Vermont Department of Libraries: Vermont Legal Decisions
    http://dol.state.vt.us/www_root/000000/html/supct.html
    Vt. Supreme Court, 1993-date.
    http://dol.state.vt.us/gopher_root5/000000/env_court/envcrt.html
    Vt. Environmental Court decisions, 1995, 1999-date.

Vermont Judiciary *www.vermontjudiciary.org*
>   Official Vt. court website

VersusLaw *www.versuslaw.com*
>   Vt. Supreme Court, from 1930. Subscription service.

WashLaw Web *www.washlaw.edu/uslaw/states/Vermont*
>   Vt. Supreme Court, July 1993-date.

Westlaw *www.westlaw.com*
>   Vt. Supreme Court, 1789-date. Subscription service or available at law libraries and other repositories. Westlaw CourtEXPRESS offers case research and document retrieval from U.S. courts.

Addison County
Founded 1785, from Rutland County

Courts

Addison Superior Court, Middlebury

Addison District Court, Middlebury
Criminal: original docket/record books and file papers; computer, 1991-date.

Addison Family Court, Middlebury
Docket/record books, file papers; original, 1973-date.

Addison Probate Court, Middlebury
Some records of estate settlements; earliest records destroyed by fire in 1852 (Addison District only).

State Archives and Records Center

Vermont State Archives, Vermont Judicial Records Program, Montpelier
Vermont State Papers. Vol. 16. *Courts.* 1778-1799.

Vermont Dept. of Buildings and General Services, Records Center, Montpelier
Vergennes City Court, 1794-1815.
Justice of the Peace: Salisbury and Shaftsbury, 1842-1855, 1891-1909.

State Historical Society

Vermont Historical Society, Barre
Addison County Court. First docket. Middlebury. #895. Manuscript copy, 1786, including humorous verse by Roswell Hopkins, clerk.
Bascom, Ortemidorus. Justice of the Peace Docket Book. MSC-199. Orwell, 1822-1830.
Kellogg, Loyal C. Court dockets. MSC-171. Including Addison Supreme Court, 1867.

Other Repositories

Henry Sheldon Museum of Vermont History, Middlebury
Extensive collection of original court and probate records, especially from Addison County, described in online catalog (*www.henrysheldonmuseum.org*), published guide

by Elizabeth H. Dow, *Treasures Gathered Here: A Guide to the Manuscript Collection of the Sheldon Museum Research Center* (Middlebury, Vt.: Sheldon Museum, 1991), and unpublished inventories and finding aids, *e.g.*:

Addison County Court: Case List, 1806-1815, 1874-1877; Dockets, 1858-1880; Hearing and Trial Notes, 1803-1805; Judge Hayward's Dockets...,1851-1853 [1995.84 (1851), 1997.70 (1852, 1853)]; Jury Lists, 1809-1855; Records of Addison and Franklin County Courts, 1793-1888; Rules and Dockets of Addison County Court, 1787-1900.

Addison County Municipal Court: Criminal File papers, Middlebury, 1917-1939.

Addison Probate Court: Distribution of estate of John Strong, 1818-1833 [F.I.C.]; Document of Guardian Assignment, 1855 [1992.32].

Addison Superior Court: Docket No. S85-80Ac, 1982. [1983.234]. Transcript of case re: right-of-way to land in E. Middlebury.

Also court and probate records in numerous collections of personal papers, *e.g.*:

Papers of Joel Boardman, 1797-1863. Middlebury and E. Middlebury court papers.

Papers of William P. Brown, ca. 1800-1860. Docket of court cases, 1827.

Papers of Abraham Holden. 1832 court proceedings re: veteran's pension. 1986.306.1-1986.306.3.

Papers of Thomas H. McLeod, 1860-1888. Addison County Court dockets, 1860-1871.

Preston family papers, 1799-1844. Deposition and court papers re: 1844 lawsuit.

Records of Roberts & Chittenden, 1860-1963. Law firm records of cases tried in Addison County Court, including witness testimony.

Papers of Horatio Seymour, 1800-1855. Court docket, 1803-1809.

Seymour family papers, 1800-1888. Court dockets and legal documents.

Harmon A. Sheldon Estate papers, 1870-1889.

Sheldon, Henry L. Scrapbook 76: Middlebury justice writs and legal documents, ca. 1880-1900.

Papers of John M. Stickney, 1869-1958. Deeds and probate records.

Family papers of Holland Weeks, 1764-1886; and Weeks family papers, 1764-1900. Court writs and estate records.

E. D. Woodbridge & Sons records, 1826-1843. Vergennes law firm, with case information and Addison County Court dockets.

Woodbridge family papers, 1794-1867. Court records, etc.

Court dockets of Emerson R. Wright, 1844-1892; Legal cases of Emerson R. Wright, 1798-1880; Papers of Middlebury lawyer and Justice of the Peace.

Shoreham Town Clerk's Office, Shoreham
Aaron Lawrence's Justice of the Peace records, 1790s-1820, re: marriages and lawsuits.

University of Vermont, Bailey/Howe Library, Burlington
Trail [sic] *of Sheldon Pond at the county court for Addison County Vermont, June term, A.D. 1855 for the murder of Decatur Cheney in Addison, September 17, 1854.* Middlebury: L.W. Clark, 1855. Special Collections Wilbur.

Microform

Probate court records
General Alphabetical Card Index to Case Files, ca. 1824-1959. Montpelier: Vt. Public Records Comm., 1959. Vergennes, New Haven District.
General Alphabetical Card Index to Case Files, 1852-January 11, 1959. Montpelier: Vt. Public Records Comm., 1959. Vergennes, Addison District.

Land Records, 1833-1883. GSU, 1968. Cornwall; includes probate records.
Land Records, 1863-1891. Vt. Dept. of Taxes, 1968. Whiting; includes probate records.
Probate Records, 1801-1851. Montpelier: n.d. Salvaged from 1852 fire.
Probate Records, 1824-1857. GSU, 1952. Vergennes, New Haven District.
Probate Records, 1824-1959. Montpelier: n.d. Restricted access.

Bennington County
Founded 1778

Courts

Note: Fires at Bennington County courthouse destroyed many Supreme or County Court records from 1790 to 1830 and after.

Bennington Superior Court, Bennington
Civil: docket/record books, file papers, appeals, index; original, 1996-date.

Bennington District Court, Bennington
Criminal: file papers, originals retained for three years, then sent to Records Center; docket books, original, 1959-1999; computer docket sheets, 1990-date; index, 1920s-1989. Search fee; need name and date of birth for criminal records check.

Bennington Family Court, Bennington
File papers with orders; originals maintained for eighteen years, then sent to Records Center; index, 1970-1991.

Probate Court
Bennington
File papers (original, 1997-date); record vols. (original, 1778-1997); some early records on microfilm; card index.
Manchester
Docket/record books, file papers, appeals, index; original, 1791-date.

State Archives and Records Center

Vermont State Archives, Vermont Judicial Records Program, Montpelier
Bennington County Court docket/record book, 1782; index.
Vermont State Papers. Vol. 12. *Courts*. 1778-1799.

Vermont Dept. of Buildings and General Services, Records Center, Montpelier
Justice of the Peace. Salisbury and Shaftsbury, 1842-1855, 1891-1909.
Naturalization. Bennington County Court, 1842-1929.

State Historical Society

Vermont Historical Society, Barre
Court Calendar for Bennington county, June term, 1868 at Manchester.... Bennington: J.I.C. Cook & Son, 1868. Pam.

Kellogg, Loyal C. Court dockets. MSC-171. Include Bennington County Court, 1854, 1861-1868.

Kellogg Papers. Doc Box 72. Include bound judge's dockets of Bennington County Supreme Court, 1865.

Probate Court Records, Manchester District, 1843-1847 and 1859-1865. MSC-185.

Other Repositories

Dorset Historical Society, Dorset
Copies of wills and inventories from the Manchester District Probate Court.

Martha Canfield Library, Arlington
Russell Collection of Vermontiana, focusing on Bennington County towns of Arlington, Sandgate and Sunderland. Legal documents include writs, deeds, sheriff attachments, wills, probate records, judgments, etc., from 1790s through 20th century. Civil cases deal primarily with debt collection, and criminal cases involve minor offenses tried before local justices.

Shaftsbury Historical Society, Shaftsbury
Fifty-four original criminal writs, ca. 1825; no index.

University of Vermont, Bailey/Howe Library, Burlington
Boorn Murder Trial. UVM-SC, Reference File.
Sketches of the Trial of Stephen and Jesse Boorn, for the Murder of Russel Colvin: Before the Supreme Court of Vermont, Held at Manchester, October 26, 1819.... Boston: Nathaniel Coverly, 1820. Special Collections Wilbur (closed stacks), KF223.B66 B66 1819. *See also* "Microform" and "Digital/Electronic Sources," *below.*
Spargo, John. Papers, 1750-1966. UVM-SC, Closed Stacks. Collection from Bennington Museum's founder; includes court records.
Vermont. County Court (Bennington County).
Court records [microform]. Microfilm 596. Record book no. 1, April 1782-Dec. 1782.
Court records: index. Typescript. Montpelier: Agency of Admin., Public Records Div., 1980. Special Collections Wilbur, Quarto KFV516.B465 A7 1782. Index to above microform records.

Books

McFarland, Gerald W. *The "Counterfeit" Man: The True Story of the Boorn-Colvin Murder Case*. New York: Pantheon Books, 1991.

Microform

Miscellaneous court records
Court Records. Montpelier: Agency of Admin., Public Records Div., 1980. Bennington County Court Record book no. 1, April 1782-Dec. 1782. *See also* "Other Repositories," *above.*

Probate court records
Bennington
General Alphabetical Card Index to Estate Files, 1778 circa thru 1915. Montpelier: Vt. Public Records Div., 1961.
Probate Records, 1778-1851. GSU, 1952.
Manchester
General Alphabetical Card Index to Records (Excluding Adoptions and Changes of Names), 1790-1960. Montpelier: Public Records Comm., 1960.
Probate Records, 1779-1850. GSU, 1953.

Early American Imprints, Series II. Shaw-Shoemaker (1801-1819). New Canaan, Conn.: Readex Microprint, in cooperation with American Antiquarian Society, 1987-1992. Microfiche. Including:
Trial of Stephen and Jesse Boorn for the murder of Russell Colvin: before an adjourned term of the Supreme Court of Vermont: to which is subjoined the particulars of the wonderful discovery thereafter of said Colvin's being alive.... Rutland: Fay & Burt, 1819. Shaw & Shoemaker, 49632.

Digital/Electronic Sources

Internet
Early American Imprints *www.readex.com/scholarl/earlamim.html*
Shaw-Shoemaker Digital Edition, Series II. Shaw-Shoemaker (1801-1819). Chester, Vt.: Readex/Newsbank, in cooperation with American Antiquarian Society, 2004. Available at academic libraries. *See also* "Microform," *above*.

Caledonia County
Founded 1792, from Orange County

Courts

Caledonia Superior Court, St. Johnsbury
Civil: docket/record books, file papers, appeals, index; original and computer, 1997-date (earlier at Records Center). Criminal: docket/record books, file papers, appeals, index; original and computer, 2000-date (earlier at Records Center).

Caledonia District Court, St. Johnsbury
Civil: docket/record books, file papers, appeals; original and computer, 1992-date. Criminal: docket/record books, file papers, appeals; original, microfilm and computer, 1995-date.

Caledonia Family Court, St. Johnsbury
Docket/record books, file papers, appeals; original and computer; domestic (1991-date), abuse (1998-date), juvenile (1996-date); indexed by card files and computer.

Caledonia Probate Court, St. Johnsbury
Docket/record books, file papers, card index; early 1700s-date.

State Archives

Vermont State Archives, Vermont Judicial Records Program, Montpelier
Vermont State Papers. Vol. 16. *Courts*. 1778-1799.

State Historical Society

Vermont Historical Society, Barre
Bartlett, Thomas. Docket, 1848-1876. MSA 163:3. Attorney's court cases in Lyndon, Vt.
Kellogg, Loyal C. Court Dockets. MSC-171. Includes Caledonia County Court, 1865.
Kellogg Papers. Doc Box 72. Includes bound judge's dockets of Caledonia Supreme
    Court, 1864.
Whitelaw, James. Papers. Doc 333, #8. Includes docket book of Justice of the Peace
    cases, before Robert Whitelaw, from 1812.

Other Repositories

Middlebury College Library, Middlebury
Docket of Caledonia County court, December term, 1847. Danville, Vt.: N. Star Press,
1847. Vermont Restrict-Special Coll. KFV52.C3 C3.

University of Vermont, Bailey/Howe Library, Burlington
Bulkeley and Loomis (law firm). Docket book, 1809-1811. UVM-SC, Sm. Bd. Mss.
    Cases in Chittenden, Orange and Caledonia counties.
Simpson, Wilder Arthur. Papers, 1930-1968. UVM-SC, Library Research Assoc. Re:
    Lyndon, Vt. legislator and public official, including court dockets.
Vermont. County Court (Caledonia County). Docket of Caledonia County Court. Spe-
    cial Collections Wilbur.

Microform

Alphabetical Card Index to Adoption Files, 1945-1973. Montpelier: Vt. Public
    Records Div., 1973.
Alphabetical Card Index to Probate Files, 1797-1973. Montpelier: Vt. Public Records
    Div., 1973. Includes estates, guardianships, name change, adoptions, before
    1945, etc.
Guardian Records, 1839-1881. GSU, 1951; Montpelier: Vt. Public Records Div., 1973.
Probate Records, 1796-1877. GSU, 1951; Montpelier: Vt. Public Records Div., 1973.

Chittenden County
Founded 1787, from Addison County

Courts

Chittenden Superior Court, Burlington
Original court records in basement vault (boxes and vols., partially inventoried),
including: Chancery Court, 1814-1963; civil, 1827-1972; County Court (warrants, verdicts, etc.), 1866-1904; criminal, 1864-1971, District Court, 1986-1989; docket books
(21 linear feet); executions, 1831-1879; fee dockets, 1923-1967; fines and costs, 1886-

1906; general index, 5 vols.; judgments, 1914-1922, 1971; land, 1792-1889; naturalization, 1843-1908; Superior Court, 1990s; Supreme Court, 1810-1944; etc.

Chittenden District Court, Burlington

Chittenden Family Court, Burlington

Chittenden Probate Court, Burlington
Original file papers, early 1800s-date; card file index. Call ahead to determine availability. Need names of decedents for search.

State Archives and Records Center

Vermont State Archives, Vermont Judicial Records Program, Montpelier
Chittenden County Court. Docket books, 1794-1836; index.
Chittenden County Supreme Court. Docket books, 1800-1834; index.
Vermont State Papers. Vol. 16. *Courts*. 1778-1799.

Vermont Dept. of Buildings and General Services, Records Center, Montpelier
Chittenden County Court. Dockets and judgments.
Naturalizations. 1869-1906, Chittenden County.

State Historical Society

Vermont Historical Society, Barre
Chittenden County (Vt.). County court. List of causes... Various imprints. Pam.
The Court Calendar for the County of Chittenden, October term, 1844. Burlington:
    Stillman Fletcher, 1844. Pam.
Kellogg, Loyal C. Court Dockets. MSC-171. Includes Chittenden Supreme Court, 1867.
Kellogg Papers. Doc Box 72. Includes bound judge's dockets of Chittenden County
    Supreme Court, 186-, 1864.
Underhill, Vt. Papers. MSS-26, #13. Includes guardianship appointment, 1814, and
    probate, 1844.
Wilbur family papers, 1830-1923. Ser. III, LaFayette Wilbur's Legal Documents. Doc.
    469-470, MSA 269. Includes court docket, 1857-1859, of cases by lawyer
    from Jericho and Burlington.

Other Repositories

Oyster Bay Historical Society, Oyster Bay, N.Y.
Court papers, 1850-1851. Case of *Hannah Townsend v. John Downer*, re: land in
Williston, Vt., including case book for Vt. Supreme Court, January term 1851.

Henry Sheldon Museum of Vermont History, Middlebury
Records of Addison County Court, 1787-1900. Includes Chittenden County Courts.

University of Vermont, Bailey/Howe Library, Burlington
Bulkeley and Loomis (law firm). Docket book, 1809-1811. UVM-SC, Sm. Bd. Mss.
    Cases in Chittenden, Orange and Caledonia counties.

Burlington Town/Burlington City records, 1800?-1900. UVM-SC, Closed Stacks. Includes legal/court records.

Butler, Franklin. *John Ward, or, The Victimized Assassin, a Narrative of Facts Connected with the Crime, Arrest, Trial, Imprisonment and Execution of the Williston Murderer,...March 20, 1868.* Windsor: Vt. Journal Print, 1869. Special Collections Wilbur HV6248.W4 A3.

Chittenden, Lucius E. Papers, 1838-1926. UVM-SC, Library Research Annex. Includes testimony and court docket books re: his Burlington law firm.

Fay, John, 1768-1809. Family papers, 1788-1860. UVM-SC. County court dockets and orders of Burlington lawyer.

Papers of Vermont Antiquarian Society, 1807-1923. UVM-SC, Closed Stacks. Includes Chittenden County deeds, 1834-1851, and court records, 1823-1842.

Vermont. County Court. (Chittenden County).
Court records [microform]. Microfilm 597. County Court, 1794-1827; Supreme Court, 1800-1834.
Court records: index. Typescript. Montpelier: Agency of Admin., Public Records Div., 1980. Special Collections Wilbur, Quarto KFV516.C56 A7 1794. Index to above microform records.
Vermont County Court docket and account book, 1806-1823. UVM-SC, Lg. Bd. Mss.
Vermont County Court Docket Book, 1829. UVM-SC, Sm. Bd. Mss. Chittenden County Court; civil and chancery cases of Judge Richard Skiller.

Vermont Supreme Court Actions on Zoning, 1968-1981. Burlington: Chittenden County Regional Planning Comm., 1982. Special Collections Wilbur, KFV458.A52 C56 1982.

Microform

Miscellaneous court records
Court Records. Montpelier: Agency of Admin., Public Records Div., 1980. Chittenden County Court and Supreme Court records, 1794-1834. Available at Univ. of Vt. Library, *above.*

Probate court records
General Alphabetical Card Index to Estate Files, 1796-1959. Montpelier: Vt. Public Records Comm., 1959.
General Alphabetical Card Index to Guardianships, 1811-1959. Montpelier: Vt. Public Records Comm., 1959.
Guardian Records, v. 1-3, 1818-1854. GSU, 1951.
Index to Probate Records of Chittenden, State of Vermont, Vol. 1. GSU, 1966, 1969.
Probate Records, 1795-1857. GSU, 1951; Montpelier: Vt. Public Records Comm., 1959.

Early American Imprints, Series II. Shaw-Shoemaker (1801-1819). New Canaan, Conn.: Readex Microprint, in cooperation with American Antiquarian Society, 1987-1992. Microfiche. Including:
The trial of Cyrus B. Dean for the murder of Jonathan Ormsby and Asa Marsh, before the Supreme Court of...Vermont...Burlington 23rd of August, A.D. 1808/ revised and corrected from the minutes of the judges. Burlington: Samuel Mills, 1808. Shaw & Shoemaker, 16344. *See also* "Digital/Electronic Sources," *below.*

Digital/Electronic Sources

Internet

Chittenden Superior Court *www.chittendensuperiorcourt.com*
> Online dockets for recent civil and small claims cases (ca. 1998-date) in
> Chittenden County. (Click "Cases.")

Early American Imprints *www.readex.com/scholarl/earlamim.html*
> Shaw-Shoemaker Digital Edition, Series II. Shaw-Shoemaker (1801-1819).
> Chester, Vt.: Readex/Newsbank, in cooperation with the American Antiquarian
> Society, 2004. Available at academic libraries. *See also* "Microform," *above*.

Essex County
Founded 1792, from Orange County

Courts

Essex Superior, District and Family Courts, Guildhall
Civil: docket/record books, file papers, appeals; original and microfilm, 1910-date.
Criminal: docket/record books, file papers, appeals; original and microfilm, 1998-
date. Family (divorce): docket/record books, file papers, appeals; original and microfilm, 1995-date. Index for records prior to May 1994.

Essex Probate Court, Island Pond
Docket/record books, file papers, index; original and microfilm, 1791-date.

State Records Center

Vermont Dept. of Buildings and General Services, Records Center, Montpelier
Naturalizations: Essex Superior Court, 1859-1958.

State Historical Society

Vermont Historical Society, Barre
Brigham, Paul W. Legal papers, 1837-1889. MSC 210:45. Deeds and probate records
> re: Norwich, Vt.
Kellogg Papers. Doc Box 72. Includes bound judge's dockets of Essex Supreme
> Court, 1864.

Microform

Pease, Janet K. *Index to Essex District, Vermont Probate Records, v. 1, 1791-1811*.
> GSU, 1979. Only 2 leaves.
Probate Records, 1791-1855. GSU, 1951.

Franklin County
Founded 1792, from Chittenden County

Courts

Franklin Superior Court, St. Albans
Civil: original file papers, some stored off premises. Small claims: original file papers, Sept. 1996-date. Advance written notice required.

Franklin District and Family Courts, St. Albans
District (criminal): docket/record books, file papers, appeals; original, stenographic tape, videotape, computer; 1994-date. Family: docket/record books, file papers, appeals; original, videotape and computer.

Franklin Probate Court, St. Albans

State Archives

Vermont State Archives, Vermont Judicial Records Program, Montpelier
Vermont State Papers.
> Vol. 16. *Courts*. 1778-1799.
> Vols. 78-79. *Miscellaneous*. 1800-1866. Includes licenses granted to tavern keepers by Franklin County Courts.

State Historical Society

Vermont Historical Society, Barre
Indexed docket for Franklin County Supreme Court and Chancery Court, 1841, 1844, 1846-1847. AC 352.0743 F 584co.
Kellogg Papers. Doc Box 72. Includes bound judge's dockets of Franklin Supreme Court, 1860, 1862, 1866.
Penniman, Jabez. #1064. Franklin County Chancery Court records re: dower rights of Ethan Allen's widow (Mrs. Penniman); Supreme Court proceedings, 1808-1809, re: murder trials of crew of smuggling boat *Black Snake*.

Other Repositories

Henry Sheldon Museum of Vermont History, Middlebury
Records of Addison County Court, 1787-1900. Includes Franklin County Court.
Records of Addison and Franklin County Courts, 1793-1888.

University of Vermont, Bailey/Howe Library, Burlington
Numerous appellate briefs and other court records re: lawsuits of Vt. & Canada Railroad Co. in Vt. Supreme Court for Franklin County. *See* Special Collections Wilbur, HE2791.V463 & V473, or search subject "Railroads-Vermont" in library catalog.

Microform

Deeds and Miscellaneous Civil Records, 1797-1883 approx. GSU, 1952, 1973; Montpelier: Vt. Public Records Div. Includes court records.
General Alphabetical Card Index to Records, ca. 1780-1970. Montpelier: Vt. Public Records Div., 1971. Includes births, estates, guardianships, name changes, etc.
Probate Records, 1796-1862; General Index to v. A-Z, 1-48. GSU, 1951.

Grand Isle County
Founded 1802, from Franklin County

Courts

Grand Isle Superior Court, N. Hero
Civil: docket/record books, file papers; original, 1986-date.

Grand Isle District Court, N. Hero
Criminal: docket/record books, file papers, appeals; original, 1997-date.

Grand Isle Family Court, N. Hero
Family: docket/record books, file papers; 1983-date.

Grand Isle Probate Court, N. Hero
Docket/record books; original, 1824-date.

State Historical Society

Vermont Historical Society, Barre
Probate records, Grand Isle District. Doc 275, 276.

Microform

Index to Grand Isle District, Vermont, Probate Records, Vols. 1-4. GSU, 1966, 1969.
     Only 3 leaves.
Probate Records, 1796-1854. GSU, 1951.

Lamoille County
Founded 1835, from Chittenden, Washington, Orleans and Franklin Counties

Courts

Lamoille Superior Court, Hyde Park

Lamoille District and Family Courts, Hyde Park
Criminal: docket/record books (original, 1973-date, computer, 1988-date, microfilm, 1955-1972 at Records Center); file papers (original, 1999-date, microfilm, 1969-1998 at Records Center); index. Fees; need name and date of birth for search. Family: docket/record books (original, 1998-date, computer, 1990-date, microfilm, 1968-1997 at Records Center); file papers (original, 1999-date, microfilm, 1969-1998 at Records Center); index.

Lamoille Probate Court, Hyde Park
Original docket/record books, file papers, appeals.

State Records Center

Vermont Dept. of Buildings and General Services, Records Center, Montpelier
See Lamoille District and Family Courts, *above.*

State Historical Society

Vermont Historical Society, Barre
Docket book for Lamoille Supreme and Chancery Courts, 1839, 1840 and 1842. AC 352.0743 L19co.
General store account book, 1809-1811. XMSC 14:12. Docket for Orleans County Court (later Lamoille County Court) in Hyde Park, by Allen Toothaker, 1811, at back of account book.
Kellogg Papers. Doc Box 72. Includes judge's dockets of· Lamoille Supreme Court, 1864.
Miscellaneous Account Books. XMSC-14. Hyde Park court docket (Lamoille County), 1811; Lawyer's day book, Hyde Park, 1811-1819, etc.
MSC-150. Includes book of justice of the peace records of Elias Chadwick, Cambridge (Lamoille County), 1860-1879.
XMSC-33. Includes day book of Morristown lawyer, 1819-1823.

Microform

Miscellaneous court records
Miscellaenous [sic] *Civil Records, 1872-1951 approx.* Montpelier: Vt. Public Records Div., 1973. Includes naturalizations, depositions, etc.
Records of the Justice of the Peace, 1814-1836. GSU, 1951. Stow.

Probate court records
General Alphabetical Card Index to Case Files, 1860 circa to January [1960]. Montpelier: Vt. Public Records Comm., 1960.
Probate Records, 1837-1875. GSU, 1973; Montpelier: Vt. Public Records Div., 1974.
Wills and Letters Testamentary, 1837-1878. GSU, 1973; Montpelier: Vt. Public Records Div. Includes guardianship records.

Orange County
Founded 1781, from Cumberland County, N.Y.

Courts

Orange Superior, District and Family Courts, Chelsea

Orange Probate Court, Chelsea
Original probate entry books, Bradford and Randolph Districts, to 1988. (Those districts combined in 1994 to create Orange Probate District.) Advance notice required.

State Archives

Vermont State Archives, Vermont Judicial Records Program, Montpelier
Vermont State Papers. Vol. 15. *Courts.* 1778-1799.

State Historical Society

Vermont Historical Society, Barre
Brock Papers. Doc. Box 196. Probate records, Newbury and Bradford area; depositions re: business dispute in early 1800s.
Docket for Orange County Justice's Court, 1831-1833. AC 352.0743 Or5j.
French, Elijah. #505. Copy of transcribed journal of Elijah French, Justice of the Peace in Braintree, 1790-1793. Court records and marriages.
Justice Docket of William Nutting of Randolph, 1842-1861, and his day book, 1843-1862. XMSC-33.

Other Repositories

Dartmouth College Library, Hanover, N.H.
Orange County Court. Hon. Daniel Cobb's docket, June term, 1843.

New England Historic Genealogical Society, Boston, Mass.
Bowman, John Elliot. Handwritten index to probate records, 1792-1808 (Orange County, Randolph). MSS C 3481.

University of Vermont, Bailey/Howe Library, Burlington
Bulkeley and Loomis (law firm). Docket book, 1809-1811. UVM-SC, Sm. Bd. Mss. Cases in Chittenden, Orange and Caledonia counties.
Philander Perrin Docket book, 1863-1876. UVM-SC, Lg. Bd. Mss. Randolph lawyer's cases before Justice of the Peace courts, Orange County.
Vermont copper mining company vs. Francis M. F. Cazin and Ely Ely-Goddard: Orange Co. Court, December term, A.D. 1883. 1883. Special Collections Wilbur, TN443.V5 V472 1883.

Microform

General Alphabetical Card Index to Case Files, 1797-1967. Montpelier: Vt. Public Records Div., 1968. Randolph District, filmed at Chelsea. Includes estates, guardianships, name changes, etc.
Probate Records, 1781-1852. GSU, 1952. Bradford District, filmed at Wells River.
Probate Records, 1792-1854. GSU, 1952. Randolph District, filmed at Chelsea.

Orleans County
Founded 1792, from Orange County

Courts

Orleans Superior Court, Newport

Orleans District Court, Newport
Criminal: original docket/record books, 1971-date; file papers and appeals, original current year and two previous years; microfilmed records, older than seven years.

Orleans Family Court, Newport
Docket/record books, file papers, appeals, index; original, 1990-date; index. *Note*: Records prior to 1990 are at Records Center, or with Superior Court records at Orleans County Courthouse. Please provide names of parties and approximate filing date, and advance notice of record requests.

Orleans Probate Court, Newport
Docket/record books, file papers, index; original, 1750-date.

State Archives

Vermont State Archives, Vermont Judicial Records Program, Montpelier
Vermont State Papers. Vols. 78-79. *Miscellaneous*. 1800-1866. Licenses granted to tavern keepers by Orleans County Courts.

State Historical Society

Vermont Historical Society, Barre
Docket book for court at Craftsbury, 1831-1851. AC 352.0743 C842.
General store account book, 1809-1811. XMSC 14:12. Docket for Orleans County Court (later Lamoille County Court) in Hyde Park, by Allen Toothaker, 1811, at back of account book.
Indexed docket for Orleans County Court, 1839. AC 352.0743 Or5co.
Kellogg Papers. Doc Box 72. Includes bound judge's dockets of Orleans Supreme Court, 1860-1864.
Miscellaneous Manuscripts. MSC 4, Folder 18. Judge Comings' docket book, June 1867.

Other Repositories

New England Historic Genealogical Society, Boston, Mass.
Hawes, Frank M. Handwritten abstract from Vol. 1 of Probate Records, Orleans County, 1797-1832. MSS A 2398.

Orleans County Historical Society, Brownington
Large collection (~20 linear feet) of criminal, juvenile, civil and small claims records, 1907-1970; some civil court records from late 1800s; no indexes.

University of Vermont, Bailey/Howe Library, Burlington
Assorted documents from the Reed and Durham ledger, 1838-1842. UVM-SC, Mss. Files. Includes petition to Chancery Court of Orleans County, *Warner Williams v. Orin Emerson and Samuel Reed*, 1841.
Vermont. County Court (Orleans County). *Bar docket of Orleans Co. Court*. Newport, Vt.: Standard Printing Co. Special Collections Wilbur.

Books

Baldwin, Frederick W. *Biography of the Bar of Orleans County, Vermont*. Montpelier: Vt. Watchman & State Journal Press, 1886.

Microform

General Alphabetical Card Index to Records, ca. 1780-1970. Montpelier: Vt. Public
    Records Div., 1971. Orleans Probate Court.
Probate Records, 1796-1855. GSU, 1951.

Rutland County
Founded 1781, from Bennington County

Courts

Rutland Superior Court, Rutland
Civil and criminal: docket/record books, file papers, appeals, some indexing; original,
1779-date. Land record books, 1779-1826. Please send requests in writing.

Rutland District Court, Rutland

Rutland Family Court, Rutland
Original record books, 1972-1993; original file papers, 1993-date; index, cards to
1993 and computer, 1993-date.

Fair Haven Probate Court, Fair Haven
Docket/record books, index; original, 1797-date.

Rutland Probate Court, Rutland

State Archives and Records Center

Vermont State Archives, Vermont Judicial Records Program, Montpelier
Vermont State Papers. Vol. 15. *Courts*. 1778-1799.

Vermont Dept. of Buildings and General Services, Records Center, Montpelier
Civil and criminal dockets, Rutland Municipal Court, 1873-1893, 1899-1907.

State Historical Society

Vermont Historical Society, Barre
Kellogg Papers. Doc Box 72. Includes judge's dockets of Rutland County Court,
    1864-1867; Rutland Supreme Court, 1862.
Kellogg, John. County Court docket and Justice Docket, Benson, 1810-1817. MSC-151.
Kellogg, John. Justice Docket, 1814-1830. MSC-153.
Kellogg, John and Loyal Papers. MS-33. Includes Rutland County jury cases, 1855;
    court docket, 1848; Supreme Court calendar, 1859; County Court calendar,
    1849.
Kellogg, Loyal C. Court Dockets. MSC-171. Including Rutland Supreme Court,
    1847-1848, 1867; Chancery Court at Rutland, 1867; Rutland County Courts,
    1845-1859, 1861-1871.
Windsor County Merchant Papers and John Kellogg of Benson Papers. MSC-58.
    Writs and executions in suits where Kellogg was attorney, 1817-1826;
    County Court dockets, 1813, 1831 and 1833.

Other Repositories

New England Historic Genealogical Society, Boston, Mass.
Bowman, John Elliot. Handwritten index to early probate records, Rutland County. MSS C 3480.

University of Vermont, Bailey/Howe Library, Burlington
Clark/Field Family Papers, 1795-1948. UVM-SC, Closed Stacks. Includes Rutland County court records.
John P. Phair; a Complete History of Vermont's Celebrated Murder Case; Containing a Report of the Trial & Conviction for the Murder of Ann E. Freeze, at Rutland.... Boston: 1879. Special Collections Wilbur.
Rutland and Burlington Railroad. *In Chancery, Rutland County, March term, A.D. 1864....* Boston: J. Wilson & Son, 1864. Special Collections Wilbur, HE2791.R953 R882 1864. Brief.
Trial of James Anthony for the murder of Joseph Green: before the Honourable Supreme Court of the state of Vermont, at their adjourned term in the county of Rutland, February 28, A.D. 1814. Rutland: Fay & Davidson, 1814. Special Collections Wilbur (closed stacks), Z209.R88 A57 1814.

Microform

Miscellaneous court records
Land Records, 1850-1898. Montpelier: Vt. Dept. of Taxes, 1968. Includes probate records re: land and property in Benson.
Naturalization Records, 1836-1906. Montpelier: Vt. Public Records Div., 1973. County Court.

Probate court records
Fair Haven
General Alphabetical Cards Index to Records (Excluding Adoptions, Change of Name), A-Z, 1797-November 1959. Montpelier: Vt. Public Records Comm., 1959.
Probate Records, 1797-1823. GSU, 1952. Some vols. not filmed, or missing.
Probate Records, 1804-1813, 1842-1851. Montpelier: Vt. Public Records Div., 1962.
Rutland
General Alphabetical Card Index to Records, 1781-1960. Montpelier: Vt. Public Records Comm., 1960. Includes estates, guardianships, name changes and adoptions.
Probate Records, 1784-1850. GSU, 1952.

Early American Imprints, Series II. Shaw-Shoemaker (1801-1819). New Canaan, Conn.: Readex Microprint, in cooperation with American Antiquarian Society, 1987-1992. Microfiche, including:
Trial of James Anthony, for the murder of Joseph Green before the Honourable Supreme Court of the State of Vermont, at their adjourned term in the county of Rutland, February 28, A.D. 1814. Rutland: Fay & Davison, 1814. Shaw & Shoemaker, 32962. *See also* "Other Repositories," *above*, and "Digital/Electronic Sources," *below*.

Digital/Electronic Sources

Internet
Early American Imprints *www.readex.com/scholarl/earlamim.html*

Shaw-Shoemaker Digital Edition, Series II. Shaw-Shoemaker (1801-1819). Chester, Vt.: Readex/Newsbank, in cooperation with American Antiquarian Society, 2004. Available at academic libraries. *See also* "Microform," *above.*

Washington County

Founded 1810, from Addison, Caledonia, Chittenden and Orange Counties; called Jefferson County until 1814

Courts

Note: Great Flood of 1927 caused substantial damage to records.

Washington Superior Court, Montpelier
Civil: docket/record books, file papers; original, 1992-date.

Washington District Court, Barre
Criminal: docket/record books, file papers, appeals, index; 1997-date.

Washington Family Court, Barre
File papers, appeals; 1990-date.

Washington Probate Court, Montpelier
Docket/record books, file papers, appeals; original, late 1800s-date.

State Archives

Vermont State Archives, Vermont Judicial Records Program, Montpelier
Jefferson County Court (now Washington County): docket books, 1811-1819; defaulted suits, 1816-1820; index.
Washington County Court: docket books, 1820-1827; deputations, 1812-1852; index.
Washington County Supreme Court, docket books, 1821-1829; index.

State Historical Society

Vermont Historical Society, Barre
E. Montpelier area, including probate records. MSA-66 (formerly MSC 188).
Kellogg Papers. Doc Box 72. Includes bound judge's dockets of Washington County Court, 1862; Washington Supreme Court, 1864.
Kellogg, John and Loyal Papers. MS-33. Includes Supreme Court docket at Montpelier, 1866.
Kellogg, Loyal C. Court dockets. MSC-171. Includes Washington County Court, 1865.
Montpelier Civil Court account book, 1920-1921. XMSC 66.
MSC-150. Includes printed Bar Docket of Washington County Court, 1904.

Other Repositories

Middlebury College Library, Middlebury
The bar docket of Wash. Co. Court, November term, 1847. Montpelier: Press of Eastman & Danforth, 1847. Vermont Restrict-Special Coll. KFV52.W3 W3.

University of Vermont, Bailey/Howe Library, Burlington
Vermont. County Court. (Washington County):
>   Court records [microform]. Microfilm 598. County Court, 1811-1827;
>   Supreme Court, 1821-1829.
>   Court records: index. Typescript. Montpelier: Agency of Admin., Public
>   Records Div., 1980. Special Collections Wilbur, Quarto KFV516.W374 A7
>   1811. Index to above microform records.

Vermont Environmental Board. *Act 250, Vermont Supreme Court cases, Environmental Board decisions, and declaratory rulings by project type.* 2 vols. Montpelier: Vt. Environmental Board, 1990-1991. Special Collections Wilbur (open stacks), KFV458.A333.

Vermont. Supreme Court (Washington County). Supreme Court Docket, Washington County, August Term, 1876. UVM-SC, Sm. Brds. W7b.W3745 1876.

Waterbury (Vt.). Appointment of a guardian for a "lunatic," April 23, 1828. UVM-SC, Mss. Files.

Microform

Miscellaneous court records
Court Records. Montpelier: Agency of Admin., Public Records Div., 1980. Washington County Court and Supreme Court records, 1811-1829. Available at Univ. of Vt. Library, *above.*

Probate court records
Alphabetical Index to Closed Estates, 1811-1988. Montpelier: Vt. Public Records Div., 1988.
Change of Name, v. 1, 1881-1924. GSU, 2002.
Guardian Licence [sic]*, v. 1, 1885-1912.* GSU, 2002.
Guardian Records, 1821-1921. GSU, 1951, 2002.
Guardians, 1885-1917. GSU, 2002.
Homestead Licenses, v. 1, 1886-1892. GSU, 2002.
Licenses Personal & Real Estate, 1870-1913. GSU, 2002.
Probate Records, 1811-1917. GSU, 1951, 2002.
Probate Records, Administrators, 1870-1913. GSU, 2002.
Probate Records, Bonds, v. 1-3, 1901-1919. GSU, 2002.
Probate Records, Insolvency, 1878-1898. GSU, 2002. Court of Insolvency.
Records Corrected by Probate Court, v. 1-4, 1940-1980. GSU, 1998. City Hall, Barre.
Records of Adoption, v. 1-2, 1882-1925. GSU, 2002.
Wills & Executors, 1871-1910. GSU, 2002.

Windham County
Founded 1781, from Cumberland County, N.Y.

Courts

Windham Superior Court, Newfane
Civil: docket/record books, file papers, appeals, index; original, 1900-date. Family: docket/record books, file papers; prior to 1972; no index. *See also* Beth T. Muskat. "Windham County Court Records, 1766-1974." Typescript, 1991. Copy at courthouse.

Windham District Court, Brattleboro
Criminal: docket books, 1970s-date; original file papers, current year plus three prior years; index cards, printed lists and computer, 1970s-date. Fees; pre-payment required.

Windham Family Court, Brattleboro
Docket/record books, file papers, appeals; originals and hearing tapes, 1990-date; no index.

Probate Court
Marlboro, Brattleboro
Docket/record books, file papers, appeals, index cards; original, transcript and microfilm (some at Records Center), 1781-date.
Westminster, Bellows Falls
Docket/record books, file papers, index; originals and microfilm (some at Records Center), 1781-date.

State Archives and Records Center

Vermont State Archives, Vermont Judicial Records Program, Montpelier
Vermont State Papers. Vol. 13. *Courts*. 1778-1799.

Vermont Dept. of Buildings and General Services, Records Center, Montpelier
Windham County court records, 1851-1906, 1808-1922.

State Historical Society

Vermont Historical Society, Barre
Bradley, Jonathan Dorr. Papers. MS-52. Includes Windham County Court reports and cases, 1849 and 1860; Vt. Supreme Court cases, 1830s; 1840 will, etc.
Kellogg Papers. Doc Box 72. Includes bound judge's dockets of Windham Supreme Court, 1864.
Kellogg, Loyal C. Court dockets. MSC-171. Includes Windham County Court, 1861, and Windham Supreme Court, 1867.
MSC-205. Includes docket book of Windham Supreme Court, 1851, under Judge Stephen Royce.
Royall Tyler collection, 1753-1935. Doc 045 (cont'd in Doc 46-52, XMSC 43, Ms Size B, C, D). Includes court dockets of Windham County, 1815-1818.
XMSC-29. Includes Windham County Court dockets, 1867-1869.
XMSC-30. Includes Windham County Court docket, 1880.

Other Repositories

Brattleboro Historical Society, Brattleboro
Brattleboro-area Municipal Court records, 1907-1941.

Massachusetts Historical Society, Boston, Mass.
Swan family. Papers, 1816-1929. Includes court calendar for Windham County Court (Mar. 1884) and Vt. Supreme Court (Feb. 1884).

University of Vermont, Bailey/Howe Library, Burlington
Vermont Valley Railroad Company of 1871 vs. Rutland Railroad Company and Central Vermont Railroad Company: In Chancery, Windham County, General term, Supreme Court, Oct. 1881. Brief for Central Vermont R.R. Co. 1881?. Special Collections Wilbur, HE2791.C463 C46 1881.

Microform

Probate court records
Marlboro
Old General Alphabetical Index to Case Files, 1781-1964. Montpelier: Vt. Public Records Div., 1965. Includes estates and guardianships, 1781-1898; name changes and adoptions, 1781-1964.
Guardian Records, v. 1-2, 1821-1849. GSU, 1952.
Probate Records, 1781-1850. GSU, 1952, 2001; Montpelier: Vt. Public Records Div., 1965.
Westminster
Alphabetical Card Index to Guardianships, 1781-1962. Montpelier: Vt. Public Records Div., 1962.
General Alphabetical Card Index to Case Files, 1781-1962. Montpelier: Vt. Public Records Div., 1962. Estates, name change, adoptions, etc.
Probate Records, 1781-1916. GSU, 1952, 2002.

Windsor County
Founded 1781, from Cumberland County, N.Y.

Courts

Windsor Superior Court, Woodstock
Civil: docket/record books, file papers, appeals; original, 1993-date.

Windsor District and Family Courts, White River Junction
District (criminal): docket/record books, file papers; original, 2000-date. Family: docket/record books, file papers; original, 1988-date (divorce), 1998-date (abuse).

Hartford Probate Court, Woodstock
Docket/record books, 1783-1995; original file papers, 2000-date; index.

Windsor Probate Court, N. Springfield
Docket/record books, 1780-1996; original file papers (some old, damaged), to date; index.

State Archives and Records Center

Vermont State Archives, Vermont Judicial Records Program, Montpelier
Vermont State Papers. Vol. 14. *Courts.* 1778-1799
Windsor County Court: record books, 1782-1786; docket books, 1788-1833; index.
Windsor County Supreme Court: docket books, 1794-1976; index.

Vermont Dept. of Buildings and General Services, Records Center, Montpelier
Naturalization: Windsor County, 1838-1958; indexes, 1888-1902, 1908-1929.

State Historical Society

Vermont Historical Society, Barre
Bail, Hamilton Vaughan. Papers re: Hartland, including court records.
Docket book of Supreme Court in Windsor County 1847. AC 352.0743 W7242co.
Early 19th-century probate records re: Allen Hayes of Windsor. AC B H325.
Kellogg Papers. Doc Box 72. Includes judge's dockets of Windsor Supreme Court, 1864.
Kellogg, Loyal C. Court dockets, including Windsor County Supreme Court, 1867. MSC-171.
Miscellaneous Manuscripts. MSC 4, Folder 3. 1770 indictment by Cumberland County grand jury re: rescue of three prisoners from sheriff at Windsor.
Court docket (Windsor County Court), 1835, and lawyer's accounts, 1846-1863. MSC-176.
Stockbridge, Vt. Papers. Probate re: estate of insane man, 1804; sheriff's writ, 1820, etc.
West-Quimby papers, 1851-1922. MSA 245. Settlement of estate, Joseph M. Quimby of Hartford, Vt. Finding aid at *www.state.vt.us/vhs/arccat/finduid/west-quim.htm.*
Windsor County Merchant Papers and John Kellogg of Benson Papers. MSC-58. Writs and executions in suits where Kellogg was attorney, 1817-1826; County Court dockets, 1813, 1831 and 1833.

Other Repositories

Billings Farm and Museum, Woodstock Foundation, Woodstock
Court records re: farm and estate of Frederick Billings; primarily 19th century.

Dartmouth College Library, Hanover, N.H.
Royalton and Woodstock Turnpike Company. Papers, 1839-1842. Records of Windsor County Court and appeal to Vt. Supreme Court.

University of Vermont, Bailey/Howe Library, Burlington
Brigham, Paul. Papers, 1730-1797. UVM-SC, Closed Stacks. Includes Windsor County Court legal papers, dockets and case transcripts.
Crosby, Dixi. *Report of a Trial for Alleged Malpractice, Against Dixi Crosby...in the Windsor County Court, at Woodstock, May Term, 1854; Verdict for Defendant.* Woodstock: Pratt, 1854. Special Collections Wilbur.
The ex-chief justice and the printer: being a report of a trial for libel, Titus Hutchinson vs. B.F. Kendall, had before the honorable county court, for the county of Windsor, and state of Vermont, May term, 1836.... Woodstock: J.B. & S.L. Chase & Co., 1836. Special Collections.
Trial for Libel. Susanna Torrey, Plaintiff. R.M. Field, Defendant. E. C. Church, 1835. Special Collections Wilbur, KF223.T6. Trial at Woodstock, 1835.

Vermont. County Court. (Windsor County):

> Court records [microform]. Microfilm 599. County Court, 1789-1833; Supreme Court, 1794-1825; Court administrators, 1782-1789.
>
> Court records: index. Typescript. Montpelier: Agency of Admin., Public Records Div., 1980. Special Collections Wilbur, Quarto KFV516.W564 A7 1789. Index to above microform records.

Washburn, Peter Thacher. Papers of Peter Thatcher Washburn, 1836-1858. UVM-SC, Closed Stacks. Governor and lawyer in Ludlow and Woodstock. Papers include county court cases, 1836-1852. *Note*: inconsistent spelling ("Thacher" and "Thatcher") in library catalog.

Books

Bartley, Scott Andrew, and Marjorie J. Bartley. *Windsor County, Vermont, Probate Index, 1778-1899*. St. Albans: Genealogical Society of Vt., 2000. More than 20,000 files in Probate Courts of Windsor and Hartford districts, indexed by party name, residence, district, type of record, year, and bound vols.

Windsor County Court Papers, 1759-1852. Burlington: Univ. of Vt., 1983. Includes records of Windsor County Court and Windsor Supreme Court.

Microform

Miscellaneous court records

Court Records. Montpelier: Agency of Admin., Public Records Div., 1980. Windsor County Court and Supreme Court records, 1789-1833. Available at Univ. of Vt. Library, *above*.

Justice of the Peace Docket, 1843-1852, Windsor County, Vermont. GSU, 1987.

Records of Births, Marriages, and Deaths, 1762-1997; Indexes to Births, Marriages, Deaths, 1762-1997. GSU, 1952, 1997; Montpelier.: Vt. Public Records Div., 1974. Vols. 1 and 9 include records of Justice's Court in Royalton, Vt.

Probate court records
Hartford

General Alphabetical Card Index to Case Files, 1783-1970. Montpelier: Vt. Public Records Div. Includes estates, guardianship, name change, adoption, etc.

Probate Records, 1783-1851. GSU, 1982.

Windsor

General Alphabetical Card Index to Estate Files, 1787-1962. Montpelier: Vt. Public Records Div., 1963.

Guardians Records, 1805-1908. GSU, 1952; Waltham, Mass.: Graphic Microfilm of New England, 1963.

Probate Files, 1779-1906. GSU, 2004.

Probate Records, 1787-1901. GSU, 1952; Waltham Mass.: Graphic Microfilm of New England, 1963.

Early American Imprints, Series II. Shaw-Shoemaker (1801-1819). New Canaan, Conn.: Readex Microprint, in cooperation with American Antiquarian Society, 1987-1992. Microfiche, including:

A sketch of the life of Samuel E. Godfrey together with an abstract of his trial on an indictment for the murder of Thomas Hewlet, keeper of the Vermont State Prison.... Windsor: s.n., 1818. Shaw & Shoemaker, 44166. *See also* "Digital/Electronic Sources," *below.*

Digital/Electronic Sources

Internet

Early American Imprints *www.readex.com/scholarl/earlamim.html*
Shaw-Shoemaker Digital Edition, Series II. Shaw-Shoemaker (1801-1819). Chester, Vt.: Readex/Newsbank, in cooperation with American Antiquarian Society, 2004. Available at academic libraries. *See also* "Microform," *above.*

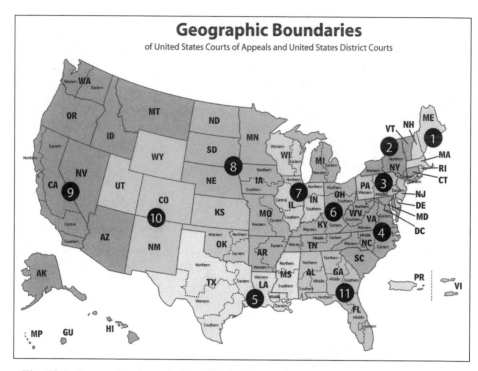

Fig. 12.1. Geographic Boundaries of U.S. Courts of Appeals and U.S. District Courts. *Courtesy of the Administrative Office of the United States Courts.*

CHAPTER 12

---·•·---

FEDERAL COURTS IN
NEW ENGLAND

Court History Timeline

1789   U.S. Congress established the federal judicial system, consisting of District Courts, Circuit Courts and Supreme Court.

U.S. District Courts, one in each New England state, served as trial courts for admiralty, maritime, and certain minor civil and criminal cases. Thirteen **federal judicial districts** consisted of the eleven states that had ratified the Constitution, plus Maine and Kentucky (which then belonged to Massachusetts and Virginia, respectively).

U.S. Circuit Courts handled trials of federal criminal cases, lawsuits between citizens of different states, and civil actions initiated by the U.S.; they also heard appeals from most admiralty and civil cases in U.S. Districts Courts. Three circuits: **Eastern** (soon including all New England states, except Maine), **Middle** and **Southern**. Circuit Courts convened in each federal judicial district, with two Supreme Court justices (later only one) and one District Court judge presiding.

U.S. Supreme Court—consisting of one chief justice and five associate justices—heard appeals of larger civil cases from lower federal courts, and cases from state courts ruling on federal statutes.

1793   Circuit Court judges appointed **Commissioners** to oversee bail in federal criminal cases.

1800   Congress enacted first Federal Bankruptcy Act. District Court judges appointed **Commissioners** to oversee **bankruptcy** cases.

1802   **U.S. Circuit Courts** were reorganized. Original three circuits were divided into six, including: **First Circuit** (New Hampshire, Massachusetts and Rhode Island) and **Second Circuit** (Connecticut, Vermont and New York). **Maine** (still part of Massachusetts) had **no circuit** assignment; Maine's District Court exercised both district and circuit court jurisdiction.

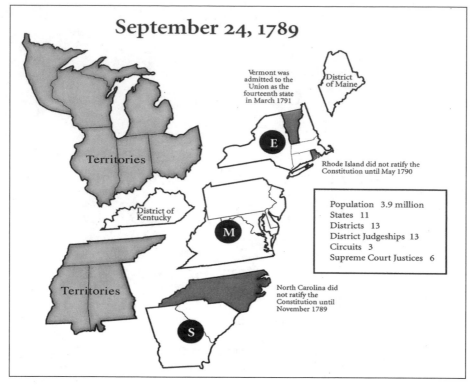

Fig. 12.2. Federal court circuits, 1789. Russell R. Wheeler and Cynthia Harrison.
Creating the Federal Judiciary System. 3rd ed. Washington, D.C.:
Federal Judicial Center, 2005, p. 5.

1803   Federal Bankruptcy Act was repealed.

1817   Duties of U.S. **Commissioners** were expanded in Circuit and District
                 Courts: taking bail, affidavits and depositions; and issuing arrest warrants.

1820   **Maine** (which had become a state) was assigned to **First Circuit**.

1841   Congress enacted Federal Bankruptcy Act of 1841 (repealed 13 months
                 later). **U.S. District Courts** had jurisdiction over all **bankruptcy**
                 proceedings.

1867   Congress enacted Federal Bankruptcy Act of 1867.

1869   Congress provided for nine **Supreme Court** justices (same number as
                 on today's court).

1878   Federal Bankruptcy Act of 1867 was repealed.

1891   **U.S. Circuit Courts of Appeals** were created to hear appeals from U.S.
                 Circuit Courts and U.S. District Courts. U.S. Circuit Courts continued to

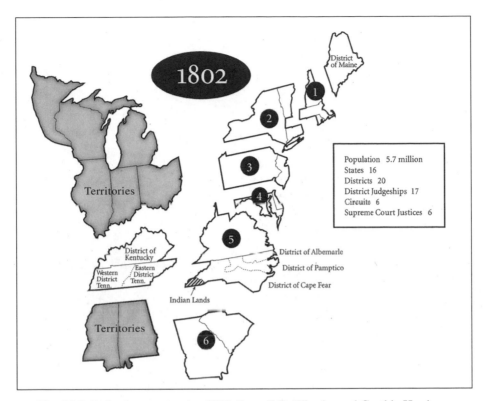

Population 5.7 million
States 16
Districts 20
District Judgeships 17
Circuits 6
Supreme Court Justices 6

Fig. 12.3. Federal court circuits, 1802. Russell R. Wheeler and Cynthia Harrison.
Creating the Federal Judiciary System. 3rd ed. Washington, D.C.:
Federal Judicial Center, 2005, p. 10.

serve as trial courts but lost appellate jurisdiction. Supreme Court justices were no longer required to serve on U.S. Circuit Courts, and appeals to Supreme Court were restricted.

1898 Federal Bankruptcy Act of 1898 confirmed U.S. District Court jurisdiction over bankruptcy cases, and created position of **Referee** to oversee **bankruptcy** cases.

1906 New **Bureau of Immigration and Naturalization** regulated naturalization procedures nationwide, creating standardized forms and collecting copies of naturalization records issued by courts. State and federal courts continued, however, to perform naturalizations.

1912 U.S. Circuit Courts were abolished. **U.S. District Courts** became the sole federal trial courts.

1968 Federal **Magistrates** replaced U.S. Commissioners.

1978 **Bankruptcy Court** was created in each judicial district, as a unit of the U.S. District Court.

1991   New federal administrative procedure was established for **naturalizations**, through Immigration and Naturalization Service, as alternative to traditional court naturalization proceeding.

Federal Courts Today

U.S. Supreme Court

Today's Supreme Court consists of a Chief Justice and eight associate justices. They hear a limited number of appeals from federal or state courts, usually involving important questions of federal law or Constitutional issues.

U.S. Courts of Appeals

There are twelve regional circuit Courts of Appeals (and one for the Federal Circuit). The two in New England are:

- **U.S. Court of Appeals for the First Circuit**, serving districts of Maine, Massachusetts, New Hampshire, Rhode Island (and Puerto Rico), and

- **U.S. Court of Appeals for the Second Circuit**, serving districts of Connecticut, Vermont (and New York).

These courts hear appeals from U.S. District Courts within the circuit, decisions of federal administrative agencies, and specialized appeals, such as those involving patent laws.

U.S. District Courts

There are ninety-four judicial districts in the United States, including one in each of the New England states: Connecticut, Maine, Massachusetts, New Hampshire, Rhode Island and Vermont. U.S. District Courts have jurisdiction over trials of most federal cases, civil and criminal.

U.S. Bankruptcy Court

Each federal judicial district has one U.S. Bankruptcy Court (one in each New England state) to hear bankruptcy matters.

Other Federal Trial Courts

Other federal trial courts include the **U.S. Court of International Trade** and **U.S. Court of Federal Claims**. Records of these courts (except for a few early Court of Claims cases) are *not covered in this book*.

Federal Courts Outside Judicial Branch

A number of federal courts operate outside the judicial branch of the U.S. government, including **Military Courts** (trial and appellate), **Court of Veterans Appeals**, **U.S. Tax**

Court and **Federal administrative agencies and boards**. Records of these courts are *not covered in this book*.

Where to Find Court Records
See Appendix for complete contact information.

General Sources

Courts

U.S. Supreme Court, Washington, D.C.
See "Federal Archives and Records Center" and other sources, *below*.

U.S. Courts of Appeals
First Circuit, Boston, Mass.
Serves districts of Maine, Mass., N.H., R.I. (and Puerto Rico).
Briefs, 1987-present, available on microfiche at 1st Circuit Library. Opinions, case files and dockets, 1992-date, available online at PACER (Public Access to Court Electronic Records): *https://pacer.ca1.uscourts.gov/main.htm*. Bankruptcy Appellate Panel decisions, from 1999, available online at PACER:
https://pacer.bap1.uscourts.gov/main.htm. See also "Digital/Electronic Sources," *below*.
Second Circuit, New York, N.Y.
Serves districts of Conn., Vt. (and N.Y.).
Recent opinions, case files and dockets available online at PACER:
https://pacer.login.uscourts.gov/cgi-bin/login.pl?court_id=02ca. See also www.ca2.uscourts.gov for recent opinions, and "Digital/Electronic Sources," *below*.

General Access Guidelines for Federal Court Records
For archived or older records (ca. **before 1970**): *See* "Federal Archives and Records Center" and "Other Repositories," *below*.
For records ca. **1970s-date**: Visit Clerk of Court, but call first (*see Appendix: Contact Information-Federal Courts*); make written request; use PACER (Public Access to Court Electronic Records, *see* "Digital/Electronic Sources, *below*); or call VCIS (Voice Case Information Service for bankruptcy cases, 1988-date).
See also "Courts" in each state section, *below*.

Federal Archives and Records Center

U.S. National Archives and Records Administration (NARA), Northeast Region-
Waltham (Boston), Mass.
Many NARA Record Groups contain federal court records, but most important include:
Record Group 21
    U.S. District Courts, including most bankruptcy records, federal court naturalizations (1790-1906); and records of U.S. Commissioners (ca. 1842-1982).
Record Group 85
    Immigration and Naturalization Service, 1787-1955, including dexigraph collection (negative photostats) of records from 301 federal and state courts

in Maine, Mass., N.H., R.I. and Vt., between 1790 and 1906. Index is available on microfilm, as *Index to New England Naturalization Petitions, 1791-1906*; *see* "Microform," *below*. Other records include Chinese Exclusion Act case files, ca. 1900-1955. *Note*: NARA-Waltham staff will search index and provide copies for a fee, if following information provided: name, residence at time of application, and birth date.

Record Group 118

U.S. Attorneys, 1866-1976. Includes bribery, civil rights, conspiracy, draft evasion, fraud, internal revenue, firearms, school desegregation cases, and criminal records from Prohibition era.

Record Group 276

U.S. Court of Appeals (1st Circuit), 1891-1978; includes appeals from U.S. District Courts in Maine, Mass., N.H. and R.I. (*See* NARA-New York office, *below*, for Second Circuit records.)

NARA-Boston Access Guidelines:

To review court records **before 1970**:

Contact NARA-Boston before visit (*see Appendix: Contact Information–Archives and Other Repositories*). *See* Archival Holdings Guide, *www.archives.gov/northeast/boston/holdings/index.html*, for details about NARA Record Groups, and Archival Research Catalog (ARC), *www.archives.gov/research/arc*. *See also* "Books and Journals," and "Microform," *below*.

To review records **after 1970**:

Court records after 1970 may be stored at NARA Records Center-Boston, but courts retain index. Contact court clerk first (*see Appendix: Contact Information–Federal Courts*), to obtain case information, *e.g.*: case name and number, transfer number, agency box number, and Records Center shelf location number. Then call NARA at 866-329-6465 to schedule appointment. *See www.archives.gov/northeast/boston/public/court-records.html* for further details.

For more information about NARA holdings of federal court records, by state, *see* "Federal Archives and Record Center" in each state section, *below*.

U.S. National Archives and Records Administration, Northeast Region-Pittsfield, Mass.
Microform of naturalization records and indexes. No original court records.

U.S. National Archives and Records Administration, **Northeast Region**-New York, N.Y.
Record Group 276: U.S. Court of Appeals (2nd Circuit), 1891-1968. Includes appeals from U.S. District Courts in Conn. and Vt.

U.S. National Archives and Records Administration, Washington, D.C., and College Park, Md.
Record Group 267: U.S. Supreme Court, 1772-1997 (bulk 1790-1984).

Other Repositories

East Providence Historical Society, E. Providence, R.I.
Pleadings and briefs from patent cases before U.S. Courts of Appeals for the 8th and 4th Circuits, 1948 and 1953, re: Hall Laboratories, Economics Laboratory, Springs

Cotton Mills, and Rumford Chemical Co. Also records of lawsuits by Rumford against other baking powder companies re: patent infringement, late 1800s and early 1900s.

Harvard Business School, Baker Library, Manuscripts Division, Boston, Mass.
U.S. Circuit Court Collection. Legal Papers, 1879-1922. U.S. Circuit Court (prior to 1911), and U.S. Court of Appeals for the 1st Circuit. 5 linear feet; unpublished finding aid.

Harvard University, Law School Library, Cambridge, Mass.
Papers of Louis D. Brandeis. Electronic finding aid, *http://nrs.harvard.edu/urn-3:HLS.LIBR:law00015*, and unpublished inventory. *See also* "Microform," *below.*
Papers of Felix Frankfurter. Electronic finding aid, *http://nrs.harvard.edu/urn-3:HLS.LIBR:law00076*, and published inventory. *See also* "Microform," *below.*
U.S. Supreme Court. Briefs, since 1881.
U.S. Court of Appeals for the 1st Circuit. Briefs.

Maine Historical Society, Portland, Maine
Clifford, Nathan. Papers, 1831-1881, Coll. 39. Legal opinions, 1858-1880, of U.S. Supreme Court Justice.

Massachusetts Historical Society, Boston, Mass.
Jenkins, Joseph. Papers, 1819-1845. Ms. N-1491. Jenkins' lawsuit against Charles H. Eldredge, 1843-1845, in U.S. Circuit Court.

Social Law Library, Boston, Mass.
U.S. Supreme Court. Briefs, since 1974-1975. Microfiche.

U.S. Citizenship and Immigration Services, U.S. Dept. of Homeland Security, Washington, D.C.
Naturalization certificate files ("C-Files"): Copies of naturalization records from state and federal courts after September 27, 1906, *e.g.*, Declaration of Intention, Petition for Naturalization, and Certificate of Naturalization.
1906-1956: Available on microfilm. Make Freedom of Information/Privacy Act (FOIA/PA) request to U.S. Citizenship and Immigration Services in Washington, D.C.
After 1956: Make FOIA/PA request to the district U.S. Citizenship and Immigration Services office that maintains the records, or office nearest your residence.
See Appendix: Contact Information-Archives and Other Repositories, Washington, D.C.

Yale University, Manuscripts and Archives, New Haven, Conn.
Clark, Charles Edward. Papers, 1907-1967 (inclusive), 1935-1963 (bulk). MS 1344. Including case and motion files, docket books, etc., as associate judge of U.S. Court of Appeals for the 2nd Circuit, 1939-1963.

Books and Journals

History

Dargo, George. *A History of the United States Court of Appeals for the First Circuit.* Boston: U.S. Court of Appeals for the 1st Circuit, 1993.

Hall, Kermit L. *The Oxford Guide to United States Supreme Court Decisions*. New York: Oxford Univ. Press, 2001.

Howard, J. Woodford. *Courts of Appeals in the Federal Judicial System: A Study of the Second, Fifth, and District of Columbia Circuits*. Princeton: Princeton Univ. Press, 1981.

Kennedy, David S., and R. Spencer Clift III. "An Historical Analysis of Insolvency Laws and Their Impact on the Role, Power, and Jurisdiction of Today's United States Bankruptcy Court and its Judicial Officers." *Journal of Bankruptcy Law and Practice* 9 (Jan/Feb 2000): 165-200.

Morris, Jeffrey B. *Federal Justice in the Second Circuit: A History of the United States Courts in New York, Connecticut, and Vermont, 1787-1987*. New York: 2nd Cir. Historical Committee, 1987.

Owens, James K. "Documenting Regional Business History: The Bankruptcy Acts of 1800 and 1841." *Prologue: Quarterly of the National Archives* 21 (1989), 3:179-185.

United States Courts in the Second Circuit: A Collection of History Lectures Delivered by Judges of the Second Circuit. New York: Federal Bar Foundation, 1992.

Zobel, Hiller B. "Those Honorable Courts—Early Days on the *First* First Circuit." 73 Federal Rules Decisions. Eagan, Minn.: West, 1977.

Law Library Resources

Case Reports: *See Chapter 17*, and *Appendix-Contact Information: Law Libraries* and *Publishers*. *See also* "Microform" and Digital/Electronic Sources," *below*.

U.S. Supreme Court

U.S. Reports. Washington, D.C.: Supreme Court of the U.S. Court opinions, 1790-date.

"Nominative Reports." 1790-1875:

Curtis 1-21	1790-1854	
Peters' Cond. Reports	1790-1827	
Dallas 1-4	1790-1800	*U.S. Reports* 1-4
Cranch 1-9	1801-1815	*U.S. Reports* 5-13
Wheaton 1-12	1816-1827	*U.S. Reports* 14-25
Peters 1-16	1828-1842	*U.S. Reports* 26-41
Howard 1-24	1843-1861	*U.S. Reports* 42-65
Black 1-2	1861-1863	*U.S. Reports* 66-67
Wallace 1-23	1863-1875	*U.S. Reports* 68-90
U.S. Reports 91-	1875-date	

Supreme Court Reporter. Eagan, Minn.: West. Court opinions, 1882-date (from Vol. 106 of *U.S. Reports*-date).

United States Supreme Court Digest. Eagan, Minn.: West. Companion set to *Supreme Court Reporter*.

United States Supreme Court Reports, Lawyers' Ed. Dayton, Ohio: Lexis-Nexis. Court opinions and summaries of attorney briefs, 1790-date.

U.S. Law Week. Washington, D.C.: Bureau of National Affairs. Current information about U.S. Supreme Court, and latest decisions.

Lower Federal Courts

Bankruptcy Reporter. Eagan, Minn.: West. Decisions of U.S. Bankruptcy Courts and bankruptcy decisions from U.S. District Courts, 1980-date.

Federal Cases. Eagan, Minn.: West. Most lower federal court decisions from more than 100 different nominative reports, alphabetically by case name, 1789-1880.

Federal Reporter. Eagan, Minn.: West. U.S. District and Circuit Courts, from 1880; U.S. Courts of Appeals only from 1932-date.

Federal Appendix. Eagan, Minn.: West. Court of Appeals decisions not selected for publication in the *Federal Reporter*, 2001-date.

Federal Rules Decisions. Eagan, Minn.: West. Selected U.S. District Court decisions re: procedural issues, 1940-date.

Federal Supplement. Eagan, Minn.: West. U.S. District Courts; also U.S. Court of International Trade and Judicial Panel on Multidistrict Litigation, 1932-date.

See also "Books and Journals" in *Chapters 6-11*. *West Digests* for each state, *e.g.*, *West's Connecticut Digest*, provide cumulative index to state and federal court decisions.

Research Guides

Cohen, Morris L., and Sharon H. O'Connor. *A Guide to the Early Reports of the Supreme Court of the United States*. Littleton, Col.: Fred B. Rothman, 1995.

Guide to Federal Records in the National Archives of the United States. 3 vols. Washington, D.C.: NARA, 1996.

Guide to Genealogical Research in the National Archives. 3d ed. Washington, D.C.: NARA, 2001.

Hickey, Walter V. "A Gold Mine of Naturalization Records in New England." *Prologue: Quarterly of the National Archives* (Fall 2004): 54-59.

Wehmann, Howard H. Rev. by Benjamin L. DeWhitt. *Guide to Pre-Federal Records in the National Archives*. Washington, D.C.: NARA, 1989.

Wilson, Don W. "Federal Court Records in the Regional Archives System." *Prologue: Quarterly of the National Archives* 21, no. 3 (1989): 176-177. Special issue re: federal court records in the National Archives.

Wonders, Peter. *Directory of Manuscript Collections Related to Federal Judges, 1789-1997*. Washington, D.C.: Federal Judicial Center, 1998. *See also* "Digital/Electronic Sources," *below*.

Microform

Law Library Microform Consortium

Court decisions on microfiche (available at libraries, but some materials priced for individual purchase). *See Appendix: Contact Information-Publishers*.

U.S. Supreme Court: all official reports; *West National Reporter System* publications, 1882-1923, and additional vols. annually; *Curtis Decisions*, vols. 1-21, 1790-1854; *Peters' Condensed Reports*, 1790-1827.

U.S. Circuit and District Courts: *Myer's Federal Decisions, 1790-1884*. St. Louis: Gilbert Book Co.; *Circuit Court of Appeals*. 63 vols. New York: Banks, 1893-1899.

LexisNexis Academic & Library Solutions

American Legal Manuscripts from the Harvard Law School Library, and other collections, on microfilm (available at libraries), including:

The Louis D. Brandeis Papers: Part I, United States Supreme Court October Terms, 1916-1931; Part II, 1932-1939.

The Felix Frankfurter Papers: Part I, Supreme Court of the United States Case Files of Opinions and Memoranda, October Terms, 1938-1952; Part II, 1953-1961.

Historical Trials Relevant to Today's Issues. British and American trials, 18th and 19th centuries.

See Appendix: Contact Information-Publishers.

National Archives and Records Administration

NARA microfilm may be viewed at NARA Records Centers and at many LDS Family History Centers (*see Appendix: Contact Information-Archives and Other Repositories* and *Publishers*), or purchase from National Archives Trust Fund (800-234-8861). Including:

Index to New England Naturalization Petitions, 1791-1906. 1983. NARA Microfilm Publications M1299. Alphabetical index of individuals naturalized, in state and federal courts of Maine, Mass., N.H., R.I. and Vt. (indicates court and certificate number).

The Revolutionary War prize cases: Records of the Court of Appeals in Cases of Capture, 1776-1787. NARA Microfilm Publications M0162.

Digital/Electronic Sources

CD-ROM

West's Federal District Court Reporter: 1st Circuit. Eagan, Minn.: West. Includes U.S. District Court decisions (Maine, Mass., N.H., R.I. and Puerto Rico) reported in *Federal Supplement,* 1925-date.

*West's Federal District Court Reporte*r: 2nd Circuit. Eagan, Minn.: West. Includes U.S. District Court decisions (Conn., Vt. and N.Y.) reported in Federal Supplement, 1925-date; also decisions reported in Bankruptcy Reporter and Federal Rules Decisions.

West's First Circuit Reporter. Eagan, Minn.: West. Includes decisions of U.S. Court of Appeals for the 1st Circuit (Maine, Mass., N.H., R.I. and Puerto Rico), reported in Federal Reporter, 1925-date.

West's Second Circuit Reporter. Eagan, Minn.: West. Includes decisions of U.S. Court of Appeals for the 2nd Circuit (Conn., Vt. and N.Y.) reported in *Federal Reporter*, 1925-date.

USSC+ CD-ROM Full Edition. Houston: InfoSynthesis, Inc. *See www.usscplus.com* or 800-784-7036. U.S. Supreme Court decisions, 1817-date, plus eighty earlier leading cases, back to 1793; semi-annual updates.

USSC+ Top 1000 CD-ROM. Houston: InfoSynthesis, Inc. *Seee www.usscplus.com* or 800-784-7036. 1,000 U.S. Supreme Court decisions most cited by court in cases from 1922-1999.

Internet

Cornell Law School's Legal Information Institute
> *http://straylight.law.cornell.edu/supct/index.html*
> U.S. Supreme Court. Decisions, 1990-date (by topic, author or party), or selected historic decisions.

FedWorld (National Technical Information Service, U.S. Dept. of Commerce)
> *www.fedworld.gov/supcourt/index.htm*
> U.S. Supreme Court. Decisions, 1937-1975. Vols. 300-422 of *U.S. Reports.*

Federal Judicial Center (FJC) *www.fjc.gov*

> Education and research agency of Federal Courts. Publications available online, in Adobe Acrobat format (PDF), include:
>
> "The *Amistad* Case and the Federal Courts." *The Court Historian* 9 (March 1998).
>
> Messinger, I. Scott. *Order in the Courts: A History of the Federal Court Clerk's Office.* Washington, D.C.: FJC, 2002.
>
> Wheeler, Russell. *Origins of the Elements of Federal Court Governance.* Washington, D.C.: FJC, 1992.
>
> Wheeler, Russell, and Cynthia Harrison. *Creating the Federal Judicial System.* 3rd ed. Washington, D.C.: FJC, 2005.
>
> Wonders, Peter. *Directory of Manuscript Collections Related to Federal Judges, 1789-1997.* Washington, D.C.: FJC, 1998.

FindLaw

> *http://supreme.lp.findlaw.com/supreme_court/decisions/index.html*
> U.S. Supreme Court. 1893-date.
> *www.findlaw.com/casecode/courts/1st.html*
> U.S. Court of Appeals for the 1st Cir. 10 years-date.
> *www.findlaw.com/casecode/courts/2nd.html*
> U.S. Court of Appeals for the 2nd Cir. 10 years-date
> *http://caselaw.lp.findlaw.com/casesummary/index.html*
> U.S. Courts of Appeals for the 1st and 2nd Cir., and U.S. Supreme Court. Decision summaries, Sept. 2000-date.

HeinOnLine *http://heinonline.org*

> U.S. Supreme Court. 1790-date. Institutional subscriptions or available at libraries.

Law Library of Congress *www.loc.gov/law/guide/usjudic.html*

> Links to web sites about federal court system and decisions.

LexisNexis *www.lexis.com*

> U.S. Supreme Court, 1790-date; U.S. Courts of Appeals and U.S. District Courts, 1912-date; U.S. Bankruptcy Court, 1979-date. Subscription service or available at law libraries and other repositories.

LexisOne *www.lexisone.com*

> Federal courts, most recent five years; U.S. Supreme Court, 1790-present. Free.

Loislaw *www.loislaw.com*

> U.S. Supreme Court, 1899-date; U. S. Courts of Appeals for the 1st and 2nd Cir., 1924-date; U.S. District Courts. Subscription service.

PACER (Public Access to Court Electronic Records)

> *http://pacer.psc.uscourts.gov/pacerdesc.html* (Overview)
> *http://pacer.uspci.uscourts.gov* (U.S. Party/Case Index)
> Low-cost online access to case and docket information from U.S. Courts of Appeals, District Courts and Bankruptcy Courts. Register at PACER website to obtain login and password, or contact PACER Service Center at 800-676-6856 or *pacer@psc.uscourts.gov*. Each court maintains own database, and date range of available records varies; *see* "Courts," *above*, and in each state section, *below*.

U.S. Court of Appeals for the 2nd Circuit *www.ca2.uscourts.gov*

> Search recent opinions.

U.S. Supreme Court

> *www.supremecourtus.gov*

Recent U.S. Supreme Court decisions
www.supremecourtus.gov/opinions/casefinder.html
Case citation finder
www.supremecourtus.gov/opinions/datesofdecisions.pdf
Note: First 107 vols. of *U.S. Reports* do not show decision dates. This report, prepared by U.S. Supreme Court Library, 1997, lists names and dates of Supreme Court decisions, 1791-1882.

USSCPlus Online *www.usscplus.com*
U.S. Supreme Court, 1855-date, with subject-matter index and keyword searching. Subscription service.

VersusLaw *www.versuslaw.com*
U.S. Supreme Court, 1886-date; U.S. Courts of Appeals (1st and 2nd Cir.), 1930-date; U.S. District Courts (*see* "Digital/Electronic Sources" in each state section, *below*). Subscription service.

Westlaw *www.westlaw.com*
U.S. Supreme Court, 1790-date; U.S. Courts of Appeals (1st and 2nd Cir.), 1891-date; federal bankruptcy cases from 1st Cir. states, 1790-date, and from 2nd Cir. states, 1797-date; U.S. District Courts (*see* "Digital/Electronic Sources" in each state section, *below*). Subscription service or available at law libraries and other repositories. Westlaw CourtEXPRESS offers case research and document retrieval from U.S. courts.

Connecticut

Courts

See "General Access Guidelines for Federal Court Records" in "General Sources: Courts," *above*.

U.S. Court of Appeals, Second Circuit, New York, N.Y.
See "General Sources: Courts," *above*.

U.S. District Court, District of Connecticut, Bridgeport, Hartford and New Haven, Conn.
Before 1993, Bridgeport Div. served Fairfield County; Hartford Div. served Hartford, Tolland and Windham Counties; and New Haven Div. served Litchfield, Middlesex, New Haven and New London Counties. From 1993-date, cases from any county may be assigned to any division.

U.S. Bankruptcy Court, District of Connecticut, Bridgeport, Hartford and New Haven, Conn.
Bridgeport Div. serves Fairfield County; Hartford Div. serves Hartford, Litchfield, Middlesex, Tolland and Windham Counties; New Haven Div. serves New Haven and New London Counties. Call 800-800-5113 and 860-240-3345 for VCIS (automated Voice Case Information Service).

Federal Archives and Record Center

U.S. National Archives and Records Administration (NARA), Northeast Region- Waltham (Boston), Mass.

Record Group 21

> **U.S. Circuit Court**, 1790-1911. Conn. records include: minute books, 1855-1911; dockets, case files and final record books, 1790-1911; naturalization, 1893-1911.
>
> **U.S. Commissioners** (appointed by Circuit or District judge). Conn. records, ca. 1897-1978, include docket/record books and file papers re: criminal cases.
>
> **U.S. District Court**, 1789-1992. Records from Hartford, New Haven, Bridgeport and Waterbury include: minute books, 1855-1955; dockets, 1789-1973; case files (civil, admiralty, general, law, equity and criminal), 1790-1977; bankruptcy, 1800-1958; final record books, 1789-1917; and naturalization, 1842-1991.

Donated Materials Group

> Naturalization Records of Non-Federal Courts in Conn. (Conn. Superior Courts, Courts of Common Pleas, District Courts, etc.) Includes city court naturalization records of: Ansonia, 1893-1906; Hartford, 1875-1876; Meriden, 1903-1940; and New Haven, 1843-1923.

Record Group 118

> Records of U.S. Attorneys. Conn., 1947-1960.

See "NARA Access Guidelines" in "General Sources: Federal Archives and Record Center," *above.*

U.S. National Archives and Records Administration, Northeast Region-New York, N.Y.
Record Group 276. U.S. Court of Appeals, 2nd Cir. 1891-1968. Includes appeals from U.S. District Court, District of Conn.

Other Repositories

Massachusetts Historical Society, Boston, Mass.
The African captives: Trial of the prisoners of the Amistad on the writ of habeas corpus, before the Circuit court of the United States, for the district of Connecticut, at Hartford, ...September term, 1839. New York: American Anti-Slavery Society, 1839. Checklist Amer. Imprints 59782.

Mystic Seaport, The Museum of America and the Sea, Mystic, Conn.
Andrew T. Judson Collection. Coll. 247. Papers and court records of Canterbury, Conn. judge of U.S. District Court, who presided over trial of the *Amistad* captives, 1839-1840. *See* overview of collection at
www.mysticseaport.org/library/manuscripts/coll/coll247/coll247.cfm.
Legal records of the Smack *L.A. Macomber*. Coll. 45. Legal briefs, probate certificates, etc. from Court of Commissioners of Alabama Claims re: destruction of Conn. vessel by Confederate warship.

Books and Journals

Cabranes, Jose A. "Notes on the History of the Federal Court of Connecticut." *Connecticut Bar Journal* 57 (1983): 351-371.
Morris, Jeffrey B. *Federal Justice in the Second Circuit: A History of the United States Courts in New York, Connecticut, and Vermont, 1787-1987.* New York: 2nd Cir. Historical Committee, 1987.

West's Connecticut Digest and *West's Atlantic Digest*. Multiple vols. Eagan, Minn.:
West. Digests of Conn. state and federal court decisions, 1764-date, organized alphabetically by topic, with headnotes, key numbers, and multiple indexes (case name, etc.). *See also* "Digital/Electronic Sources," *below*.

Microform

Index to Naturalization Petitions 1895-1988 (Waterbury, Connecticut). GSU, 2003-2004. Includes U.S. District Court, Waterbury, 1972-1988.

Index to Naturalization Petitions, 1963-1992 (Bridgeport, Connecticut). GSU, 2004. U.S. District Court, Bridgeport.

Index to Naturalization Records, 1906-1992, Hartford [Connecticut]. GSU, 2004. U.S. Circuit Court and U.S. District Court, Hartford.

Index to Naturalization Records, New Haven, CT, 1851-1926. GSU, 2004. U.S. Circuit Court and U.S. District Court, New Haven.

Naturalization Record Books, 1842-1903. GSU, 1984. U.S. District Court.

Naturalization Record Books, 1893-1906. GSU, 1984. U.S. Circuit Court.

Records Relating to the Various Cases Involving the Spanish Schoooner Amistad; *and Appellate Case File No. 2161, U.S. v. the* Amistad, *40 US 518*. National Archives microfilm publications M1753 and M2012.

Digital/Electronic Sources

CD-ROM

West's Connecticut Digest. Eagan, Minn.: West. Digest of state and federal appellate court decisions, 1764-date.

Internet

PACER (Public Access to Court Electronic Records)
https://ecf.ctd.uscourts.gov
U.S. District Court, Conn. Decisions, case files, dockets: civil, 1961-date; criminal, 1972-date.
https://ecf.ctb.uscourts.gov
U.S. Bankruptcy Court, Conn. Decisions, case files, dockets: 1997-date.

U.S. Bankruptcy Court, District of Connecticut
www.ctd.uscourts.gov/Bankruptcy%20Opinions.htm
Selected bankruptcy decisions, 2000-date.

U.S. District Court, District of Connecticut
www.ctd.uscourts.gov/Civil%20Opinions.htm
Selected civil decisions, 1999-date.
www.ctd.uscourts.gov/Criminal%20Opinions.htm
Selected criminal decisions, 2000-date.

VersusLaw *www.versuslaw.com*
U.S. District Courts. Conn., 1932-date. Subscription service. *See also* "General Sources: Digital/Electronic Sources," *above*.

Westlaw *www.westlaw.com*
U.S. District Courts. Conn., 1799-date. Subscription service, or available at law libraries and other repositories. *See also* "General Sources: Digital/Electronic Sources," *above*.

Maine

Courts

See "General Access Guidelines for Federal Court Records" in "General Sources: Courts," *above.*

U.S. Court of Appeals, First Circuit, Boston, Mass.
See "General Sources: Courts," *above.*

U.S. District Court, District of Maine, Portland and Bangor, Maine
Portland Div. serves Androscoggin, Cumberland, Knox, Lincoln, Oxford, Sagadahoc and York Counties; Bangor Div. serves Aroostook, Franklin, Hancock, Kennebec, Penobscot, Piscataquis, Somerset, Waldo and Washington Counties.

U.S. Bankruptcy Court, District of Maine, Portland and Bangor, Maine
Portland Div. serves Androscoggin, Cumberland, Oxford, Sagadahoc and York Counties. Bangor Div. serves Aroostook, Franklin, Hancock, Kennebec, Knox, Lincoln, Penobscot, Piscataquis, Somerset, Waldo and Washington Counties. Call 800-650-7253 and 207-780-3755 for VCIS (automated Voice Case Information Service).

Federal Archives and Record Center

U.S. National Archives and Records Administration (NARA), Northeast Region-Waltham (Boston), Mass.
Record Group 21

> **U.S. Circuit Court**, 1820-1911. Maine records include: dockets and case files, 1820-1911; and naturalization, 1850-1911. (Before 1820, appeals from the District Court in Maine went to the U.S. Circuit Court for the District of Massachusetts.)
>
> **U.S. Commissioners** (appointed by Circuit or District judge). Maine records, ca. 1891-1971. Docket/record books and file papers re: criminal cases.
>
> **U.S. District Court**. N. Div. (Bangor) and S. Div. (Portland). Including: dockets, 1789-1916; indexes, 1790-1886; case files, 1790-1906; bankruptcy records, 1800-1878; naturalization, 1850-1991; and clerk of court records, 1819-1912.

Record Group 118

> Records of U.S. Attorneys. Maine, 1866-1945.

See "NARA Access Guidelines" in "General Sources: Federal Archives and Record Center," *above.*

Other Repositories

Maine Historical Society, Portland, Maine
Sewall, David, 1735-1825. Court Docket Book, 1800-1803. Coll. 1475. Judge of U.S. District Court, Maine, 1800-1803.
John W. Jones, et als. in equity, vs. Rufus K. Sewall, Administrator of Henry Clark. Portland: Stephen Berry, printer, 1872?. M 347.9 J718. Circuit Court, Maine District, re: patent rights to method of canning corn.

The opinion of Judge Story in the case of William Allen vs. Joseph McKeen, treasurer of Bowdoin College: decided in the Circuit Court of the United States, at the May term at Portland, 1833. Boston: Printed at the office of the Daily Advertiser and Patriot, 1833. Stacks 378 B674C.

Jane S. Robison, complainant v. The Female Orphan Asylum of Portland et als., respondents: pleadings and proofs. Portland: Printed under direction of clerk, 1882, 1883. *Jane S. Robison, appellant, v. The Female Orphan Asylum of Portland and others: brief for respondents.* Mt P837.r2a. Brief to U.S. Supreme Court, 1887. Stacks Mt P837.r2. Appeal to U.S. Supreme Court from decision of Circuit Court of the United States, District of Maine, In Equity, contesting will of Robert I. Robison.

Massachusetts Historical Society, Boston, Mass.

A charge delivered to the grand jury of the Circuit court of the United States: at its first session in Portland, for the judicial district of Maine, May 8, 1820.... Portland: A. Shirley, 1820.

Books

West's Maine Digest and *West's Atlantic Digest*. Multiple vols. Eagan, Minn.: West. Digests of Maine state and federal appellate court decisions, 1820-date, organized alphabetically by topic, with headnotes, key numbers, and multiple indexes (case name, etc.).

Microform

Court Records, 1898-1928. GSU, 1991. FHL computer #570947. U.S. District Court records from Androscoggin County Building, Auburn, Maine.

Index to Declarations of Intention and Index to Naturalization Petitions [Maine], 1906-1955. GSU, 2004.

Digital/Electronic Sources

Internet

PACER (Public Access to Court Electronic Records)

https://ecf.med.uscourts.gov

U.S. District Court, Maine. Decisions, case files, dockets: civil, 1972-date; criminal, 1975-date.

https://ecf.meb.uscourts.gov

U.S. Bankruptcy Court, Maine. Decisions, case files, dockets: 1982-date.

VersusLaw *www.versuslaw.com*

U.S. District Courts. Maine, 1934-date. Subscription service. *See also* "General Sources: Digital/Electronic Sources," *above.*

Westlaw *www.westlaw.com*

U.S. District Courts. Maine, 1821-date. Subscription service, or available at law libraries and other repositories. *See also* "General Sources: Digital/Electronic Sources," *above.*

Massachusetts

Courts

See "General Access Guidelines for Federal Court Records" in "General Sources: Courts," *above*.

U.S. Court of Appeals, First Circuit, Boston, Mass.
See "General Sources: Courts," *above*.

U.S. District Court, District of Massachusetts, Boston, Springfield and Worcester, Mass.
Boston Div. serves Barnstable, Bristol, Dukes, Essex, Middlesex, Nantucket, Norfolk, Plymouth and Suffolk Counties; Springfield Div. serves Berkshire, Franklin, Hampden and Hampshire Counties; and Worcester Div. serves Worcester County.

U.S. Bankruptcy Court for the District of Massachusetts, Boston and Worcester, Mass.
Boston Div. serves counties of Barnstable, Bristol, Dukes, Essex (except towns assigned to Worcester Div.), Nantucket, Norfolk (except towns assigned to Worcester Div.), Plymouth, Suffolk, and following towns in Middlesex County: Arlington, Belmont, Burlington, Everett, Lexington, Malden, Medford, Melrose, Newton, North Reading, Reading, Stoneham, Wakefield, Waltham, Watertown, Wilmington, Winchester and Woburn. Worcester Div. serves counties of Berkshire, Franklin, Hampden, Hampshire, Middlesex (except towns assigned to Boston Div.), Worcester County and following towns: in Essex County—Andover, Haverhill, Lawrence, Methuen and North Andover; in Norfolk County—Bellingham, Franklin, Medway, Millis and Norfolk. Call 888-201-3572 and 617-565-6025 for VCIS (automated Voice Case Information Service).

Federal Archives and Record Center

U.S. National Archives and Records Administration (NARA), Northeast Region- Waltham (Boston), Mass.
Record Group 21
> **U.S. Circuit Court**, 1790-1911. Mass. records include: minute books, 1853-1859; dockets, 1800-1911; case files and final record books, 1790-1911; indexes, 1790-1847; equity and criminal case records, 1834-1911; naturalization, 1845-1911; and clerk of court records, 1832-1911.
> **U.S. Commissioners** (appointed by Circuit or District judge). Mass. records, ca. 1842-1967. Docket/record books and file papers re: criminal cases.
> **U.S. District Court**. Mass. records include: dockets, 1790-1977; case files, 1790-1978; final record books, 1789-1918; indexes, 1806-1979; bankruptcy, 1801-1973; admiralty, equity and criminal cases, 1812-1965; naturalization, 1790-1991; customs and Internal Revenue, 1803-1880; seamen, 1872-1956; and clerk of court records, 1803-1954.

Record Group 118
> U.S. Attorneys. Mass., 1928-1976.

See "NARA Access Guidelines" in "General Sources: Federal Archives and Record Center," *above*.

Other Repositories

Boston Athenaeum, Boston, Mass.
Manuscript collection includes:
Davis, John, 1761-1847.
> Circuit Court Dockets: Boston, 1804-1831. Mss S2 pt. 1. U.S. Circuit Court; some cases summarized in detail.
> District Court Dockets: Boston, 1810-1833. Mss S2 pt. 2. U.S. District Court, Mass.; some cases summarized in detail.
> Judge Davis's decree: Mass. District, Special District Court, May 31, 1805, re: Ship *Hazard*.
Rare book collection includes:
Report of a Trial for Violation of the Patent Right of the 'American Air-Tight' Cooking Stove: in the Circuit Court of the United States Within and For the District of Massachusetts: Wherein Elias Johnson and David B. Cox, were Plaintiffs, and Peter Low and George W. Hicks, were Defendants. Boston: Dickinson Printing, Damrell & Moore, 1848. Rare Book (LC) KF228.B67 1848.

Massachusetts Historical Society, Boston, Mass.
Davis, John. Judicial Opinions, 1811-1836. Ms. N-1098. Maritime cases before John Davis, Judge of the U.S. District Court, Mass.
The Trial of John Williams, Francis Frederick, John P. Rog, Nils Peterson, and Nathaniel White, on an Indictment for Murder on the High Seas; Before the Circuit Court of the United States; Holden for the District of Massachusetts, at Boston, on the 28th of December, 1818. Boston: Russell & Gardner, 1819. Box 1819.
The Trial of Theodore Parker, for the "Misdemeanor" of a Speech in Faneuil Hall against kidnapping, before the Circuit Court of the United States, at Boston, April 3, 1855. Boston: By author, 1855. B Parker.
The trial of William Holmes, Thomas Warrington, and Edward Rosewain, on an indictment for murder on the high seas: before the Circuit Court of the United States, holden for the district of Massachusetts, at Boston, on the 4th Jan. 1819. Boston: Joseph C. Spear, 1820. Box 1820.

Peabody-Essex Museum, Phillips Library, Salem, Mass.
Peleg W. Chandler papers. 1829-1908; bulk: 1852-1866. MH-55. Includes legal papers from U.S. District Court (Mass.), etc.
French spoliation claims records, 1796-1927. MSS 160. U.S. Court of Claims cases by heirs of U.S. merchants, shipowners, etc., whose vessels or cargo were captured and condemned by the French from 1794 to 1801.

University of Massachusetts, Archives and Special Collections Dept., Boston, Mass.
Garrity, W. Arthur. Papers on the Boston Schools Desegregation Case, 1972-1997 (1974-1982). Chambers papers of Judge Garrity, U.S. District Court, District of Mass., in *Morgan v. Hennigan*, 379 F. Supp. 410 (1974). 84 linear feet; finding aid available.

Books and Journals

"Pillar of the Political Fabric: Federal Courts in Massachusetts, 1789-1815." *Massachusetts Law Review* 74 (December 1989): 197-205.

West's Massachusetts Digest. Multiple vols. Eagan, Minn.: West. Digest of Mass. state and federal appellate court decisions, 1761-date, organized by topic and key number, and indexed by case name, etc. *See also* "Digital/Electronic Sources," *below*.

Microform

Naturalization records

Index to Declaration of Intentions [Massachusetts], 1943-1955. GSU, 2004. U.S. District Court, Mass.

Index to Naturalization Petitions and Records of the U.S. District Court, 1906-66, and the U.S. Circuit Court, 1906-11, for the District of Massachusetts. National Archives microfilm publications M1545.

Naturalization Index Cards, 1790-1926. GSU, 1985. U.S. Circuit Court and U.S. District Court, Mass.

Petitions and Records of Naturalization of the U.S. District Court and Circuit Courts of the District of Massachusetts, 1906-1929. National Archives microfilm publications M1368.

Early American Imprints, Series II. Shaw-Shoemaker, 1801-1819. New Canaan, Conn.: Readex Microprint, in cooperation with American Antiquarian Society, 1987-1992. Microfiche. Including:

A charge delivered to the grand juries of the Circuit Court at October terms, 1819, in Boston, and at November term, 1819, in Providence...by Joseph Story. Shaw & Shoemaker, 49743.

A report of the trial of Samuel Tully & John Dalton, on an indictment for piracy, committed January 21st, 1812 before the Circuit Court of the United States, at Boston, 28th October, 1812..... Boston: J. Belcher, 1812, 1813, 1814. Shaw & Shoemaker, 26595, 29972, 32965.

The trial of John Williams, Francis Frederick, John P. Rog, Nils Peterson, and Nathaniel White, on an indictment for murder on the high seas: before the Circuit Court of the United States, holden for the District of Massachusetts, at Boston, on the 28th of December, 1818. Boston: Russell & Gardner, 1819. Shaw & Shoemaker, 49630.

Digital/Electronic Sources

CD-ROM

West's Massachusetts Digest, 2d. Eagan, Minn.: West. Digest of state and federal appellate court decisions, 1933-date.

Internet

Early American Imprints: *www.readex.com/scholarl/earlamim.html*
    Shaw-Shoemaker Digital Edition, Series II. Shaw-Shoemaker, 1801-1819. Chester, Vt.: Readex/Newsbank, in cooperation with American Antiquarian Society, 2004. Available at academic libraries. *See also* "Microform," *above*.

PACER (Public Access to Court Electronic Records)
> *https://ecf.mad.uscourts.gov*
> U. S. District Court, Mass. Decisions, case files, dockets: civil, 1961-date; criminal, 1970-date.
> *https://ecf.mab.uscourts.gov*
> U.S. Bankruptcy Court, Mass. Decisions, case files, dockets: 1966-date.

VersusLaw *www.versuslaw.com*
> U.S. District Courts. Mass., 1931-date. Subscription service. *See also* "General Sources: Digital/Electronic Sources," *above.*

Westlaw *www.westlaw.com*
> U.S. District Courts. Mass., 1792-date. Subscription service, or available at law libraries and other repositories. *See also* "General Sources: Digital/Electronic Sources," *above.*

New Hampshire

Courts

See "General Access Guidelines for Federal Court Records" in "General Sources: Courts," *above.*

U.S. Court of Appeals, First Circuit, Boston, Mass.
See "General Sources: Courts," *above.*

U.S. District Court, District of New Hampshire, Concord, N.H.

U.S. Bankruptcy Court, District of New Hampshire, Manchester, N.H.
Call 800-851-8954 or 603-666-7424 for VCIS (automated Voice Case Information Service).

Federal Archives and Record Center

U.S. National Archives and Records Administration (NARA), Northeast Region-Waltham (Boston), Mass.
Record Group 21
> **U.S. Circuit Court**, 1790-1911. N.H. records include: journals or minute books, 1892-1911; dockets, case files, final record books and miscellaneous, 1790-1911; naturalization, 1849-1911.
> **U.S. Commissioners** (appointed by Circuit or District judge). N.H. records, 1901-1957. Docket/record books and file papers re: criminal cases.
> **U.S. District Court**, 1789-1977. N.H. records include: journals or minute books, 1892-1977; dockets, 1795-1972; case files, 1802-1969; final record books, 1789-1946; bankruptcy, 1842-1968; naturalization, 1805-1977; clerk of court records, 1791-1958; and miscellaneous, 1789-1960.

Record Group 118
> U.S. Attorneys. N.H., 1903-1966.

See "NARA Access Guidelines" in "General Sources: Federal Archives and Record Center," *above.*

Other Repositories

New Hampshire Division of Archives and Records Management, Concord, N.H.
Condemnation cases, U.S. District Court, ca. 1910-1920, 1930-1969. #689112-3.

Books

West's New Hampshire Digest and *West's Atlantic Digest*. Multiple vols. Eagan,
    Minn.: West. Digests of N.H. state and federal appellate court decisions, ear-
    liest to date, organized alphabetically by topic, with headnotes, key numbers,
    and multiple indexes.
Wilder, Brad, et al., coordinated by James R. Starr. *History of the New Hampshire
    Federal Courts*. Concord, N.H.: U.S. Dist. Court, Dist. of N.H., 1991. *See
    also* "Digital/Electronic Sources," *below.*

Digital/Electronic Sources

Internet
PACER (Public Access to Computer Electronic Records)
    https://ecf.nhd.uscourts.gov
    U.S. District Court, N.H. Decisions, case files, dockets: civil, 1974-date.
    https://ecf.nhb.uscourts.gov
    U.S. Bankruptcy Court, N.H. Decisions, case files, dockets, 1986-date.
U.S. District Court, District of New Hampshire
    www.nhd.uscourts.gov/oo/oo_index.asp
    Decisions, 1989-date. Free searchable database.
    www.nhd.uscourts.gov/ci/history/historyindex.asp
    Wilder, Brad, et al. *History of the New Hampshire Federal Courts. See also*
    "Books," *above.*
VersusLaw *www.versuslaw.com*
    U.S. District Courts. N.H., 1932-date. Subscription service. *See also* "Gen-
    eral Sources: Digital/Electronic Sources," *above.*
Westlaw *www.westlaw.com*
    U.S. District Courts. N.H. 1798-date. Subscription service or available at law
    libraries and other repositories. *See also* "General Sources: Digital/Electronic
    Sources," *above.*

Rhode Island

Courts

See "General Access Guidelines for Federal Court Records" in "General Sources:
Courts," *above.*

U.S. Court of Appeals, First Circuit, Boston, Mass.
See "General Sources: Courts," *above.*

U.S. District Court, District of Rhode Island, Providence, R.I.

U.S. Bankruptcy Court, District of Rhode Island, Providence, R.I.
Call 800-843-2841 or 401-528-4476 for VCIS (automated Voice Case Information Service).

Federal Archives and Record Center

U.S. National Archives and Records Administration (NARA), Northeast Region- Waltham (Boston), Mass.
Record Group 21
>   **U.S. Circuit Court**, 1790-1911. R.I. records include: minute books, dockets, case files and final record books, 1790-1911; indexes, 1790-1890; naturalization, 1802-1911; and miscellaneous, 1791-1911.
>   **U.S. Commissioners** (appointed by Circuit or District judge). R.I. records, 1891-1939. Docket/record books and file papers re: criminal cases.
>   **U.S. District Court**. R.I. records include: minute books, 1790-1969; dockets, 1800-1972; case files, 1790-1978; final record books, 1791-1922; indexes, 1791-1888; bankruptcy, 1800-1972; naturalization, 1842-1991; clerk of court records, 1790-1928; and miscellaneous, 1790-1959.

Record Group 118
>   U.S. Attorneys. R.I., 1943-1965.

See "NARA Access Guidelines" in "General Sources: Federal Archives and Record Center," *above*.

Other Repositories

University of Rhode Island Library, Kingston, R.I.
Dismissed with Prejudice. Series I. Court Documents, 1957-1960. MSG #146. *Commerce Oil Refining Corp. v. William W. Miner, et al.* Alleged conspiracy to obstruct development of refinery. Superior Court, Newport; U.S. District Court, District of R.I.; U.S. Court of Appeals.
Rhode Island Circuit Court, Providence. Opinion, *Tyler v. Wilkinson*. MSG #20, Box 5, Folder 60.

Books

West's Rhode Island Digest. Eagan, Minn.: West. 1783-date. *West's Atlantic Digest*. Eagan, Minn.: West. 1764-date. Digests of R.I. state and federal appellate court decisions, organized alphabetically by topic, with headnotes, key numbers, and multiple indexes (case name, etc.).

Microform

Index to Declarations of Intentions [Rhode Island], 1906-1984. GSU, 2004. U.S. District Court, R.I.
Index to Naturalization Petitions, 1906-1991 (Rhode Island). GSU, 2004. U.S. Circuit Court (Eastern), 1906-1911; U.S. District Court, R.I., Providence, 1906-1991.
Index to Rhode Island Naturalizations, 1918-1968. GSU, 2004. U.S. District Court, R.I.

Early American Imprints, Series II. Shaw-Shoemaker, 1801-1819. New Canaan, Conn.: Readex Microprint, in cooperation with American Antiquarian Society, 1987-1992. Microfiche. Including: *A charge delivered to the grand juries* *of the Circuit Court at October terms, 1819, in Boston, and at November term, 1819, in Providence...by Joseph Story.* Shaw & Shoemaker, 49743.

Digital/Electronic Sources

Internet
PACER (Public Access to Computer Electronic Records)
> *http://pacer.rid.uscourts.gov*
> U.S. District Court, R.I. Decisions, case files, dockets: civil, 1991-date; criminal, 1993-date.
> *https://ecf.rib.uscourts.gov*
> U.S. Bankruptcy Court, R.I. Decisions, case files, dockets, 1980-date.

U.S. District Court, District of Rhode Island
> *www.rid.uscourts.gov/Judges%20Opinions.asp*
> Decisions within sixty days, and selected earlier opinions, from 1992.

VersusLaw *www.versuslaw.com*
> U.S. District Courts. R.I., 1934-date. Subscription service. *See also* "General Sources: Digital/Electronic Sources," *above.*

Westlaw *www.westlaw.com*
> U.S. District Courts. R.I., 1812-date. Subscription service, or available at law libraries and other repositories. *See also* "General Sources: Digital/Electronic Sources," *above.*

Vermont

Courts

See "General Access Guidelines for Federal Court Records" in "General Sources: Courts," *above.*

U.S. Court of Appeals, Second Circuit, New York, N.Y.
See "General Sources: Courts," *above.*

U.S. District Court for the District of Vermont, Burlington and Rutland, Vt.
Burlington Div. serves Caledonia, Chittenden, Essex, Franklin, Grand Isle, Lamoille, Orleans and Washington counties; Rutland Div. serves Addison, Bennington, Orange, Rutland, Windsor and Windham counties.

U.S. Bankruptcy Court for the District of Vermont, Rutland, Vt.
Call 800-260-9956 for VCIS (automated Voice Case Information Service).

Federal Archives and Record Center

U.S. National Archives and Records Administration (NARA), Northeast Region- Waltham (Boston), Mass.
Record Group 21
> **U.S. Circuit Court**, 1792-1911. Vt. records include: dockets and case files, 1792-1911; and miscellaneous records re: chancery, civil, law and criminal cases, 1809-1911.

U.S. Commissioners (appointed by Circuit or District judge). Vt. records, ca. 1872-1982. Docket/record books and file papers re: criminal cases.
U.S. District Court, 1791-1983. Vt. records include: dockets, 1798-1974; case files, 1791-1967; indexes, 1906-1983; journals, 1894-1954; bankruptcy, 1802-1963; naturalization, 1801-1983; records of District Judge Hoyt H. Wheeler, 1877-1905.
Record Group 118
U.S. Attorneys. Vt., 1909-1967.
See "NARA Access Guidelines" in "General Sources: Federal Archives and Record Center," *above.*

U.S. National Archives and Records Administration, **Northeast Region**-New York, N.Y.
Record Group 276: U.S. Court of Appeals, 2nd Cir., 1891-1968. Includes appeals from U.S. District Courts in Vt.

Other Repositories

Middlebury College Library, Middlebury, Vt.
Smalley, David Allen. *U.S. Circuit court, for the district of Vermont, at Rutland, October term, 1862: in the matter ex parte Anson Field. Application for habeas corpus...Decision of his honor Judge Smalley, adjudging the marshal guilty of comtempt....* Burlington: W.H. & C.A. Hoyt & Co., 1862. Bailey's collection of Vermont pamphlets; vol. 11, no. 5. Vermont Restrict-Special Coll. KFV548.A54 S62 1862.

Henry Sheldon Museum of Vermont History, Middlebury, Vt.
Records of Addison County Court, and Rules and dockets of Addison County Court, 1787-1900. Includes records of U.S. Circuit and District courts.

University of Vermont, Bailey/Howe Library, Burlington, Vt.
Circuit court of the United States, district of Vermont, in equity: Robert B. Chisholm, complainant, vs. Trenor W. Bark and H. Henry Baxter.... 1871?. Special Collections Wilbur, TN433.U8 C47 1871. Re: Utah silver mine.
In the United States Circuit Court of appeals for the Second Circuit: Claude R. Wickard, Secretary of Agriculture of the U.S., defendant-appellant v. New England Dairies, Inc., plaintiff-appellee, on appeal from the District Court of the United States for the District of Vermont: brief for the appellee. 1940. Special Collections Wilbur, KF228.N48 F43 1940.
In the United States Circuit Court of Appeals for the Second Circuit, United States of America, appellant, v. Percy W. Muzzey, appellee, on appeal from the District Court of the United States for the District of Vermont.... 193-?. Special Collections Wilbur, KFV502.6 .A545 1930z. Disabled veterans case.
Transcript of record, Supreme court of the United States: no. 225, the Rutland Marble Company...vs. William Y. Ripley and William F. Barnes...April 17, 1869. 1869. Special Collections Wilbur, TN277.R87 1869. Appeal of case re: Vt. quarrying, from U.S. Circuit Court, District of Vt.
U.S. Circuit court, for the district of Vermont, at Rutland, October term, 1862: in the matter ex parte Anson Field. Application for habeas corpus.... Burlington: W.H. & C.A. Hoyt & Co., 1862. Special Collections Wilbur, KFV548.A54 S62 1862. Court opinion.

United States of America, defendant-appellant v. George W. Hill, plaintiff-appellee, on appeal from the District court of the United States for the district of Vermont.... 1939. Special Collections Wilbur, KF228.H54 B34 1939. *See also* related court briefs re: WWI military pensions, at: Special Collections Wilbur, UB373.H54 1938, UB383.U5 1938.

United States Circuit Court, Vermont District in Equity. Riley Burdett vs. Jacob Estey and others.... New York: George F. Nesbitt & Co., 1876. Special Collections Wilbur. Court brief; other related briefs in collection.

Books and Journals

Coffrin, Albert W. "The United States District Court for the District of Vermont—Its Background, History, and Judicial Heritage." *Second Circuit Redbook, 1985-1986.* New York: Federal Bar Council, 1986.

Gorham, Alan "Federal Court Records Pertaining to Vermont: Sources for Study." *Vermont History* 39 (Summer/Fall 1971).

Morris, Jeffrey B. *Federal Justice in the Second Circuit: A History of the United States Courts in New York, Connecticut, and Vermont, 1787-1987.* New York: 2nd Cir. Historical Committee, 1987.

West's Vermont Digest. Eagan, Minn.: West. 1764-date. *West's Atlantic Digest.* Eagan, Minn.: West. 1789-date. Digests of Vt. state and federal court decisions, organized alphabetically by topic, with headnotes, key numbers, and multiple indexes (case name, etc.). *See also* "Digital/Electronic Sources," *below.*

Digital/Electronic Sources

CD-ROM

West's Vermont Digest. Eagan, Minn.: West. Digests of state and federal court decisions, 1789-date.

Internet

PACER (Public Access to Computer Electronic Records)
   https://ecf.vtd.uscourts.gov
   U.S. District Court, Vt. Decisions, case files, dockets: civil, 1974-date; criminal, 1976-date.
   https://ecf.vtb.uscourts.gov
   U.S. Bankruptcy Court, Vt. Decisions, case files, dockets, 1979-date.

U.S. Bankruptcy Court, District of Vermont *www.vtb.uscourts.gov/opinions.html*
   Decisions, 1985-date.

U.S. District Court, District of Vermont *www.vtd.uscourts.gov*
   Search recent opinions and filings of interest.

VersusLaw *www.versuslaw.com*
   U.S. District Courts. Vt. 1960-date. Subscription service. *See also* "Digital/Electronic Sources" in "General" section, *above.*

Westlaw *www.westlaw.com*
   U.S. District Courts. Vt. 1798-date. Subscription service or available at law libraries and other repositories. *See also* "Digital/Electronic Sources" in "General" section, *above.*

PART III

SAMPLING

THE SOURCES

Court House, Pittsfield, Mass.

The image on the preceding page, from the author's collection of vintage picture postcards, depicts the courthouse in Pittsfield, Massachusetts, ca. 1911.

CHAPTER 13

INDEXES TO COURT RECORDS:
People of Color in Colonial *Rhode Island*

People on the margins of colonial society—slaves and servants, transient sailors, fishermen and laborers—can be difficult to trace. When I began my own research about seventeenth-century Scottish war prisoners in New England, I soon realized that most primary sources—church records, land deeds and tax lists, for example—documented the lives of the more-prosperous English settlers, and offered few clues about other people who lived among them.

Court records provided the best evidence of what happened to the unwilling Scottish immigrants. Some Scotsmen tried using colonial law to their advantage, petitioning the courts for release from servitude. Scottish war prisoners wound up in court for resisting their fate—assaulting their masters, refusing to work, cursing—or for violating other Puritan rules and regulations. Sometimes Scotsmen testified as trial witnesses, their words preserved almost-verbatim in the old court records. Probate inventories, which included Scotsmen in lists of land, barns, cattle and farm equipment, contained information about the identities of these men and their English masters.

I culled most of this data in laborious page-by-page review of court records from the 1600s, or by scanning the few available indexes to court records, looking for mention of "Scots" or names that appeared Scottish. Researchers seeking people of color in colonial New England have similar difficulties, compounded by the fact that few Africans or Native Americans appeared with surnames in the old court records. Although I ran across many entries about "Negro" slaves and "Indians" in the seventeenth-century court records, while searching for Scotsmen, few of those cases were indexed or readily accessible to other researchers.

Finding people of color in colonial New England remains challenging, but Rhode Island research is becoming easier, thanks to the meticulous work of scholars who recently indexed original records. This chapter samples two of the best-indexed sources—Rhode Island colonial court records, transcribed and abstracted by Jane Fletcher Fiske, and original manuscripts archived at the Rhode Island Historical Society. Both of these sources help genealogists and historians to locate people of color in the old court records and offer a glimpse of the surprisingly diverse and multi-cultural world of colonial Rhode Island.

Books by Jane Fletcher Fiske

From 1647 to 1729, Rhode Island's General Court of Trials met primarily in Newport, for civil and criminal trials. In 1730, two new courts assumed trial jurisdiction in the counties of Newport, King's and Providence: the Inferior Courts of Common Pleas for civil cases, and the Courts of General Sessions of the Peace for criminal cases. Although some of those original records still exist and can be reviewed at the Rhode Island State Archives in Providence and at the Judicial Records Center in Pawtucket (*see Chapter 10*), Jane Fletcher Fiske brings selected records to researchers in two recent books. *Gleanings from Newport Court Files, 1659-1783* abstracts file papers and dockets. *Rhode Island General Court of Trials, 1671-1704* transcribes part of the record book known as "Book A," or "Newport Court Book A," which covers the entire colony, not just Newport.

Indexes at the back of each book locate numerous cases involving people of color. In *Gleanings from Newport Court Files*, Fiske compiles a separate list of more than one hundred people identified in the court records as "Indian," "Mulatto," "Mustee," or "Negro," with the page numbers of their cases.[6] Similarly, the Index to Names for *Rhode Island General Court of Trials* lists approximately eighty "Indians" and several "Negroes."[7] These cases include much information of historical and genealogical interest, as the following highlights suggest:

Windmill Burning
At the General Court of Trials in Newport, in the spring of 1677, two Africans—Joseph and Salvadore—faced trial for burning Thomas Gould's windmill and cutting the sails from his boat. The "General Attorney" also indicted a ten-year-old girl, Mary Gerrad, for participating in the boat vandalism. All three defendants denied the charges, and a jury found them "not guilty."[8]

"Ale and Punch at Silverwoods"
Mary Silverwood invited several local African and Native American servants to her Newport home for "ale and punch" on "Cristmas Day night" in 1724. Local baker John Davis "was passing by," heard noise and disturbance in an upstairs chamber, and entered the house to investigate. There he found "Indian Dick, a servant of Peleg Smith," arguing about a squaw with "Tom, a Negro belonging to Major Brown." The candle was out, so no one could see well, and Dick lunged for Tom with a knife, accidentally cutting Davis on the left hand. Mrs. Silverwood implored "James Cadman a free Negro to walk up in the chamber" to stop the quarreling. Dick was indicted for the assault.[9]

---

[6] Jane Fletcher Fiske, *Gleanings from Newport Court Files, 1659-1783* (Boxford, Mass: By author, 1998), 579-580. *Note*: References in *Gleanings* are to item number, rather than page number.

[7] Fiske, *Rhode Island General Court of Trials, 1671-1704* (Boxford, Mass.: By author, 1998), 250-251, 253-254.

[8] Ibid., 54.

[9] Fiske, *Gleanings*, 198.

Infanticide

In 1729, "Indian Sarah Faraoh" was "indicted for murdering her child" in South Kingstown. Other Indian women testified, including Mary Sambo and Indian Hannah, "who commonly lives with Robert Potter in South Kingstown." According to Hannah, Sarah had "come to her...in...mowing time, and told her y^t she was not well and was much out of order and desired s^d Hannah to get some roots for her to take but s^d Hannah...told her she thought she was with child and if so the taking s^d roots would kill ye child...."[10]

Runaway Servants

"Isaac Anthony, a molatto" laborer from Newport, was accused in 1731 of helping two African slaves—Jupiter and "Tomas alias Tom"—to escape from their Newport masters. Anthony provided both slaves with forged travel passes, and they managed to reach New London before authorities apprehended them. Anthony admitted his role: "I gave them each one [a pass] and they gave me a pair of striped satin britches and a Bible for it, which I was very sorry for and I hope God will forgive me and I hope never to be guilty of ye like again."[11]

Slave Insurrection

In 1766, Newport merchants Samuel and William Vernon sued the master of the brig *Othello*, Thomas Rogers, when he returned to port without his full cargo of seventy African slaves. Rogers testified that the "slaves made an Insurrection upon the ship's crew" outside Barbados, beating and wounding Rogers "with billets of wood," and fracturing another man's skull. Rogers managed to get behind a "Barricade and endeavoured for near two hours by fair words and persuasion to pacify sd slaves." They "shouted, laughed and made a great noise in their savage manner," until finally, "near sunset and no hopes left of quelling them," Rogers ordered his men to fire on the Africans. "[O]ne of the slaves was killed on the spot, three wounded, thirteen jumped overboard or swam away and refused to return or be taken up, voluntarily drowning."[12]

Manuscripts at Rhode Island Historical Society

As many researchers know, the Rhode Island Historical Society in Providence maintains an extensive collection of manuscripts, including court records detailed in *Chapter 10* of this book. Historians and genealogists interested in people of color will want to pay special attention to a useful finding aid compiled by the Society, "Guide to Manuscripts at the Rhode Island Historical Society Library Relating to People of Color" (Providence: Rhode Island Historical Society, Manuscripts Division, 1988-2004). That guide is now available online, at *www.rihs.org/mssinv/PeopleofColorweb.htm*.

Over the past twenty years, Society staff collected any references that they happened to find about people of color in the manuscript collection, notations from varied sources—account books, letters, diaries, and court records. Although the Society cautions that this Guide is a "working draft," not a comprehensive list, it may serve as

---

[10] Ibid., 428.
[11] Ibid., 540.
[12] Ibid., 1070.

"a starting point into the collections containing information about people of color." The following sampling of entries from the Guide can only suggest the rich research potential for genealogists and historians:

Mss 9001-A	Arnold, Richard (d. 1710). Providence. Will dated 1708, making provision for "Negro servent" Toby.
Mss 75	Stephen Arnold Papers. East Greenwich. Estate inventory, 1734, includes "one negro girl."
Mss 9001-B	Bayley, William. Middletown. Will, 1770, re: slave Prince.
Mss 109	Beriah Brown Papers, 1696-1874. Kings/Washington County lawsuit re: 1779 sale of slaves to North Carolina.
Mss 9001-C	Carr, Mary. Newport. Estate inventory, 1746, naming "1 Negro man named Tom, 1 Negro woman named Phillis and Negro child named Violet."
Mss 680, pp. 16-20	Thomas Rice. Warwick. Depositions, 1741/2-1744, re: death of Capt. John Rice's servant Sharper.
Mss 9001-S	Samuel. Portsmouth. Coroner's inquest and jury verdict, 1670, re: Indian found dead in Anthony Emry's well.

CHAPTER 14

---◦•◦---

COMPUTER DATABASE:
Slander in Nineteenth-Century *Maine*

In 1826, at a small town north of Augusta, Maine, blacksmith John Ladd accused neighbor Isaac Cowan of "swindling and cheating people" and "stealing timber." Ladd's voice was loud enough to attract the attention of "other good citizens," who also heard Ladd declare that Cowan "would commit highway robbery and steal and forge notes." Cowan, outraged at these "false, scandalous and defamatory words," filed a slander[13] suit against Ladd in the Court of Common Pleas for Kennebec County. The records of this case, and many other slander lawsuits, can be found at the Maine State Archives.

Finding Cases with a Computer Database

Locating original court records about a particular type of case, like slander, usually means paging through docket or record books for the time period that interests you. If the volume contains an index, you may find party names listed alphabetically, but finding specific subject matter may require reading the clerk's entries one by one. At the Maine State Archives, however, a helpful computer database makes research much easier.

The *Index of Early Maine Court Records* allows you to search records from the York County Court of Common Pleas (1696-1760), the Kennebec County Supreme Judicial Court (1799-1854), and the Washington County District Court (1839-1846). Check the Maine State Archives website to download the free index in Microsoft Access format—*www.state.me.us/sos/arc/files/dbinfo.html#CTS*—or use a computer at the Archives reading room. Like most archival finding aids, the *Index of Early Maine Court Records* sorts cases by party name, but two additional options make the index especially useful: you can search by the party's place of residence, and also by type of lawsuit. Although this database covers only a small portion of the court records at the Archives, it is well worth checking if your research topic involves Maine in the 1700s or early 1800s.

---

[13] "Slander" means a false oral statement that harms the reputation of another person.

I decided to look for slander cases at the Maine State Archives, and to prepare for my trip, I searched the *Index of Early Maine Court Records* from my home computer. I clicked on the *Index* search screen for a list of "causes of action,"[14] to see if "slander" was in the database. The index offered hundreds of search possibilities, but several topics, in addition to "slander," looked possibly relevant to my project:

Abusive speech
Assault, Profanity
Cursing
Defamation
Perjury
Profane Actions
Profanity
Profanity, Drunk
Rudeness
Scandalous speech
Scandelous speech (misspelled—a common problem with computer databases!)
Scolding
Slander
Swearing
Threatening
Threatening speech
Uncivil behavior

I clicked the "cause of action" search button, typed in "slander," and seconds later I had an alphabetical list of eighty-seven people—each entry providing the name of the court, date, case number, type of case (slander), type of party (plaintiff or defendant), town of residence, and archives box number.

Sampling File Papers at the Maine State Archives

I chose four cases to sample, appeals from Kennebec County:

COWAN, ISAAC JR
Kennebec County Supreme Judicial Court
Jun 1828
7-143-5574   SLANDER   PLT   Sidney   75-25

LOOMIS, ERASTUS
Kennebec County Supreme Judicial Court
Oct 1832
8-59-6060   SLANDER   PLT   Hallowell   82-29

---

[14] "Cause of action" is specialized legal terminology, referring to the facts that form the basis for a claim. Lawyers analyze factual situations to determine whether a person has a "cause of action," or a right to sue. The *Index* list contains an assortment of topics, but they are not all "causes of action" as a lawyer would use the term.

KILBURN, WILLIAM
Kennebec County Supreme Judicial Court
<u>Oct 1836</u>
8-449-6636   SLANDER   PLT   Temple   91-16

COWAN, ISAAC
Kennebec County Supreme Judicial Court
<u>Oct 1837</u>
9-96-6889   SLANDER   PLT   Sidney   93-50

When I arrived at the Maine State Archives, I gave this identifying case information to Archives staff, and within minutes I was opening boxes and folders of original court records. I realized that I was, perhaps, the first person to read these faded ink-splotched papers in nearly two hundred years.

Understanding the Context

To make sense of file papers like these, you need to know what courts operated in the jurisdiction at the time of the lawsuits. My four sample cases all occurred during the decade from the 1820s to the 1830s. By the mid 1820s, most civil trials in Maine—such as these slander cases—took place on the county level at the Court of Common Pleas. Appeals went to Maine's Supreme Judicial Court, which met three times per year in each county. *See* Maine's "Court History Timeline" in *Chapter 7*.

Understanding basic facts about courts at the trial and appellate levels helped me to reconstruct what happened in each of the four cases, since the file papers were not arranged in chronological order, and some documents undoubtedly were missing. The original records reveal colorful details about community life, business affairs and surprising connections between small-town Mainers and the rest of New England. Here are a few highlights:

Isaac Cowan, Jr. v. John Ladd

Isaac Cowan, a "trader," and John Ladd, a blacksmith, both lived in Sidney, Maine, a small Kennebec River town north of Augusta. When townspeople gathered at the blacksmith's shop, they gossiped about their neighbors, and Ladd voiced some provocative opinions, calling Cowan "a great scoundrel and…villain." Over a period of several months, Ladd repeated a variety of charges about Cowan to many different people: Cowan forged financial documents, then paid the Furbish family a "considerable sum…to hush…up" the charges and prevent a prosecution. Cowan "went up and down the river stealing timber" and "swindling and cheating people out of their property."

Finally Cowan took action to stop this defamatory talk. In 1827, he sued Ladd for slander in the Kennebec County Court of Common Pleas at Augusta. Cowan's complaint against Ladd appears as part of a *writ of attachment* issued by the court to the county sheriff. *See Fig. 14.1*. As was typical practice, the court ordered the sheriff to *attach* or seize property of John Ladd, or to take Ladd himself into custody, to ensure his appearance at trial. (Sometimes separate file papers mark the start of a lawsuit—a *complaint*,

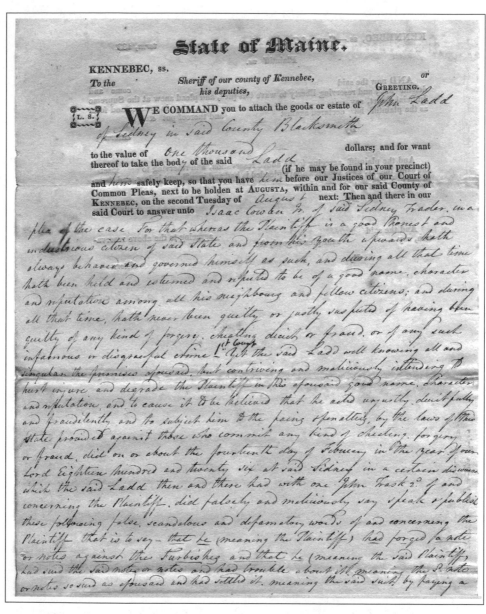

Fig. 14.1. Detail from writ of attachment, commencing case of *Isaac Cowan, Jr. v. John Ladd*, Court of Common Pleas, Kennebec County, Maine, 1827. File papers of Supreme Judicial Court, Kennebec County, June 1828, 7-143-5574, 75-25. *Courtesy of Maine State Archives.*

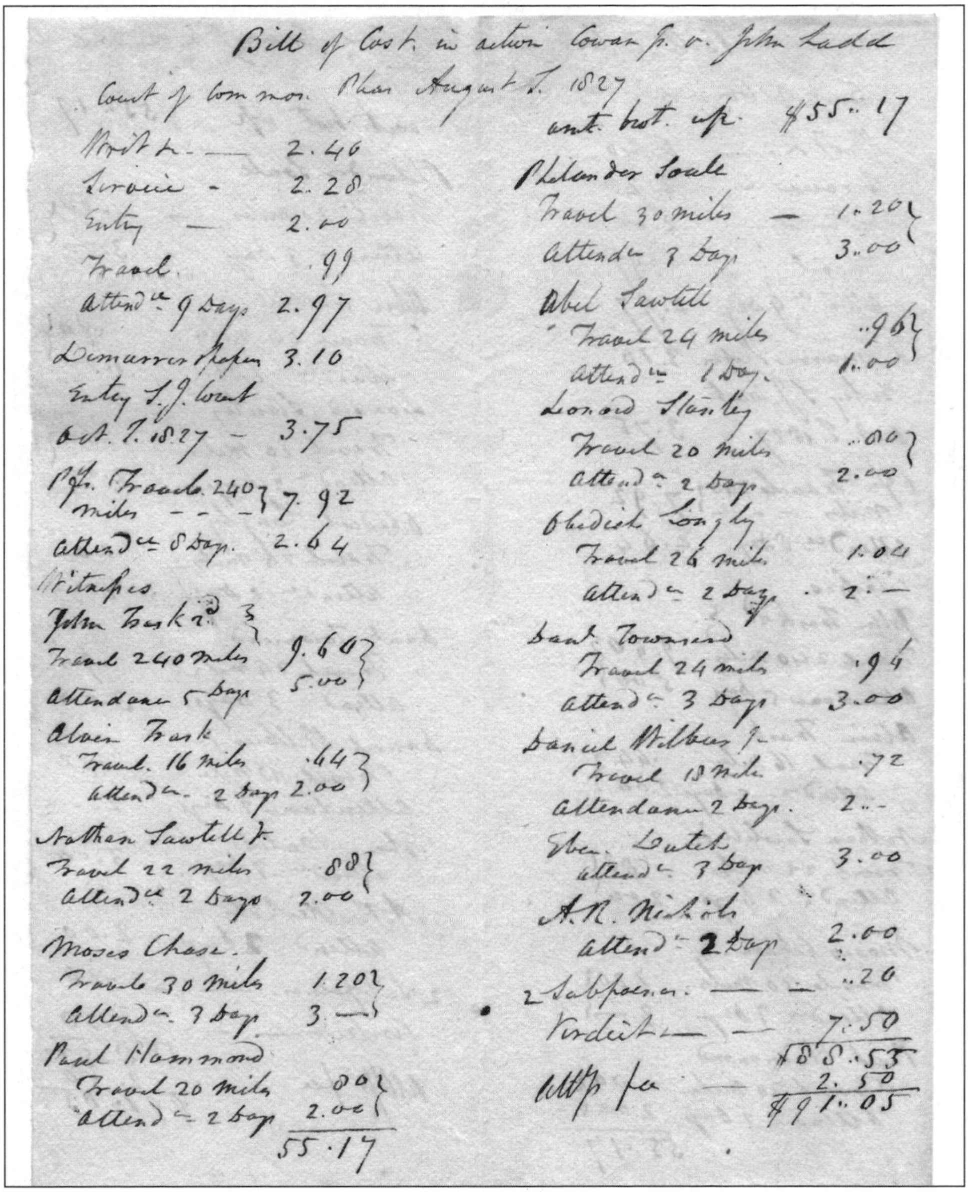

Bill of Cost in action Cowan Jr. v. John Ladd

Court of Common Pleas August T. 1827

Writ &c —	2.46
Service —	2.28
Entry —	2.00
Travel	.99
Attend.ce 9 Days	2.97
Demurrer paper	3.10
Entry L.J. cont	
Oct. T. 1827 —	3.75
Pff. Travel 240 miles — }	7.92
Attend.ce 8 Days	2.64

Witnesses.

John Baker 2d }	
Travel 240 miles	9.60 }
Attendance 5 Days	5.00 }
Alvin Trask	
Travel 16 miles	.64 }
Attend.ce 2 Days	2.00 }
Nathan Sawtell Jr.	
Travel 22 miles	.88 }
Attend.ce 2 Days	2.00 }
Moses Chase.	
Travel 30 miles	1.20 }
Attend.ce 3 Days	3.— }
Paul Hammond	
Travel 20 miles	.80 }
Attend.ce 2 Days	2.00 }
	55.17

amt. brot. up $55.17

Philander Soule	
Travel 30 miles —	1.20 }
Attend.ce 3 Days	3.00 }
Abel Sawtell	
Travel 24 miles	.96 }
Attend.ce 1 Day.	1.00 }
Leonard Stanley	
Travel 20 miles	.80 }
Attend.ce 2 Days	2.00 }
Obadiah Longly	
Travel 26 miles	1.04
Attend.ce 2 Days	2.—
Saml. Townsend	
Travel 24 miles	.96
Attend.ce 3 Days	3.00
Daniel Wilbur Jr.	
Travel 18 miles	.72
Attendance 2 Days.	2.—
Eben. Cutch	
Attend.ce 3 Day	3.00
A.R. Nichols	
Attend.ce 2 Day	2.00
2 Subpoenas —	.20
Verdict —	7.50
	$88.55
Attys fee —	2.50
	$91.05

Fig. 14.2. Bill of costs in case of *Isaac Cowan, Jr. v. John Ladd*, Court of Common Pleas, Kennebec County, Maine, 1827. From file papers of Supreme Judicial Court, Kennebec County, June 1828, 7-143-5574, 75-25. *Courtesy of Maine State Archives.*

a *summons* and a *writ of attachment*—but in this case the writ contained all of the essential information. *See Chapter 3* for more detail about types of file papers.)

Cowan described himself as a "good honest and industrious citizen," who "from his youth upwards hath always behaved and governed himself as such." During all that time, he never engaged in "any kind of forgery, cheating, deceit or fraud, or…any such infamous or disgraceful crime." Until Ladd's false accusations, Cowan enjoyed a "good name, character and reputation among all his neighbors and fellow citizens."

To prove his good character, and the damage caused by Ladd's slander, Cowan subpoenaed thirteen witnesses. Their names appear on various documents in the court file, including a "bill of costs" (*Fig. 14.2*), in which Cowan itemized all of his trial expenses. One witness, John Trask, traveled 240 miles and spent five days in court; others, who apparently lived closer, reported trips of up to thirty miles, and waits of one or more days before giving testimony. As required by court rules, Cowan paid witness fees (Trask, for example, received $14.60), based upon mileage and days in attendance.

The witness testimony must have been persuasive. Despite Ladd's denials, the jury found him "guilty" and calculated the damage to Cowan's reputation as worth $125. Ladd, represented by attorney "P. Sprague," took his appeal to the Supreme Judicial Court for Kennebec County, which finally heard the case in June 1828. (Unfortunately, since I did not have time to read all of the file papers during my visit to the Maine State Archives, I cannot report the result!)

Erastus Loomis v. Daniel Stevens

The case of Erastus Loomis, innkeeper at the town of Hallowell, involved slander of a different sort. A stranger arrived at the "forks of the road in Hallowell" and asked farmer Daniel Stevens, "Who keeps a public house here?" Stevens purportedly replied, "[O]ne Loomis keeps a whore house." People also heard Stevens tell another traveler "not to stop there as it would by and by cost him his oxen as it had another man his horse." Heeding that advice, the traveler moved on to the next town, and Loomis lost a customer. Loomis sued Stevens, and the Court of Common Pleas heard the trial in Augusta during the summer of 1831.

Although testimony confirmed that Stevens "kept constantly slandering Loomis," the innkeeper ran into problems with his case. Several witnesses raised doubts about Loomis's reputation and suggested that the whorehouse allegation might be true. When asked, "What is the general character of said Loomis," witness Isaac Moore answered: "It is bad." Other witnesses testified that Loomis "kept a loud, noisy & irregular tavern," and that "loose girls were kept there, & that young men met them there."

Despite this troubling evidence, the jury returned a verdict in favor of Loomis, for $254.16, plus costs of $207.92. Stevens appealed the case to the Supreme Judicial Court. The Court of Common Pleas clerk prepared a beautiful handwritten summary of the trial court proceedings—"A true copy as of Record"—for the appellate judges in Augusta. *See Fig. 14.3.*

Instead of arguing the case before the Supreme Judicial Court, however, Stevens and Loomis resolved the appeal out of court. They chose three "referees" to review the

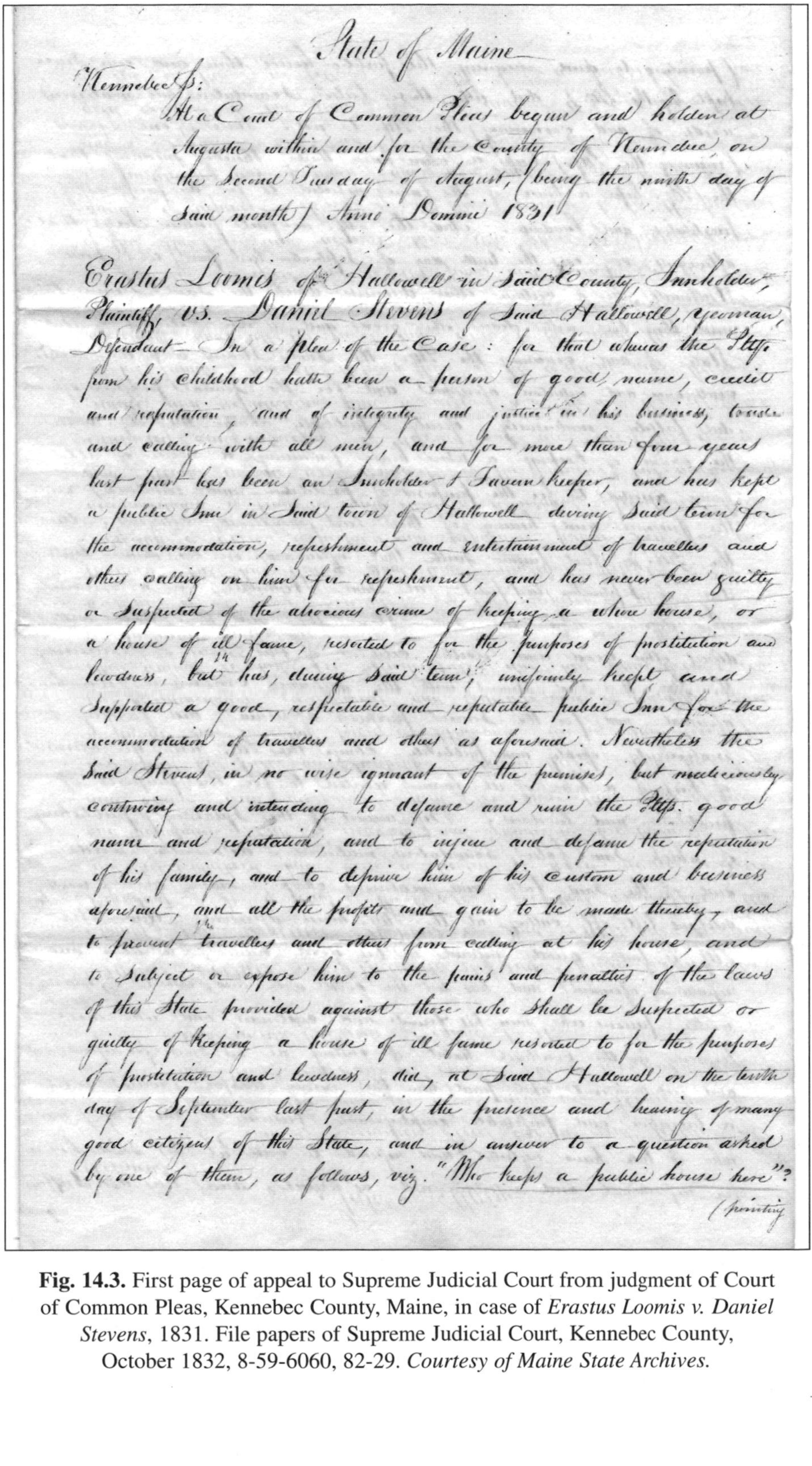

State of Maine

Kennebec ss:

At a Court of Common Pleas begun and holden at Augusta within and for the County of Kennebec, on the Second Tuesday of August, (being the ninth day of said month) Anno Domini 1831

Erastus Loomis of Hallowell in said County, Innholder, Plaintiff, vs. Daniel Stevens of said Hallowell, yeoman, Defendant — In a plea of the Case: for that whereas the Plff. from his childhood hath been a person of good name, credit and reputation, and of integrity and justice in his business, trade and calling with all men, and for more than four years last past has been an Innholder & Tavern keeper, and has kept a public Inn in said town of Hallowell during said term for the accommodation, refreshment and entertainment of travellers and others calling on him for refreshment, and has never been guilty or suspected of the atrocious crime of keeping a whore house, or a house of ill fame, resorted to for the purposes of prostitution and lewdness, but has, during said term, uniformly kept and supported a good, respectable and reputable public Inn for the accommodation of travellers and others as aforesaid. Nevertheless the said Stevens, in no wise ignorant of the premises, but maliciously contriving and intending to defame and ruin the Plff. good name and reputation, and to injure and defame the reputation of his family, and to deprive him of his custom and business aforesaid, and all the profits and gain to be made thereby, and to prevent travellers and others from calling at his house, and to subject or expose him to the pains and penalties of the laws of this State provided against those who shall be suspected or guilty of keeping a house of ill fame resorted to for the purposes of prostitution and lewdness, did, at said Hallowell on the tenth day of September last past, in the presence and hearing of many good citizens of this State, and in answer to a question asked by one of them, as follows, viz. "Who keeps a public house here"?

(printing)

Fig. 14.3. First page of appeal to Supreme Judicial Court from judgment of Court of Common Pleas, Kennebec County, Maine, in case of *Erastus Loomis v. Daniel Stevens*, 1831. File papers of Supreme Judicial Court, Kennebec County, October 1832, 8-59-6060, 82-29. *Courtesy of Maine State Archives.*

record and make a binding decision. (Why Stevens and Loomis opted for private arbitration at this point is uncertain. Perhaps arbitration was quicker and less expensive than paying attorneys to argue the case in court; maybe the parties wanted to minimize publicity, or they had little confidence in the Supreme Judicial Court judges who would decide the appeal.) The referees devised a compromise. They affirmed the trial court's judgment—agreeing that Stevens slandered Loomis—but they also reduced the award, perhaps concluding that Loomis never had much reputation for Stevens to damage.

William Kilburn v. Phineas Dinsmore

William Kilburn, plaintiff in the next slander case, lived more than forty miles northwest of Augusta, in the tiny village of Temple (originally founded in 1796 by a community of Quakers). The court documents do not specify whether Kilburn was a Quaker, but he "received [the] degree of Doctor of medicine from Middlebury College, Vermont, and had been physician and surgeon" at Temple for two years before his case came to trial in 1835.

Remarks by "yeoman" farmer Phineas Dinsmore, also of Temple, prompted Kilburn to sue. Dinsmore told people that Kilburn "never attended to a regular course of studies as a physician," and if he had any credentials, "they are forged." Dinsmore also hinted that Kilburn had a criminal past. If Kilburn ever studied medicine, he "got an old doctor book, and studied while in [a Vermont] jail, and as soon as he…got out, he…run away down here…." Kilburn was a "grossly intemperate man when he lived at the West," and a "lying imposter."

At a trial in Augusta's Court of Common Pleas, the jury concluded that Dinsmore's statements were false and defamatory. The damages amounted only to $75, plus court costs of $62.27. Dinsmore appealed to Supreme Judicial Court.

Isaac Cowan v. Samuel A. Bradley

A few years after *Cowan v. Ladd*, Isaac Cowan returned to court with another slander case.[15] This time, the Sidney resident alleged that Portland businessman Samuel Bradley had called him a "thief" and a "pirate." The main witness, housewright Peter C. Virgin, lived far away in Massachusetts, and Cowan had no power to force him to attend a trial in Maine. Cowan traveled to Virgin, instead, and took Virgin's testimony by deposition before an Essex County justice of the peace in Lynn, Massachusetts.

That deposition, preserved as four pages of densely-packed script in the case files of the Kennebec County Supreme Judicial Court, offers an extraordinary glimpse into the world of land speculators and lumber barons. The document also demonstrates that nineteenth-century litigation was remarkably sophisticated; the detailed "interrogatories" (*Fig. 14.4*) that Cowan asked Virgin to answer are so carefully drafted that they could have been prepared by a twenty-first century lawyer.

---

[15] Probably the same Cowan who sued John Ladd a few years before, this Isaac Cowan also lived in Sidney, although the court records refer to him as "yeoman" rather than "trader," and no "Jr." appears after his name.

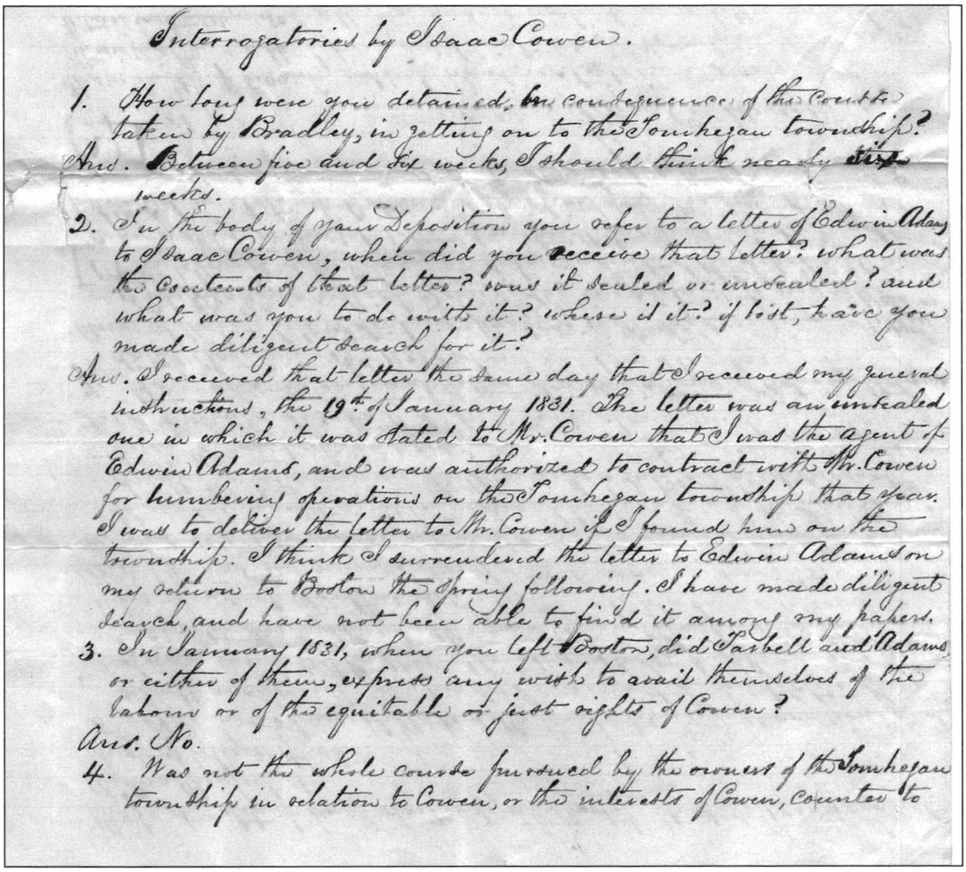

Interrogatories by Isaac Cowen.

1. How long were you detained, in consequence of the course taken by Bradley, in getting on to the Souhegan township?

Ans. Between five and six weeks, I should think nearly ~~six~~ weeks.

2. In the body of your Deposition you refer to a letter of Edwin Adams to Isaac Cowen, when did you receive that letter? what was the contents of that letter? was it sealed or unsealed? and what was you to do with it? where is it? if lost, have you made diligent search for it?

Ans. I received that letter the same day that I received my general instructions, the 19th of January 1831. The letter was an unsealed one in which it was stated to Mr. Cowen that I was the agent of Edwin Adams, and was authorized to contract with Mr. Cowen for lumbering operations on the Souhegan township that year. I was to deliver the letter to Mr. Cowen if I found him on the township. I think I surrendered the letter to Edwin Adams on my return to Boston the Spring following. I have made diligent search, and have not been able to find it among my papers.

3. In January 1831, when you left Boston, did Tarbell and Adams, or either of them, express any wish to avail themselves of the labour or of the equitable or just rights of Cowen?

Ans. No.

4. Was not the whole course pursued by the owners of the Souhegan township in relation to Cowen, or the interests of Cowen, counter to

Fig. 14.4. Detail from p. 3 of Isaac Cowan's interrogatories to witness Peter Virgin, 1836, in case of *Isaac Cowan v. Samuel A. Bradley*. File papers of Supreme Judicial Court, Kennebec County, October 1837, 9-96-6889, 93-50. *Courtesy of Maine State Archives.*

Virgin's deposition recounts how he traveled to remote Moosehead Lake north of Sidney, as an agent for one of the men who owned that township, to negotiate a timber-cutting deal with Cowan. On the way, Virgin met with Bradley in Portland, Maine, who warned against "going into the township alone" saying that Cowan "and his associates would murder" him. When Virgin "replied that [he] was not afraid," Bradley persisted, saying that "they were a lot of pirates, plunderers and depredators, and would lie [Virgin] out of [his] Christian name." The rest of the story is too convoluted for summary here, but the result of Bradley's interference was considerable lost business for Cowan at Moosehead Lake.

Cowan won his slander case—and a verdict for the large sum of $326.50. The Supreme Judicial Court, however, deducted more than $200 that Cowan owed Bradley from another court judgment. Perhaps Bradley's nasty remarks about Cowan had their origin in that previous dispute?

My research time was limited, so I never learned more about the Bradley feud with Cowan, although someday I hope to find that earlier *Bradley v. Cowan* case among the court records at the Maine State Archives. Many more boxes of court records await researchers there—cases about slander and countless other topics. I hope that historians and genealogists will try the *Index of Early Maine Court Records* and continue the search.

CHAPTER 15

FEDERAL COURT RECORDS:
Bankruptcy in Post-Civil War *Vermont*

Federal bankruptcy records may hold the key to your New England research project, yet few people ever consider this goldmine of original case files. Who would expect, for example, to find a rural Vermont ancestor in federal court? Yet thousands of ordinary New Englanders—farmers to big-city merchants—walked into federal court seeking debt relief after Congress enacted the first bankruptcy legislation in 1800. Over the past two centuries, U.S. District Courts in every New England state gathered reams of personal detail about individuals and their business affairs, and most of that bankruptcy paperwork is now consolidated at the National Archives-Northeast Region in Waltham, Massachusetts.[16]

Finding Bankruptcy Cases at the National Archives

I decided to sample bankruptcy records from nineteenth-century Vermont, so I contacted the National Archives to plan my research strategy. (Always call ahead, at the National Archives and other archival repositories, to confirm research hours and make sure that the records you need are available.) Archives personnel reminded me that four different federal bankruptcy acts—1800, 1841, 1867 and 1898—applied at varying times during the nineteenth century.[17] I opted not to review the largest and most recent collection of federal bankruptcies in Vermont—more than eight thousand cases from 1898 to 1963—because those records feature a two-volume index and pose fewer challenges. Instead, I focused on the earlier cases, which lie virtually untouched in row after row of Archives boxes.

The Bankruptcy Act of 1800

When I arrived at the Archives, a few bankruptcy files and docket books awaited my review in the document reading room. The smallest group of Vermont bankruptcies,

---

[16] This regional facility of the U.S. National Archives and Records Administration maintains archival federal records and microfilm from all six New England states—Connecticut, Maine, Massachusetts, New Hampshire, Rhode Island and Vermont. The federal bankruptcy files are part of Record Group 21, Records of the District Courts of the United States.

[17] *See also Chapter 3.*

twenty-four cases from the Act of 1800, fit entirely into two document boxes—folders of loose file papers, and a bound "final record" book. That yellowed volume, where the clerk copied important documents, was surprisingly easy to read, thanks to elegant calligraphy and scarcely-faded ink. A short list of names at the front of the record book served as an index, and nearly half of the pages at the back were blank; apparently the court clerk never managed to fill the book before 1803, when Congress repealed that first federal bankruptcy act. Although these early records looked interesting, I returned the oldest Vermont bankruptcy files to their document boxes, and opened a docket book from the 1841 act.

The Bankruptcy Act of 1841

The second federal bankruptcy law lasted just thirteen months before its repeal, but Vermont's U.S. District Court handled 1,732 cases, far more than under the previous act. Part of the reason was the 1841 act's expansive scope, which encouraged more people to seek its protections. Unlike the act of 1800, which covered only *involuntary* bankruptcies forced by unpaid creditors, the 1841 act also allowed insolvent debtors to file *voluntary* petitions.

When someone arrived at court with a bankruptcy petition, the clerk assigned the case a number, and entered the party's name, usually on a new page in the docket or record book, where subsequent document filings and actions in the case would be recorded. Usually the clerk also wrote the name (and page number) in an alphabetical index at the front or back of the volume. Today's researchers can look for particular names in these volume indexes, or they can page through the books chronologically, to find a case of interest. Then, with the party name and case number, Archives staff can retrieve file papers from the archival boxes. I decided, however, to look at the 1867 docket books before I selected cases for closer review.

The Bankruptcy Act of 1867

Congress passed the Bankruptcy Act of 1867 just after the Civil War, when all regions of the United States faced economic ruin. In Vermont, the U.S. District Court saw 993 bankruptcy filings, voluntary and involuntary, during those post-war years before the act's 1878 repeal. These cases are particularly interesting from a genealogical and historical standpoint, because so many collateral sources are available to supplement the information in bankruptcy filings. Researchers can compare census records from 1860 and 1870, for example, to see how a late-1860s bankruptcy affected a person's economic status. Civil War tax records also may provide clues to explain post-war financial problems.

I picked up an old leather-bound volume labeled "District Court Docket 1867 to… Petitions 1-412," the first Vermont docket book under the federal bankruptcy act of 1867. A handwritten name index began the book, apparently entered chronologically under each letter of the alphabet as a case was filed. Most were names of people, but businesses also appeared in the index, such as American Marble Co., Green Mountain Marble Co. and The Howe Scale Co. Following the index, each page of the book recorded a new petition, consecutively numbered, with the party's name, the type of bankruptcy (voluntary or involuntary), the attorney's name (if any), and a list of documents filed and other actions taken in the case.

Page 26, for example, shows the following entry, for the involuntary bankruptcy of Daniel Snow. The law firm of Fields & Tyler, which apparently represented Snow's creditor, filed the *petition* on October 17, 1867, together with *depositions* (written testimony) about the claim:

In the matter of   Fields & Tyler
Daniel Snow against whom a petition
in bankruptcy is filed

1867
October 17 at 5 p.m.   Filed petition of John Stearns
                          Deposition of petitioning creditor
                          Deposition as to petitioning claim, [etc.]

As the Snow case proceeded over the next three years, the clerk continued to write short summaries of documents filed or actions taken, until he filled that page and continued the Snow docket on page 127. Snow's bankruptcy must have been especially complicated; most other cases in the book required only one page for entries, and were resolved after only a few months.

The Bankruptcies of Pearl Blodgett and Anna Crandall

As I paged through the docket book, men's names predominated. I wondered whether any Vermont women were forced into bankruptcy or filed petitions under the 1867 act. The front index did not help to find women—only a last name and first initial appeared in most cases—so I began searching for women's names at the top of each docket page. I found two: the voluntary bankruptcy petition of Pearl D. Blodgett (case number 146, on page 152—*see Fig. 15.1*), and an involuntary filing against Anna E. Crandall (case number 400, on page 579). I asked the Archives to pull those case files, so that I could learn Pearl's and Anna's stories.

An Archives staff member returned with two dusty bundles of paper, tri-folded and tied into tight packages, as was the custom in courthouses until recent years. I watched as he unwrapped these files, unfolding and flattening each sheet, one by one—printed forms and handwritten papers of various sizes, some glued together at the top margin to form multi-page booklets. Anna Crandall's file was the smallest, so I began reading that while the archivist finished opening the Blodgett packet.

Anna E. Crandall

Someone named O. E. Butterfield filed a petition against Anna E. Crandall on July 4, 1873, at 4:00 P.M. (apparently the Fourth of July was an ordinary working day for the U.S. District Court). *See Fig. 15.2.* Reading on, I learned that Butterfield represented the estate of Wilmington, Vermont resident Sylvanus Clark, whose own bankruptcy case was in progress. Anna owed the very large sum of $2,200 to Clark. By forcing Anna into bankruptcy, Butterfield hoped to collect money for the benefit of Clark's creditors.

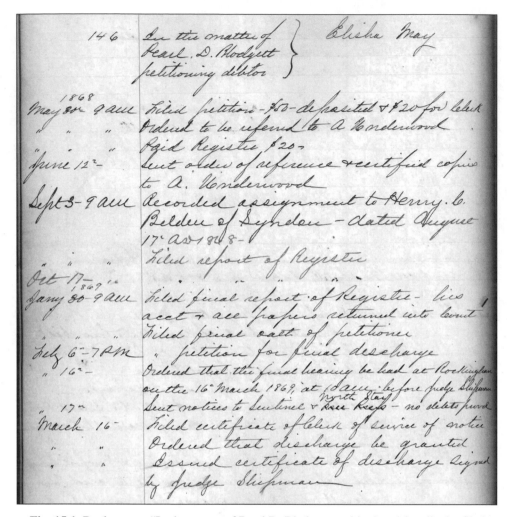

Fig. 15.1. Docket page "In the matter of Pearl D. Blodgett, petitioning debtor," who filed
for bankruptcy, May 1868. U.S. District Court for the District of Vermont. "District
Court Docket 1867 to… Petitions 1-412," p. 152, Case #146. NARA Record Group 21.
Courtesy of U.S. National Archives and Records Administration, Northeast Region.

How did Anna amass such an enormous debt? She purchased "dry goods" (textiles,
clothing, etc.) from Clark in Vermont, to resell at her small store over the border
in Bernardston, Massachusetts. Unfortunately Anna's business did not succeed, and
she never paid Clark—she "neglects and refuses so to do," according to the petition—
contributing to his own financial collapse.

Butterfield's bankruptcy case against Anna did not last long, probably because he filed
it in the wrong court. Anna sent a handwritten response to the petition, pointing out
that she had been a Massachusetts resident for the preceding two years and had just
moved to Troy, New Hampshire. Shortly thereafter, in October 1873, attorneys
for Anna and Butterfield agreed to "discontinue" the Vermont case. I wondered what

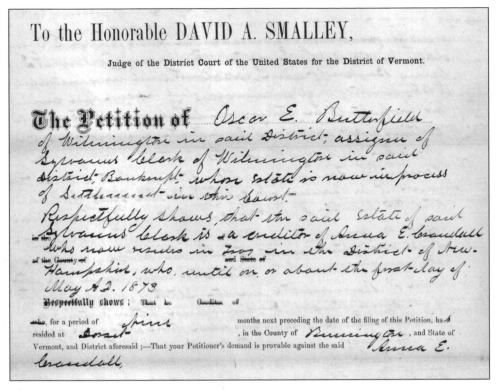

Fig. 15.2. Detail from first page of bankruptcy petition against Anna E. Crandall, filed July 4, 1873. U.S. District Court for the District of Vermont, Case #400. NARA Record Group 21. *Courtesy of U.S. National Archives and Records Administration, Northeast Region.*

happened next. Possibly Butterfield filed a new bankruptcy petition against Anna in the U.S. District Courts of Massachusetts or New Hampshire; other docket books at the Archives might reveal her fate, if I had time to look, but I decided to turn my attention to Pearl Blodgett.

Pearl D. Blodgett

First Step in Voluntary Bankruptcy: the Petition

The Blodgett file was larger, and I secured the stack of newly-unfolded documents with small sandbag paperweights that the Archives provided. I began to read the first document: "The Petition of Pearl Davis Blodgett of the Town of St. Johnsbury, in the county of Caledonia and State of Vermont…," which was signed by Pearl and attorney Elisha May and dated May 30, 1868.

Most of the petition's text was pre-printed, and with spaces to fill in names and other information. (Interestingly, this was a Massachusetts form, but the attorney had crossed out "Massachusetts" and substituted "Vermont.") I read on: "[Petitioner] Respectfully Represents, That he has resided and carried on the business of an Insurance Agent…at

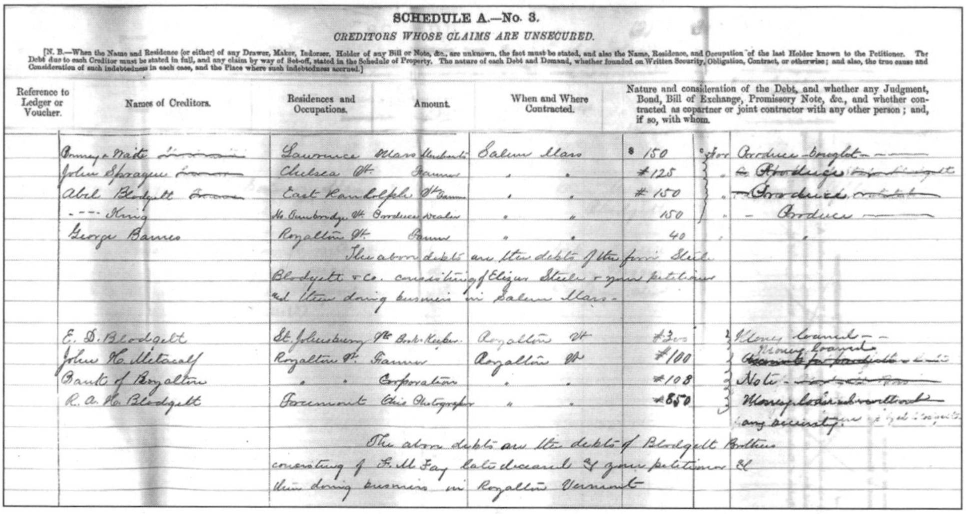

Fig. 15.3. Detail from Schedule A, #3, "Creditors Whose Claims are Unsecured,"
in bankruptcy file papers of Pearl D. Blodgett. U.S. District Court for the
District of Vermont, Case #146. NARA Record Group 21.
Courtesy of U.S. National Archives and Records Administration, Northeast Region.

said St. Johnsbury…." While the word "he" did not surprise me ("he" was pre-printed, with no "he/she" option as modern forms might provide), I stopped short at "Insurance Agent." A female insurance agent in mid-nineteenth-century Vermont? The petition continued, asserting that Pearl D. Blodgett, "a partner in the firm of…Steel & Blodgett & Co.…and of the late firm of Blodgett Bros…, owes Debts exceeding the amount of *Three Hundred Dollars*, and is unable to pay all of the same in full; that he is willing to surrender all his Estate and Effects for the benefit of his Creditors…."

"Blodgett *Brothers*"? I wondered: was Pearl a man? Continuing to review the file, I guessed that Pearl was a widow, perhaps the successor to her late husband's business affairs.

The next sheets, attached to the petition, listed Pearl's debts and assets. **Schedule A** (*Fig. 15.3*) detailed more than $1,200 owed by Steele & Blodgett for a business in Salem, Massachusetts—a large loan—and goods purchased from Vermont farmers. Did Steele & Blodgett supply produce to grocery stores in Massachusetts? Other debts on Schedule A reflected efforts by Blodgett Brothers to start a business in Royalton, Vermont; Pearl owed $1,353 for that venture, borrowed from the Bank of Royalton and from various people named Blodgett (including a Vermont farmer and book-keeper, and an Ohio photographer).

Schedule B confirmed that Pearl owned no real estate but lived "at sufferance" (without a lease or other legal interest) in a house belonging to E. L. Blodgett, probably a relative. The next page, listing personal property, solved the puzzle of Pearl's name. Pearl D. Blodgett was not a pioneering Vermont businesswoman; he was a husband and father, whose worldly assets now included about $400 in "household furniture & wearing apparel" for "self wife & children," a barrel of flour and potatoes, five cords of wood, a

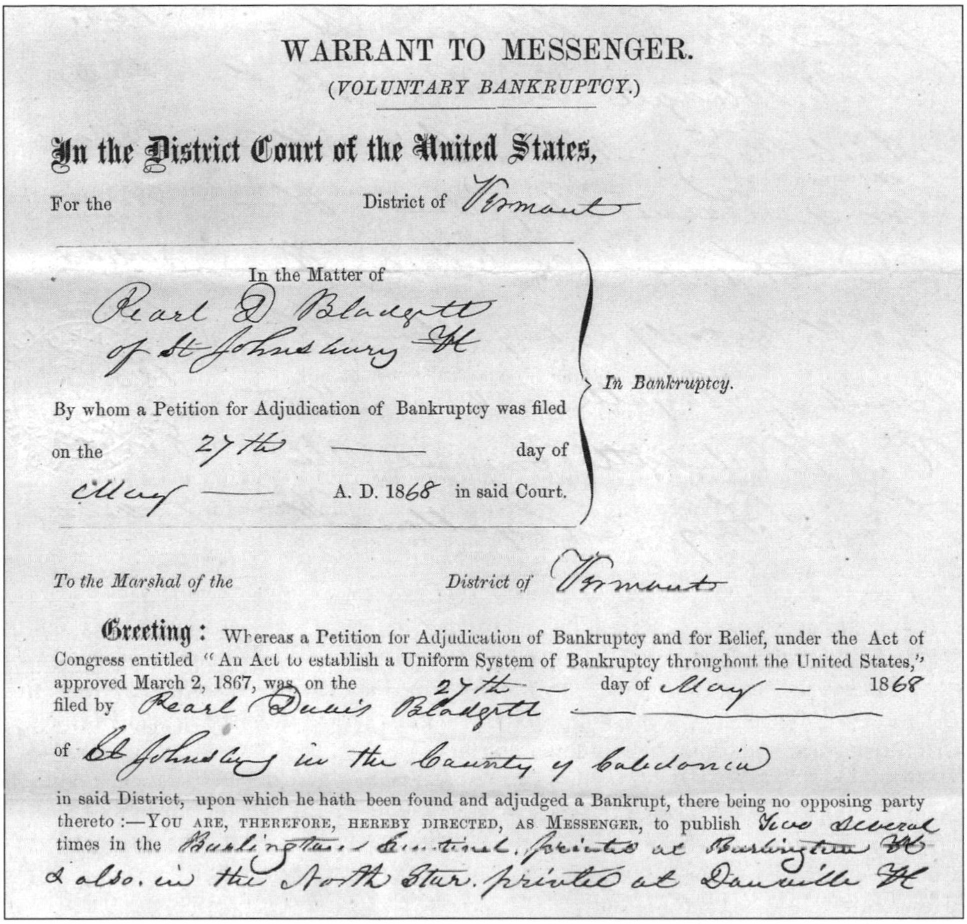

WARRANT TO MESSENGER.
(VOLUNTARY BANKRUPTCY.)

In the District Court of the United States,

For the   District of *Vermont*

In the Matter of

Pearl D. Blodgett
of St. Johnsbury Vt

⎫
⎬ *In Bankruptcy.*
⎭

By whom a Petition for Adjudication of Bankruptcy was filed

on the   *27th*   day of

May   A. D. 18*68*   in said Court.

To the Marshal of the   District of *Vermont*

Greeting : Whereas a Petition for Adjudication of Bankruptcy and for Relief, under the Act of Congress entitled "An Act to establish a Uniform System of Bankruptcy throughout the United States," approved March 2, 1867, was, on the   *27th*   day of *May* —   18*68* filed by *Pearl Davis Blodgett* —

of *St Johnsbury in the County of Caledonia*

in said District, upon which he hath been found and adjudged a Bankrupt, there being no opposing party thereto :—YOU ARE, THEREFORE, HEREBY DIRECTED, AS MESSENGER, to publish *two several* times in the *Burlington Sentinel, printed at Burlington Vt & also in the North Star printed at Danville Vt*

Fig. 15.4. Detail from Warrant to Messenger, in bankruptcy file papers of Pearl D. Blodgett. U.S. District Court for the District of Vermont, Case #146. NARA Record Group 21. *Courtesy of U.S. National Archives and Records Administration, Northeast Region.*

few books, a watch, and a $3000 life insurance policy for the benefit of his wife Laura. He also held $5,000 in failed investments—demand notes—now "deemed worthless."

Adjudication of Bankruptcy and Notice to Creditors

On the same day that Pearl filed his bankruptcy petition, U.S. District Court Judge David Smalley ordered the case transferred to another court official, called a "Register in Bankruptcy." Mr. A. Underwood, the Register for Pearl's case, quickly reviewed the file, and took the usual next steps, issuing two documents:

Adjudication of Bankruptcy, declaring Pearl D. Blodgett "a "bankrupt" person, and

Warrant to Messenger (*Fig. 15.4*), ordering the U.S. Marshal to notify Pearl's creditors of his bankruptcy and an upcoming meeting of creditors.

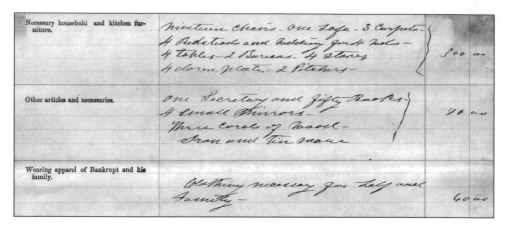

Fig. 15.5. Detail from Schedule of Exempted Property, in bankruptcy file papers of Pearl D. Blodgett. U.S. District Court for the District of Vermont, Case #146. NARA Record Group 21. *Courtesy of U.S. National Archives and Records Administration, Northeast Region.*

Two methods of notice—publication and *service* (delivery)—were required. The Warrant specified that the marshal should publish a bankruptcy notice in two newspapers, the *Burlington Sentinel*, and the *North Star* (printed at Danville, near St. Johnsbury). Although Montpelier was the state capital and closer to St. Johnsbury than Burlington, the Warrant did not order publication in a Montpelier newspaper. (Perhaps the editorial policies of *Sentinel* and the *North Star* matched Register Underwood's political leanings, and he favored those newspapers with the advertising business.) U.S. Marshal George Gale also reported on the "Return of Messenger" that he traveled 352 miles, apparently to serve notice on each of the known creditors (whose names and towns were listed on the warrant).

Meetings of Creditors and Discharge of Debts

Other file papers told the rest of the story:

Certified Memorandum of First Meeting of Creditors, dated July 24, 1868, was a printed form, which stated that Register Underwood held a creditors meeting in Lyndon, Vermont. Perhaps no creditors showed up, because "no debts were proven." Underwood appointed attorney Henry Belcher of Lyndon to be "assignee of the Estate & effects of said Bankrupt." Normally, the assignee would take charge of the bankrupt person's property, dispose of it, and distribute the proceeds to creditors who had proved their claims. Pearl Blodgett, however, owned almost no property, and he had no real estate to sell; there was virtually nothing left for creditors (and many were relatives), so they had little motivation to attend a meeting.

Schedule of Exempted Property (*Fig. 15.5*), dated January 5, 1869, was another printed form, partially handwritten, probably by the assignee or Pearl's attorney. The bankruptcy law allowed Pearl to keep up to $500 of personal property. Pearl retained $300 in "necessary household and kitchen furniture," including nineteen chairs, a sofa, three carpets, four beds, four tables, two bureaus, plates and pitchers. "Other articles and necessaries," valued at $70, included one "secretary and fifty Books," four "small mirrors," and three "cords of wood." The Blodgett family also kept $60 worth of clothing.

Finally, on March 16, 1869, the U.S. District Court judge issued a certificate discharging Pearl D. Blodgett of his debts. The bankruptcy case was over, nearly ten months after it started.

Postscript

Archives staff suggested checking the U.S. census records for 1860 and 1870, to provide a "before" and "after" look at Pearl D. Blodgett's financial status. A few minutes later, I had two oversized photocopies from the census schedules and new information about Pearl—definitely a match. The 1860 census for Salem, Massachusetts listed "Perley T. Blodgett," a thirty-one-year-old flour dealer, his wife Laura, and two-year-old son Perley. Reasonably well-off, they owned real estate valued at $6,000, and $5,000 in personal property.

Ten years later, in the 1870 census, forty-two-year-old "Pearl D. Blodgett" appeared in the list for St. Johnsbury, Vermont, again with wife Laura, now-eleven-year-old son Pearl, and two younger children: Hattie, six, and Ernest, four. And how was the family managing, only one year after the bankruptcy? Amazingly, they now owned $3,000 worth of real estate, plus personal property of $500. Somehow, through good luck or friends in high places, Pearl had landed a lucrative new job with the federal government. He now boasted the impressive title of "U.S. Assistant Assessor"—probably collecting taxes from his neighbors.

CHAPTER 16

JUSTICE OF THE PEACE RECORDS:
Local Justice in Cornwall, *Connecticut*

One of the richest sources for historical and genealogical research—justice of the peace records—remains underutilized, perhaps because these files are scattered in so many places around New England. Until now, researchers wanting to view these records of early local courts had no easy way to find them. *Part II* of this book, however, lists dozens of archival collections, in public and private repositories, where justice of the peace records are waiting for researchers to unlock their secrets.

This chapter highlights one of those collections, from the Cornwall Historical Society at the small town of Cornwall, in Litchfield County, Connecticut. There, in a box marked "Court Summons," the Society holds hundreds of original records dated from about 1760 to 1825, of civil lawsuits tried before local judges—Cornwall justices of the peace. Years ago, someone recognized the value of these old files and started to index them, but the collection remained untouched and nearly forgotten for decades, until my inquiries prompted the Cornwall town historian to take a closer look.

Important Role of Local Judges

Throughout New England, into the twentieth century, the local Justice of the Peace ("JP")[18] played an extraordinarily important role in the legal system. For many people, the JP was the first, or only, court official they encountered. He (they all were men, until recently) handled minor civil and criminal matters—trying cases without a jury, imposing fines for wrongdoing, ordering sheriffs to seize property in payment of debts. He took depositions and prepared written summaries of testimony for cases pending in the county courts. He performed marriage ceremonies, drafted wills, witnessed contracts, and performed many other duties requiring a local legal authority. Sometimes the JP was a trained lawyer, but not always, and he often held court at his own home, where he kept his records.

This home-based informality is part of the reason why justice of the peace records can be so hard to find today. Unless the JP (or his descendants) passed the records on for

---

[18] Also called a "magistrate" or "commissioner for small causes" in colonial days.

safekeeping at the town hall, local library, or a historical society, the files might wind up with other family papers in a home attic or basement. Unfortunately, some records have not survived. For example, I heard the story of one New Hampshire JP from the early 1900s, known locally as "Old Grandpa Johnson," who worked at home. His wife assisted with correspondence and paperwork, and periodically she reorganized the office, throwing away files that did not look important. Many years later, a property dispute arose, in which Old Grandpa Johnson's written opinion would have proven valuable, but the file could not be found, probably purged during one of those home office cleanups.

Although justices of the peace still exist in New England, they no longer serve a central role in the court system. In the 1980s, for example, Maine merged the office of JP with that of the Notary Public (who administers oaths and certifies or notarizes documents). New England JPs still perform marriages, but they have few other official duties. Their predecessors from the seventeenth to twentieth centuries, however, left records well worth reviewing—if you can find them.

Examples from the Cornwall Collection

This chapter highlights four file papers, selected at random from the box marked "Court Summons" at the Cornwall Historical Society. These samples, all involving actions to collect small debts, illustrate the types of data that researchers can glean from justice of the peace records. Debt-collection cases were a routine part of the JP's court docket, so common that he often entered information about the claims on pre-printed forms.

Nathan Bristol, Jr. v. Isaac Knickerbacher

Nathan Bristol's case against Isaac Knickerbacher is a good example of a pre-printed *summons* form, with handwritten entries on both sides (reproduced in *Chapter 3* as *Figs. 3.6* and *3.11*). The front is an order directed to the Litchfield County sheriff:

> [Y]ou are hereby commanded to Summon Isaac Knickerbacher of Salisbury in said County to appear before Edward Rogers, Esq., Justice of the Peace for the County of Litchfield, at his Dwelling-House in Cornwall...on Wednesday ye 10th Day of April Next at two of the Clock in the afternoon, then and there to answer unto Nathan Bristol Junr of Cornwall...in a Plea, that to the Plaintiff the Defendant render the sum of Eleven Shillings and Nine pence Silver Money which...the Defendant justly owes by Book...; Which Debt the Defendant hath never paid (though often requested and demanded)....And for the Recovery thereof with just Costs, the Plaintiff brings this Suit. ... Dated at Cornwall the twenty fifth Day of March...1782.

> Edward Rogers Justice of the Peace

On the back (wasting no paper) is an account of what happened next. A sheriff's deputy wrote his *return*, confirming that he went to Salisbury and carried out his instructions: "I read the within suit in the hearing of the within named Defendant." Then, as was customary, the deputy brought the paper back to the Justice of the Peace. At the April 10th hearing, Nathan Bristol proved his case, or Isaac Knickerbacher admitted the debt, because JP Rogers wrote that Bristol "Recovered Judgment against Isaac Knickerbacher."

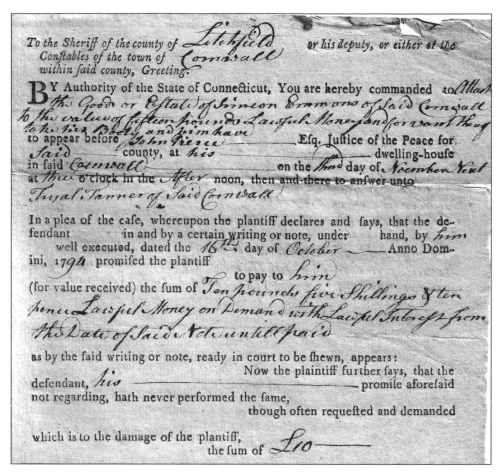

Fig. 16.1. Detail from summons and writ of attachment issued by John Pierce, Justice of the Peace for Cornwall, Connecticut, in case of *Tryal Tanner v. Simeon Emmons*, October 20, 1794. "Court Summons" box, Unsorted, Document 1. *Courtesy of Cornwall (Connecticut) Historical Society.*

Judgment meant that JP Rogers ordered Knickerbacher to pay the debt, but payment was not automatic. Whether Bristol actually received the money is not clear from this document alone. Perhaps other papers in the Cornwall collection tell whether Knickerbacher handed over the "Eleven Shillings and Nine pence Silver Money," or whether Bristol took further legal action to satisfy the judgment.

Tryal Tanner v. Simeon Emmons

The next document (*Fig. 16.1*) is similar—an order dated October 20, 1794, by Justice of the Peace John Pierce, summoning a defendant to trial—but this time the form also includes a *writ of attachment*. Tryal Tanner's lawsuit claimed a debt owed by Simeon Emmons (£10 due on a note). To ensure Emmons's appearance at trial and to provide Tanner with security, Pierce ordered seizure of property worth £15.

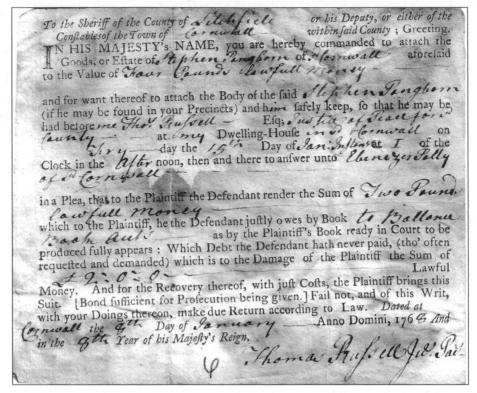

Fig. 16.2. Summons and writ of attachment issued by Justice of the Peace for Cornwall, Connecticut, in case of *Ebenezer Polly v. Stephen Pangborn*, January 8, 1768.
"Court Summons" box, Folder 1, Document 6.
Courtesy of Cornwall (Connecticut) Historical Society.

On the reverse side, the constable's *return* states that he "attached two pieces of Land lying in said Cornwall and owned by the Defendant." This record is particularly interesting, and potentially useful for researchers, because the constable described the location in great detail, with names of adjoining landowners:

> …one of said pieces of Land Bounds North on Asa Emmon's Land East on a Highway in part & part on Land owned by Simeon Emmons and Mary Ann Emmons, South on a Highway & West on said Asa Emmon's Land in part & part on Land said to be owned by George Dibble—the other piece Bounds East on Hezekiah Gold's land North on Asa Emmon's Land and Westerly and Southerly on a Highway—the first piece Contains about Six Acres of Land the other piece Contains about 11 Acres of Land, and both pieces are a part of the Land which Mr Woodruff Emmons gave to the within named Simeon Emmons by his last Will and Testament.

Coincidentally, the constable making this attachment was Solomon Emmons, probably one of Simeon's relatives.

Constable Emmons also wrote that his return was "a true Coppy of the Original writ." Another notation on the back of the paper states: "Copy of Attachment Recd in the

Town Clerks office in Cornwall." Perhaps the town clerk received a copy because the attachment affected title to land, or maybe Cornwall justices of the peace routinely filed copies at the town hall. In the late eighteenth century, of course, copies were made with quill pen and ink, by hand.

Ebenezer Polly v. Stephen Pangborn

In 1768, another Cornwall justice of the peace issued a summons and writ of attachment to initiate a lawsuit for plaintiff Ebenezer Polly, who claimed that Stephen Pangborn owed "Two Pounds lawfull Money." This partially-printed form (*Fig. 16.2*, from pre-Revolutionary days) started out:

> Greeting In His Majesty's Name, you are hereby commanded to attach the Goods, or Estate of Stephen Pangborn...and for want thereof to attach the Body of the said Stephen Pangborn (if he may be found in your Precincts) and him safely keep, so that he may be had before me....

A constable named Edward Rogers (possibly the same as the justice of the peace in *Bristol v. Knickerbacher*) served the writ on Pangborn. The back of the writ is faded and difficult to read, but Rogers apparently found a black cow and other goods, which he seized instead of "the Body of...Pangborn."

John Wright v. David Jewell

The fourth sample writ from the Cornwall collection, *Wright v. Jewell*, bears the latest date, November 10, 1802, and an Edward Rogers signed it again as Justice of the Peace. While the other writs were *pre*-trial orders (summons and writs of attachment), this was a *post*-trial document (a *writ of execution*). See *Figs. 16.3* and *16.4*.
John Wright obtained a judgment of $17.57 against David Jewell in 1799, but Jewell still had not paid by 1802. JP Rogers issued a writ of execution, commanding the constable to seize "money, goods, chattles or land," or to imprison Jewell until he satisfied the judgment. Constable William Kelley "went to the debtor's place of abode in Cornwall," but Jewell owned no land and little property. According to the back of the writ, Jewell surrendered his meager possessions: "...4 1/2 Cords of Wood, a quantity of White Beans on the Ground, a quantity of Potatoes in the ground and the Corn grown and standing on about 3/4th of an Acre of Land."

The constable returned to Cornwall and posted a notice on the "public signpost" that Jewell's goods would be sold on November 30. The day before the auction, however, the creditor apparently had a change of heart. John Wright directed the constable to return Jewell's goods and cancel the sale. A further notation, signed by Wright on the back of the writ, confirms that he gave up enforcing the judgment. Instead, the parties agreed to private arbitration, probably to work out long-term payment of a lesser amount, saving Jewell from the poorhouse.

If these four justice of the peace documents are any indication, the rest of the Cornwall collection is a remarkable untapped resource for genealogists and historians. Similar records, at a multitude of archives listed in *Part II*, undoubtedly offer fascinating insights—up close and personal—about daily life in bygone New England. Many more boxes of justice of the peace records, like those in Cornwall, may be waiting for you to discover in your own town or library.

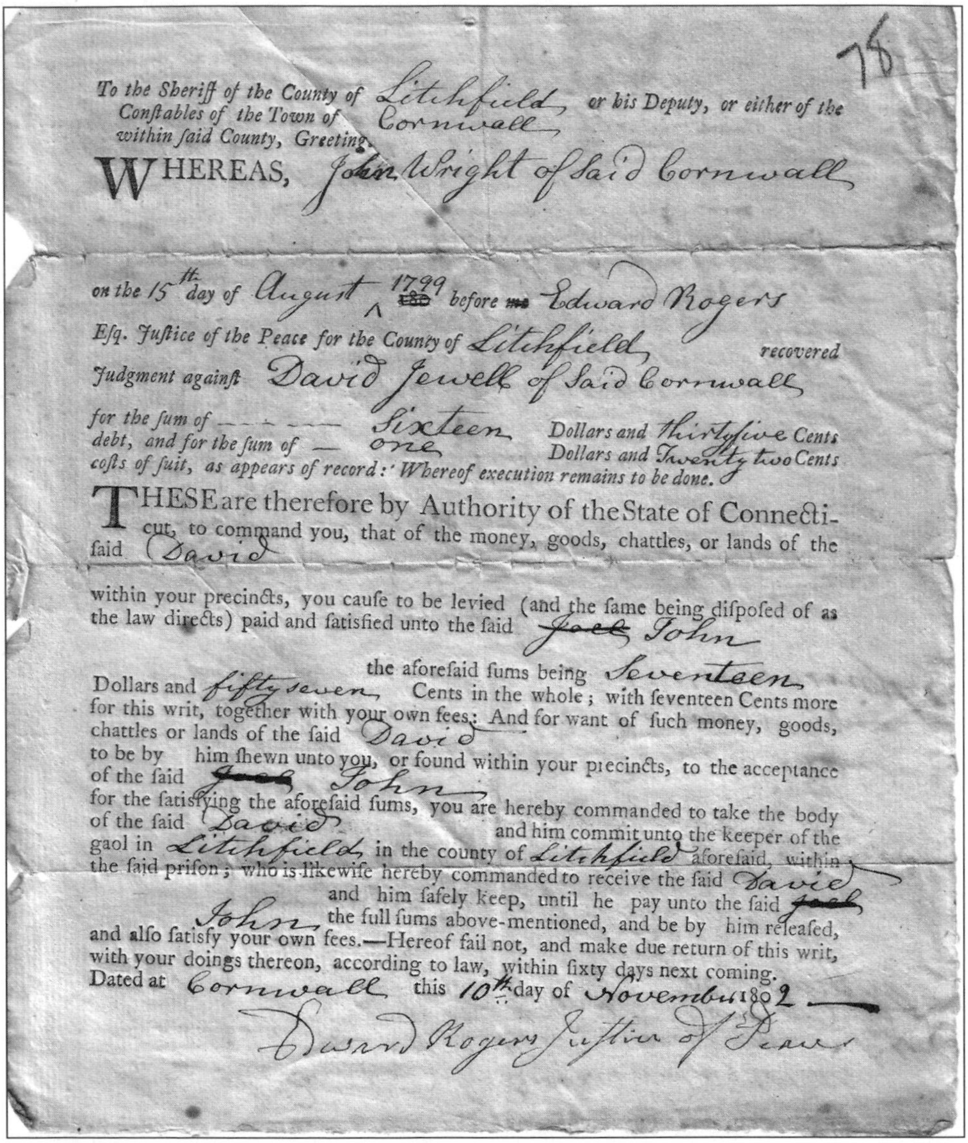

78

To the Sheriff of the County of Litchfield, *or his Deputy, or either of the Constables of the Town of* Cornwall *within said County, Greeting.*

WHEREAS, John Wright of Said Cornwall

on the 15th day of August 1799 before ~~me~~ Edward Rogers Esq. Justice of the Peace for the County of Litchfield recovered Judgment against David Jewell of Said Cornwall for the sum of Sixteen Dollars and thirtyfive Cents debt, and for the sum of one Dollars and Twenty two Cents costs of suit, as appears of record: Whereof execution remains to be done.

THESE are therefore by Authority of the State of Connecticut, to command you, that of the money, goods, chattles, or lands of the said David

within your precincts, you cause to be levied (and the same being disposed of as the law directs) paid and satisfied unto the said ~~Joel~~ John

the aforesaid sums being Seventeen Dollars and fiftyseven Cents in the whole; with seventeen Cents more for this writ, together with your own fees: And for want of such money, goods, chattles or lands of the said David to be by him shewn unto you, or found within your precincts, to the acceptance of the said ~~Joel~~ John for the satisfying the aforesaid sums, you are hereby commanded to take the body of the said David and him commit unto the keeper of the gaol in Litchfield in the county of Litchfield aforesaid, within the said prison; who is likewise hereby commanded to receive the said David and him safely keep, until he pay unto the said ~~Joel~~ John the full sums above-mentioned, and be by him released, and also satisfy your own fees.—Hereof fail not, and make due return of this writ, with your doings thereon, according to law, within sixty days next coming. Dated at Cornwall this 10th day of November 1802 —

Edward Rogers Justice of Peace

Fig. 16.3. Writ of execution issued by Edward Rogers, Justice of the Peace for Cornwall, Connecticut, in case of *John Wright v. David Jewell*, November 10, 1802. "Court Summons" box, Folder 3, Document 78. *Courtesy of Cornwall (Connecticut) Historical Society.*

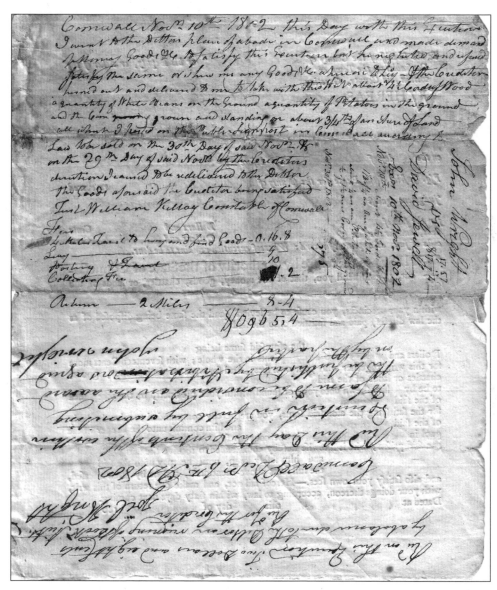

Fig. 16.4. Reverse side of *Fig. 16.3*, back of writ of execution, showing sheriff's return and other notations. "Court Summons" box, Folder 3, Document 78.
Courtesy of Cornwall (Connecticut) Historical Society.

CHAPTER 17

LAW LIBRARY RESOURCES:
Will Contest in Twentieth-Century
New Hampshire

Law libraries can be intimidating places, even for lawyers. Specialized legal tomes crowd the shelves—a bewildering array of multi-volume reporters, citators, digests, treatises, statutes, codes, casebooks, and rules, with odd-sounding titles like *Corpus Juris Secondum*, *ALR Federal*, or *Prosser on Torts*. Few lawyers are familiar with all of the books in a law library, or the many computer databases for legal research, like *Westlaw* and *LexisNexis*. Law students spend years learning how to use these resources, and lawyers hone their research skills in day-to-day legal practice and continuing-education classes.

So why include a chapter about law libraries in a book for genealogists and historians? Because law library resources can lead you to court records, if you know where to look. This chapter identifies basic sources that may help genealogists and historians, showing you how to read and use them, so that you can decide whether to visit a law library for your own research.

I decided to sample New Hampshire law library sources for this chapter. Although I could have visited a library in New Hampshire, I chose a law library closer to my Boston-area home, instead—the library of the Middlesex County courthouse in Cambridge, Massachusetts. (*See Appendix: Contact Information-Law Libraries*, for a list of locations.) Larger law libraries, like the one in Cambridge, carry materials about other states, so I did not call ahead to confirm availability of research sources—which turned out to be a mistake. When I drove up to the courthouse on a Friday morning, I found a roadblock and "detour" signs. To my surprise, the policeman directing traffic informed me that the building was closed for the entire day due to roof repairs!

Luckily, I had other options, so I drove on into Boston, to the Social Law Library at the beautiful (and newly-renovated) John Adams Courthouse. I called from my cell phone on the way, to confirm that the library was open, and that I could obtain a non-member "day pass" to do research. When I arrived, I looked for the state materials—ask a reference librarian to direct you—and I began to work.

Reporters and Digests

At the Social Law Library, I focused on New Hampshire "Law Library Resources" listed in the "Where to Find Court Records" section of *Chapter 9,* under "Statewide or General Sources: Books or Journals." Follow along with this sample research project, and you will be ready to review similar reference materials for any of the other New England states. (*See* "Books: Law Library Resources" in each chapter of *Part II*.)

Reporters

For more than two hundred years, many state and federal appeals court decisions have been published in books called *reporters*. Decisions of the New Hampshire Supreme Court (and its predecessors) appear in two sources:

New Hampshire Reports have been published by the New Hampshire Supreme Court since 1816.

Atlantic Reporter, one of the regional reporters in the "West National Reporter System," is published by legal publisher West and includes appellate decisions of nine eastern states, including New Hampshire.[19] The full texts of New Hampshire Supreme Court opinions from 1886 appear in the *Atlantic Reporter*, enhanced with synopses and West "headnotes" or "key numbers," for research in accompanying *digest* volumes.

Digests

Digests are special finding aids published by West, to locate cases in the state and federal court reporters. These volumes, organized alphabetically by topic, also feature "headnotes" and "key numbers," and multiple index systems allow search by case name, descriptive word, etc. The two digests relevant to New Hampshire research are: *West's New Hampshire Digest* and *West's Atlantic Digest*.

Finding a Case in the West Digests

I located those two digests—*West's New Hampshire Digest* and *West's Atlantic Digest*—on the second floor of the Social Law Library's expansive collection. (Some libraries maintain only the digests of their own state or region.) Both digests are multi-volume sets, but the *Atlantic* (already into its second series of volumes, titled *West's Atlantic Digest 2d*), is much larger, because it covers several states, not just New Hampshire. The *Atlantic* set at the library also looked much newer, but the publisher keeps both sets equally current, with pocket-part updates in each volume.

I decided to look for New Hampshire Supreme Court cases involving will contests—disputes about whether a deceased person's will is valid—from the early-to-mid 1900s. My research goal could be accomplished using either of the digests, because both contained the same information about New Hampshire cases.

---

[19] The only New England state whose appellate decisions are not covered in the *Atlantic Reporter* is Massachusetts; West publishes Massachusetts cases in the *North Eastern Reporter*. (*See Chapter 8*.)

Searching for a Case by Name

If I already knew the name of a case,[20] I could start looking in the alphabetical Table of Cases offered by either digest. Most digests provide entries under either of the parties' names, facilitating research if you do not know the complete case name. Then, you can find the case citation and proceed directly to the relevant reporter volume. Computerized database services, such as *Westlaw* or *LexisNexis* (available at law libraries and listed in the "Where to Find Court Records" sections of *Part II* chapters under "Statewide or General Sources: "Digital/Electronic Sources") also provide quick access to appellate court opinions when the name is known.

Searching for a Case by Topic

Not having a particular case in mind, I tried another approach to my will contest research. Each of the West digests is organized alphabetically by subject—more than 400 different topics, from "Abandoned and Lost Property" to "Zoning and Planning"—and each topic is further subdivided into numbered sections ("key numbers") about specific points of law. Under each key number, the digest provides brief summaries ("headnotes") about relevant cases, with case citations to the reporter volumes where the decisions are published.

You can scan the list of topics, A to Z, until you find one of interest. For my research project, the obvious topic was "Wills." Social historians might check cases under topics like "Marriage" or "Parent and Child;" economic historians tracing the lumber industry might focus on "Logs and Logging" or "Woods and Forests." Researchers can also search a Descriptive Word Index in each West digest series, to help identify relevant topics.

I turned to Volume 9A of *West's New Hampshire Digest*, which contained citations to cases about "Wills." Many of the numbered sections under "Wills" focused on narrow legal issues, of interest only to lawyers researching the common law, but I scanned the headings until I found one that looked promising: "Mistake, Undue Influence, and Fraud," beginning at key number 152.

Right away I saw a case that looked interesting, under key number 155, about "Mistake, Undue Influence, and Fraud—In General." As shown in *Fig. 17.1, below*, one of the headnotes stated:

> **N.H. 1938.** If testator was induced by fear of his stepmother and made will in her favor because testator did not dare to do otherwise, will was void.
>
> *Ford v. Ford's Estate*, 197 A. 824, 89 N.H. 292.

"N.H. 1938" means that the case was decided by the New Hampshire Supreme Court in 1938. The headnote summarizes one point of law decided by the court in *Ford v.*

---

[20] Court cases are identified with the party names, the *plaintiff* versus the *defendant*; *e.g.*, *Brown v. Board of Education*. When a case is appealed, the case name may be reversed, putting the defendant's name in front of the "v," if the defendant is appealing the trial court judgment.

For references to other topics, see Descriptive-Word Index

N.H. 1853. Verbal directions and instructions for drawing up a written will, although spoken in the presence of the proper number of witnesses required to bear witness thereto, and reduced to writing, and offered for probate according to the statute, do not constitute a nuncupative will.

Dockum v. Robinson, 26 N.H. 372, 6 Fost. 372.

⟋**137–144.** *See Topic Analysis for scope.*
Library references

C.J.S. Wills § 210 et seq.

⟋**142. Attestation.**
Library references

C.J.S. Wills § 214 et seq.

⟋**145. —— Request to witnesses.**
N.H. 1853. That the words of a decedent may be proved as a nuncupative will, Rev.St. c. 156, § 15, requires that three witnesses present must be requested to bear witness to the will of the testator.

Dockum v. Robinson, 26 N.H. 372, 6 Fost. 372.

⟋**146–151.** *See Topic Analysis for scope.*
Library references

C.J.S. Wills §§ 210, 217–219, 221.

(F) MISTAKE, UNDUE INFLUENCE, AND FRAUD.

⟋**152. Mistake.**
Library references

C.J.S. Wills § 223.

N.H. 1944. If testator knew and approved contents of will, it is immaterial if he mistook legal effect of the language used or that he acted upon mistaken advice of counsel, provided that advice was given in an honest belief that it was sound.

Leonard v. Stanton, 36 A.2d 271, 93 N.H. 113.

Generally, if in drawing up a will by testator's instructions, the draughtsman, without reason or special directions, but in good faith introduces words the effect of which testator does not intelligently appreciate when will is read over to him, the words must stand as part of the will.

Leonard v. Stanton, 36 A.2d 271, 93 N.H. 113.

⟋**153. Fraud.**
Library references

C.J.S. Wills § 222.

N.H. 1944. To invalidate will, misrepresentation must have been such as to induce testator to make some disposal of his property that he would not otherwise have made.

Leonard v. Stanton, 36 A.2d 271, 93 N.H. 113.

N.H. 1933. Fraud necessary to invalidate will does not differ from that required to vitiate ordinary contract.

Knox v. Perkins, 163 A. 497, 86 N.H. 66.

"Fraud" which invalidates will may consist in intentional concealment of material fact as well as in false statement of fact.

Knox v. Perkins, 163 A. 497, 86 N.H. 66.

To invalidate will, deception must be such as to induce testator to make disposition of his property that he would not otherwise have made.

Knox v. Perkins, 163 A. 497, 86 N.H. 66.

⟋**154. Undue influence.**
Library references

C.J.S. Wills § 224 et seq.

⟋**155. —— In general.**
⟋**155(1). Nature and degree in general.**
N.H. 1938. If testator was induced by fear of his stepmother and made will in her favor because testator did not dare to do otherwise, will was void.

Ford v. Ford's Estate, 197 A. 824, 89 N.H. 292.

N.H. 1933. To justify disallowance of will on ground of undue influence, it must appear influence overpowered volition and substituted another's will for that of testator.

Knox v. Perkins, 163 A. 497, 86 N.H. 66.

N.H. 1923. To justify disallowance of a will for undue influence, there must be evidence sufficient to permit the inference that testatrix was misled or coerced; that her mind was so subjugated to that of another as to destroy her free agency; the mere influence of affection or desire to gratify another being insufficient, in the absence of imposition or fraud.

Bartlett v. McKay, 120 A. 627, 80 N.H. 574.

N.H. 1921. Undue influence invalidating a will must be something destroying the testator's free agency, and in effect substituting another's will.

Loveren v. Eaton, 113 A. 206, 80 N.H. 62.

⟋**155(2)–155(3).** *See Topic Analysis for scope.*
Library references

C.J.S. Wills §§ 225, 226.

Fig. 17.1. Page from "Wills" section of *West's New Hampshire Digest* (Eagan, Minn.: West), Vol. 9A, p. 179. *Courtesy of West.*

Ford's Estate (the case may have dealt with other legal issues, listed under other key numbers in the digest). The full opinion was published in the West *Atlantic Reporter* (197 A. 824 means volume 197, page 824) and in the *New Hampshire Reports* (89 N.H. 292 means volume 89, page 292).

Reading the Reporters

I was ready to use the other major law library resource—reporters—where the full appeals court opinions are published. I looked for volume 197 of the *Atlantic Reporter* in the library shelves but discovered that Social Law Library maintained only the *Atlantic Reporter 2d* series, starting in the late 1930s, just after the New Hampshire Supreme Court decided *Ford v. Ford's Estate*. I could have gone online to find the decision by computer, through a service like *Westlaw*, but that probably would mean an access fee. When I checked the parallel citation, 89 N.H. 292, however, I was in luck. Volume 89 of *New Hampshire Reports* was on the shelves, and the court's decision in *Ford v. Ford's Estate* appeared at page 292.

This reported case (excerpted in *Figs. 17.2* and *17.3, below*) paints a vivid picture of the sad life for a "mentally deficient" young farmer and his stepmother from Dover, New Hampshire, in the years just before World War II. Baker Ford was nineteen when his mother died, and a woman named Kari came to "visit" his father Hollis. A few months later, Hollis married Kari. From all accounts, Kari treated her stepson badly, yelling at him and calling him "crazy," and Baker was so afraid of her that "he would jump to whatever she wanted him to do." When Hollis died, Kari pressured Baker to sign a will leaving his entire estate to her, and shortly thereafter, she also convinced him to petition the court for appointment of a conservator to manage his property. Baker told neighbors that Kari wanted him committed to the state hospital for the insane, and that he "couldn't stand any longer the way things were going at home." When Baker confronted Kari about his concerns, she flew into a rage, and he committed suicide. After Baker's death, his uncle challenged the will.

Ford v. Ford's Estate provides a good example of the types of information that researchers can find in a reported appeals court decision, including:

Place of Appeal and Decision Date
In this case, Strafford County, March 1, 1938.

Names of Parties
Lorenzo D. H. Ford (*appellant*), the party dissatisfied with the trial court decision, who appealed to the New Hampshire Supreme Court, and Kari L. Ford (*appellee*), the party defending the result at trial.

Legal Issues Decided by the Court
These technical points are of most interest to lawyers or judges studying the common law, to determine how a court would decide future cases. *Note:* Decisions published in the *Atlantic Reporter* also assign key numbers to each of the legal points, corresponding with the topics listed in *West's Atlantic Digest*.

all be overruled, with only the one relating to the amount of the award remaining in abeyance.

Case discharged.

All concurred.

Strafford, }
March 1, 1938. }

LORENZO D. H. FORD, *Ap't*

v.

KARI L. FORD, *Ap'ee*

On the issue of *devisavit vel non* the fact that the person charged with procurement of the will by undue influence was not present at its execution does not conclusively establish his non-coercion of the testator.

On such issue evidence of the petition of the testator for appointment of a conservator was properly admitted where the obtaining of that petition is attributable to the person charged with procuring the will.

The statement of the person so charged to the effect that the testator's father was only a life tenant on whose death the declarant would be left penniless is admissible to prove motive though not to prove title.

A will induced by the testator's fear of another person and the fact that he made the will because he did not dare to do otherwise is void.

On such issue the executor has the ultimate burden of proving that the will was the free and voluntary act of the testator.

On such issue the quality of the testator's mind is relevant.

As to such fact, witnesses found by the court to be competent to form valuable opinions on the subject may testify.

The latitude allowed to counsel in examining his own witness is within the discretion of the trial court.

And so of the exclusion of a question previously answered.

And so of statements to show the feelings, purposes and actions of the parties both before and after the fact in issue where such statements are relevant.

And so of a ruling permitting a witness to state conclusions which he drew from facts.

PROBATE APPEAL, from the allowance of the will of Charles Baker Ford. The appellant, who was the testator's uncle and sole heir-at-law, charged that the execution of the will was procured by undue influence on the part of the appellee, who was the testator's step-

---

Fig. 17.2. First page of New Hampshire Supreme Court's opinion in Ford v. Ford, 89 N.H. 292 (1938), *New Hampshire Reports. Courtesy of Reporter, Supreme Court of New Hampshire.*

mother. The issue of undue influence was tried by jury with a verdict for the appellant. The appellee excepted to the denial of her motions to withdraw the issue from the jury, to dismiss the appeal, and to affirm the decree of the Probate Court. She also excepted to the admission and exclusion of certain evidence and to portions of the charge. The material facts are stated in the opinion.

Transferred by *Lorimer*, J.

Thorp & Branch (*Mr. Branch* orally), for the appellant.

Hughes & Burns, Charles F. Hartnett and *Dwight Hall* (*Mr. Burns* orally), for the appellee.

MARBLE, J. The testator, Charles Baker Ford (referred to in the testimony as Baker Ford), was the son of Hollis and Alice Ford of Dover. His mother died in January, 1931, when he was nineteen years old. After his mother's death he lived on the home farm with his father. The appellee came to the farm for a visit in August, 1931, and remained "visiting there" (to quote her own testimony) until she married Hollis Ford on February 25, 1932.

She herself characterized the testator as a supersensitive boy. A witness, called in her behalf, stated on cross-examination that "the poor boy had never decided anything for himself," that he had "never been allowed to have" any initiative. Another witness, who had known him ever since he was born, expressed the opinion that "he was a boy that was mentally deficient." A clergyman, whose church the testator attended "rather frequently" (called as a witness by the appellee), agreed that the testator was "different at least" and thought that "his deficiency" consisted in the fact that "he was so very easily influenced." One of the testator's former schoolmates stated that he could "be led very easily to do practically anything anyone wanted him to do."

There was evidence tending to prove that he disliked his stepmother and was afraid of her. The last-mentioned witness said: " . . . before she came there we used to have good times together, afterwards it was all stopped. . . . He was extremely nervous and jumpy and the minute she spoke he would jump to whatever she wanted him to do." The witness added that the testator's attitude toward his stepmother was one of fear.

Nancy Ford, the wife of the appellant, testified: "When she would tell Baker to do things if he didn't move instantly she'd tell him that

Fig. 17.3. Second page of New Hampshire Supreme Court's opinion in Ford v. Ford, 89 N.H. 292 (1938), *New Hampshire Reports. Courtesy of Reporter, Supreme Court of New Hampshire.*

Brief Synopsis of Case

A short paragraph tells what happened at trial and the reasons for the appeal. Here, the deceased's uncle and heir, Lorenzo Ford, objected to the will, claiming that Kari Ford, the deceased's stepmother, "procured" the will "by undue influence." The jury agreed with the uncle, but the trial judge nonetheless allowed the will. Lorenzo appealed the case to the New Hampshire Supreme Court, seeking to declare the will void.

Name of Trial Judge

J. (Judge) Lorimer.

Attorneys for the Parties

The law firm of Thorp & Branch represented Lorenzo Ford; "Mr. Branch orally" means that he handled the oral argument before the New Hampshire Supreme Court. The law firm of Hughes & Burns, Charles F. Hartnett and Dwight Hall represented Kari Ford, and Mr. Burns argued the appeal. Undoubtedly, these attorneys also filed written briefs, explaining their legal arguments.

Name of Supreme Court Judge Who Wrote Opinion

J. (Judge) Marble.

Opinion (Decision)

In several pages, Judge Marble summarized the facts of the case and the evidence presented at trial (quoting from transcripts of testimony and documents admitted as exhibits). He concluded that "the verdict of the jury was entirely warranted," and then he explained how the New Hampshire Supreme Court arrived at that decision, applying the law to the facts and citing earlier cases that the court found persuasive.

Action Taken

The will was disallowed.

Decision of Other Judges on the Panel

One New Hampshire Supreme Court judge (Judge Branch) "did not sit," meaning that he did not participate in the decision. "[T]he others concurred," or agreed , with Judge Marble's written opinion.

Beyond the Reported Case

The case of *Ford v. Ford's Estate* not only settles some technical legal issues about what constitutes "undue influence"—of interest to lawyers and judges concerned with the validity of wills—but it also reveals numerous bits of information useful for genealogists. Judge Marble's opinion mentions dates of death (of Baker and his parents), names of Baker's aunt and uncle, references to other court actions, and the type of title held by Baker to the farm property.

More details about *Ford v. Ford's Estate* may appear in original court records—the docket book, record book and file papers from the trial in Strafford County Probate Court, for instance—if those documents still exist. The Probate Court in Dover maintains original record books and file papers from as far back as 1770. LDS Family History Centers offer microfilmed Strafford County probate records from 1773 to the late 1900s.[21] Perhaps the original *Ford* briefs and appeal records remain in the New Hampshire Law Library basement, where Supreme Court papers from 1849 to 1970 are preserved in hundreds of bound volumes.[22]

Law library resources are not just for lawyers. Case digests and reporters open up a new world of research possibilities for historians and genealogists, too, particularly for nineteenth and twentieth-century topics. Use the tips in this chapter to make effective use of these powerful research tools, and enter a law library with confidence.

---

[21] *See* the "Strafford County" section of "Where to Find Court Records" in *Chapter 9*.

[22] *See* "Statewide and General Sources: State Archives and Law Library" under "Where to Find Court Records" in *Chapter 9*.

CHAPTER 18

---•◆•---

OLD-FASHIONED RESEARCH:
Scandal in Seventeenth-Century *Massachusetts*

In the *Preface*, I promised to revisit *Row v. Bacon*, one of my favorite finds from the old court records. *Row v. Bacon* provides an entertaining look at rural Massachusetts of the 1600s, as well as a treasure trove of information about the parties to the lawsuit. And this discovery led me to something else—a long-hidden family secret, tucked away in the Massachusetts Archives.

I began with a very simple research objective—to find court records about one particular person in a seventeenth-century Massachusetts county. Your research might be similar. Perhaps you are tracing an ancestor, a figure in local history, or a famous person. The following account of my own quest will not provide you with an exact roadmap for your own research, because every project is different. I hope, however, that my story will encourage you to be persistent and patient as you look for court records, even when your research tools are old-fashioned index cards and an ancient microfilm reader. I also share this experience as a reminder: court records may lead you to places and people that you never expected to find.

The Search for William Munro

My research focused on William Munro, a former Scottish war prisoner who lived in Lexington, Massachusetts (then a part of Cambridge, in Middlesex County) between the late 1650s and 1719. Generations of genealogists and town historians had already researched Munro and his family, so I had no particular reason to expect that I would find anything "new." But I decided to look for court records about Munro at the Judicial Archives of the Supreme Judicial Court, located at the Massachusetts Archives building in Boston.

Helpful staff directed me to an alphabetical card file, which contained index cards for the "Middlesex County Court Folio Collection,"[23] listing each case by the party's last name. I flipped through the cards to "Mu" and found two possibilities:

---

[23] These Middlesex County index cards are also available on microfilm: *Folio index cards, 1650-1800* (Salt Lake City: Genealogical Society of Utah, 1986). *See* the "Middlesex County" section of "Where to Find Court Records" in *Chapter 8,* and *Appendix: Contact Information- Publishers.*

Munroe, William. Lexington v. David Comee. Ejectment. 1737-195A, Reel #6.
This, I knew, was too late in time, probably "my" William's son. I recorded the reference in my research notes but continued looking for something more relevant.

Munroe, William v. Michael Bacon. Debt for a cow. 1676-72-2, Reel #3.
I looked for Reel #3 in the microfilm cabinet, but to my disappointment, it was missing—maybe someone else was viewing it. When I checked with the Archives staff, they informed me that Reel #3 was lost! Boxes of the original folio documents, from which Reel #3 had been microfilmed, were in the vault but not immediately available.

Not ready to give up, I returned to the card file and considered what to do next. I wondered whether Munro's last name could have been spelled in some other way (no uniform spelling rules applied during the seventeenth century). I tried "Monroe" and other similar variants, with no luck. Then I remembered seeing the name spelled "Row" in an old Lexington town history; a quick check of the "R" index cards brought a possible candidate: *Row, William and Michael Bacon. Re: taking away swine. 1672-59-2, Reel #2.* This time, the microfilm reel was in the cabinet where it belonged. I loaded the microfilm reader, feeling a bit silly to be so excited about viewing a swine case, not even sure that this William Row would be the right man. Fast-forwarding the tape to Folio 1672-59-2, I stopped, and there it was: *Row v. Bacon.*

Old-style script crowded page after page of documents, seemingly microfilmed in no particular order. First came "William Rows bill of costs agt Michael Bacon," then "testimony of Benjamin and John Russell." More written testimony followed, signed by William Row with his mark. This document mentioned "Martha his wife," and since William Munro's first wife was named Martha, I cheered (silently, of course, as I was not alone in the Archives reading room). Almost certainly I had found my William Munro, and other details in the court records confirmed his identity. I read on and on, some pages requiring several tries to decipher the seventeenth-century handwriting.

One of the court documents (*see Fig. 3.5* in *Chapter 3*), sets forth William Munro's complaint against neighbor Michael Bacon, for taking away the Munro family's pigs. When I read this, I could visualize Munro standing before the local magistrate, telling what had happened, pausing occasionally in his narrative as the magistrate recorded it all with quill pen. Many other documents in the *Row v. Bacon* file contain similar testimony, bringing this seventeenth-century neighborhood dispute to life in vivid (and amusing) detail. The file papers, too numerous to reproduce here in their entirety, tell the following story (excerpted from my article about the case, published in *New England Ancestors* magazine):[24]

---

[24] Diane Rapaport, "Tales From the Courthouse: The Case of the Purloined Pigs," *New England Ancestors* 5 (Winter 2004): 54-55, with permission of the New England Historic Genealogical Society. For more information about *New England Ancestors* magazine and the New England Historic Genealogical Society, please visit *NewEnglandAncestors.org*.

The Case of the Purloined Pigs

The problems started on a Monday in late November 1671, after a heavy snowfall in a remote corner of Cambridge Farms, near today's intersection of Lowell and Woburn Streets in Lexington. Here, at the house where William Munro lived with his wife Martha and three small children, a neighbor arrived looking for his hogs.

Michael Bacon (his real name!) had a reputation for letting his hogs run wild, and this time they had wandered all the way from Bacon's house (in present-day Bedford, Massachusetts) to enjoy the companionship of Munro's own pigs. Munro and his wife, wanting only to be rid of the uninvited swine-guests who were depleting their meager forage, helped Bacon to separate his hogs from their own. Bacon then headed off through the woods with his swine, and the Munros returned to their daily chores.

But Bacon's hogs apparently did not want to leave their friends, and they soon came back. This time, when Bacon returned to retrieve them, he did not bother to sort them out; he just drove the whole lot off, his and the Munro pigs. Seeing most of the family's worldly wealth hoofing away, Martha shouted at Bacon to stop, but he ignored her. William, who was occupied feeding the oxen or fetching firewood, had to drop everything, strap on snowshoes and take off in pursuit.

Munro was not a man to be trifled with. He had endured many hardships—on the battlefield as a Scottish soldier, in a prison camp after his capture by Cromwell's army, during a long winter voyage across the Atlantic, and as an unpaid servant, little more than a slave. Now he was free to farm his own piece of land, and those pigs were crucial to his family's survival. Hogs meant meat on the table and income to buy other necessities of life, and Munro could not afford to lose a single animal.

He also knew that Michael Bacon could not be trusted. Bacon was known throughout the county for making trouble. His hogs had damaged crops for miles around, but he always denied responsibility, blaming others for failing to keep their fences in repair or claiming that the hogs belonged to someone else. Bacon's name appeared repeatedly in land disputes, cases of wandering horses and cattle, slander and forgery accusations, and breach of contract. Thus, when Munro set off in the snow after Bacon and his pigs, he had good reason to expect problems.

Munro trudged north through three miles of drifted snow, following hog tracks until he finally overtook Bacon and found most of his livestock. One pregnant sow was "so tired and spent that shee could not come back," and he had to leave her with Bacon. Another sow, also "big with pig," was missing. Munro was angry, but nothing more could be done before nightfall. He drove the rest of his hogs back home.

The next day, Munro sought out constable's deputy John Gleison and his brother William. He showed them the hoof-trodden farmyard and the path through the woods, and together they trekked back to Bacon's house to retrieve the last two swine. Bacon's response was predictable. First he pretended the incident never happened. Then, when the Gleisons clearly were not accepting that story, he "confessed that William Rows swine was with him in the drift the day before, but ... he did them no wrong," and he had none of them "in his hands" now. "If Row lost them, he must go look for them." Bacon, of course, did not offer to help.

On Wednesday, the weary Munro turned to his neighbors John and Benjamin Russell, and together they scoured the woods for the missing hogs. They found one, stuck in a drift, amazingly still alive, and with "much difficulty" they brought her home.

One sow was still missing, and Munro's patience was running out. He took the law-abiding next step, which required yet another long journey on foot through the snow. He walked to Cambridge, to magistrate Thomas Danforth's house overlooking Harvard College, where he filed a claim against Bacon. Danforth took up quill pen to issue a warrant, ordering Michael Bacon "to appeare before me at my house, the last day of the weeke at 12. of the clock to answear the complaint of William Row, for violence done him in taking away his swine out of his yard, & driving them away...."

At the appointed time, six people—William and Martha Munro, the Russells, the Gleison brothers—crowded into the magistrate's study to testify. Danforth recorded the evidence with careful penmanship, and the witnesses all signed with their marks. Michael Bacon was not there, and he lost the case. The constable's deputy set out to seize a "branded steere" from Bacon to ensure payment of Munro's damages.

Shortly thereafter, before Munro could collect a single shilling, his missing sow reappeared at his door. She was "lamed and went but upon three legs," delivered by a man who claimed that he "found" her and was asked by Bacon to bring her home.

Bacon probably hoped that returning the sow would get him off the hook for damages, but Munro stood firm. In late December, Bacon asked for a rehearing, which Danforth granted on January 29. The result was the same, only now Bacon owed more, reflecting the added costs for witness time and constable's fees.

Still Bacon refused to pay, and he mounted a vigorous appeal, seeking a jury trial in the Middlesex County Court. He hired Concord lawyer John Hoare to draft a tedious petition with a long series of technical arguments, from improper service of the attachment on his steer to misfeasance by Danforth. The trial took place in Cambridge on April 2, 1672, probably at the local Blue Anchor Tavern (as was customary in those days, since only Boston had courtroom facilities). Someone apparently represented Munro at the trial (although his identity is not known), for an elegantly-written legal argument appeared in the court records on Munro's behalf.

The final result, after more than four months of legal wrangling, was judgment again in favor of Munro: "One Pound sixteen shillings & foure pence," plus court costs, a goodly sum, but probably less a financial boost than a moral victory for the dogged Scotsman. Presumably Bacon paid up, for here the paper trail of *Row v. Bacon* ends.

Secrets Revealed

At the very end of the microfilmed documents in Folio 1672-59-2, I found one cryptic scrap of paper, seemingly out of place and unrelated to *Row v. Bacon*. I almost disregarded it, almost rewound the film and moved on to other research, but luckily I paused for a closer look. I realized that it was an index card, written by some early archivist to identify a 1672 court document, a bill of costs in yet another case involving Michael Bacon:

> 1672 April 2 … (Mary Ball)
> Michael Bacon … & a woman:
> William Hudson's bill of charges for taking care of a woman at childbirth.
> The reputed father was Michael Bacon …

I knew that Mary Ball was the name of William Munro's *second* wife, and that he married her sometime in 1672 (probably after Martha died in childbirth, leaving Munro with three small children and an infant). But this index card, misfiled with the *Row v. Bacon* papers, linked Mary Ball with Michael Bacon in 1672. What was *this* all about? Did Mary Ball have Michael Bacon's child shortly before she married William Munro?

I scrolled back and forth through the microfilm reel, hoping to find that "bill of charges," but the original document was nowhere to be seen, either lost or filed with other court papers. I returned to the card file for the Middlesex County Court Folio Collection, looking for other references to Michael Bacon and Mary Ball, too intrigued to let this go—and gradually I uncovered a poignant story long hidden in the old court records.

With the help of Elizabeth Bouvier, head of the Judicial Archives, I found pieces of the story scattered on other microfilm reels and in boxes of original folio papers. What emerged was the stuff of romance novels, yet all of it was true—a secret love affair between a married man and his teenage servant, Mary's desperate flight to Rhode Island, her illegitimate child, Michael's arrest and jailbreak, a courtroom confession, bitter betrayal, and the resolute Scots widower who gave Mary (and himself) another chance at happiness.

This case must have been the talk of the county, in every tavern, at Sunday meeting, anyplace where people gathered to share the news. Yet the scandal faded from memory, finally forgotten or deliberately suppressed by later generations. No record of Mary's first child appeared in any of the Bacon, Ball or Munro genealogies, although she went on to have ten more children (and to raise four stepchildren) as William Munro's wife. I might never have stumbled across this case, or learned of Mary's troubled past, had it not been for Munro's "purloined pigs."

The court records did not reveal the entire story. I am still searching for the child (whose fate was unclear), although I think that I may have found him in another surprising source. But there is always more research—more detective work—to do. I hope that your own research in the New England court records will be as rewarding.

APPENDIX

Nashua, N.H. Court House.

The image on the preceding page, from the author's collection of vintage picture postcards, depicts the courthouse in Nashua, New Hampshire, ca. pre-1907.

Contact Information

State Courts

Connecticut
www.jud.state.ct.us

Connecticut Supreme Court
231 Capitol Ave., **Hartford**, CT 06106; Tel. 860-757-2200

Connecticut Appellate Court
95 Washington St., **Hartford**, CT 06106

FAIRFIELD COUNTY

Superior Court—Judicial Districts
Danbury: 146 White St., Danbury, CT 06810; Tel. 203-207-8600
Fairfield: 1061 Main St., Bridgeport, CT 06604; Tel. 203-579-6527; Fax 203-382-8406
Stamford-Norwalk: 123 Hoyt St., Stamford, CT 06905; Tel. 203-965-5308; Fax 203-965-5370

Superior Court—Geographical Areas
Area #1: 123 Hoyt St., **Stamford**, CT 06905-5794; Tel. 203-965-5208; Fax 203-965-5355
Area #2: 172 Golden Hill St., **Bridgeport**, CT 06604; Tel. 203-579-6568; Fax 203-382-8408
Area #3: 146 White St., **Danbury**, CT 06810; Tel. 203-207-8600; Fax 203-207-8642
Area #20: 17 Belden Ave., **Norwalk**, CT 06850; Tel. 203-846-3237; Fax 203-847-8710

Probate District Courts
Bethel: 1 School St., PO Box 144, Bethel, CT 06801; Tel. 203-794-8508; Fax 203-794-8587
Bridgeport: 202 State St., McLevy Hall, 3rd Floor, Bridgeport, CT 06604; Tel. 203-576-3945; Fax 203-576-7898
Brookfield: Town Hall, 100 Pocono Rd., PO Box 5192, Brookfield, CT 06804; Tel. 203-775-3700; Fax 203-775-5246
Danbury: City Hall Bldg., 155 Deer Hill Ave., Danbury, CT 06810; Tel. 203-797-4521; Fax 203-796-1526
Darien: Town Hall, 2 Renshaw Rd., Darien, CT 06820; Tel. 203-656-7342; Fax 203-656-0774
Fairfield: Independence Hall, 725 Old Post Rd., Fairfield, CT 06824; Tel. 203-256-3041; Fax 203-256-3044
Greenwich: Town Hall, 101 Field Point Rd., PO Box 2540, Greenwich, CT 06836-2540; Tel. 203-622-3766; Fax 203-622-6451
New Canaan: Town Hall, 77 Main St., New Canaan, CT 06840; Tel. 203-594-3050; Fax 203-594-3128
New Fairfield: 4 Brush Hill Rd., New Fairfield, CT 06812; Tel./Fax 203-312-5627
Newtown: Edmond Town Hall, 45 Main St., Newtown, CT 06470-2157; Tel. 203-270-4280; Fax 203-270-4283
Norwalk: 125 East Ave., PO Box 2009, Norwalk, CT 06852-2009; Tel. 203-854-7737; Fax 203-854-7825

Redding: Town Hall, 100 Hill Hall, PO Box 1125, Redding, CT 06875-1125; Tel. 203-938-2326; Fax 203-938-8816

Ridgefield: Town Hall, 400 Main St., Ridgefield, CT 06877; Tel. 203-431-2776, 2733; Fax 203-431-2722

Shelton: 40 White St., PO Box 127, Shelton, CT 06484; Tel. 203-924-8462; Fax 203-924-8943

Stamford: 888 Washington Blvd., 8th Floor, PO Box 10152, Stamford, CT 06904-2152; Tel. 203-323-2149; Fax 203-964-1830

Stratford: 468 Birdseye St., 2nd Floor, Stratford, CT 06615; Tel. 203-385-4023; Fax 203-375-6253

Trumbull: Town Hall, 5866 Main St., Trumbull, CT 06611-5416; Tel. 203-452-5068; Fax 203-452-5092

Westport: Town Hall, 110 Myrtle Ave., Westport, CT 06880; Tel. 203-341-1100; Fax 203-341-1102

HARTFORD COUNTY

Superior Court—Judicial Districts

Hartford: 95 Washington St., Hartford, CT 06106; Tel: 860-548-2700; Fax 860-548-2711

New Britain: 20 Franklin Sq., New Britain, CT 06051; Tel. 860-515-5180; Fax 860-515-5185

Superior Court—Geographical Areas

Area #12: 410 Center St., **Manchester**, CT 06040; Tel. 860-647-1091; Fax 860-645-7540

Area #13: 111 Phoenix, **Enfield**, CT 06082; Tel: 860-741-3727; Fax 860-741-3474

Area #14: 101 Lafayette St., **Hartford**, CT 06106; Tel. 860-566-1630; Fax 860-566-1983

Area #15: 20 Franklin Sq., **New Britain**, CT 06051; Tel. 860-515-5080; Fax 860-515-5103

Area #17: 131 N. Main St., **Bristol**, CT 06010; Tel. 860-582-8111

Probate District Courts

Avon: 60 W. Main St., Avon, CT 06001-0578; Tel. 860-409-4348; Fax 860-409-4368

Berlin: 1 Liberty Sq., PO Box 400, New Britain, CT 06050-0400; Tel. 860-826-2696; Fax 860-826-2695

Bloomfield: Town Hall, 800 Bloomfield Ave., Bloomfield, CT 06002; Tel. 860-769-3548; Fax 860-242-1167

Bristol: 111 N. Main St., City Hall, 3rd Floor, Bristol, CT 06010; Tel. 860-584-6230; Fax 860-584-3818

Burlington: Town Hall, 200 Spielman Highway, Burlington, CT 06013; Tel. 860-673-2108; Fax 860-673-8607

Canton: Town Hall, 4 Market St., PO Box 175, Collinsville, CT 06022-0175; Tel. 860-693-7851; Fax 860-693-7889

E. Granby: Town Hall, 9 Center St., PO Box 542, E. Granby, CT 06026-0542; Tel. 860-653-3434; Fax 860-653-7085

E. Hartford: Town Hall, 740 Main St., E. Hartford, CT 06108; Tel. 860-291-7278; Fax 860-291-7211

E. Windsor: Town Hall, 1540 Sullivan Ave., S. Windsor, CT 06074-2786; Tel. 860-644-2511; Fax 860-648-5047

Enfield: 820 Enfield St., Enfield, CT 06082; Tel. 860-253-6305; Fax 860-253-6388

Farmington: 1 Monteith Dr., Farmington, CT 06032; Tel. 860-675-2360; Fax 860-673-8262

Glastonbury: 2155 Main St., PO Box 6523, Glastonbury, CT 06033-6523; Tel. 860-652-7629; Fax 860-368-2520

Granby: Town Hall, 15 N. Granby Rd., PO Box 240, Granby, CT 06035-0240; Tel. 860-653-8944; Fax 860-844-5325

Hartford: 250 Constitution Plaza, Hartford, CT 06103-2814; Tel. 860-757-9150; Fax 860-724-1503

Manchester: 66 Center St., Manchester, CT 06040; Tel. 860-647-3227; Fax 860-647-3236

Marlborough: 26 N. Main St., PO Box 29, Marlborough, CT 06447; Tel. 860-295-6239; Fax 860-295-0317

New Hartford: Town Hall, 530 Main St., PO Box 308, New Hartford, CT 06057-0308; Tel. 860-379-3254; Fax 860-379-8560

Newington: 66 Cedar St., Rear, Newington, CT 06111; Tel. 860-665-1285; Fax 860-665-1331

Plainville: 1 Central Sq., Plainville, CT 06062; Tel. 860-793-0221; Fax 860-793-2424

Simsbury: 933 Hopmeadow St., PO Box 495, Simsbury, CT 06070-0495; Tel. 860-658-3277; Fax 860-658-3204; *http://simsburyct.virtualtownhall.net/Public_Documents/SimsburyCT_Probate/index*

Southington: Town Hall, 75 Main St., PO Box 165, Southington, CT 06489-0165; Tel. 860-276-6253; Fax 860-276-6255

Suffield: Town Hall, 83 Mountain Rd., PO Box 234, Suffield, CT 06078-0234; Tel. 860-668-3835; Fax 860-668-3029; *probate@suffieldtownhall.com*

W. Hartford: 50 S. Main St., W. Hartford, CT 06107; Tel. 860-523-3174; Fax 860-236-8352

Windsor: 275 Broad St., PO Box 342, Windsor, CT 06095; Tel. 860-285-1976; Fax 860-285-1909

Windsor Locks: Town Office Building, 50 Church St., Windsor Locks, CT 06096; Tel. 860-627-1450; Fax 860-627-1451

LITCHFIELD COUNTY
Superior Court

Litchfield Judicial District: 15 West St., PO Box 247, Litchfield, CT 06759; Tel. 860-567-0885; Fax 860-567-4779

Geographical Area #18: 80 Doyle Rd., PO Box 667, **Bantam**, CT 06750; Tel. 860-567-3942; Fax 860-567-3934

Probate District Courts

Canaan: Town Hall, 100 Pease St., PO Box 905, Canaan, CT 06018-0905; Tel. 860-824-7114; Fax 860-824-3139

Cornwall: Town Office Bldg., 26 Pine St., PO Box 157, Cornwall, CT 06753-0157; Tel/Fax 860-672-2677

Harwinton: Town Hall, 100 Bentley Dr., Harwinton, CT 06791; Tel. 860-485-1403; Fax 860-485-0051

Kent: Town Hall, 41 Kent Green Blvd., PO Box 185, Kent, CT 06757-0185; Tel. 860-927-3729; Fax 860-927-1313

Litchfield: 74 West St., PO Box 505, Litchfield, CT 06759; Tel. 860-567-8065; Fax 806-567-2538

New Milford: 10 Main St., New Milford, CT 06776; Tel. 860-355-6029; Fax 860-355-6002

Norfolk: 19 Maple Ave., PO Box 648, Norfolk, CT 06058-0648; Tel. 860-542-5134; Fax 860-542-5876

Plymouth: 80 Main St., Terryville, CT 06786; Tel. 860-585-4014; Fax 860-585-4099; *probatecourt@plymouthct.us*

Roxbury: Town Hall, 29 North St., PO Box 203, Roxbury, CT 06783; Tel. 860-354-1184; Fax 860-355-3091

Salisbury: Town Hall, 27 Main St., PO Box 525, Salisbury, CT 06068; Tel. 860-435-5183; Fax 860-435-5172

Sharon: 63 Main St., PO Box 1177, Sharon, CT 06069-1177; Tel. 860-364-5514; Fax 860-364-5789

Thomaston: Town Hall Bldg., 158 Main St., PO Box 136, Thomaston, CT 06787; Tel. 860-283-4874; Fax 860-283-1013

Torrington: Municipal Bldg., 140 Main St., Torrington, CT 06790; Tel. 860-489-2215; Fax 860-496-5910

Washington: Town Hall, 2 Bryan Memorial Plaza, PO Box 295, Washington Depot, CT 06794-0295; Tel. 860-868-7974; Fax 860-868-0512

Winchester: 338 Main St., PO Box 625, Winsted, CT 06098-0625; Tel. 860-379-5576; Fax 860-738-7053

Watertown: Town Hall, 38 DeForest St., Watertown, CT 06795; Tel. 860-945-5230

Woodbury: 281 Main St., S., PO Box 84, Woodbury, CT 06798; Tel. 203-263-2417; Fax 203-263-2748

MIDDLESEX COUNTY

Superior Court

Middlesex Judicial District: 1 Court St., Middletown, CT 06457-3374; Tel. 860-343-6400; Fax 860-343-6423

Geographical Area #9: 1 Court St., **Middletown**, CT 06457-3377; Tel. 860-343-6445; Fax 860-343-6566

Probate District Courts

Clinton: Eliott House, 50 E. Main St., PO Box 130, Clinton, CT 06413-0130; Tel./Fax 860-669-6447

Deep River: Town Hall, 174 Main St., PO Box 391, Deep River, CT 06417; Tel. 860-526-6026; Fax 860-526-6094; *probate@DeepRiverCT.com*

E. Haddam: Goodspeed Plaza, PO Box 217, E. Haddam, CT 06423; Tel. 860-873-5028; Fax 860-873-5025

E. Hampton: Town Hall, 20 E. High St., Annex, E. Hampton, CT 06424; Tel. 860-267-9262; Fax 860-267-6453

Essex: Town Hall, 29 West Ave., Essex, CT 06426; Tel. 860-767-4340; Fax 860-767-2538

Haddam: 30 Field Park Dr., Haddam, CT 06438; Tel. 860-345-8531; Fax 860-345-3730

Killingworth: Town Office Bldg., 323 Rt. 81, Killingworth, CT 06419-1298; Tel. 860-663-2304; Fax 860-663-3305

Middletown: 94 Court St., Middletown, CT 06457; Tel. 860-347-7424; Fax 860-346-1520

Old Saybrook: 251 Main St., Old Saybrook, CT 06475; Tel./Fax 860-395-3128

Portland: 33 E. Main St., PO Box 71, Portland, CT 06480-0071; Tel. 860-342-6739; Fax 860-342-0001

Saybrook: 65 Main St., PO Box 628, Chester, CT 06412; Tel. 860-526-0013 x221; Fax 860-526-0004

Westbrook: 866 Boston Post Rd., PO Box 676, Westbrook, CT 06498; Tel. 860-399-5661; Fax 860-399-3092

NEW HAVEN COUNTY

Superior Court—Judicial Districts

Ansonia-Milford:

14 W. River St., PO Box 210, **Milford**, CT 06460; Tel. 203-877-4293; Fax 203-876-8640

106 Elizabeth St., **Derby**, CT 06418; Tel. 203-735-7438; Fax 203-735-2047

New Haven:

54 W. Main St., **Meriden**, CT 06451; Tel. 203-238-6666; Fax 203-238-6322

235 Church St., **New Haven**, CT 06510; Tel. 203-503-6800; Fax 203-789-6424

Waterbury: 300 Grand St., Waterbury, CT 06702; Tel. 203-591-3300; Fax 203-596-4032

Superior Court—Geographical Areas

Area #4: 400 Grand St., **Waterbury**, CT 06702; Tel. 203-236-8100; Fax 203-236-8090

Area #5: 106 Elizabeth St., **Derby**, CT 06418; Tel. 203-735-7438; Fax 203-735-2047

Area #7: 54 W. Main St., **Meriden**, CT 06451; Tel. 203-238-6130; Fax 203-238-6016

Area #22: 14 W. River St., **Milford**, CT 06460; Tel. 203-874-1116; Fax 203-874-5233

Area #23: 121 Elm St., **New Haven**, CT 06510; Tel. 203-789-7461; Fax 203-789-7492

Probate District Courts

Bethany: Town Hall, 40 Peck Rd., Bethany, CT 06524; Tel. 203-393-3744; Fax 203-393-0821

Branford: 1019 Main St., PO Box 638, Branford, CT 06405-0638; Tel. 203-488-0318; Fax 203-315-4715

Cheshire: 84 S. Main St., Cheshire, CT 06410; Tel. 203-271-6608; Fax 203-271-6628

Derby: City Hall, 253 Main St., Ansonia, CT 06401; Tel. 203-734-1277; Fax 203-736-1434

E. Haven: Town Hall, 250 Main St., E. Haven, CT 06512; Tel. 203-468-3895; Fax 203-468-5155

Guilford: Town Hall, 31 Park St., Guilford, CT 06437; Tel. 203-453-8006; Fax 203-453-8132

Hamden: Govt. Center, 2750 Dixwell Ave., Hamden, CT 06518; Tel. 203-287-7082; Fax 203-287-7087

Madison: 8 Campus Dr., Madison, CT 06443; Tel. 203-245-5661; Fax 203-245-5653

Meriden: City Hall, Room 113, 142 E. Main St., Meriden, CT 06450; Tel. 203-630-4150; Fax 203-630-4043

Milford: Parsons Govt. Office Complex, 70 W. River St., PO Box 414, Milford, CT 06460; Tel. 203-783-3205; Fax 203-783-3364

Naugatuck: Town Hall, 229 Church St., Naugatuck, CT 06770; Tel. 203-720-7046; Fax 203-720-5476

New Haven: 200 Orange St., PO Box 905, New Haven, CT 06504-0905; Tel. 203-946-4880; Fax 203-946-5962

N. Branford: 909 Foxon Rd., N. Branford, CT 06471; Tel. 203-484-6007; Fax 203-484-6017

N. Haven: 18 Church St., PO Box 175, N. Haven, CT 06473-0175; Tel. 203-239-5321; Fax 203-239-1874

Orange: 525 Orange Center Rd., Orange, CT 06477; Tel. 203-891-2160; Fax 203-891-2161

Oxford: Town Hall, Rt. 67, Oxford, CT 06478; Tel. 203-888-2543 x3014; Fax 203-888-2136

Southbury: Townhall Annex, 421 Main St., S., PO Box 674, Southbury, CT 06488-0674; Tel. 203-262-0641; Fax 203-264-9310

Wallingford: Town Hall, 45 S. Main St., Wallingford, CT 06492; Tel. 203-294-2100; Fax 203-294-2109

Waterbury: 236 Grand St., Waterbury, CT 06702; Tel. 203-755-1127; Fax 203-597-0824

W. Haven: 355 Main St., PO Box 127, W. Haven, CT 06516; Tel. 203-937-3552; Fax 203-937-3556

Woodbridge: Town Hall, 11 Meetinghouse Lane, Woodbridge, CT 06525-1597; Tel. 203-389-3410; Fax 203-389-3480

NEW LONDON COUNTY

Superior Court—Judicial Districts

70 Huntington St., PO Box 671, **New London**, CT 06320; Tel. 860-443-5363; Fax 860-442-7703

1 Courthouse Sq., **Norwich**, CT 06360; Tel. 860-887-3515; Fax 860-887-8643

Superior Court—Geographical Areas

Area #10: 112 Broad St., **New London**, CT 06320; Tel. 860-443-8343; Fax 860-437-1168

Area #21: 1 Courthouse Sq., **Norwich**, CT 06360; Tel. 860-889-7338; Fax 860-885-0509

Probate District Courts

> **Bozrah**: Town Hall, 1 River Rd., Bozrah, CT 06334; Tel. 860-889-2958; Fax 860-887-7571
>
> **Colchester**: Town Hall, 127 Norwich Ave., Colchester, CT 06415; Tel. 860-537-7290; Fax 860-537-7298
>
> **E. Lyme**: 108 Pennsylvania Ave., PO Box 519, Niantic, CT 06357; Tel. 860-739-6931; Fax 860-739-6930
>
> **Griswold**: 28 Main St., Jewett City, CT 06351; Tel. 860-376-7060; Fax 860-376-0216
>
> **Groton**: Town Hall, 45 Fort Hill Rd., Groton, CT 06340-4394; Tel. 860-441-6655; Fax 860-441-6657
>
> **Ledyard**: 741 Colonel Ledyard Highway, Rt. 117, Ledyard, CT 06339; Tel. 860-464-3219; Fax 860-464-8531
>
> **Lyme**: Town Hall, 480 Hamburg Rd., Lyme, CT 06371; Tel. 860-434-7733; Fax 860-434-2989
>
> **Montville**: 310 Norwich-New London Turnpike, Uncasville, CT 06382; Tel. 860-848-9847 x319; Fax 860-848-2116
>
> **New London**: 181 Captain's Walk, Municipal Bldg., PO Box 148, New London, CT 06320; Tel. 860-443-7121; Fax 860-437-8155
>
> **N. Stonington**: 391 Norwich Westerly Rd., Rt. 2, PO Box 204, N. Stonington, CT 06359-0204; Tel./Fax 860-535-8441
>
> **Norwich**: 100 Broadway, PO Box 38, Norwich, CT 06360-0038; Tel. 860-887-2160; Fax 860-887-2401
>
> **Old Lyme**: Memorial Town Hall, 52 Lyme St., Old Lyme, CT 06371; Tel. 860-434-1605; Fax 860-434-9283
>
> **Salem**: 270 Hartford Rd., Salem, CT 06420; Tel. 860-859-3873; Fax 860-537-1433
>
> **Stonington**: 152 Elm St., PO Box 312, Stonington, CT 06378-0312; Tel. 860-535-5090; Fax 860-535-0520

TOLLAND COUNTY

Superior Court

> **Tolland Judicial District**: 69 Brooklyn St., **Rockville**, CT 06066; Tel. 860-896-4920; Fax 860-875-0777
>
> **Geographical Area #19**: 20 Park St., PO Box 980, **Rockville**, CT 06066-0980; Tel. 860-870-3200; Fax 860-870-3290

Probate District Courts

> **Andover**: Bolton Town Hall, 222 Bolton Center Rd., Bolton, CT 06043; Tel. 860-647-7979; Fax 860-649-3187
>
> **Ellington**: 14 Park Place, PO Box 268, Rockville, CT 06066-0268; Tel. 860-872-0519; Fax 860-870-5140
>
> **Hebron**: 15 Gilead St., Hebron, CT 06248; Tel. 860-228-5971; Fax 860-228-4859
>
> **Mansfield**: Municipal Bldg., 4 S. Eagleville Rd., Storrs, CT 06268; Tel. 860-429-3313; Fax 860-429-4088
>
> **Stafford**: Town Hall, 1 Main St., PO Box 63, Stafford Springs, CT 06076-0063; Tel. 860-684-1783; Fax 860-684-7173
>
> **Tolland**: 21 Tolland Green, Tolland, CT 06084; Tel. 860-871-3640; Fax 860-871-3641

WINDHAM COUNTY

Superior Court

> **Windham Judicial District**:
> 120 School St., **Danielson**, CT 06239; Fax 860-779-8511
> 155 Church St., **Putnam**, CT 06260-1515; Tel. 860-928-7749; Fax 860-928-7076
> 108 Valley St., **Willimantic**, CT 06226; Tel. 860-423-8491; Fax 860-423-3749
> **Geographical Area #11**: 120 School St., **Danielson**, CT 06239; Tel. 860-779-8480; Fax 860-779-8488

Probate District Courts

> **Ashford**: 20 Pompey Hollow Rd., PO Box 61, Ashford, CT 06278; Tel. 860-429-4986; Fax 860-429-1114

Brooklyn: Town Hall, 4 Wolf Den Rd., PO Box 356, Brooklyn, CT 06234-0356; Tel. 860-774-5973; Fax 860-779-3744

Eastford: PO Box 207, Eastford, CT 06242-0207; Tel. 860-974-3024; Fax 860-974-0624

Hampton: Town Hall, 164 Main St., PO Box 143, Hampton, CT 06247; Tel. 860-455-9132; Fax 860-445-0517

Killingly: 172 Main St., Danielson, CT 06239; Tel. 860-779-5319; Fax 860-779-5394

Plainfield: Town Hall, 8 Community Ave., Plainfield, CT 06374; Tel. 860-230-3031; Fax 860-230-3033

Pomfret: 5 Haven Rd., Rt. 44, Pomfret Center, CT 06259; Tel. 860-974-0186; Fax 860-974-3950

Putnam: Town Hall, 126 Church St., PO Box 548, Putnam, CT 06260; Tel. 860-963-6868; Fax 860-963-6814

Thompson: Town Hall, 815 Riverside Dr., PO Box 74, N. Grosvenordale, CT 06255; Tel. 860-923-2203; Fax 860-923-3836

Windham: 979 Main St., PO Box 34, Willimantic, CT 06226; Tel. 860-465-3049; Fax 860-465-2162; *probateclerk@snet.net*

Woodstock: 415 Rt. 169, Woodstock, CT 06281; Tel. 860-928-2223; Fax 860-963-7557; *probate@townofwoodstock.com*

Maine

www.courts.state.me.us

Supreme Judicial Court

Clerk's Office, 205 Newbury St., PO Box 368, **Portland**, ME 04112-0368; Tel. 207-822-4146

ANDROSCOGGIN COUNTY

Superior Court

2 Turner St., PO Box 3660, **Auburn**, ME 04212-3660; Tel. 207-783-5150

District Court

71 Lisbon St., PO Box 1345, **Lewiston**, ME 04243-1345; Tel. 207-795-4801

Probate Court

2 Turner St., **Auburn**, ME 02410; Tel. 207-782-0281/3410; Fax 207-782-1135

AROOSTOOK COUNTY

Superior Court

144 Sweden St., **Caribou**, ME 04736; Tel. 207-498-8125

26 Court St., PO Box 457, **Houlton**, ME 04730 (not open to public); Tel. 207-532-6563

District Court

144 Sweden St., **Caribou**, ME 04736; Tel. 207-493-3144

139 Market St., PO Box 473, **Fort Kent**, ME 04743; Tel. 207-834-5003

25 School St., PO Box 457, **Houlton**, ME 04730; Tel. 207-532-2147

645 Main St., PO Box 127, **Madawaska**, ME 04756; Tel. 207-728-4700

27 Riverside Dr., **Presque Isle**, ME 04769; Tel. 207-764-2055

Probate Court

26 Court St., Suite 103, **Houlton**, ME 04730; Tel. 207-532-1502; *www.aroostook.me.us/probate.html*

CUMBERLAND COUNTY

Superior Court

142 Federal St., PO Box 287, **Portland**, ME 04101-0287; Tel. 207-822-4109 (Civil), 4113 (Criminal)

District Court

3 Chase St., **Bridgton**, ME 04009; Tel. 207-647-3535

142 Federal St., PO Box 412, **Portland**, ME 04112; Tel. 207-822-4200/822-4193

Probate Court

142 Federal St., Portland, ME 04101 (*Mail*: PO Box 15277, **Portland**, ME 04112); Tel. 207-871-8382; Fax 207-791-2658; *www.CumberlandCounty.org/PROmain.html*

FRANKLIN COUNTY
Superior Court
> 140 Main St., **Farmington**, ME 04938; Tel. 207-778-3346; Fax 207-778-8261

District Court
> 129 Main St. , **Farmington**, ME 04938-1992; Tel. 207-778-8200

Probate Court
> 140 Main St., **Farmington**, ME 04938; Tel. 207-778-5888; Fax 207-778-5899;
> *fcprobate@midmaine.com*

HANCOCK COUNTY
Superior Court
> 50 State St., **Ellsworth**, ME 04605-1926; Tel. 207-667-7176

District Court
> **Bar Harbor**, ME (Closed permanently, July 2005). Contact Ellsworth District Court.
> 50 State St., **Ellsworth**, ME 04605-1992; Tel. 207-667-7141

Probate Court
> 50 State St., **Ellsworth**, ME 04605; Tel. 207-667-8434

KENNEBEC COUNTY
Superior Court
> 95 State St., **Augusta**, ME 04330; Tel. 207-624-5800

District Court
> 145 State St., **Augusta**, ME 04330-7495; Tel. 207-287-8075
> 18 Colby St., **Waterville**, ME 04903; Tel. 207-873-2103

Probate Court
> 95 State St., **Augusta**, ME 04330; Tel. 207-622-7558, 722-7559; Fax 207-621-1639;
> *www.datamaine.com/probate*; *kenprob@gwi.net*

KNOX COUNTY
Superior, District and Probate Courts
> 62 Union St., **Rockland**, ME 04841
> **Superior**: Tel. 207-594-2576
> **District**: Tel. 207-596-2240
> **Probate**: Tel. 207-594-0427; Fax 207-594-0443;
> *knoxcounty.midcoast.com/probate/index.html*; *probate@knoxcounty.midcoast.com*

LINCOLN COUNTY
Superior, District and Probate Courts
> 32 High St., PO Box 249, **Wiscasset**, ME 04578
> **Superior**: Tel. 207-882-7517; Fax 207-882-7741
> **District**: Tel. 207-882-6363; Fax 207-882-5980
> **Probate**: Tel. 207-882-7392; Fax 207-882-4324;
> *www.co.lincoln.me.us/dep.html*; *lincprob@co.lincoln.me.us*
> **Register of Deeds**: Tel. 207-882-7431 (For access to archived court records in vault)

OXFORD COUNTY
Superior Court
> 26 Western Ave., PO Box 179, **S. Paris**, ME 04281-0179; Tel. 207-743-8936; Fax
> 207-743-0544

District Court
> Municipal Bldg., 145 Congress St., **Rumford**, ME 04276; Tel. 207-364-7171
> 26 Western Ave., **S. Paris**, ME 04281; Tel. 207-743-8942

Probate Court
> 26 Western Ave., PO Box 179, **S. Paris**, ME 04281; Tel. 207-743-6671; Fax 207-743-
> 2656; *oxprob@megalink.net*

PENOBSCOT COUNTY
Superior Court
> 97 Hammond St., **Bangor**, ME 04401; Tel. 207-561-2300

District Court
> 73 Hammond St., **Bangor**, ME 04401; Tel. 207-941-3040

    52 Maine St., **Lincoln**, ME 04457; Tel. 207-794-8512

    207 Penobscot Ave., **Millinocket**, ME 04462; Tel. 207-723-4786

    12 Water St., **Newport**, ME 04953; Tel. 207-368-5778

Probate Court

    97 Hammond St., **Bangor**, ME 04401-4996; Tel. 207-942-8769; Fax 207-941-8499; *penpro@midmaine.com*

PISCATAQUIS COUNTY

Superior Court

    159 E. Main St., **Dover-Foxcroft**, ME 04426; Tel. 207-564-8419; Fax 207-564-3363

District Court

    163 E. Main St., **Dover-Foxcroft**, ME 04426; Tel. 207-564-2240

Probate Court

    159 E. Main St., **Dover-Foxcroft**, ME 04426; Tel. 207-564-2431; Fax 207-564-3022; *piscourt@Foxcroft.pvt.K12.me.us*

SAGADAHOC COUNTY

Superior Court

    752 High St., **Bath**, ME 04530; Tel. 207-443-9733

District Court

    147 New Meadows Rd., **W. Bath**, ME 04530; Tel. 207-442-0200

Probate Court

    752 High St., **Bath**, ME 04530; Tel. 207-443-8218; Fax 207-443-8217; *sagprob@gwi.net*

SOMERSET COUNTY

Superior Court

    41 Court St., PO Box 725, **Skowhegan**, ME 04976; Tel. 207-474-5161

District Court

    47 Court St., PO Box 525, **Skowhegan**, ME 04976; Tel. 207-474-9518

Probate Court

    41 Court St., **Skowhegan**, ME 04976; Tel. 207-474-3322

WALDO COUNTY

Superior Court

    137 Church St., PO Box 188, **Belfast**, ME 04915; Tel. 207-338-1940

District Court

    103 Church St., PO Box 382, **Belfast**, ME 04915; Tel. 207-338-3107

Probate Court

    39A Spring St., PO Box 323, **Belfast**, ME 04915-0323; Tel. 207-338-2780/2963; Fax 207-338-2360; *www.waldocountyme.gov*; *registerofprobate@waldocountyme.gov*

WASHINGTON COUNTY

Superior Court

    47 Court St., PO Box 526, **Machias**, ME 04654; Tel. 207-255-3326

District Court

    382 South St., **Calais**, ME 04619; Tel: 207-454-2055

    47 Court St., PO Box 297, **Machias**, ME 04654; Tel. 207-255-3044

Probate Court

    47 Court St., PO Box 297, **Machias**, ME 04654; Tel. 207-255-6591

YORK COUNTY

Superior Court

    45 Kennebunk St., PO Box 160, **Alfred**, ME 04002-0160; Tel. 207-324-5122

District Court

    25 Adams St., **Biddeford**, ME 04005; Tel. 207-283-1147

    447 Main St., **Springvale**, ME 04083; Tel. 207-459-1400

    11 Chase's Pond Rd., **York**, ME 03909; Tel. 207-363-1230

Probate Court

    45 Kennebunk Rd., PO Box 399, **Alfred**, ME 04002; Tel. 207-324-1577; Fax 207-324-0163; *probate@co.york.me.us*

Massachusetts

www.mass.gov/courts

Supreme Judicial Court

1 Pemberton Sq., **Boston**, MA 02108; Tel. 617-557-1020; Fax 617-557-1145; *sjccommclerk@sjc.state.ma.us*. **Head of Archives**, 3 Pemberton Sq. High Rise, 16th Flr., Boston, MA 02108-1701; Tel. 617-577-1082

Appeals Court

John Adams Courthouse, 1 Pemberton Sq., **Boston**, MA 02108; Tel. 617-725-8106; Fax 617-523-2845

Land Court

226 Causeway St., **Boston**, MA 02114; Tel. 617-788-7470; Fax 617-788-8953

BARNSTABLE COUNTY

Superior Court

3195 Main St., PO Box 425, **Barnstable**, MA 02630; Tel. 508-375-6684; Fax 508-362-7754 (civil), 362-1658 (criminal)

District Court

Courthouse, Main Street, Route 6A, PO Box 427, **Barnstable**, MA 02630; Tel. 508-375-6600, 508-375-6773

161 Jones Rd., **Falmouth**, MA 02540; Tel. 508-495-1500; Fax 508-495-0992

237 Rock Harbor Rd., **Orleans**, MA 02653; Tel. 508-255-4700

Probate and Family Court

3195 Main St., PO Box 346, **Barnstable**, MA 02630; Tel. 508-362-2511/375-6709; Fax 508-362-3662

BERKSHIRE COUNTY

Superior Court

76 East St., **Pittsfield**, MA 01201; Tel. 413-499-7487; Fax 413-442-9190

District Court

111 Holden St., **N. Adams**, MA 01247; Tel. 413-663-5339; Fax 413-664-7209

24 Wendell Ave., PO Box 875, **Pittsfield**, MA 01201; Tel. 413-442-5468; Fax 413-499-7327

9 Gilmore Ave., **Great Barrington**, MA 01230; Tel. 413-528-3520; Fax 413-528-0757

Probate and Family Court

44 Bank Row, **Pittsfield**, MA 01201; Tel. 413-442-6941; Fax 413-443-3430

BRISTOL COUNTY

Superior Court

9 Court St., PO Box 547, **Taunton**, MA 02780-3244; Tel. 508-823-6588

441 N. Main St., **Fall River**, MA 02720; Tel. 508-672-4464

441 County St., **New Bedford**, MA 02740; Tel. 508-996-2051

District Court

88 N. Main St., **Attleboro**, MA 02703; Tel. 508-222-5900

45 Rock St., **Fall River**, MA 02720; Tel. 508-679-8161; Fax 508-675-5477

75 N. Sixth St., **New Bedford**, MA 02740; Tel. 508-999-9700, 990-9352; Fax 508-990-8094

120 Cohannet St., **Taunton**, MA 02780; Tel. 508-824-4032; Fax 508-824-2282

Probate and Family Court

11 Court St., PO Box 567, **Taunton**, MA 02780-0567; Tel. 508-824-4004; Fax 508-821-4630

DUKES COUNTY

Superior, District, and Probate and Family Courts

81 Main St., **Edgartown**, MA 02539

Superior: PO Box 1267; Tel. 508-627-4668; Fax 508-627-7571

District: PO Box 1284; Tel. 508-627-3751; Fax 508-627-7070

Probate and Family: PO Box 237; Tel. 508-627-4703; Fax 508-627-7664

ESSEX COUNTY
Superior Court
> 34 Federal St., **Salem**, MA 01970; Tel. 978-744-5500; Fax 978-741-0691
> 43 Appleton Way, **Lawrence**, MA 01841; Tel. 978-687-7463; Fax 978-687-7869
> High St., **Newburyport**, MA 01950; Tel. 978-462-4474; Fax 978-462-0432

District Court
> 197 Main St., **Gloucester**, MA 01930; Tel. 978-283-2620; Fax 978-283-8784
> James P. Ginty Blvd., PO Box 1389, **Haverhill**, MA 01831; Tel. 978-373-4151; Fax 978-521-6886
> 188 State St., **Newburyport**, MA 01950; Tel. 978-462-2652; Fax 978-462-5641 (**Ipswich** District Court)
> Fenton Judicial Center, 2 Appleton St., **Lawrence**, MA 01840-1525; Tel. 978-687-7184; Fax 978-687-0794
> 580 Essex St., **Lynn**, MA 01901; Tel. 781-598-5200; Fax 781-598-4350
> 188 State St., Rt. 1 Traffic Circle, **Newburyport**, MA 01950-6637; Tel. 978-462-2652; Fax 978-463-0438 (**Newburyport** District Court)
> 1 Lowell St., PO Box 666, **Peabody**, MA 01960; Tel. 978-532-3100; Fax 978-531-8524
> 65 Washington St., **Salem**, MA 01970; Tel. 978-744-1167; Fax 978-744-3211

Probate and Family Court
> 36 Federal St., **Salem**, MA 01970; Tel. 978-744-1020; Fax 978-741-2957
> Fenton Judicial Center, 2 Appleton St., **Lawrence**, MA 01840; Tel. 978-686-9692; Fax 978-687-3694

FRANKLIN COUNTY
Superior Court
> 425 Main St., PO Box 1573, **Greenfield**, MA 01302; Tel. 413-774-5535; Fax 413-774-4770

District Court
> 425 Main St., **Greenfield**, MA 01301; Tel. 413-774-5533, 34; Fax 413-774-5328
> 1 Court Sq., **Orange**, MA 01364-1232; Tel. 978-544-8277; Fax 978-544-5204

Probate and Family Court
> 425 Main St., PO Box 590, **Greenfield**, MA 01302; Tel. 413-774-7011; Fax 413-774-3829

HAMPDEN COUNTY
Superior Court
> 50 State St., PO Box 559, **Springfield**, MA 01102-0559; Tel. 413-735-6016/17; Fax 413-737-1611

District Court
> 30 Church St., **Chicopee**, MA 01020; Tel. 413-598-0099; Fax 413-594-6187
> 20 Court Plaza, **Holyoke**, MA 01040; Tel. 413-538-9710
> 235 Sykes St., **Palmer**, MA 01069; Tel. 413-283-8916; Fax 413-283-6775
> 50 State St., PO Box 2421, **Springfield**, MA 01101-2421; Tel. 413-748-8600; Fax 413-747-4841
> 224 Elm St., **Westfield**, MA 01085; Tel. 413-568-8946; Fax 413-568-4863

Probate and Family Court
> 50 State St., PO Box 559, **Springfield**, MA 01102-0559; Tel. 413-748-7786; Fax 413-781-5605

HAMPSHIRE COUNTY
Superior Court
> 15 Gothic St., PO Box 1119, **Northampton**, MA 01061; Tel. 413-584-5810; Fax 413-586-8217

District Court
> 15 Gothic St., **Northampton**, MA 01060; Tel. 413-584-7400; Fax 413-586-1980
> 71 South St., PO Box 300, **Ware**, MA 01082; Tel. 413-967-3301, 7911; Fax 413-967-7986

Probate and Family Court

33 King St., **Northampton**, MA 01060-3297; Tel. 413-586-8500; Fax 413-584-1132; *www.hampshireprobate.com* (excellent website, with forms, research links, glossary, etc.)

MIDDLESEX COUNTY

Superior Court

40 Thorndike St., **Cambridge**, MA 02141; Tel. 617-494-4010

360 Gorham St., **Lowell**, MA 01852; Tel. 978-453-0201 (Civil), 453-4181 (Criminal)

District Court

25 E. Main St., **Ayer**, MA 01432; Tel. 978-772-2100; Fax 978-772-5345

40 Thorndike St., PO Box 338, **Cambridge**, MA 02141; Tel. 617-494-4300/4310; Fax 617-494-9129

205 Walden St., **Concord**, MA 01742-3616; Tel. 978-369-0500; Fax 978-369-8976

600 Concord St., PO Box 1969, **Framingham**, MA 01701; Tel. 508-875-7461, 62; Fax 508-626-2503

41 Hurd St., **Lowell**, MA 01852; Tel. 978-459-4101; Fax 978-937-2846

89 Summer St., **Malden**, MA 02148; Tel. 781-322-7500; Fax 781-821-7521

45 Williams St., **Marlborough**, MA 01752; Tel. 508-485-3700; Fax 508-485-1575

117 E. Central St., **Natick**, MA 01760; Tel. 508-653-8100; Fax 508-655-8196

1309 Washington St., **W. Newton**, MA 02465-2011; Tel. 617-244-3600; Fax 617-243-7291

175 Fellsway, **Somerville**, MA 02145; Tel. 617-666-8000

38 Linden St., **Waltham**, MA 02452; Tel. 781-894-4500

30 Pleasant St., **Woburn**, MA 01801-4184; Tel. 781-935-4000; Fax 781-933-4404

Probate and Family Court

208 Cambridge St., PO Box 410480, **Cambridge**, MA 02141-0005; Tel. 617-768-5808; Fax 617-225-0781

NANTUCKET COUNTY

Superior, District, and Probate and Family Courts

Town and County Bldg., 16 Broad Street, **Nantucket**, MA 02554

Superior: PO Box 967; Tel. 508-228-2559

District: PO Box 1800; Tel. 508-228-0460; Fax 508-228-5759

Probate and Family: PO Box 1116; Tel. 508-228-2669; Fax 508-228-3662

NORFOLK COUNTY

Superior Court

650 High St., **Dedham**, MA 02026; Tel. 781-326-1600; Fax 781-326-3871 (Civil), 320-9726 (Criminal)

District Court

360 Washington St., **Brookline**, MA 02445; Tel. 617-232-4660; Fax 617-232-7905

631 High St., **Dedham**, MA 02026; Tel. 781-329-4777; Fax 781-329-8640

One Dennis Ryan Parkway, **Quincy**, MA 02169; Tel. 617-471-1650

1288 Central St., **Stoughton**, MA 02072; Tel. 781-344-2131, 4200; Fax 781-341-8744

60 East St., **Wrentham**, MA 02093; Tel. 508-384-3106; Fax 508-384-9454 (civil), 384-5052 (criminal)

Probate and Family Court

35 Shawmut Rd., **Canton**, MA 02021; Tel. 781-830-1200; Fax 781-830-4310

PLYMOUTH COUNTY

Superior Court

Courthouse, Court St., **Plymouth**, MA 02360; Tel. 508-747-6911; Fax 508-830-0676 Criminal sessions also held at: 72 Belmont Street, **Brockton**, MA 02301; Tel. 508-583-8250; Fax 508-584-5639

District Court

215 Main St., **Brockton**, MA 02301 (*Mail*: PO Box 7610, Brockton, MA 02303-7610); Tel. 508-587-8000

28 George Washington Blvd., **Hingham**, MA 02043; Tel. 781-749-7000; Fax 781-740-8390

Russell St., **Plymouth**, MA 02360; Tel. 508-747-0500; Fax 508-830-9303

2200 Cranberry Hwy, **W. Wareham**, MA 02576; Tel. 508-295-8300; Fax 508-291-6376

Probate and Family Court

7 Russell St., PO Box 3640, **Plymouth**, MA 02361; Tel. 508-747-6204; Fax 508-746-6846

215 Main St., PO Box 7277, **Brockton**, MA 02303-7277; Tel. 508-897-5400; Fax 508-584-4142

SUFFOLK COUNTY

Superior Court

3 Pemberton Sq., **Boston**, MA 02108; Tel. 617-788-8175 (Civil), 617-788-8160 (Criminal); Fax 617-788-7798

Boston Municipal Court

24 New Chardon St., **Boston**, MA 02114; Tel. 617-788-8700 (**Central** Division)

52 Academy Hill Rd., **Brighton**, MA 02135; Tel. 617-782-6521, 782-6540; Fax 617-254-2127

3 City Sq., **Charlestown**, MA 02129; Tel. 617-242-5400; Fax 617-242-1677

510 Washington St., **Dorchester**, MA 02124; Tel. 617-288-9500; Fax 617-436-8250

37 Meridian St., **E. Boston**, MA 02128; Tel. 617-569-7550, 51; Fax 617-561-4988

85 Warren St., **Roxbury**, MA 02119; Tel. 617-427-7000; Fax 617-541-0286

535 E. Broadway, **S. Boston**, MA 02127; Tel. 617-268-9292, 93; Fax 617-286-7321

445 Arborway, **Jamaica Plain**, MA 02130; Tel. 617-971-1200; Fax 617-983-0243 (**W. Roxbury** Div.)

District Court

120 Broadway, **Chelsea**, MA 02150; Tel. 617-660-9200; Fax 617-660-9215

Probate and Family Court

24 New Chardon St., PO Box 9667, **Boston**, MA 02114, Tel. 617-788-8300; Fax 617-788-8961; *www.probatecourtiannella.com* (excellent *unofficial* website of Register of Probate); *rpi@gis.net*

WORCESTER COUNTY

Superior Court

2 Main St., **Worcester**, MA 01608; Tel. 508-770-1899; Fax 508-754-9365

District Court

Rt. 62 & 70, 300 Boylston St., **Clinton**, MA 01510-4209; Tel. 978-368-7811; Fax 978-368-7827

W. Main St., PO Box 100, **Dudley**, MA 01571; Tel. 508-943-7123; Fax 508-949-0015

544 E. Main St., **E. Brookfield**, MA 01515; Tel. 508-885-6305, 06; Fax 508-885-7623

100 Elm St., **Fitchburg**, MA 01420; Tel. 978-345-2111; Fax 978-342-2461

108 Matthews St., **Gardner**, MA 01440; Tel. 978-632-2373; Fax 978-630-3902

25 School St., **Leominster**, MA 01453; Tel. 978-537-3722; Fax 978-537-3970

161 West St., Rt. 140, PO Box 370, **Milford**, MA 01757-0370; Tel. 508-473-1260; Fax 508-634-8477

261 S. Main St., **Uxbridge**, MA 01569-1690; Tel. 508-278-2454, 55; Fax 508-278-2929

175 Milk St., **Westborough**, MA 01581; Tel. 508-366-8266; Fax 508-366-8268

80 Central St., **Winchendon**, MA 01475; Tel. 978-297-0156; Fax 978-297-0161

50 Harvard St., **Worcester**, MA 01608; Tel. 508-747-8350

Probate and Family Court

2 Main St., **Worcester**, MA 01608; Tel. 508-770-0825; Fax 508-752-6138

New Hampshire

www.courts.state.nh.us

New Hampshire Supreme Court

1 Noble Dr., **Concord**, NH 03301; Tel. 603-271-2646

BELKNAP COUNTY
Superior Court
 64 Court St., **Laconia**, NH 03246; Tel. 603-524-3570
District Court
 26 Academy St., PO Box 1010, **Laconia**, NH 03247-3639; Tel. 603-524-4128
Probate Court
 64 Court St., PO Box 1343, **Laconia**, NH 03247-1343; Tel. 603-524-0903
CARROLL COUNTY
Superior Court
 Rt. 171, Courthouse Sq., PO Box 433, **Ossipee**, NH 03864-0433; Tel. 603-539-2201
District Court
 E. Conway Rd., Rt. 302, **N. Conway**, NH (*Mail*: PO Box 940, Conway, NH 03818-0940); Tel. 603-356-7710 (Northern Carroll County)
 96 Watervillage Rd., Box 2, **Ossipee**, NH 03864; Tel. 603-539-4561 (Southern Carroll County)
Probate Court
 96 Water Village Rd., Box 1, **Ossipee**, NH 03864; Tel. 603-539-4123; Fax 603-539-4761; *carroll.probate@courts.state.nh.us*
CHESHIRE COUNTY
Superior Court
 12 Court St., **Keene**, NH 03431-0444; Tel. 603-352-6902
District Court
 84 Peterborough St., PO Box 39, **Jaffrey**, NH 03452-0039; Tel. 603-532-8698 (Jaffrey-Peterborough District Court)
 3 Washington St., PO Box 364, **Keene**, NH 03431-0364; Tel. 603-352-2559
Probate Court
 12 Court St., **Keene**, NH 03431; Tel. 603-357-7786
COOS COUNTY
Superior Court
 55 School St., **Lancaster**, NH 03584; Tel. 603-788-4702
District Court
 220 Main St., **Berlin**, NH 03570; Tel. 603-752-3160; Fax 603-752-7361
 10 Bridge St., PO Box 5, **Colebrook**, NH 03576-0005; Tel. 603-237-4229
 Town Bldg., 20 Park St., PO Box 176, **Gorham**, NH 03581-0076; Tel. 603-466-2454
 55 School St., **Lancaster**, NH 03584; Tel. 603-788-4485
Probate Court
 55 School St., **Lancaster**, NH 03584; Tel. 603-788-2001;
 coos.probate@courts.state.nh.us
GRAFTON COUNTY
Superior Court
 3785 Dartmouth College Hwy., **N. Haverhill**, NH 03774-9708; Tel. 603-787-6961
District Court
 3785 Dartmouth College Hwy., Box 10, **N. Haverhill**, NH 03774; Tel. 603-787-6626
 38 Centerra Parkway, **Lebanon**, NH 03766-0247; Tel. 603-643-3555
 134 Main St., **Littleton**, NH 03561; Tel. 603-444-7750
 26 Green St., **Plymouth**, NH 03264; Tel. 603-536-3326
Probate Court
 3785 Dartmouth College Hwy., Box 3, **N. Haverhill**, NH 03774-4936; Tel. 603-787-6931
Family Court *www.nh.gov/judiciary/fdpp/index.htm*
 38 Centerra Parkway, **Lebanon**, NH 03766-0768; Tel. 603-343-3666, 343-1469
 134 Main St., **Littleton**, NH 03561; Tel. 603-444-3187
 3785 Dartmouth College Hwy., Box 9, **N. Haverhill**, NH 03774; Tel. 603-787-6820
 26 Green St., **Plymouth**, NH 03264; Tel. 603-536-7609, 536-7280

HILLSBOROUGH COUNTY
Superior Court
>**North**: 300 Chestnut St., **Manchester**, NH 03101-2490; Tel. 603-669-7410
>**South**: 30 Spring St., PO Box 2072, **Nashua**, NH 03061-2072; Tel. 603-883-6461

District Court
>16 Main St., PO Box 129, **Goffstown**, NH 03045-0129; Tel. 603-497-2597
>27 School St., PO Box 763, **Hillsborough**, NH 03244-0763; Tel. 603-464-5811
>35 Amherst St., PO Box 456, **Manchester**, NH 03105-0456; Tel. 603-624-6510
>Town Office Building, Baboosic Lake Rd., PO Box 324, **Merrimack**, NH 03054-0324; Tel. 603-424-9916
>180 Elm St., **Milford**, NH 03055-4735; Tel. 603-673-2900
>25 Walnut St., PO Box 310, **Nashua**, NH 03060; Tel. 603-880-3333

Probate Court
>PO Box P, **Nashua**, NH 03061-6015; Tel. 603-882-1231

MERRIMACK COUNTY
Superior Court
>163 N. Main St., PO Box 2880, **Concord**, NH 03302-2880; Tel. 603-225-5501

District Court
>32 Clinton St., PO Box 3420, **Concord**, NH 03302-3420; Tel. 603-271-6400
>7 Hancock Terrace, PO Box 172, **Franklin**, NH 03235-0172; Tel. 603-934-3290
>2 Depot St., **Henniker**, NH 03242; Tel. 603-428-3214
>101 Merrimack St., PO Box 16309, **Hooksett**, NH 03106-6309; Tel. 603-485-9901
>Main St., PO Box 1966, **New London**, NH 03257-1966; Tel. 603-526-6519

Probate Court
>163 N. Main St., **Concord**, NH 03301; Tel. 603-224-9589; Fax 603-225-0179; *merrimack.probate@courts.state.nh.us*

ROCKINGHAM COUNTY
Superior Court
>10 Rt. 125, **Brentwood**, NH 03833 (*Mail*: PO Box 1258, Kingston, NH 03848-1258); Tel. 603-642-5256

District Court
>5 Priscilla Lane, **Auburn**, NH 03032; Tel. 603-624-2084
>10 Manning St., **Derry**, NH 03038; Tel. 603-434-4676
>120 Water St., PO Box 394, **Exeter**, NH 03833-0394; Tel. 603-772-2931
>132 Winnacunnet Rd., PO Box 10, **Hampton**, NH 03843-0010; Tel. 603-926-8817
>14 Elm St., PO Box 129, **Plaistow**, NH 03865-0129; Tel. 603-382-4651; Fax 603-382-4952
>111 Parrott Ave., **Portsmouth**, NH 03801-4490; Tel. 603-431-2192
>35 Geremonty Dr., **Salem**, NH 03079; Tel. 603-893-4483

Probate Court
>10 Rt. 125, **Brentwood**, NH 03833 (*Mail*: PO Box 789, Kingston, NH 03842-0789); Tel. 603-642-7117

Family Court *www.nh.gov/judiciary/fdpp/index.htm*
>10 Rt. 125, **Brentwood**, NH (*Mail*: PO Box 1208, Kingston, NH 03848-9998); Tel. 603-642-6314, 642-6371
>10 Manning St., **Derry**, NH 03038; Tel. 603-421-0077, 421-0088
>111 Parrott Ave., **Portsmouth**, NH 03801-4490; Tel. 603-433-8518, 436-5039
>35 Geremonty Dr., **Salem**, NH 03079; Tel. 603-893-2084

STRAFFORD COUNTY
Superior Court
>279 County Farm Rd., PO Box 799, **Dover**, NH 03820-0799; Tel. 603-742-3065

District Court
>30 St. Thomas St., **Dover**, NH 03820; Tel. 603-742-7202; Fax 603-742-5956
>1 Main St., **Durham**, NH 03824; Tel. 603-868-2323
>76 N. Main St., **Rochester**, NH 03867-1905; Tel. 603-332-3516

Probate Court

> County Farm Rd., PO Box 799, **Dover**, NH 03820-0799; Tel. 603-742-2550

SULLIVAN COUNTY
Superior Court

> 22 Main St., **Newport**, NH 03773; Tel. 603-863-3450

District Court

> Tremont Sq., PO Box 313, **Claremont**, NH 03743-0313; Tel. 603-542-6064
> 55 Main St., **Newport**, NH 03773-0581; Tel. 603-863-1832

Probate Court

> 22 Main St., PO Box 417, **Newport**, NH 03773-0417; Tel. 603-863-3150

Rhode Island

www.courts.state.ri.us

Rhode Island Supreme Court

> Licht Judicial Complex, 250 Benefit St., **Providence**, RI 02903; Tel. 401-222-3272

Rhode Island Workers' Compensation Court

> One Dorrance Plaza, **Providence**, RI 02903-3973; Tel. 401-458-5000; Fax 401-222-3121

BRISTOL COUNTY
Town Courts

> **Barrington Probate Court**, Barrington Town Hall, 283 County Rd., Barrington, RI 02806; Tel. 401-247-1900; Fax 401-245-5003;
> *www.ci.barrington.ri.us*; *barrtownclerk@hotmail.com*
> **Bristol Probate Court**, Bristol Town Hall, 10 Court St., Bristol, RI 02809-2208; Tel: 401-253-7000; Fax 401-253-1570/253-3080; *www.onlinebristol.com*
> **Bristol Municipal Court**, Burnside Building, 400 Hope St., Bristol, RI 02809; Tel: 401-253-7000; Fax 401-253-1570/253-3080; *www.onlinebristol.com*
> **Warren Probate Court and Municipal Court**, Warren Town Hall, 514 Main St., Warren, RI 02885; Tel. 401-245-7340; Fax 401-245-7421

KENT COUNTY
Note: New Kent County courthouse to open late 2005.
Superior, District and Family Courts

> Leighton Judicial Complex, 222 Quaker Lane, **Warwick**, RI 02886-0107
> **Superior**: Tel. 401-822-1311
> **District** (3rd Div.): Tel. 401-822-1771
> **Family**: Tel. 401-822-1600

Town Courts

> **Coventry Probate Court and Municipal Court**, Coventry Town Hall, 1670 Flat River Rd., Coventry, RI 02816; Tel. 401-822-9173 (Probate), 401-822-9187 (Municipal); Fax 401-822-9132; *www.town.coventry.ri.us*; *covmuni@town.coventry.ri.us* (Municipal)
> **E. Greenwich Probate Court**, E. Greenwich Town Hall, 125 Main St., PO Box 111, E. Greenwich, RI 02818; Tel. 401-886-8604; Fax 401-886-8625;
> *www.eastgreenwichri.com*
> **Warwick Probate Court**, Warwick City Hall, 3275 Post Rd., Warwick, RI 02886; Tel. 401-738-2000; Fax 401-738-6639;
> *www.warwickri.com*; *Probate.court@warwickri.com*
> **Warwick Municipal Court**, 99 Veterans Memorial Dr., Warwick, RI 02886; Tel. 401-738-2000;
> *www.warwickri.gov*; *municipal.court@warwickri.com*
> **W. Greenwich Probate Court**, W. Greenwich Town Hall, 280 Victory Hwy., W. Greenwich, RI 02817; Tel. 401-392-3800; Fax 401-392-3805; *www.wgtownri.org*
> **W. Warwick Probate Court**, W. Warwick Town Hall, 1170 Main St., W. Warwick, RI 02893-4829; Tel. 401-822-9200; Fax 401-822-9266; *www.westwarwickri.org*

NEWPORT COUNTY

Superior, District and Family Courts

> Florence K. Murray Judicial Complex, 45 Washington Sq., **Newport**, RI 02840
> **Superior**: Tel. 401-841-8330; Fax 401-846-1673
> **District** (2nd Div.): Tel. 401-841-8350
> **Family**: Tel. 401-841-8340

Town Courts

> **Jamestown Probate Court**, Jamestown Town Hall, 93 Narragansett Ave., Jamestown, RI 02835; Tel. 401-423-7200; Fax 401-423-7230; *www.jamestownri.net*
> **Little Compton Probate Court**, Little Compton Town Hall, 40 Commons, PO Box 226, Little Compton, RI 02837; Tel. 401-635-4400; Fax 401-635-2470
> **Middletown Probate Court and Municipal Court**, Middletown Town Hall, 350 E. Main Rd., Middletown, RI 02842; Tel. 401-847-0009; Fax 401-845-0406; *www.middletownri.com*; *townclerk@ci.middletown.ri.us*
> **Newport Probate Court and Municipal Court**, Newport City Hall, 43 Broadway, Newport, RI 02840; Tel. 401-846-9600; Fax 401-849-8757/848-5750; *www.cityofnewport.com*
> **Portsmouth Probate Court**, Portsmouth Town Hall, 2200 E. Main Rd., PO Box 155, Portsmouth, RI 02871; Tel. 401-683-2101; Fax 401-683-6804
> **Tiverton Probate Court and Municipal Court**, Tiverton Town Hall, 343 Highland Rd., Tiverton, RI 02878; Tel. 401-625-6703 (Probate), 6720 (Municipal), Fax 401-625-6705; *www.tiverton.org*; *townclerk@tiverton.org*

PROVIDENCE COUNTY

Superior Court

> Frank Licht Judicial Complex, 250 Benefit St., **Providence**, RI 02903; Tel. 401-222-3250

District Court (6th Div.) and **Family Court**

> Garrahy Judicial Court House, 1 Dorrance Plaza, **Providence**, RI 02903
> **District**: Tel. 401-458-5400
> **Family**: Tel. 401-458-3200 (Domestic)/458-3290 (Juvenile)

Town Courts

> **Burrillville Probate Court**, Burrillville Town Hall, 105 Harrisville Main St., Harrisville, RI 02830; Tel. 401-568-4300; Fax 401-568-0490; *www.burrillville.org*; *townclerk@burrillville.org*
> **Central Falls Probate Court**, Central Falls City Hall, 580 Broad St., Central Falls, RI 02863; Tel. 401-727-7400; Fax 401-727-7406; *www.centralfallsri.us*
> **Cranston Probate Court**, Cranston City Hall, 869 Park Ave. Cranston, RI 02910; Tel. 401-461-1000 x3198; Fax 401-780-3170; *www.cranstonri.com*
> **Cranston Municipal Court**, 275 Atwood Ave., Cranston, RI 02920; Tel. 401-942-2211; *www.cranstonri.com*
> **Cumberland Probate Court and Municipal Court**, Cumberland Town Hall, 45 Broad St., PO Box 7, Cumberland, RI 02864; Tel. 401-728-2400; Fax 401-724-3311; *www.cumberlandri.org*
> **E. Providence Municipal Court**, 610 Waterman Ave., E. Providence, RI 02914; Tel. 401-435-7540; Fax 401-431-4023; *www.eastprovidence.com*
> **E. Providence Probate Court**, E. Providence City Hall, 145 Taunton Ave., E. Providence, RI 02914; Tel. 401-435-7590; Fax 401-435-6530; *www.eastprovidence.com*
> **Foster Probate Court**, Foster Town Hall, 181 Howard Hill Rd., Foster, RI 02825; Tel. 401-392-9200; Fax 401-392-9201
> **Glocester Probate Court**, Glocester Town Hall, 1145 Putnam Pike, PO Box B, Glocester/Chepachet, RI 02814-0702; Tel. 401-568-6206; Fax 401-568-5850; *www.glocesterri.org*
> **Johnston Municipal Court**, 1395 Atwood Ave., Johnston, RI 02919; Tel. 401-946-7150; Fax 401-946-7153; *johnstonmunicipalcourt@yahoo.com*

Johnston Probate Court, Johnston Town Hall, 1385 Hartford Ave., Johnston, RI 02919; Tel. 401-351-6618 (Probate), 946-7150 (Municipal); Fax 401-553-8835

Lincoln Probate Court, Lincoln Town Hall, 100 Old River Rd., PO Box 100, Lincoln, RI 02865; Tel. 401-333-8451; Fax 401-333-3648; *www.lincolnri.org*

N. Providence Probate Court and Municipal Court, N. Providence Town Hall, 2000 Smith St., N. Providence, RI 02911; Tel. 401-232-0900; Fax 401-233-1409; *www.northprovidenceri.com*

N. Smithfield Probate Court, N. Smithfield Town Hall, Municipal Annex, 575 Smithfield Rd., N. Smithfield, RI 02896; Tel. 401-767-2200; Fax 401-356-4057; *www.northsmithfieldri.com*

Pawtucket Probate Court and Municipal Court, Pawtucket City Hall, 137 Roosevelt Ave., Pawtucket, RI 02860; Tel. 401-728-0500; Fax 401-728-8932; *www.pawtucketri.com*

Providence Municipal Court, 25 Washington St., Providence, RI 02903-1726; Tel. 401-272-1111; *www.providenceri.com*

Providence Probate Court, Providence City Hall, 25 Dorrance St., Providence, RI 02903; Tel. 401-421-7740; Fax 401-861-6208; *www.providenceri.com*

Scituate Probate Court, Scituate Town Hall, 195 Danielson Pike, PO Box 328, N. Scituate, RI 02857-0328; Tel. 401-647-2822; Fax 401-647-7220; *www.scituateri.org*; *Scitclerk@aol.com*

Smithfield Probate Court, Smithfield Town Hall, 64 Farnum Pike, Esmond, RI 02917; Tel. 401-233-1000; Fax 401-232-7244; *www.smithfieldri.com*; *clerk@smithfieldri.com*

Woonsocket Probate Court and Municipal Court, 169 Main St., Woonsocket, RI 02895; Tel. 401-767-9248/49 (Probate), 9250 (Municipal); Fax 401-765-0022 (Probate), 766-8368 (Municipal); *www.ci.woonsocket.ri.us*

WASHINGTON COUNTY
Superior, District and Family Courts
McGrath Judicial Complex, 4800 Towerhill Rd., **Wakefield**, RI 02879
Superior: Tel. 401-782-4121
District (4th Div.): Tel. 401-782-4131
Family: Tel. 401-782-4111
Town Courts
Charlestown Probate Court, Charlestown Town Hall, 4540 S. County Trail, Charlestown, RI 02813; Tel. 401-364-1200; Fax 401-364-1238; *www.charlestownri.org*; *clerk@charlestownri.org*

Exeter Probate Court, Exeter Town Hall, 675 Ten Rod Rd., Exeter, RI 02822; Tel. 401-294-3891/295-7500; Fax 401-295-1248; *www.town.exeter.ri.us*; *clerk@town.exeter.ri.us*

Hopkinton Probate Court, Hopkinton Town Hall, 1 Town House Rd., Hopkinton, RI 02833-0038; Tel. 401-377-7777; Fax 401-377-7788

Narragansett Probate Court and Municipal Court, Narragansett Town Hall, 25 5th Ave., Narragansett, RI 02882; Tel. 401-782-0603; Fax 401-783-9637; *www.narragansettri.com/townhall/index.htm*; *Townclerk@NarragansettRI.com*; *Narraclerk@netsense.net*

New Shoreham Probate Court, New Shoreham Town Hall, Old Town Rd., PO Box 220, Block Island, RI 02807; Tel. 401-466-3200; Fax 401-466-3219

N. Kingstown Probate Court, N. Kingstown Town Hall, 80 Boston Neck Rd., N. Kingstown, RI 02852-5762; Tel. 401-294-3331; Fax 401-885-7373; *www.northkingstown.org*

Richmond Probate Court, Richmond Town Hall, 5 Richmond Townhouse Rd., Wyoming, RI 02898; Tel. 401-539-2497; Fax 401-539-1089; *www.richmondri.com*; *townclerk@richmondri.com*

S. Kingstown Probate Court, S. Kingstown Town Hall, 180 High St., Wakefield, RI 02879; Tel. 401-789-9331; Fax 401-788-9792; *www.southkingstownri.com*

Westerly Probate Court and Municipal Court, Westerly Town Hall, 45 Broad St., Westerly, RI 02891; Tel. 401-348-2506 (Probate), 596-7374/348-2535; Fax 401-348-2571 (Probate), 348-2318 (Municipal); *www.townofwesterly.com*

Vermont
www.vermontjudiciary.org

Supreme Court of Vermont
Supreme Court Bldg., 111 State St., Drawer 9, **Montpelier**, VT 05609; Tel. 802-828-3278

Vermont Environmental Court
2418 Airport Rd., **Barre**, VT 05641; Tel. 802-828-1660

ADDISON COUNTY

Superior, District, Family and Probate Courts
7 Mahady Ct., **Middlebury**, VT 05753
Superior: Tel. 802-388-7741; Fax 802-388-4621
District: Tel. 802-388-4237; Fax 802-388-4643
Family: Tel. 802 388 4605; Fax 802 388 4643
Probate: Tel. 802-388-2612

BENNINGTON COUNTY

Superior Court
207 South St., PO Box 4157, **Bennington**, VT 05201; Tel. 802-447-2700; Fax 802-447-2703

District and Family Courts
200 Veterans Memorial Dr., **Bennington**, VT 05201
District: Tel. 802-447-2727; Fax 802-447-2750
Family: Tel. 802-447-2729; Fax 802-447-2794

Probate Court
207 South St., PO Box 65, **Bennington**, VT 05201-0065; Tel. 802-447-2705; *bnprobat@mail.state.vt.us*
PO Box 446, **Manchester**, VT 05254; Tel. 802-447-1410; Fax 802-362-2205

CALEDONIA COUNTY

Superior, District and Family Courts
1126 Main St., Suite #1, **St. Johnsbury**, VT 05819; Tel. 802-748-6600; Fax 802-748-6603

Probate Court
1126 Main St., PO Box 406, **St. Johnsbury**, VT 05819-0406; Tel. 802-748-6605; Fax 802-748-6603

CHITTENDEN COUNTY

Superior Court
175 Main St., PO Box 187, **Burlington**, VT 05402; Tel. 802-863-3467; Fax 802-863-7250; *www.chittendensuperiorcourt.com/index.htm*; *cscourt@vbimail.champlain.edu*

District and Family Courts
32 Cherry St., **Burlington**, VT 05401
District: Tel. 802-651-1800; Fax 802-651-1740
Family: Tel. 802-651-1709; Fax 802-651-1740

Probate Court
175 Main St., PO Box 511, **Burlington**, VT 05402; Tel. 802-651-1518

ESSEX COUNTY

Superior, District and Family Courts
Box 75, **Guildhall**, VT 05905; Tel. 802-676-3910; Fax 802-676-3463

Probate Court
PO Box 426, **Island Pond**, VT 05846; Tel./Fax 802-723-4770

FRANKLIN COUNTY

Superior Court
17 Church St., PO Box 808, **St. Albans**, VT 05478; Tel. 802-524-3863

District and Family Courts

     36 Lake St., **St. Albans**, VT 05478; Tel. 802-524-7997; Fax 802-524-7946

Probate Court

     17 Church St., **St. Albans**, VT 05478; Tel. 802-524-7948

GRAND ISLE COUNTY

Superior, District, Family and Probate Courts

     Courthouse, PO Box 7, **N. Hero**, VT 05474; Tel. 802-372-8350; Fax 802-372-3221

LAMOILLE COUNTY

Superior, District, Family and Probate Courts

     154 Main St., **Hyde Park**, VT 05655

     Superior: PO Box 490; Tel. 802-888-2207; Fax 802-888-1347

     District and Family: PO Box 489; Tel. 802-888-3887; Fax 802-888-2591

     Probate: PO Box 102; Tel. 802-888-3306; Fax 802-888-0669

ORANGE COUNTY

Superior, District, Family and Probate Courts

     5 Court St., **Chelsea**, VT 05038-9746; Tel. 802-685-4610; Fax 802-685-3246

ORLEANS COUNTY

Superior Court

     247 Main St., **Newport**, VT 05855-1203; Tel. 802-334-3344; Fax 802-334-3385

District Court

     217 Main St., **Newport**, VT 05855; Tel. 802-334-3325

Family Court

     247 Main St., **Newport**, VT 05855; Tel. 802-334-3305; Fax 802-334-3385

Probate Court

     247 Main St., **Newport**, VT 05855; Tel. 802-334-3366; Fax 802-334-3385

RUTLAND COUNTY

Superior Court

     83 Center St., **Rutland**, VT 05701; Tel. 802-775-4394

District Court

     92 State St., **Rutland**, VT 05701-2886; Tel. 802-786-5880; Fax 802-786-5888

Family Court

     83 Center St., **Rutland**, VT 05701; Tel. 802-775-5856; Fax 802-775-5871

Probate Court

     3 N. Park Place, **Fair Haven**, VT 05743; Tel. 802-265-3380; Fax 802-265-3380; *fhprobat@mail.crt.state.vt.us*

     83 Center St., **Rutland**, VT 05701; Tel. 802-775-0114

WASHINGTON COUNTY

Superior Court

     65 State St., **Montpelier**, VT 05602-3594; Tel. 802-828-2091

District and Family Courts

     255 N. Main St., **Barre**, VT 05641-4164

     District: Tel. 802-479-4252

     Family: Tel. 802-479-4205; Fax 802-479-4423

Probate Court

     10 Elm St., **Montpelier**, VT 05602; Tel. 802-828-3405

WINDHAM COUNTY

Superior Court

     PO Box 207, **Newfane**, VT 05345; Tel. 802-365-7979; Fax 802-365-4360

District and Family Courts

     30 Putney Rd., **Brattleboro**, VT 05301

     District: Tel. 802-257-2800, 251-2009; Fax 802-257-2853

     Family: Tel. 802-257-2830; Fax 802-257-2869

Probate Court

     Marlboro Probate Court, W. River Rd., PO Box 523, **Brattleboro**, VT 05302; Tel. 802-257-2898

Westminster Probate Court, PO Box 47, **Bellows Falls**, VT 05101-0047; Tel. 802-463-3019; Fax 802-463-0144; *weprobat@mail.state.vt.us*

WINDSOR COUNTY

Superior Court

12 The Green, PO Box 458, **Woodstock**, VT 05091; Tel. 802-457-2121; Fax 802-457-3446

District and Family Courts

82 Railroad Row, **White River Junction**, VT 05001-1962; Tel. 802-295-8865; Fax 802-295-8897

Probate Court

Hartford Probate Court, PO Box 275, **Woodstock**, VT 05091; Tel. 802-457-1503; Fax 802-457-3446

Windsor Probate Court, 65 Rt. 106, Cota Fuel Bldg., PO Box 402, **N. Springfield**, VT 05150, Tel. 802-886-2284; *wrprobat@mail.state.vt.us*

Federal Courts

Connecticut

U.S. Court of Appeals for the Second Circuit (*see* **New York**)

U.S. District Court for the District of Connecticut

www.ctd.uscourts.gov; *CTOpinions@ctd.uscourts.gov*

915 Lafayette Blvd., **Bridgeport**, CT 06604; Tel. 203-579-5861; Fax 203-579-5867

450 Main St., **Hartford**, CT 06103; Tel. 860-240-3200; Fax 860-240-3211

141 Church St., **New Haven**, CT 06510; Tel. 203-773-2140; Fax 203-773-2334

14 Cottage Place, **Waterbury**, CT 06702. (No clerk at Waterbury courthouse. Questions referred to New Haven Clerk.)

U.S. Bankruptcy Court for the District of Connecticut

www.ctb.uscourts.gov

915 Lafayette Blvd., **Bridgeport**, CT 06604; Tel. 203-579-5808

450 Main St., **Hartford**, CT 06103; Tel. 860-240-3675

157 Church St., **New Haven**, CT 06510; Tel. 203-773-2009

Maine

U.S. Court of Appeals for the First Circuit (*see* **Massachusetts**)

U.S. District Court for the District of Maine

www.med.uscourts.gov

156 Federal St., **Portland**, ME 04101; Tel. 207-780-3356; Fax 207-780-3772

202 Harlow St., **Bangor**, ME 04401 (*Mail:* PO Box 1007, Bangor, ME 04402-1007); Tel. 207-945-0575; Fax 207-945-0362

U.S. Bankruptcy Court for the District of Maine

www.meb.uscourts.gov

537 Congress St., **Portland**, ME 04101; (*Mail:* PO Box 17575, Portland, ME 04112-8575); Tel. 207-780-3482; Fax 207-780-3679

202 Harlow St., **Bangor**, ME 04401; (*Mail:* PO Box 1109, Bangor, ME 04402-1109); Tel. 207-945-0348; Fax 207-945-0304

Massachusetts

U.S. Court of Appeals for the First Circuit

1 Courthouse Way, Boston, MA 02210; Tel. 617-748-9057 (Clerk), 748-9567 (Records Room); *www.ca1.uscourts.gov*

U.S. District Court for the District of Massachusetts

www.mad.uscourts.gov

1 Courthouse Way, **Boston**, MA 02210; Tel. 617-748-9152

1550 Main St., **Springfield**, MA 01103; Tel. 413-785-0015

595 Main St., **Worcester**, MA 01608-2076; Tel. 508-929-9900

U.S. Bankruptcy Court for the District of Massachusetts

www.mab.uscourts.gov

1101 Thomas P. O'Neill, Jr. Federal Building, 10 Causeway St., **Boston**, MA 02222-1074; Tel. 617-565-8950; Fax 617-565-6650

595 Main St., **Worcester**, MA 01608-2076; Tel. 508-770-8900; Fax 508-793-0189

New Hampshire

U.S. Court of Appeals for the First Circuit (*see* **Massachusetts**)

U.S. District Court for the District of New Hampshire

55 Pleasant St., **Concord**, NH 03001; Tel. 603-225-1423; *www.nhd.uscourts.gov*

U.S. Bankruptcy Court for the District of New Hampshire

275 Chestnut St., **Manchester**, NH 03101; Tel. 603-222-2600, 666-7626 (Record Room); Fax 603-666-7408; *www.nhb.uscourts.gov*

New York

U.S. Court of Appeals for the Second Circuit

40 Foley Sq., New York, NY 10007; Tel. 212-857-8500; *www.ca2.uscourts.gov*

Rhode Island

U.S. Court of Appeals for the First Circuit (*see* **Massachusetts**)

U.S. District Court for the District of Rhode Island

1 Exchange Terrace, Federal Bldg., **Providence**, RI 02903; Tel. 401-752-7200; Fax 401-752-7247; *www.rid.uscourts.gov*

U.S. Bankruptcy Court for the District of Rhode Island

380 Westminster St., Providence, RI 02903; Tel. 401-528-4477; Fax 401-528-4470; *www.rib.uscourts.gov*

Vermont

U.S. Court of Appeals for the Second Circuit (*see* **New York**)

U.S. District Court for the District of Vermont

www.vtd.uscourts.gov

11 Elmwood Ave., **Burlington**, VT 05401; (*Mail*: PO Box 945, Burlington, VT 05402-0945); Tel. 802-951-6301

151 West St., **Rutland**, VT 05701; (*Mail*: PO Box 607, Rutland, VT 05702-0607); Tel. 802-773-0245

U.S. Bankruptcy Court for the District of Vermont

67 Merchants Row, **Rutland**, VT 05701 (*Mail*: PO Box 6648, Rutland, VT 05702-6648); Tel. 802-776-2000; Fax 802-776-2020; *www.vtb.uscourts.gov*

Washington, D.C.

Supreme Court of the United States

Washington, DC.; *www.supremecourtus.gov*

Archives and Other Repositories

Connecticut

STATE ARCHIVES AND RECORDS CENTER

Connecticut State Library

231 Capitol Ave., Hartford, CT 06106; *www.cslib.org*

Connecticut State Archives

Tel. 860-757-6511; Fax 860-757-6542;

www.cslib.org/archives.htm; *www.cslib.org/judicial.pdf*; *isref@cslib.org*

History and Genealogy, Information Services Division

Tel. 860-757-6580; Fax 860-757-6677; *www.cslib.org/handg.htm*; *H&G@cslib.org*

Law and Legislative Reference Unit

Tel. 860-757-6590; Fax 860-757-6539; *www.cslib.org/llru.htm*

State of Connecticut, Judicial Dept., Superior Court Records Center

111 Phoenix Ave., Enfield, CT 06082; Tel. 860-741-3741; Fax 860-741-2478

STATE HISTORICAL SOCIETY

Connecticut Historical Society

1 Elizabeth St., Hartford, CT 06105; Tel. 860-236-5621;

www.chs.org; *ask_us@chs.org*

OTHER REPOSITORIES

James Blackstone Memorial Library

758 Main St., Branford, CT 06405; Tel. 203-488-1441;

www.blackstonelibrary.org; *library@blackstone.lioninc.org*

Canton Historical Museum

11 Front St., Collinsville, CT 06019; Tel. 860-693-2793; *www.cantonmuseum.org*

Cornwall Historical Society

7 Pine St., Box 115, Cornwall, CT 06753

Danbury Historical Society

43 Main St., Danbury, CT 06810; Tel. 203-743-5200; Fax 203-743-1131;

www.danburyhistorical.org; dmhs@danburyhistorical.org

E. Granby Public Library

PO Box G, E. Granby, CT 06026; Tel. 860-653-3002

Fairfield Historical Society

636 Old Post Rd., Fairfield, CT 06824; Tel. 203-259-1598; Fax 203-255-2716;

www.fairfieldhistoricalsociety.org; *info@fairfieldhs.org*

Guilford Keeping Society

PO Box 363, 171 Boston St., Guilford, CT 06437; Tel. 203-453-3167;

www.guilfordkeepingsociety.com; info@guilfordkeepingsociety.com

Historical Society of Glastonbury

Museum on the Green, 1944 Main St., PO Box 46, Glastonbury, CT 06033; Tel./Fax.

860-633-6890; *http://town.glasct.org/hissoc/index.html; HSGlastonbury@netzero.net*

Killingly Historical Society

196 Main St., Danielson, CT 06239; Tel. 860-779-7250;

www.killinglyhistory.org; information@killinglyhistory.org

Litchfield Historical Society

7 South St., PO Box 385, Litchfield, CT 06759; Tel. 860-567-4501; Fax 860-567-

3565; *www.litchfieldhistoricalsociety.org*; *archivist@litchfieldhistoricalsociety.org*

Mansfield Historical Society

PO Box 145, Storrs, CT 06268; Tel. 860-429-6575; *http://mansfield-history.org*;

info@mansfield-history.org

Mashantucket Pequot Museum and Research Center

Archives and Special Collections, 110 Pequot Trail, PO Box 3180, Mashantucket, CT

06338-3180; Tel. 860-396-7001; *www.pequotmuseum.org; Archive@mptn.org*

Middlesex County Historical Society

151 Main St., Middletown, CT 06457; Tel. 860-346-0746

Mystic River Historical Society

74 High St., PO Box 245, Mystic, CT 06355-0245; Tel. 860-536-4779;

www.mystichistory.org; info@mystichistory.org

Mystic Seaport, The Museum of America and the Sea
>G. W. Blunt White Library, Manuscripts and Archives, 75 Greenmanville Ave., PO Box 6000, Mystic, CT 06355-0990; Tel. 860-572-0711; Fax 860-572-5394; *www.mysticseaport.org*

New Hartford Historical Society
>367 Main St., Pine Meadow, CT 06061 (*Mail*: PO Box 41, New Hartford, CT 06057); Tel. 860-379-6894

New Haven Colony Historical Society
>14 Whitney Ave., New Haven, CT 06510; Tel. 203-562-4183; Fax 203-562-2002

New London County Historical Society
>11 Blinman St., New London, CT 06320; Tel. 860-443-1209; *www.newlondonhistory.org*; *info@newlondonhistory.org*

Russell Library
>123 Broad St., Middletown, CT 06457; Tel. 860-347-2528; *http://russelllibrary.org*; *infodept@russell.lioninc.org*

Salmon Brook Historical Society
>208 Salmon Brook St., PO Box 840, Granby, CT 06035; Tel. 860-653-9713; *www.salmonbrookhistorical.org*

Sharon Historical Society
>Gay-Hoyt House Museum, 18 Main St., PO Box 511, Sharon, CT 06069-0511; Tel. 860-364-5688; *www.sharonhist.org*; *director@sharonhist.org.*

Simsbury Historical Society
>800 Hopmeadow St., PO Box 2, Simsbury, CT 06070; Tel. 860-658-2500; *www.simsburyhistory.org; info@simsburyhistory.org; SHSLibrarian@aol.com*

Somers Historical Society, Inc.
>11 Battle St., PO Box 652, Somers, CT 06071; Tel. 860-749-6437, 749-6311; Fax 860-749-0753; *www.SomersNow.com/HistoricalSociety; HistoricalSociety@SomersNow.com*

Stonington Historical Society
>R. W. Woolworth Library, PO Box 103, 40 Palmer St. , Stonington, CT 06378; Tel. 860-535-8445, 535-1131 (Library); *www.stoningtonhistory.org; stonhistlib@snet.net; library@stoningtonhistory.org*

Trumbull Historical Society
>1856 Huntington Turnpike (Rt. 108), PO Box 312, Trumbull, CT 06611-0312; Tel. 203-377-6620; *www.trumbullhistory.org*

University of Connecticut
>Thomas J. Dodd Research Center, Archives & Special Collections, 405 Babbidge Rd., Unit 1205, Storrs, CT 06269-1205; Tel. 860-468-4500; *www.lib.uconn.edu/online/research/speclib/ASC*

Windsor Historical Society
>96 Palisado Ave., Windsor, CT 06095; Tel. 860-688-3813; Fax 860-687-1633; *www.windsorhistoricalsociety.org; info@windsorhistoricalsociety.org*

Woodstock Historical Society
>523 Scenic Rt. 169, PO Box 65, Woodstock, CT 06281; Tel. 860-928-1035; *www.woodstockhistoricalsociety.org*

Yale University
>Beinecke Rare Book & Manuscript Library, 121 Wall St., PO Box 208240, New Haven, CT 06520-2840; Tel. 203-432-2972; Fax 203-432-4047; *www.library.yale.edu/beinecke*; *Beinecke.Library@yale.edu*

Yale Law School
>Lillian Goldman Law Library, Sterling Law Bldg., 127 Wall St., PO Box 208215, New Haven, CT 06520; Tel. 203-432-1606 (Reference); *www.law.yale.edu/library; lawref@pantheon.yale.edu*

Delaware

Hagley Museum and Library

> Manuscripts & Archives Dept., 298 Buck Rd. E., Wilmington, DE 19807-0630; Tel. 302-658-0545; *www.hagley.lib.de.us*

Illinois

University of Chicago

> Joseph Regenstein Library, 1100 E. 57th St., Chicago, IL 60637; Tel. 773-702-4685; *www.lib.uchicago.edu/e/reg*

Maine

STATE ARCHIVES

Maine State Archives

> Cultural Bldg., 84 State House Station, Augusta, ME 04333-0084; Tel. 207-287-5790; Fax 207-287-5739; *www.maine.gov/sos/arc*

STATE HISTORICAL SOCIETY

Maine Historical Society

> 485 Congress St., Portland, ME 04101; Tel. 207-774-1822; Fax 207-775-4301; *www.mainehistory.com*; *www.mainehistory.org/library_search.shtml* (online library catalog); *rdesk@mainehistory.org*

OTHER REPOSITORIES

Androscoggin Historical Society

> Androscoggin County Bldg., 2 Turner St., Court St. Door, Auburn, ME 04210-5978; Tel. 207-784-0586; *www.rootsweb.com/~meandrhs*; *androhs@verizon.net*

Bangor Museum & Center for History

> 6 State St., Bangor, ME 04401; Tel. 207-942-1900; Fax 207-941-0266; *www.bangormuseum.org*; *info@bangormuseum.org*

Boothbay Region Historical Society

> 72 Oak St., PO Box 272, Boothbay Harbor, ME 04538-0272; Tel. 207-633-0820; *www.boothbayhistorical.org*; *brhs@gwi.net*

Dover-Foxcroft Historical Society

> 28 Orchard Rd., Dover-Foxcroft, ME 04426; *www.geocities.com/dfhistory*; *dfhistorical@yahoo.com*

Freeport Historical Society

> 45 Main St., Freeport, ME 04032; Tel. 207-865-3170; *www.freeporthistoricalsociety.org*; *info@freeporthistoricalsociety.org*

Hamlin Memorial Library

> Hannibal Hamlin Dr., PO Box 43, Paris, ME 04271; Tel. 207-743-2980; *www.sad17.k12.me.us/libraries/paris.htm*; *amcdonald@hamlin.lib.me.us*

Hampden Historical Society

> PO Box 456, Hampden, ME 04444; Tel. 207-862-2027

Jefferson Historical Society

> 430 Sennett Rd., Jefferson, ME 04348; Tel. 207-549-3415

New Gloucester Historical Society

> PO Box 531, New Gloucester, ME 04260

Old Berwick Historical Society

> The Counting House, PO Box 296, S. Berwick, ME 03908; Tel. 207-384-0000; *www.obhs.net/Museum.html; info@obhs.net*

Old York Historical Society

> 207 York St., PO Box 312, York, ME 03909-0312; Tel. 207-363-4974; Fax 207-363-4021; *www.oldyork.org*; *oyhs@oldyork.org*

Pejepscot Historical Society

> 159 Park Row, Brunswick, ME 04011; Tel. 207-729-6606; Fax 207-729-6012; *www.curtislibrary.com/pejepscot.htm*; *pejepscot@gwi.net*; *phs@suscom-maine.net*

Poland Historical Society
>1229 Maine St., Poland, ME 04274

Sanford Historical Committee
>c/o Sanford-Springvale Historical Society, 919 Main St., Sanford, ME 04073; *www.sanfordhistory.org; pauger@sanford.org* (include "Sanford Historical Committee" in subject of email)

Standish Historical Society
>55 Oak Hill Rd., PO Box 28, Standish, ME 04084; Tel. 207-642-5170

Thomaston Historical Society
>Knox St., PO Box 384, Thomaston, ME 04861; Tel. 207-354-8835; *www.thomastonhistoricalsociety.com*; *katsmeow@adelphia.net*

University of Maine at Orono
>Special Collections, 5729 Raymond H. Fogler Library, Orono, ME 04469-5729; Tel. 207-581-1661; Fax 207-581-1653; *www.library.umaine.edu*

Windham Historical Society
>22 Montgomery Rd., Windham, ME 04062; *www.rootsweb.com/~mewhs*; *mainegen@aol.com*

Winter Harbor Historical Society
>PO Box 93, Winter Harbor, ME 04693; Tel. 207-963-7244

Maryland

FEDERAL ARCHIVES

U.S. National Archives and Records Administration (NARA) at College Park
>8601 Adelphi Rd., College Park, MD 20740-6001; Tel. 866-272-6272, 301-713-6800; *www.archives.gov/facilities/md/archives_2.html*

Massachusetts

STATE ARCHIVES AND LIBRARY

Massachusetts Archives
>Columbia Point, 220 Morrissey Blvd., Boston, MA 02125; Tel. 617-727-2816; Fax 617-288-8429; *www.sec.state.ma.us/arc/arcidx.htm; archives@sec.state.ma.us.* For questions re: **Judicial Archives** (located at the Massachusetts Archives), contact: Head of Archives, Supreme Judicial Court, Div. of Archives Records Preservation, 3 Pemberton Sq. High Rise, 16th Flr., Boston, MA 02108-1701; Tel. 617-577-1082

State Library of Massachusetts
>George Fingold Library, State House Rm. 341, Boston, MA 02133; Tel. 617-727-2590; Fax 617-727-5819; *www.mass.gov/lib*; *Reference.Department@state.ma.us*

FEDERAL ARCHIVES

U.S. National Archives and Records Administration (NARA), Northeast Region-Waltham (Boston)
>Frederick C. Murphy Federal Center, 380 Trapelo Rd., Waltham, MA 02452-6399; Tel. 781-663-0130, 866-406-2379, 866-329-6465 (court records); Fax 781-663-0154; *www.archives.gov/northeast/waltham*; *www.archives.gov/research/arc* (online catalog); *waltham.archives@nara.gov*; *waltham courts@nara.gov*

U.S. National Archives and Records Administration, Northeast Region-Pittsfield
>10 Conte Dr., Pittsfield, MA 01201-8230; Tel. 413-236-3600; Fax 413-236-3609; *www.archives.gov/northeast/pittsfield; pittsfield.archives@nara.gov*

STATE HISTORICAL SOCIETY

Massachusetts Historical Society
>1154 Boylston St., Boston, MA 02215; Tel. 617-536-1608; Fax 617-859-0074; *www.masshist.org*

OTHER REPOSITORIES

American Antiquarian Society
>185 Salisbury St., Worcester, MA 01609-1634; Tel. 508-755-5221; Fax 508-753-3311; *www.americanantiquarian.org*

American Textile History Museum
> Osborne Library, Manuscript Collection, 491 Dutton St., Lowell, MA 01854; Tel. 978-441-0400; Fax 978-441-1412; *www.athm.org*

Berkshire Athenaeum
> Pittsfield Public Library, 1 Wendell Ave., Pittsfield, MA 01201-6385; Tel. 413-499-9488; Fax 413-499-9489;
> *www.berkshire.net/PittsfieldLibrary/index.html*; *pittsref@cwmars.org*

Bolton Historical Society
> Box 211, 676 Main St., Bolton, MA 01740-1306; Tel. 978-779-6495

Boston Athenaeum
> 10¹/₂ Beacon St., Boston, MA 02108-3777; Tel. 617-227-0270;
> *www.bostonathenaeum.org*; *reference@bostonathenaeum.org*

Boston College Law School Library
> 885 Centre St., Newton Centre, MA 02459; Tel. 617-552-4434;
> *www.bc.edu/schools/law/library*

Boston University Law School Library
> 765 Commonwealth Ave., Boston, MA 02215; Tel. 617-353-3151; Fax 617-353-5995; *www.bu.edu/lawlibrary*

Boston Historical Society and Museum
> 206 Washington St., Boston, MA 02109; Tel. 617-720-1713; Fax 617-720-3289; *www.bostonhistory.org*; *library@bostonhistory.org*

Boston Public Library
> 700 Boylston St., Boston, MA 02116; Tel. 617-536-5400; *www.bpl.org*; *info@bpl.org*

Bourne Archives
> Jonathan Bourne Historical Center, 30 Keene St., Bourne, MA 02532; Tel. 508-759-8167; *www.bournehistoricalsoc.org/histctr.htm*

Cape Cod Community College
> Library-Learning Resources Center, 2240 Iyanough Rd, W. Barnstable, MA 02668; Tel. 508-362-2131; *www.capecod.mass.edu*

Concord Free Public Library
> Special Collections, 129 Main St., Concord, MA 01742; Tel. 978-318-3300; *www.concordnet.org/library*

Dedham Historical Society
> Box 215, 612 High St., Dedham, MA 02027-0215; Tel. 781-326-1385;
> *www.DedhamHistorical.org*; *Society@DedhamHistorical.org*

Falmouth Historical Society
> PO Box 174, 55-65 Palmer Ave. Falmouth, MA 02541;
> *www.falmouthhistoricalsociety.org*; *Archives@cape.com*

Fitchburg Historical Society
> 50 Grove St., PO Box 953, Fitchburg, MA 01420; Tel. 978-345-1157; Fax 978-345-2229; *http://fitchburghistory.fsc.edu*; *FitchburgHistory@verizon.net*

City of Gloucester, Massachusetts, Archives Committee
> City Hall, 9 Dale Ave., Gloucester, MA 01930; Tel. 978-282-3043; Fax 978-281-8472; *www.gloucester-ma.gov; archives@ci.gloucester.ma.us*

Harvard University
> **Harvard Business School, Baker Library**, Historical Collections, Soldiers Field, Boston, MA 02163; Tel. 617-495-6411; *www.library.hbs.edu*; *histcollref@hbs.edu*
> **Harvard Law School Library**, Langdell Hall, 1545 Massachusetts Ave., Cambridge, MA 02138; Tel. 617-495-3170; *www.law.harvard.edu/library*
> **Houghton Library**, Dept. of Manuscripts, Cambridge, MA 02138; Tel. 617-495-2449; Fax 617-495-1376; *http://hcl.harvard.edu/houghton*;
> *Houghton_Manuscripts@harvard.edu*
> **Lamont Library**, Harvard Yard, Cambridge, MA 02138; Tel. 617-495-2451; Fax 617-496-3692; *http://hcl.harvard.edu/lamont*; *lamref@fas.harvard.edu*

Widener Library, Harvard Yard, Cambridge, MA 02138; Tel. 617-495-2411;
http://hcl.harvard.edu/widener
Hingham Historical Society
PO Box 434, Hingham, MA 02043; Tel. 617-749-7721
Historic Northampton Museum & Education Center
46 Bridge St., Northampton, MA 01060; Tel. 413-584-6011; Fax 413-584-7956;
www.historic-northampton.org
Lexington Historical Society
PO Box 514, Lexington, MA 02420; Tel. 781-862-1703; Fax 781-862-4920;
www.lexingtonhistory.org; *info@lexingtonhistory.org*
Lincoln Public Library
Bedford Rd., Lincoln, MA 01773; Tel. 781-259-8465; Fax 781-259-1056;
www.lincolnpl.org; *esisco@minlib.net*
Lynn Museum & Historical Society
Lynn Heritage State Park, 590 Washington St., Lynn, MA 01901; Tel. 781-592-2465;
Fax 781-592-0012; *www.lynnmuseum.org*
Martha's Vineyard Historical Society
Huntington Reference Library, PO Box 1310, Edgartown, MA 02539;
www.marthasvineyardhistory.org; info@marthasvineyardhistory.org;
mvhist@vineyard.net
Memorial Libraries
PO Box 53, Deerfield, MA 01342; Tel. 413-775-7125; Fax 413-775-7223;
http://library.historic-deerfield.org; *library@historic-deerfield.org*
Nantucket Historical Association Research Library
PO Box 1016, 7 Fair St., Nantucket, MA 02554; Tel. 508-228-1655; Fax 508-325-
7968; *www.nha.org*
Newburyport Archival Center
Newburyport Public Library, 94 State St., Newburyport, MA 01950; Tel. 978-465-
4428, x229; Fax 978-463-0394; *www.newburyportpl.org/archival.html*
New England Historic Genealogical Society
R. Stanton Avery Special Collections Dept., 101 Newbury St., Boston, MA 02116-
3007; Tel. 617-536-5740; *www.NewEnglandAncestors.org*
N. Andover Historical Society
153 Academy Rd., N. Andover, MA 01845; Tel. 978-686-4035; Fax 978-686-6616;
*www.essexheritage.org/visiting/placestovisit/listofsitesbycommunity/north_andover_*
hist_soc.shtml; nahistory@juno.com
Old Colony Historical Society
66 Church Green, Taunton, MA 02780; Tel. 508-822-1622;
www.oldcolonyhistoricalsociety.org; Oldcolony@oldcolonyhistoricalsociety.org
Old Dartmouth Historical Society, New Bedford Whaling Museum
Kendall Institute, Research Library, 18 Johnny Cake Hill, New Bedford, MA 02740-
6398; Tel. 508-997-0046; Fax 508-997-1018, 994-4350 (Library);
www.whalingmuseum.org
Peabody-Essex Museum, Phillips Library
E. India Sq., 132 Essex St., Salem, MA 01970; Tel. 978-745-9500/800-745-4054;
www.pem.org/museum/library.php. Fees waived for probate searches only.
Plymouth County Commissioner
11 S. Russell St., Plymouth, MA 02360
Shelburne Historical Society
PO Box 86, Shelburne Falls, MA 01370; Tel. 413-625-6150;
www.merrill.olm.net/shs; *merrill@crocker.com*
Social Law Library
Joan Adams Courthouse, 1 Pemberton Sq., Boston, MA 02108-1792; Tel. 617-226-
1500; Fax 617-523-2458; *www.sociallaw.com*

Stockbridge Library Association
>   Main St., PO Box 119, Stockbridge, MA 01262-0119; Tel. 413-298-5501; Fax 413-298-0218

Supreme Judicial Court Historical Society
>   1200 New Court House, Boston, Massachusetts 02108; Tel. 617-742-6090; *www.sjchs-history.org*

Topsfield Historical Society
>   1 Howlett St., PO Box 323, Topsfield, MA 01983; Tel. 978-887-3998; *www.topsfieldhistory.org*; *webmaster@topsfieldhistory.org*

University of Massachusetts, Amherst
>   W. E. B. Du Bois Library, Special Collections & Archives, Amherst, MA 01003; Tel. 413-545-2780; Fax 413-577-1399; *www.library.umass.edu/spcoll/spec.html*; *askanarc@library.umass.edu*

University of Massachusetts, Boston
>   Healey Library, Archives & Special Collections, 100 Morrissey Blvd., Boston, MA 02125-3393; Tel. 617-287-5940; *www.lib.umb.edu*

Waltham Public Library
>   735 Main St., Waltham, MA 02451; Tel. 781-314-3425; Fax 781-314-3439; *www.waltham.lib.ma.us*

Wayland Historical Society
>   12 Cochituate Rd., PO Box 56, Wayland, MA 01778; Tel. 508-358-7959; *http://j.w.d.home.comcast.net/whs*

Wellesley Historical Society
>   Dadmun-McNamara House, 229 Washington St., PO Box 81142, Wellesley Hills, MA 02481-0001; Tel. 617-235-6690; Fax 617-239-0660; *www.wellesleyhsoc.com*

Westford Museum & Historical Society
>   2-4 Boston Rd., Westford, MA 01886; Tel/Fax 978-692-5550; *www.westford.com/museum/index.shtml*; *museum@westford.com*

Westford (Town of)
>   Town Clerk, 55 Main St., Westford, MA 01886; Tel. 978-692-5515; Fax 978-399-2555

Westminster Historical Society
>   PO Box 177, 110 Main St., Westminster, MA 01473-1444; Tel./Fax 978-874-0544; *www.westminsterhistoricalsociety.org*; *curator@westminsterhistoricalsociety.org*

Weston Historical Society Museum
>   Josiah Smith Tavern, PO Box 343, 626 Boston Post Road, Weston, MA 02193; Tel. 781-893-8870

Winthrop Public Library & Museum
>   2 Metcalf Sq., Winthrop, MA 02152; Tel. 617-846-1703

New Hampshire

STATE ARCHIVES

New Hampshire Division of Archives and Records Management
>   71 S. Fruit St., Concord, NH 03301; Tel. 603-271-2236; Fax 603-271-2272; *www.sos.nh.gov/archives/default.html*; *archives@sos.state.nh.us*

STATE HISTORICAL SOCIETY

New Hampshire Historical Society
>   Tuck Library, 30 Park St., Concord, NH 03301-6384; Tel. 603-228-6688; Fax 602-224-0463; *www.nhhistory.org*; *library@nhhistory.org*

OTHER REPOSITORIES

Chesterfield Historical Society
>   PO Box 204, Main St. (Rt. 63), Chesterfield, NH 03443; Tel. 603-636-8018

Dartmouth College Library
>   Hanover, NH 03755-3525; Tel. 603-646-2560; *http://diglib.dartmouth.edu*

Goffstown Historical Society
>   PO Box 284, 18 Parker Station Rd., Goffstown, NH 03045; Tel. 603-497-4306

Hampton Historical Society
>   Tuck Museum, Meeting House Green, 40 Park Ave., PO Box 1601, Hampton, NH 03843-1601; Tel. 603-929-0781; *www.hamptonhistoricalsociety.org*; *info@hamptonhistoricalsociety.org*

Historical Society of Cheshire County
>   PO Box 803, 246 Main St., Keene, NH 03431; Tel. 603-352-1895; *www.hsccnh.org*; *hscc@hsccnh.org*

Historical Society of Seabrook
>   PO Box 500, 109 Washington St., Seabrook, NH 03874; Tel. 603-474-3538

Kensington Historical Society
>   c/o Kensington Public Library, 126 Amesbury Rd., Kensington, NH 03833; Tel. 603-772-5022

Laconia Historical and Museum Society
>   PO Box 1126, Laconia, NH 03247; Tel. 603-527-1278; Fax 603-527-1277; *lhm-slpl@metrocast.net*

Manchester City Archives & Records Center
>   City Clerk, 1 City Hall Plaza, Manchester, NH 03101; Tel. 603-624-6455; Fax 603-624-6481; *http://ci.manchester.nh.us/CityGov/CLK/archives/home.html; CityClerk@ci.manchester.nh.us*

New Hampshire Law Library
>   Supreme Court Bldg., 1 Noble Dr., Concord, NH 03301; Tel. 603-271-3777; Fax 603-271-2168; *www.courts.state.nh.us/lawlibrary/index.htm*

Portsmouth Athenaeum
>   9 Market Sq., Portsmouth, NH 03801; Tel. 603-431-2538; Fax 603-431-7180; *athenaeum@juno.com*

Rye Historical Society
>   PO Box 583, 10 Old Parish Rd., Rye, NH 03870; Tel. 603-964-7730

University of New Hampshire Library
>   Milne Special Collections & Archives, 18 Library Way, Durham, NH 03824; Tel. 603-862-2714; Fax 603-862-1919; *www.izaak.unh.edu; library.special.collections@unh.edu; archives@unhh.unh.edu*

New York

FEDERAL ARCHIVES

U.S. National Archives and Records Administration (NARA), Northeast Region–New York
>   201 Varick St., 12th Flr., New York, NY 10014; Tel. 212-401-1620; Fax 212-401-1638; *www.archives.gov/northeast/nyc/new_york.html*; *newyork.archives@nara.gov*

OTHER REPOSITORIES

Oyster Bay Historical Society
>   PO Box 297, 20 Summit St., Oyster Bay, NY 11771-0297; Tel. 516-922-5032; Fax 516-922-6892; *http://members.aol.com/OBHistory/index.html*; *OBHistory@aol.com*

Syracuse University Law Library
>   222 Waverly Ave., Syracuse, NY 13244; Tel. 315-443-2093; *www.law.syr.edu/lawlibrary*

Ohio

Western Reserve Historical Society Library
>   10825 East Blvd., Cleveland, OH 44106-1788; Tel. 216-721-5722; *www.wrhs.org/library*; *reference@wrhs.org*

Pennsylvania

American Philosophical Society Library
> 105 S. 5th St., Philadelphia, PA 19106-3386; Tel. 215-440-3400;
> *www.amphilsoc.org/library*

Rosenbach Museum & Library
> 2008-2010 Delancey Place, Philadelphia, PA 19103; Tel. 215-732-1600;
> *www.rosenbach.org*; *info@rosenbach.org*

University of Pennsylvania
> Van Pelt Library, 3420 Walnut St., Philadelphia, PA 19104-6206; Tel. 215-898-7556;
> *www.library.upenn.edu/vanpelt; library@pobox.upenn.edu*

Rhode Island

STATE ARCHIVES, RECORDS CENTER AND LIBRARY

Rhode Island, Supreme Judicial Court, Judicial Records Center
> 5 Hill St., Pawtucket, RI 02860; Tel. 401-721-2640; Fax 401-721-2653;
> *www.courts.ri.gov/records/forms.htm*; *www.courts.ri.gov/records/locations.htm;*
> *archives@courts.state.ri.us*

Rhode Island State Archives
> 337 Westminster St., Providence, RI 02903; Tel. 401-222-2353; Fax 401-222-3199;
> *www.sec.state.ri.us/archives*; *reference@sec.state.ri.us*

Rhode Island State Law Library
> Frank Licht Judicial Complex, 250 Benefit St., Providence, RI 02903; Tel. 401-222-
> 3275; Fax 401-222-3865; *www.courts.state.ri.us/library/defaultlibrary.htm*

STATE HISTORICAL SOCIETY

Rhode Island Historical Society
> Research Library, 121 Hope St., Providence, RI 02906; Tel. 401-273-8109; Fax 401-
> 751-7930; *www.rihs.org/libraryhome.htm*

OTHER REPOSITORIES

Brown University Library, Special Collections Department
> Box A, John Hay Library, 20 Prospect St., Providence, RI 02912; Tel. 401-863-3723;
> Fax 401-863-2093;
> *www.brown.edu/Facilities/University_Library/libs/hay*; *hay@brown.edu*

E. Providence Historical Society
> John Hunt House Museum, Hunts Mills Rd., PO Box 4774, E. Providence, RI 02916;
> Tel. 401-438-1750; *http://ephist.org; info@ephist.org*

Newport Historical Society
> 82 Touro St., Newport, RI 02840; Tel. 401-846-0813; Fax 401-846-1853;
> *www.newporthistorical.org*

Pettaquamscutt Historical Society
> 2636 Kingstown Rd., Kingston, RI 02881; Tel. 401-783-1328;
> *www.freewebs.com/pettaquamscutt; pettaquamscutt@yahoo.com*

Providence City Archives
> City Hall, City Clerk, 25 Dorrance St., Providence, RI 02903; Tel. 401-421-7740;
> *www.providenceri.com/government/citydir.html*

Providence College
> Phillips Memorial Library, 549 River Av., Providence, RI 02918-0001; Tel. 401-865-
> 2581; *www.providence.edu/Academics/Phillips+Memorial+Library*

University of Rhode Island Library
> 15 Lippitt Rd., Kingston, RI 02881-0803; Tel. 401-874-2594, 4632; Fax 401-874-
> 4608; *www.uri.edu/library/special_collections*

Vermont

STATE ARCHIVES AND RECORDS CENTER

Vermont State Archives, Vermont Judicial Records Program
> Redstone Bldg., 26 Terrace St., Montpelier, VT 05609-1135; Tel. 802-828-2397 or
> 802-828-2308; *www.vermont-archives.org*

Vermont Dept. of Buildings & General Services, Records Center
US Rt. 2, Middlesex, Drawer 33, Montpelier, VT 05633-7601; Tel. 802-828-1005; Fax 802-828-3710; *www.bgs.state.vt.us/gsc/pubrec/referen/index.html*; *bgs-recordscenter@state.vt.us*

STATE HISTORICAL SOCIETY
Vermont Historical Society
Vermont History Center, 60 Washington St., Barre, VT 05641-4209; Tel. 802-479-8500; Fax 802-479-8510; *www.vermonthistory.org*; *library@vhs.state.vt.us*

OTHER REPOSITORIES
Billings Farm and Museum
Woodstock Foundation, Inc., Rt. 12 & River Rd., Woodstock, VT 05091-0489; Tel. 802-475-2355; Fax 802-457-4663; *www.billingsfarm.org; billings.farm@valley.net*

Brattleboro Historical Society
PO Box 6392, Brattleboro, VT 05301-6392; Tel. 802-258-4957

Dorset Historical Society
PO Box 52, Dorset, VT 05251; Tel. 802-867-0331

Martha Canfield Library
P. O. Box 267, 528 E. Arlington Rd., Arlington, VT 05250; Tel. (802) 375-6153; *russell_vermontiana_collection@hotmail.com*

Middlebury College Library
110 Storrs Ave., Middlebury, VT 05753; Tel. 802-443-5494; Fax 802-443-5698; *www.middlebury.edu/academics/lis/lib*

Orleans County Historical Society, Inc.
28 Old Stone House Rd., Brownington, VT 05860-9557; Tel. 802-754-2022; *oldstonehousemuseum.org; information@oldstonehousemuseum.org*

Shaftsbury Historical Society
PO Box 401, Shaftsbury, VT 05262

Henry Sheldon Museum of Vermont History
Stewart-Swift Research Center, 1 Park St., Middlebury, VT 05753; Tel. 802-388-2117; *www.henrysheldonmuseum.org*; *info@henrysheldonmuseum.org*

Shoreham Town Clerk's Office
297 Main St., Shoreham, VT 05770; Tel. 802-897-5841; Fax 897-2545

University of Vermont
Bailey/Howe Library, Burlington, VT 05405-0036; Tel. 802-656-2022; *http://library.uvm.edu*; *bhref@uvm.edu*

Vermont Department of Libraries
Law Library, 109 State St., Montpelier, VT 05609-0601; Tel. 802-828-3268; Fax 802-828-1481; *http://dol.state.vt.us*

Virginia

University of Virginia Library
Special Collections, PO Box 400113, Charlottesville, VA 22904-4113; Tel. 434-924-3021; Fax 434-924-1431; *www.lib.virginia.edu*

Washington, D. C.

FEDERAL ARCHIVES
U.S. National Archives and Records Administration (NARA)
700 Pennsylvania Ave., NW, Washington, DC 20408; Tel. 866-325-7208, 202-501-5400; *www.archives.gov/dc-metro/washington/index.html*

OTHER REPOSITORIES
Library of Congress
101 Independence Ave., SE, Washington, DC 20540; Tel. 202-707-5000;

www.loc.gov; *www.loc.gov/rr/askalib* ("Ask a Librarian" online reference service); *http://catalog.loc.gov* (online catalog)

U.S. Citizenship and Immigration Services, U.S. Department of Homeland Security

Washington, D.C. Freedom of Information/Privacy Act (FOIA/PA) request: For naturalization records 1906-1956, contact: Director, Freedom of Information Act/Privacy Act Program, 111 Massachusetts Ave., N.W., 2nd Floor, ULLICO Bldg., Washington, DC 20529; Tel. 202-272-8269

For naturalization records after 1956, contact district office that maintains records, or office near your home: *http://uscis.gov/graphics/aboutus/foia/ADDRESS.HTM*

Law Libraries

Many law libraries offer access to computer databases such as *Westlaw* or *LexisNexis*, and to other published appellate case reporters and digests. This Appendix lists public law libraries in the New England states (most located at courthouses), and other selected libraries with legal collections (where restrictions on access may apply). Researchers may also find legal reference resources at general public libraries and at law libraries in other states. Contact a librarian first to determine access requirements and availability of research materials.

Connecticut

STATE LIBRARY

Connecticut State Library

Law and Legislative Reference Unit, 231 Capitol Ave., **Hartford**, CT 06106; Tel. 860-757-6590; Fax 860-757-6539; *www.cslib.org*; *www.cslib.org/llru.htm*; *isref@cslib.org*

COURTHOUSE LAW LIBRARIES

1061 Main St., **Bridgeport**, CT 06604; Tel. 203-579-6237; Fax 203-579-6512

146 White St., **Danbury**, CT 06810; Tel. 203-207-8625; Fax 203-207-8627

95 Washington St., **Hartford**, CT 06106; Tel. 860-548-2866; Fax 860-548-2868

15 West St., **Litchfield**, CT 06759; Tel. 860-567-0598; Fax 860-567-4533

1 Court St., **Middletown**, CT 06457; Tel. 860-343-6560; Fax 860-343-6568

14 W. River St., **Milford**, CT 06460; Tel. 203-283-8235; Fax 203-283-8267

20 Franklin Sq., **New Britain**, CT 06051; Tel. 860-515-5110; Fax 860-515-5111

235 Church St., **New Haven**, CT 06510; Tel. 203-503-6828; Fax 203-789-6499

70 Huntington St., **New London**, CT 06320; Tel. 860-442-7561; Fax 860-442-9416

1 Courthouse Sq., **Norwich**, CT 06360; Tel. 860-887-2398; Fax 860-823-1752

155 Church St., **Putnam**, CT 06260; Tel. 860-928-3716; Fax 860-963-7531

69 Brooklyn St., **Rockville**, CT 06066; Tel. 860-896-4955; Fax 860-875-3213

123 Hoyt St., **Stamford**, CT 06905; Tel. 203-965-5250; Fax 203-965-5784

300 Grand St., **Waterbury**, CT 06702; Tel. 203-591-3338; Fax 203-596-4317

108 Valley St., **Willimantic**, CT 06226; Tel. 860-450-0627; Fax 860-423-0772

OTHER LAW LIBRARIES

Quinnipiac University School of Law Library

275 Mt. Carmel Ave., **Hamden**, CT 06518-1951; Tel. 203-582-3303; *http://law.quinnipiac.edu/x24.xml*; *lawlibrary@quinnipiac.edu*

University of Connecticut School of Law Library

39 Elizabeth St., **Hartford**, CT 06105; Tel. 860-570-5200; *www.law.uconn.edu/library*

Yale Law School, Lillian Goldman Law Library

Sterling Law Bldg., 127 Wall St., PO Box 208215, **New Haven**, CT 06520; Tel. 203-432-1606; *www.law.yale.edu/library*; *lawref@pantheon.yale.edu*

Maine

STATE LIBRARY
Maine State Library
>230 State St., **Augusta**, ME 04333-0064; (*Mail*: 64 State House Station, Augusta, ME 04333-0064); Tel. 207-287-5600; *www.state.me.us/msl*; *reference.desk@maine.gov*

Maine State Law and Legislative Reference Library
>43 State House Station, **Augusta**, ME 04333-0043; Tel. 207-287-1600;
>*www.state.me.us/legis/lawlib/homepage.htm*;
>*www.state.me.us/legis/lawlib/refemail.htm*

COURTHOUSE LAW LIBRARIES
York County Courthouse, Court St., **Alfred**, ME 040021
Androscoggin County Courthouse, 2 Turner Street, **Auburn**, ME 04212
Kennebec County Courthouse, 95 State St., **Augusta**, ME 04330
Penobscot County Courthouse, 97 Hammond St., **Bangor**, ME 04401
Sagadahoc County Courthouse, 752 High St., **Bath**, ME 04530
Waldo County Courthouse, 147 Church St., **Belfast**, ME 04915
Caribou District Courthouse, 144 Sweden St., **Caribou**, ME 04736
Piscataquis County Courthouse, 51 E. Main St., **Dover-Foxcroft**, ME 04426
Hancock County Courthouse, 60 State St., **Ellsworth**, ME 04605
Franklin County Courthouse, 140 Main St., **Farmington**, ME 04938
Aroostook County Courthouse, 26 Court St., **Houlton**, ME 04736
Washington County Courthouse, 47 Court St., **Machias**, ME 04654
Cumberland County Courthouse, Cleaves Law Library, 142 Federal St., **Portland**, ME 04112;
>Tel. 207-773-9712; Fax 207-773-2155; *www.cleaves.org; info@cleaves.org*

Knox County Courthouse, 62 Union St., **Rockland**, ME 04841
Somerset County Courthouse, Court St., **Skowhegan**, ME 04976
Oxford County Courthouse, 26 Western Ave., **S. Paris**, ME 04281
Lincoln County Courthouse, High St., **Wiscasset**, ME 04578

OTHER LAW LIBRARIES
University of Maine School of Law
>Donald L. Garbrecht Law Library, 246 Deering Ave., **Portland**, ME 04102; Tel. 207-780-4350; *http://mainelaw.maine.edu/library/general.htm*

Massachusetts

FEDERAL COURT LIBRARY
Library of the U.S. Courts in the First Circuit
>John Joseph Moakley U.S. Courthouse, 1 Courthouse Way, Suite 9400, **Boston**, MA 02210; Tel. 617-748-9044; Fax 617-748-9358; *www.ca1.uscourts.gov*

STATE LIBRARY
State Library of Massachusetts
>George Fingold Library, State House, **Boston**, MA 02133; Tel. 617-727-2590; Fax 617-727-5819; *www.mass.gov/lib*; *Reference.Department@state.ma.us*

TRIAL COURT LIBRARIES
>Tel. 800-445-8989 (toll-free number staffed on rotating basis by reference librarians)
>*www.lawlib.state.ma.us*

First Dist. Court House, Main St., PO Box 427, **Barnstable**, MA 02630; Tel. 508-362-8539;
>Fax 408-362-1374; *barnlaw45@hotmail.com*

Superior Courthouse, 72 Belmont St., **Brockton**, MA 02301; Tel. 508-586-7110; Fax 508-588-8483; *brocklaw72@hotmail.com*

Courthouse, 40 Thorndike St., **Cambridge**, MA 02141; Tel. 617-494-4148; Fax 617-225-0026;
>*midlawlib@yahoo.com*

Superior Court House, 441 N. Main St., **Fall River**, MA 02720; Tel. 508-676-8971; Fax 508-677-2966; *fallriver.lawlib@verizon.net*

Superior Court House, 84 Elm St., **Fitchburg**, MA 01420; Tel. 978-345-6726; Fax 978-345-7334

Courthouse, 425 Main St., **Greenfield**, MA 01301; Tel. 413-772-6580; Fax 413-772-0743; *franklinlawlib@hotmail.com*

Fenton Judicial Center, 2nd Floor, 2 Appleton St., **Lawrence**, MA 01840-1525; Tel. 978-687-7608; Fax 978-688-2346; *lawrencelawlibrary@yahoo.com*

Superior Court House, 360 Gorham St., **Lowell**, MA 01852; Tel. 978-452-9301; Fax 978-970-2000; *lowlaw@meganet.net*

Superior Court House, 441 County St., **New Bedford**, MA 02740; Tel. 508-992-8077; Fax 508-991-7411

Courthouse, 99 Main St., **Northampton**, MA 01060; Tel. 413-586-2297; Fax 413-584-0870

57 Providence Hwy., **Norwood**, MA 02062; Tel. 781-769-7483; Fax 781-769-7836; *norfolk-lawlibrary@hotmail.com*

Courthouse, 76 East St., **Pittsfield**, MA 01201; Tel. 413-442-5059; Fax 413-448-2474; *berk-shirelawlib@hotmail.com*

County Commissioners' Bldg., 11 S. Russell St., **Plymouth**, MA 02360; Tel. 508-747-4796, 747-0500; Fax 508-746-9788; *plymouthlawlibrary@hotmail.com*

Superior Court House, 34 Federal St., **Salem**, MA 01970; Tel. 978-741-0674; Fax 978-745-7224

50 State St., PO Box 559, **Springfield**, MA 01102-0559; Tel. 413-748-7923; Fax 413-734-2973; *hampdenlawlibrary@yahoo.com*

Superior Court House, 9 Court St., **Taunton**, MA 02780; Tel. 508-824-7632; Fax 508-824-4723; *bristollawlibrary@yahoo.com*

4th Middlesex Law Library, District Court, 30 Pleasant St., **Woburn**, MA 01801; Tel. 781-935-4000

Courthouse, 2 Main St., **Worcester**, MA 01608; Tel. 508-770-1899, Ext. 185; Fax 508-754-9933; *worcesterlaw@yahoo.com*

OTHER LAW LIBRARIES

Massachusetts School of Law Library
500 Federal St., **Andover**, MA 01810; Tel. 508-681-6330; *http://msl.edu/Library*

Boston Public Library
Government Documents Rm., 666 Boylston St., **Boston**, MA 02116; Tel. 617-536-5400; *www.bpl.org*

Boston University Law School Library
765 Commonwealth Ave., **Boston**, MA 02215; Tel. 617-353-3151; Fax 617-353-5995; *www.bu.edu/lawlibrary*

New England School of Law Library
154 Stuart St., **Boston**, MA 02116; Tel. 617-422-7299, ext. 299; *www.nesl.edu/library*

Northeastern University School of Law Library
400 Huntington Ave., **Boston**, MA 02115; Tel. 617-373-3594; *www.slaw.neu.edu/library*

Social Law Library of Boston
John Adams Courthouse, 1 Pemberton Square, **Boston**, MA 02108-1792; Tel. 617-226-1500; Fax 617-523-2458; *www.sociallaw.com*; *reference@sociallaw.com*

Suffolk University Law School, John Joseph Moakley Law Library
120 Tremont St., **Boston**, MA 02108; Tel. 617-573-8177; *www.law.suffolk.edu/library/index.cfm*; *lawref@suffolk.edu*

Harvard Law School Library
Langdell Hall, 1545 Massachusetts Ave., **Cambridge**, MA 02138; Tel. 617-495-3170; *www.law.harvard.edu/library*

Southern New England School of Law Library
874 Purchase St., **New Bedford**, MA 02740; Tel. 508-998-9600; *www.snesl.edu*

Boston College Law School Library
> 885 Centre St., **Newton Centre**, MA 02459; Tel. 617-552-4434;
> *www.bc.edu/schools/law/library*

Western New England School of Law Library
> 1215 Wilbraham Rd., **Springfield**, MA 01119; Tel. 413-782-1457;
> *www1.law.wnec.edu/library*

New Hampshire

STATE LIBRARIES

New Hampshire Law Library
> Supreme Court Building, 1 Noble Dr., **Concord**, NH 03301; Tel. 603-271-3777; Fax
> 603-271-2168; *www.courts.state.nh.us/lawlibrary/index.htm*

New Hampshire State Library
> 20 Park St., **Concord**, NH 03301; Tel. 603-271-2144; Fax 603-271-6826;
> *www.state.nh.us/nhsl*

OTHER LIBRARIES

Franklin Pierce Law Center
> 2 White St., **Concord**, NH 03301; Tel. 603-228-1541, ext. 1130;
> *www.library.piercelaw.edu/library.htm*

Rhode Island

STATE LIBRARIES

Rhode Island State Law Library
> Frank Licht Judicial Complex, 250 Benefit St., **Providence**, RI 02903; Tel. 401-222-
> 3275; Fax 401-222-3865; *www.courts.state.ri.us/library/defaultlibrary.htm*

Rhode Island State Library
> State House, **Providence**, RI 02903; Tel. 401-222-2473; Fax 401-222-3034;
> *www.sec.state.ri.us/library*; *tatelibrary@sec.state.ri.us*

OTHER LIBRARIES

Roger Williams University
> Ralph R. Papitto School of Law Library, 10 Metacom Ave., **Bristol**, RI 02809; Tel.
> (401) 254-4546; *http://law.rwu.edu/Law+Library*

Vermont

STATE LIBRARY

Vermont Dept. of Libraries, Law Library
> 109 State St., **Montpelier**, VT 05609-0601; Tel. 802-828-3268; Fax 802-828-1481;
> *http://dol.state.vt.us*

OTHER LIBRARIES

Vermont Law School, Julien and Virginia Cornell Library
> PO Box 96, Chelsea St., **S. Royalton**, VT 05068; Tel. 800-227-1395;
> *http://julien.vermontlaw.edu*

Publishers

Part II cites many published sources—books, microform and digital/electronic—too numerous for inclusion of all publishers in this *Appendix*. The following contact information features only selected major publishers or specialized sources.

Family History Library
> 35 N. W. Temple St., Salt Lake City, UT 84150-3400; Tel. 801-240-2584, 800-346-
> 6044; Fax 801-240-3718; *www.familysearch.org*
> World's largest genealogical library, founded in 1894 by The Church of Jesus Christ of
> Latter-day Saints (LDS); more than 5,000 branch **Family History Centers** worldwide,

open to the public, where researchers can access microform and other library resources. Call for locations, hours of service and fees. Search microform and other resources published by **Genealogical Society of Utah** (and other publishers) at the Family History Library (FHL) Catalog online. Most microform titles in this book appear exactly as listed in the FHL catalog. Obtain more information about a particular title (including the FHL numbers and contents of reels or fiche) by doing a "title" search in the online FHL catalog or by contacting a Family History Center. (*Note*: If a "title" search does not yield information—due to occasional typographical errors in FHL catalog— try a "keyword" or "place" search instead, or omit hyphens or apostrophes.)

Genealogical Society of Utah

50 E. N. Temple St., Salt Lake City, UT 84150; Tel. 801-538-2978; Fax 801-240-1448; *www.gensocietyofutah.org*; *society@gensocietyofutah.org*

The microfilming arm of the LDS Family and Church History Dept., which filmed most of the microform listed in this book. (*Note:* In *Part II*, Genealogical Society of Utah microform is identified with the abbreviation "GSU.")

Law Library Microform Consortium

PO Box 1599, Kaneohe, HI 96744; Tel. 800-235-4446, 808-235-2200; Fax 808-235-1755; *www.llmc.com*; *llmc-digital@hawaii.rr.com*

Court decisions on microfiche (available at libraries, but some materials are priced within range for individual purchase).

LexisNexis Academic & Library Solutions

7500 Old Georgetown Rd., Bethesda, MD 20814-6126; Tel. 800-638-8380, 301-654-1550; Fax 301-657-3203; *www.lexisnexis.com/academic*

Readex/Newsbank

Microform

Early American Imprints, Series I. Evans (1639-1800). New York: Readex Microprint, in cooperation with American Antiquarian Society, 1985. Microfiche. *See www.readex.com/scholarl/eai_micro.html.*

Early American Imprints, Series II. Shaw-Shoemaker (1801-1819). New Canaan, Conn.: Readex Microprint, in cooperation with American Antiquarian Society, 1987-1992. Microfiche. *See www.readex.com/scholarl/eai_ser2_micro.html.*

Digital/Electronic

Evans Digital Edition. Early American Imprints, Series I. Evans (1639-1800). Chester, Vt.: Readex/Newsbank, in cooperation with American Antiquarian Society, 2003. Searchable Internet-based digital collection, with expanded database converted from microform version; available at academic libraries.

See www.readex.com/scholarl/eai_digi.html.

Shaw-Shoemaker Digital Edition. Early American Imprints, Series II. Shaw-Shoemaker (1801-1819). Chester, Vt.: Readex/Newsbank, in cooperation with American Antiquarian Society, 2004. Searchable Internet-based digital collection, with expanded database converted from microform version, released in monthly segments over 3-year period beginning August 2004; available at academic libraries. *See www.readex.com/scholarl/earlamim.html.*

West (Thomson Legal & Regulatory)

610 Opperman Dr., Eagan, MN 55123; Tel. 651-687-7000; *http://west.thomson.com*

Foremost legal publisher: West National Reporter System, Westlaw, etc.

Glossary

Since court records often contain specialized terminology, this glossary features definitions of common legal terms that researchers are likely to encounter. For more help with unfamiliar words and phrases, consult *Black's Law Dictionary* (the standard reference, available at many libraries), or other dictionaries and online glossaries:

Law Dictionaries

Garner, Bryan A. *Black's Law Dictionary*. 8th ed. Eagan, Minn.: West, 2004.

Gifis, Steven H. *Dictionary of Legal Terms: A Simplified Guide to the Language of the Law*. 3rd ed. Hauppauge, N.Y.: Barron's, 1998.

_____. *Law Dictionary*. 5th ed. Hauppauge, N.Y.: Barron's, 2003.

Hill, Gerald N., and Kathleen Thompson Hill. *Real Life Dictionary of the Law: Taking the Mystery Out of Legal Language*. Reprint. Toronto: Stoddart Publishing Co., 1997.

Merriam-Webster's Dictionary of Law. Springfield, Mass.: Merriam-Webster, 1996.

Oran, Daniel. *Oran's Law Dictionary for Non-Lawyers*. 4th ed. Clifton Park, N.Y.: Thomson Delmar Learning, 2000.

Rothenberg, Robert E. *The Plain-Language Law Dictionary*. 2nd ed. New York: Signet, 1996.

Free Online Glossaries

www.legal-definitions.com

www.lectlaw.com/def.htm

Common Legal Terms

Abstract of Title

Document summarizing history of title to a parcel of real estate, with prior owners, *liens* (claims) by creditors against the property, *mortgages*, etc., often including maps and boundary descriptions (plot plans or surveys).

Acquit

To find the accused "not guilty" in a criminal case.

Action

Court case or lawsuit. *Action on the case* is archaic term for a type of lawsuit seeking damages; *see also trespass on the case*.

Administrator

Person appointed by court to oversee settlement of estate when someone dies without leaving a will.

Admiralty

Court for maritime contracts, torts, injuries or offenses. Today admiralty matters are handled by the federal courts; before 1789, royal admiralty courts operated in the New England colonies.

Adjudication

Decision or sentence by judge.

Affidavit

Written statement of facts given under oath.

Alimony

In divorce case, money that one spouse is ordered to pay the other for support.

Allegation

Saying that something is true.

Answer

First document filed by *defendant* in lawsuit, answering or denying *plaintiff's* claims, and stating defenses or counterclaims.

Appeal

Asking higher court to review lower court's decision, because of alleged error or injustice. *Appellant* is the party appealing the decision. *Appellee* is the party against whom an appeal is taken.

Arbitration

Method of resolving dispute out of court, where parties choose one or more neutral *arbitrators* who hear evidence and decide case.

Arraignment

First court appearance of person accused of a crime, when plea is entered.

Arrest

Police officer takes person into custody and charges him with a crime.

Assault and Battery

Threat or use of force with intent to cause injury.

Assize

Archaic term, referring to a court session.

Assumpsit

Archaic term for lawsuit to collect debt, or for breach of a contract.

Attachment

Seizing goods or title to real estate by court order, to satisfy *judgment* or to guarantee person's appearance in court.

Attorney

Person licensed to practice law (*lawyer*), who performs professional services such as representing clients in court, preparing written contracts and other legal documents, advising clients about the law, etc.

Bail

Money paid to court to allow release of prisoner and secure his return to court at a later time.

Bankruptcy

Court proceeding to deal with party who is *insolvent* (unable to pay debts). *Voluntary bankruptcy*: Initiated by an insolvent person or company, asking to be relieved of most debts and to undergo a liquidation or reorganization in favor of creditors. *Involuntary bankruptcy*: Initiated by creditors, to force debtor into bankruptcy.

Bequest

Property (usually *personal property*, *i.e.*, not real estate) disposed of in a *will*.

Beneficiary

Person who benefits or receives something due to a legal arrangement (*e.g.*, *bequest* in a *will* or proceeds of life insurance). *See also Trust.*

Bill of Costs

Itemized statement of expenses incurred by one party in lawsuit, *e.g.*, filing fees, sheriff's service fees, witness fees.

Bond

Written promise to do some act or to pay money to court for specific purpose, such as *appeal* or *bail*. Other examples: *bastardy bond*, paid by alleged father, to guarantee that illegitimate child did not become a public charge; *executor's bond*, to assure faithful administration of estate in probate case.

Brief

Written arguments submitted to court by parties or their lawyers, debating applicable law and summarizing relevant trial evidence. On appeal from a lower court judgment, the *appellant's* brief usually argues that the trial court made an error of law in deciding the case. The *respondent's* brief answers the appellant's arguments, and usually requests that the judgment be *affirmed* (allowed to stand).

Burglary

Breaking and entering a dwelling at night with intent to commit a crime. *See Felony.*

Calendar

See Docket.

Cause of Action

General term for a type of claim, or the facts that give someone the right to file a lawsuit, *e.g.*, the employee who was fired from his job had a cause of action for wrongful termination.

Certificate of Naturalization

Document issued by court in *naturalization* proceeding, when citizenship is granted.

Certiorari

Writ of certiorari, issued by U.S. Supreme Court when it decides to take a case, orders lower court to deliver case record for review.

Chancery Court

Court of *equity*.

Chattel

See Personal Property.

Civil Action

Lawsuit to enforce, redress, or protect private or individual right; *not* a *criminal* case.

Claimant

See Plaintiff.

Clerk of Court

Court officer who keeps records of court proceedings; in probate court, clerk is often called a *register* or *registrar*.

Codicil

Document that amends or supplements a *will*.

Common Law

Body of court decisions from individual cases, creating rules to guide resolution of future disputes.

Complaint

(1) Document that starts *civil action*, stating the basis for the plaintiff's claim, and a demand for relief. (2) Formal charge in *criminal action*, accusing person of an offense, often after evidence presented to *grand jury* (*see also indictment*).

Conservator

Person appointed by court to manage someone's property or affairs. *See also Guardian*.

Contempt of Court

Refusing to obey court order or authority, sometimes punishable by fine or imprisonment.

Continuance

Adjourning or postponing a court case to a later date.

Contract

Binding agreement between two or more parties.

Conveyance

See Deed.

Conviction

Court *judgment* that person is guilty of a crime.

Court of Gaol Delivery

Archaic name for a court with authority to try prisoners held in jail ("gaol") for various offenses.

Criminal Action

Lawsuit by government to punish offenses against the public.

Cross-Examination

Questioning a witness called by the opposing party (or a hostile witness) at trial. The cross-examiner tries to discredit the witness, show inconsistencies in the witness's testimony, etc.

Damages

Money to compensate *plaintiff* for loss or injury caused by *defendant*.

Decedent

Person who died.

Declaration of Intention

Naturalization document, also known as *first papers* or *primaries*, often filed at court in port of entry shortly after arrival; required until 1950s.

Deed

Also known as a *conveyance*, transferring title to *real estate*.

Defamation

False statement that harms reputation of another person. *Libel* is written defamation. *Slander* is oral defamation.

Default

Failure to perform a legal duty; *e.g.*, when *defendant* fails to answer *plaintiff's complaint* or fails to appear at trial.

Defendant

One being sued (in a *civil* case) or being prosecuted by the government (in a *criminal* case).

Demurrer

Special *pleading* filed by *defendant* asking court to dismiss *plaintiff's complaint*, because the facts, even if true, do not state a valid claim or require an answer; also called *motion to dismiss*.

Deposition

Sworn testimony taken outside of court and put into writing, to be used as evidence in a court case. One who gives deposition testimony is a *deponent. Note*: Modern depositions are verbatim transcripts of testimony, recorded by a court reporter or stenographer. In colonial days, depositions were written summaries, generally prepared by magistrates or other officials, paraphrasing the testimony of witnesses, similar to today's *affidavit*.

Devise

Property (usually *real estate*) disposed of in a *will*.

Discovery

One party may obtain information relevant to a lawsuit from the other party before trial (by *interrogatories*, *depositions*, *requests for admission* and *requests for production of documents*), to prevent surprise trial evidence. After trial, the winning party may conduct discovery about the other party's assets to satisfy the *judgment*.

Dismissal

Court order ending a lawsuit before *judgment*. If the case is *dismissed with prejudice*, the *plaintiff* may not file a later suit about the same claim. *Dismissal without prejudice* means that the *plaintiff* is free to file the suit again.

Docket

(1) Schedule of pending court cases; also called *court calendar.* (2) *Docket book* contains chronological entries by the court clerk about each court session or case. These entries include the case number, court term and date (useful in locating *file papers*), presiding judges, jury members, etc.

Dower

Wife's *common-law* right, upon her husband's death, to possess one-third of his land for the rest of her life.

Easement

Right to use another person's land for a specific limited purpose, *e.g.* to pass through the land (a right-of-way) to reach a public road.

Ejectment

Causing owner or occupier of property to leave. Early common law *writ of ejectment* was a lawsuit to recover possession of land.

Eminent Domain

Government's right to take private property for a public use, upon paying owner a reasonable price.

Equity

An action in equity seeks *equitable relief,* where money cannot redress an injury or the *common law* does not provide an adequate remedy; *e.g.*, a court may order the *defendant* to do something (*specific performance*), or to stop or refrain from doing something (*injunction*).

Estate

Property—*real* or *personal*—owned by person or entity.

Eviction

Legally forcing a person to leave land or rental property.

Evidence

Testimony, documents or tangible objects offered at trial to prove or disprove a fact.

Ex Parte

Done without notice to, or argument by, an affected party, *e.g.*, a court order issued at one party's request without advance notice to the other.

Execution

Carrying out a court order, *e.g.*, seizing and selling property of a *defendant* to satisfy a *judgment* (to pay the *plaintiff*). *See also Writ.*

Executor

Person chosen to carry out provisions of a *will*.

Felony

Serious crime—usually punished by more than one year in prison or death—such as murder, burglary, rape, arson, etc.

Fiduciary

Someone who owes another a high standard of care, in the management of money or property, *e.g. administrator* of estate.

File Papers

Documents filed with the court in a civil or criminal case, *e.g.*, *summons*, *complaint*, *answer*, *deposition*, etc.

Finding

Determination of a fact (also called *finding of fact*) by judge or jury, based upon evidence at trial.

Foreclosure

Action by lender to terminate debtor's ownership of property, usually to force sale in order to pay off mortgage debt.

Guardian

Person with legal authority and duty to care for someone else (an infant, disabled person, etc.). *Guardian ad litem* is a person appointed by the court to represent a *minor* or incompetent person in lawsuit.

Habeas Corpus

Court order (*writ*) to bring a person before the court, to determine whether arrest or imprisonment is legal.

Hearsay

Testimony given by a witness who has no personal knowledge about a fact and is merely reporting what others have said.

Homicide

Killing someone. *Murder* is an intentional killing, planned ahead of time. *Manslaughter* is an unplanned killing, *e.g.*, done in the "heat of passion." *See also Felony.*

Indictment

Formal charge (issued by a *grand jury* to the court) accusing someone of a crime.

Infant

See Minor.

Injunction

Court order to stop, prevent or require a specific act.

Inquest

Official investigation of a death by coroner or medical examiner, sometimes with a jury.

Interrogatories

Written questions directed by one party in a lawsuit to another, which must be answered as part of *discovery* in a case.

Intestate

Person who dies without a valid *will*.

Issue

Child or offspring.

Judgment

Court's final decision in a case.

Jurisdiction

Court's power to decide a case, which may be limited by geographical or political boundaries. *General* jurisdiction is authority to hear wide range of cases—civil or criminal. Courts of *limited* jurisdiction, *e.g.* probate court, bankruptcy court, etc., decide only particular kinds of cases.

Jury

Grand jury considers whether evidence is sufficient to *indict* (accuse) someone of an offense, to start a *criminal action*. *Petit jury* or *trial jury* decides questions of fact in a *civil* or *criminal* trial.

Justice of the Peace

Local judge whose *jurisdiction* is limited to minor civil and criminal matters, performing marriage ceremonies, etc. In early New England colonies, often called a *magistrate. See Chapter 16.*

Lawyer

See Attorney.

Lease

Similar to a *deed*, transferring limited rights to *real estate* for a period of time, creating a landlord/tenant relationship.

Legacy

Gift of *personal property* (often money) by *will.*

Libel

(1) False written statement that harms reputation of another person; *see Defamation.*
(2) In Admiralty Court, initial complaint by *libellant*, the party who filed lawsuit.

Lien

A legal right or interest in someone else's property, which lasts until the debt is paid.

Lis Pendens

Notice filed with local authorities some jurisdictions, warning that certain *real property* is the subject matter of a lawsuit that could affect title.

Litigation

Process of a lawsuit. A *litigant—e.g., plaintiff* or *defendant*—is a party to a lawsuit.

Minor

Person who has not reached legal age.

Minute Book

See Record Book.

Misdemeanor

A crime less serious than a *felony*, usually punishable by a fine or brief confinement.

Mittimus

Court order directing sheriff to deliver a person to jail.

Mortgage

Document giving house or property as security for repayment of loan. Lender/creditor is the *mortgagee* and borrower/debtor is the *mortgagor.*

Motion

Written (or oral) request that the court make a specific ruling or order. Parties communicate with the court by filing motions before, during and after a trial, on a variety of matters, *e.g.*:
Motion to amend a document previously filed. The plaintiff, for example, may want to correct errors or add new claims to a complaint.
Motion to compel discovery, to force the opponent to answer interrogatories or provide other information.

Motion to dismiss the case, before trial, because of settlement or a procedural defect (lack of jurisdiction, failure to state a claim, etc.). *See Demurrer.*

Motion in limine, asking to exclude certain evidence, before trial.

Motion to continue (postpone) some action in the case.

Naturalization

Procedure granting citizenship to a foreign-born person.

Non Suit

Dismissal or termination of a lawsuit without judging the merits, *e.g.*, when the *plaintiff* voluntarily withdraws a *complaint*.

Notary Public

Person (sometimes called a *notary*) authorized to administer oaths, to certify or *notarize* documents, and to perform other official acts.

Opinion

Written decision or ruling of court, usually summarizing facts and explaining reasons for outcome of case.

Oyer and Terminer

Special royal courts for serious cases in the New England colonies, *e.g.* in 1692, for Massachusetts witchcraft cases.

Partition

Court order dividing land between two or more persons.

Party

Plaintiff or *defendant* in a lawsuit (can be a person or a business entity, such as a corporation).

Per Capita

Property distributed equally among all beneficiaries.

Per Stirpes

Property distributed proportionally among beneficiaries, depending upon their deceased ancestor's share. For example, Mr. A's *will* left property to his three children: B, C and D. D died before Mr. A, but left two children, D1 and D2 (Mr. A's grandchildren). Mr. A's property, divided into three equal parts, is distributed as follows: one part to B, one part to C, and the third part divided equally between D1 and D2.

Perjury

Making false statement under oath.

Personal Property

Property that can be moved or transferred, *e.g.*, household furnishings, clothing, cars, bank accounts, stocks and bonds—*not real property*.

Plaintiff

One who starts a *civil* lawsuit by filing a *complaint*.

Plea

Answer to a *criminal* charge, *i.e.*, guilty, not guilty, or no contest (*nolo contendere*).

Pleading

Written statements filed in court by a party to lawsuit, setting forth or responding to claims, denials, defenses, *e.g.*, *complaint*, *answer*, etc.

Power of Attorney

Authority to act as agent for another person, usually granted in writing.

Presentment

See Indictment.

Probate

Court proceedings to establish that a *will* is valid and to administer a *decedent*'s estate. *Probate* courts also typically have jurisdiction over other types of matters, such as guardianship, trusts, adoptions, name change, etc.

Pro Se

Representing oneself in court, without a lawyer.

Prosecutor

Lawyer for the government in a *criminal* case.

Real Property

Real estate such as land, a home, a farm, or ownership of a condominium unit.

Receiver

Person appointed by court to protect or collect property, as in *bankruptcy* case.

Recognizance

Written obligation to perform particular act, *e.g.*, to keep the peace for a specified period of time, appear in court on a certain date, etc., or otherwise to pay money or suffer penalty, *e.g.*, a *bail bond*.

Record Book

Book (also called *minute book*) in which a court clerk enters basic facts about case, *e.g.*, dates of hearing, parties, orders, judgments, etc. Record books generally contain more detail than *docket books*, summarizing testimony and other information from file papers, or copying full text of court orders and judgments.

Register

Government official who keeps official records. In *probate* court, clerk is often called a *register* or *registrar*.

Relict

Widow.

Remand

Higher court sends case back to lower court for further proceedings.

Replevin

Lawsuit seeking return of *personal property* wrongfully detained by another. In colonial times, plaintiff often started lawsuit with a *writ of replevin* or *writ of detinue*.

Reporter

(1) Court opinions or case reports published in volumes such as "West National Reporter System" (*see Chapter 17*). (2) *Court reporter* is a stenographer who makes verbatim record of court proceedings.

Request for Admission

Written factual statement prepared by one party to lawsuit, asking other party to admit a fact. If admitted (and not denied or objected to), the fact need not be proved at trial.

Request for Production of Documents

Written request by one party to lawsuit during pre-trial *discovery*, asking other party to provide certain documents for inspection and copying.

Respondent

Appellee or *defendant*. See Appeal.

Return

Judicial document returned to court by sheriff or other official, with written statement of what he did or found; *e.g.*, *return* may be written on back of *summons*, describing when and how sheriff made *service* or delivery of papers, or on back of *writ of attachment* or *writ of execution*, describing property seized.

Robbery

Taking item of value by force.

Sentence

Court's *judgment* in a *criminal* case, finding *defendant* guilty and specifying the legal consequences, *e.g.*, amount of monetary fine, length of time to be served in prison, etc.

Service

Legal method for giving or delivering a copy of court papers to other parties in lawsuit.

Slander

See Defamation.

Slip Opinion

Written court decision, issued publicly before official publication.

Specific Performance

Court order requiring specific act, *e.g.*, to enforce a contractual obligation.

Statute

Law enacted by legislative branch of government.

Statute of Limitations

Time allowed by law for filing a civil lawsuit or prosecuting a crime.

Stay

Temporarily stopping a court proceeding or enforcement of a *judgment*.

Stipulation

Agreement between parties to a lawsuit about some issue in the case.

Subpoena

Court order (*writ*) ordering a witness to appear in court. *Subpoena duces tecum* orders witness to appear and bring certain documents.

Summons

Court order telling person to appear in court, usually delivered (*served*) by sheriff or constable.

Surety

Person who is liable to pay another's debt or to perform another's obligation.

Testator

Person who makes a *will*.

Testimony

Evidence given by a witness under oath at trial, or in an *affidavit* or *deposition*.

Tort

A *civil* (not criminal) wrong, for which injured party may seek money *damages* in court. *Tort* cases include *defamation*, negligence, trespass, etc.

Transcript

Verbatim written record of court proceedings or *testimony*, usually recorded by stenographer or *court reporter*.

Trespass

Unlawful interference with another's person, property, or rights, *e.g.* wrongfully entering someone's property. Archaic uses include: *Trespass with force and arms*, which usually involved violence, *e.g.*, assault, destruction of land (cutting down trees, destroying crops, etc.), or theft of animals and personal property. *Trespass on the case* (sometimes simply called *action on the case*), was precursor to modern *tort* action, seeking damages for wrongful act, *e.g.* slander, failure to deliver goods, medical malpractice, etc.

Trial

Judicial proceeding to examine evidence and resolve legal claims. In a *bench trial*, which takes place before a judge without a jury, the judge decides all questions of fact and of law. In a *jury trial*, the judge decides legal questions, and the jury resolves factual disputes.

Trover

Lawsuit seeking damages for *personal property* wrongfully taken.

Trust

Property held by one person (*trustee*) at request of another (*settlor*) for benefit of third party (*beneficiary*).

Vacate

To cancel or invalidate; *e.g.*, court *vacates a judgment*.

Venire

(1) Court order telling sheriff or constable to summon a *jury*. (2) Panel of people from whom *jury* will be selected.

Verdict

Decision by *jury* on factual issues of case.

Venue

Place where *trial* may be held.

Voir Dire

Questions directed by judge or lawyer to prospective jurors, to determine qualifications for serving on *jury*.

Warrant

Court order requiring sheriff or constable to arrest a person and bring him to court for questioning about an alleged offense.

Waste Book

Book in which judge or court clerk makes rough entries before posting them in official *docket book* or *record book*.

Will

Document directing how *testator* wants *estate* distributed after death.

Witness

Person who gives *evidence* under oath at *trial*, or in an *affidavit* or *deposition*.

Writ

Written court order, *e.g.*, *writ of attachment* or *writ of execution* (directing sheriff or constable to seize *defendant's* property to guarantee appearance in court or to satisfy a *judgment*). *Writ of error* is *appeal* to higher court for alleged mistake of law by lower court.

Recommended Reading

Each chapter in *Part II* lists published reference sources about New England state and federal courts. The following titles supplement the sources in *Part II*, providing general information about the American legal system, state and federal courts, and research with court records.

American Courts and Law

Baum, Lawrence. *American Courts: Process and Policy*. 5th ed. Boston: Houghton Mifflin, 2001.

Burnham, William. *Introduction to the Law and Legal System of the United States*. 3rd ed. Eagan, Minn.: Thomson West, 2002.

Calvi, James V., and Susan Coleman. *American Law and Legal Systems*. 5th ed. Upper Saddle River, N.J.: Prentice Hall, 2003.

Clark, David S., and Tugrul Ansay. *Introduction to the Law of the United States*. 2nd ed. The Hague, Netherlands: Kluwer Law International, 2001.

Farnsworth, E. Allan. *An Introduction to the Legal System of the United States*. 3rd ed. Dobbs Ferry, N.Y.: Oceana Publications, 1996.

Feinman, Jay M. *Law 101: Everything You Need to Know About the American Legal System*. New York: Oxford Univ. Press, 2000.

Friedman, Lawrence M. *A History of American Law*. 3rd ed. Carmichael, Cal.: Touchstone Books, 2005.

_____. *Law in America: A Short History*. New York: Modern Library, 2002.

Glendon, Mary Ann, Michael Wallace Gordon, and Paolo G. Carozza. *Comparative Legal Traditions in a Nutshell*. 2nd ed. Eagan, Minn.: Thomson West, 1999.

Horwitz, Morton J. *The Transformation of American Law, 1780-1860*. Cambridge, Mass.: 1977; New York: Oxford Univ. Press, 1994.

Kempin, Frederick G., Jr. *Historical Introduction to Anglo-American Law in a Nutshell*. 3rd ed. Eagan, Minn.: Thomson West, 1990.

Kurian, George T., and Joseph P. Harahan. *A Historical Guide to the U.S. Government*. New York: Oxford Univ. Press, 1998.

Meador, Daniel John. *American Courts*. 2nd ed. Eagan, Minn.: Thomson West, 2000.

Meador, Daniel John, and Jordana Simone Bernstein. *Appellate Courts in the United States.* Eagan, Minn.: Thomson West, 1994.

Morrison, Alan B. *Fundamentals of American Law.* New York: Oxford Univ. Press, 1996, 2000.

Patrick, John J., Richard M. Pious, and Donald A. Ritchie. *The Oxford Guide to the United States Government.* New York: Oxford Univ. Press, 2001.

Schubert, Frank A. *Introduction to Law and the Legal System.* 8th ed. Boston: Houghton-Mifflin Co., 2004.

Bankruptcy and Insolvency

Balleisen, Edward J. *Navigating Failure: Bankruptcy and Commercial Society in Antebellum America.* Chapel Hill, N.C.: Univ. of N. Carolina Press, 2001.

Coleman, Peter J. *Debtors and Creditors in America: Insolvency, Imprisonment for Debt, and Bankruptcy, 1607-1900.* Madison, Wisc.: State Historical Society of Wisc., 1974; Beard Books, 1999.

Eisenberg, Theodore. *Bankruptcy and Debtor-Creditor Law: Cases and Materials.* 3rd ed. Eagan, Minn.: Foundation Press, 2004.

Mann, Bruce H. *Republic of Debtors: Bankruptcy in the Age of American Independence.* Cambridge, Mass.: Harvard Univ. Press, 2003.

Regis, F. *A History of the Bankruptcy Law.* Buffalo, N.Y.: William S. Hein & Co., 2002.

Warren, Charles. *Bankruptcy in United States History.* 1935; Cambridge, Mass.: Da Capo Press, 1972.

Colonial Courts and Law

Bilder, Mary Sarah. *The Transatlantic Constitution: Colonial Legal Culture and the Empire.* Boston: Harvard Univ. Press, 2004.

Billias, George A., ed. *Law and Authority in Colonial America: Selected Essays.* Barre, Mass.: Barre Publishers, 1965.

McManus, Edgar J. *Law and Liberty in Early New England: Criminal Justice and Due Process 1620-1692.* Amherst, Mass.: Univ. of Mass. Press, 1993.

Land

Crandall, Ralph J. *Shaking Your Family Tree: A Basic Guide to Tracing Your Family's Genealogy.* 2nd ed. Boston: New England Historic Genealogical Society, 2001, pp. 113-128.

Hatcher, Patricia Law. *Locating Your Roots: Discover Your Ancestors Using Land Records.* Cincinnati, Ohio: Betterway Books, 2003.

Rose, Christine. *Courthouse Research for Family Historians: Your Guide to Genealogical Treasures.* San Jose, Cal.: CR Publications, 2004, pp. 27-65.

Naturalization

Bockstruck, Lloyd deWitt. *Denizations and Naturalizations in the British Colonies in America, 1607-1775.* Baltimore, Md.: Genealogical Publishing Co., 2005.

Schaefer, Christina K. *Guide to Naturalization Records of the United States.* Baltimore, Md.: Genealogical Publishing Co., 1997, 2004.

U.S. Citizenship and Immigration Services, a bureau of the U.S. Department of Homeland Security:
   "Historical Articles." *http://uscis.gov/graphics/aboutus/history/articles/arti.html.*
   "Historical Research Tools."
   http://uscis.gov/graphics/aboutus/history/tools.html#tooljump.

Probate

Crandall, Ralph J. *Shaking Your Family Tree: A Basic Guide to Tracing Your Family's Genealogy.* 2nd ed. Boston: New England Historic Genealogical Society, 2001, pp. 91-104.

Rose, Christine. *Courthouse Research for Family Historians: Your Guide to Genealogical Treasures.* San Jose, Cal.: CR Publications, 2004, pp. 65-111.

Research

Chiorazzi, Michael, and Margaret Most, eds. *Prestatehood Legal Materials: A Fifty State Research Guide*. 2 vols. Binghamton, N.Y.: Haworth Press, 2006.

Cohen, Morris L. *Bibliography of Early American Law*. 6 vols. Buffalo, N.Y.: William S. Hein & Co. 1998; also CD-ROM version.

Cohen, Morris L., and Kent C. Olson. *Legal Research in a Nutshell*. 8th ed. Eagan, Minn.: Thomson West, 2003.

Elias, Stephen R., and Susan Levinkind. *Legal Research: How to Find & Understand the Law*. 13th ed. Berkeley, Cal.: Nolo, 2005.

Olson, Kent C. *Legal Information: How to Find It, How to Use It*. Phoenix, Ariz.: Oryx Press, 1999.

On Trial series. Santa Barbara, Cal.: 2001-. Handbooks with cases, laws and excerpts from court documents re: controversial legal topics in America, *e.g.*: *Death Penalty on Trial*; *Marriage on Trial*; etc. *See www.abc-clio.com.*

Singer, Suzan Herskowitz. *Legal Research Made Easy*. 3rd ed. Naperville, Ill.: Sphinx Publishing, 2002.

Sperry, Kip. *Reading Early American Handwriting*. Baltimore, Md.: Genealogical Publishing Co., 1998.

INDEX

———✦———

EAST BOSTON, MASS. DISTRICT COURT AND PUBLIC LIBRARY BRANCH

The image on the preceding page, from the author's collection
of vintage picture postcards, depicts the District Court
in East Boston, ca. 1908.

INDEX

A

Abell, Allice, 90
Abbot, Edward F., 240
Abington, Mass., 208, 209
Acton, Mass., 195
Acushnet, Mass., 172, 174, 203
Acworth, N.H., 255
Adam family, 218
Adams
    Benjamin, 224
    Elijah, 205, 214
    Family, 75
    George W., 108
    Henry, 205, 214
    Jeremiah, 77, 85
    John, 163, 214
    Moses, 131
    Nathaniel, 251
Adams, Mass., 16, 171
Addison County, Vt., 16, 286, 293-295, 298, 319, 339, 413
Addison, Vt., 294
Adlow, Elijah, 216
admiralty, 9, 10
    Conn., 64, 329
    Maine, 116
    Mass., 153, 155, 161, 213-216, 220, 333
    N.H., 230, 233
    R.I., 258, 259, 261, 264
    U.S. courts, 317
adoption, 8, 12, 31, 59
    Conn., 66, 109
    Maine, 119, 130
    Mass., 38, 152, 156, 158, 159
    N.H., 231, 243
    R.I., 260
    Vt., 287, 297, 298, 308, 310, 312, 314
Africans/African Americans, 329, 346-348
    Attucks, Crispus, 215, 222
    Cadman, James, 346
    Conn., 87, 91, 101, 103, 105, 107
    Joseph, 346
    Jupiter, 347
    Mass., 215, 222
    Pegg, 75
    Phillis, 348
    Prince, 348
    R.I., 262, 346-368
    Salvadore, 346
    Sharper, 348
    Toby, 348
    Tom, 347, 348
    Tomas, alias Tom, 347
    Venus, 98
    Violet, 348

Agawam, Mass., 188, 192
Albany County, N.Y., 285
Albro, John, 263
Alcock, Samuel, 250
Alford, Mass., 169
Alfred, Maine, 147, 148, 403, 428
Allen
    Charles, 196
    Ethan, 302
    William, 332
    William Pitt, 207
    William, Jr., 144
Allenstown, N.H., 248
Alley, Benjamin, Jr., 179
Allyn
    Family, 81
    Henry, 81, 83
    Matthew, 82
American Antiquarian Society, 100, 103, 105, 131-133, 163, 172, 184, 185, 189, 192, 194, 197, 207, 208, 215, 222-224, 276, 278, 297, 300, 301, 308, 309, 314, 315, 335, 338, 420, 431
American Marble Co., 360
American Philosophical Society, 233, 425
American Textile History Museum, 197, 215, 421
Ames family, 206
Amesbury, Mass., 178, 183
Amherst, Mass., 162, 170, 191, 218, 423
Amherst, N.H., 245, 246, 251
Amistad, 327, 329, 330
Andover, Conn., 70, 106-108, 400
Andover, Mass., 178, 181, 333, 429
Andrew, Charles Bartlett, 89
Andrews
    Family, 75
    John, 173
Andros, Edmond (Gov.), 64, 68, 163, 258, 261
Androscoggin Historical Society, 124, 125, 419
Androscoggin County, Maine, 118, 123-125, 331, 332, 401, 428
Angell, Benjamin, 274
Anson, Maine, 143
Ansonia, Conn., 95-97, 99, 329, 398, 399
Anthony
    Isaac, 347
    James, 308
Aquidneck, 257, 263
Aquinnah (Gay Head), Mass., 177
Archbill/Archibald, John, 174
Arlington, Mass., 195, 333
Arlington, Vt., 296, 426
Armstrong
    Charles, 134
    Elijah, 262
Arnold, Richard and Stephen, 348

Aroostook County, Maine, 118, 125, 126, 331, 401, 428
Ashburnham, Mass., 224
Ashby, Mass., 195
Ashfield, Mass., 186, 187
Ashford, Conn., 70, 109, 112, 400
Ashland, Maine, 126
Ashland, Mass., 195
Aspinwall, William, 218, 220
Athens, Maine, 143
Atherton, Joshua, 245
Athol, Mass., 186
Atkins, Delia, 216
Atkinson, Sarah and Simeon, 248
Attleboro, Mass., 172, 175, 176, 404
Attucks, Crispus, 215, 222
Auburn, Maine, 123, 124, 332, 401, 419, 428
Auburn, Mass., 224
Auburn, N.H., 249, 409
Augusta, Maine, 118-120, 124, 126, 129-133, 135, 138, 140-145, 147, 351, 356, 402, 419, 428
Avery
    Ephraim K. (Rev.), 262
    James, 136
Avon, Conn., 70, 78, 80, 396
Avon, Mass., 205
Ayer, Anna, 246
Ayer, Mass., 195, 406

B

Babcock, Adam, 100, 105
Bacheler, Origen, 217
Bacon
    Lavinia, 67
    Michael, 20, 26, 387-391
Bail, Hamilton Vaughan, 313
Bailey, George E., 160
Baileyville, Maine, 145
Baker
    Family, 167
    Nellie, 136
    Orville Dewey, 140
    Samuel, 192
    Sarah, 192
Ball, Mary (Mrs. William Munro), 26, 391
Ballentine, John, 216
Bangor, Maine, 118, 139-141, 331, 402-403, 415, 419, 428
bankruptcy, 10, 33, 317-321, 324, 326, 328, 359-367, 433, 442
    Conn., 93, 328, 329, 415
    Maine, 331, 332, 415
    Mass., 198, 333, 336, 416
    N.H., 336, 416
    R.I., 338, 339, 416
    Vt., 339-341, 359-367, 416
Banks family, 75
Bantam, Conn., 86, 397
Bar Harbor, Maine, 130, 402
Barbados, 347
Bark, Trenor W., 340
Barkhamsted, Conn., 70, 86, 87
Barnes, William F., 340

Barnstable County, Mass., 154, 159, 166-169, 333, 404
Barnstable, Mass., 167, 404, 428
Barre, Mass., 223, 226
Barre, Vt., 182, 234, 286, 288, 289, 293, 295, 299, 301-307, 309, 311, 313, 413, 426
Barrington, R.I., 259, 266, 267, 273, 410
Barron, John Wilson, 140
Bartis, John C. and Stanley J., 46
Bartlett
    Family, 143, 250
    Levi, 250
Barton
    Cyrus, 233
    Elijah, 132
Bascom, Ortemidorus, 293
Bass
    Joseph P., 140
    Perkins, 232
Bassett, Henry, 187
Batchelder & Snyder Co., 147
Bath, Maine, 142, 403, 428
Baxter, H. Henry, 340
Bayley, William, 348
Baylies, Francis, 173
Beacon Falls, Conn., 95
Beals, George B., 217
Bean, Alamanzo, 30
Beath family, 136
Becket, Mass., 169
Bedford, Mass., 195
Bedford, N.H., 246, 247
Beers family, 75
Belcher
    Henry, 366
    Joseph, 218
Belchertown, Mass., 191
Belfast, Maine, 144, 403, 428
Belknap County, N.H., 237, 238, 408
Bell
    Edward B., 149
    William H., 93
Bellingham, Richard (Gov.), 218
Bellingham, Mass., 223, 333
Bellows, Josiah G., 240
Bellows Falls, Vt., 286, 311, 415
Belmont, Mass., 195, 333
Bennet, Peter, 180
Bennett, George, 97
Bennett (Bennitt) family, 75
Bennington County, Vt., 285, 286, 290, 295-297, 307, 339, 413
Bennington, Vt., 285, 286, 295, 297, 413
Benson, Vt., 307, 308
Berkley, Mass., 173
Berkshire Athenaeum, 170, 421
Berkshire County, Mass., 38, 169-172, 333, 404
Berkshire, Vt., 289
Berlin, Conn., 78, 80, 83, 84, 396
Berlin, Mass., 223
Berlin, N.H., 241, 408
Bernardston, Mass., 186, 362
Berwick, Maine, 147-149
Best, John C., 160

Bethany, Conn., 71, 95, 97, 99, 399
Bethel, Conn., 70, 72-74, 76, 395
Bethel, Maine, 138
Bethlehem, Conn., 86
Beverly, Mass., 179
Bickness, John, 217
Biddeford, Maine, 117, 147, 403
Billerica, Mass., 195
Billings
    Coddington, 103
    Family, 107
    Frederick, 313
    Sanford, 107
Billings Farm and Museum, 313, 426
Bingham, Maine, 143
Black Snake (boat), 302
Blackstone family, 98
Blackstone (James) Memorial Library, 98, 417
Blackstone, Mass., 224
Blair, Henry W., 243
Blake
    Family, 136
    Samuel, 217
Blakeman, Rufus, 75
Blandford, Mass., 188
Block Island, R.I., 279
Blodgett
    E. L., 364
    Ernest, 367
    Hattie, 367
    Laura, 365, 367
    Pearl D., 361-367
    Perley, 367
Blodgett Brothers, 364
Bloomfield, Conn., 78, 80, 396
Blue Hill, Maine, 130
Boardman
    Family, 84
    Joel, 294
    William F. J., 84
Boies, Jane and John, 207
Boise, Patrick, 189
Bolton, Conn., 106, 400
Bolton, Mass., 223, 225, 421
Boorn, Jesse and Stephen, 296, 297
Boothbay Harbor, Maine, 136, 419
Boscawen, N.H., 248
Boston Athenaeum, 167, 180, 206, 215, 240, 262, 334, 421
Boston College Law School, 161, 421, 430
Boston Gas Light Co., 216
Boston Historical Society, 148, 173, 197, 216, 421
Boston Massacre, 160, 214, 215, 222
Boston Public Library, 216, 421, 429
Boston University Law School, 161, 421, 429
Boston, Mass., 76, 81, 82, 93, 97, 104, 116, 120, 127, 130, 132, 134, 136, 139, 145, 148, 155-161, 167, 168, 170, 173, 177, 179-181, 186-188, 191, 192, 196-198, 202, 203, 205, 206, 208, 209, 212-222, 224, 225, 234, 238, 240, 241, 243, 251, 253, 262, 267, 271, 275, 280, 289, 305, 306, 308, 311, 321, 323, 328, 329, 331-339, 377, 387, 404, 407, 415, 416, 420-423, 428, 429

Bourne, Mass., 167, 421
Bouton, Nathaniel, 234
Bowditch, Joseph, 181
Bowdoin, James, 214
Bowdoin College, 332
Bowlan, Elizabeth (Mrs.), 222
Bowman, Jonathan, 136
Boxborough, Mass., 195
Boxford, Mass., 178
Boylston, Mass., 223
Bozrah, Conn., 70, 100-102, 104, 400
Bradford, Mass., 178
Bradford, Vt., 304, 305
Bradley
    Edward E., 88
    Family, 75
    Henry, 75
    Jonathan Dorr, 234, 311
    Joshua, 100
    Samuel A., 356, 358
    William, 75
Bradstreet, Simon, 216
Brainard family, 93
Braintree, Mass., 205, 217
Braintree, Vt., 305
Braman, Jason, 214
Branch, (Judge) and (Mr.), 384
Brandeis, Louis D., 323, 325
Branford, Conn., 95-99, 399, 417
Brattleboro, Vt., 286, 311, 414, 426
Braynard, Selden, 216
Brayton, George A., 262
Breed & Mumford, 75
Breed & Susquehannah Co., 75
Brentwood, N.H., 249, 409
Brewer, Maine, 140
Brewster, Caleb, 75
Brewster, Mass., 167
Bridge, William F., 240
Bridgeport, Conn., 72-74, 76, 328, 330, 395, 415, 427
Bridges, Delores, 232
Bridgewater, Conn., 86
Bridgewater, Mass., 208
Bridgton, Maine, 126, 127, 401
Briggs, James Franklin, 245
Brigham
    Elijah, 225
    Paul, 313
    Paul W., 301
Brighton, Mass., 212, 407
Brighton, Vt., 286
Brimfield, Mass., 188
Bristol, Nathan, 21, 26, 370
Bristol, Conn., 70, 78, 80, 84, 396
Bristol County, Mass., 154, 172-176, 266, 333, 404
Bristol County, R.I., 259, 260, 266, 267, 410
Bristol, R.I., 259, 266, 267, 273, 410, 430
Brock family, 305
Brockett, Miron C., 82
Brockton, Mass., 208, 209, 211, 406, 407, 428
Brookfield, Conn., 73, 74, 76, 395
Brookfield, Mass., 223, 226
Brookline, Mass., 205, 406

Brooklyn, Conn., 70, 71, 109, 110, 112, 401
Brooks
    Isaac, 245
    Nathan, 197
Brow, Emily, 174
Brown
    (Maj.), 346
    Beriah, 280, 348
    Family, 182, 199
    J. Bundy, 127
    Nelson Pierce, 161
    Philip H., 127
    Samuel, 214
    William P., 294
Brown University, 67, 110, 275, 425
Brownfield, Maine, 138
Brownington, Vt., 306, 426
Brunswick, Maine, 124, 127, 128, 419
Buckfield, Maine, 138
Buckingham, J.T., 27, 215
Buckland, Mass., 186
Bucksport, Maine, 130
Buffum, Jonathan, 179
Bulfinch, John, 135
Bulkeley family, 75
Bulkeley & Loomis (law firm), 298, 299, 305
Bunker, Lauriston & Winslow, 203
Burbank, Caleb, 181
Burdett, Riley, 341
Burgess, James H., 141
Burlington Sentinel, 366
Burlington, Conn., 70, 71, 78, 80, 81, 84, 396
Burlington, Mass., 196, 333
Burlington, Vt., 286, 290, 294, 296, 298-300, 302,
    306, 308, 310, 312, 313, 339, 340, 366, 413,
    416, 426
Burnap, Daniel, 107
Burnell, Barker, 203
Burns
    Anthony, 215
    (Mr.), 384
Burnside, Ambrose E., 280
Burr family, 75
Burrell, Samuel, 217
Burrillville, R.I., 273, 276, 411
Burritt Family, 75
Burt, Abel, 174
Butler
    Deborah, 44
    J., 44
    John, 29, 43
Butterfield, O. E., 361-363
Butts, Josiah, 38
Buxton, Maine, 147, 148

C

Cadman, James, 346
Calais, Maine, 145, 403
Calden, William, 144
Caledonia County, Vt., 22, 23, 30, 286, 297, 298,
    309, 339, 363, 413
Calhoun, John, 89
Call, Moses, 135

Camata, Mary, 174
Cambridge Farms, Mass., 389
Cambridge, Mass., 148, 161, 192, 195-197, 206,
    234, 275, 323, 377, 387, 389, 390, 406, 421,
    422, 428
Cambridge, Vt., 304
Canaan, Conn., 70, 71, 86, 87, 90, 397
Canterbury, Conn., 70, 109, 111, 112, 329
Canton Historical Museum, 82, 417
Canton, Conn., 70, 71, 78, 80-82, 84, 396
Canton, Mass., 205, 206, 406
Cape Cod Community College, 167, 421
Cape Elizabeth, Maine, 127
Cape Porpoise, Maine, 115, 148, 154
Capen family, 127
capital cases
    Maine, 116, 117, 121
    Mass., 153, 154, 156, 161
Card, Lester, 74, 76, 77, 93
Caribou, Maine, 125, 126, 401
Carlisle, Mass., 195
Carr, Mary, 348
Carroll County, N.H., 231, 239, 408
Carver, Mass., 208
Carville family, 199
Casco, Maine, 106, 154
Case
    John S., 134
    Seymour, 82
Cazin, Francis M. F., 305
Central Falls, R.I., 273, 276, 411
Central Vermont Railroad Co., 312
Chadwick
    Elias, 304
    Paul, 132
Chamberlayne, Charles Frederic, 168
Champion, Henry, 103
Chandler
    Charles Parsons, 142
    Peleg W., 128, 217, 334
    Zachariah, 214
Chaplin, Conn., 70, 71, 109
Chapman, Thomas (Capt.), 180
Charlemont, Mass., 186
Charlestown, Mass., 17, 196-199, 213-215, 407
Charlestown, R.I., 279-281, 412
Charlotte County, Vt., 285
Charlton, Mass., 223
Chatham, Conn., 92, 94
Chatham, Mass., 167
Checkley, John, 219
Chelmsford, Mass., 195
Chelsea, Mass., 157, 213, 218, 407
Chelsea, Vt., 304, 414
Cheney, Decatur, 294
Chepachet, R.I., 273
Cheshire County, N.H., 50, 240, 241, 254, 408, 424
Cheshire, Conn., 70, 71, 95, 97, 399
Cheshire, Mass., 169
Chesley, Samuel, 233
Chester, Conn., 91, 92, 398
Chester, John, 82
Chester, Mass., 188
Chester, N.H., 252

Chesterfield, Mass., 191
Chesterfield, N.H., 240, 423
Chicopee, Mass., 188, 189, 405
Child, David Lee, 198
Childs, Jonathan R., 189
Chinese Exclusion Act, 19, 322
Chisholm, Robert B., 340
Chittenden, Lucius E., 300
Chittenden County, Vt., 290, 298-301, 309, 339, 413
Chubb family, 218
Church family, 270
Church of Jesus Christ of Latter-day Saints. *See* LDS
Churchill, Edwin A., 149
Cilley, Jonathan, 134
Cinnemon, Thomas, 103
Clagett, Wyseman, 245
Claghorn
    Benjamin (Capt.), 174
    Shubal, 44
Clap, Thomas, 174
Claremont, N.H., 254, 410
Clark
    Charles Edward, 323
    Family, 308
    Henry, 331
    Sylvanus, 361, 362
    Thomas, 139
    Thomas Chester, 83
Clarksburg, Mass., 169
Clawson, Elizabeth, 76
Cleeve family, 149
Clifford, Nathan, 323
Clift family, 103
Clinton, Conn., 91, 94, 398
Clinton, Mass., 223, 407
Clough, Ebenezer, 215
Cobb
    Daniel, 305
    William, 148
Coddington, William, 257, 263
Coffin, Isaac, 203
Cogswell, Dorothea Bates, 180
Cohasset, Mass., 205
Colby, Joseph, 232
Colchester, Conn., 70, 71, 94, 100-102, 104, 400
Colcord, Elihu and Munroe, 250
Colebrook, Conn., 86, 90
Colebrook, N.H., 242, 408
Collinsville, Conn., 78, 396, 417
Colonial Society of Mass., 218, 220, 263
Colrain, Mass., 186
Colt, Samuel P., 280
Columbia, Conn., 103, 106, 107
Colvin, Russell, 296, 297
Comee, David, 388
Comings, (Judge), 306
Commerce Oil Refining Corp., 271, 338
Concord, Mass., 195-197, 390, 406, 421
Concord, N.H., 198, 232, 233, 238, 240, 243, 245, 247, 248, 250, 253, 255, 336, 337, 407, 409, 416, 423, 424, 430
Congdon, George W., 269

Connecticut courts, 62-113, 395-401
    Appellate, 65, 66, 71, 72, 395
    Assistants, 63, 64, 66
    Circuit, 65, 70
    Common Pleas, 64, 65, 67, 73, 76, 79, 84, 87, 90, 96, 101, 103, 104, 109
    County, 64, 69, 73, 79, 84, 87, 89, 91-94, 96, 98, 101, 104-106, 108, 109, 111
    District, 64, 67, 74, 80, 92, 96, 101, 106, 109
    Equity, 101
    Justices of the Peace, 21, 26, 27, 64, 66, 67, 74, 75, 80-83, 87-90, 92, 93, 96-98, 107, 109-111, 369-375
    Juvenile, 64, 65, 75
    Magistrates, 63
    Maritime, 64, 73, 79, 87, 96, 101
    Mashantucket Pequot Tribal, 72
    Mohegan Gaming Disputes, 72
    Municipal (City), 64, 64, 80, 81, 84, 87, 92, 96-99, 101, 106, 108
    Oyer and Terminer, 64, 67
    Particular, 63, 68
    Plantation Court, 63
    Probate, 63, 64, 66, 67, 69, 73-99, 101-112, 395-401
    Quarter, 63
    Superior, 64, 65, 67, 68, 70, 72-76, 78-80, 82-96, 98-104, 106-109, 111, 395-400
    Supreme, 58, 65-67, 69-72, 395
    Supreme, of Errors, 64, 65, 69, 73, 79, 87, 92, 101, 106, 109
    Town, 63, 64
    Trial Justices, 64, 65
    Vice-Admiralty, 64
Connecticut Historical Society, viii, 61, 67, 68, 75, 81, 82, 88, 93, 97, 103, 107, 110, 417
Connecticut State Library (State Archives), xiii, 66, 67, 69-71, 73, 74, 79-81, 83, 87, 88, 91-93, 96, 97, 101-103, 105-107, 109, 110, 176, 416, 417, 427
Connecticut, Superior Court Records Center, 67, 417
Connor, Samuel, 238
Conway, Mass., 186
Cook, Charles L., 216
Cooke
    Family, 218
    Josiah Parsons, 214
Cooke & Whitmore, 82
Cookson, John, 180
Coolidge, Valorous P., 132
Cooper
    Family, 218
    Samuel, 220
Coos County, N.H., 231, 241, 242, 408
Copley, John Singleton, 217
Cornell
    George, 174
    Sarah M., 262
Cornell University Law School, 292, 326
Cornwall, Conn., xiv, 21, 26, 50, 86-88, 90, 369-375, 397, 417
Cornwall, Vt., 295
coroners, 15

Conn., 74, 80, 87, 92, 97, 102, 107, 109
Maine, 125
R.I., 279, 348
Couch family, 75
Coventry, Conn., 70, 71, 106-108
Coventry, R.I., 269, 410
Cowan, Isaac, 349-354, 356-358
Cown, Ng Yuk, 19
Cox, David B., 334
Craftsbury, Vt., 306
Crandall
     Anna E., 361-363
     Prudence, 110
Cranston, Samuel, 280
Cranston, R.I., 273, 274, 276, 277, 411
Creek, John, 217
Croade, Edmund R. and Lydia, 275
Cromwell, Oliver, 140
Cromwell, Conn., 91
Crosby, Dixi, 313
Crossman, Robert, 174
Cumberland County, Maine, 53, 54, 117, 118, 123,
     126-128, 131, 138, 331, 401
Cumberland County, N.Y., 285, 304, 310, 312
Cumberland County, Vt., 285
Cumberland, R.I., 259, 273, 277, 411
Cummings, Oliver, 198
Cummington, Mass., 191
Cunningham, Nathaniel and Susannah, 217
Currier family, 243
Curtiss, Reuben B., 98
Curwen
     Family, 148, 181
     George (Capt.), 148, 181
     George (Rev.), 181
     Samuel, 181
Cushing, Maine, 133
Cushing, William, 148, 160
Cutting, Jonas, 140

D

Daley, Dominic, 194
Dalton, John, 335
Dalton, Mass., 169
Dana
     Francis and Richard, 214
     John Adams, 225
Danbury, Conn., 71-77, 395, 417, 427
Dane, Nathan, 179
Danforth, Maine, 145
Danforth, Thomas, 174, 390
Danielson, Conn., 108, 109, 400, 401, 417
Danvers, Mass., 179, 181, 183
Danversport, Mass., 181
Danville, Vt., 366
Darien, Conn., 72, 73, 395
Darling, Joshua, 245
Dartmouth College, 160, 180, 233, 234, 240, 243,
     245, 250, 305, 313, 424
Dartmouth, Mass., 172, 174, 203
Davenport, Bennett Franklin, 161
Davis
     James, 253

John, 89, 214, 334, 346
Dawes, Thomas, 218
Day, Rebecca, 207
Dean
     Cyrus B., 300
     Hannah (Mrs. Isaac), 174
Dedham, Mass., 88, 204-207, 406, 421
Deep River, Conn., 91, 92, 94, 398
Deer Isle, Maine, 137
Deerfield, Mass., 186, 187, 422
Deering
     Frank C., 147
     Roger, 149
DeGregory, Hugo, 233
Delany, Henry William, 42
Dennegri, Gaspard, 222
Dennis, Mass., 167
Derby, Conn., 71, 95-97, 99, 398, 399
Derry, N.H., 249, 409
Devens, Charles, 160
Devens Regional Enterprise Zone, Mass., 195
Dexter, Maine, 140
Dibble, George, 372
Dighton, Mass., 173
Dike, Nicholas, 225
Dimon family, 75
Dinsmore, Phineas, 356
divorce, 31, 39
     Conn., 63, 65, 66, 68, 83-85, 90, 91, 93, 97,
          98, 104, 107, 111
     Maine, 118, 119, 123, 126, 129, 131, 138, 143
     Mass., 39, 153-156, 158-160, 164, 167, 169-
          173, 175, 177, 179, 186-189, 191, 193,
          195, 196, 204, 205, 207-209, 212, 213,
          220, 223, 224, 226
     N.H., 231, 243, 244, 249
     R.I., 258, 260, 261, 267, 280
     Vt., 285, 287, 291, 301, 312
Dixmont, Maine, 140
Doe
     Charles, 233
     Joseph, 250
Dole, Richard, Sr., 184
Donnell family, 143, 148
Dorchester, Mass., 213, 217, 407
Dorr family, 214
Dorrance, John, 275, 276
Dorset, Vt., 296, 426
Douglas, Mass., 224
Dover & Portsmouth County, 229
Dover, Maine, 141
Dover, Mass., 205
Dover, N.H., 136, 154, 178, 229, 230, 252-254,
     383, 384, 409, 410
Dover-Foxcroft, Maine, 141, 142, 403, 419, 428
Downer, John, 299
Doyle, John, 207
Dracut, Mass., 195
Dresden, Maine, 136
Dublin, N.H., 240
Dudley
     John, 233
     Joseph, 163
Dudley, Mass., 223, 224, 407

Dukes County, Mass., 29, 44, 45, 157, 159, 177, 178, 202, 333, 404
Duncan, Laurence I., 233
Dunlap, Andrew, 181
Dunn, Charles J., 141
Dunstable, Mass., 195, 198
Durham, Conn., 91, 93
Durham, N.H., 149, 238, 253, 409, 424
Duxbury, Mass., 208
Dyer family, 218

E

E. D. Woodbridge & Sons (law firm), 294
Early American Imprints, 94, 99, 100, 105, 106, 131-133, 172, 184, 185, 194, 208, 222, 223, 276, 278, 297, 300, 301, 308, 309, 314, 315, 335, 338, 339, 431
East Boston Co., 219
East Boston, Mass., 213, 221, 407
East Bridgewater, Mass., 208
East Brookfield, Mass., 223, 407
East Cambridge, Mass., 195
East Granby, Conn., 78, 80, 82, 84, 396, 417
East Granby Public Library, 82, 417
East Greenwich, R.I., 268, 269, 410
East Haddam, Conn., 91, 92, 94, 398
East Hampton, Conn., 92, 94, 398
East Hartford, Conn., 78-81, 85, 396
East Haven, Conn., 95-97, 399
East Longmeadow, Mass., 188
East Lyme, Conn., 70, 71, 100-102, 105, 400
East Machias, Maine, 145
East Middlebury, Vt., 294
East Montpelier, Vt., 309
East Providence Historical Society, 322, 323, 425
East Providence, R.I., 259, 273, 277, 322, 323, 411, 425
East Windsor, Conn., 70, 71, 78-80, 85, 396
Eastern (Paucatuck) Pequots, 103
Eastford, Conn., 70, 71, 109, 112, 401
Eastham, Mass., 167
Easthampton, Mass., 191
Easton, Conn., 70-72, 74
Easton, Mass., 173
Eastport, Maine, 145, 146
Eaton
    Lisle, 149
    Nathan, 250
    Stephen, 250
Economics Laboratory, 322
Edgartown, Mass., 43, 177, 404, 422
Egremont, Mass., 169
Eldred/Eldredge families, 168
Eldredge, Charles H., 323
Elizabeth Isl., Mass., 177
Ellington, Conn., 70, 71, 107, 108, 400
Ellis, James P., 174
Ellms, John B., 206
Ellsworth, Maine, 130, 402
Ely-Goddard, Ely, 305
Emerson, Orin, 306
Emmery, Abigail and John, 39
Emmons

Asa, 372
Mary Ann, 372
Simeon, 371, 372
Solomon, 372
Woodruff, 372
Emry, Anthony, 348
Endicott, William C., Sr., 160
Enfield, Conn., 70, 71, 78-80, 85, 396
English, Phillip, 180
Epping, N.H., 251
equity, 5, 435
    Conn., 93, 101, 329
    Maine, 116, 135, 147, 333
    Mass., 153, 154, 156-158, 172, 195, 212, 220, 333
    N.H., 230, 239-242, 244-249, 251, 252, 254
    R.I., 258, 261, 263, 265
    Vt., 285, 286, 301, 339
Erving, Mass., 186
Esmond, R.I., 274, 412
Essex County, Mass., 56, 58-60, 154, 159, 178-185, 333, 356, 405
Essex County, Vt., 301, 339, 413
Essex, Conn., 91, 92, 94, 398
Essex, Mass., 178
Estey, Jacob, 341
Everett, Ebenezer, 127
Everett, Mass., 195, 333
Exeter, N.H., 154, 178, 229, 249-252, 409
Exeter, R.I., 279-281, 412

F

Fair Haven, Vt., 307, 308
Fairbanks, Jason, 207
Fairfield (Conn.) Historical Society, 75, 417
Fairfield County, Conn., 63, 71-77, 86, 328, 395-396
Fairfield, Conn., 63, 71-77, 395, 417
Fairfield, Maine, 143
Fairhaven, Mass., 172, 174, 203
Fales, Elizabeth, 207
Fall River, Mass., 172, 176, 404, 428
Falmouth, Maine, 116, 117
Falmouth, Mass., 167, 168, 404, 421
Faraoh, Sarah, 347
Farmer, Daniel Davis, 246
Farmington, Conn., 70, 71, 78-82, 85, 396
Farmington, Maine, 128-130, 402, 428
Farrar, Timothy, 234, 251
Faxon, John, 145, 146
Fay, John, 300
Female Orphan Asylum of Portland, 332
Fenner, Arthur, 275, 276
Field
    Anson, 340
    Family, 170, 308
    R.M., 313
Fields & Tyler (law firm), 361
Fisher family, 206
Fiske, William, 198, 201
Fitch, Theophilus, 76
Fitchburg, Mass., 223-225, 407, 421, 429
Flagg, Samuel, 225

Florida, Mass., 169
Folger, Walter, Jr., 203
Foot, Lucius H., 88
Force, Peter, 177
Ford
    Alice, 383
    Charles Baker, 381-384
    Family, 379-385
    Hollis, 381, 383
    Kari L., 381-384
    Lorenzo D. H., 381, 382, 384
Fort Fairfield, Maine, 126
Fort Kent, Maine, 126, 401
Foster, R.I., 273, 274, 277, 411
Fowl family, 199
Fowler, Simeon, 141
Foxborough, Mass., 205
Foxcroft, Maine, 142
Framingham, Mass., 195, 197, 198, 200, 406
Frankfurter, Felix, 323, 326
Franklin County, Maine, 118, 128, 129, 331, 402, 428
Franklin County, Mass., 185-188, 333, 405
Franklin County, Vt., 301-303, 339, 413, 414
Franklin Pierce Law Center, 430
Franklin, Conn., 100
Franklin, Mass., 205, 333
Franklin, N.H., 247, 409
Frederick, Francis, 334, 335
Freedom of Information/Privacy Act, 68, 121, 162, 234, 263, 290, 323, 427
Freeman
    Nathaniel, 167
    Samuel, 127
Freeport, Maine, 127, 419
Freetown, Mass., 172, 174, 203
Freeze, Ann E., 308
French
    Elijah, 305
    George, 22
French spoliation claims, 174, 203, 214, 225, 334
Frost, William, 147
Frothingham, John, 127
Fryeburg, Maine, 138
Fuller, Amos, 217

G

Gage, Asa, 232
Gale, George, 366
Gallup, Benadam, 103
Galpin, Samuel, 89
Gardiner, Maine, 132
Gardner, Mass., 220, 407
Garrity, W. Arthur, 334
Gault, William, 216
Gay Head (Aquinnah), Mass., 177
Genealogical Society of Utah, xiii, 48, 49, 58, 70, 71, 76, 77, 84, 85, 90, 91, 93, 94, 98, 99, 104, 105, 108, 111, 112, 122, 124-126, 128, 129, 131, 132, 134, 137, 139, 141-144, 146, 150, 164, 165, 168, 171, 175, 176, 178, 183, 184, 187, 189, 190, 193, 194, 197, 200, 201, 204, 207, 210, 211, 220, 221, 226, 227, 236, 238,

239, 241-244, 246-249, 251-255, 264, 265, 267, 269, 270, 272, 273, 276-278, 281, 282, 295, 297, 298, 300-302, 304, 305, 307, 310, 312, 314, 330, 332, 335, 338, 388, 430
General Court (General Assembly), 8, 31
    Conn., 63, 65, 68, 104
    Maine, 115, 116
    Mass., 38, 153, 154, 159, 164, 165
    N.H., 232
    Plymouth Colony, 153
    R.I., 258, 261, 265
    Vt., 286
George Tavern, 217
Georgetown, Maine, 136, 143, 148
Georgetown, Mass., 178
Gerrad, Mary, 346
Gibson family, 199
Giddings family, 182
Gifford family, 168
Gill, Mass., 186
Gilmanton, N.H., 238
Giveen, Thomas M., 128
Glastonbury, Conn., 78-82, 396, 417
Gleison, John and William, 389, 390
Glocester, R.I., 273, 277, 411
Gloucester County, Vt., 285, 291
Gloucester, Mass., 178-180, 405, 421
Glover
    Nathan Holbrook, 161
    William B., 75
Godard, George Seymour, 67, 70
Godfrey
    Richard, 173
    Samuel E., 315
Goffstown, N.H., 245, 246, 409, 424
Gold, Hezekiah, 372
Goldthwait, Ezekiel, 180, 216
Goodridge, Elijah Putnam, 184
Gorgeana (York), Maine, 115, 154
Gorges, Ferdinando, 115, 116
Gorham, N.H., 242, 408
Gorman, Edward, 82
Goshen, Conn., 86, 87
Goshen, Mass., 191
Goslee family, 81
Gosnold, Mass., 177
Gould
    Sarah, 216
    Thomas, 346
Gouldsboro, Maine, 130
Gove
    Family, 199
    Jonathan, 255
Grafton County, N.H., 231, 239, 241-244, 247, 408
Grafton, Mass., 224
Granby, Conn., 70, 71, 78-80, 83, 85, 396, 418
Granby, Mass., 191
Grand Isle County, Vt., 303, 339, 414
Grand Isle, Vt., 303
Grant, Roswell, 81
Granville, Mass., 188
Gray, Samuel, 110
Gray, Maine, 127
Great Barrington, Mass., 169-171, 404

Greek families, 226
Green, Joseph, 308
Green Mountain Marble Co., 360
Greenbush, Maine, 141
Greenfield, Mass., 185-188, 405, 429
Greenwich, Conn., 70, 72-74, 77, 395
Greenwood, John and Thomas, 198
Greenwoods Co., 89
Griswold, Conn., 100, 101, 400
Griswold, George and John, 82
Groton, Conn., 100, 103, 107, 400
Groton, Mass., 195, 196
Groveland, Mass., 178
GSU. *See* Genealogical Society of Utah
Guildhall, Vt., 301, 413
Guilford, Conn., 71, 91, 92, 95-99, 399, 417

H

Haddam, Conn., 70, 71, 91-94, 398
Hadley, Mass., 191, 192
Hagley Museum and Library, 180, 419
Hail family, 176
Hale
    Benjamin, 233
    Jonathan, 80
    Nathan, 261
Halifax, Mass., 208
Hall
    Albert, 134
    Dwight, 383, 384
    Family, 107
    Hannah, 271
    Lucian, 67, 93
Hall Laboratories, 322
Hallett, Henry L., 28
Halligan, James, 194
Hallowell, Maine, 117, 132, 350, 354
Hamden, Conn., 95, 96, 399, 427
Hamlin Memorial Library, 139, 419
Hammond
    Benjamin, 174
    John Wilkes, 162
Hampden County, Mass., 188-190, 333, 405
Hampden, Maine, 140, 419
Hampden, Mass., 188, 189
Hampshire County, Mass., 40, 81, 170, 188, 190-194, 333, 407
Hampton, Conn., 70, 71, 109, 110, 112, 401
Hampton, N.H., 154, 178, 229, 230, 249-252, 409, 424
Hancock County, Maine, 117, 118, 129-131, 139, 144, 331, 402, 418
Hancock, Mass., 169
Handley, Simon, 135
Hanover, Mass., 208
Hanover, N.H., 161, 180, 233, 240, 243, 245, 250, 305, 313, 423
Hanscom, John, 252
Hanson, Mass., 208
Hardwick, Mass., 223, 225
Hardy, William, 225
Harmony, Maine, 143
Harper, John Adams, 238

Harris
    Family, 103
    Nathaniel, 197, 200
Harrison, Katherine, 82
Harrisville, R.I., 273
Hart, Thomas, 82
Hartford County, Conn., 27, 56-61, 63, 64, 69, 78-86, 91, 328, 396, 397
Hartford, Conn., 56-61, 63, 65-67, 69-71, 73, 75, 78-81, 84, 85, 87, 88, 91-93, 96, 97, 101, 103, 106, 107, 109, 110, 328-330, 395-397, 415-417, 427
Hartford, Vt., 287, 312-314
Hartland, Conn., 70, 71, 80, 81, 85, 86
Hartland, Vt., 313
Hart-Meservey murder, 134
Hartnett, Charles F., 383, 384
Harvard, Mass., 223
Harvard University, 390, 421
    Business School, 180, 217, 323, 421
    Houghton Library, 161, 421
    Lamont Library, 197, 421
    Law School, 148, 161, 192, 197, 206, 207, 234, 323, 325, 421, 429
    Widener Library, 275, 422
Harvey, Joseph, 191
Harwich, Mass., 167
Harwinton, Conn., 70, 71, 86, 87, 90, 397
Haskins, William, 174
Hatfield, Mass., 191
Haverhill, Mass., 154, 178, 229, 333, 405
Haverhill, N.H., 242, 243
Hawkes, Micajah, 145, 146
Hawley
    Family, 75
    Joseph, 191
Hawley, Mass., 186
Hayes, Allen, 313
Haynes, Aaron, 141
Hayward
    (Judge), 294
    George (Mrs.), 214
Hazard, C. J., 261
Hazard (ship), 334
Hazleton, Charles, 93
Heard
    David, 18, 198
    Horace, 198
Heath, Mass., 186
Hebron, Conn., 70, 71, 106-108, 400
Hempstead, Joshua, 104
Hennigan family, 334
Henniker, N.H., 247, 409
Henry Sheldon Museum of Vermont History. *See* Sheldon (Henry) Museum of Vermont History
Herrick, William H., 265
Hersey, George C., 215
Hewlet, Thomas, 315
Heywood, Abiel, 197
Heywood
    Abiel, 197
    S.R., 22
Hicks, George W., 334
Higley, Silas, 83

Hildreth, Charles L., 199
Hill
    Arthur Dehon, 206, 217
    Family, 75, 149, 206, 217
    George W., 341
    Isaac, 233
Hill & Barton, 250, 251
Hillard, Heddle, 141
Hillsborough Bridge, N.H., 245
Hillsborough County, N.H., 231, 244-247, 409
Hillsborough, N.H., 245, 409
Hinckley, Gustavus Adolphus, 168
Hingham, Mass., 208, 209, 407, 422
Hinsdale, Mass., 169
Hinsdale, N.H., 240
Historic Deerfield Library, 186, 192
Historic Northampton Museum, 192, 422
Historical Society of Cheshire County, 241, 424
Historical Society of Glastonbury, 82, 417
Historical Society of Seabrook, 250, 424
Hoadly, Charles J., 67, 68, 98
Hoar/Hoare
    John, 197, 390
    Samuel, Jr., 226
Hodgdon family, 136
Holbrook, Mass., 205
Holden, Abraham, 294
Holden, Mass., 224
Holland, Mass., 188
Holliston, Mass., 195, 197
Holmes
    John, 132, 144
    Mercy, 36, 37
    Oliver Wendell, 162
    William, 334
    Zacheus, 218
Holyoke, Mass., 188, 190, 405
Hooksett, N.H., 248, 409
Hooper, Robert, 180
Hopedale, Mass., 223
Hopkins
    Family, 75
    Roswell, 293
Hopkinton, Mass., 195
Hopkinton, R.I., 279, 281, 412
Hopson, David, 23
Hornick family, 174
Houlton, Maine, 126, 401, 428
Howe Scale Co., 360
Hubbard
    Ebenezer, 197
    Henry, 233
    Joshua, 147
Hubbardston, Mass., 223
Hudson
    Family, 181
    William, 391
Hudson, Mass., 195
Hughes & Burns (law firm), 383, 384
Hull
    Benjamin, 280
    Family, 75
Hull, Mass., 208
Hunt

Chester, 110
    Ephraim, 217
Huntington
    Family, 75
    Isaac, 104, 111
Huntington, Conn., 77
Huntington, Mass., 191
Hurlbutt
    Ralph, 103
    Roger, 101
Hutchinson
    Anne, 162, 257
    Thomas, 182
    Titus, 313
Hyde (Hide) family, 75
Hyde Park, Vt., 303, 304, 414

I

Indians. See Native Americans
Inglee, Moses, 214
Ingraham, Joseph, 134
Ipswich, Mass., 153, 155, 178-182, 184, 405
Island Pond, Vt., 301, 413
Ives, R. H., 261

J

Jacobus, Donald L., 90, 102, 105
Jaffrey, N.H., 240, 408
Jamaica Plain, Mass., 213, 407
Jamestown, R.I., 270, 272, 411
Jefferies family, 143, 148
Jefferson County, Vt., 309
Jefferson, Maine, 136, 419
Jenkins, Joseph, 323
Jenks, Stephen, 275
Jennings family, 75
Jennison family, 160
Jericho, Vt., 299
Jewell, David, 373-375
Jewett City, Conn., 101, 400
Jews, R.I., 276
Jobe, Experience, 43
Johnson
    Elias, 334
    William Samuel, 68
Johnston, R.I., 273, 274, 277, 411, 412
Jones
    John W., 331
    William, 250
Jonesboro, Maine, 145
Judicial Archives, Mass. See Massachusetts Judi-
    cial Archives
Judson, Andrew T., 329
justices of the peace, 369-375. See also Connecti-
    cut courts, Maine courts, Massachusetts courts,
    New Hampshire courts, Rhode Island courts
    and Vermont courts

K

Keene, N.H., 240, 241, 408, 424
Kein, Prince, 132

Kelley
    Family, 136
    William, 373
Kellogg
    Family, 289, 296, 298, 299, 302, 304, 306,
        307, 309, 311, 313
    John, 289, 307, 309, 313
    Loyal, 289, 293, 296, 298, 299, 307, 309, 311,
        313
Kendall, B.F., 313
Kenison, Frank R., 233
Kennebec County, Maine, 117, 118, 123, 128,
    131-133, 143, 349-357, 402, 428
Kennebunk, Maine, 147
Kennedy, Timothy, 215
Kenniston, Laban and Levi, 184
Kensington, N.H., 251, 424
Kent County, R.I., 267-270, 410
Kent, Conn., 70, 71, 86, 87, 89, 90, 397
Keyes, John, 198
Kibbe, Daniel, 107
Kilbourne, Dwight D., 88
Kilburn, William, 351, 356
Killingly, Conn., 70, 71, 109-112, 401, 417
Killingworth, Conn., 70, 71, 91, 92, 94, 398
King Philip's war, 210, 258
King's County, R.I., 258, 280, 346, 348
Kingsbury, Sanford, 120, 136
Kingston, Mass., 208
Kingston, N.H., 250
Kingston, R.I., 263, 271, 275, 280, 338, 425
Kinney, George I., 216
Kittery, Maine, 115, 116, 147, 159
Knapp, John Francis, 160
Knickerbacher, Isaac, 21, 26, 370, 371
Knight, George, 124
Knox
    Henry (Maj.Gen.), 134
    Joseph, 225
Knox County, Maine, 118, 133, 134, 331, 402, 428
Knurow, Edward R., 170
Kollock, Cornelius, 206

L

L.A. Macomber (ship), 103, 329
Lacey family, 75
Laconia, N.H., 238, 408, 424
Lad, David, 173
Ladd, John, 349, 351-354
Lakeville, Mass., 208
Lamoille County, Vt., 303, 304, 339, 414
Lancaster, Mass., 223
Lancaster, N.H., 241, 242, 408
Lanesborough, Mass., 169
Law Library of Congress, 72, 123, 292, 327
Law Library Microform Consortium, 431
law library resources, 35, 48, 58, 69-72, 121-123,
    163-166, 235-237, 264-266, 291-293, 324-328,
    330, 332, 335-339, 341, 377-385, 427-431
Lawrence, Aaron, 294
Lawrence, Mass., 178, 179, 184, 333, 405, 429

LDS (Church of Jesus Christ of Latter-day Saints),
    48, 49, 58, 430. *See also* Genealogical Society
    of Utah
LDS Family History Centers, xiii, 48, 49, 58, 430-
    431
LDS Family History Library, 49, 93, 430-431
Leach, Edward, 233
Lebanon, Conn., 70, 71, 100, 102, 105
Lebanon, Maine, 147
Lebanon, N.H., 242, 293, 408
Lechford, Thomas, 215, 218
Ledyard, Conn., 70, 71, 100-102, 105, 400
Lee, Mass., 169
Leicester, Mass., 223, 225
Leland, S., 174
Lemmon, Joseph, 197
Lenox, Mass., 169, 172
Leominster, Mass., 223, 407
Leonard
    Hannah (Mrs. Isaac Dean), 174
    James, 174
    Phillip, 174
    Samuel, 173, 174
    Uriah, 174
Leverett, Mass., 186
Lewis family, 127
    John, 127
    Media, 174
    Peleg, 103
Lewiston, Maine, 124, 401
Lexington, Mass., xi, 195, 198, 333, 387-389, 422
LexisNexis, 431
Leyden, Mass., 186
Liacos, Paul M., 162
Libby, Charles Thornton, 120-122
Library of Congress, 168, 178, 198, 269, 271, 275,
    426
Library of U.S. Courts in First Circuit, 428
Limerick, Maine, 147, 148
Limestone, Maine, 126
Limington, Maine, 147
Lincoln County, Maine, 50, 51, 117, 118, 120,
    122, 123, 128, 129, 133, 135-139, 142, 145,
    331, 403, 428
Lincoln, Maine, 139, 140, 403
Lincoln, Mass., 195, 197, 198, 422
Lincoln, R.I., 273, 274, 277, 412
Lisbon, Conn., 100
Lisbon, Maine, 124
Litchfield County, Conn., 86-90, 328, 369-375,
    397-398
Litchfield Historical Society, 89, 417
Litchfield Law School, 88
Litchfield, Conn., 70, 71, 86-90, 397, 417, 427
Little
    Marcia E., 180
    Moses, 128
Little Compton, R.I., 259, 270-273, 411
Littleton, Mass., 195
Littleton, N.H., 243, 408
Livermore Falls, Maine, 124
Livius, Peter, 251
Livius family, 234
Longley, Edmund, 214

Longmeadow, Mass., 188
Loomis, Erastus, 350, 354-356
Lorimer, (Judge), 383, 384
Loring, George Bailey, 181
Loucks, Elizabeth, 90
Low, Peter, 334
Lowell
    Charles, 145, 146
    John, 161
Lowell, Maine, 140
Lowell, Mass., 195, 197, 215, 406, 421, 429
Ludlow, Mass., 188
Ludlow, Vt., 289, 314
Lunenburg, Mass., 223
Lung, Peter, 100
Lyman, Theodore, Jr., 160, 215
Lyman, Maine, 147
Lyme, Conn., 70, 71, 100-103, 105, 400
Lyndon, Vt., 298, 366
Lynn, David and Nathaniel, 132
Lynn, Mass., 178-180, 182, 184, 217, 289, 356, 405, 422
Lynnfield, Mass., 178
Lyon
    Family, 75
    Marcus, 194

M

M'Donnough, Elizabeth and William, 222
Machias, Maine, 145, 403, 428
Mackworth, Family, 149
Macomber, Thomas, 173
Madawaska, Maine, 126, 143, 401
Madison, Conn., 95-97, 99, 399
Madison, Maine, 129
Maine Central R. R. Co., 124
Maine courts, 115-151, 401, 403
    Associates, 115, 116
    Common Pleas, 117, 118, 120, 128, 132, 137, 146, 147, 150, 349, 351-356
    Common Pleas, Circuit Court of, 116, 117, 136, 144, 149
    Common Pleas, Inferior Court of, 116, 117, 149, 150
    Common Pleas, Superior Court of, 116
    County, 116, 117, 125, 149
    County Commissioners, 118, 128, 134, 136, 142, 144, 148
    District, 118-119, 124-126, 129-131, 133, 135, 138-147, 349, 401-403
    District, Family Div., 119, 124
    General Sessions of the Peace, 116, 117, 128
    Inferior, 115
    Insolvency, 124, 125, 134
    Justices of the Peace, 115-118, 123, 126-130, 132-141, 143-145, 147-149
    Juvenile, 119
    Municipal, 117, 123, 124, 126, 127, 129, 130, 132, 133, 135, 138, 140-145, 147, 150
    Passamaquoddy Tribal, 123
    Pleas, 116
    Police, 117
    Probate, 116-119, 121, 124, 150, 401-403
    Quarter Sessions, 116, 150
    Sessions, 116, 118
    Sessions of the Peace, 116, 150
    Superior, 118, 119, 122, 123, 125, 126, 128, 129, 131, 133, 135, 138, 139, 141-146
    Superior Court of Judicature, Court of Assize and General Gaol Delivery, 116, 117
    Supreme, 121, 132, 133, 141, 147
    Supreme Judicial, 117-125, 127, 130-132, 134-140, 143, 145-149, 349-358, 401-403
    Town, 118, 133
    Vice-Admiralty, 116
Maine Historical Society, 121-124, 127, 130, 132, 134, 138, 140, 142-145, 147-150, 323, 331, 419
Maine State Archives, xiv, 120, 123, 124, 126, 127, 129, 130, 132, 133, 135, 136, 138, 140-147, 150, 349-358, 419
Maine State Law & Legislative Reference Library, 428
Maine State Library, 135, 428
Majory, Samuel, 180
Malcolm, James, 133
Malden, Mass., 195, 333, 406
Manchester by the Sea, Mass., 179
Manchester, Conn., 78-80, 85, 396, 397
Manchester, N.H., 244-246, 336, 408, 416, 424
Manchester, Vt., 287, 295-297, 413
Mann, Horace, 88, 206
Manning, Elizabeth, 133
Mansfield, Conn., 70, 71, 106-108, 400
Mansfield Historical Society, 107, 417
Mansfield, Mass., 172
Manwaring, Charles William, 68, 70, 81, 83, 85, 86
Marble, (Judge), 383, 384
Marblehead, Mass., 178, 180, 181
Marion, Mass., 208
Marlboro, Vt., 287, 311, 312, 414
Marlborough, Conn., 70, 71, 78-81, 85, 397
Marlborough, Mass., 195, 406
Marlborough, N.H., 240
Mars Hill, Maine, 126
Marsh, Asa, 300
Marshfield, Mass., 208
Martha Canfield Library, 296, 426
Martha's Vineyard, Mass., 177, 178, 422
Martin, Michael, 197
Mashantucket, Conn., 89, 103, 111, 417
Mashantucket Pequot Museum, 89, 103, 111, 417
Mashpee, Mass., 167
Mason
    Ebenezer, 207
    Family, 176
Massachusetts Archives, xi, xiv, 17, 20, 24, 26, 36-41, 120, 127, 130, 136, 145, 148, 159, 160, 164-167, 170, 173, 177, 179, 186, 188, 191, 196, 197, 202, 203, 205, 208, 209, 213, 224, 387, 388, 420
Massachusetts courts, 153-227, 404-407
    Admiralty, 162, 216, 220, 222
    Appeals, 157-159, 161, 163-166, 404
    Assistants, 153, 154, 162, 163, 165, 183, 198, 199, 216
    Boston, Common Pleas, 155

Boston, Municipal, 156, 157, 159, 212, 216, 407
Common Pleas, 44, 154-156, 161, 167, 168, 170, 171, 173, 175-177, 179-181, 183, 186, 187, 189-193, 196, 202-204, 207, 208, 210, 211, 213-215, 220, 221, 224-226, 234
Common Pleas, Circuit Court of, 175, 180, 200, 207
Common Pleas, Inferior Court of, 24, 45, 155, 177, 183, 187, 192, 193, 200, 209, 215-217, 219, 226
County, 17, 154, 168, 181-185, 189, 193, 194, 196-198, 200, 202, 213, 218, 220, 222, 229, 251, 387
District, 155-157, 159, 164, 166, 167, 169, 171-173, 175-179, 186-191, 193, 195, 196, 199, 202, 205, 208, 213, 221, 223, 224, 404, 407
District, Appellate Div., 164-166
General Sessions, 154, 155, 175, 197, 203, 217
General Sessions of the Peace, 29, 155, 167, 170, 173, 177, 179, 181-183, 186, 189, 191, 193, 194, 196, 200, 202, 204, 207, 209, 210, 212, 216-218, 220, 224, 226
Governor and Council, 39, 154, 155
Housing, 156, 158
Insolvency, 156, 171, 184, 190
Justices of the Peace, 18, 155, 156, 159, 161, 168, 173, 174, 181, 186, 187, 189, 191, 192, 197, 198, 200, 201, 205, 214, 215, 224-226
Juvenile, 156, 158
Land, xiv, 34, 156, 158, 159, 162, 166, 176, 180, 181, 185, 187, 190, 195, 198, 202, 204, 206, 200, 217, 219, 223, 227, 404
Land Registration, 156, 219
Magistrates, 153 155
Maritime, 155, 161
Municipal, 155, 159
Municipal, Town of Boston, 155, 156, 213, 215-217, 222
Oyer and Terminer, 154, 181-183, 185
Police, 155, 156, 173, 180, 181, 189, 190, 211
Probate/Probate and Family/Probate and Insolvency, 36, 37, 155-159, 161, 162, 167-171, 173-188, 190-192, 194, 196-214, 218, 219, 221, 224-227, 404-407
Quarter/Quarterly, 153, 154, 163, 181-183, 185
Registration, 156
Superior, 40, 41, 156, 157, 159-161, 164, 166-173, 175-179, 183-191, 193, 195, 196, 200-209, 211-213, 216-218, 221, 223, 224, 226, 404-407
Superior Court of Judicature, 44, 45, 154, 155, 161, 162, 180, 183, 217, 218, 220
Superior Court of Judicature, Court of Assize and General Gaol Delivery, 154, 222
Supreme Judicial, 120, 121, 155-167, 169-173, 175-179, 184, 186-191, 193-198, 200, 205-209, 211-216, 218-224, 226, 227, 404, 420
Trial, 157-159, 166
Vice-Admiralty, 155
Massachusetts Historical Society, 132, 139, 145, 148, 160, 162, 163, 179, 180, 191, 196, 197,

199, 203, 205, 206, 209, 214, 215, 218, 224, 241, 311, 323, 329, 332, 334, 420
Massachusetts Judicial Archives (Supreme Judicial Court), xiv, 17, 20, 24, 26, 36, 37, 60, 120, 127, 130, 136, 145, 148, 159, 167, 170, 173, 177, 179, 186, 188, 191, 196, 197, 202, 203, 205, 208, 209, 213, 224, 387, 388, 390, 391, 420
Massachusetts School of Law, 429
Massachusetts State Library, 169, 214, 420, 428
Mather family, 162
Mathews, Edward, 132
Mattapoisett, Mass., 208
Maule, Thomas, 174
May, Elisha, 362, 363
Mayflower families, 168, 169, 175, 178, 203, 204, 210-212
Maynard, Jonathan, 197
Maynard, Mass., 195
McClary (brigantine), 233
McCleary, Family, 214
McClellan, John, 110
McDaniel, John, 120
McGuire family, 143
McKeen, Joseph, 332
McLeod, Thomas H., 294
Medfield, Mass., 205
Medford, Mass., 195, 333
Medway, Mass., 205, 333
Meeker family, 75
Megquier family, 124
Meiggs, Anson amd Jabex, 132
Melrose, Mass., 195, 333
Memorial Libraries, 186, 187, 189, 422
Mendon, Mass., 223, 225
Mercer, Maine, 129, 143
Meredith Bridge, N.H., 238
Meriden, Conn., 95-97, 99, 329, 398, 399
Merrill, Phinehas, 250
Merrill, Maine, 126
Merrimac, Mass., 178
Merrimack County, N.H., 232, 247-249, 409
Merrimack, N.H., 245, 409
Merwin family, 75
Methuen, Mass., 178, 333
Middleboro, Mass., 208
Middlebury College, 298, 309, 340, 426
Middlebury, Conn., 96
Middlebury, Vt., 68, 293, 294, 298, 299, 302, 309, 340, 413, 426
Middlefield, Conn., 91
Middlefield, Mass., 191
Middlesex County, Conn., 91-94, 328, 398
Middlesex County (Conn.) Historical Society, 93, 417
Middlesex County, Mass., 17, 20, 24, 26, 154, 190, 195-202, 223, 333, 377, 387, 390, 406
Middleton, Mass., 179
Middletown, Conn., 70, 71, 91-94, 398, 417, 418, 427
Middletown, R.I., 270, 272, 348, 411
Milford, Conn., 70, 71, 95-97, 99, 398, 399, 427
Milford, Mass., 223, 407
Milford, N.H., 245, 409
Millbury, Mass., 224

Miller, Charles, 93
Milliken
    Elizabeth, 148
    (Justice), 127
Millinocket, Maine, 139, 140, 403
Millis, Mass., 205, 333
Mills
    A. O., 82
    Ephraim (Dr.), 82
    Jane, 82
Millville, Mass., 224
Milton, Mass., 205
Miner
    Amos, 275
    William W., 271, 338
Minor, William Thomas, 74, 97, 102, 109
Minot
    Family, 199
    Stephen, 217
Mistick, Mass., 198
Mohegan tribe, 103
Monroe, Conn., 72, 74
Monroe, Mass., 186
Monson, Mass., 188
Montague, Mass., 181
Monterey, Mass., 169
Montgomery, Mass., 188
Montpelier, Vt., 286, 288-290, 293, 295, 298, 299,
    301, 302, 304, 306, 307, 309, 311-313, 366,
    413, 414, 425, 426, 430
Montville, Conn., 70, 71, 100-102, 105, 400
Moody Beach, Maine, 149
Moore
    Abel, 197
    Isaac, 354
Moosehead Lake, Maine, 358
Morehouse family, 75
Morgan
    Family, 107, 334
    Jonathan, 127
Mormon Church. See LDS
Morris, Robert, 215
Morris, Conn., 86
Morristown, Vt., 304
Morrow, John, 203
Moses, Martha T., 252
Mt. Washington, Mass., 169
Mulatto, 346
    Anthony, Isaac, 347
Munro/Row
    Martha, 20, 388-391
    Mary (Ball), 391
    William, xi, xii, 20, 387-391
Murphy, Stephen, 207
Muzzey, Percy W., 340
Mystic, Conn., 103, 329, 417, 418

N

Nahant, Mass., 178
Nahant Bank, 180, 217
Nantucket County, Mass., 157, 159, 202-204, 333,
    406
Nantucket Historical Assoc., 203, 422

Nantucket, Mass., 174, 202, 203, 406, 422
Narragansett, R.I., 279, 281, 412
Nashua, N.H., 245, 393, 394, 409
Natick, Mass., 18, 195, 198, 406
Native Americans
    Conn., 87, 89, 91, 101, 103, 105, 111, 417
    Dick, 346
    Faraoh, Sarah, 347
    Hannah, 347
    Jobe, Experience, 43
    Mass., 43, 45, 177, 203, 224
    Papemeck, Zachariah, 45
    Patompan, Josiah, 45
    Paul, Thomas, 45
    R.I., 262, 345-348
    Sambo, Mary, 347
    Samuel, 348
    Squaw Sachem, 198
naturalization, 9, 10, 32, 33, 40, 41, 321, 323, 326,
    427, 438, 442
    Conn., 66-68, 76, 81, 84, 90, 94, 99, 104, 108,
        111, 329, 330
    Maine, 51, 120-122, 125, 126, 331, 332
    Mass., 40, 41, 42, 159, 160, 162, 165, 167-
        173, 175-177, 179, 180, 183, 184, 186-191,
        193-196, 201, 203-205, 207-209, 211-213,
        216, 221, 223, 224, 226, 333, 335
    N.H., 233, 236-245, 247-252, 254, 255, 336
    R.I., 262, 263, 265, 267, 269, 272, 276, 281,
        338
    Vt., 289, 290, 292, 295, 299, 301, 304, 308,
        313, 340
Naugatuck, Conn., 95-97, 99, 399
Neal, William K., 127
Needham, Mass., 205, 206
Nelson, James, 217
Nevin, James, 251
New Ashford, Mass., 169
New Bedford, Mass., 172-174, 176, 203, 404, 422,
    429
New Braintree, Mass., 223
New Britain, Conn., 71, 78, 80, 83, 84, 396, 427
New Canaan, Conn., 72-74, 395
New England Dairies, Inc., 342
New England Historic Genealogical Society, xi,
    xiii, 27, 29, 42-45, 57, 69, 70, 76, 77, 83, 93,
    104, 106, 123, 133, 134, 136, 138, 146, 148,
    150, 161, 164, 168, 169, 176-178, 180, 187,
    192, 194, 198, 200, 202, 204, 206, 211, 212,
    217, 225, 227, 234, 238, 241, 243, 246, 251,
    253, 262, 265, 267, 269, 271, 273, 275, 278,
    280, 292, 305, 306, 308, 388, 422, 442
New England School of Law, 429
New Fairfield, Conn., 72, 73, 77, 395
New Gloucester, Maine, 128, 419
New Hampshire courts, 229-255, 407-410
    Appeals, 236
    Associates, 229
    Chancery, 230
    Circuit, 238, 239, 241, 243, 244, 246-248, 254,
        255
    Common Pleas, 161, 230, 231, 234, 238, 241,
        243-248, 250, 251, 254, 255
    Common Pleas, Circuit Court of, 238, 251

Common Pleas, Inferior Court of, 230, 236
County, 229
District, 231, 232, 238-242, 245, 247-249, 253, 254, 408-410
Equity, 248
Family, 231, 232, 243, 249, 408, 409
General Quarter Sessions, 236
General Sessions of the Peace, 230
Inferior, 251
Justices of the Peace, 230, 232, 234, 240, 241, 245-247, 250-252, 255
Municipal, 231, 232, 238, 240, 243, 246, 248, 250
Pleas, 230, 234
Police, 230, 238, 246, 247, 254
Probate, 231, 232, 235-255, 377-385, 408-410
Quarter, 229, 230
Quarter Sessions, 230
Quarter Sessions of the Peace, 234
Sessions, 234, 248
Sessions, Quarter Court of , 230
Superior, 231, 233, 235-249, 252-255, 408-410
Superior Court of Judicature, 230, 231, 233, 234, 236, 244, 246-248, 250, 251, 254, 255
Supreme, 46, 231-239, 242-244, 246, 248, 251, 253, 255, 378-385, 407
Supreme Court of Judicature, 230, 231, 241
Supreme Judicial, 231, 233, 238-241, 243, 244, 246-251, 254, 255
Town, 229, 253
Vice-Admiralty, 230
New Hampshire Div. of Archives and Records Management, xiv, 232, 237, 238, 240, 243, 245, 248, 250, 253, 255, 337, 423
New Hampshire Historical Society, 190, 233, 243, 245, 248, 250, 253, 255, 423
New Hampshire Law Library, 233, 285, 424, 430
New Hampshire State Library, 430
New Hartford, Conn., 86, 87, 89, 397, 418
New Haven Colony Historical Society, 98, 418
New Haven County, Conn., 63, 64, 95-100, 328, 398, 399
New Haven, Conn., 1, 2, 63-65, 68, 70, 71, 83, 89, 95-100, 104, 111, 192, 323, 328-330, 398, 399, 415, 418, 427
New Haven, Vt., 294, 295
New London County, Conn., 63, 64, 100-107, 328, 399, 400
New London, Conn., 63, 64, 72, 91, 93, 100-105, 399, 400, 418, 427
New London, N.H., 248, 409
New Marlborough, Mass., 169
New Milford, Conn., 71, 86, 88-90, 397
New Salem, Mass., 186
New Sharon, Maine, 129
New Shoreham, R.I., 279, 412
New Somersetshire, Maine, 115
New York, N.Y., 321, 322, 328, 329, 339, 340, 416, 424
Newbury, Mass., 39, 178-180, 184, 416, 424
Newbury, Vt., 305, 306
Newburyport, Mass., 178, 180, 181, 405, 422
Newburyport Public Library, 180, 422
Newfane, Vt., 310, 414

Newhall, Solomon, 180
Newington, Conn., 78-80, 397
Newmarket, N.H., 250
Newport (R.I.) Historical Society, 271, 425
Newport County, R.I., 258, 263, 270-273, 279, 346-348, 411
Newport, Maine, 140, 403
Newport, N.H., 250, 410
Newport, R.I., 257, 258, 263, 270-273, 346-348, 411, 425
Newport, Vt., 305, 306, 414
Newton Centre, Mass., 161, 421, 430
Newton, Mass., 195, 198, 333
Newton, N.H., 250
Newtown, Conn., 71-74, 77, 395
Newtown, Mass., 153
Niantic, Conn., 101, 400
Nichols family, 75
Norfolk County (Old), Mass., 154, 178, 182-184, 229, 235, 236, 251, 252
Norfolk County, Mass., 204-208, 223, 333, 406
Norfolk, Conn., 71, 86-88, 390, 397
Norfolk, Mass., 205, 333
Norridgewock, Maine, 132, 136, 143, 144
North Adams, Mass., 169, 404
North Andover, Mass., 178, 181, 333, 422
North Attleboro, Mass., 172
North Branford, Conn., 95, 96, 399
North Brookfield, Mass., 223
North Canaan, Conn., 86
North Conway, N.H., 239, 408
North Grosvenordale, Conn., 109, 401
North Haven, Conn., 95, 96, 100, 399
North Haverhill, N.H., 242, 243, 408
North Hero, Vt., 303, 414
North Kingstown, R.I., 279-281, 412
North Providence, R.I., 273-275, 277, 412
North Reading, Mass., 196, 333
North Scituate, R.I., 274, 412
North Smithfield, R.I., 274, 277, 412
North Springfield, Vt., 312, 415
North Star (Vt. newspaper), 366
North Stonington, Conn., 71, 100-102, 105, 400
North Yarmouth, Maine, 127, 155
Northampton, Mass., 190-192, 194, 405, 406, 422, 429
Northborough, Mass., 224
Northbridge, Mass., 224
Northeastern University School of Law, 429
Northend family, 180
Northfield, Mass., 186
Northford, Conn., 95
Norton
     Henry and Lewis, 88
     Thomas, 82
Norton, Mass., 172, 174
Norwalk, Conn., 65, 72-74, 76, 77, 395
Norway, Maine, 138
Norwell, Mass., 208
Norwich, Conn., 71, 100-106, 110, 399, 400, 427
Norwich, Vt., 301
Norwood, Mass., 205, 429
Notary Public
     Maine, 127, 370

Mass., 183, 197, 203, 211, 215, 220
N.H., 232, 252
R.I., 261, 265
Nutter, Frank W., 147
Nutting, William, 305

O

O'Brian family, 127
O'Brien, Raymond, 174
Oak Bluffs, Mass., 177
Oakes, Abner, 148
Oakham, Mass., 223
Ogden family, 75
Old Berwick Historical Society, 148, 419
Old Colony Historical Society, 173, 174, 206, 422
Old Dartmouth Historical Society, 174, 203, 422
Old Lyme, Conn., 71, 100-102, 105, 400
Old Orchard Beach, Maine, 147
Old Saybrook, Conn., 71, 91-94, 398
Old Town, Maine, 140
Old York Historical Society, 148, 419
Orange County, Vt., 297, 301, 304, 305, 309, 339, 414
Orange, Conn., 95, 96, 399
Orange, Mass., 186, 187, 405
Oriental Bank, 180, 217
Orleans County Historical Society, 306, 426
Orleans County, Vt., 286, 305-307, 339, 414
Orleans, Mass., 167, 404
Ormsby, Jonathan, 300
Orono, Maine, 134, 137, 139, 141, 149, 420
Orrington, Maine, 141
Osborn family, 75
Osgood family, 181
Ossipee, N.H., 239, 408
Othello (brig), 347
Otis, Harrison Gray, 217
Otis, Mass., 169
Overbaugh family, 75
Oxford County, Maine, 117, 123, 128, 138, 139, 331, 402, 428
Oxford, Conn., 71, 95-99, 399
Oxford, Mass., 108, 223, 225
Oyster Bay Historical Society, 299, 424

P

PACER (Public Access to Court Electronic Records), 321, 327, 330, 332, 336, 337, 339, 341
Page, Samuel, 181
Paige family, 218
Paine
    Family, 225
    Robert Treat, 160
Palmer, Jonathan, Jr., 81
Palmer, Mass., 188, 189, 405
Pangborn, Stephen, 372, 373
Papemeck, Zachariah, 45
Paris, Maine, 139, 419
Parker
    Isaac, 145
    Theodore, 334

Parkman, George (Dr.), 216
Parmenter, Addison and Louisa, 18
Parris, Albion K., 147
Parsons
    Family, 107
    Theophilus, 194
    William, 147
Passadumkeag, Maine, 141
Patompan, Josiah, 45
Patten, Matthew, 246, 247
Patterson
    Joseph, 246, 251
    William D., 136-138
Paul, Thomas, 45
Pawtucket, R.I., 261, 266, 268, 270, 274, 277, 280, 346, 412, 425
Paxton, Mass., 223
Peabody, Mass., 178, 405
Peabody-Essex Museum, 60, 128, 148, 179, 181, 217, 334, 422
Pearson, Ebenezer, 184
Pease family, 107
Peck, Asahel, 289
Peirce, Daniel, 251
Pejepscot Historical Society, 124, 419
Pelham, Mass., 191
Pembroke, Maine, 145
Pembroke, Mass., 208
Penhallow, Samuel, 251
Penniman, Jabez, 302
Penobscot County, Maine, 118, 125, 139-141, 331, 402, 403, 428
Pepperell, Mass., 195
Pepperrell, William, 147
Pequots. *See* Mashantucket Pequot Museum & Research Center
Perkins
    Charles Lorenzo, 147
    William J., 135
Perley, Ira, 233
Perrin, Philander, 305
Peru, Mass., 169
Petersham, Mass., 223
Peterson, Nils, 334, 335
Pettaquamscutt Historical Society, 280, 425
Phair, John P., 308
Phelps
    Charles, 289
    Elisha, 82
    Noah, 82
    Timothy, 289
Phillips
    Henry, 222
    Philip, 187
Phillipston, Mass., 224
Pickering
    John, 179, 246, 251
    Valentine, 251
    William, 251
Pickett family, 75
Pickman, Benjamin, 181
Pierce, John, 371
Pigsley, Abigal, 25
Pilgrims, 153

Pine Meadow, Conn., 89, 418
Pinkham, Benjamin and James, 136
Piscataqua County, N.H., 229, 235
Piscataquis County, Maine, 118, 141, 142, 331, 403, 428
Pitts, Adam, 132
Pittsfield, Maine, 143
Pittsfield, Mass., 169, 170, 322, 343, 344, 404, 421, 429
Plainfield, Conn., 71, 109, 110, 112, 401
Plainfield, Mass., 191
Plainville, Conn., 78-81, 85, 397
Plainville, Mass., 205
Plaistow, N.H., 249, 409
Plymouth Colony, 153, 154, 166, 172, 208-212
Plymouth County, Mass., 36, 37, 45, 154, 208-212, 333, 406
Plymouth County (Mass.) Commissioner, 209, 422
Plymouth, Conn., 71, 78, 86, 88, 90, 397
Plymouth, Mass., 153, 154, 208-212, 406, 407, 422, 429
Plymouth, N.H., 242, 243, 408
Plympton, Mass., 208
Pocasset, R.I., 257
Pocumtuck Valley Memorial Assn. Library, 186, 192
Poland, Maine, 124, 420
Polly, Ebenezer, 372, 373
Pomfret, Conn., 71, 109-112, 401
Pond
    Preston (Gen.), 206
    Sheldon, 294
Portland, Conn., 91-93, 398
Portland, Maine, 53, 54, 117-119, 124, 126, 127, 129, 130, 132, 134-136, 138, 140, 142-143, 147, 148, 234, 323, 331, 332, 356, 358, 401, 415, 428
Portsmouth & Concord Railroad, 250
Portsmouth Athenaeum, 149, 206, 217, 251, 424
Portsmouth, N.H., 149, 178, 206, 217, 229, 230, 246, 249-251, 409, 424
Portsmouth, R.I., 257, 270-273, 348, 411
Potter
    Robert, 347
    William, 128
Powars, Michael, 215
Pownalborough, Maine, 117, 136, 137
Pratt, Micah, 174
Prentiss, Joshua, 197
Prescott family, 248
Presque Isle, Maine, 126, 401
Preston family, 294
Preston, Conn., 100, 102
Price, Ezekiel, 180, 215, 216
Prince
    Family, 181
    Hezekiah, 137
    John, 181
Princeton, Mass., 223
Prospect, Conn., 95
Providence College, 262, 425
Providence County, R.I., 258, 259, 266-268, 273-278, 346, 411, 412

Providence Plantations, 258, 261, 263-265, 275, 276, 278
Providence, R.I., 67, 110, 257, 258, 260-262, 266-268, 270, 271, 273-277, 337, 338, 346-348, 410-412, 416, 426, 436
Provincetown, Mass., 167
Pudeater family, 180
Putnam, George W. S., 148
Putnam, Conn., 108-110, 112, 400, 401, 427
Putney, Henry M., 232
Pynchon, John, 189, 192-194

Q

Quabbin (Mass.) Reservoir, 191
Quakers, 179, 356
Quelch, John (Capt.), 214
Quimby, Joseph M., 313
Quincy, Edmund, 217
Quincy, Mass., 205, 207, 406
Quinnipiac University School of Law, 427
Quirico, Francis, 161

R

Rackly, Martha, 147
Rand, John, 127
Randolph family, 162
Randolph, Mass., 205
Randolph, Vt., 304, 305
Rankin, Jennett and Joseph, 88
Rawson
    Charles I., 108
    Edward, 217
Ray family, 218
Raynham, Mass., 173
Read
    Benjamin, 225
    John, 75
Readfield, Maine, 132
Reading, Mass., 196, 333
Redding, Conn., 71-75, 77, 396
Reed, Samuel, 306
Reed and Durham, 306
Reeves, Jacob, 198
Rehoboth, Mass., 173
Revere, Mass., 213
Rex family, 218
Reynolds family, 267
Rhode Island courts, 257-283, 410-413
    Admiralty, 258, 259, 264
    Commissioners, 271
    Common Pleas, 259, 263, 266, 268-272, 274-276, 280, 281
    Common Pleas, Inferior Court of, 258, 259, 272, 280, 281, 346
    District, 259, 262, 268, 270, 273, 279, 410-412
    Equity, 258, 261, 263, 265
    Family, 260, 268, 270, 273, 279, 410-412
    General Court of Trials, 258, 261, 263-265, 271, 346
    General Court of Trials and General Gaol Delivery, 258, 264
    General Quarter Sessions, 258

General Sessions of the Peace, 258, 259, 266, 270, 274, 346
Justices of the Peace, 258, 262, 268, 272, 274, 275, 280, 281
Magistrates, 261, 270
Municipal, 260, 266, 268, 270, 273, 274, 279, 281, 410-413
Particular, 257
Police, 260
Probate, 259-261, 263-282, 410-413
Probate, General Council of, 258, 261
Quarter/Quarter Sessions, 257, 263
Superior, 259, 265, 266, 268-273, 276, 279, 281, 410-412
Superior Court of Judicature, 258, 259, 281
Superior Court of Judicature, Court of Assize and General Gaol Delivery, 259, 264, 265
Superior Court of Trials, 261
Supreme Court, 259-263, 264-266, 268-272, 274-276, 280, 410
Supreme Court (General Council) of Probate, 259, 261
Supreme Judicial Court, 259, 261, 262, 265, 276
Town Councils, 258, 259, 267, 269, 272, 281
Town Courts, 258, 260
Traffic Tribunal, 260
Vice-Admiralty, 258, 264
Workers' Compensation, 260, 410
Rhode Island Historical Society, 262, 263, 265, 268, 271, 274, 275, 277, 280, 347, 348, 425
Rhode Island Jewish Historical Assoc., 276
Rhode Island Judicial Records Center, xiv, 261, 266, 268, 270-274, 280, 346, 425
Rhode Island State Archives, xiv, 261, 266, 268, 270, 274, 279, 346, 425
Rhode Island State Law Library, 262, 425, 430
Rhode Island State Library, 430
Rice
    Family, 199
    John (Capt.), 348
    Thomas, 348
Richards,
    Fred E., 130
    Joseph, 225
Richardson
    Edward, 132, 139
    Family, 199
Richmond, Mass., 169
Richmond, R.I., 279-281, 412
Ridgefield, Conn., 72-74, 77, 396
Rigby, Alexander, 115
Riggs, Benjamin, 136, 137
Rindge, Isaac, 234
Ripley, William Y., 340
Robert and John (brigantine), 216
Roberts
    Bethuel, 93
    C.P., 140
    Tobias L., 130
Roberts & Chittenden (law firm), 294
Robinson, Judith, 174
Robison, Jane S. and Robert I., 332
Roby, (Justice), 198

Rochester, Mass., 208
Rochester, N.H., 253, 409
Rockingham County, N.H., 231, 247, 249-252, 409
Rockland, Maine, 133, 134, 402, 428
Rockland, Mass., 208
Rockport, Mass., 178
Rockville, Conn., 106, 107, 400, 427
Rockwell
    Elijah, 90
    Forbes, 181
Rocky Hill, Conn., 78, 80
Rog, John P., 334, 335
Roger Williams University, 430
Rogers
    Ebenezer (Roggers), 45
    Edward, 21, 26, 370, 371, 373, 374
    Eli F., 98
    Family, 98
    Thomas, 347
Rolfe, Benjamin, 180
Rosenbach Museum & Library, 89, 425
Rosewain, Edward, 334
Round Porcupine Island, Maine, 130
Rounds, Joseph, 120
Row. See Munro
Rowe, Mass., 186
Rowland
    Andrew, 75
    Family, 75
Rowley, Mass., 178, 180
Roxbury, Conn., 71, 86, 88, 90, 397
Roxbury, Mass., 213, 214, 217, 407
Royalston, Mass., 224
Royalton & Woodstock Turnpike Co., 313
Royalton, Vt., 364
Royce
    Family, 182
    Stephen, 289, 311
Ruggles family, 134
Rumford Chemical Co., 322
Rumford, Maine, 138, 402
Russell
    Benjamin, 390
    Family, 180
    James, 196
    John, 390
    Thomas, 214
Russell Collection of Vermontiana, 296
Russell Library, 93, 418
Russell, Mass., 188
Rutland and Burlington Railroad, 308
Rutland County, Vt., 287, 289, 293, 307-309, 339, 414
Rutland Marble Co., 340
Rutland Railroad Co., 312
Rutland, Mass., 223
Rutland, Vt., 286, 287, 307, 339, 340, 414, 416
Rye, N.H., 251, 424

S

Sacco, Nicola, 206, 207
Saco Savings Bank, 147
Saco, Maine, 115, 127, 147, 148, 154

Saffin family, 218
Sagadahoc County, Maine, 142, 143, 331, 403, 428
Salem Village, Mass., 183
Salem, Conn., 71, 100-102, 105, 400
Salem, Mass., 56-61, 128, 148, 153, 155, 178-185,
    217, 234, 339, 364, 367, 405, 412, 429
Salem, N.H., 249, 409
Salisbury, Conn., 86-88, 90, 370, 397
Salisbury, Mass., 154, 178, 183, 229
Salisbury, Vt., 293
Salmon Brook Historical Society, 82, 83, 418
Salt Lake City, Utah, 430, 431
Saltonstall, Leverett, 181
Sambo, Mary, 347
Sanborn, Cyrus King, 253
Sanderson, Elijah and Jacob, 181
Sandgate, Vt., 296
Sandisfield, Mass., 169
Sandwich, Mass., 167
Sanford
    Emily Judson, 75
    Family, 75
    Joseph, 271
Sanford, Maine, 147, 149, 420
Sargent, William, 147
Sassamon, John, 210
Saugus, Mass., 178
Savage family, 196
Savoy, Mass., 169
Saybrook, Conn., 63, 92, 94, 398
Scarborough, Maine, 115, 127, 148
Scituate, Mass., 208
Scituate, R.I., 273, 274, 278, 412
Scottish war prisoners, xi, xii, 345, 387
Seabrook, N.H., 250, 424
Sears, Francis and Philip, 161
Seaver, Dolly, 250
Seavey family, 136
Seekonk, Mass., 173
Seeley family, 75
Seely, Ephraim, 89
Selden, Richard Ely, 103
Sewall
    David, 331
    Jacob S., 143
    Rufus K., 331
    Samuel, 214
Seymour
    Family, 84, 294
    Horatio, 294
Seymour, Conn., 95
Shaftsbury, Vt., 295, 296, 426
Sharon, Conn., 71, 86, 88-90, 397, 418
Sharon, Mass., 205
Sharon, Vt., 25
Shaw, Benjamin, 179
Shawomet, R.I., 257
Sheepscot, Maine, 135
Sheffield, Mass., 169
Shelburne Falls, Mass., 187, 422
Shelburne, Mass., 186
Sheldon
    Henry L., 68, 294
    Joseph, 97

Sheldon (Henry) Museum of Vermont History, 68,
    293, 294, 299, 302, 340, 426
Shelton, Conn., 73, 74, 77, 95, 396
Shepard, Elmer, 176
Shepherd family, 199
Shepley, Ether, 127, 148
Sherborn, Mass., 195, 198
Sherman, Conn., 71, 72, 74, 77
Sherman, Roger Minott, 75, 87, 89
Sherwood family, 75
Shirley, Mass., 195
Shoreham, Vt., 294, 426
Shrewsbury, Mass., 224, 225
Shutesbury, Mass., 186
Sidney, Maine, 351, 352, 356
Silliman family, 75
Silloway, John, 250
Silverwood, Mary, 346
Simmons, George, Jr., 37
Simms family, 143
Simonds, Sarah J. and William E., 82
Simpson, Wilder Arthur, 298
Simsbury, Conn., 71, 78, 79, 81-83, 85, 99, 397,
    418
Sisson family, 270
Skaghticoke tribe, 89
Skidmore, Thomas, 77, 85
Skiller, Richard, 300
Skowhegan, Maine, 143, 151, 403, 428
Slater, Samuel, 275
Slosson, Barzillai, 89
Smalley
    David, 363, 365
    David Allen, 340
Smart, Thomas (Capt.), 217
Smith
    Bertram L., 140
    Hannah B., 280
    Jeremiah, 235
    John, 253, 275
    Josiah, 83
    Justin Webber, 136
    Peleg, 346
    Regard, 174
    Richard, 77, 85
    Samuel E., 136
    Samuel Emerson, 120
    Seth Samuel, 75
    William, 251
Smithfield, R.I., 273-275, 278, 412
Snow, Daniel, 361
Social Law Library, 161, 166, 219, 323, 377, 378,
    381, 422, 429
Solon, Maine, 143
Somers, Conn., 71, 106-108, 418
Somerset County, Maine, 117, 118, 128, 136, 141,
    143, 144, 331, 403, 428
Somerset, Mass., 172
Somerville, Mass., 195, 196, 406
South Berwick, Maine, 147-149, 419
South Boston, Mass., 213, 407
South Hadley, Mass., 191
South Kingstown, R.I., 279-281, 347, 412
South Paris, Maine, 138, 402, 428

South Portland, Maine, 127
South Royalton, Vt., 430
South Windsor, Conn., 78-80, 396
Southampton, Mass., 186
Southborough, Mass., 220
Southbridge, Mass., 220, 221
Southbury, Conn., 86, 87, 88, 387
Souther, Daniel, 212
Southern New England School of Law, 420
Southington, Conn., 60, 67-70, 72, 75, 385
Southwick, Mass., 183
Spargo, John, 296
Spencer, Mass., 223
Sprague
    Family, 181
    P., 354
    Preserved, 179
Sprague, Conn., 100
Spratt, Jonathan M., 252
Springfield, Mass., 19, 156, 188, 190, 192, 194,
    333, 405, 416, 429, 430
Springfield, Vt., 286
Springs Cotton Mills, 322
Springvale, Maine, 147, 403
Squaw Sachem, 198
St. Albans, Vt., 286, 302, 413, 414
St. George, Bridie Claire, 40, 41
St. Johnsbury, Vt., 297, 363, 365-367, 413
Stafford Springs, Conn., 106, 400
Stafford, Conn., 71, 106-108, 400
Stain, David L., 140
Stamford, Conn., 65, 71-74, 76, 77, 396, 427
Standish, Maine, 128, 420
Stanley, George W., 93
Stanton, Phineas, 100, 105
Staples, William R., 263
Starks, Maine, 143
Stearns
    Family, 181
    Isaac, 196
    John, 361
Steele & Blodgett, 364
Stegeman family, 75
Sterling, Conn., 71, 110, 112
Sterling, Mass., 223
Stevens
    Daniel, 354-356
    George, 130
    Henry, 288, 291
    Henry W., 233
Stickney, John M., 294
Stockbridge, Mass., 169, 423
Stockbridge, Vt., 313
Stoddard & Lovering, 215
Stone
    Daniel, 198, 199
    John, 198
    William Eben, 198
Stoneham, Mass., 196, 333
Stonington, Conn., 71, 100-105, 400, 418
Stonington, Maine, 130
Storrs, Conn., 83, 107, 400, 417, 418
Story
    Joseph (Judge), 332, 335, 339

Stratton &, 214
Stoughton, Mass., 205, 406
Stow, Mass., 195, 198
Stow, Vt., 304
Strafford County, N.H., 237, 239, 252-254, 382,
    384, 385, 409, 410
Strange, Lott, 174
Stratford, Conn., 71-74, 77, 396
Stratton & Story, 218
Strawbery Banke, N.H., 229, 251
Strong
    (Gov.), 194
    John, 294
    Lewis, 226
    (Mr.), 174
    Simeon, 192
Sturbridge, Mass., 223
Sturges, Mary A., 75
Sudbury, Mass., 195, 197, 198
Suffield, Conn., 71, 78-81, 85, 397
Suffolk County, Mass., 24, 64, 68, 154, 155, 157,
    159, 162, 165, 204, 206, 209, 212-223, 333, 407
Suffolk University Law School, 429
Sullivan, John L., 214
Sullivan County, N.H., 232, 254, 255, 410
Summers family, 75
Sumner, Increase, 214
Sunderland, Mass., 186
Sunderland, Vt., 296
Supreme Judicial Court (Mass.) Historical Society,
    121, 155, 161, 162, 423
Susanna (brigantine), 233
Sutton, Mass., 224
Swampscott, Mass., 178
Swan
    Family, 311
    William, 196
Swansea, Mass., 172
Swift, Zephaniah, 9
Symonds, Samuel, 182
Syracuse University Law School, 239, 424

T

Talcott, Matthew, 93
Tanner, Tryal, 371
Tapping Reeves Law School, 88
Taunton, Mass., 172-176, 206, 404, 422, 429
Taylor
    Charles J., 170
    William, 82
Temple, Maine, 351, 356
Templeton, Mass., 224
Terry, Eli, 88
Terryville, Conn., 86, 397
Tervet (Trevett) family, 261, 271
Tewksbury, Henry and John, 218
Tewksbury, Mass., 195
Thacher
    (Judge), 215
    Peter O., 217
Thatcher
    Ebenezer, 120, 136, 144
    Moses (Rev.), 206

Thayer, Henry Otis, 143, 148
Thing (Thwing?), Nathaniel, 238. *See also* Thwing
Thomas
    Seth, 88
    William, Jr., 174
Thomaston, Conn., 87, 88, 91, 397
Thomaston, Maine, xiv, 133, 134, 420
Thompson, Edwin P., 238
Thompson, Conn., 71, 109, 110, 112, 401
Thompsonville Carpet Manufacturing Co., 82
Thorp family, 75
Thorp & Branch (law firm), 383, 384
Thrasher, Ebenezer, 127
Thwing, Nathaniel, 135. *See also* Thing
Tirrell, Betsy Frances, 215
Tisbury, Mass., 45, 177
Tisdale, James, 174
Tiverton, R.I., 259, 270, 273, 411
Tolland County, Conn., 106-108, 328, 400
Tolland, Conn., 71, 106-108, 400
Tolland, Mass., 188
Toothaker, Allen, 304, 307
Toppan, Jane, 167
Topsfield, Mass., 181, 423
Topsham, Maine, 136
Torrey, Susanna, 313
Torrington, Conn., 71, 86-88, 91, 398
Townsend, Hannah, 299
Townsend, Mass., 195
Trask, John, 353, 354
Treadwell, John, 81
Trelawny Papers, 149
Trevett family. *See* Trevet
Trinity Church, 75
Trowbridge, Edmund, 179
Troy, N.H., 362
Trumbull
    J. Hammond, 68, 70
    Jonathan, Sr., 67
Trumbull, Conn., 72, 73, 76, 396, 418
Truro, Mass., 167
Tully, Samuel, 335
Turell family, 218
Turney family, 75
Tuttle, John, 253
Tyler
    Royall, 311
    Thomas, 216
Tyley, Samuel, 180, 216
Tyngsboro, Mass., 195
Tyringham, Mass., 169

U

U.S. Attorneys, 322, 329, 331, 333, 336, 338, 340, 341
U.S. Bankruptcy Courts, 9, 33, 319, 320, 324, 325, 327
    Conn., 328-330, 415
    Maine, 331, 332, 415
    Mass., 333, 336, 416
    N.H., 336, 337, 416
    R.I., 338, 339, 416
    Vt., 339-341, 416

U.S. Circuit Courts, 317-319, 323-325
    Conn., 329, 330
    Maine, 331, 332
    Mass., 28, 333-335
    N.H., 336
    R.I., 338, 339
    Vt., 339-341
U.S. Citizenship & Immigration Services, 32, 68, 120, 121, 162, 234, 263, 290, 323, 427, 442
U.S. Commissioners, 19, 28, 317-319, 321, 329, 331, 333, 336, 338, 340
U.S. Court of Claims, 334
U.S. Court of Federal Claims, 320
U.S. Court of International Trade, 320, 325
U.S. Courts of Appeals, 9, 316, 318, 320-322, 325-328
    First Circuit, 320-328, 331, 333, 336, 337, 339, 415
    Second Circuit, 320-330, 339-341, 415
U.S. Dept. of Homeland Security, 32, 68, 120, 121, 162, 234, 263, 290, 323, 427, 442
U.S. District Courts, 9, 33, 155, 316-322, 324-328, 359, 360
    Conn., 328-330, 415
    Maine, 331, 332, 415
    Mass., 42, 333-336, 415, 416
    N.H., 336-337, 416
    R.I., 337-339, 416
    Vt., 339-342, 359-367, 416
U.S. Immigration & Naturalization Service, 32, 320
U.S. Magistrates, 319
U.S. National Archives and Records Admin., xiii, xiv, 19, 28, 33, 67, 81, 97, 120, 122, 160, 165, 233, 236, 262, 265, 289, 292, 321, 322, 326, 328-331, 333-336, 338-340, 359, 362-366, 420, 424, 426
U.S. Supreme Court, 9, 10, 232, 234, 317-328, 416
U.S. Tax Court, 320, 321
Ulmar, John, 216
Uncasville, Conn., 101, 400
Underhill, Vt., 299
Underwood, A., 365, 366
Union, Conn., 106, 107
University of Chicago, 217, 418
University of Connecticut, 83, 418, 427
University of Maine School of Law, 428
University of Maine, Orono, 121, 128, 134, 137, 139, 141, 149, 420
University of Massachusetts, Amherst, 162, 170, 218, 423
University of Massachusetts, Boston, 334, 423
University of New Hampshire 149, 238, 253, 424
University of Pennsylvania, 111, 425
University of Rhode Island, 263, 271, 275, 280, 338, 425
University of Vermont, 290, 294, 296, 298-300, 302, 305, 306, 308, 310, 312, 313, 340, 341, 466
University of Virginia, 89, 426
Upham, Timothy, 250, 251
Upton, Mass., 223
Ursuline (Charlestown, Mass.) Convent, 214
Uxbridge, Mass., 224, 407

V

Van Buren, Maine, 126
Vanceboro, Maine, 145
Vanderbilt, Cornelius J., 280
Vanzetti, Bartolomeo, 206, 207
Vaughn
    Eliot, 148
    Family, 132
Vergennes, Vt., 286, 293-295
Vermont & Canada Railroad Co., 302
Vermont Antiquarian Society, 300
Vermont Copper Mining Co., 305
Vermont courts, 285-315, 413-415
    Chancery, 286, 289, 298, 302, 304, 306, 308
    City, 293
    Common Pleas, 285
    Confiscations, 285, 288
    County, 285, 286, 289, 290, 293-295, 298-300, 302, 304-315
    District, 287, 292, 293, 295, 297, 299, 302-305, 307, 309, 311, 312, 413-415
    Environmental, 34, 287, 288, 292, 310, 413
    Family, 287, 292, 293, 295, 297, 299, 301, 303, 304, 306, 307, 309, 311, 312, 413-415
    General Sessions of the Peace, 285
    Insolvency, 310
    Judicial Bureau, 287
    Justices of the Peace, 16, 286, 289, 293-296, 304, 306, 307, 314
    Municipal, 286, 294, 300, 307, 311
    Probate, 285-287, 289, 292-314, 413-415
    Superior, 285, 286, 292-295, 297, 299, 301-305, 307, 309, 310, 312, 413-415
    Supreme, 285, 286, 288-302, 304, 307-314, 413
Vermont Dept. of Buildings & General Services (Records Center), 288, 289, 293, 295, 299, 301, 304, 307, 311, 313, 426
Vermont Dept. of Libraries, xiv, 290, 292, 426, 430
Vermont Historical Society, xiv, 182, 234, 289, 290, 293, 295, 296, 298, 301, 302, 304-307, 309, 311, 313, 314, 426
Vermont State Archives (Judicial Records Program), xiv, 16, 22, 23, 25, 30, 288, 289, 291, 293, 295, 298, 299, 302, 304, 306, 307, 309, 311, 312, 425
Vermont Law School, 430
Vermont Valley Railroad Co., 312
Vernon, Samuel and William, 347
Vernon, Conn., 106
Vickum, Levina, 216
Village Water Co., 89
Virgin, Peter C., 356-358
Voluntown, Conn., 71, 100, 102
Vose, Frederick, 233, 240

W

Wade, John, 206
Wadley family, 251
Wadsworth, Alfred, 136
Wadsworth Papers, 97

Wait
    Family, 191
    John Turner, 102
    Thomas, 173
Wakefield, Mass., 195, 333
Wakefield, R.I., 279, 412
Wakeman family, 75
Waldo, (Judge), 97
Waldo County, Maine, 118, 133, 144, 331, 403, 428
Waldoboro, Maine, 117, 135
Waldron, Isaac, 216
Wales, Maine, 124
Wales, Mass., 188
Wallingford, Conn., 71, 95-97, 99, 399
Walpole, Mass., 205
Walpole, N.H., 240
Waltham, Mass., 33, 67, 81, 97, 120, 160, 196, 198, 201, 233, 262, 289, 322, 323, 328, 329, 331, 333, 336, 338, 339, 359, 406, 420, 423
Wamesit Power Co., 197
Ward
    Family, 107
    John, 300
Ware, Mass., 191, 193, 405
Wareham, Mass., 208, 211
Warner, Benjamin F. and George B., 124
Wallace, R. B., 22, 23
Warren, Conn., 86
Warren, Mass., 223
Warren, R.I., 259, 266, 267, 273, 410
Warrington, Thomas, 334
Warwick, Mass., 186
Warwick, R.I., 257, 268-270, 275, 348, 410
Washburn
    (Judge), 203
    Peter Thacher/Thatcher, 314
    Reuben, 182, 289
Washington County, Maine, 117, 118, 123, 125, 145, 146, 331, 403, 428
Washington County, R.I., 279-282, 348, 412, 413
Washington County, Vt., 290, 303, 309, 310, 339, 414
Washington Depot, Conn., 87, 398
Washington, Conn., 86-89, 91, 398
Washington, D.C., 68, 120, 121, 162, 168, 177, 198, 234, 263, 269, 271, 275, 290, 321-323, 416, 426, 427
Washington, Mass., 169
Waterboro, Maine, 117
Waterbury, Conn., 65, 71, 95-97, 99, 113, 329, 330, 398, 399, 415, 427
Waterbury, Vt., 310
Waterford, Conn., 100, 101
Waterford, Maine, 138
Waters, John and Joseph G., 181
Watertown, Conn., 87, 88, 91, 95, 398
Watertown, Mass., 196, 200, 333
Waterville, Maine, 132, 402
Watkins, Oliver, 110
Wayland, Mass., 18, 195, 198, 423
Ways, Richard, 217
Webb, Nathan, 127
Webster
    Daniel, 160, 215, 234, 235

John A., 250
John H., 144
John W., 216
John White, 214
Webster, Mass., 223, 224
Weeden family, 261, 271
Weeks, Holland, 294
Wellesley, Mass., 205, 206, 423
Wellfleet, Mass., 167
Wells
    Daniel, 196
    Nathaniel, 148
Wells Beach, Maine, 149
Wells, Maine, 115, 116, 147-149, 154, 181
Wemms, William, 222
Wendell, Mass., 186
Wentworth, John (Gov.), 234
West (Thompson Legal & Regulatory), 431
West Barnstable, Mass., 167, 421
West Bath, Maine, 142, 403
West Boylston, Mass., 223
West Bridgewater, Mass., 208
West Brookfield, Mass., 223
West family, 313
West Greenwich, R.I., 268-270, 410
West Hartford, Conn., 78-80, 85, 397
West Haven, Conn., 95, 96, 399
West National Reporter System, 35, 46, 48, 58,
    378, 431. *See also* West (Thompson Legal &
    Regulatory) and Westlaw
West Newbury, Mass., 178
West Newton, Mass., 195, 406
West Roxbury, Mass., 213, 407
West Springfield, Mass., 188
West Stockbridge, Mass., 169
West Tisbury, Mass., 177
West Wareham, Mass., 208, 407
West Warwick, R.I., 268, 270, 410
Westborough, Mass., 224, 407
Westbrook, Conn., 91-94, 398
Westbrook, Maine, 127
Westerly, R.I., 279, 280, 282, 413
Western New England School of Law, 430
Western Reserve Historical Society, 89, 93, 424
Westfield, Mass., 188, 405
Westford, Conn., 71
Westford, Mass., xiv, 50, 195, 197, 199, 423
Westhampton, Mass., 191
Westlaw, 72, 123, 166, 237, 266, 293, 328, 330,
    332, 336, 337, 339, 341, 377, 379, 381, 427,
    431
Westminster, Mass., 223, 225, 423
Westminster, Vt., 287, 311, 312, 415
Westmoreland County, Conn., 90
Weston, Nathan, 136, 144
Weston, Conn., 72, 74
Weston, Mass., 196, 198, 423
Westport, Conn., 72-74, 77, 396
Westport, Mass., 172, 174, 203
Westwood, Mass., 205
Wethersfield, Conn., 78, 80-82, 84
Weymouth, Mass., 205
Whately, Mass., 186
Wheeler

Betsy, 172
Ephraim, 170, 172
Family, 75
Hoyt H., 340
Wheeler's Porcupine Isl., Maine, 130
White
    Family, 75
    John, 162
    Joseph, 160
    Nathaniel, 334, 335
    Samuel, 173
    Thomas, Jr., 217
White River Junction, Vt., 312, 415
Whiting, Vt., 295
Whitman, Mass., 208
Whittier, Benjamin, 129
Wickard, Claude R., 340
Wiggin, Andrew, 250
Wilbour, Benjamin F., 173, 176
Wilbraham, Mass., 188
Wilbur, LaFayette, 299
Wilcox
    Christopher G., 269
    Leonard, 233
Williams
    Ebenezer, 25
    George W., 265
    John, 174, 187, 192, 265, 334, 335
    Roger, 257
    Seth, 173
    Warner, 306
    William, 103, 107
    Zebedee, 265
Williamsburg, Mass., 191
Williamstown, Mass., 169
Willimantic, Conn., 108, 109, 400, 401, 427
Willington, Conn., 106
Williston, Vt., 300
Wilmington, Mass., 196, 333
Wilmington, Vt., 361
Wilson family, 206
Wilton, David, 192
Wilton, Conn., 72, 73
Winchendon, Mass., 224, 226, 407
Winchester, Conn., 71, 86-88, 91, 398
Winchester, Mass., 196, 333
Windham County, Conn., 106, 108-112, 328, 400,
    401
Windham County, Vt., 287, 310-312, 339, 414,
    415
Windham, Conn., 71, 109, 110, 401
Windham, Maine, 128, 420
Windsor County, Vt., 287, 290, 312-315, 339, 415
Windsor Locks, Conn., 78-81, 397
Windsor, Conn., 78-83, 85, 397, 418
Windsor, Mass., 169
Windsor, Vt., 313
Winooski, Vt., 286
Winslow, Edward and Josiah, 209
Winsted, Conn., 86, 87, 398
Winter family, 149
Winter Harbor, Maine, 130, 420
Winthrop, Maine, 132
Winthrop, Mass., 213, 218, 423

Wiscasset, Maine, 51, 117, 120, 135, 402, 428
witchcraft
    Conn., 64, 67, 69, 76, 82
    Mass., 155, 179, 181, 183, 185
Withington family, 214
Woburn, Mass., 196, 333, 406, 429
Wolcott
    Frederick, 89
    Roger, 82
Wolcott, Conn., 95, 97
Wood
    Family, 75
    Oliver, 136
Woodbridge family, 294
Woodbridge, Conn., 95, 96, 399
Woodbury, Levi, 233
Woodbury, Conn., 71, 87, 88, 91, 95, 99, 398
Woodman family, 148
Woodruff, George Catlin, 88
Woodstock, Conn., 71, 109-112, 401, 418
Woodstock, Vt., 290, 312, 314, 415, 426
Woodward
    Family, 243
    William H., 234
Wooley, George W., 82
Woonsocket, R.I., 273, 274, 278, 283, 412
Worcester County, Mass., 223-227, 333, 407

Worcester, Mass., 103, 156, 189, 192, 197, 215, 223-227, 333, 407, 416, 420, 429
Worth, Henry Barnard, 174, 203, 204
Worthington, Mass., 191
Wrentham, Mass., 205, 406
Wright
    Andrew, 194
    Emerson R., 294
    John, 373-375
    Josiah, 93
Wyllys, Samuel, 67
Wyman
    Lewis, 144
    Louis C., 232
    Thomas Bellows, 198
    William, 196, 198
Wyoming Valley, 90
Wyoming, R.I., 279, 412

Y

Yale Law School, 68, 89, 104, 418, 427
Yale University, 83, 104, 111, 192, 323, 418
Yarmouth, Mass., 167
York County, Maine, 115-118, 123, 126, 135, 138, 146-150, 331, 403, 419, 428
York, Maine, 115-117, 147-149, 154, 403, 419